LEGAL AID HAN

1998/99

C000183255

AUSTRALIA
LBC Information Services
Sydney

CANADA and USA
Carswell
Toronto

NEW ZEALAND
Brooker's
Auckland

SINGAPORE and MALAYSIA
Thomson Information (S.E. Asia)
Singapore

LEGAL AID HANDBOOK
1998/99

Prepared by

The Legal Aid Board

LONDON   SWEET & MAXWELL   1998

Published in 1998 by
Sweet & Maxwell Limited of
100 Avenue Road, London NW3 3PF.
(http://www.smlawpub.co.uk)
Phototypeset by MFK Information Services Ltd, Hitchin, Herts.
Printed and bound in Great Britain by Butler & Tanner,
Frome and London

No natural forests were destroyed to make this product;
only farmed timber was used and replanted

British Library Cataloguing in Publication Data

A CIP catalogue record for this book
is available from the British Library

ISBN 0-421-641-002

All rights reserved. UK statutory material in this publication is acknowl-
edged as Crown copyright.

No part of this publication may be reproduced or transmitted, in any form or
by any means, or stored in any retrieval system of any nature without prior
written permission, except for permitted fair dealing under the Copyright,
Designs and Patents Act 1988, or in accordance with the terms of a licence
issued by the Copyright Licensing Agency in respect of photocopying and/or
reprographic reproduction. Application for permission for other use of copyright material including permission to reproduce extracts in other published
works shall be made to the publishers. Full acknowledgment of author,
publisher and source must be given.

©
Legal Aid Board

Preface

I hope all users of the legal aid system will find the Board's *Legal Aid Handbook* helpful. While the *Handbook* came into being principally as a reference tool for practitioners using the system, I hope that its contents will also help individuals generally as well as those legal advisers who are not familiar with the various types of "legal aid" and the workings of the Legal Aid Board.

The starting point is obviously the statutory material and the *Handbook* includes not only the Legal Aid Act 1988 but all the Regulations made under it as well as the Arrangements which have been made by the Board, covering Duty Solicitors, Multi-Party Actions, Area Committees and the new Regional Legal Services Committees.

In addition to the statutory material, the *Handbook* contains the Board's Notes for Guidance which give a summary of the important decision making points and includes the Board's Standards on the Consistency of Decision Making in connection with the statutory charge. While legal aid is a statutory system the Act and Regulations contain many areas where the decision of the Area Director or the Area Committee is discretionary. The Board takes the view that guidance on the factors to be taken into account when exercising a discretion may help to minimise variations and it is concerned that discretionary decisions should be both justifiable and consistent.

Finally, the *Handbook* includes a detailed reference section which gives practical information on eligibility and remuneration, as well as information on the Board's Customer Service Standards and reproduces checklists regarding the completion of the Board's principal application and costs claim forms.

The Board holds corporate accreditation to what is now ISO 9002 and all its staff are working to a documented quality management system. The *Handbook* with its Notes for Guidance complements our internal systems in promoting consistency and improvement.

The Lord Chancellor's announcements about his reform programme for legal aid focused our work on legal aid reform in 1997–98. The various pilot projects are now being managed within the context of his request to the Board to prepare an implementation plan to deliver all civil advice and assistance and family civil legal aid under contracts by the end of 1999. The Civil Non-Family Contracting Pilot involving solicitors' offices was successfully launched in the summer of 1997. The Not-for-Profit Sector Pilot has been expanded and the Family Mediation Pilot is moving into its second phase. A criminal contracting pilot, including police station work, both duty and own solicitor, court duty solicitor work and criminal green form work has also been launched. Documentation and guidance to help all those participating in the pilots is issued to supplement conventional legal aid guidance set out in this *Handbook*.

Significant progress has been made with the implementation of a new Corporate Information System. It represents a significant move towards the increased use of modern technology in the Board's area offices and has some outwardly visible implications for our users. In particular, we have introduced new forms to complement the system changes. Implementation has been phased in the area offices to minimise the effect of the transition on those who deal with us. We are continuing to keep practitioners informed of any changes through mail-shots and our Newsletter, *Focus*. Implementation will be complete by the end of 1998.

SIR TIM CHESSELLS, CHAIRMAN
LEGAL AID BOARD

NOTE
Unless stated otherwise, remuneration rates are those applicable for work done from April 1, 1996 onwards. Eligibility limits are those in force on April 6, 1998.

The law is stated as at September 1, 1998.

Changes/additions to the Notes for Guidance contained in Part One from the previous edition are marked with a downward line in the margin. In relation to legal advice and assistance, references to the "green form" have been reduced to reflect the fact that the application form is now white rather than green.

Contents

PART THREE

REFERENCE MATERIAL

Table of Cases

Table of Points of Principle of General Importance

ABWOR

CIVIL

CRIMINAL

Part One

Part One

Notes for Guidance

---

1. INTRODUCTION TO LEGAL AID AND NOTES FOR GUIDANCE ISSUED BY THE LEGAL AID BOARD

WHAT IS LEGAL AID?

Legal aid is a system of Government funding for those who cannot afford to pay for legal advice, assistance, mediation and representation.

THE DIFFERENT KINDS OF LEGAL AID

(a) Legal Advice and Assistance (also known as the green form scheme). This covers advice and help with any legal problems (see NFG 2, para. 2–01) and, in some cases, under Assistance by Way of Representation (ABWOR) (see NFG 3, paras 3–01 to 3–31).

(b) Civil Legal Aid. This covers representation in court proceedings including assistance in the steps preliminary or incidental to proceedings (see NFGs 4 to 17, paras 4–01 to 17–07).

(c) Criminal Legal Aid for criminal offences (see NFG 18, paras 18–01 to 18–96).

(d) In addition, duty solicitors are available at most magistrates' courts and police stations and offer free legal advice (see Duty Solicitor Arrangements, p. 601).

(e) A court may grant non means tested representation for some contempt proceedings (see NFG 19, paras 19–01 to 19–02).

(f) Mediation. In family cases the Legal Aid Board may enter into contracts for the provision of mediation (see NFG 1–12).

HOW LEGAL AID IS ADMINISTERED IN ENGLAND AND WALES

The Legal Aid Board administers legal advice and assistance (including ABWOR) and legal aid for civil proceedings under the general guidance of the Lord Chancellor. Its Customer Service Standards are reproduced at p. 691. The Board is based in London and a list of Board members appears on p. 744. Legal Aid Head Office, which is also based in London, consists of the Chief Executive, the Secretariat—which services the Board—and the Legal Department as well as the Finance and Information Systems Departments. For administrative purposes, England and Wales are divided into a number of areas. Each area has a legal aid area office, run by an Area Manager, and an area committee made up of practising solicitors and barristers. The Board has implemented a new computerised administration system called the Corporate Information System (CIS). The text of the Board's introductory leaflet about CIS is reproduced at p. 700.

The area office decides on applications for civil legal aid (see NFG 4). The area office can either grant or refuse legal aid. The area committee deals with appeals against refusals of legal aid by the area office. Area offices are also responsible for legal advice and assistance (see NFG 2, paras. 2–01 to 2–70).

Complaints by individuals or solicitors (*e.g.* regarding delay) should be addressed to the area office. The name of the assisted person and the area office reference should be clearly stated at the top of any written complaint which should be boldly marked "Complaint" and addressed to the Customer Services Manager (see also the Board's leaflet to help clients who wish to complain, reproduced at p. 695). Complaints will be fully investigated and any appropriate action taken. The Board's published Customer Service Standards (see p. 691) include a commitment to address complaints promptly and efficiently. If a complaint is made an explanation will be given and, if the Board is at fault, an apology and information also given on what has been done to put things right.

Representations against the grant/continuation of civil legal aid should be made to the area office concerned. They may be on means and/or merits grounds. The name of the assisted person and the area office reference, if known should be clearly stated at the top of any letter which should also be boldly marked "Representations" (see NFG 13, para. 13–05).

The administration of criminal legal aid is the responsibility of the Lord Chancellor (see NFG 18, paras 18–01 to 18–96), although the Board's area offices assess claims for payment for magistrates' court work and deal with some aspects of criminal legal aid.

1–04 | FRANCHISING

The Board's objectives for the franchise scheme are fundamentally the same now as when the initiative was launched in 1994. The Board wishes to work in partnership with the suppliers of legal services to provide an accessible and quality assured service to clients, while at the same time delivering improving value for money to the taxpayer.

There are four essential elements to the scheme:

- the specification of standards of quality assurance that the Board would expect suppliers to meet;
- audits by the Board to ensure that standards are being achieved and maintained;
- continuous improvement in the service offered by suppliers of legal services to their clients and reduction of their administration costs;
- the control of case costs.

The detailed requirements of the scheme can be found in the Board's publication, *Franchising Specification* (second ed., March 1995) which is available from any of the Board's 13 area offices, free of charge. The third edition, to be renamed the *Legal Aid Franchising Quality Assurance Standard*, due for implementation in July 1999, will be published in late 1998.

A franchise contract can be issued for the following categories of legal aid work:

- Matrimonial/Family
- Employment
- Debt
- Consumer and General Contract
- Housing
- Immigration and Nationality
- Welfare Benefits
- Crime
- Mental Health
- Personal Injury.

A Medical Negligence category is being developed to meet the needs of proposed legal aid reforms. This will be an exclusive area of work in which only those holding a medical negligence franchise will be eligible to carry out legal aid work.

It is likely that further new categories will evolve.

1–05

WHO CAN APPLY

Any solicitors' firm may apply (to their local legal aid area office) for a franchise, as can any law centre or independent advice agency employing a solicitor with a current practising certificate and complying with the Solicitors' Practice Rules and other principles of conduct. In addition there is a limited research pilot which has allowed for an extension of block funding to not-for-profit agencies meeting the Board's contracting criteria and franchise requirements.

1–06

THE MAIN ELEMENTS OF FRANCHISING

The franchise scheme enables the Board to seek assurance that the main elements in the delivery of legal services, such as practice management, individual case management, cost control/financial management and client care will be effectively measured and controlled. The criteria in the *Franchising Specification* are designed to ensure that franchised organisations are able to meet the objectives of the scheme which are stated at para. 1–04 above.

The Board is continuing its research on outcome measures and other audit tools which will, when used in conjunction with transaction criteria, be applied to franchised organisations.

1–07

MANAGEMENT REQUIREMENTS

The first of these requirements is embodied in the management requirements outlined in Section 3 of *Franchising Specification*. This sets out the mandatory requirements for a franchise, covering the systems and controls the Board expects to be in place in a quality assured legal services practice. The Board does not want to control the detail of the management systems adopted, but it does need to be satisfied that systems embodying general principles of good management are in place and operating effectively. The management requirements in the specification include references, where appropriate, to the relevant Law Society Practice Management Standard; explanatory notes are also provided to give helpful background information and to give general or specific guidance on how requirements might or must be met, as appropriate.

The major elements on which the Board requires assurance, and for which mandatory requirements apply, are:

(a) *Strategic management*. In the current economic environment, business planning is essential. For franchisees, this means having a written outline strategy to provide background against which the organisation can assess its own performance and make decisions about the future. It also means having a written services plan which covers the various elements of service provision, including services to be offered and methods of provision, clients to be served, and the organisation's approach to marketing. The Board does not assess the content or feasibility of such plans, but seeks merely to ensure that they exist and are regularly reviewed.

(b) *Financial management*. The Board sets requirements to assure itself that there are proper financial controls in place within a practice. These include detailed requirements to demonstrate that the organisation has the management and financial information necessary to monitor income, expenditure and cost, and for forward planning. Organisations must also be able to show who exercises responsibility for financial affairs, and must have systems in place to ensure that time spent on casework can be accurately recorded and attributed and that they can provide a running record of costs incurred for each legal aid case. All of these requirements can be met by manual systems, although computerisation may assist the firm. It is not a requirement that the Board examines a firm's accounts, as an accountant's certificate confirming that all the requirements are in place will be accepted.

(c) *Personnel management*. Here the Board is looking to ensure that firms think about the skills, knowledge and experience required of all staff. The delivery of legal services is a knowledge-based, interpersonal process, and the skills and performance of all staff involved directly or indirectly in delivering the service are crucial factors. The requirements which cover this area of work include the need for documented procedures to record and monitor recruitment, induction, training and appraisal, as well as responsibilities and objectives of all personnel. There are also requirements for organisations to demonstrate practice in accordance with the relevant legislation covering equal opportunities and non-discrimination.

There is also a need for franchisees to manage day-to-day supervision and file review, as a way of assuring themselves about the quality of work being done by their staff. Requirements set out to achieve this cover the qualifying criteria for supervisors as well as procedures for ensuring that supervision and file review is carried out effectively. In addition to day-to-day supervision, which includes arrangements for incoming and outgoing post, case management and reviewing the exercise of devolved powers, there needs to be a procedure for the reg-

ular review of files. File reviews need to cover both procedural and
substantive issues, and a central record must be kept.

(d) *File and case management.* Day-to-day file management is fundamental to the delivery of legal services, and the requirements outlined in the specification are designed to ensure that these are handled
in the most effective and efficient manner. For instance, the requirements include procedures to maintain orderly files, to be able to trace
documents and correspondence and to monitor actions which need to
be followed-up. If a file is kept in an orderly way with key information
shown clearly, then anyone who picks it up can see what stages have
been reached. Equally, if key dates are recorded and monitored, then
the organisation is taking steps to guard against potentially costly
mistakes. This aspect of the specification also covers requirements
such as procedures to identify legal aid cases and their status, to check
for conflicts of interest, to manage linked cases, to authorise and
monitor undertakings, and to record details about the exercise of
devolved powers.

The specification also seeks to assure the quality of case management, setting out detailed requirements for managing various
elements at the outset, during the progress, and at the end of a case.
For example, the Board requires firms to confirm certain information
to the client, including the instructions received, advice given, action
to be taken, who will have responsibility, an estimate of the likely
total cost of the case, and the possible effect of the solicitor's or statutory charge. Throughout the case, clients must also be kept informed
of progress, as well as costs incurred to date, and the validity of the
original estimate, or a revised estimate if appropriate. Finally, there
must be procedures in place to ensure that at the end of the case, it is
effectively closed, original documents are returned, and the matter is
concluded.

(e) *Supplier management.* As the Board seeks, through the franchising
initiative, to assure itself about the quality of suppliers providing
legal aid, so franchisees need to be aware of the services being provided to them by others. Franchisees need to have a documented procedure for using outside suppliers, such as counsel, agents, experts,
etc. This includes the use of selection criteria, defined by the firm,
together with requirements covering instructions, payment and
appraisal of suppliers, as well as a requirement to consult with and
advise the client about the selection of a supplier where appropriate.

(f) *Client care.* This covers compliance with Solicitors Practice Rule 15
or any equivalent complaints procedure specified, *e.g.* by NACAB,
and seeks to ensure that organisations both have a complaints procedure, and use it to improve the service they provide. The requirements include arrangements to record and respond appropriately to
complaints, to identify the causes of complaint and to take corrective
action where necessary.

(g) *Welfare benefits.* Even where an organisation does not hold or apply
for a franchise in the welfare benefits category, the Board requires that
it must have at least one employee suitably qualified to recognise the
need for welfare benefits advice, and to train all other legal aid case-

workers to be able to recognise the need for welfare benefits advice and refer clients to an appropriate source of advice.

1–08 TRANSACTION CRITERIA

Transaction criteria are now a well-established means of assessing the extent to which legal aid files demonstrate that the basic issues essential to the provision of a competent service have been addressed by franchisees. The Board uses transaction criteria to verify that appropriate information has been gathered, advice given and steps taken in a sample of files relevant to the franchise category. While they are based on best practice seen on existing case files and developed with input from the profession, transaction criteria are an audit tool for the Board which practitioners are not expected to adopt as file checklists or follow in every case. Meeting the requirements of transaction criteria should not add to the work that franchisees have to do. Most practitioners accept that transaction criteria are an accurate indicator of good quality work.

Criteria have been introduced and subsequently revised for every category of work with the exception of family and matrimonial, which will be revised in late 1998.

While maintaining the underlying principles given above, the Board has developed, revised and updated transaction criteria since their introduction and it is proposed that this process will be continuous.

The Board is developing additional uses for the transaction criteria, by identifying the case issues or questions that are fundamental to the effective handling of the case and then using them as audit performance indicators, to improve the value of the file audit.

Copies of the transaction criteria may be obtained from the Board's area offices.

1–09 MONITORING

The final element is monitoring, which covers the work submitted by firms to the Board's area office. This assessment allows the Board, at the same time as awarding a franchise contract, to devolve some of its powers to firms. Devolved powers currently include the ability to extend green forms, issue and amend emergency certificates, proceed to grant ABWOR, and amend civil certificates in specific circumstances. During the franchising process, the Board provides organisations with guidance in the exercise of devolved powers and works with firms to ensure that the applications it submits are correct, and if not, to identify ways in which they can be improved. This helps to improve the efficiency of both the firm and the Board, as well as helping to improve the service to clients. Monitoring is ongoing throughout the duration of the franchise contract and is explained in detail in the *Franchising Specification*.

1–10 HOW TO APPLY FOR A FRANCHISE

The first step to obtaining a franchise is to request a copy of *Franchising Speci-*

fication from the area office, and to become familiar with the requirements and guidance that are set out.

Prospective applicants should be aware that the Franchising Specification is due to be replaced by the Legal Aid Quality Assurance Franchise Specification in 1999 and that copies will be available from late 1998. The procedures explained below relate to applications processed within the current (Franchising Specification) requirements.

Starting the formal process towards obtaining a franchise simply requires a completed application form (for each office to be franchised) to be submitted to the area office; however, to help organisations assess their readiness to apply, the Board has developed a "self assessment checklist", which must be completed and sent, together with supporting documentation, with the application form. Once the application is accepted by the Board, it is assessed against the self assessment checklist and supporting documentation. If the Board is satisfied that the application should proceed, it is allocated to a trained Liaison Manager who will play a key role in progressing the application from this stage. The initial phase starts with a visit by the Liaison Manager to the applicant's office to carry out a preliminary audit. Providing the Liaison Manager if satisfied at that stage, there is then an interim period, usually of four to six months, for the monitoring process to be undertaken. This period also helps a firm build up objective evidence that its systems and procedures are working effectively. At the end of this period, the Liaison Manager and a small team of auditors (usually two) will carry out a pre-contract audit against both management criteria and the transaction criteria. Depending upon the number of categories applied for, this usually takes two days. The results of these audits are discussed with the firm, and then reviewed by the Liaison Manager, who recommends to the Area Manager, whether or not a franchise should be granted (this may be for all or some of the categories applied for) and whether or not certain powers should be devolved. Detailed guidance covering the application, monitoring, audit processes and appeal procedures is contained in Sections 4 to 7 of *Franchise Specification*.

Separate detailed notes for guidance, including guidance on the exercise of devolved powers, have been prepared, and are issued to all organisations on successful completion of the preliminary audit. The aim of this is to provide all the information necessary to enable franchisees to exercise devolved powers in the same way that the Board currently exercises its statutory powers. Guidance on making claims for costs under a franchise are also included, covering the financial incentives and arrangements for franchisees.

Once the contract documentation is complete, the firm can use and display the franchise logo. It can be used in both advertising and letterheads. In addition, the Board also provides a certificate for display at the office. During the life of the contract, the Board will carry out regular audits, usually annually, in a similar format as the pre-contract audit.

LEGAL AID REFORM   1–11

This *Handbook* is essentially concerned with the legal aid scheme in its present form, rather than any future reforms of the system or the Woolf reforms, due to be implemented in April 1999, which may necessitate changes to the Board's guidance and/or processes. However, the Board has already set up a number of pilot schemes and initiatives, based on the foundation of the quality assurance provided by legal aid franchising, which will affect a growing number of practitioners over the next year, as well as having an important influence on the future development of the legal aid scheme.

In October 1997 the Lord Chancellor announced Government support for moves to a fully contracted legal aid scheme, together with proposed changes in the scope of the scheme and the merits test. At the time of writing we await decisions on scope and merits changes but explain below our approach to developments in contracting through the various pilot schemes we are already running, and our proposals for introducing exclusive contracts in the civil sphere.

1–12 | **Family Mediation: the pilot, availability and funding**

Part III of the Family Law Act 1996 enables the Board to secure, through franchise contracts, provision of family mediation services for clients eligible for legal aid throughout England and Wales. The Act does not create a general entitlement to mediation.

Initially the availability of legally assisted mediation (*i.e.* under the Legal Aid Act) will be limited as the Board tests out the contracting arrangements by way of pilot schemes in limited areas of the country before expanding the pilots to develop eventually into a national network of quality assured mediators working under the legal aid arrangements. Initial contracts were let in Birmingham, Bristol, Bromley, Cambridge, Cardiff, Coventry, Durham, London (certain locations), Manchester, Newcastle upon Tyne, Northampton and Peterborough in June 1997 to 33 mediation suppliers. The pilot is now being extended and approximately a further 70 services are under contract. Details of the Board's approach to the pilot are set out in *Franchising Family Mediation Services,* available from The Family Mediation Project, Legal Aid Head Office, 85 Gray's Inn Road, London WC1X 8AA.

The rules on eligibility for legally assisted mediation are contained in the Legal Aid (Mediation in Family Matters) Regulations 1997. Eligibility levels are set at the upper income and capital limits for ABWOR, but no contribution or statutory charge applies at this stage. As well as dealing with financial eligibility, section 13B(3) Legal Aid Act 1998 provides that a person may not be granted mediation in relation to any dispute unless mediation appears to the mediator suitable to the dispute and the parties and all the circumstances. This assessment of suitability is known as the "intake" assessment and takes place prior to substantive mediation.

Section 29 Family Law Act 1996 introduced amendments to section 15 Legal Aid Act to the effect that, subject to important prescribed exceptions, civil legal aid will not be available for family matters (as defined) until an applicant has attended a mediator for assessment. The regulations contain an exception that legal aid need not be refused if there is no "recognised" mediator available to the applicant (see Civil Legal Aid (General) Regulations 1989, reg. 26A). In the Phase I areas listed above, there are 150 mediators recognised for the purposes of this regulation. A further 400 mediators across other geographical areas will be recognised by December 1998. For a full list of areas please contact the Family Mediation Project.

Section 29 is currently being piloted in the following areas: Bristol, Northamptonshire, Birmingham, Coventry, Greater Manchester, Cambridge and Peterborough.

Further progressive implementation will take place by April 1999 in those parts of the country where legally assisted mediation (*i.e.* under the Legal Aid Act 1998) is available. The Board will notify all firms affected once there is a "recognised" mediator in their area and section 29 is implemented.

Contracts have also been let to solicitors in the section 29 pilot areas to provide legal services to support the mediation process (*i.e.* where the client qualifies for mediation but is outside the financial eligibility limits for advice and assistance) and these will be extended as the pilot progresses.

The pilot and the Family Law Act 1996 do not affect the general position in relation to mediation, ADR and conciliation themselves, which is that civil legal aid, ABWOR and advice and assistance are not available (save that the Board will, under legal advice and assistance, meet a fixed fee for a report from a recognised conciliation service following referral by a solicitor (see p. 690).

Exclusive contracting for civil advice and assistance and family civil legal aid   **1–13**

In response to an invitation from the Lord Chancellor the Board published a consultation paper in April 1998 containing proposals aimed at delivering all civil advice and assistance under contracts with franchised suppliers by the end of 1999. The Board proposed that the initial contracts in the exclusive scheme should be based on payments for time up to a maximum amount. The proposal is for contracts to be let exclusively to franchised firms and firms which have passed a preliminary audit, based on recommendations for priorities identified by the Regional Legal Services Committees. In the longer term, the block contracting pilots (see below) are designed to determine how best to move away from payment for time to payment at fixed prices for units of work. The Lord Chancellor has since determined that contracts which are exclusive to franchised firms should be extended to all family certificated work in the same timescale.

Advice from the not-for-profit sector   **1–14**

Although legal aid is primarily delivered by lawyers, the Board has power under Part II of the Act to provide advice, assistance and representation by means of grants, loans or contracts with non-lawyers. In 1994 the Board began a pilot project with 42 non-solicitor advice agencies. The agencies reached full compliance with the franchise requirements at the end of the initial pilot year. The Board has since expanded the scheme as part of its block contracting pilots to include further contracts for agencies in the not-for-profit sector, including law centres and other solicitor agencies. Under these arrangements organisations which can meet the contract and franchise requirements by the end of an initial 12-month pre-franchise contract qualify for longer-term contracts. By the summer of 1998 more than 130 contracts had been signed based on the cost of the caseworker time that a caseworker provides annually. Work

11

carried out under these contracts is being studied as part of the research being carried out by the Institute of Advanced Legal Studies (IALS).

1–15 | **Contracts with solicitors for civil advice and assistance**

The Board has also established block contracting pilots in four area offices looking at the delivery of civil non-family advice and assistance under contract with franchised solicitors in private practice. Firms taking part in the pilot receive payment under the contract instead of payment assessed on individual green forms. Contracts were signed with 100 solicitors' offices in the pilot aimed at establishing the most effective way of introducing block contracting for this work. The initial two-year contracts began in August and September 1997. The contracts are divided into different research groups aimed at exploring the effect of different payment arrangements. Some contracts are based on payment for work done at an hourly rate, others pay a fixed sum, while others are for a specified number of cases. The IALS research project (see above) is also studying these contracts. The Board expects to publish reports on this research in 1999.

1–16 | **Contracts for criminal advice and assistance and duty solicitor work**

The Board has commenced a pilot for the delivery of what is presently covered under criminal advice and assistance, as well as court and police station duty and own solicitor work through contracts with criminal franchisees. The pilot has commenced in six areas with two-year contracts being let to 68 franchisees during June 1998. The contract includes additional quality requirements in order to enhance the services offered. This pilot is the subject of research by a team at Warwick University.

In October 1998 the Board will be extending the contracts for criminal advice and assistance to cover representation in the youth courts. The Board will consult with the firms in the pilot areas and expects to enter into youth contracts by January 1999. This work will also be evaluated by the research team at Warwick University.

The Home Office and the Lord Chancellor's Department are also piloting requirements set out in the Crime and Disorder Act 1998 aimed at reducing delays at court. These include the introduction of two new hearings, 'Early First Hearings' and 'Early Administrative Hearings', which will deal with cases bailed to the next available court day which could be as soon as the day following charge. Duty solicitors will be remunerated for representing clients at the new hearings. An evaluation of the pilot will be conducted by Home Office appointed researchers Ernst & Young and this will include interviews with defence solicitors which will help to inform national implementation.

1–17 | **Multi-party actions and high-cost civil cases**

The Lord Chancellor has asked the Board to implement the main recommendations in the Board's report "When the Price is High", published in June 1997. This report proposed reform of the Board's contracting arrangements for multi-party actions, including the introduction of price tendering and control of costs through price ceilings and hourly rates fixed by the contract. Contracts may also be awarded to any firm with an interest in the action, whether or not they have legally-aided clients. The Board will also establish a panel of firms with expertise in group litigation to whom preference will be given in awarding contracts. Contracts may also be awarded to any firm with an interest in the action, whether or not they have legally-aided clients. The Board will be implementing these proposals in 1999 and will be considering the role of contracting in very high cost individual civil claims. Copies of "When the Price is High" may be obtained from the Legal Aid Board Secretariat at 85 Gray's Inn Road, London, WC1X 8AA.

New Franchising Quality Assurance Standard   1–18

The current edition of the *Franchise Specification* was published in March 1995 and the third edition, to be renamed the *Legal Aid Franchising Quality Assurance Standard*, due for implementation in July 1999, will be published in late 1998. Its focus is on improving supervisor standards, making franchisees' internal file review procedures more rigorous, and requiring franchised suppliers to take a more robust approach to business planning, financial management and cost control, so as to provide an appropriate foundation for contracting.

Medical negligence   1–19

The Board in establishing a new medical negligence franchise with effect from January 31, 1999. The new franchise will include membership of either the Law Society accreditation or AVMA (Action for Victims of Medical Negligence) referral panels as a supervisor standard. New guidance and procedures on the application of the merits test will also be introduced. Advice, assistance and representation in new medical negligence cases will be restricted to holders of the medical negligence franchise (but firms with an existing personal injury franchise will be able to carry out medical negligence work for a period of six months after the medical negligence franchise is established, *i.e.* until July 31, 1999).

REGIONAL LEGAL SERVICES COMMITTEES (RLSCs)

Tasks and timetable for RLSCs   1–20

The Legal Aid Board has agreed Arrangements and Directions for the operation of RLSCs. These are reproduced in Part Two (pages 655 to 659).

The role of the 13 RLSCs (one for each of the Board's area offices) will be as advisory committees to provide an independent element in the Board's planning process.

The key tasks of the RLSCs will be to:

(a) assess the need for legal and related services;

(b) gather information on the supply of legal and related services;

(c) identify regional priorities according to geographical area, category of work and client group need for such services;

(d) develop a regional strategy for approval by the Board to meet, as far as possible within the available budget, the priorities and needs for legal aid services; and

(e) monitor implementation of the regional strategy approved by the Board.

In their first year of operation, RLSCs will focus on advice and assistance in order to support the move to exclusive contracting for the year 1999/2000. The RLSCs should now be consulting on the first draft regional strategies. Consultation will take place both in open conferences and in writing. The final version of the regional strategies will be completed and submitted to the Board in February 1999 for approval.

1–21 | **Constitution of RLSCs**

Each of the 13 Committees is headed by a Chair who is also a member of the Legal Aid Board, and is comprised of external members recruited from the wider community, including suppliers of legal services and those involved in the advice sector. The role of the external members in bringing experience and expertise to bear on the recommendations that the RLSCs will make is seen as crucial to the process. The Board's Area Managers also take part as ex officio members and support is provided in each area by a Regional Legal Services Adviser.

Practitioners and others with an interest in legal services who do not wish to apply to become external members of RLSCs can participate in the process by joining their local Network—an informal body which will be closely involved in the consultation process. Details of how to apply to become a RLSC member or of how to join the Network can be obtained from the Regional Legal Services Adviser at each area office.

1–22 **LEGAL AID IN SCOTLAND AND NORTHERN IRELAND**

There are similar legal aid schemes in Scotland and Northern Ireland. For information about legal aid in Scotland, contact The Scottish Legal Aid Board, 44 Drumsheugh Gardens, Edinburgh EH3 7SW (tel: 0131–226 7061, fax: 0131–220 4879).

For information about legal aid in Northern Ireland, contact the Incorporated Law Society of Northern Ireland, Legal Aid Department, Bedford House, 16–22 Bedford Street, Belfast BT2 7FL (tel: 01232–246441, fax: 01232–332548).

1–23 **LEGAL AID ABROAD**

Many foreign countries have legal aid schemes but some are not as comprehensive as the system in England and Wales. Limited information about legal aid abroad is available from the Policy and Legal Department, Legal Aid Head

Office, 85 Gray's Inn Road, London WC1X 8AA (tel: 0171–813 1000), (see also Note for Guidance 20, p. 268), although more detailed information may be available from the United Kingdom representative (*i.e.* embassy, consulate) of the country concerned.

LEGAL AID LEAFLETS AND OTHER INFORMATION   1–24

A series of leaflets is produced about legal aid. "How to Get Free or Low Cost Legal Help" gives a general explanation in jargon free English. "A Practical Guide to Legal Aid" is a more detailed explanation of the schemes and supplies full details of financial eligibility. In addition, the Board publishes a criminal legal aid leaflet entitled "Criminal Legal Aid at the Police Station and in the Court". There are also leaflets regarding the statutory charge, customer service (see pp. 698 and 695 respectively) and representations, as well as about franchising. A new booklet, "MEANS 1 – The Guide", has been produced to assist in the completion of the civil legal and financial application form MEANS 1. A copy should be handed to all clients whenever a MEANS 1 form is to be completed. Supplies are available from the Board's area offices. The Board also issues specific information leaflets to applicants/assisted persons at key stages in the civil legal aid process.

Other publications by the Board include "Guidance: Exercise of Devolved Powers" ("GEDP") issued to franchisees and subscribers and *Legal Aid Focus*—a newsletter for legal aid practitioners. *Focus* is sent automatically to all legal aid account holders. It is important to circulate *Focus* to all staff who do legal aid work as it contains important guidance material and legal updates. The Board also publishes an Annual Report in June detailing the organisation's performance on bill payment and decision times on civil legal aid applications.

The Solicitors Regional Directory is published in eight volumes (North West, North East, Midlands, Eastern, South East, South West, Wales, Greater London) by the Law Society and lists all local solicitors firms, giving details of categories of work they do, opening hours and languages spoken. Copies of the Directory are available in the majority of libraries, town halls and most advice centres. Further information and copies are available from the Directories Section, The Law Society, Ipsley Court, Berrington Close, Redditch, Worcestershire B98 0TD (tel: 0171–242 1222 ext. 3091). The Directories list solicitors who offer a free or fixed fee interview as well as indicating whether they undertake legal aid work.

The Law Society also accredits solicitors for family law proceedings, Mental Health Review Tribunal cases, proceedings involving personal injury and medical negligence claims and the representation of children; for information contact Regulatory and Information Services, The Law Society, Ipsley Court, Berrington Close, Redditch, Worcester B98 8TD (tel: 01527 504448 for family law proceedings (from January 1999), mental health, children panel and medical negligence claims) and The Accident Line (tel: 0500 192939) for personal injury.

THE PURPOSE OF THE NOTES FOR GUIDANCE   1–25

One of the aims of the Legal Aid Board is to produce a consistent quality of decision-making throughout the legal aid offices. The Act and Regulations contain many cases where the decision of the area office or area committee is discretionary. It is in these cases particularly that variations creep in.

While the exercise of discretion is always a judgment for the person concerned, so that there is always likely to be a variation between individuals, the Board takes the view that guidance on the questions and factors to be considered when exercising a discretion may help to minimise variations. Such guidance appears in these Notes for Guidance and the "Guidance: Exercise of Devolved Powers". Standards to be applied when considering the statutory charge have also been issued to the area offices and are included in these Notes for Guidance.

These and other standards, to help ensure consistency of decision-making, form part of the Board's ISO 9002 quality procedures. The Legal Aid Board achieved corporate accreditation in late 1993.

1–26   THE JUSTIFIABILITY OF DECISION-MAKING

It is particularly important in legal aid that discretionary decisions are justifiable. Legal aid serves a number of masters, who may have conflicting interests. These have been defined as "stakeholders", each of whom has to be borne in mind when a decision is made. The stakeholders are the applicants for legal aid and those granted legal aid, the Government (as represented by the Lord Chancellor and his Department), the suppliers of legal aid, the judicial system and the opponents, or potential opponents, of legally aided individuals. The interests of these stakeholders differ—and sometimes compete—and the relationships and contact that the Board has with them also differ. The Board recognises these differing relationships and interests and, in its dealings with its stakeholders, seeks to ensure that its decisions are consistent and justifiable to all of them. What is the right decision for the applicant may not be the right decision for the court or taxpayer if legal aid is granted when it should not be; what may be the right decision for the taxpayer may not be right for the applicant if legal aid is refused when it should be granted. What is necessary is that the decision can be justified to the stakeholders in any particular case. The standards on the consistency of decision-making which are included in the Notes for Guidance (see NFG 16, para. 16–17) address justifiability.

1–27   ADVANTAGES OF OPENNESS

The Legal Aid Board is convinced that the more is known about the grounds on which a decision is reached, the greater the chance that the decision will be justifiable to, and understood by, the various stakeholders. In addition, there will be more understanding about the information which it is necessary for area offices and franchisees to have in order to reach correct decisions.

1–28   THE FORMAT OF THE NOTES FOR GUIDANCE

The general principles are set out in the Legal Aid Act 1988 (see p. 277).

16

Detailed procedures are contained in various sets of regulations made by the Lord Chancellor. Each type of legal aid has different sets of regulations: advice and assistance, assistance by way of representation (ABWOR), civil legal aid and criminal legal aid. There are also different regulations governing financial eligibility for each type of legal aid.

The format of these Notes for Guidance highlights the most common points of decision-making as they affect the profession and the public and indicates what matters are taken into account when decisions are made. The Notes also include the standards on the consistency of decision making which have been issued to the Board's area offices. The Notes are not intended to be a substitute for the Act or the Regulations which must always be the first points of reference when seeking information about the system.

INVESTIGATION AND FRAUD CONTROL   1–29

The Board's Investigations Section and Area Office Investigation Liaison Officers work together to identify claims which cause concern and to investigate whether impropriety is involved.

Where the Board has evidence of impropriety in relation to legal aid claims its primary duty is to protect public funds. During the period of any enquiry into potential abuse the Board must ensure that its potential losses are identified and steps taken to recover them, in addition to ensuring that future claims are bona fide. The temporary stopping of a firm's account (known as a vendor hold) whether in whole or in part may be necessary to protect the fund in those circumstances. It is inconceivable to envisage that the Board would knowingly allow payments to be made for what are believed to be potentially fraudulent claims simply because the investigations have not concluded or the matter has not proceeded to court.

Given the drastic effect of such a measure on a firm's business the decision is taken by the Chief Executive and reviewed regularly. It is a temporary measure to protect the Board's position pending an investigation and possible resolution of the issues. All efforts are made to determine the Board's loss and resolve the matter expeditiously.

Where there is evidence of wrongful claiming and a likely claim for fraud or restitution, the Board considers it has the power to impose a vendor hold as a temporary measure, to reopen old paid claims and to recoup quantified sums by way of set off against sums due to the firm concerned in respect of other cases.

This approach was accepted by the Divisional Court in *R. v. Legal Aid Board, ex p. Rafina* (February 12, 1998, *New Law Journal* February 27, 1998—see also NFG 2, para. 2–51).

2. LEGAL ADVICE AND ASSISTANCE (THE GREEN FORM SCHEME)

WHAT DOES LEGAL ADVICE AND ASSISTANCE COVER?   2–01

Giving general advice, writing letters, negotiating, obtaining counsel's opinion and preparing a written case to go before a tribunal. It extends to all assistance short of actual representation (*i.e.* advocacy) (see *R. v. Legal Aid Board ex. p. Higgins*, unreported, QBD, October 15, 1993). It can cover most legal problems concerning English law such as divorce or maintenance and, in certain circumstances, the making of a will.

It enables people who are financially eligible to get help from a solicitor, subject to the operation of the solicitor's charge in respect of his/her costs, until the solicitor's charges reach a total of two hours' worth of work, or three hours' worth of work in matrimonial cases involving the preparation of a petition. Solicitors cannot claim more without the authority of the area office unless they exercise their devolved powers under a franchise.

If a client may need to go to court in civil proceedings it will usually be necessary to apply for civil legal aid (see NFGs 4 to 16) or ABWOR (see NFG 3, paras. 3–01 to 3–31). If the client has to go to court in a criminal case, it will usually be necessary to apply for criminal legal aid (see NFG 18, paras. 18–01 to 18–96).

Legal advice and assistance is available in England and Wales and applies only to questions of English law. It does not cover the law of Scotland or Northern Ireland, nor that of any other country.

2–02 HOW TO APPLY FOR LEGAL ADVICE AND ASSISTANCE

Generally clients should call at a solicitor's office—the application form (previously known as the green form) can only be sent by post by franchise solicitors or, with area office authority, by other solicitors to clients resident outside England and Wales (see para. 2–11, below). If clients live too far away or cannot travel, they should ask someone to call at the solicitor's office for them (see para. 2–12, below)—or the solicitor may be able to visit them (see also para. 2–07 below regarding distant solicitors). The solicitor will ask about the client's capital and income and whether the client has had previous advice and assistance. The relevant financial information must be provided at the same time as the completion, including signing and dating, of the form (see para. 2–08 below). He/she should then fill in the application form. Using the key card (which is re-issued when financial eligibility is changed) the solicitor will be able to tell clients whether they qualify on financial grounds. If the client wants the solicitor to advise, the client should sign the application form. Only at that stage can the solicitor start to give advice and assistance under the scheme—costs incurred prior to the assessment of means and the signature of the completed form will not be met out of the legal aid fund (this is subject only to a minor exception for franchisees). The solicitor cannot collect any administration fee, *e.g.* for opening a file. A solicitor can refuse to give legal advice and assistance. He/she need not give the client a reason but may be asked by the area office to explain the reason(s) for refusal.

2–03 CHILDREN

Children are eligible for legal advice and assistance. In most cases where a child under school-leaving age (at present 16) requires the help of a solicitor, a parent or guardian should apply on his/her behalf. A solicitor can, however, ask the legal aid area office for permission to advise a child direct in special circumstances and can even do so without authority in certain limited circumstances (see paras 2–08/15 and 2–09, below). Where a solicitor advises a child direct it is unlikely to be appropriate for the resources of any adult to be taken into account in assessing financial eligibility.

DOES THE CLIENT QUALIFY FINANCIALLY? (See also para. 2–08, below)   2–04

A client's disposable income and disposable capital must both be within the eligibility limits in force at the time the application form is signed (see Eligibility Tables, p. 667).

Provided both disposable income and disposable capital are within the limits no contribution can be called for. A client receiving income support, income-based Jobseeker's Allowance, family credit or disability working allowance or with an income of £80 or below per week will be eligible on income for free legal advice and assistance.

Note that there is no longer any system of contributions, except for assistance by way of representation (see NFG 3). Note also that for applications from June 1, 1996 the treatment of a client's home, which previously was wholly exempt for eligibility purposes, was amended so that:

(a) the capital value of the property (that is market value less amount outstanding on any mortgage debt or charge) is taken into account in so far as it exceeds £100,000;

(b) the capital amount allowed in respect of a mortgage debt or charge over the property cannot exceed £100,000;

(c) there are provisions for second and subsequent dwellings which provide that the total amount of mortgage debt to be allowed for all the client's dwellings cannot exceed £100,000.

This means that for capital assessment, the value of an assisted person's home is reduced by the amount of the mortgage or by £100,000, whichever is the less, to produce a net equity figure. If this net equity figure exceeds £100,000, the excess over £100,000 is taken into account as capital for assessment purposes.

If either disposable income or disposable capital is above the limit, the client will not be eligible for legal advice and assistance.

WHAT HAPPENS IF MONEY OR PROPERTY IS RECOVERED OR PRESERVED AND HOW DOES THE SOLICITOR GET PAID?   2–05

Where money or property is recovered or preserved under legal advice and assistance, the solicitor must use this to pay his/her bill (subject to para. 2–34 below). The solicitor's bill, less the value of any property which has been recovered or preserved, will be considered for payment by the area office where there is a deficiency. There is no system of payments on account of the solicitor's costs/disbursements prior to the submission of any costs claim for payment once the advice and assistance has been completed. The solicitor must take reasonable steps to protect his/her charge because where there is a recovery or preservation there will be no, or a reduced, deficiency for payment

19

out of the legal aid fund. This means that where the charge is lost the solicitor will bear that loss.

2–06 STATUTORY FRAMEWORK AND CONDITIONS

The statutory framework for advice and assistance is contained in Parts I and III, sections 1, 2 and 8–13 of the Legal Aid Act 1988 (see p. 277).

Details of the system are set out in the Legal Advice and Assistance (Scope) Regulations 1989 (p. 333); the Legal Advice and Assistance Regulations 1989 (p. 339); the Legal Advice and Assistance (Duty Solicitor) Remuneration Regulations 1990 (p. 590); and the Legal Advice and Assistance at Police Stations (Remuneration) Regulations 1989 (p. 594).

The general principle of Part III of the Legal Aid Act 1988 is that advice and assistance is available to any person whose financial resources make him/her eligible, subject to exclusions and conditions contained in regulations.

NOTE: *The regulations use the phrase "application for advice and assistance." This "application" is made by the client to the solicitor by signing the application form, which also includes the assessment of the client's means and the solicitor's claim for costs.*

SOLICITOR'S DECISIONS

2–07 Is advice and assistance available?

The rule is that where a solicitor has carried out work under the green form which does not require any additional authority from the area office, payment can be refused if the advice and assistance does not come within the basic requirements of the Legal Aid Act 1988 and the regulations. Before agreeing to give a client advice and assistance therefore the solicitor must ensure:

(a) *The matter is one of English law.* Advice or assistance may be given on matters relating to the application of English law, which are not excluded by regulation. Assisting in administrative steps (*e.g.* form filling) which have no legal element may not be remunerated. Advice cannot be given on matters of foreign law (including applications to the European Commission of Human Rights so long as that is not part of English law) but advice is available on the transmission of applications for legal aid to some other countries under the *European Agreement on the Transmission of Applications for Legal Aid*, Strasbourg, January 27, 1977 (see NFG 20).

(b) *The matter is not excluded from the scheme.* Matters excluded by the Legal Advice and Assistance (Scope) Regulations 1989 are:

(i) conveyancing services, except rental purchase agreements or conditional sale agreements for the sale of land and any conveyancing necessary to give effect to an order of court or the terms of a matrimonial agreement (see p. 334);

(ii) wills, except where the client is aged 70 or over, or suffers from a mental or physical handicap or illness, or is a parent or guardian in certain circumstances (for full details, see Legal Advice and Assistance (Scope) Regulations 1989, reg. 4, p. 334, and for further comment, see para. 2–29).

(c) *The matter does not constitute representation.* Advice and assistance is not available for representation (save under ABWOR). However, the solicitor can advise and assist a client who is a litigant in person. The most common example is in undefended matrimonial proceedings where the client is a litigant in person, advised and assisted by the solicitor with the client's address for service of documents being care of that solicitor. Another example is a client pursuing a claim in a tribunal where the solicitor can assist the client in the proceedings, *e.g.* by drafting documents and taking other steps short of representing the client at a hearing. Advice and assistance is not available for obtaining a grant of representation to an estate, since a grant is an order of the court for which application must be made to the court (but see para. 2–32 for advice and assistance leading to a grant). (See also para. 2–27 regarding advice and assistance from a McKenzie adviser.)

NOTE: *If advice and assistance relates to excluded matters or matters not involving the application of English law, payment will not be made out of the legal aid fund for the work done, even if the cost is within the prospective cost limit.*

The solicitor must also consider whether he has the necessary expertise or is prepared to accept the cost of acquiring it as an overhead, unless the use of counsel is justified (see para. 2–47).

Even where the solicitor would otherwise be prepared to accept the matter and provide advice and assistance he should consider the guidance given on distant solicitors which appeared in Focus 23 *(April 1998) and is reproduced from the "Guidance: Exercise of Devolved Powers" below. This is relevant to both the acceptance of instructions and costs assessment.*

"1.5 Distant Solicitors
1.5.1 Clients may be at a distance from the solicitor/adviser.

1.5.2 Special arrangements are available to franchisees (but not other practitioners) which make it administratively easier to accept an application for advice and assistance where issues of access can be demonstrated. These are postal applications, telephone advice and the payment of outward travel disbursements but not travelling time. General guidance on the use of these special arrangements is given at Section 1, General – Advice & Assistance – paragraph 9.2.

1.5.3 Franchisees considering using one of these arrangements, as well as other practitioners generally, should consider whether it is, in all the circumstances appropriate to accept instructions having regard to the service to be provided to the client and the costs of providing that service. Factors in favour of accepting instructions will include:

(a) any legitimate expectation of the client of specialist assistance *i.e.* by an adviser with appropriate expertise, particularly in an unusual subject area;

(b) the lack of availability (including, if necessary, at short notice) of that expertise in the client's geographical area;

(c) the nature, complexity and/or significance of the subject matter such as to justify the involvement of a distant solicitor;

(d) for franchisees only, the possibility of advising without the need for personal attendances; and

(e) significant previous knowledge/dealings with the client such as to justify renewed involvement even though the client is at a distance.

These factors need to be balanced against the distance between the client and solicitor/adviser in terms of accessibility for the client and increased costs of travel/travelling time. The greater the distance the greater the justification which will be required.

1.5.4 It is unlikely to be justified for a solicitor/adviser to travel to attend on a client at a significant distance from his office, involving say a one way travelling time of more than 2 hours, on the basis that it would be more appropriate for the matter to be dealt with by a solicitor/adviser local to the client. This will, however, depend on all the circumstances of the case. Even where a longer time could be apportioned between a number of clients on a particular occasion this will not justify a longer travelling time because it will not necessarily always be possible to apportion in the same way on all occasions.

1.5.5 Where a franchisee does consider a longer travelling time to be justified in a particular case (*e.g.* possibly where a client moves (or is moved) away but the franchisee's continued personal involvement is justified) an appropriate note should be made and retained on the file. Where the franchisee does not consider this to be justified he should consider what assistance he can provide in ensuring that the client is referred to an appropriate source of information regarding advisers with relevant expertise, who are more local to the client."

2–08   Is the client financially eligible? How are the means assessed?

The financial limits for eligibility for advice and assistance are fixed in regulations produced by the Lord Chancellor's Department. There are both income and capital limits which are different from those for assistance by way of representation (ABWOR) and legal aid. The assessment of means for advice and assistance is the responsibility of the solicitor who also collects any contribution due in respect of ABWOR (see para. 3–04). A key card, for use with the advice and assistance application form (and giving the up-to-date figures for allowances, etc.), is issued by the Legal Aid Board to legal aid practitioners.

Some cases are exempt from the requirement to assess the client's means:

(a) advice and assistance at police stations;

(b) advice and assistance or ABWOR given under the Court Duty Solicitor Scheme;

(c) ABWOR for applications for warrants of further detention; and

(d) ABWOR for representation in Mental Health Review Tribunal proceedings.

In all other cases, however, the solicitor has, as a first step, to determine the client's financial eligibility on information provided by the client. Except where a postal application is possible (see para. 2–11, below) or the client is represented by another person authorised by the client (see para. 2–12, below), the client has to make the application for advice and assistance in person, at which time the solicitor must carry out the assessment of means, *before* giving advice and assistance. This is a mandatory requirement under the Legal Advice and Assistance Regulations 1989. Where the capital or income details in the application form are not completed or are incomplete (which includes striking through or leaving boxes blank—see para. 2–67 below), then a claim for costs will be assessed at nil. The solicitor must also ask whether the client has received previous legal advice and assistance in the same matter and ensure the application form is fully completed in that respect (see para. 2–13 below).

Reasonable steps, for instance requesting sight of a pay slip, must be taken to verify the information about income and capital provided by the client. It is good practice for clients to have the importance of giving a full and fair picture emphasised to them when they are applying for advice and assistance.

Schedule 2 of the Legal Advice and Assistance Regulations 1989 sets out the detailed rules as to assessment of eligibility. Regard should be had to the following guidance in the application of those rules.

Aggregation of means   2–08/1

Schedule 2 contains a general rule that if a person is married or living with someone as husband and wife in the same household, then the income and capital of the partner must be taken into account and added to those of the client (paragraphs 2 and 6 of Schedule 2).

However, there are important exceptions to this rule and means are not aggregated in the following circumstances:

(a) Where the partner has a contrary interest in the matter in respect of which the client is seeking advice and assistance.

Contrary interest in the most obvious sense will mean that the partner is the opponent or potential opponent in proceedings. However, this will not necessarily be the case—the client and their partner could in theory have a contrary interest in a claim made by a third party, such as in the case of a mortgagee seeking possession where undue influence by the partner may be a defence.

In disputes between divorcing or separating couples, whether as to children or property, one partner will by definition have a contrary interest to the other. However, if an applicant has left his or her spouse and has gone to live with a new partner as husband and wife in the same household, then the means of the new partner should be aggregated with those of the applicant.

(b) The client and their partner are living separate and apart.

In general, this refers to physical separation, *i.e.* the parties are living in separate properties. However, this may not always be the case. It is possible for former partners to live separate and apart in the same household. This would be the case if they regarded their relationship as at an end and no longer pooled their financial resources.

An example of this would be where a couple have decided to part and have separated their finances and are now simply waiting for the property to be sold before going their separate ways. Further, even if they are physically separated, *i.e.* they live in separate properties, this does not necessarily mean that they are living separate and apart for the purpose of the regulations. The fact that both terms are used (*i.e.* "separate" and "apart") means that more than mere physical separation is required if the partners' means are not to be aggregated. Living separate and apart is well defined in the context of matrimonial law and refers to a breakdown in the relationship. In other words, the parties must be living separate and apart because at least one of them regards the relationship as at an end and not due purely to financial or practical reasons, *e.g.* job location or the fact that one of the parties is in prison, hospital, residential care, etc.

(c) In all the circumstances of the case it would be inequitable or impractical to aggregate.

Since the normal rule is that partners' means are aggregated, the onus must be on the client to show that this exception applies. An example of where it may be impracticable or inequitable to aggregate means might be a client seeking advice and assistance on an immigration matter where their partner remains in the country of origin and is genuinely unable to make resources available due to currency restrictions.

2–08/2 | Assessing income

If the client or their partner (if aggregated) is in receipt of certain state benefits, namely income support, income-based Jobseeker's Allowance, family credit or disability working allowance they qualify automatically on income (by virtue of regulation 13(2)), but their capital must still be assessed to see if they are eligible. In the case of an application for ABWOR to which regulation 9 applies, those in receipt of income support or income-based Jobseeker's Allowance also qualify automatically on capital (by virtue of Regulation 13(3)).

If the client or their partner (if aggregated) is in receipt of none of these benefits, both income and capital must be assessed and the client will only be eligible if both income and capital are within the limits.

"Income" means the total income from all sources which a person has received or may reasonably expect to receive in respect of the seven days up to and including the date of the application for advice and assistance. There are a number of specific disregards and allowances from income which are set out below, but otherwise all income must be included, whether from employment, state benefits or elsewhere, *i.e.* foster allowances. To calculate weekly income, multiply by 12 and divide by 52 if payment is by calendar month and divide by 4 if payment is four-weekly.

Note that, unlike certain other types of "legal aid", there are no deductions or allowances for rent, mortgage repayments, hire purchase repayments, etc.

Contributions towards private pensions are not an allowable disregard against income for means assessment. Income cannot be disregarded merely because the client has incurred liabilities and expenses which must be repaid.

Erratic income (including the self-employed) 2–08/3

Where a client's income is erratic (because of bonuses, commission, nature of employment or payment, etc.) they may be ineligible for advice and assistance one week, but eligible the next as it is the income a client has received or can reasonably expect to receive in respect of the seven days prior to the application that is taken into account.

As long as there is no question of the client having deprived themselves of income with a view to qualifying, then there would be nothing to stop them from delaying their application for advice and assistance until the next week. In these situations, the client should be made aware of the basis of the assessment and the effect of good/bad weeks. It will be for the client to decide if they wish to proceed immediately on a private fee-paying basis if on the previous seven days income they are ineligible.

It is important to remember that this situation differs from deprivation of income or capital. This is not allowed and the resources which have been disposed of must still be taken into account in the assessment.

The income that should be taken into account should include any that is due or will become due for the seven day period prior to the application for legally aided advice and assistance. If a client has become entitled to money in the previous seven days which he has not yet received (*e.g.* he has earned a commission), then that income too must be included in the assessment.

In relation to students, grants should be treated as income by reference to the number of weeks the particular grant is intended to cover and attributed to those weeks. Student loans should be treated as capital.

In the case of a self-employed client, it is the gross amount due to the business for the work carried out in the preceding seven days which will count as the client's income. In the case of a shopkeeper, for example, the income would be the gross sum due from sales in that period, or in the case of a painter and decorator, the amount which he is entitled to be paid in respect of work carried out in that period, even if not yet actually paid or even billed.

Note that in self-employed cases, expenses such as cost of materials or staff costs are not deductible from income. The regulations deal only with gross income, not net profit. Only income tax and the other allowances specified in the regulations should be deducted. There are no special deductions for the self-employed.

For the self-employed, a deduction of £6.35 per week can be made for National Insurance contributions (the weekly class 2 payment). A notional income tax figure should be based on 1/52nd of the client's income tax liability for the preceding year (*i.e.* of their last income tax bill). If the client does not have the information (*e.g.* because they have not submitted any returns), then no allowance should be made.

"No income" 2–08/4

Situations may arise, especially in the family/matrimonial context, where a client has not received or become entitled to any direct income at all in the preceding seven days. This may be so where the client is living separate and apart from their spouse in the same home, with the client not being employed but the spouse still meeting all outgoings. In these circumstances the client can be assessed as having no income. If, however, the client is receiving money from the partner, to pay bills or as maintenance, this must be shown as income.

2–08/5 | **Disregarded income**

Certain state benefits are disregarded as income in the assessment. They are:

  (a) The following payments under the Social Security Contributions and Benefits Act 1992, namely:
    — disability living allowance;
    — attendance allowance paid under section 64 or Schedule 8 to the Act;
    — constant attendance allowance paid under section 104 as an increase to disability pension;
    — any payment made out of the social fund.
  (b) Any back to work bonus under section 26 of the Jobseekers Act 1995;
  (c) Payments under the Earnings Top-Up Scheme 1996; and
  (d) Payments under the Community Care (Direct Payments) Act 1996.

ALLOWANCES AGAINST INCOME

2–08/6 | **Dependants' allowances**

£28.65 is allowed against income if the applicant has a spouse or partner. Note this allowance applies provided the couple are living together, regardless of whether there is a contrary interest, but a couple should not be treated as living together if they have been treated as living separate and apart for aggregation purposes.

£17.30 is allowed for each dependent child (including a foster child) or dependent relative of the applicant who is living in the same household and is aged up to 11.

£25.35 is allowed for each such dependant aged 11 to 16.

£30.30 is allowed for each such dependant aged 16 or over.

Where a dependant child or relative is aged 11 or 16, the allowance depends on when their birthday falls (see below).

2–08/7 | **Allowances for dependants aged 11 or 16**

The allowances of dependants with these ages are tied to certain benefit regulations which relate to school years. The rules are as follows:

11-year-olds
Use the higher rate of "11–16" if the child became 11 before September 7, 1998 and the lower rate "up to 11" if the child became 11 on or after that date.

16-year-olds
Use the higher rate of "16–18" if the child became 16 before September 7, 1998 and the lower rate "11–16" if they became 16 on or after that date. The "16–18" allowance is to be used from the September following the child's sixteenth birthday until the day before their nineteenth birthday.

19 and over
Where a dependant child/relative is 19 or over, use the "16–18" allowance.

Other allowances against income
2–08/8

Apart from dependants' allowances, the following sums should be deducted from total income for the preceding seven days:

(a) any income tax paid or payable on that income;

(b) any National Insurance contributions paid or payable on that income under the Social Security Acts 1975 to 1998; and

(c) bona fide maintenance payments to a spouse or former spouse, a child or relative, who is not in any such case a member of the household of the applicant. An allowance can be made whether the payments are being made under a court order, CSA ruling or voluntary agreement. Only payments actually made can be taken into account.

Assessing capital
2–08/9

"Capital" means the amount or value of every resource of a capital nature, including all savings and any other capital assets (other than the exceptions listed below). Capital derived from a bank loan or borrowing facilities should be taken into account. There are special rules about assessing the value of the client's dwelling which are set out below.

The only items of capital which are not taken into account are the following:

- household furniture and effects;
- clothes;
- tools and implements of trade;
- back-to-work bonus received under section 26 of the Jobseekers Act 1995; and
- payments under the Community Care (Direct Payments) Act 1996.

The client's share of joint assets when the partner is the opponent
2–08/10

There will often be assets which are jointly owned by the parties or to which both parties have access. In deciding what should be taken into account for the client a key question is whether the client has access to or control of the asset. For example, if the client has free access to money in a bank account, then that money should be included in the client's assets. There is, however, some scope for discretion. If the client establishes that there is an agreement or understanding about certain assets being split equally, then it would be reasonable only to take into account half the value of the asset.

2–08/11 | **Subject matter of the dispute**

Under the regulations the value of the subject matter of any claim in respect of which a person is seeking advice and assistance is required to be left out of account in computing the capital and income of that person.

This situation is more likely to arise in practice in relation to capital assets. It is a very important rule in the context of family/matrimonial advice and assistance. It means that assets which are being fought over in relation to the dispute for which advice and assistance is required must not be taken into account when assessing income or capital.

Sometimes it will be obvious that a particular asset is in dispute between the parties, but in the family/matrimonial context the point is more difficult to consider if parties seek advice and assistance at an early stage and there is a range of assets which may or may not be at issue. The general approach should be that an asset should **not** be disregarded as the subject matter of the dispute if the other party has made no specific claim against it and if in practice it is available to the applicant to use as his or her own and could be used to fund legal costs.

If the advice and assistance is on issues about a child/children, then assets cannot be treated as subject matter of the dispute, even if the parties are litigating or otherwise in dispute over those assets (although the assets may be disregarded under any other appropriate heading and the means of partners are unlikely to be aggregated—as the parties are living separate and apart).

2–08/12 | **Value of the home**

Provided it is not disregarded as subject matter of the dispute, a client's main or only dwelling in which he resides must be taken into account as capital subject to the following rules:

(a) the dwelling should be valued at the amount for which it could be sold on the open market;

(b) the first £100,000 of the value of the client's interest must be disregarded; and

(c) the amount of any mortgage or charge registered on the property must also be deducted, but the maximum amount that can be deducted for such a mortgage or charge is £100,000.

Example
The applicant has a home worth £215,000 and the mortgage is £200,000:

Value of home	£215,000
Deduct mortgage up to maximum allowable	£100,000
Deduct exemption allowance	£100,000
Amount to be taken into account in assessing financial eligibility	£15,000

In this example the client is ineligible on capital for advice and assistance.

Where the applicant has more than one dwelling the value of all other dwellings should be taken into account, but the total amount which can be allowed in respect of mortgages and charges on all the properties cannot exceed £100,000. There is no equity disregard for second properties.

Example
The client has a main dwelling worth £150,000 and a second dwelling worth £100,000. Each has a mortgage of £80,000.

The main dwelling after allowing for the mortgage has a net equity of £70,000 which is below the exempt limit. The value of the second property must be taken into account as £80,000. This is because £80,000 of mortgage has already been taken into account on the main dwelling, leaving only £20,000 (of the £100,000 allowable maximum) to be allowed against the second dwelling. The client would not be eligible for advice and assistance.

Value of main dwelling	£150,000
Deduct mortgage up to maximum allowable	£ 80,000
Amount of equity	£ 70,000
less disregard (up to £100,000)	£nil
Add value of second dwelling	£100,000
Deduct mortgage up to outstanding amount of the maximum allowable	£ 20,000
Amount to be taken into account in assessing financial eligibility	£ 80,000

The £100,000 maximum allowable mortgage and the £100,000 disregard (for the main home) only apply to the client's dwellings in which he resides. The client's interest in other properties should be taken into account and valued at market value less the amount of any mortgage/charge or relevant part of such mortgage/charge.

Deduction for dependants
2–08/13

A fixed deduction from capital is allowable if the client has living with him a spouse/partner whose resources are aggregated, or a dependent child or a dependent relative whom he wholly maintains. The deduction is £335 in respect of the first person, £200 in respect of the second and £100 in respect of each further person.

Intentional deprivation of resources
2–08/14

Occasionally a person will deliberately transfer assets to another person in order to make themselves eligible. This is not permitted. If it appears that a person applying for advice and assistance has directly or indirectly deprived himself or herself of any resources or has converted any part of his resources into resources which are to be left out of account wholly or partly under the regulations, the resources which have been transferred or converted must still be taken into account in the assessment. This will normally mean that such a person will not qualify for advice and assistance.

Note that this rule applies where it appears to the solicitor that the person concerned has transferred or deprived himself of assets with the intention of reducing the amount of his disposable income or disposable capital, whether for the purpose of becoming eligible or otherwise. Obviously this rule would not apply if the person had lost assets or money without intending to do so.

2–08/15 | **Eligibility of children**

A child may apply for advice and assistance in the circumstances set out in regulation 14 (see p. 346). When assessing the means of a child, the resources of any person who is liable to maintain the child or who usually contributes substantially to the child's maintenance or who has care and control of the child (other than on a temporary basis) should be taken into account, as well as any assets of the child. There is a discretion not to aggregate assets in this way if it appears inequitable to do so, having regard to all the circumstances including the age and resources of the child and any conflict of interest between the child and the carer. (See also paras 2–09 and 2–10, below.)

2–08/16 | **Mistakes in assessment**

Sometimes a mistake will be made in assessing a person's financial eligibility or new information will come to light which suggests that an earlier assessment was inaccurate. Where this happens the assessment can and should be reopened and a new assessment carried out, which may mean that a person previously eligible is no longer so. If any dishonesty or improper conduct in relation to disclosure of assets is discovered, the details should be reported to the area office.

2–08/17 | **Changes in circumstances**

Where on an accurate assessment a client is found financially eligible for advice and assistance, there is no subsequent reassessment of means if the client's circumstances change. There is therefore no duty on the client to report improvements in means, except in relation to any fresh application for advice and assistance (but see NFG 3, para. 3–17(h)).

Where a client is initially ineligible there is nothing to prevent a further application and assessment where a change in circumstances makes him eligible. However, the cover only runs from the date the application form was fully completed and the client was assessed as eligible.

AREA OFFICE DECISIONS

2–09 | **Is it reasonable for the solicitor to accept an application personally from a child?**
(Legal Advice and Assistance Regulations 1989, reg. 14)

The rule is that (except where the child is at a police station) a solicitor can only accept an application for advice and assistance direct from a child (*i.e.* a person under the age of 16) in relation to proceedings which that child is entitled to begin, prosecute or defend without a next friend or guardian *ad litem* or where he has been authorised to do so by the area office. (He can accept an application on behalf of a child by the persons specified in regulation 14(3)(a) and (c) of the Legal Advice and Assistance Regulations 1989 but see para. 2–10 regarding authority under regulation 14(3)(d).)

Authority to advise a child direct will be given if:

(a) there is a good reason why the parent or guardian is not applying (*e.g.* conflict of interest, or the child is in care and needs separate representation); and

(b) the child is old enough to give instructions and understand the nature of the advice and assistance.

Where authority is given or is not required, the child will sign the application form himself and the solicitor may well consider it just and equitable **not** to aggregate the child's means with those of the person liable to maintain him (para. 5, Schedule 2 Legal Advice and Assistance Regulations 1989). Note that the starting point is that there should be aggregation but the solicitor can decide not to aggregate (and assess only the child's means) if, having regard to all the circumstances, including the age and resources of the child, and to any conflict of interest, it appears just and equitable to do so. This is a question for the solicitor and, although (unlike for civil legal aid) the starting point is aggregation, non-aggregation is likely to be justified where there is a conflict and/or where the child is older.

Is it reasonable for the solicitor to accept an application from "any other   **2–10**
person" acting on behalf of a child or patient?
(Legal Advice and Assistance Regulations 1989, reg. 14(3)(d))

The rule is that a solicitor can accept an application for advice and assistance on behalf of a child (*i.e.* a person under the age of 16) by a parent or guardian, and on behalf of a patient (*i.e.* under the Mental Health Act 1983) by either a receiver or the nearest relative or guardian.

A solicitor can only accept an application for advice and assistance from "any other person" where he has received prior authority from the area office. The Board's application form CLAIM 10 should be used to apply.

Such authority will be given if:

(a) there is good reason why the parent or guardian cannot make the application (*e.g.* conflict of interest); and

(b) there is sufficient connection between the child or patient and the other person to ensure that the other person is likely to act responsibly in the interests of the child/patient; and

(c) the other person has sufficient knowledge of the child or patient, the problem and the financial circumstances, to give proper instructions to the solicitor.

Where an application for legal advice and assistance is accepted within regulation 14(3), either with or without authority, the application will be for the child or patient but made on his/her behalf. The application form CLAIM10 should be completed in the name of the child or patient but signed by the person who is applying on behalf of the child or patient with an annotation to that effect, indicating his or her full name and the capacity in which the form is signed within regulation 14(3) (*e.g.* "signed by John Joseph Brown, parent"). The appropriate means must be taken into account in the means assessment—that is, those of the patient or, in the case of applications on behalf of a child, those of the child and, where appropriate, any person who has care and control or is liable to maintain him or her or usually contributes substantially to his or her maintenance. Failure to complete the application form (green form) appropriately or to annotate a signature (other than the client's) with the relevant details may lead to queries or to costs claims being disallowed.

(See paras. 2–12 and 2–62 regarding attendances on behalf of the client under Legal Advice and Assistance Regulations, reg. 10.)

2–11 **Is it reasonable for the solicitor to accept a postal application from a person residing outside England and Wales?**
(Legal Advice and Assistance Regulations 1989, reg. 15)

The rule is that where a client resides outside England and Wales, a solicitor can, with the prior authority of the area office, accept a postal application for advice and assistance. This will be exceptional and the solicitor should consider whether advice and assistance on the same matter could be applied for by a person resident in England and Wales. The Board's application form should be used to apply for authority.

Such authority will be given where there is good reason why the client cannot attend personally but not where the client's residence is purely temporary and the solicitor can, without disadvantage to the client, postpone giving advice and assistance until the client returns to England and Wales. Franchised solicitors, can, in their franchised categories of work, send the application form by post for completion by a client in any event.

NOTE: *The solicitor should not start work until he has received the completed application form from the client, to ensure that the client is financially eligible. See also para. 2–07 regarding distant solicitors.*

2–12 **Is it reasonable for the solicitor to accept an application made by another person on behalf of the client?**
(Legal Advice and Assistance Regulations 1989, reg.10)

The rule is that where a client cannot for good reason attend on the solicitor in order to apply for advice and assistance, another person may be authorised to attend on the client's behalf. The application is completed in the name of the client and the means assessment is based on the client's means. The form is signed by the authorised person on the client's behalf and the signature should be annotated indicating the full name of the person signing and to also make it clear that the application was signed in accordance with regulation 10 (*e.g.* "signed by Mary Louise Smith with the client's authority").

Failure to complete the application form (green form) appropriately or to annotate a signature (other than the client's) with the relevant details may lead to queries or to costs claims being disallowed.

Good reason is likely to be established where the client is physically unable to attend due to detention in an institution such as a prison, mental hospital or immigration detention centre. It may include other circumstances such as hospitalisation or inability to travel due to disability. The reason relied upon should always be noted by the solicitor. Good reason is unlikely to be established if the incapacity is temporary and the provision of advice and assistance could be postponed without prejudice to the client.

The person who attends on behalf of the client should normally be independent of the solicitor's firm providing the advice and assistance, *e.g.* a friend or relative. In certain limited circumstances the authorised person may be an employee of the firm, other than the solicitor who is to provide the advice. Solicitors are expected to first make enquiries of the client as to the availability of a friend or relative. If the client does not wish to authorise a friend or relative, he or she should be asked to give reasons. Temporary unavailability is not a sufficient reason.

The person authorised must physically attend on the solicitor who is to provide the advice. The authorised person must provide the client's details, brief facts of the case and sufficient information to enable the client's financial eligibility to be determined. This information must be provided at the same time that the form is completed and signed by the authorised person.

If an employee of the solicitor's firm is the authorised person then a full note of the authorisation and the physical attendance should be kept on file. Work in respect of the authorisation and the attendance note should not be included in the solicitor's claim for costs. If the client provides written authority, a copy should be kept by the solicitor. If the authorisation was by telephone, a full telephone attendance note should be made. See also NFG 2–62 below.

If the client resides outside England and Wales, another person may be authorised to make the application provided that the relevant criteria are satisfied. Alternatively, an application form for advice and assistance may be sent by post to a client resident outside England and Wales. See also para. 2–11 above.

See also para. 2–07 regarding distant solicitors.

Advice and assistance from more than one solicitor   2–13

Except where advice and assistance is given at a police station or by a duty solicitor at a magistrates' court or by a franchised solicitor exercising devolved powers, advice and assistance cannot be given on *the same matter* by more than one solicitor without authority from the area office. "One solicitor" is for practical purposes generally treated as one firm of solicitors. If a client changes solicitor within the same firm, or the solicitor changes firm and continues to advise/assist the client, no authority is needed. However, if the client changes firms and the same solicitor does not continue to advise/ assist the client, authority is needed.

Authority will not be required where the "new" solicitor knows that the previous solicitor(s) will not make any claim for payment from the legal aid fund. Nor will authority be required where the matter is treated by the Board as a separate matter.

Care should be exercised when establishing whether previous advice has been given. If there is any indication that previous advice has been given, the solicitor should make enquiries about who gave the advice and whether it was given under the legal advice and assistance (green form) scheme. If in doubt, the solicitor should assume that an application form has already been signed and apply for authority from the area office. The onus is on the solicitor to satisfy the Board that no green form has been previously signed and he must ensure the application is fully completed in that respect before providing advice and assistance.

Authority may be given on such terms and conditions as the area office may in its discretion see fit to impose (regulation 16(1) Legal Advice and Assistance Regulations 1989). This means that the area office can, for example, fix a costs limit (*i.e.* lower than the usual initial limit) to reflect the advice and assistance which has already been given and the work which reasonably remains to be done on the client's behalf.

2–14   *Authority will be given if:*

(a) there is a gap in time and circumstances have changed materially between the first and second occasions when advice and assistance is sought, *e.g.* a reconciliation which has failed;

(b) the client has reasonable cause to be dissatisfied with the service provided by the first solicitor (but see 2–15(a) below);

(c) the client has moved a distance away from the first solicitor and communication is difficult.

2–15   *Authority will not be given if:*

(a) the client merely finds the first advice unpalatable and wants a second opinion;

(b) there is only a short time between the first and second occasion when advice and assistance is sought and no material change of circumstances has occurred;

(c) there has already been one authority granted, *i.e.* the change requested is from a second to a third solicitor (unless there is good reason for a further change); or

(d) there is no reasonable explanation for the client seeking advice and assistance from a new solicitor.

Where authority is required it will not be granted or operate retrospectively, but the application form may be signed and dated in anticipation of the authority being granted. Work done before the grant of authority cannot be remunerated and should be disregarded in the calculation of the work already done for the purposes of fixing the amount of any extension to the costs limit. (See Costs Appeals Committee decision LAA 1, as amended.)

2–16   Separate matters, separate forms—when are matters separate?

The rule under regulation 17 Legal Advice and Assistance Regulations 1989 is that, where two or more separate matters are involved (this includes where one matter is treated as two separate matters) each matter must be the subject of a separate application form (green form). There is an exception for matters connected with or arising from proceedings for divorce or judicial separation, actual or prospective. Whether matters are (or are treated as) separate is an issue of fact and not one where the area office can give an authority.

A single application form (green form) should be used to identify the issues and provide general, preliminary advice. If one issue is identified then the original, single form should be used for the provision of further advice and assistance. If other separate legal issues *are identified or subsequently arise* requiring separate progression, then a further form or forms should be used.

Whether single or multiple forms are used, the solicitor must justify the work done and costs incurred. Duplicated work should not be remunerated and work undertaken under one form (or previously under the same form) may affect the reasonableness of subsequent work under the same or separate forms (reflecting, *e.g.* the solicitor's existing knowledge of the client and circumstances).

Separate matters—advice about more than one category of work

2–17

(a) Where the two matters are genuinely different problems requiring separate advice and assistance, albeit at the same time, these are probably separate matters justifying separate forms.

(b) Where two or more matters arise from the same set of circumstances, the chances of them being separate matters diminish.

(c) Where two matters or more lead to one single action, cause or matter one form should be used.

(d) Where two or more matters would be dealt with under one legal aid certificate, one form should be used.

(e) Where advice and assistance is given as to enforcement, a review or appeal in a matter on which advice was previously given, the same form should be used, *e.g.* to enforce an order obtained, to appeal against a refusal of legal aid or to appeal at any stage in the immigration appeal process (including by way of judicial review) but see below at para. 2–18 for referrals to the Criminal Cases Review Commission.

(f) If a client seeks advice as to whether (s)he should change solicitor from a solicitor already providing advice and assistance, it is not justified to consider this as separate to the advice being given by the previous solicitor. Regulation 16 authority is required before any advice is given under a fresh form.

Separate matters—Non-matrimonial

2–18

(a) *Debt.* As a general rule each individual debt does not justify the use of a separate form but where separate proceedings have been issued in respect of different debts, separate forms in respect of each set of proceedings may be justified.

(b) *Welfare benefits.* Advice and assistance in relation to various or separate benefits including those administered by local government *may* justify the use of separate forms where they are administered by different bodies under different legal regimes and the issues involved/

work to be undertaken are separate. It is, however, reasonable to expect that a single form will be used to provide general, preliminary advice, including checking any benefit currently paid, providing a report on entitlement to welfare benefits generally and advising on applying for particular benefits. Where a separate problem is identified or subsequently arises this may justify the use of a separate, additional form, *e.g.* general benefits advice followed by a particular housing benefit problem such as a specific query regarding the particular client's entitlement, including a review/appeal (two forms unless the original form continued to be used) or followed by particular housing benefit and income support problems (three forms unless the original form continued to be used). (See Costs Appeals Committee decision LAA16, para. 2–68, below.)

Where preliminary, general advice as to welfare benefits is triggered by advice in another legal subject area (*e.g.* for the solicitor to recognise the need for benefits advice or to indicate benefits available to the client in the particular matrimonial or personal injury context) this will not normally constitute a separate matter justifying the signature of a fresh form unless/until more specific detailed advice is given, *e.g.* as to the individual client's particular entitlement (including a check of benefit in payment or entitlement report) or as to a specific problem.

Benefit entitlement advice which arises from advice on a child maintenance assessment by the Child Support Agency (and vice versa) should be dealt with under one form unless/until they become separate matters.

(c) *Child maintenance assessment.* Unless the six months' rule applies (see para. 2–20 below), a single form must be used for advice on child maintenance assessments by the Child Support Agency. This will, where applicable, be the form used for matrimonial advice and/or benefit entitlement.

(d) *Housing problems.* Problems or remedies arising out of housing difficulties (possession/disrepair, rehousing) would not normally justify the use of separate forms. However, once a separate problem requiring separate preliminary work, *e.g.* following a decision to institute proceedings (for example under the Environmental Protection Act 1990) has been identified, a separate form can be signed for that matter (unless the original form continues to be used).

(e) *Crime.* Charges laid at the same time which are likely to be dealt with under one legal aid order, or are likely to be heard together, should be dealt with under one form.

Advice given on a similar matter which could be considered to be a "series of offences" should be dealt with by way of the original form, rather than separate forms. See NFG 18–22 for guidance on "series of offences".

Advice and assistance in respect of a referral to the Criminal Cases Review Commission constitutes a separate matter from advice and assistance given in respect of the case itself including any other appeal.

(f) *Employment.* All issues in relation to the same employer should be dealt with under one form, unless as a result of clearly separate incidents, separate proceedings are to be taken.

(g) *Personal injuries.* A separate form is appropriate for each set of proceedings or potential set of proceedings. However, the same form should be used for one incident (even though various opponents may be involved).

(h) *Immigration.* One form is appropriate for all aspects of immigration advice, including asylum applications, applications for a work permit, visa/leave to enter, etc. Any appeal against refusal both in the immigration appeal process and by way of any judicial review should also be dealt with under the original form.

Advice in relation to related matters such as welfare benefits and housing advice may constitute a separate matter justifying the signature of a fresh form if specific, detailed advice, *e.g.* as to a specific problem, is given.

(i) *Consumer/general contract.* Only if genuinely different problems requiring separate advice and assistance arise, will this justify separate forms. If a similar problem arises involving the same legal issues but various opponents, the same form should be used unless and until separate proceedings are issued.

(j) *Family breakdown.* See also para. 2–19, below. Unmarried clients may have family breakdown problems and require advice and assistance regarding, *e.g.* the children, an injunction, maintenance and property. A single form should be used, including for advice on these and related matters, *e.g.* debts and housing, unless and until they become separate problems which require separate progression. Where proceedings are likely to be necessary under the Trusts of Land and Appointment of Trustees Act 1996 this may justify the use of a separate green form, bearing in mind that they cannot be taken forward in the same proceedings or under the same civil legal aid certificate as say an injunction and/or Children Act application, which should be dealt with under the original form. (See para. 2–16, above.)

Advice on welfare benefits in the context of family breakdown may constitute a separate matter justifying the signature of a fresh form if specific, detailed advice, *e.g.* as to the individual client's particular entitlement or as to a specific problem, is given. This could include a check or entitlement report (rather than merely preliminary, general advice).

(k) *Family wills.* Advice and assistance in making a will (where available) justifies the signature of a separate form. See also NFG 2–29 below.

(l) *Mental health.* A single application form (green form) should be used to identify the issues and provide general, preliminary advice. If one issue is identified then the original, single form, should be used for the provision of further advice and assistance. If other separate legal issues are identified or subsequently arise requiring separate progression, then a further form or forms should be used. For example, where in the context of giving advice regarding a client's treatment it becomes clear that he requires advice and assistance in relation to welfare benefits, or a complaint or a possible claim for *e.g.* medical negligence, this would justify the completion of a further form or forms where that legal issue or issues required separate progression. Issues regarding after care would be unlikely to constitute a separate matter as they would be likely to form part of the main issue (*e.g.* an application to the Mental Health Review Tribunal) and be taken forward in that context. Whether single or multiple forms are used, the solicitor must justify the work done and costs incurred. Duplicated work will not be remunerated and work undertaken under one form (or previously under the same form) may affect the reasonableness of subsequent work under the same or separate forms (reflecting *e.g.* the solicitor's existing knowledge of the client and circumstances).

Where the solicitor advising on a mental health matter identifies a separate legal issue upon which the client needs advice, but which is outside his expertise then he should seek to ensure that the client is referred to an appropriate adviser who may or may not be within the solicitor's own firm.

A separate application for advice and assistance may be made where the client requires advice/assistance in relation to a fresh application or automatic referral to the Mental Health Review Tribunal. This means that a client may sign a number of applications in succession over a period of time. The solicitor should ensure that details of the basis of the application/referral (*i.e.* the section of the Mental Health Act 1983 and the trigger for the application/referral) are retained in the file.

Where the client may pursue a review by the hospital managers and/or an application for the Mental Health Review Tribunal the use of a second application form may be justified. Costs are subject to assessment and the costs of a review are unlikely to be justified where a very recent Tribunal application has been unsuccessful and there have been no apparent changes in circumstances to justify re-examination of the case. It may initially not be clear whether the client will pursue both routes for reviewing his detention. A single application form should be used up until the point of decision. Where both options are to be pursued and there will be future legal advice and assistance (as opposed to ABWOR) costs in respect of the Mental Health Review Tribunal, a separate application form should be signed in respect of the managers' review. Costs incurred in relation to that review should then be claimed under that form where they are separate from the costs of taking forward the Mental Health Review Tribunal case. This may mean that at any one time the client may have two current applications for legal advice and assistance in respect of the managers' review and the Tribunal respectively, or an application for advice and assistance and an ABWOR in respect of the review and the Tribunal respectively.

Where more than one form is used, there may be work undertaken which is of relevance to more than one aspect. Generally, where there is an application for legal advice and assistance and an ABWOR the ABWOR should only be used for Mental Health Review Tribunal work. However, some preparation work will be relevant to both a Tribunal hearing and a managers' review and such work can be claimed under the ABWOR covering the Tribunal application/referral.

In any event, care must be taken to ensure that costs incurred are claimed only under one form and are not duplicated. Generally, it will be possible to identify the main purpose and relevance of the work and claim accordingly.

The solicitor should not generally accept applications for advice and assistance from both the patient and nearest relative simultaneously on the same matter (although it may be possible for the solicitor to advise them both where there is no conflict of interest between them—see below). Either the patient or the nearest relative may apply for advice and assistance although there may be particular circumstances where there is no conflict between the patient and nearest relative and they each require advice and assistance on separate legal issues. If the advice relates to the nearest relative's right to apply for the patient's discharge, this would normally fall within the advice for the patient. Where, however, the nearest relative wishes to apply for a MHRT in his/her own right, this should be the subject of a separate application for advice and assistance/ABWOR.

Separate matters—Matrimonial (divorce and judicial separation) 2–19

(a) One application form (green form) relates to the whole proceedings, *i.e.* decree proceedings and all ancillaries are treated as one matter. It will also cover advice on related matters, *e.g.* welfare benefits, debts and housing unless and until they become genuinely separate problems which are no longer connected with or arising from the matrimonial advice. A separate form should, however, be completed for advice and assistance in making a will (although the original matrimonial form can be used to draw attention to the advisability of making a will).

(b) Advice on child maintenance, including advice in connection with an application for assessment by the Child Support Agency, is not a separate matter and must be dealt with under the form signed in respect of matrimonial advice or proceedings.

(c) Even where there are two sets of proceedings, *e.g.* judicial separation followed by divorce proceedings or two sets of divorce proceedings, provided that they relate to the same marriage, they are still to be treated as one matter for the purposes of legal advice and assistance.

(d) Magistrates' court proceedings relating to the marriage do not come within (c) above and can therefore be treated as separate matters for the purposes of legal advice and assistance, although child maintenance and Child Support Agency assessments will not constitute another separate matter.

Separate matters—All cases (including divorce and judicial separation)— 2–20 advice and assistance given to the same client six months or more after submission of the claim for costs

(a) Where a client seeks further advice and assistance on the same matter six months (or more) after the claim for the earlier advice and assistance has been submitted for payment, the further advice and assistance is treated as being for a separate matter. (There are two factors behind this approach. First, an application for legal advice and assistance does not terminate on submission of a claim for payment, and second, particularly in intermittent, long-running matters, it is difficult to say when circumstances stop being one matter and start being another.)

(b) This means that, if the earlier form was submitted for payment six or more months previously, the client must make a fresh application for advice and assistance in the usual way (so a fresh assessment of means must be carried out and a fresh initial cost limit will apply) and, if the further advice and assistance is sought from a fresh solicitor, no prior authority from the area office is required. For the position where the further advice and assistance is given, within six months of the submission of the claim for costs, see para. 2–21, below.

2–21   **Separate matters—All cases (including divorce and judicial separation)—advice and assistance given to the same client within six months of submission of the claim for costs**

(a) It is only when further advice and assistance on the same matter is given six months (or more) after the claim for costs for the earlier advice and assistance is treated as being for a separate matter. If it is given within six months, it is the same matter and must be given under the original form even though this has been submitted to the area office for payment.

(b) Where a client goes to a new solicitor (on the same matter) within the six months' period, authority from the area office will be required and a fresh application for advice and assistance will have to be made (see para. 2–13, above). The new solicitor will claim his/her costs on the form in the usual way.

(c) Where the client returns to the same solicitor (on the same matter) within the six months' period, the further advice and assistance must be given under the form already submitted for payment. It is likely, therefore, that the solicitor will have to apply for an extension to the form as otherwise only the balance of the old limit (including any extensions) will be available. When the solicitor later wishes to claim payment for the further advice and assistance, he/she will not have the original form and the procedure set out below should be followed.

(d) The solicitor should complete the front of an application form to show the client's name and address and should clearly strike through the rest of the form, writing boldly in the space on the left-hand side "CLAIM SENT BY US [FIRM NAME] FOR PAYMENT ON [DATE]. FURTHER WORK CARRIED OUT". The claim section should then be completed and the form submitted in the usual way.

2–22   **Is it reasonable to grant authority to exceed the prescribed limit (*i.e.* grant an extension)? (Legal Advice and Assistance Regulations 1989, reg. 21)**

The rule is that (except where advice and assistance at police stations or in criminal proceedings in magistrates' courts are concerned) a solicitor cannot exceed the initial legal advice and assistance costs limit without obtaining an extension from the area office.

The area office has to be satisfied that it is reasonable for the advice and assistance to be given *and* that the estimate of costs to be incurred in giving it is reasonable.

Costs Guidelines appeared in the April 1996 issue of the Board's *Focus* newsletter. These give an indication of the units of time (and therefore the costs) which are likely to be considered reasonable. They will be updated/amended from time to time and published through *Focus*. They are indicators only and where the circumstances of the case/client mean that the guidelines are inappropriate the solicitor should explain why.

NOTE:

1. *The solicitor must submit with the application for an extension sufficient information to enable the office to make a decision about what the problem is, what work has already been done, what needs to be done and why, and the estimated cost of the work to be done.*

2. *Every application must be considered by reference to the relevant statutory provisions and on its own facts and merits.*

3. *All applications must be considered objectively on the information which is made available. If insufficient information is provided to justify granting the application or granting it in full then it must be refused or partially refused.*

Will the extension be granted?   **2–23**

Before dealing with the reasonableness of the extension, the area office has to answer some basic questions:

(a) *Is the problem one of English law?* (Legal Aid Act 1988, s.2. See p. 280 and para. 2–07, above.) If not, the extension will not be granted, and any costs claim for advice and assistance cannot be paid.

(b) *Is the problem one which is excluded from the advice and assistance provisions?* (Legal Advice and Assistance (Scope) Regulations 1989. See p. 333 and para. 2–07, above.) If it is, the extension will not be granted and any costs claim for advice and assistance cannot be paid.

(c) *Is legal aid available for the matter?*

   (i) If not, this is not a bar in itself to an extension being granted.
   (ii) If it is, the questions (d) to (g) below need to be answered.

(d) *Has legal aid (whether civil or criminal) or ABWOR already been granted covering the work required?* If it has, the extension will not be granted but the bill for the required advice and assistance will be paid (not under the application for legal advice and assistance but under the certificate, order or approval granted).

(e) *Has legal aid (whether civil or criminal) or ABWOR already been refused?* If it has, the extension may still be granted. In particular limited extension may be granted to prepare an appeal against refusal to an area committee in the case of civil legal aid provided the appeal is not in connection with repeated applications for legal aid.

(f) *Has legal aid (whether civil or criminal) or ABWOR already been applied for?* If it has, the extension may still be granted if there is likely to be delay before the application is determined and further work needs to be done without which the client's position would be prejudiced. Note, however, that the availability of civil legal aid on an emergency basis is a factor which would be taken into account in deciding whether an extension should be granted.

(g) *Does the applicant have no alternative source of finance for the legal costs, e.g.* Union financed advice? If he does, it may well be unreasonable to grant an extension. The element of hardship will be an important consideration.

2–24 Once the basic questions have been answered in the affirmative, the reasonableness of the extension in the particular case can be considered. The greater the extension sought, the more compelling will need to be the reasons for granting it.

(a) *Do the prospects of success justify the expenditure?* If not, it is unlikely that an extension will be granted although in some cases further work will be necessary for the prospects to be assessed.

(b) *For a monetary claim, is the opponent worth pursuing?* If not, it will be unreasonable to authorise further expenditure.

(c) *Does the money or benefit at stake justify the expenditure?* If not, it is unlikely that an extension will be granted and indeed this is an issue which the area office will consider on costs assessment in any event. In extreme cases such work may be disallowed when a costs claim is submitted, notwithstanding the fact that an extension had been approved.

(d) *Does the application relate to compensation from the Criminal Injuries Compensation Authority (CICA)?* If so, an extension to the financial limit will not normally be granted for assistance up to and including consideration of and advice on the CICA decision. However, when the CICA either refuses an application or makes an award, it may be reasonable to grant an extension to enable the solicitor to advise and assist the client in applying for a review or, subsequently, an appeal.

(e) *Is it reasonable for the client to deal with some of the steps involved himself having regard to all the circumstances of the case?* If so, the application for an extension may be refused or a reduced extension may be granted. In deciding this question regard will be had to whether the client could adequately deal with some aspects of the matter with a view to avoiding unnecessary costs being incurred for which, in certain circumstances, the client may become liable through the operation of the solicitor's charge. For example, the client will probably be able to complete the Child Support Agency's application and enquiry forms without assistance, save for advice as to any legal implications.

(f) *In cases where proceedings are a possibility, should the matter be dealt with by way of an application for legal aid or ABWOR, if avail-*

able and likely to be granted, rather than an extension of advice and assistance?

(i) Where the proceedings are anticipated or likely, given the circumstances of the case, it usually should, in which case, an extension will be granted only for a limited amount to enable an application to be prepared if that work cannot be done within the original limit.

(ii) Where the solicitor can show real prospects of settling without having to issue proceedings, the area office may be prepared to authorise one extension but, if further work is necessary thereafter, may require an application for legal aid to be submitted. A legal aid application should be made at an early stage unless there is a clear indication of settlement.

(g) *Should an extension be granted to obtain an opinion of counsel?*

(i) Where the application relates to potential litigation, generally not. The matter should be dealt with by applying for legal aid at the earliest opportunity (see (f) above).

(ii) Where there is no potential litigation and the matter appears to be beyond the expertise of a reasonably competent solicitor, or advice is needed on the format or type of litigation, it may be reasonable to grant an extension to cover obtaining counsel's opinion.

(h) *In matrimonial cases, does the upper limit apply, and if so, why is that limit not sufficient?* (Legal Advice and Assistance Regulations 1989, reg. 4(1)(b), p. 342). The upper limit (three hours' work) only applies to a petitioner for divorce or judicial separation who has had advice or assistance in the preparation of a petition. Unless a need is shown it will not be reasonable to grant an extension.

The following are examples of the work that a solicitor may be expected to carry out under a green form and within the upper limit: **2–25**

(a) Preliminary advice on the grounds for divorce or judicial separation, the effects of a decree on status, the future arrangements for the children, the income and assets of the family (including child maintenance and assessment by the Child Support Agency) and matters relating to housing and the matrimonial home.

(b) Drafting the petition and the statement of the arrangements for the children and, where necessary, typing or writing the entries on the forms.

(c) Advising on filing the documents at court and the consequential procedure, including service if no acknowledgment of service is filed.

(d) Advising a client when the acknowledgment of service is received as to the procedure for applying for directions for trial, and typing or writing the entries on the form of affidavit of evidence.

(e) Advising as to the court's powers under the Children Act 1989 and the circumstances in which a court attendance by the client may be required regarding the arrangements for the children of the family.

(f) Advising on the decree absolute.

Special cases

2–26   *Tribunal hearing/preparation*

The green form does not extend to representation (no matter what the circumstances of the client and/or the case), and where an extension to the costs limit is sought for representation then it must be refused.

The definitions of "advice" and "assistance" were considered in *R. v. Legal Aid Board, ex p. Higgins* (unreported, QBD, October 15, 1993) when the Divisional Court considered that assistance, as defined, extends to all assistance short of actual representation (*i.e.* advocacy).

Assisting the client in the gathering of evidence may be justified in the particular case. It may also be reasonable for the solicitor to advise the client in relation to conducting the hearing him or herself, including preparing a written submission.

Costs which arise *directly* and only as a result of representing the client at a hearing would not normally be allowed—it would not normally be reasonable to meet them in the absence of particular circumstances which would justify them. That is to say, preparing a brief or papers (including any letter of instruction and supporting papers) for privately funded counsel, a Free Representation Unit or other *pro bono* (*i.e.* free) advocate would not normally be covered, although assistance to the client in gathering evidence and advice to the client regarding the hearing could be more easily justified as reasonable.

Although costs which arise directly out of representation would not normally be met, work such as preparing a chronology, rationalising documents or preparing a written submission suitable for the client's own use at a hearing can sometimes be justified according to individual circumstances of the particular case. Such costs can still be covered even if the work is passed to an advocate by the client who subsequently decides to obtain representation. Such costs would not, however, normally be allowed where they are undertaken only for the purpose of the client being represented at the hearing.

2–27   *McKenzie advisers*

Following the principles laid down by the case of *McKenzie v. McKenzie* [1971] P. 33 counsel has advised that the definition of advice and assistance in the Legal Aid Act 1988 includes a solicitor advising a client informally without actually representing that client in any proceedings. There is accordingly jurisdiction to grant an extension under the legal advice and assistance scheme for this purpose and to pay appropriate costs out of the legal aid fund. The client must attend the relevant hearing having regard to the nature of a McKenzie adviser.

An application for an extension to the costs limit to enable a solicitor to act as a McKenzie adviser falls within the general principles laid down by regulation 21 of the Legal Advice and Assistance Regulations 1989.

The use of a solicitor McKenzie adviser (as opposed to a friend or other supporter) must be justified. An extension application will usually be necessary, as the initial limit is unlikely to suffice.

When considering whether it is reasonable for advice and assistance to be given in these circumstances, the area office will bear in mind that it will normally be unreasonable to grant an extension:

(a) where full legal aid is available for the proceedings and the client would be better served by being fully represented in such proceedings;

(b) unless the solicitor can satisfy the area office that, by reason of either the difficulty of the case or the importance to the client or the inability of the client to act on his or her own without **legal** help, it is necessary for the client to have the services of a **solicitor** acting as a McKenzie adviser.

The presence of any of the following factors may make the case one of difficulty or importance or inability on the part of the client so as to justify an extension:

(a) *Difficulty.* Does the case turn on a point of law or assessment of quantum with which the client could not reasonably be expected to deal without the assistance of a McKenzie adviser?

(b) *Importance.* Is the case of such importance to the client that the costs of a McKenzie adviser are justified when applying the test of the fee-paying client of moderate means?

(c) *Inability of the client.* Has the client got particular characteristics which justify **the use of a solicitor** as a McKenzie adviser? Learning difficulties, a material disability, or insufficient knowledge of English for the client to adequately present his or her case will not suffice to justify a McKenzie adviser under legal advice and assistance unless **legal help**, rather than other support/help, *e.g.* from a social worker, relative or friend, is justified.

In deciding whether a McKenzie adviser is justified under legal advice and assistance, regard should be had as to whether a legally qualified McKenzie adviser is needed and to the possibililty of the solicitor assisting the client with his or her preparation of the case including written submissions.

As the role of the McKenzie adviser is to advise the client without actually representing him or her, the client must be present at the relevant hearing. If the application for an extension indicates that the client will not be present then it should be refused (or part refused, to enable the solicitor to advise the client outside the hearing, *e.g.* by writing a letter). Note also that a solicitor agent or counsel cannot be a McKenzie adviser, although the solicitor can delegate the case in accordance with regulation 20 Legal Advice and Assistance Regulations 1989.

When a costs claim for legal advice and assistance which includes costs for a solicitor acting as a McKenzie adviser is submitted, the area office will call for the solicitor's file. This will enable the area office to be satisfied, before payment is authorised, that there is no element of representation claimed.

Conveyancing 2–28
Advice and assistance for conveyancing services is excluded except for (a) advice or assistance relating to a rental purchase agreement or a conditional sale agreement for the sale of land and (b) such conveyancing services as are necessary to give effect to an order of the court or matrimonial agreement (Legal Advice and Assistance (Scope) Regulations 1989, reg. 3, p. 334).

Extensions will therefore only be available for the cases which are not excluded and costs claims will not be paid where they relate to excluded work.

Wills (see also para 2–29/1 regarding living wills) 2–29
Advice and assistance in the making of a will are excluded from legal advice

and assistance except where the client is aged 70 or over, or suffers from a physical or mental handicap or illness (as defined in regulation 4 of the Legal Advice and Assistance (Scope) Regulations 1989, p. 334) or is the parent or guardian of such a person for whom the client wishes to provide in the will, or is the mother or father of a minor who is living with the client, where the client is not living with the minor's other parent and the client wishes to appoint a guardian for that minor (Legal Advice and Assistance (Scope) Regulations, reg. 4).

Extensions will therefore only be available for the cases which are not excluded and costs claims will not be paid where they relate to excluded work. Work done and time spent must be justified on assessment of costs in the usual way.

2–29/1

Living wills (see also para. 2–29 regarding wills)
The Legal Aid Board's Costs Appeals Committee considers that advice and assistance is available in respect of living wills (also known as advance directives about medical treatment decisions) but particular circumstances must have arisen requiring advice to be given (see para. 2–69, Costs Appeals Committee decision LAA 17). The Committee has given the following guidance.

An advance directive enables a competent person to give instructions about what is to be done if he or she should subsequently lose the capacity to decide or to communicate. It may cover any matter on which the individual has decided views but most commonly arises in relation to decisions about medical treatment, particularly when a person has a serious life-threatening condition.

In advance directive may also be referred to as a "living will", "treatment refusal" or "refusal/release". It should include an informed authorisation or refusal of specific treatments. It cannot, however insist on a specific treatment or require medical professionals to act contrary to the law, *e.g.* active euthanasia.

The Costs Appeals Committee considers that legal advice and assistance in relation to an advance directive can be provided as long as the requirements in section 2(2) and (3) of the Legal Aid Act 1988 are satisfied, *i.e.* that particular circumstances have arisen in relation to the person seeking the advice.

Particular circumstances will only arise at the point when the individual realises that there is a real probability of suffering some form of future incapacity by virtue of a current condition, *e.g.* extreme age or terminal illness or diagnosis of a degenerative disease, which will prevent that person from expressing his or her wishes.

Particular circumstances may also arise where an individual holds a strong religious or moral belief, *e.g.* a Jehovah's Witness who wishes to decline a blood transfusion.

The crucial point is that the need for legal advice and assistance must stem from the particular circumstances of the individual and these circumstances should already have arisen when legal advice is sought. A person facing a hypothetical risk would not satisfy this test and would therefore not be eligible for advice under the scheme, *e.g.* a person who was concerned about the possible threat of sudden incapacity or death through a freak accident.

A minor illness or recurring minor medical condition would not generally satisfy this test as such circumstances would not normally justify the preparation of an advance directive. In other words, there must be some relationship between the particular circumstances which have arisen and the need for legal advice and assistance in relation to an advance directive.

It is considered that the preparation of an advance directive would be unlikely in all but exceptional cases to take more than one hour in total (including taking instructions/attending on the client).

Welfare law

2–30

Advice and assistance can be given about assessment of a client's entitlement to welfare benefits and for verifying an assessment by the Benefits Agency or other benefit-granting bodies such as local authorities.

Child Support Agency

2–31

Advice and assistance can be given about child maintenance and assessment/ enforcement by the Child Support Agency. A single form will usually be used for this, including where advice is to be given on matrimonial proceedings (actual or prospective) and/or entitlement to welfare benefits (see paras. 2–18(b) and 2–19(a)). Note also that form filling will only be remunerated so far as it has a legal element and therefore it is reasonable for the solicitor (as opposed to the client) to do the work. In the case of freestanding assessments it is expected that the solicitor will be able to undertake the work necessary to assist in obtaining an assessment and to advise on it within the initial limit.

Grant of representation to an estate

2–32

A solicitor may give advice and assistance to a client to enable that client to make a personal application for a grant of representation but the client will be responsible for payment of the court fees.

Mental Health

2–33

Detailed guidance on mental health matters has been given to support the mental health franchise category—see *Focus* 22, January 1998.

Criminal Cases Review Commission

2–33/1

The following guidance has been given on the Criminal Cases Review Commission in the Board's Guidance: Exercise of Devolved Powers (GEDP), reproduced in *Focus* 22 (April 1998):

> "**1.4.5 Should an extension be allowed where solicitors say there has been a miscarriage of justice?**
>> 1.4.5.1 The Criminal Cases Review Commission has the power to refer cases back to the Court of Appeal under the Criminal Appeals Act 1995 where it considers that there is a real possibility that a conviction, verdict, finding or sentence would not be upheld. The Commission's role is to review and investigate suspected miscarriages of justice, and to determine in each case whether or not a referral to the Court of Appeal is appropriate.
>> 1.4.5.2 In most cases, the solicitor considering the making of the application to the Commission will not be the solicitor who handled the defence preparation work/trial. In order that the convicted defendant can be given advice on the possibility and merits of the application it is likely to be necessary for the new solicitor to obtain and consider a transcript of the judge's summing up (in Crown Court cases) and the defence solicitor's file of papers.
>> 1.4.5.3 These cases will often involve novel or unusual kinds of

evidence. Some investigation may be necessary on behalf of the convicted defendant before any application is made, possibly including further forensic testing, the obtaining of witness statements and counsel's opinion. If an application is to be made to the Commission, then the solicitor will be involved in gathering and rationalising the material, preparing a chronology of events, and preparing the submission of any legal arguments required.

1.4.5.4 The solicitor is also likely to need to advise and assist the convicted defendant after the application is submitted to the Commission by assisting the Commission with specific queries, making further submissions (if appropriate) arising from material disclosed by the Commission in the course of the review and investigation, liaising with the Commission as to its approach and progress and advising the client in relation to any decisions made by the Commission in the case. It may be necessary for the solicitor to meet the Commission's representatives on more than one occasion in a complex case.

1.4.5.5 It may be necessary to allow more than **10 hours (100 units)** depending on the individual circumstances of the case. There is no other form of legal aid available for this type of work although the Commission will, in considering the application, make what further enquiries it considers appropriate to enable it to investigate the case and reach a decision. It is suggested that cases of this nature should be referred up to a solicitor/senior member of staff."

2–34   Is it reasonable to grant a solicitor authority not to enforce the solicitor's charge?
(Legal Advice and Assistance Regulations 1989, reg. 33)

The rule is that in paying for advice and assistance the legal aid fund is only responsible for the deficiency after taking into account the client's contribution (ABWOR only), costs paid by the other side and the solicitor's charge on property recovered or preserved for the legally assisted person in connection with that matter (Legal Aid Act 1988, s.11, p. 286). It may be necessary to look at the solicitor's file to decide whether the charge applies in any particular case.

Paragraph (f) of Schedule 4 to the Legal Advice and Assistance Regulations 1989 creates an exception from the solicitor's charge in respect of any sum, payment or benefit which by virtue of any provision of or made under an Act of Parliament, cannot be assigned or charged. The trigger to bring the exception into play is that the provision of or made under an Act of Parliament must prevent the monies in question from being assigned or charged. The most common category of cases to which the exception applies is state benefits, whether contributory, non-contributory or income related but awards by the Criminal Injuries Compensation Authority are also excepted.

NOTE: *The green form solicitor's charge is different from the legal aid statutory charge because:*

1. *There are different exemptions (see Legal Advice and Assistance Regulations 1989, Sched. 4, p. 358, compared to the Civil Legal Aid (General) Regulations, reg. 94, p. 407).*

2. *The green form charge is wholly handled by the solicitor who must take reasonable steps to protect his or her charge to ensure he or she receives money or property recovered or preserved and sets it off against any deficiency he/she is claiming out of the legal aid fund. This contrasts with the legal aid charge which involves payments in and out of the legal aid fund. The solicitor must take reasonable steps to protect his/her charge because where there is a recovery or preservation there will be no, or a reduced, deficiency for payment out of the legal aid fund. This means that where the charge is lost the solicitor will bear that loss.*

3. *The area office has power to authorise the solicitor not to enforce his or her charge (whereas there is no power to waive the legal aid charge). The grounds are grave hardship or distress to the client or unreasonable difficulty in enforcement because of the nature of the property. See Legal Advice and Assistance Regulations 1989, reg. 33 and below.*

Grave hardship   2–35

(a) *What are the personal or financial circumstances of the client compared with the value of the money or property recovered or preserved?* Since the hardship must be grave, the lower the value of the money or property recovered or preserved the less chance there is of grave hardship being suffered.

(b) *What are the personal or financial circumstances of the client?* If the client is on a low income, or income support/income based Jobseeker's Allowance, authority will usually be given where the client has suffered a financial loss and the compensation is to remedy that loss, but not where the compensation has an element of profit.

If the client is on a higher income any hardship may not be so grave as to justify authority.

(c) *What is the value of the money or property recovered or preserved?* If it is so low that enforcement would substantially diminish or wholly extinguish the benefit to the client, authority might be justified. In such circumstances, however, the area office might consider whether to disallow the solicitor's costs on the grounds that he should have advised the client from the outset that the work would not be cost effective.

(d) *What is the nature of any property recovered or preserved?* If the property is an essential item such as a cooker, refrigerator or furniture, authority will be granted. If the property is a luxury item such as jewellery, a video or television, authority will usually be refused.

Grave distress   2–36

Does the property itself have any special meaning for the client? If the item is of genuine sentimental value, for example, a wedding ring, authority may be granted.

Difficulty in enforcement due to nature of property   2–37

What are the problems in enforcement? Authority will be given only where there is real difficulty as opposed to inconvenience or delay, for example where the property is outside the jurisdiction (but query should the advice and assistance have been given in the first place if difficulty in enforcement could be foreseen?).

Payment to a client by mistake and the difficulty of recovering the money are not matters for authority under regulation 33. They are matters for the area office to consider when assessing the solicitor's costs.

2–38 ADVICE AND ASSISTANCE AT POLICE STATIONS

The Board cannot pay for any legal advice and assistance at police stations by a non-solicitor representative unless the representative is on the Board's register of representatives. Representatives may be registered as accredited or as probationers. Probationers will be restricted to advising on summary and either way cases. Probationers have 12 months in which to obtain accreditation. Accreditation consists of three stages:

(a) submitting a portfolio of nine cases to a testing organisation which must notify the Board within six months of the probationer's registration that a complete portfolio has been received;

(b) once a satisfactory portfolio has been submitted, the probationer must pass a written test on criminal law and procedure, his/her role at the police station and the skills necessary to perform that role;

(c) the critical incidents test which simulates police station situations on an audio tape. The candidate will have to respond on tape to a given situation in a limited time.

If the probationer does not complete the three stage accreditation process within 12 months the Board will not pay for any further work done by that representative (on either a duty solicitor or own solicitor basis) until he/she has obtained full accreditation. Similar arrangements covering immigration advice have also been introduced.

The operation of the register of representatives is covered by the Board's Legal Advice and Assistance at Police Stations Register Arrangements 1995 (see p. 635) and the Duty Solicitor Arrangements 1997 (see p. 601) (the latter concern the application of the registration requirements to duty solicitor representatives).

The following information may be useful:

(a) An information pack can be obtained from Practice Advice Service, Library and Information Services, The Law Society, 50 Chancery Lane, London WC2A 1SX; DX 56 Lond/Chancery Ln. Tel: 0171 242 1222.

(b) Law Society Training Kit "Police Station Skills for Legal Advisers" £137.75 from the Law Society Business Centre, 113 Chancery Lane, London WC2A 1PL. Telephone orders: 01235 465656.

(c) The Register application form is available from the Secretariat Department, Legal Aid Head Office, 85 Gray's Inn Road, London WC1X 8AA, DX 450 London. Tel: 0171 813 1000 ext. 8561/2.

Is it reasonable to grant an extension to the costs limit in respect of a claim by a solicitor attending a police station? (Legal Advice and Assistance Regulations 1989, reg. 4(2)(a))   2–39

The options are to:

(a) grant an extension in whole or in part; or

(b) refuse an extension.

The following questions must be answered:

(a) Is the client a person who has either been arrested or is a volunteer or is being interviewed in connection with a serious service offence? The definition of "volunteer" does not exclude a person who is not under suspicion him/herself (see para. 2–43).

(b) Was there an adequate reason that "the interests of justice required advice and assistance to be given as matter of urgency" (*e.g.* continuing interview/age of client/physical or mental capability/language difficulties)?

(c) Was the extent of advice given necessary? (The solicitor's interview notes may be requested.)

(d) In an "own solicitor" case where there is a considerable distance between the solicitor's office and police station, should the duty solicitor have been used (*e.g.* where the claim for an extension to the upper limit has to be made only because of a large travelling costs claim)?

ASSESSMENT OF POLICE STATION AND COURT DUTY SOLICITOR COSTS CLAIMS   2–40

(See Note for Guidance 18, para. 18–23 which deals with claims queries and late claims for advice and assistance at police stations and court duty solicitor work.)

The Legal Aid Board has decided the following points of principle in connection with the assessment of police station costs claims:

When the duty solicitor rate is payable   2–41

Duty solicitor rates rather than own solicitor rates are only payable when a solicitor is advising as a duty solicitor within the Duty Solicitor Arrangements or when advice is commenced in a duty period and continues without interruption beyond the end of the duty period. (Legal Aid Board reference DS 1.)

NOTE: *The above decision relates to the pre-1994 Duty Solicitor Arrange-*

ments and it is unlikely that claims would now be submitted to which the decision would apply. In respect of the Duty Solicitor Arrangements 1994 and 1997 the Board considers that:

> The duty solicitor rate of remuneration will be paid for all work undertaken following receipt of the case from the Board's duty solicitor call centre until the latest of the following:

> **rota duty solicitor:** all assistance provided during the rota period (and any advice which continues without interruption beyond the end of the duty period) or, after the expiration of the rota period, the end of the first attendance at the police station to give advice or the first police interview or identity parade, group identification or confrontation.

> **panel duty solicitor:** the end of the first attendance at the police station to give advice or the first police interview or identity parade, group identification or confrontation.

2–42 Solicitor to justify use of interpreter

Where a solicitor employs an interpreter to assist in his advising a client at the police station it will be for the solicitor to justify the interpreter's fees taking into account all the circumstances of the case, including the need to preserve confidentiality of advice given to a suspect and information received from a suspect and/or the particular characteristics of the language spoken and the need for accurate interpretation. (Legal Aid Board reference DS 2.) See also Note for Guidance 18–22 regarding interpreters.

2–43 Volunteer: interpretation of definition

The definition of "volunteer" set out in regulation 2 of the Legal Advice and Assistance at Police Stations (Remuneration) Regulations 1989 does not exclude a person assisting police with enquiries at a police station or at any other place where a constable is present who is not at that time under suspicion themselves.

A legal representative may be remunerated for attending such persons providing that the conditions set out in regulation 5(2) of the Legal Advice and Assistance at Police Stations (Remuneration) Regulations 1989 are satisfied. (Legal Aid Board reference DS 3.)

2–44 Abortive visit to police station

A legal representative who attends by prior appointment at a police station for the purpose of giving advice and assistance is entitled to be paid for work actually and reasonably done even though the purpose of the attendance is thwarted, for example because the client does not attend or the appointment has been cancelled without notice. (Legal Aid Board reference DS 4.)

2–45 Panel duty solicitor rates under the 1992 Arrangements

Where a claim falls under the 1992 Duty Solicitor Arrangements the payment to a panel duty solicitor shall be at duty solicitor rates until the suspect's initial period of detention at the police station ends. (Legal Aid Board reference DS 5.)

Interviews during an investigation by a non-police agency 2–46

A solicitor attending a client making a voluntary attendance at a place other than a police station in connection with an investigation by an agency other than the police force is not covered by the advice and assistance at the police station scheme unless a constable is present and taking part in the proceedings. (Legal Aid Board reference DS 6.)

Advising and assisting over the telephone 2–46/1

The expression "advising and assisting over the telephone" in regulation 5(1)(d) of the Legal Advice and Assistance at Police Stations (Remuneration) Regulations 1989 covers any telephone attendance actually and reasonably made which is not a routine call and which materially progresses the case.

The onus is on the solicitor to satisfy the assessing officer that the work did progress the case, was actually and reasonably done, and that the amount of time spent was reasonable. The solicitor should be able to supply an attendance note to justify a claim for advising and assisting over the telephone, if required to do so by the assessing officer. (Legal Aid Board reference DS 7.).

DISBURSEMENTS 2–47

Problems have arisen for practitioners, area committees, and area office staff in determining which disbursements can, subject to the appropriate limit on the costs to be incurred, be recovered under the legal advice and assistance scheme. Technically, the question of determining whether a disbursement is recoverable can be difficult, but it is in the interests of the public and practitioners that guidance be kept as simple as possible. Therefore, there follows a list of those disbursements which will normally be treated as recoverable under the scheme, provided:

(a) it is reasonable for the solicitor to incur the disbursement *for the purpose of giving advice or assistance* to the client, and

(b) the amount of the disbursement is reasonable.

There also follows a list of those disbursements which are unlikely ever to be properly recoverable. In connection with disbursements which are in neither list practitioners are advised to seek advice and authority from the relevant area office. The House of Lords held in *R. v. Legal Aid Board, ex p. Bruce* [1992] 1 W.L.R. 694; [1992] 3 All E.R. 321 that the cost of legal advice by a person who is not a lawyer or supervised by a lawyer cannot be claimed as a disbursement. The assistance of a non lawyer can be sought but must be absorbed as an overhead, rather than charged as a disbursement. Furthermore, the House of Lords accepted that a solicitor agent *cannot* be used under legal advice and assistance (either as a disbursement or an element of profit costs)—see also para. 2–70, Costs Appeals Committee decision LAA 18. The

Board does, however, accept that solicitor agents can be used in ABWOR cases (as opposed to legal advice and assistance). See also para. 2–51.

See also NFG 11, para. 11–06 for the position regarding disbursements where a solicitor, his partner or employee is involved in the provision of non-legal services.

Recoverable Disbursements	*Irrecoverable Disbursements*
Accident report fees.	*Ad valorem* stamp duties.
Birth and other certificates.	
Conciliation referral fees to approved services. (See also below.)	Capital duty.
Counsel's fees.	Client's travelling and accommodation expenses.
	Contact centre fees.
Enquiry agents' and interpreters' fees.	Discharge of debts owed by the client, *e.g.* rent or mortgage arrears.
Experts' fees including for medical reports.	Mortgagees' or lessors' solicitors costs and disbursements.
Newspaper advertisements.	Passport fees.
Fees recoverable on oaths.	Fee payable on voluntary petitions in bankruptcy.
Photographers' accounts.	Court fees (unless for a search/ photocopies/bailiff service).
Search fees.	Probate fees.
Stamp duties of a nominal amount, *e.g.* the fee paid on a power of attorney.	
Travelling expenses of a solicitor, including a solicitor in the capacity of McKenzie friend.	

If an extension is sought in respect of an item which appears in neither list then the area office must consider whether the disbursement is recoverable or not by reference to its purpose (*i.e.* is it for the purpose of giving advice or assistance?). For example, an accountant's fees for the preparation of outstanding accounts will not be recoverable, as they are incurred not for the purpose of giving advice and assistance but for the purpose of putting the client's outstanding records in order. This contrasts with the position where the accountant is providing a report as an expert.

Occasionally clients wish to use legal advice and assistance as a vehicle to obtain the funding of disbursements. Where the only work to be undertaken by the solicitor is incurring the disbursement and passing the service provided (normally a report) to the client, the costs should not be allowed. Although the system of legal advice and assistance is intended to cover advice and assistance rather than representation, it would not be reasonable for it to be used in such a way that the client receives no oral or written legal advice in relation to the particular circumstances that have arisen.

In deciding whether the amount sought is reasonable, regard must be had to all the circumstances, including the purpose of the disbursement in the context of the particular case (*i.e.* having regard to the justification/need for it, as against the value/importance of the case), the particular service involved, the extent to which there is a choice of alternative service providers and whether all elements of the service are justified in the particular case/at the particular time (*e.g.* proofs or limited prints of photographs, rather than a larger number of prints).

Where a solicitor refers a client to a recognised conciliation service outside the mediation pilot scheme (see NFG 1, para. 1–12), a fixed amount can be allowed under legal advice and assistance. This is currently £33.13 (£33.00 for non-franchisees), which is broken down as to £23.35 for the report (*i.e.* the disbursement for the service's fee) and £9.78 (£9.65 for non-franchisees) for the solicitor's costs. An extension to the costs limit may or may not be needed to undertake this work, depending on the work already reasonably undertaken when the referral is to be made. (See also NFG 1, para. 1–12 regarding mediation generally.)

Blood tests including DNA—immigration cases   2–48

There are two principal classes of cases in which solicitors apply for an extension of the financial limit to cover the cost of blood tests to resolve an issue of paternity:

(1) *To avoid court proceedings.* An extension may be granted, provided that the area office is satisfied that the parties have agreed the identity of the test agency (to minimise the possibility of further tests), no alternative funding, *e.g.* by the Child Support Agency is reasonably available and the costs are reasonable.

(2) *Immigration cases.* In principle, the cost of blood tests is an expense which may be incurred in connection with the giving of advice and assistance to a sponsor here, whose alleged child or children abroad have applied for leave to enter the United Kingdom. The following points must be carefully noted:

   (a) Entry Clearance Officers employ an extended interview procedure for dealing with difficult applications, for instance where acceptable marriage or birth certificates are not available. An extension will not normally be granted to cover the cost of obtaining blood tests at that stage, therefore, unless the solicitor certifies that, without blood tests, the available evidence is likely to be insufficient to satisfy the Entry Clearance Officer as to an alleged blood relationship upon which the application for entry hinges.

   (b) Where the blood tests are required for any appeal following the refusal of an application for entry clearance, the extension will be granted if the solicitor certifies that the blood tests are necessary to establish a blood relationship upon which the outcome of the appeal hinges, and that there are reasonable prospects that any other grounds for refusing entry can be overcome.

   (c) In the case of blood samples taken abroad, the Immigration Authorities will only accept blood tests where the samples are taken in accordance with a strict procedure. On the Indian sub-continent, facilities which comply with that procedure are only at present available in Islamabad in Pakistan and Dhaka in Bangladesh. Unless and until facilities become available in other places, applications will be refused as fruitless unless the person resident abroad can take advantage of the facilities at Islamabad or Dhaka.

(d) Blood samples from a person who has gained entry to the United Kingdom, or who has been stopped at the port of entry, must be taken by a consultant haematologist, a medical practitioner in a Regional Blood Transfusion Centre, or an appointed blood tester. The Immigration Authorities have laid down a detailed procedure which the person taking the sample must follow.

2–49 Medical reports

In personal injury cases an extension for a medical report will only be granted where there is a reasonable case on liability *and* there is a real prospect of the solicitor being able to settle the case without having to issue proceedings (and hence the solicitor would not propose applying for legal aid). Where an application for legal aid has been made or is intended to be made an extension will not be granted, unless the circumstances are exceptional, as a medical report is seldom required merely for the purpose of ascertaining whether the likely *quantum* of damages justifies the issue of proceedings.

2–50 Photographs

Where a solicitor seeks an extension to take photographs in a personal injury case, in a normal "pavement trip" case it is reasonable to expect someone from the solicitor's office or the client or a friend or relative to take photographs. Such a case does not justify employing a professional photographer. A more complex case, *e.g.* a serious road or industrial accident might justify employing a professional, although this would almost invariably be done once a legal aid certificate has been issued. It would only be reasonable to justify an extension to the legal advice and assistance costs limit if, for example, there was a real risk that the evidence to be photographed might disappear.

2–51 ASSESSMENT OF COSTS—GENERAL PRINCIPLES

The solicitor is limited as to the amount of costs he can incur without obtaining an extension from the area office—£90 for advice and assistance in police stations, three hours' work at current rates of remuneration for petitioners for divorce or judicial separation, and two hours' work at current remuneration rates in other cases.

The costs of giving advice and assistance include disbursements as well as legal fees but solicitor agents may not be employed (see paras. 2–47 and 2–70, Costs Appeals Committee decision LAA 18). The effect of the House of Lords' ruling in *R. v. Legal Aid Board, ex p. Bruce* [1992] 1 W.L.R. 694; [1992] 3 All E.R. 321 is that all legal advice under legal advice and assistance (green form) must be provided by legal representatives (which at present means only solicitors or barristers).

The ruling does not prevent solicitors from obtaining experts' reports on matters other than law, notwithstanding that those reports may be given with the legal issues in mind.

Solicitors are not prevented from seeking legal advice from non-lawyers but the cost cannot be charged as a disbursement and must be absorbed by the solicitors as part of their overheads. If a solicitor chooses to seek advice elsewhere, he or she must then give the advice to the client direct as the solicitor's own advice. Any claim under legal advice and assistance will then be assessed on the basis of what would have been a reasonable time for a solicitor who was competent in that field of law to spend giving the advice to the client.

The House of Lords also accepted that the use of solicitor agents is not permitted under legal advice and assistance. If solicitors who are advising a client under legal advice and assistance decide that they are no longer able to deal with the matter, either for geographical reasons or because of a lack of relevant expertise, any new solicitors who wish to advise the client should not do so as agents of the first firm but should apply for prior authority from the appropriate area office to give advice and assistance to the client on the same matter.

Where solicitors lack the necessary expertise to advise a client under legal advice and assistance and the use of counsel is not justified, they should either refer the client to another firm of solicitors who are able to advise or alternatively accept that the cost of acquiring the relevant expertise must be treated as an office overhead and cannot be charged as a disbursement under legal advice and assistance.

Solicitors are permitted (under regulation 20 of the Legal Advice and Assistance Regulations 1989) to entrust work to someone under their immediate supervision who is not legally qualified, provided that person is competent to give the advice. Solicitors may not be paid under the legal advice and assistance scheme for the cost of obtaining *legal* advice for their clients from anyone who is not a solicitor or barrister. Note also that for work to be delegated within regulation 20 the solicitor's representative must be competent and responsible and either employed in the solicitor's office under a contract of service or be under the solicitor's immediate supervision.

It may be possible for a self-employed contractor engaged by a solicitor to fit these requirements but the mere fact of being engaged by a firm of solicitors is not of itself sufficient.

Whether a representative is under the immediate supervision of a solicitor will depend upon all the relevant facts. Practitioners should note the decision of the Divisional Court in *R. v. Legal Aid Board, ex p. Rafina* (February 12, 1998, *New Law Journal*, February 27, 1998) which involved an application for judicial review by a firm of solicitors which specialised in immigration work.

The Board had concerns about the use of unsupervised representatives by the firm to provide immigration advice under the Legal Advice and Assistance Scheme. The Board placed a temporary stop on the firm's legal aid account while it investigated. The area office disallowed a number of claims after determining that the firm's supervisory arrangements did not satisfy regulation 20 of the Legal Advice and Assistance Regulations 1989. The area committee upheld the decision of the area office on appeal. The solicitors appealed to the Costs Appeals Committee which certified a point of principle of general importance known as LAA12. (See para. 2–64, below).

The solicitors challenged the Board's interpretation of regulation 20, the failure of the area committee to give proper reasons for its decision and the

Board's decision to impose a temporary stop on the solicitor's account. The firm's application for judicial review was dismissed by the Court.

Mr Justice Latham upheld the Costs Appeals Committee's interpretation of regulation 20 as set out in the point of principle. This means that if unqualified representatives undertake work under the Legal Advice and Assistance Scheme, they must be competent and responsible, and either be employed in a solicitor's office under a contract of service or be under the immediate supervision of a solicitor. It is not sufficient for an unqualified person to be employed in a solicitor's office as an independent contractor unless the person is being immediately supervised by a solicitor.

The Court adopted an interpretation of "immediate supervision" put forward by the Law Society, which is as follows:

> "The Society's interpretation of 'immediate supervision' is that it requires the solicitor be empowered to direct the work of the clerk and to review it as necessary. If the solicitor is able to direct the work of the representative, is able to monitor its quality, and to take immediate and effective action if the quality is unsatisfactory as well as being able to insist that the representative cease to act as necessary then in the Society's view adequate and immediate supervision has taken place."

This should be read in conjunction with the Board's views below.

The Court confirmed that the consequences of a breach of regulation 20 are that there will be no entitlement to any payment under the Legal Advice and Assistance Scheme. It prevents payment of both profit costs and disbursements, for example interpreter's fees.

This case also determined that area committees have an obligation to provide reasons for their decisions on appeals.

The Board took action in the interests of the fund, the tax-payer and the legally-aided client. The judgment implicitly accepts that the Board has power to impose a temporary stop (a "vendor hold") on a solicitor's account where appropriate (see also NFG 1, para. 1–29).

The Board considers:

(a) that it may be easier to demonstrate supervision of the representative for the purpose of the regulation when it can be shown to take place on a general, and not merely an individual case, basis;

(b) that it is more difficult to exercise supervision at a distance;

(c) that the less contact the solicitor has with the representative or "welfare officer" the more difficult it will be for him to exercise supervision; and

(d) that "immediate" means that there must be no third party between the solicitor and the representative, *i.e.* the solicitor's contract must be with the representative and not with an agency or organisation on behalf of the representative.

Solicitors need to ensure that, if they do entrust any of their legal advice and assistance work to another person, the arrangements and the person properly fit within the requirements of regulation 20. (See the *Law Society's Gazette*, January 27, 1993, p. 32 and *R. v. Legal Aid Board, ex p. Rafina*.)

See also para. 2–07 above regarding distant solicitors and NFG 11, para. 11–06 for the position regarding disbursements where a solicitor, his partner or employee is involved in the provision of non-legal services.

Costs are assessed by the area office in accordance with the Legal Aid Act 1988, The Legal Advice and Assistance (Scope) Regulations 1989 and the Legal Advice and Assistance Regulations 1989. Note, however, that the test for the costs assessor determining a costs claim is whether the work appears to have been reasonably done and the time as claimed (excluding time spent on routine letters and calls) is reasonable. Whilst solicitors may adopt units for time recording purposes the determining officer will allow such time as is considered reasonable rather than notional time with reference to units.

Time spent carrying out the means assessment and completing the green form is undertaken prior to the signature of the green form and cannot be remunerated.

The opening of a file, maintenance of time/costing records and the preparation/submission of extension applications and costs claims are not chargeable work but are overheads and cannot be remunerated. A client care letter can be remunerated.

Generally, letters written and telephone calls are paid at the routine rate set out in Schedule 6 to the Legal Advice and Assistance Regulations 1989. Where a letter written is substantial in length (more than one page) and content, or where a telephone call is lengthy and of such substance as to constitute an attendance, then it may be reasonable for the preparation rate to be used. If so the claim should be the actual time spent calculated at the preparation rate.

It is not permissible to claim both the preparation rate and the routine letter or routine telephone rate in respect of the same letter or telephone call.

It should be noted that there is no separate charge for routine letters received. The rate set for routine letters written includes the perusal and consideration of such letters received and therefore no sepeate charge can be made for such letters.

Where a letter is produced using modern technology, then the routine letter rate should be used (*e.g.* where details are inserted into a format by the use of a word processor), even where a number of letters using fundamentally the same text are produced on the same file. Time spent inputting information to a word processed document/computer package to generate a letter is not preparation by a fee-earner but is akin to typing and is an overhead. To that extent the solicitor gains the benefit of modern technology and he is not expected to dictate or redraft the text of the letter each time it is used.

Letters are subject to costs assessment in the usual way and where a number of separate letters are produced to deal with matters which could reasonably, conveniently and appropriately have been dealt with in a single letter, then the costs of the additional, subsequent, letters are liable to be disallowed on costs assessment. This also applies to client care letters.

The area office may call for the solicitor's file to carry out its costs assessment. Payment is made to the solicitor in order of priority of the solicitor's charge on costs recovered from the other side and property recovered or preserved (collected by solicitor) and the balance (paid out of the legal aid fund).

If conditions as to availability of advice and assistance are not met (*e.g.* that the matter must be one of English law not specifically excluded by the regulations), costs out of the legal aid fund will be refused even if the amount of costs claimed is under the prospective cost limit. The assessment is based on work actually and reasonably done.

The original application form (green form) signed by the client must be submitted to the area office where a claim for payment out of the legal aid fund is made. The income and capital details must be fully completed at the time that the application (green form) is signed. To comply with the mandatory requirements set out in the regulations, words or figures should be inserted as appropriate. Solicitors should not complete the income and capital details using either a dash or a strike through. This will result in a claim for payment being refused by the area office on the grounds that the relevant information has not been furnished.

Where the form has been lost the solicitor should complete a fresh form (unsigned by the applicant) and submit it with a photocopy of the original form (if available), together with a letter signed by a partner confirming the loss, the accuracy of the contents of the fresh form, and that the costs have not been claimed previously nor will be claimed in the future. The area office will then decide whether the existence and contents of the original form have been sufficiently proved to justify payment of the claim.

The solicitor's charge can in certain circumstances be waived by the area office (see para. 2–34). If, however, the basis of the application for waiver is that enforcement would substantially diminish or wholly extinguish the benefit to the client of any property or money recovered or preserved, the area office, even if authorising the waiver, might consider disallowing some or all the costs on the grounds that the solicitor should have advised the client from the outset (or subsequently) that the work would not be cost effective.

What happens if the limit is exceeded? The Legal Aid Board considers that a solicitor who exceeds the prescribed financial limit cannot obtain payment of the balance from the legal aid fund. Nor can payment be obtained from the client on a private basis unless there has first been an application to the area office for an extension which has been refused, and the client, having been informed of such refusal, elects to instruct the solicitor on a private basis. It is not possible for a client to retain the solicitor on a legal advice and assistance, *i.e.* statutory, basis and private basis at the same time (*Joyce v. Kammac (1988) Ltd* [1996] 1 All E.R. 923). See also Legal Aid and Solicitors' Professional Conduct, p. 740.

2–52   Legal Aid Board decisions as to assessment of legal advice and assistance (green form) costs

The Legal Aid Board has issued the following decisions as a point of principle of general importance in connection with the assessment of legal advice and assistance costs:

2–53   Authority for the signature of a fresh green form

There is no power to grant retrospective authority to give advice and assistance under a fresh green form where such authority is required and there is also no power to allow costs in green form or ABWOR cases where such authority is required but has not been obtained. An approval of ABWOR by the area office does not alter the position. A client *may* complete an application for advice and assistance in anticipation of such authority under regulation 16 being granted. (Legal Aid Board reference LAA1 as amended.)

Costs of supervision

A claim for costs for time spent supervising a fee earner may be remunerated if such supervision falls within the description of preparation of the case, as opposed to practical instruction or practice management. A fee earner should ordinarily be competent to deal with cases allocated to him.

Where costs of supervision are claimed an explanation of the reasons why the nature of the case made the supervisor's participation necessary and of the occasions, duration and circumstances of his participation must be provided in the claim. (Legal Aid Board reference LAA2.)

Advice by more than one solicitor on same matter: requirement for prior authority

By regulation 16(1) of the Legal Advice and Assistance Regulations 1989 a solicitor requires prior authority from the Area Director to advise on the same matter if advice has previously been given by another solicitor. Where advice has been previously given but no charge is to be made for that advice, it is deemed not to be advice to which the Legal Advice and Assistance Regulations 1989 apply and no prior authority under regulation 16(1) of the Legal Advice and Assistance Regulations 1989 is required. (Legal Aid Board reference LAA3.)

Work undertaken following detention at a police station

The Legal Advice and Assistance Scheme is available for work reasonably and necessarily done for a client following on his/her detention at a police station. (Legal Aid Board reference LAA4.)

Costs guidelines: Guidance on the Exercise of Devolved Powers: interim edition

The costs guidelines contained in "Guidance on the Exercise of Devolved Powers—interim edition" are indicators only. Payment in each case should be made for work actually and reasonably undertaken. (Legal Aid Board reference LAA5.)

(This edition has been superseded.)

Preparation of brief to counsel for Immigration Appeal Tribunal hearing

Legal Aid Board reference LAA6—*this decision has been withdrawn.*

Application for advice and assistance under the Legal Advice and Assistance Regulations 1989

The combined effect of regulations 9(1), 9(3), 9(4) and 9(6) of the Legal Advice and Assistance Regulations 1989 is that the making of the application for advice and assistance includes the provision of the financial information, both capital and income, as required by regulation 9(4). The application must be made in person and the information which is part of that application must be provided at the same time as the completion, including signing and dating, of a form approved by the Board.

On attendance on behalf of the client under regulation 10 of the Legal Advice and Assistance Regulations 1989 the person so authorised should attend to make the application on behalf of a client. The making of that application must include a personal attendance by the person so authorised, the provision of the information required by the Regulations and completion of the form approved by the Board.

If the date inserted on the signing of the form is incorrectly recorded or omitted, it shall be permissible to provide to the Board satisfactory evidence to show the date on which the form was actually signed. Extraneous evidence cannot be provided in respect of the mandatory information required by the Regulations. (Legal Aid Board reference LAA7 as amended.)

2–60 Application of English law

A solicitor who discovers during the course of the preliminary interview that the matter concerns a foreign jurisdiction cannot claim under the Green Form Scheme the cost of identifying that the matter is foreign or of advising the client to seek legal advice of the relevant jurisdiction. (Legal Aid Board reference LAA8.)

2–61 The exercise and recording of devolved powers

Solicitors may charge for work done in the exercise of devolved powers and the recording of such exercise. (Legal Aid Board reference LAA9.)

2–62 Regulation 10 attendance on behalf of a client

Whilst it may be usual for the "another person" authorised under regulation 10 of the Legal Advice and Assistance Regulations 1989 to be independent of the solicitor's firm undertaking the advice and assistance, there may be circumstances in which the "another person" may be an employee of the firm other than the fee-earner advising. In such circumstances a full record of the authorisation (written or otherwise) and the physical attendance on the solicitor should be made. The cost for authorisation of work done prior to the physical attendance by the "another person" should not form part of the solicitor's claim for costs. (Legal Aid Board reference LAA10.) See also para. 2–12 above.

2–63 No previous green form

Where an applicant has deliberately misled his solicitor that no green form has been signed previously, or that any previous advice was not provided by a solicitor and even though the solicitor has no information that a green form has been signed, no payment is able to be made, given the mandatory nature of regulation 16(1) of the Legal Advice and Assistance Regulations 1989.

Solicitors should exercise great care when questioning the client whether previous advice has been given. If a solicitor has received any indication that any previous advice has been given, it would be reasonable to expect the solicitor to check whether it was a solicitor who previously provided that advice and how such advice was funded. If there is any indication previous advice may have been given, or if in doubt, the solicitor should assume one has been signed. The onus will be on the solicitor advising to satisfy the Board that no green form has previously been signed.

If, after providing advice, it becomes clear that the applicant has deliberately misled his solicitor and the solicitor has taken all reasonable steps, payment may not be made under the Legal Advice and Assistance Regulations but it may be appropriate for an extra-statutory payment to be made. (Legal Aid Board Reference LAA11.)

Regulation 20 and supervision   2–64

The words "employed in his office" within regulation 20 refer to those persons employed by the solicitor or firm under the normal principles of employment, including payment of PAYE. Those persons who carry out some work within a solicitor's office who are, for example, self-employed, or those who work outside of the office must be under the solicitor's immediate supervision.

A breach of regulation 20 of the Legal Advice and Assistance Regulations prevents payment for the advice and assistance work undertaken including any disbursements directly connected with it, *e.g.* interpreter's fees. Costs claims for such work will thus be disallowed. (Legal Aid Board Reference LAA12.)

Persons resident outside of England and Wales and the interaction   2–65
between regulations 10–15 of the Legal Advice and Assistance
Regulations 1989

Notwithstanding the provisions of regulation 15 of the Legal Advice and Assistance Regulations, if a person who resides outside England and Wales is able to satisfy the criteria under regulation 10, "another person" may be instructed to attend upon the solicitor on his or her behalf. (Legal Aid Board Reference LAA13.)

Error or mistake in assessment   2–66

Paragraph 11 of Schedule 2 to the Legal Advice and Assistance Regulations 1989 indicates that if it appears there has been some error or mistake the solicitor may, but not must, amend the means assessment but is not obliged to do so. If the solicitor decides not to amend, he/she must specify when submitting their claim for costs precisely why that decision was made and may have regard in respect of a spouse to whether in all the circumstances of the case it would be inequitable or impractical to do so. (Legal Aid Board Reference LAA14.)

2–67 Insertion of capital and income details on the green form

The combined effect of regulations 9(4) and 9(6) of the Legal Advice and Assistance Regulations 1989 are to make it mandatory for a solicitor to obtain capital and income details from the person applying to be assisted and to furnish that information on the green form.

In order to comply with those mandatory requirements solicitors must ensure that both sections for income and capital details are completed on the green form using words and/or figures as appropriate. A tick or striking through of the income or capital detail boxes does not furnish information as required by the Regulations. (Legal Aid Board Reference LAA15.)

2–68 Advice and assistance on welfare benefits

A single form should be used where general, preliminary advice and assistance is provided in relation to various or separate welfare benefits, including checking any benefit currently paid, advice on application procedures for particular benefits and providing a report on entitlement to welfare benefits generally.

Where a separate problem is identified or subsequently arises, this may justify the use of a separate, additional form, *e.g.* general benefits advice followed by, say, a particular housing benefit problem, such as a specific query regarding the client's entitlement (two green forms unless the original green form continued to be used) or followed by housing benefit and income support problems (three green forms, unless the original green form continued to be used). (Legal Aid Board reference LAA16.)

2–69 Advice and assistance on living wills

It may be reasonable to provide legal advice and assistance in connection with preparing an "advance directive" where the individual concerned can satisfy the requirement in section 2(2) and (3) of the Legal Aid Act 1988 that particular circumstances have arisen requiring such advice to be given.

This requirement might be satisfied if it can be shown that such a directive may be needed, *i.e.* that by virtue of the individual's current medical state there is a real probability of medical treatment being required in the future. (Legal Aid Board reference LAA17.) See also para. 2–29/1 for guidance.

2–70 Solicitor agents and the legal advice and assistance scheme

Section 32(10) of the Legal Aid Act 1988 authorises the use of solicitor agents for representation only. A solicitor cannot therefore delegate the provision of advice and assistance to a solicitor agent. (Legal Aid Board reference LAA18.)

3. ASSISTANCE BY WAY OF REPRESENTATION (ABWOR)

WHAT DOES ABWOR COVER?   3–01

ABWOR covers the cost of a solicitor preparing the client's case and representing him/her in most civil cases in magistrates' courts. These cases include separation, maintenance and defended adoption proceedings and the scope of an approval includes giving notice of appeal. It is also available for hearings before Mental Health Review Tribunals, the Parole Board (Discretionary Lifer Panel and Her Majesty's Pleasure Panel), for prison disciplinary hearings (where permission has been given for the prisoner to be represented) for proceedings under section 47 of the National Assistance Act 1948 and for proceedings in the magistrates' court where a fine or other defaulter is at risk of imprisonment. All proceedings under the Children Act 1989 are covered by civil legal aid.

NOTE: *Approvals of ABWOR do not operate retrospectively.*

HOW DOES A CLIENT APPLY FOR ABWOR?   3–02

The solicitor should assess the client's means (except for proceedings before Mental Health Review Tribunals) and fill in the application form and send it to the area office. Note that there is now no need to fill in a legal advice and assistance application form (a green form) when applying for ABWOR but see the guidance at NFG 2, para. 2–07 regarding the acceptance of instructions by distant solicitors.

The area office will then decide whether it is reasonable for the client to receive ABWOR. The area office can either grant or refuse ABWOR but, if the application is refused, the client can appeal to the area committee.

Following the implementation of the Board's computer system (CIS) in each area office, costs conditions will no longer be imposed on the grant of legal aid. A costs limitation will be imposed for the work authorised under each ABWOR approval/certificate issued in any case including matrimonial/family cases. This will be a true limitation rather than merely a condition requiring a report once a certain level of costs has been reached. In other words solicitors will only have legal aid/ABWOR cover to carry out work up to the costs limitation imposed. The limitation limits the costs to be incurred under the approval/certificate and/or any linked/related certificate(s) to a figure including disbursements and any counsel's fees but excluding any VAT. (See NFG 9–14 and 9–15, p. 154.)

DOES THE CLIENT QUALIFY FINANCIALLY?   3–03

The assessment of means for ABWOR is carried out by the solicitor, preparatory to applying for ABWOR (as opposed to through an assessment of means carried out by/on behalf of the Legal Aid Board). ABWOR for proceedings before Mental Health Review Tribunals is not subject to a means test.

The income eligibility limits for assistance by way of representation are different to advice and assistance (although the basis of means assessment is the same—see NFG 2 and the Legal Advice and Assistance Regulations 1989, pp. 339, *et seq.*). The capital limit for ABWOR is higher than for advice and assistance (but not as high as for civil legal aid) and it does not give rise to any contribution from capital. Detailed guidance on means assessment which applies to both legal advice and assistance and ABWOR appears at NFG 2, para. 2–08.

If the capital assessed is above the ABWOR limit but within that of civil legal aid, an application for civil legal aid may be made, if it is available for the proceedings, in which case a means assessment will be needed which may include a capital contribution element (see NFG 4).

The procedure is that:

(a) the solicitor assesses means;

(b) if the client is within the ABWOR limits and the solicitor wishes to apply for ABWOR (rather than for civil legal aid where it is available), he prepares and submits the application for ABWOR;

(c) if the client is outside the ABWOR capital limit but within the maximum civil legal aid limit, an application for civil legal aid has to be submitted to the area office with a civil legal aid means form. The matter will then be dealt with on a legal aid basis and not under ABWOR (provided civil legal aid is available for the particular proceedings).

NOTE: *If the proceedings involve making an application under the Children Act 1989 civil legal aid should be applied for.*

A client's eligibility for ABWOR differs from other forms of advice and assistance. A client's disposable income and disposable capital must both be within the eligibility limits in force at the time ABWOR is applied for (although those in receipt of income support/income-based Jobseeker's Allowance qualify automatically on both capital and income) (see Eligibility Tables p. 667). Provided both disposable income and disposable capital are within those limits:

(a) no contribution can be called for from capital;

(b) a client receiving income support, income-based Jobseeker's Allowance family credit or disability working allowance, or with a disposable income of £72 or below per week will be eligible for free ABWOR;

(c) a client with disposable income in excess of £72 and up to £172 per week will be liable to pay a weekly contribution of one third of the excess over £72. So if disposable income is £102 per week, *i.e.* £30 over the lower limit, the contribution will be £10 per week.

3–04 CONTRIBUTIONS

Contributions for ABWOR are calculated on a weekly basis. Such contributions are due from the date that ABWOR is approved (see para. 3–02 above) until either the proceedings are concluded or ABWOR is withdrawn (see para. 3–17). The solicitor and client may agree on the most convenient method for making contribution payments. There are no powers to reassess the contribution.

AMENDMENT

3–05

An ABWOR approval can be amended, for example, to amend or delete a limitation or alter the proceedings covered. Note however that an ABWOR approval cannot be amended to show a change of solicitor. Instead the client must make a fresh ABWOR application. If the client is financially eligible, the proposed new solicitor will need to obtain prior authority to provide any advice and assistance before applying for ABWOR.

WHAT HAPPENS IF MONEY OR PROPERTY IS RECOVERED OR PRESERVED?

3–06

The same rules apply as for legal advice and assistance (see NFG 2, para. 2–34).

HOW DOES THE SOLICITOR GET PAID?

3–07

The solicitor's bill, less the total contribution due from the client while ABWOR has been in force and the value of any property which is recovered or preserved, will be considered for payment by the area office. Full details of the contribution history must be provided when costs are being claimed. There are powers to assess a global sum for division between solicitors and counsel where counsel has not been authorised. See also NFG 2, para. 2–07 regarding distant solicitors.

The solicitor may apply for a payment on account of disbursements incurred or about to be incurred in connection with proceedings covered by an ABWOR approval. Where such a payment is made the solicitor must report to the area office on the conclusion of the case in any event (*i.e.* even if he is not making a claim for payment).

STATUTORY FRAMEWORK AND CONDITIONS

3–08

The statutory framework for assistance by way of representation is contained in Parts I and III, sections 1, 2 and 8–13 of the Legal Aid Act 1988 (see pp. xxx *et seq.*).

Details of the system are contained in the Legal Advice and Assistance (Scope) Regulations 1989 (see pp. 333 *et seq.*); the Legal Advice and Assistance Regulations 1989 (pp. 339 *et seq.*); the Legal Advice and Assistance (Duty Solicitor) Remuneration Regulations 1989 (pp. 590 *et seq.*); and the Legal Advice and Assistance at Police Stations (Remuneration) Regulations 1989 (pp. 594 *et seq.*). Assistance by way of representation is a half-way house between advice and assistance and civil legal aid.

AVAILABILITY OF ABWOR

3–09

ABWOR is available if the proceedings are specified in Part III of the Legal

Advice and Assistance (Scope) Regulations 1989 (see p. 337). (Re-enactments of provisions specified in the Schedule are automatically effective in relation to this list by virtue of the Interpretation Act 1978. For example, ABWOR is available for proceedings under section 106 of the Social Security Administration Act 1992 which replaced section 24 of the Social Security Act 1986 and also for proceedings under Part IV of the Family Law Act 1996 where Part IV replaces the provisions for protection/exclusion orders under Part I of the Domestic Proceedings and Magistrates' Courts Act 1978.)

ABWOR is available for certain domestic and criminal proceedings in the magistrates' court, including those relating to fine and other defaulters at risk of imprisonment; hearings in relation to application for warrants of further detention; hearings before Mental Health Review Tribunals, the Parole Board (Discretionary Lifer Panel and Her Majesty's Pleasure Panel), prison disciplinary hearings (in the case of prisoners permitted to be represented) and hearings in the magistrates' court or county court where authority is given by the court.

NOTE:

1. *The approval of ABWOR includes the cost of giving notice of appeal or applying for a case to be stated within the ordinary time limit and matters preliminary to that.*
2. *ABWOR (save court approved ABWOR) is not available for representation on enforcement/arrears proceedings under the Child Support Act 1991. Nor is ABWOR available in respect of an order made (and to be enforced) in the county court (as ABWOR covers magistrates' court proceedings only).*
3. *Detailed guidance has been given by the Board to support the mental health franchise category—see Focus 22, January 1998.*

3–10   IS THE APPROVAL OF THE LEGAL AID BOARD REQUIRED?
(Legal Advice and Assistance Regulations 1989, reg. 22)

Legal Aid Board approval is required except for:

(a) duty solicitor representation which is dealt with by the Legal Aid Board under general arrangements (see p. xxx). ABWOR is not available under regulation 7(2) or 7(4) of the Legal Advice and Assistance (Scope) Regulations other than under the duty solicitor arrangements made by the Board;

(b) cases where either a magistrates' court or county court requests (or endorses a request from) a solicitor within the precincts of the court to represent a client at a hearing that day (see the Legal Advice and Assistance (Scope) Regulations 1989, pp. xxx and xxx);

(c) application for warrants of further detention or extensions of such warrants.

Otherwise an application has to be made to the appropriate area office for approval. Approvals issued by an area office will include scope and costs limitations (for more information on costs limitations see NFG 9, para. 9–15).

Note that the magistrates' court or county court can only grant ABWOR under (b) above where:

(a) the individual concerned is a party who is not receiving and has not been refused representation in connection with proceedings;

(b) the court is satisfied the hearing should proceed that day;

(c) the court is satisfied that the party would not otherwise be represented; and

(d) the court requests, or approves a proposal from, a solicitor (who must be at court other than to provide court granted ABWOR) to provide ABWOR.

Unless these requirements are all satisfied any court granted ABWOR will not be valid (as it will be *ultra vires* the powers of the court). The client must also qualify financially.

The court may confirm the grant by endorsing a completed ABWOR application form, although no statement of case is required. Any endorsement should be in the following or similar terms:

I confirm that this court requested/approved a proposal that ABWOR be provided pursuant to regulation 7(1)(b)/8 of the Legal Advice and Assistance (Scope) Regulations 1989 in respect of a hearing on (insert date).
Signed _____
Clerk to the justices/of the court
Dated _____

Alternatively, the grant may be confirmed by a county court order or a letter from the court in appropriate terms and appropriately signed. An ABWOR application form must be completed and signed by the client in all cases (to confirm the client's financial eligibility) although no statement of case is required. The confirmation of grant must be forwarded to the area office with the claim for payment which is made using an ABWOR claim form.

Note that the advice and assistance (green form) costs limit (two hours at the appropriate preparation rate) applies to this form of ABWOR (but the Board accepts that this is irrespective of any previous advice and assistance (green form) costs incurred).

WHEN WILL APPROVAL OF THE AREA OFFICE BE REFUSED?   3–11
(Legal Advice and Assistance Regulations 1989, regs. 22(5) and (6))

Unless the client has reasonable grounds for taking, defending or being a party to the proceedings to which the application relates, an application for approval will be refused by the area office.

NOTE: *This is the legal merits test which is applied in the same way as for civil legal aid (see NFG 7, para. 7–02).*

An application for approval may also be refused if it appears unreasonable to grant it in the particular circumstances of the case.

NOTE: *This is the reasonableness test, which is also applied in the same way as in civil legal aid (see NFG 7, para. 7–03).*

Subject to the following exceptions, both tests have to be satisfied as in civil legal aid. The legal merits test does not, however, apply to ABWOR for Mental Health Review Tribunal or Parole Board (Discretionary Lifer Panel or Her

Majesty's Pleasure Panel) proceedings, but area office approval is still necessary and is subject to the reasonableness test. Applications for representation by fine and other defaulters in proceedings where they are at risk of imprisonment are subject to a different "interests of justice" test.

3–12   EXAMPLES OF DECISIONS IN ABWOR CASES

Matrimonial/family cases

Examples of decisions in ABWOR cases involving matrimonial/family cases are given in the Board's Guidance: Exercise of Devolved Powers which was reproduced in the May 1997 issue of the Board's *Focus* newsletter (*Focus* 19) and, for domestic violence under Part IV of the Family Law Act, 1996, in the September 1997 issue (*Focus* 21).

Mental Health Review Tribunal, prison disciplinary proceedings and, for discretionary life prisoners/those detained as juveniles at Her Majesty's Pleasure, Parole Board (Discretionary Lifer Panel/Her Majesty's Pleasure Panel)

ABWOR will be granted unless:

it appears unreasonable that approval should be granted.

The applicant for ABWOR does not have to show that he has reasonable grounds in the proceedings but, in the case of prison disciplinary proceedings, ABWOR is only available where permission has been given for the prisoner to be represented.

ABWOR for fine and other defaulters in the Magistrates' Court

ABWOR has been made available for those facing proceedings in the Magistrates' Court for fine/other default which are likely to lead to imprisonment. These proceedings fall within the debt franchise category and the usual ABWOR application form is used to apply.

In deciding whether ABWOR is likely to be granted the guidance below should be applied.

1.   *Is the applicant before the court as a result of a failure:*
      (a) to pay a fine or other sum which he was ordered to pay or;
      (b) to obey an order of the court
      where such failure is likely to lead to the applicant being at risk of imprisonment?

1.1   If "no", the application should be refused as the case is not within the scope of the new regulations. If "yes", go on to the next question.

NOTE: *The Regulations apply equally to civil and criminal proceedings. In criminal cases, such as non-payment of fines ordered on conviction, the applicant has the alternative of applying to the court for a criminal legal aid order, but ABWOR should not be refused simply on the grounds that criminal legal aid is also available.*

2.   *Could the case be dealt with by the duty solicitor?*

2.1   If it appears that the duty solicitor could deal with the case by providing the degree of representation needed by the applicant, ABWOR should normally be refused.

2.2   Clearly if the court in question has no duty solicitor scheme, or if no duty solicitor will be available for the hearing, ABWOR should not be refused on this ground. The courts are being issued with guidance to encourage these cases to be listed at times when the duty solicitor will be available.

2.3   It should be assumed that duty solicitors are experienced in helping people regarding non-payment of fines and assisting people in explaining their financial position to the court or putting forward mitigation for any failure. Therefore ABWOR should only be granted in preference to allowing the duty solicitor to deal with the case if the case is unusual, particularly in the sense that the case raises complicated issues of fact, law or procedure.

2.4   The fact that the applicant may have many debts or complicated finances would not make ABWOR necessary, unless the whole circumstances of the case were so complex that it would not be feasible to expect a duty solicitor to assimilate all the facts to present a necessary defence or mitigation to the court.

2.5   ABWOR should generally be granted if the case genuinely raises some new or complex issue of law.

2.6   If the case is not suitable for the duty solicitor, consider the next question.

3.   *Is it in the interests of justice for ABWOR to be granted?*

3.1   The interests of justice test is the same as the merits test for criminal legal aid. See the guidance on the test set out at p. 659. Once the legal and factual complexity of the case has been considered as above, in practice the most important element of the interests of justice test will be the likelihood of imprisonment.

3.2   The mere fact that at the hearing in question the applicant could in theory be committed to prison for non-payment should not automatically lead to the grant of ABWOR. The issue is whether there is a real risk of imprisonment. It is for the solicitor to explain on the application form that there is such a risk. As a general rule a person is unlikely to be committed to prison on the first occasion they are brought before the court for failure to pay a fine or obey an order. Imprisonment will become more likely in cases where there have been a number of appearances, or where the court has issued a clear warning that the applicant is likely to be sent to prison.

3.3   If it is concluded that it is not in the interests of justice for ABWOR to be granted, the application should be refused. Otherwise consider the next question.

4.   *Is it reasonable in all the circumstances for ABWOR to be granted?*

4.1   If it is decided to be in the interests of justice for ABWOR to be granted, it will almost certainly be reasonable in all the circumstances for ABWOR to be granted. However, each case must be considered on its own facts and one cannot identify in advance every possible factor which may be relevant to the reasonableness of the grant.

4.2   For example, in some cases, it may be clear that the applicant is before the court solely because of his deliberate decision not to pay or to obey an order, as opposed to a case where the applicant feels unable to comply or has a legal defence to the allegation against him. If, for example, an applicant was refusing to pay a particular charge solely because he felt on moral grounds that the charge or tax was wrongful, it might not be reasonable for ABWOR to be granted if this would lead to public funds being spent to argue a political or moral point of view rather than a legal defence.

4.3   If the case is not one that can appropriately be dealt with by the duty solicitor, it is in the interests of justice for ABWOR to be granted and there is nothing about the case which shows that it is unreasonable for ABWOR to be granted, the application for approval of ABWOR should be granted.

3–13 APPEAL AGAINST REFUSAL OF AN APPLICATION BY AN AREA OFFICE
(Legal Advice and Assistance Regulations 1989, reg. 26(1))

The client has a right of appeal by written notice/submissions to the appropriate area committee. There is no right of representation before the committee. The appeal is by way of reconsideration of the application for approval. The area committee can dismiss the appeal or grant the application with or without conditions. It must give reasons for its decision, from which there is no appeal.

3–14 IS IT REASONABLE TO PERMIT EXPENDITURE FOR EXPERTS OR FOR UNUSUAL/UNUSUALLY EXPENSIVE ACTS?
(Legal Advice and Assistance Regulations 1989, reg. 22(7))

The rule is that prior permission must be obtained from the area office before expenditure is incurred on any of the following:

(a) obtaining a report or opinion of an expert;

(b) tendering expert evidence;

(c) taking some action which is either unusual or involves unusually large expenditure.

NOTE:

1. *This provision is mandatory and the Board's appropriate application*

form must be used (a separate form is necessary for each application). Even if the court has ordered the work to be done, e.g. taking a blood test (including DNA), permission from the area office is required. See para. 3–22 below, decision ABWOR 1.

2. Permission cannot be granted retrospectively. It must be obtained in advance of any work being done but can be granted at the same time as the ABWOR itself.

3. If no prior permission has been obtained, payment will not be made out of the legal aid fund. Where permission has been obtained, the expenditure will still always be subject to costs assessment as the permission is not a binding authority but rather a pre-requisite for incurring the expenditure.

4. See also NFG 11, para. 11–06 for the position regarding disbursements where a solicitor, his partner or employee is involved in the provision of non-legal services.

Permission will be given if the expense is necessary and reasonable having regard to the nature of the proceedings and the likely benefit to the applicant but not if a privately funded client would be advised:

(a) not to incur the expense; or

(b) to use a cheaper alternative, e.g. obtaining a report from a GP rather than a consultant; making enquiries himself rather than employing an inquiry agent.

NOTE: *If such permission is given:*

1. An upper limit may be stated in the permission, although it will always be subject to costs assessment in any event.

2. Sometimes area offices will, as well as stating the upper limit for obtaining a report or opinion of an expert, indicate the daily or half-daily rate which would be allowed for such an expert to tender evidence. This is intended to help the solicitor to avoid a situation where he might become committed to an expert whose fee for a report is reasonable but whose fee for court attendance may turn out later to be unreasonable.

Special cases   3–15

Enquiry agents and interpreters.   Normally an enquiry agent's fees or interpreter's charges will not require prior permission. He is not an expert, nor are his services unusual in their nature. The only category within which such fees would require prior permission is where unusually large expenditure (of more than £200) is involved, for example in tracing the whereabouts of a respondent or for interpreter's charges.

Blood tests, including DNA.   See para. 3–22 below, decision ABWOR 1.

Mental Health Review Tribunal.   Detailed guidance has been given by the Board to support the mental health franchise category—see *Focus* 22, January 1998.

Parole Board (Discretionary Lifer Panel/Her Majesty's Pleasure Panel). The solicitor may wish to apply for authority for an independent psychiatric or other expert report when applying for the ABWOR approval, or subsequently. The area office will in any event need to know the reasons for, and likely cost of, the report.

3–16 DOES THE PROPER CONDUCT OF THE PROCEEDINGS REQUIRE COUNSEL?
(Legal Advice and Assistance Regulations 1989, reg. 23)

The rule is that where assistance by way of representation has been granted and the solicitor thinks that the proper conduct of proceedings requires counsel, he may instruct counsel and may apply to the area office for permission under regulation 23 of the Legal Advice and Assistance Regulations 1989 (but is not obliged to do so). The issue under regulation 23 is not so much whether the matter should be dealt with by a solicitor or by counsel but whether the nature or circumstances of the particular case justifies the payment of an additional lawyer.

NOTE: *The result of not obtaining permission or of having permission refused is that costs will be assessed on the basis of the solicitor having conducted the case on his own, rather than on a separate assessment of counsel's fee as would happen where approval has been given (Legal Advice and Assistance Regulations 1989, reg. 29(5) and (6), p. 351). This will be the case unless the area office consider at the time of assessing costs that the proper conduct of proceedings required counsel in which case full payment may be made (see para. 3–19).*

Approval will be given if the case poses *unusually complex evidential problems or novel or difficult points of law,* but *not* if:

(a) the reason for instructing counsel is:

(i) that the case is contested, protracted or involves the cross-examination of witnesses or arguments on points of law;
(ii) the personal circumstances or convenience of the solicitor;
(iii) that the other side is represented by counsel; or

(b) it would be more appropriate to instruct a solicitor agent.

In Mental Health Review Tribunal cases approval of the instruction of counsel is likely to be exceptional and it is generally considered that a solicitor should be able to deal with the matter.

Where the solicitor instructed is unable, *e.g.* through illness, to deal with the matter himself (as required by membership of the Law Society's Mental Health Review Tribunal Panel) it would generally be more appropriate to consider instructing an appropriately qualified solicitor agent rather than counsel. This could be a mental health franchisee or an MHRT panel member.

The instruction of counsel based on either the complexity of the case or the fact that the solicitor is unavailable would therefore be exceptional in a Mental Health Review Tribunal case. (See *Focus* 22, January 1998.)

SHOULD ABWOR BE WITHDRAWN?   3–17
(Legal Advice and Assistance Regulations 1989, reg. 25)

The rule is that the area office are required to withdraw approval of ABWOR where they consider that the client no longer has reasonable grounds for taking, defending or being a party to the proceedings or continuing to do so; or that the client has required the proceedings to be conducted unreasonably so as to incur an unjustifiable expense to the legal aid fund; or that it is unreasonable for ABWOR to continue.

NOTE: *On withdrawal the solicitor has to serve notice on his client, the court and other parties to the proceedings but withdrawal is no bar to future applications for assistance by way of representation.*
There is a right of appeal to the area committee (Legal Advice and Assistance Regulations 1989, reg. 26, p. 350). If the appeal is successful the solicitor has to serve another notice on the court and other parties to the proceedings.
The area office can act on information from any source—including the opponent. These grounds are the equivalent to the legal aid powers to discharge on merits (Civil Legal Aid (General) Regulations 1989, reg. 77, p. 399). There is no equivalent in ABWOR to the legal aid system of revocation or to the legal aid "show cause" procedure.

ABWOR will be withdrawn if:

(a) information comes to light which if known at the time would have meant that the original application for ABWOR would have been refused;

(b) circumstances have changed so that the applicant no longer has reasonable grounds for continuing or reasonable prospects of success;

(c) the client is dead;

(d) the solicitor is without instructions (but in Mental Health Review Tribunal cases there may be special circumstances);

(e) the client has had a reconciliation with the other party;

(f) the client refuses to accept advice not to proceed;

(g) in means tested cases, the client has failed to pay his contribution (contributions remain payable until the conclusion of the proceedings or until ABWOR is withdrawn);

(h) in means tested cases, the client has had a financial windfall and can afford to continue the proceedings at his own expense;

(i) the client consents; or

(j) there is any other good reason.

Appeal against refusal by the area office to grant authority or against a decision to withdraw ABWOR should be made to the area committee on the same conditions as for an appeal against refusal of approval (see para. 3–13 above).

ASSESSMENT OF COSTS

(See also NFG 2, para. 2–07 regarding distant solicitors).

3–18 Where no counsel instructed

The area office assesses the solicitor's claims for costs and pays to the solicitor the balance after deducting the client's contribution and the amount of the costs ("the assessed deficiency"). There is a special rate for Mental Health Review Tribunal and Parole Board (Discretionary Lifer Panel/Her Majesty's Pleasure Panel) cases but legal advice and assistance (green form) work in those cases must still be claimed at the legal advice and assistance (green form) rate (see *Law Society's Gazette*, November 6, 1991, p. 16).

3–19 Where counsel instructed and allowed or authorised

Where counsel has been instructed, and the area office consider that the proper conduct of the proceedings required counsel, or the instruction of counsel has been authorised, the solicitor's costs are assessed excluding counsel's fees. The solicitor is paid the assessed deficiency. Counsel's fee is then assessed and paid after deduction of the amount, if any, by which the client's contribution and the charge exceed the amount allowed to the solicitor, *e.g.* solicitor's profit costs, including disbursements, allowed at £500, counsel's fees assessed at £200 in a case where the solicitor's charge and the client's contribution total £550. Counsel is paid £150 by the Board and £50 by the solicitor.

3–20 Where counsel instructed but not allowed or authorised

The costs are assessed in total by the area office on the basis that the solicitor had conducted the case. The amount which would have been allowed to counsel if authorised is deducted from the total and paid to counsel. The balance is paid to the solicitor, again after taking into account the contribution and the charge.

3–21 Appeals against costs assessments

There is an appeal to the area committee against area office costs assessments and, on a certified point of principle of general importance, to the Board's Costs Appeals Committee. On a review of an assessment the area committee has the power to confirm, increase or reduce the assessment. Reviews are by way of written representations but see NFG 14, para. 14–05.

Legal Aid Board decisions as to assessment of ABWOR costs

The Legal Aid Board has issued the following decisions on matters of principle of general importance in connection with ABWOR costs:

Disbursements: blood tests   3–22

The obtaining of blood tests is a matter requiring prior permission pursuant to regulation 17(4) of the Legal Advice and Assistance Regulations (No. 2) 1980 (now regulation 22(7) of the Legal Advice and Assistance Regulations 1989) unless such permission has been included in the approval of ABWOR itself. The position is not affected by any adjournment or order of the court relating to the obtaining of blood tests. (Legal Aid Board reference ABWOR 1.)

Scope of ABWOR approval   3–23

The scope of an ABWOR approval includes negotiations for settlement of the proceedings covered, provided that the negotiations reasonably relate to the scope of the particular ABWOR approval. The scope does not include implementation of any settlement save to obtain a final order within the scope of the ABWOR approval. (Legal Aid Board reference ABWOR 2.)

Enhanced rates in ABWOR cases   3–24

The provisions of regulation 30(1) of the Legal Advice and Assistance Regu-lations 1989 permitted the payment of enhanced rates in appropriate ABWOR cases assessed or reviewed prior to April 8, 1991 when the Legal Advice and Assistance (Amendment) Regulations 1991 came into force (amending regu-lation 30(1) so as to clearly exclude the payment of enhanced rates). (Legal Aid Board reference ABWOR 3.)

ABWOR: nullity without green form   3–25

Where the Area Director or Area Committee grants an approval of an ABWOR application made by a solicitor without any misrepresentation of the facts the ABWOR approval is nevertheless a nullity if there is no green form. No estop-pel arises. (Legal Aid Board reference ABWOR 4—no longer applicable.) *This decision does not apply to applications made on or after April 12, 1993—see para. 3–02.*

Costs claim where green form not available   3–26

If the original signed green form is not available when a costs claim is made and it can be proved to the reasonable satisfaction of the Board, by submission of a copy or otherwise, that the signed and correctly completed green form existed at the relevant time, the Board may assess the claim and authorise payment notwithstanding the absence of the original green form. (Legal Aid Board reference ABWOR 5—no longer applicable.)

**Custodianship proceedings: prior authority for certificates of general   3–27
health**

A certificate of general health by a general practitioner obtained for the purpose of proceedings under the Magistrates' Courts (Custodianship Orders) Rules 1985 is not a report or opinion of an expert requiring prior authority under regulation 22(7) of the Legal Advice and Assistance Regulations 1989. (Legal Aid Board reference ABWOR 6.)

3–28   Travel by Mental Health Review Tribunal panel members

In deciding whether, in a case involving Mental Health Review Tribunal proceedings work, a claim for travel is reasonable, the appropriate authority shall consider all the relevant circumstances of the case, including:

(a) any legitimate expectation of the assisted person of specialist representation, *i.e.* Mental Health Review Tribunal panel member;

(b) the availability of Mental Health Review Tribunal panel members; and

(c) the undertaking which is required to be given by a Mental Health Review Tribunal panel member to conduct such cases personally. (Legal Aid Board Reference ABWOR 7.)

3–29   Allowance for checking and signing the Report on Case

On the assessment of an ABWOR claim for costs, where a claim is made for preparing and signing the Report on Case, consideration should be given to making a small allowance for the solicitor's time in checking and signing the Report on Case. Normally an allowance of 5–10 minutes would be appropriate. (Legal Aid Board reference ABWOR 8.)

3–30   ABWOR: Mental Health Review Tribunals

ABWOR approval for Mental Health Tribunal work does not cover work only carried out for a Hospital Manager's Appeal including representation on the appeal itself. However, if work is properly carried out in preparation for the representation on the Mental Health Review Tribunal it should not be disallowed if it incidentally assists on the Hospital Manager's Appeal. The ABWOR approval does not cover representation on the Hospital Manager's Appeal in any event. (Legal Aid Board reference ABWOR 9.)

3–31   Deferred conditional discharge in Mental Health Review Tribunal Proceedings

On a deferred conditional discharge, the Mental Health Review Tribunal proceedings are not concluded when the deferred conditional discharge decision is given, but when either the Tribunal is reconvened to consider the discharge arrangements and makes a final determination or the recommendation lapses by expiry of time. The ABWOR approval will continue until either the date on which the Tribunal makes a final determination, or the date of expiry, whichever is the earlier. (Legal Aid Board reference ABWOR 10.)

4. CIVIL LEGAL AID

STATUTORY FRAMEWORK AND CONDITIONS   4–01

The statutory framework for civil legal aid is contained in Parts I and IV, sections 1, 2, and 14–18 of the Legal Aid Act 1988 (see pp. 277 *et seq.*).

Details of the system are set out in the Civil Legal Aid (General) Regulations 1989 (see pp. 367 *et seq.*); and the Civil Legal Aid (Assessment of Resources) Regulation 1989 (see pp. 439 *et seq.*).

The general principle of Part IV of the Legal Aid Act 1988 is that representation for specific proceedings is available to any person whose financial resources make him/her eligible, subject to such person satisfying the Board that he/she has reasonable grounds for taking, defending or being a party to proceedings which come within the Act, and that it is reasonable for representation to be granted (see NFG 7). Representation is, however, available on a non-means, non-merits tested or means tested only basis to certain applicants in specified proceedings under the Children Act 1989 (see NFG 8).

Schedule 2 to the Act specifies the proceedings for which legal aid is available (see p. 318). The Act defines the general scope of civil legal aid. Details of the system are set out in the regulations.

The Act uses different terminology when compared with the Legal Aid Act 1974. It specifies "representation" in civil courts and criminal courts instead of civil legal aid and criminal legal aid. The latter descriptions have been retained from the previous system for the purposes of these Notes for Guidance (and they still appear in the Act in the headings to Parts IV and V).

The administrative framework requires an application which, if granted, will lead to the issue of a certificate. While that certificate is in existence, certain duties and responsibilities are imposed on the assisted person and his/her solicitor and counsel, in return for the assurance of payment of legal costs out of the legal aid fund. Failure to comply with those duties or responsibilities may lead to premature termination of the legal aid certificate. Termination, whether premature or otherwise, is by discharge or revocation, after which payment of costs can be made (see NFG 13). There are some provisions for payment on account of costs and disbursements during the life of a certificate (see NFG 14, para. 14–15).

AVAILABILITY—WHAT KIND OF COURTS AND CASES ARE COVERED?   4–02

Civil legal aid is available for cases in:

    (a) the House of Lords;

    (b) the High Court and the Court of Appeal;

(c) county courts (but not judgment summonses nor, usually, the decree proceedings for undefended divorce and judicial separation);

(d) magistrates' courts for cases about marriage and the family, including separation, maintenance and defended adoption proceedings. Civil legal aid is also available for proceedings under the Children Act 1989 (see NFG 8);

(e) the Employment Appeal Tribunal;

(f) the Lands Tribunal;

(g) the Commons Commissioners;

(h) the Restrictive Practices Court (for some cases); and

(i) appeals to the Court of Appeal on points of law from Social Security Commissioners.

Civil legal aid is not available for proceedings before a coroner's court and most tribunals (except those listed above), nor normally for proceedings involving libel and slander. However, advice may be given about these proceedings under legal advice and assistance (see NFG 2, above). Civil legal aid is not available for court cases outside England and Wales (including applications to the European Commission of Human Rights) except on a reference to the Court of Justice of the European Communities for a preliminary ruling. Note, however, that the availability of legal aid may, in exceptional circumstances, be a relevant consideration for the court when dealing with an application for a stay of proceedings in England and Wales on the grounds of *forum non conveniens* (see *Connelly v. RTZ Corporation Plc and Another*, HL, July 24, 1996 and NFG 20, para. 20–01).

4–03   Is civil legal aid available for the proceedings? (Legal Aid Act 1988, s.14)

The rule is that civil legal aid is a statutory system. Unless the application comes within the statutory provisions, civil legal aid will not be available. So the first basic question which every caseworker in an area office asks on receipt of an application is whether it comes within the system.

The availability of civil legal aid is defined normally by the court or other body which hears the proceedings. It is a matter which a solicitor should consider before submitting an application for legal aid.

4–04   *Civil legal aid is available if:*

(a) the proceedings are in courts specified in Part I, paras. 1 and 2 of Schedule 2 to the Legal Aid Act 1988 (see p. 318) but note that civil legal aid is only available for certain, specified proceedings in a magistrates' court;

(b) the proceedings are before any of the tribunals specified in Part I of Schedule 2 to the Legal Aid Act 1988 (see p. 319), namely Employment Appeal Tribunal, Lands Tribunal and Commons Commissioners;

(c) the proceedings are before the Restrictive Practices Court under Part III of the Fair Trading Act 1973 (Part I, para. 6 of Schedule 2 to the Legal Aid Act 1988: see p. 319).

Civil legal aid is not available if: **4–05**

(a) the proceedings (and proceedings incidental to them) are excepted under Part II of Schedule 2 to the Legal Aid Act 1988 (see p. 319) namely, defamation (apart from defending a counterclaim); relator actions; recovery of penalties; election petitions; county court (as opposed to High Court) judgment summonses and other county court matters where only the time and mode of payment are in issue;

(b) the proceedings are before a Coroner's Court or the Court of Protection (not part of the court system mentioned in Part I of Schedule 2 to the Legal Aid Act 1988 (above);

(c) the application is for a grant of representation to an estate unless it is necessary to enable a legally aided action to be brought (Civil Legal Aid (General) Regulations 1989, reg. 46, p. 390);

(d) proceedings are before an arbitrator except for a county court reference to arbitration (although the existence, in an insurance policy, of an arbitration clause which will not be enforced is not a bar to the grant of legal aid for court proceedings).

(e) generally the proceedings are for undefended divorce (Part I, para. 5A of Schedule 2 to the Legal Aid Act 1988), p. 319.

Legal aid is not available for undefended divorce or judicial separation decree proceedings. It may only be granted for such decree proceedings (a) if they become defended (either to the respondent to defend or to the petitioner to continue the proceedings after an answer has been filed); or (b) if the district judge directs the petition to be heard in open court (for example where he is not satisfied on the merits of the case or on other matters such as domicile); or (c) if by reason of physical or mental incapacity it is impracticable for the applicant to proceed without legal aid.

See also NFG 9, para. 9–11.

Is the applicant a person to whom legal aid can be granted?   **4–06**
(Legal Aid Act 1988, s.15)

The rule is that civil legal aid is available to "any person" subject to and in accordance with the Act. Legal aid is not available to guardians *ad litem* for the purposes of any proceedings under the Children Act 1989 although applications for legal aid for minors may be made by a guardian *ad litem* or, in some circumstances, a solicitor on the minor's behalf (see NFG 8, para. 8–09).

The second general question which area office staff have to answer therefore is whether the applicant is a person to whom legal aid can be granted. This is another matter the solicitor should bear in mind when submitting an application for legal aid since the application must be refused if the applicant is not within this category.

Legal aid can be granted if the applicant is:

(a) an individual;

(b) a partner or member of a firm since a firm or partnership is not a body corporate or incorporate.

Legal aid cannot be granted if the applicant:

(a) is a body of persons corporate or unincorporate unless that body is concerned only in a representative, fiduciary or official capacity (Legal Aid Act 1988, s.2(10), p. 281), *i.e.* where such a body would be exempt from any assessment of means. Note that a company which assigns the benefit of a cause of action to an individual is not thereby acting in a fiduciary capacity, and is not entitled to legal aid (see *R. v. Legal Aid Board, ex p. Floods of Queensferry Ltd*, CO/3472/97, October 16, 1997, Popplewell J. and December 18, 1997, CA; see paras 7–03.36 to 7–03.39 below);

(b) in the case of any proceedings under the Children Act 1989, is a local authority, any other body acting in a representative, fiduciary or official capacity or a guardian *ad litem.*

4–07 IS THE APPLICANT WITHIN THE FINANCIAL ELIGIBILITY LIMITS?

See Eligibility Tables and Guide to Assessing Financial Eligibility, p. 667.

4–08 APPLICATIONS FOR CIVIL LEGAL AID

The solicitor or applicant should complete the Board's application form which is appropriate for the particular type of case together with the appropriate means form, and with form L17 completed by the employer where the applicant and/or his/her partner is in employment (or form L30 for company directors). The forms should then be sent to the area office. (For a list of addresses of area offices, see p. 745.)

For a complete list of legal aid forms and table of civil legal aid forms, see pp. 702 *et seq.* For circumstances where a minor may instruct a solicitor direct, see NFG 8.

It is important that the relevant application form is completed fully and correctly—it must be signed, dated and have all the relevant parts completed otherwise it will be rejected. Enclosures should be securely attached. A badly completed form which is not rejected but contains insufficient information may result in the application being refused.

In the case of applicants who receive a "passported" benefit (income support or income-based Jobseeker's Allowance), it would be helpful if the solicitor confirms entitlement to income support or income-based Jobseeker's Allowance before the application is submitted. Confirmation may be obtained by requesting sight of either a letter of entitlement provided by the Benefits Agency or their order book. The documentary evidence should not be forwarded to the area office as positive confirmation will be obtained directly from the Benefits Agency once the application has been submitted. This check is recommended, as sometimes applicants are uncertain what benefit they receive and incorrectly state they receive one of the above benefits. Where this happens it results in delays for the applicant in that their application has to be rejected.

A solicitor can be paid for filling in the application form under legal advice and assistance (if the applicant qualifies financially).

An assessment officer at the area office will work out whether the client qualifies financially (see the Assessment Guide at p. 670 and NFG 5). Under

CIS the area office will decide whether the merits test is satisfied in the particular case before the means decision is made. Means queries/out of scope decisions may, therefore, only arise after the submission of a merits appeal.

EMERGENCY APPLICATIONS 4–09

If the case is urgent, an applicant can apply for emergency legal aid. This can be granted at once but will only cover the most urgent and immediate steps. Emergency legal aid certificates are limited as to their scope and as to both costs and time.

When an applicant applies for emergency legal aid, he/she must agree to co-operate with the assessment officer in the enquiry into the applicant's financial position and must also agree to pay any contribution that is assessed. The applicant will also have to agree to pay the full costs of any steps taken under the emergency certificate if it is found that he/she does not qualify for civil legal aid or if an offer of a full certificate is refused. (See also NFG 6 for detailed guidance on emergency applications/certificates.)

CONSIDERATION OF APPLICATIONS FOR CIVIL LEGAL AID 4–10

Except in the case of some applicants in certain Children Act proceedings, the applicant must:

(a) qualify financially (see Eligibility Tables, p. 667).

(b) show that he/she has reasonable grounds for taking or defending a court action and that it is reasonable to grant legal aid in the circumstances of the case.

The application will be considered by the area office who will consider all questions of fact and law arising out of the application. They may decide to grant a certificate with limited scope, for example, for the purpose of obtaining counsel's opinion. They may also refuse legal aid, in which case there is a right of appeal to the area committee in most cases.

WHAT HAPPENS WHEN AN APPLICATION HAS BEEN GRANTED? 4–11

If the means test applies and the applicant is found by the assessment officer to be within financial scope, either a certificate will be issued immediately or, if the applicant has a financial contribution, an offer will be sent to the applicant. This will need to be accepted and processed, with any instalment of contribution paid, before the certificate is issued.

As the Board implements CIS, some changes have affected the offer and contribution process. Where there is an aggregated assessment for applicants who are married or cohabiting, contribution payments will be divided between each person and no longer notionally paid under one "master" case. Where an assisted person has several certificates, contribution payments will be spread equally across all the ongoing certificates.

NOTE: *Legal aid does not commence until the date of the legal aid certificate (see NFG 9 for effects of certificate).*

4–12 IS THERE A RIGHT OF APPEAL IF THE APPLICATION IS REFUSED BY THE AREA OFFICE?

If the application has been refused by the area office, a notice of refusal giving reasons will be sent to the applicant and the solicitor. Except in the case of a financial refusal based on the amount of income, there will be right of appeal to the appropriate area committee for the decision to be reviewed (see Civil Legal Aid (General) Regulations 1989, reg. 34 on p. 386 for details of grounds of refusal). The notice of refusal incorporates a notice of appeal where there is a right of appeal.

There is a right of representation on an appeal but the legal aid fund may only pay for the preparatory work under legal advice and assistance where the client qualifies financially (and not for representation at the appeal hearing).

The form of the appeal is by way of reconsideration of the application. The area committee will consider any new or extra information which may be available as well as the documentation considered by the area office. The area committee may dismiss the appeal for a different reason or reasons from the area office refusal.

4–13 WHAT CAN THE AREA COMMITTEE DO?

The area committee may:

    (a) dismiss the appeal;

    (b) direct a certificate to be offered on whatever terms and conditions it thinks fit;

    (c) direct the area office to settle terms and conditions of a possible offer;

    (d) adjourn the appeal.

NOTE: *It must give reasons for its decision.*

There is no appeal from the decision of the area committee which is final.

4–14 LIMITS ON LEGAL AID APPLICATIONS

If there have been three refusals of civil legal aid and the area office think there is an abuse of legal aid, the area committee can recommend to the Board that a prohibitory direction be made (Civil Legal Aid (General) Regulations 1989, reg. 40).

The Board may prohibit further applications for legal aid for up to five years generally or in respect of any particular matter. Such decisions must be notified to the Lord Chancellor.

There is no right of appeal against the Board's decision but the Board has power to vary or revoke any prohibitory direction in whole or in part at any time.

5.   CIVIL LEGAL AID—MEANS ASSESSMENT

See Notes in file

ASSESSMENT OF AN APPLICANT'S MEANS   **5–01**

The Board took over formal responsibility for civil means assessment from the Benefits Agency on April 1, 1997. The Legal Aid Assessment Office (part of the Benefits Agency) closed on March 31, 1998. The function of means assessment is now undertaken by each of the Board's area offices. Assessment officers employed by the Board will assess the applicant's disposable income and capital and the contribution, if any (see Eligibility Tables, p. 667).

There is an Assessment Guide at p. 670 but, although means are assessed in accordance with the Civil Legal Aid (Assessment of Resources) Regulations 1989, there are elements of discretion so that an entirely accurate means assessment can only be obtained by submitting an application.

Comprehensive guidance has been issued to assessment officers regarding all aspects of the means assessment decision-making process. This guidance will help ensure consistency of approach in decisions relating to means assessment undertaken by the Board. As part of the Board's continued commitment to creating transparency in the decision making process, the key parts of the guidance have been published and can be purchased so that practitioners have access to the available guidance. Further details regarding this published document can be obtained from the documentation team at the following address, Legal Aid Board, Quality Assurance Department, 85 Gray's Inn Road, London WC1X 8AA, DX328 LON/CH'RY LN WC2, Fax: 0171 813 8647.

The following notes also provide guidance on some of the main issues in means assessment.

The value of the subject matter of the particular dispute is disregarded from the assessment. This reflects the fact that it would be illogical to expect an applicant to utilise an asset towards the cost of the litigation, if in fact the case is about whether the applicant is entitled to the asset at all. The test for whether an item is the subject matter of dispute is the same test as to whether that item is in issue in the proceedings for statutory charge purposes (see NFG16).

For applications from June 1, 1996 the treatment of an applicant's dwelling house, which was previously wholly exempt for eligibility purposes, was amended so that:

(a) the capital value of the property (that is market value less amount outstanding on any mortgage debt or charge) will be taken into account in so far as it exceeds £100,000;

(b) the capital amount allowed in respect of a mortgage debt or charge over the property cannot exceed £100,000;

(c) as regards allowances against income for mortgage payments, if the mortgage debt exceeds £100,000 the amount allowed will be reduced in proportion (for example, if mortgage debt is £200,000, only half the amount actually paid will be taken into account);

(d) there are also provisions for second and subsequent dwellings which provide that the total amount of mortgage debt to be allowed for all the properties cannot exceed £100,000.

This means that for capital assessment, the value of an applicant's home is reduced by the amount of the mortgage or by £100,000, whichever is the less, to produce a net equity figure. If this net equity figure exceeds £100,000, the excess over £100,000 is taken into account as the capital of the assisted person. For pensioners (men and women aged 60 and over), the usual disregards of capital can be applied if appropriate.

Note that the above changes apply to applications for legal aid made on or after June 1, 1996 but do not apply to further assessments or amended assessments on existing certificates applied for before June 1, 1996, nor do they affect those in receipt of/continuing to receive passported benefits.

An additional discretionary power was also introduced for applications made on or after June 1, 1996 which allows the assessment officer to take into account the assets of persons other than the applicant for legal aid. The regulation may be applied where the other person has transferred resources to the assisted person, has been maintaining the assisted person in the proceedings, or where any of the resources of the other person have been made available to the assisted person. If this happens, the resources of the other person can be treated as those of the assisted person. This discretionary power can be invoked on an application for legal aid, but is also likely to be used where the assisted person has complex financial affairs which have been brought to the Board's attention by representations. Applications made and certificates in force before June 1, 1996 are not affected.

From October 1, 1996 the rule regarding the treatment of any capital payment received in relation to the incident giving rise to the dispute for which the legal aid application had been made was abolished. The rule provided that any such capital would be wholly disregarded in the assessment. This applied to make exempt interim awards and payments from, amongst other sources, compensation funds or insurance policies taken out by the applicant to cover personal injuries. The abolition of this rule means that such capital received after October 1, 1996 is no longer required to be disregarded in the assessment. The general discretion under the regulations does, however, remain and may apply to the payment in the particular circumstances of each case.

The present relevance of the rule is on reassessments where the original assessment was made before October 1, 1996. In such a case, if a sum was disregarded under the previous rule on the original assessment, then any capital remaining from that sum will continue to be disregarded on the reassessment. However, any further sums received after that date will be taken into account in the reassessment.

The position of interim payments (formerly exempted by the above rule) calls for special comment here. Certain interim payments are exempt from the statutory charge by virtue of regulation 94(a) of the Civil Legal Aid (General) Regulations 1989. The purpose of this exemption (*i.e.* to allow the assisted person to receive the interim payment whilst the case is going on) will be defeated if the Board collects the payment by way of a capital contribution. Further, in a personal injury case, (the most common example) interim payments are often made to meet an applicant's immediate needs.

Therefore, in general, interim payments should be disregarded, unless, having regard to the amount of the payment, the assessment officer is of the view that the assisted person can afford to proceed without the benefit of legal aid.

If an applicant applies in a representative, fiduciary or official capacity it will be the value of any property or estate out of which the applicant is entitled to be indemnified and the assets of any beneficiaries from the proceedings which will be taken into account. The applicant's own personal finances will not be relevant unless he is also a beneficiary.

If the applicant's income changes, he marries, remarries or starts living with a partner as husband and wife or he comes into money (for example, on selling his house or winning the pools) while a legal aid certificate is in force, a further assessment may be carried out (see regulation 12 of the Civil Legal Aid (Assessment of Resources) Regulations 1989 for amounts triggering reassessment—p. 444). Changes in circumstances should be notified to the area office without delay.

A Special Investigations Unit has been established as an integral part of means assessment. The Unit which operates from the Board's London area office deals with applications to any of the area offices from applicants with complex financial affairs whose circumstances warrant particularly close scrutiny. This includes those who appear to have access to wealth, but who nevertheless consider they qualify for legal aid. Cases may be referred to the Unit by the Board or by assessment officers either before or after legal aid has been granted. This initiative is intended to ensure that those who do not qualify financially are excluded from the legal aid scheme.

THE FINANCIAL LIMITS 5–02

Children (including applicants over 16 but in full time education or undergoing vocational training) are assessed in their own right and not on their parent's financial position. The current financial limits apply to children and adults alike, although legal aid for some Children Act proceedings is not means tested and pensioners on a low income are given some allowances against capital. If a person is granted civil legal aid and his/her finances, liabilities or dependants change, he/she must inform the area office.

ACCEPTANCE OF OFFERS 5–03

If the client qualifies financially and the area office decides that the civil legal aid merits test is satisfied (see para. 4–10, above) the area office will either issue a certificate if the applicant does not have to pay a contribution, or an offer of a certificate if a contribution is payable. The area office will also automatically provide a breakdown of the financial assessment to the applicant in all cases where legal aid has been refused on means, or a contribution is payable.

Once the offer has been accepted, a contribution from capital is normally paid immediately. Contributions from income are calculated on a monthly basis and the first contribution must be paid on acceptance of the offer. A certificate will be issued and only then can the solicitor start to deal with the case under civil legal aid. Note that there is no longer a system of "maximum" and "actual" contributions. Following the implementation of the Board's Corporate Information System (CIS), applicants who are married or cohabiting will have their contribution payments divided between each application and they will no longer be payable in relation to one of the offers only. Where one person has several certificates, contribution payments will be spread equally across all the ongoing certificates. Applicants can elect to make payments by direct debit.

5–04 PAYMENT OF CONTRIBUTION AND FURTHER ASSESSMENTS

From April 1993 a new system of legal aid contributions was introduced. Instead of contributions from income being paid over a 12 month period, legal aid contributions became payable for the lifetime of the certificate. Disposable income is assessed on an annual basis, but this is used to calculate an ongoing monthly contribution liability.

On acceptance of an offer an applicant must pay any contribution from capital together with the first monthly income contribution. Subject to any reassessment, contributions in respect of income must be made every month until the certificate is discharged or revoked. The following points should be noted:

(a) Solicitors should ensure that certificates are discharged as soon as the proceedings are concluded, or the work covered by them has been completed. If there is a delay in applying to discharge a certificate, the client will continue to be liable to pay contributions. A solicitor can still be paid for work done in the taxation proceedings after discharge of a certificate.

(b) There is no annual or minimum contribution from income due under the new system, so if a certificate lasts only for six months, only the initial instalment and six monthly contributions are payable.

(c) Further assessments of income or capital under the new system can take place at any time while the certificate is in force. Further assessments on change of means will look at likely income and capital in the 12 months following either the request to reassess or the change in circumstances, rather than being referred back to the original period of computation.

(d) Because the system of a "maximum" and an "actual" contribution no longer applies the full assessed initial contribution must be paid on acceptance of the offer. However, a point may come where the contributions paid exceed the likely total costs of the proceedings. If so, a solicitor may apply to the area office for future contributions to be waived under regulation 52(2) of the General Regulations as amended. An example of where this power might be used is a case where proceedings have become dormant pending the outcome of some other test case or generic trial. Note that there is no power to waive contributions on general grounds such as hardship. Further, it is not enough if total contributions paid are likely to exceed costs to date; further contributions can only be waived if those already paid appear to the area office to exceed the likely total costs of the proceedings. If contributions are waived an appropriate costs condition will be inserted in the certificate (see NFG 9, para. 9–13). Waived contributions may be revived.

(e) When a person (including spouses or cohabitees) has more than one certificate in force, those certificates will be linked and only one contribution will be sought. The monthly contribution will continue to be payable until the last certificate is discharged. When a second certificate is applied for, means will be further assessed and the contribution may be amended, but only if means have changed beyond the limits set out in regulation 12 of the Civil Legal Aid (Assessment of Resources) Regulations 1989.

(f) Note that the above system applies to certificates where the original period of computation for assessment of means commences on or after April 12, 1993. For certificates issued under the old system, contributions are payable only during the initial period of computation, and that period is used for the purpose of any reassessments following change of means within that period of computation (regulation 12 of the Assessment of Resources Regulations in its unamended form).

If the applicant has a contribution to pay by instalments, it is important that the payments are kept up. If they are not, the legal aid certificate (and any linked certificate) may be discharged.

A letter is sent to the assisted person 10 days after an unpaid instalment falls due. From that point only two courses of action are available. They are:

(a) the contribution can be brought up to date within 14 days;

(b) means can be further assessed in appropriate cases.

If neither of these courses of action is taken the certificate will be discharged after a further 21 days.

The letter sent to the assisted person makes it clear how to apply for a further assessment and in what circumstances a further assessment would be appropriate. At the same time as the letter goes to the assisted person a letter is sent to the solicitor. This sets out the same details and requests the solicitor to incur no further costs without reference to the area office. Area offices will give guidance to solicitors about the appropriateness of further assessment or of continuing work, for example if a hearing is imminent. In appropriate cases the Board will use its power under regulation 51 of the Civil Legal Aid (General) Regulations 1989 to amend certificates to prevent further work.

While a further or reassessment is being carried out, no steps will be taken to pursue any arrears of contribution or to discharge or revoke the certificate on that ground. However, ongoing contributions will continue to be payable while further or reassessment is taking place, unless and until such contributions are amended as a result of the further or reassessment. Any person having his/her means further or reassessed should therefore continue to pay contributions (or to put money aside), as the full amount due during the period of further or reassessment may be called for as soon as the process is complete.

WHAT COSTS ARE PAYABLE BY A SUCCESSFUL ASSISTED PERSON? 5–05

The amount the applicant will have to pay will depend on whether:

(a) the other side is ordered to pay costs and in fact does so;

(b) the applicant is awarded any money by the court or recovers or preserves any property as a result of the proceedings.

If the other side does pay the costs *in full* such that there is no claim or a deficiency to the fund, the applicant will receive a refund of any contribution.

If the other side does not pay the costs in full, the assisted person's contribution (or part of it) will not be refunded and the area office may deduct from any moneys ordered by the court to be paid to the assisted person (and actually paid) sufficient to cover those costs. This deduction is known as the statutory charge and it will also apply to any property recovered or preserved in the case. Maintenance and the first £2,500 of any money or property recovered or preserved in matrimonial or Children Act proceedings are exempt from the statutory charge—and so are state benefits (see p. 407).

5–06 WHAT COSTS ARE PAYABLE BY AN UNSUCCESSFUL ASSISTED PERSON?

The most the applicant will normally have to pay towards the solicitor's costs and counsel's fees will be the contribution, if any, due under his certificate. The court may also order the applicant to pay part or all of the opponent's costs. The court decides how much should be paid towards those costs and this will depend on the applicant's means and conduct in connection with the dispute (the amount is often equal to the applicant's contribution).

6. EMERGENCY APPLICATIONS/CERTIFICATES

6.1.1 OVERALL APPROACH

6.1.1.1. The emergency certificate procedure is an important part of the legal aid scheme in that it allows a person in need of legal aid as a matter of urgency to apply for, and receive if the statutory tests are met, civil legal aid more quickly than would normally be the case.

6.1.1.2 This very quick decision-making is possible because the area office can grant emergency legal aid without a full means assessment being carried out before the certificate is issued.

6.1.1.3 This is a significant benefit to applicants but creates a high risk to the legal aid fund. This is because emergency legal aid is granted without certainty that the applicant is financially eligible, will co-operate with the means assessment or accept an offer should a contribution be required.

6.1.1.4 The Legal Aid Board recognises this risk and aims to minimise it by controlling emergency certificates tightly, both at the time initial decisions are made and subsequently throughout their existence.

6.1.1.5 When considering applications, and controlling emergency certificates, the area offices will consider all the circumstances of the application, including the means of the applicant, the merits of the application, the urgency of the matter, potential cost, potential risk to the legal aid fund and the nature of the case. Overall the area offices must seek to reach decisions that are in accordance with the Legal Aid Act, Regulations and Guidance and justifiable to all the Board's stakeholders.

6.1.1.6 Applications should be made by written postal application, fax or telephone depending on the urgency of the case. Area offices will initially decide whether the urgency of the case justifies the method of application used. Telephone applications will rarely be justified as they will only be necessary where work must be undertaken within a few hours including where the solicitor does not have immediate access to a fax machine. Fax applications will only be justified where work must be undertaken within a working day (3 pm to 3 pm for this purpose). Written postal applications should be submitted in all other circumstances.

6.1.1.7 The client must be advised by the solicitor about the nature and consequences of emergency legal aid. He or she must be told

(a) an emergency certificate will only help an applicant about urgent matters and will not be a substitute for full legal aid;

(b) the applicant's means will still have to be assessed by the assessment office so:
   (i) if the applicant does not co-operate, this may result not only in no grant of full legal aid but also in withdrawal of the emergency certificate. This could mean the applicant having to pay all the legal costs personally;
   (ii) if the applicant turns out to be outside the eligibility limits or fails to accept an offer of legal aid and pay any contribution, again the emergency legal aid may be withdrawn and the applicant may have to pay; and

(c) the emergency certificate will only cover urgent legal work. It is no use the applicant expecting the solicitor to run the whole case on emergency legal aid.

6.2 INITIAL GRANT DECISION—BASIC TESTS

6.2.1 INITIAL DECISION

6.2.1.1 The rules relating to decision-making of an application for emergency legal aid are set out in regulations 19 and 20 of the Civil Legal Aid (General) Regulations 1989. They require that an applicant must provide the information, and any supporting documents, necessary for the area office to determine the nature of the proceedings for which legal aid is sought, and the circumstances in which it is required and to determine:

(a) whether the applicant is likely to be financially eligible for legal aid, co-operating in the means assessment process and accepting any offer made;

(b)   whether the case passes the usual merits test; and

(c)   whether it is in the interests of justice that the applicant should as a matter of urgency be granted legal aid.

6.2.1.2   Save in relation to means tested only Children Act applications, all of these tests must be applied by the area office and passed before an emergency certificate can be granted. Guidance on the application of these three tests is set out below. Means tested only Children Act applications have to satisfy the financial eligibility test and urgency test.

6.2.1.3   Applications are considered in the light of all the circumstances of the case. It is necessary to consider the degree of likelihood that the applicant is financially eligible for legal aid.

6.2.2   FINANCIAL ELIGIBILITY TEST

6.2.2.1   The Guide to Assessing Financial Eligibility and fax emergency application means form should be used to assist in applying the test to emergency applications. However, the ultimate decision on the application of the regulations (including the application of discretionary powers) and complex calculations to administer the means test will rest with the assessment officer.

6.2.2.2   Most legal aid applicants organise their financial affairs in such a way that assessing their likely entitlement can be completed relatively quickly. However, there are cases where further information or investigation are needed before the means test can be concluded. Such cases will include those from applicants with complex financial affairs or with properties/resources overseas. When considering such emergency applications, area office staff will be particularly concerned that an application is likely to qualify on means before granting an emergency certificate (see 6.2.11 for more details).

6.2.3   URGENT APPLICATIONS (Decision required that day)

6.2.3.1   For applications by fax the fax emergency application form and means form are designed to take solicitors through an assessment process which will generally allow an informed decision to be made on the **likelihood** of entitlement being established on a full means assessment. Only in the extreme cases will applications be accepted by telephone (*i.e.* where work is required within a few hours, probably on the same day the application is made, including where the solicitor does not have immediate access to a fax machine) and then the area office will obtain the information contained in the fax emergency application and, if appropriate, means form from the solicitor.

6.2.4   AGGREGATION

6.2.4.1   The resources of spouses and partners are required to be aggregated and taken into account, subject only to certain limited exceptions (contrary interest in the dispute or living separate and apart, in a legal and not merely physical sense).

6.2.5   INCOME SUPPORT AND INCOME BASED JOBSEEKER'S ALLOWANCE

6.2.5.1   Applicants on income support or income-based Jobseeker's Allowance should be given a full certificate if the case passes the merits test as the receipt of benefit is a "passport" to civil legal aid, free of contribution.

There are two ways to check eligibility:

(a)   sight of the full notification from the Benefits Agency— this will be in the form of a letter of entitlement (issues when income support/income-based jobseeker's allowance was awarded or when benefit was uprated in April);

(b)   proof of payment—either from bank statements showing the benefit paid in, or by sight of the orderbook.

6.2.6   FAMILY CREDIT AND DISABILITY WORKING ALLOWANCE

6.2.6.1   Applicants in receipt of either of the above benefits are likely to be eligible on income. However, these benefits are not a passport to legal aid and income and capital should be checked before an emergency certificate is granted.

6.2.7   INCOME

6.2.7.1   The figures used to decide eligibility are on a weekly basis and may need to be converted. For example, if the applicant's salary is paid monthly, the net salary should be converted to a weekly figure (multiply by 12 and divide by 52). Similarly where interest is paid yearly or half yearly, this should be divided by either 52 or 26 respectively.

6.2.8   EXPENDITURE

6.2.8.1   Again figures should, if necessary, be converted to a weekly basis as for income. Care should be taken to ensure housing costs are net of housing benefit, *i.e.* rent £50, housing benefit £10, net rent £40.

6.2.8.2   Area offices will not generally make allowances which would be dependent upon the exercise of the assessment officer's discretion in accordance with the Civil Legal Aid (Assessment of Resources) Regulations 1989. However, an area office may in a borderline case, where the exercise of discretion would be likely to materially affect eligibility and which otherwise satisfies all the tests for the issue of an emergency certificate, seek a view from the assessment officer as to the likely exercise of any relevant discretion.

6.2.8.3   Area office staff will either check financial eligibility on receipt of a postal or fax application or, in the case of telephone applications, determine the applicant's eligibility based on the information in the fax emergency application means form. Details of the financial limits and relevant allowances are contained in both the current Legal Aid Handbook and in the Guidance: Exercise of Devolved Powers (GEDP).

6.2.9   MERITS TEST INCLUDING REASONABLENESS

6.2.9.1   The merits test is dealt with at Note for Guidance 7 and must be applied in accordance with that guidance. Paragraph 7–03.33 deals with the applicant's legal aid history which is relevant and could lead the area office to refuse an emergency certificate (having regard to a previous non co-operation/revocation).

6.2.10   URGENCY TEST

6.2.10.1   The urgency test may be met in any of the following circumstances if there is insufficient time for an application for substantive legal aid to be processed:

(a)   representation (or other urgent work for which civil legal aid would be needed) justified in injunction or other emergency proceedings;

(b)   representation (or other urgent work for which civil legal aid would be needed) justified in relation to an imminent hearing in existing proceedings; or

(c)   a limitation period is about to expire.

6.2.10.2   However, failure by the applicant/solicitor to apply for legal aid at the earliest appropriate opportunity, including in a court action which has been ongoing for some time, will not constitute grounds for granting an application for emergency legal aid where there has been an unjustifiable delay which has created or helped to create the emergency.

6.2.10.3   The area office must be satisfied that it is in the interests of justice that the applicant should, as a matter of urgency, be granted legal aid before issuing an emergency certificate. The following general matters will fall to be considered under this head:

(a)   Is there a hearing date before expiry of the time a full legal aid application would take to process, and, if so, would an adjournment be possible without undue difficulty to the applicant, the opponent or the court? If so, an emergency certificate is not appropriate; the adjournment should be arranged and the full application for a substantive certificate take its course.

(b)   Has there been any unjustifiable delay on the part of the solicitor or the applicant which has helped to create the emergency? If there has, it is not reasonable to grant an emergency certificate.

(c) Is the applicant's liberty threatened? If it is, it is likely to be in the interests of justice for the emergency certificate to be granted.

(d) Would any delay cause a significant risk of miscarriage of justice, or unreasonable hardship to the applicant, or irretrievable problems in handling the case? If it will, it is likely to be in the interests of justice for the emergency certificate to be granted.

(e) The imminence of a court hearing does not of itself constitute an emergency situation sufficient to satisfy the urgency test. The area office must be satisfied that all reasonable steps were taken to obtain legal aid at the earliest appropriate opportunity and that there has been no unjustifiable delay taking all the circumstances into account.

6.2.10.4 All the circumstances of the particular case must be considered but the following are among the factors which will usually fall to be considered in balancing the absence of a means assessment and the urgency of the case:

(a) Unless the nature of the case and the work envisaged is urgent as against the time which a substantive application would be likely to take to process, the test will not be satisfied. For example an emergency certificate would not be granted for work to be carried out in a period of weeks rather than days, to cover commencing proceedings for a contact order or defending ancillary relief proceedings short of a final hearing. The time limit for applying for leave for judicial review would not of itself justify a grant—this will depend on the remaining time available, the urgency of the case and the time it is likely to take for the ordinary application to be processed.

(b) Unless the significance of the work envisaged and the consequences of not undertaking it are serious, the test will not be satisfied. For example, the likely loss of an applicant's liberty, the nature of the particular case, including the real risk of significant harm to mental or physical health, the irretrievable loss of significant evidence (*e.g.* through destruction, deterioration or repair) or the inability to pursue a claim due to the limitation period would be likely to satisfy the test. A delay in undertaking work which would have lesser consequences would not (*e.g.* undertaking a particular item of preparation which could be delayed or interviewing a particular witness who would continue to remain available or taking proceedings to seek the return of a child to a parent who normally has care of the child where the child is not at significant risk of harm serious enough to justify immediate proceedings).

(c) Unless no other appropriate options would be available to deal with the emergency, the test will not be satisfied. Other options include:

— Seeking an adjournment of a hearing or an extension of time.
— Dealing with an outstanding matter by way of agreement (*e.g.* directions by consent between the parties).
— Dealing with the urgent work in person (with assistance under the green form if appropriate).
— Entering into correspondence to seek to resolve the matter.

(d) The conduct of the applicant in relation to the case will be relevant. If there has been an unreasonable delay on his or her part which has created or helped to create the emergency then the application is likely to be refused.

6.2.10.5 If an application is refused but the matter becomes more urgent due to a change of circumstances (which may include the passage of time) then the application, supported by relevant information/documents, can be renewed. In addition to the usual tests/factors, any failure to submit a full application, the position in any on-going means assessment as well as the applicant's conduct in co-operating with that process would be relevant.

6.2.11 APPLICANTS WITH COMPLEX MEANS/ACCESS TO ASSETS

6.2.11.1 Before an emergency certificate will be granted an applicant will need to satisfy the area office that they are likely to be financially eligible for legal aid. The procedures applied by the area office in assessing this are set out in 6.2.2 above.

6.2.11.2 Applicants for legal aid can be broadly grouped into the following categories:

(a) applicants on income support/income-based Jobseeker's Allowance;

(b) non-passported applicants with very simple financial affairs, *e.g.* employed people with regular salaries and straightforward capital assets or those in receipt of family credit with low capital assets;

(c) people with slightly more complex financial affairs, *e.g.* self-employed people with small, simple, businesses and straightforward capital assets;

(d) people with complex financial affairs, *e.g.* people with company directorships, several businesses, beneficiaries of trust funds, those whose capital assets are not straightforward etc.;

(e) applicants with extremely complex financial affairs of the type that would be referred to the Special Investigations Unit for means assessment.

6.2.11.3 In general the more complex an applicant's financial affairs, the less likely the area office will be able to satisfy itself that the applicant is likely to be financially eligible. The means assessment process involves the inclusion of all assets of the applicant including aggregation of a spouse/partner (as well as the resources of others in some circumstances), subject to mandatory and discretionary allowances and disregards. Where an applicant has significant capital/income or complex means the likelihood increases that the applicant would be unlikely to qualify unless the assessment officer exercised his or her powers as to allowances/disregards in the particular case. See para. 6.2.8.2 above.

6.2.11.4 Applicants with access to or control of resources such as apparently substantial capital, a significant income (albeit potentially off-set by significant outgoings) and/or whose means involve complex issues such as interests in companies, trusts or the assessment of third party assets would be likely to have their applications refused as the area office would consider them unlikely to satisfy the means test. Where assets are frozen by injunction the area office would look at the monies available to the applicant under the order (both generally and for legal costs) and, as to scope, would consider whether an application should be made to vary the order.

6.2.11.5 It has to be remembered that a revocation based on an out of scope means assessment or non co-operation renders the former assisted person fully liable for his solicitor's costs. Generally the interests of an applicant in obtaining an emergency certificate must be weighed with the consequences for him/her of a subsequent revocation and area offices will not grant emergency certificates where the applicant is unlikely to qualify financially.

6.2.12   HIGH COST CASES

6.2.12.1 The majority of cases for which emergency legal aid is sought are short in duration and relatively low in cost. However, there are a small number of applications where because of the work involved the area office is being asked to commit substantial sums immediately and with little opportunity of controlling the costs incurred once the emergency certificate has been granted. These cases often arise where an application for emergency legal aid is received shortly before an expensive and/or lengthy hearing (often in the High Court) is about to commence.

6.2.12.2 The imminence of a hearing, even a High Court hearing, is not of itself enough to meet the "urgency" test for the grant of an emergency certificate (see 6.2.10 above). Even if it is considered that the urgency test is met it is necessary—in considering whether it is reasonable in all the circumstances of the case to grant legal aid—to consider the relationship between the potential cost to the fund if the application is granted alongside the timing of the application and the degree of likelihood about whether the applicant is likely to be financially eligible for legal aid.

97

6.2.12.3 Every application will be judged against the statutory tests and having regard to all its circumstances but if the application is in respect of an action where to grant would immediately involve significant costs which would be incurred under the emergency certificate, the area office will exercise particular care in considering the means test. It is in the interests of the applicant that an emergency certificate is not subsequently revoked (as it must be if it transpires he or she does not qualify financially).

6.2.12.4 If the area office considers that the applicant is unlikely to qualify or that it would be unreasonable to grant, it will refuse the application. The likelihood of a refusal increases with the complexity of the applicant's means as the area office may conclude that the applicant is unlikely to qualify.

6.2.12.5 In a high cost case clearly involving costs in excess of the standard costs limitation but where, in the view of the area office, an applicant is unlikely to qualify financially but nonetheless wishes to pursue his/her application which otherwise satisfies all the tests for the issue of an emergency certificate (*i.e.* both as to urgency and merits), the area office may refer such means information as is available to the assessment officer for a view as to whether the applicant is likely to qualify financially. In that small minority of cases where such a referral is made and the assessment officer considers that the applicant is likely to qualify, then the area office may issue an emergency certificate. In such cases, however, the area office will limit the duration of the certificate to a short period only, usually a week, extendable on application by further limited periods (again usually of a week). This will go towards ensuring that the assisted person co-operates as speedily as possible in the means assessment and will give the area office an opportunity to check the position with the assessment officer.

6.2.13 INCOMPLETE INFORMATION

6.2.13.1 It is the responsibility of the applicant and/or the solicitor to submit the correct forms, fully and correctly completed and supported by relevant documentation, before the area office can decide whether to grant an emergency legal aid certificate.

6.2.13.2 If the urgency or the nature of the situation dictates that the applicant or solicitor is unable to submit the forms **fully completed** then the following exceptions can be made:

(a) The urgency of a situation will sometimes prevent the applicant from being able to produce a form L17 (employer's statement). In those circumstances, wage slips will be acceptable but it/they must cover, as a minimum, the immediately previous 6-week period, *i.e.* the previous 6 slips if the applicant is paid weekly or the last 2 slips if paid monthly. Fewer slips will normally be acceptable only if it/they contain cumulative information covering the previous 6 weeks. Where fewer or no wage slips are speed-

ily available having regard to the circumstances of the case
(*e.g.* the applicant cannot get access to the place where they
are kept and copies could not be quickly obtained), then
emergency legal aid will only be granted when justified by
the urgency, gravity and all the other circumstances of the
case.

(b) It will sometimes be reasonable to entertain an application
by fax or telephone.

6.2.13.3 These are the only exceptions to the rule that the correct forms
must be submitted fully and correctly completed.

6.2.14 UPGRADES WHEN AN ORDINARY APPLICATION IS PENDING

6.2.14.1 It may become necessary to make an emergency application in
a case where an ordinary application has already been submitted. The general guidance in this section will apply subject to
the following paragraphs.

6.2.14.2 The emergency application should be made by postal forms, fax
or telephone depending on the urgency of the case. The emergency application should be made by postal forms, fax or telephone, depending on the urgency of the case. A further
application form APP1 or APP2 should be submitted. This
should be marked with the date of submission of the earlier
substantive application and should be completed only as to the
applicant's details, the back page headed "Emergency details"
and any other parts of the form where the information will be
different from that set out in the earlier substantive application. The applicant must sign the declaration on page 11. The
fax emergency application form should not be used (even for
faxed applications) as the relevant merits information will have
already been provided in the full application previously
submitted.

6.2.14.3 In relation to means, where the ordinary application was submitted less than two working weeks previously and the applicant is not in receipt of income support or income-based
Jobseeker's Allowance, a fax emergency application means
form duly completed as to his/her means must be submitted for
both postal and faxed applications. In the case of a telephone
upgrade, the information covered by the fax emergency means
form must be provided over the telephone.

6.2.14.4 Where the ordinary application was submitted two working
weeks or more previously, a fax emergency means form need
not be submitted in the first instance as the area office may, if
otherwise minded to grant the emergency application, contact
the assessment section for information regarding the means
assessment outcome/applicant's co-operation in the means
assessment process to date. Where the assessment outcome is
not imminent but the applicant has co-operated up to the submission of the emergency application, it may then be necessary

for the area office to obtain the means information contained in the fax emergency means form (by fax or otherwise) to decide whether the applicant is likely to qualify financially.

6.3   METHODS OF APPLYING

6.3.1   POSTAL APPLICATIONS

6.3.1.1   Incorrect, unsigned or incorrectly dated forms will be returned to the solicitor. Where the solicitor has a fax number the area office will send a fax to the solicitor to notify him. If the solicitor faxes or telephones an application to the area office, pending receipt and return of the corrected forms, the area office will start from the premise that the application should be refused on the basis that the urgency is self created. The area office may, however, decide to grant an application, by fax or telephone particularly in cases where the applicant is at immediate personal risk.

6.3.1.2   Where postal application forms (APP1/2/3 and MEANS 1/2/3/4) have been completed but the legal application form is incomplete *e.g.* if the solicitor has failed to estimate costs or prospects of success, or supporting documentation has not been provided, the application will be accepted for processing.

6.3.1.3   The area office should telephone (or fax) the solicitor to obtain missing information. However, if sufficient information cannot be gathered the application will be refused. The decision will be faxed to the solicitor.

6.3.1.4   Where the means form is incomplete, for example, if the applicant has failed to tick a box or to confirm how much he/she pays in rent or no L17 or insufficient wage slips have been supplied, the forms will be returned to the solicitor. Where the solicitor has a fax number the area office will send a fax to the solicitor to notify him. If the solicitor faxes or telephones an application to the area office, pending receipt and return of the corrected forms, the area office will start from the premise that the application should be refused on the basis the urgency is self created. The area office may, however, decide to grant an application by fax or telephone, particularly in cases where the applicant is at immediate personal risk. Exceptionally, where insufficient wage slips are speedily available having regard to the circumstances of the case (*e.g.* the applicant cannot get access to the place where they are kept and copies could not be quickly obtained), then emergency legal aid will only be granted when justified by the urgency, gravity and all the other circumstances of the case.

6.3.1.5   The area office should, where the urgency of the case justifies it, telephone the solicitor to clarify information relevant to means, for example if the missing/unclear information is limited, such as *e.g.* the address of the local benefits office, dates of birth of dependent children rather than means information itself.

6.3.2 FAXED APPLICATIONS

6.3.2.1 Standard Faxed Emergency Application Forms

6.3.2.1.1 Faxed emergency applications will only be accepted if submitted on the fax emergency application form and, unless the applicant is in receipt of a benefit which constitutes a passport (*i.e.* income support or income-based Jobseeker's Allowance), the fax emergency means form. The intention of the forms is to assist the solicitor in providing the information (concerning the urgency of the situation, the merits of the case and the means of the applicant) necessary to determine an emergency application. The supporting statement should be succinct but cover all the relevant points. Documents should not be sent in support.

6.3.2.1.2 Where postal application forms have been completed these should form a postal application, and must not be faxed to the area office. In circumstances where the postal forms have been completed but the urgency of the situation is such that a faxed emergency application can be justified, the fax emergency application form will still be required and postal application forms must not be faxed. Any postal applications which are incorrectly faxed to the area office will be destroyed on receipt and not actioned. However, any statement prepared for submission with a postal application can be submitted in support of the fax emergency application form (and vice versa).

6.3.2.1.3 A pending substantive application can, if appropriate on the basis of increased urgency, be upgraded by a faxed application. Paragraph 6.2.14 (and not this Section) deals with upgraded applications.

6.3.2.2 Urgency criteria

6.3.2.2.1 A faxed emergency should only be made in circumstances where it meets both of the following urgency criteria:

(a) to justify making an emergency application (see para. 6.2.10.1 *et seq.*) and

(b) to justify consideration of that emergency application without a fully completed postal application being made (*i.e.* the urgency of the situation is such that a decision is required before a postal application could reasonably be processed). Generally a fax application will only be justified where work must be undertaken within a working day (3 pm to 3 pm for this purpose).

6.3.2.2.2 Only in circumstances where a faxed application can be justified, should the fax emergency application form and, if appropriate, means form be completed in full (by the solicitor) and faxed to the area office.

6.3.2.3 Means and Merits criteria

6.3.2.3.1 If, on consideration of the information provided, the area office is not satisfied that the matter is sufficiently urgent to justify a faxed emergency application or that the applicant is likely to satisfy the means or merits tests, the application will be refused (see para. 6.3.2.5).

6.3.2.3.2 Where the solicitor is unable to provide all of the income or capital information necessary to complete the fax emergency means form in full, it is for the solicitor to satisfy the area office that the client is, nonetheless, likely to be financially eligible for civil legal aid, *e.g.* an applicant with low capital and on low earnings who is unable to provide full details on water rates, council tax etc. immediately but who can provide full details of capital and income is likely to qualify whereas the area office cannot be satisfied of this if full details of capital and income are not available.

6.3.2.4 Returning faxed emergency applications

6.3.2.4.1 Applications which have not been signed by the solicitor will be returned to the solicitor and postal applications incorrectly faxed to the area office will be destroyed on receipt. However, where the area office is not satisfied that sufficient information has been provided on which to base a decision about the urgency of the situation, or the merits of the case (*e.g.* where the information requested in the fax emergency application form is incomplete) further information should be sought by telephoning the solicitor in the first instance, or if unsuccessful, by returning the fax indicating the information required. A decision will not be made until all outstanding information has been obtained. See also para. 6.3.1.4 regarding means information.

6.3.2.4.2 If the fax emergency application form remains incomplete despite a request for further information or means information is omitted then the application must be returned to the solicitor. No faxed emergency should be allowed to remain outstanding for longer than 5 working days (as a postal emergency application could have been submitted in this time).

6.3.2.5 Refusing faxed emergency applications

6.3.2.5.1 Where the area office is satisfied that sufficient information has been provided (*i.e.* all information requested in the fax emergency application form including, if appropriate, the means form) but on the basis of that information the application does not satisfy all the tests, including for a faxed application, the application will be refused.

6.3.2.5.2 The refusal decision will be faxed back to the solicitor, giving details of the reason(s) for refusal. There is no appeal against the refusal of an emergency application. Further applications including by post can be made in the same matter and any previous decision to refuse will have no bearing on a further application (although in the absence of a change of circumstances the application would again be refused).

6.3.2.6 Granting faxed emergency applications

6.3.2.6.1 A copy of the decision form, confirming the description and limitation wordings, will be faxed back to the solicitor within a working day from receipt (3 pm to 3 pm for this purpose).

6.3.3 TELEPHONE APPLICATIONS

6.3.3.1 Determining Applications

6.3.3.1.1 Emergency applications for legal aid will not be considered over the telephone unless the area office is satisfied that a decision is required before a faxed or written application could reasonably be processed (see para. 6.3.2.2.1) or very urgent work is required and the solicitor does not have immediate access to a fax machine (*i.e.* he is away from his office and could not be expected to get access to a fax machine). This means that in **all** instances where the solicitor has time to do so having regard to the urgency of the case, an emergency application should be made in writing to the area office or by fax rather than by telephone.

6.3.3.1.2 Telephone applications will only be accepted in rare and extremely urgent circumstances (*e.g.* where work must be undertaken within a few hours, probably on the same day the application is made including where the solicitor is telephoning from the court) and where the solicitor is able to provide the area office with adequate information relating to the means of the applicant and the merits of the case.

6.3.3.1.3 In circumstances where the urgency of the situation is such that a telephone application can be justified, the information contained in the fax emergency application form and, if appropriate, the fax emergency means form must be provided to the area office caseworker over the telephone. Where telephone emergency legal aid is granted a copy of the decision will be faxed to the solicitor as confirmation.

6.3.3.2 Urgency criteria

6.3.3.2.1 In circumstances where a telephone emergency application can

103

be justified (see para. 6.3.3.1.2), the information required by the fax emergency application form and, if appropriate, the fax emergency means form should be obtained in as much detail as possible, by the area office caseworker. Consideration will then be given to the application on the basis of the information provided over the telephone. The caseworker will consider the urgency of the case first as, if the urgency test for a telephone application is not met, the application will not be granted and the rest of the information need not be obtained.

6.3.3.2.2 A telephone application will not be justified only on the basis that previous forms have been returned by the area office. Where application forms have been returned, if the solicitor makes a telephone (or fax) application pending receipt and return of the corrected forms the area office will start from the premise that the application should be refused on the basis that the urgency is self created. The area office may, however, decide to grant an application by fax or telephone in exceptional circumstances, particularly where the applicant is at immediate personal risk.

6.3.3.3   Means and Merits criteria

6.3.3.3.1 If, on consideration of the information provided, the area office is not satisfied that the applicant is likely to satisfy the means and merits tests, the application will be refused.

6.3.3.3.2 Where the solicitor is unable to provide all of the income and/or capital information which would be necessary to complete a fax emergency application form in full the application will be refused unless the area office can otherwise be satisfied that the application is likely to meet the means test, *e.g.* applicants with low capital and on low earnings who are unable to provide full details on water rates, council tax etc. immediately.

6.3.3.4   Refusing telephone emergency applications

6.3.3.4.1 Where the caseworker has accepted the telephone emergency application as meeting the urgency criteria, but is not satisfied that sufficient information has been provided on which to base a decision, either about the means of the client or the merits of the case (*i.e.* where the information requested on the fax emergency application form cannot be completed and/or the caseworker has not been otherwise satisfied as to eligibility) the application will not be granted.

6.3.3.4.2 Information will be obtained in as much detail as possible up until the point at which the lack of material information becomes clear. At that point the solicitor will be advised about the information which is needed and of the options to call again within the same day or make another application once the information is available. The fact that a telephone emergency application has previously been refused on the basis of lack of information is not in itself justification for a further application by telephone.

6.3.3.4.3 Where the caseworker is satisfied that sufficient information has been provided (*i.e.* all of the information requested in the fax emergency application form) but on the basis of that information the urgency test for the grant of an emergency certificate has not been met or a substantive application would not be granted, the application will be refused.

6.3.3.4.4 Where the application is refused, the solicitor will be informed of the reason for refusal. There is no appeal against the refusal of an emergency application. However, a further postal application or application by fax can, if appropriate, be made in the same matter depending on the urgency of the case.

6.3.3.5 Granting telephone emergency applications

6.3.3.5.1 Where the area office grants a certificate the solicitor will be given the description and limitation wordings over the telephone, and asked to agree to the conditions applied (as quoted from the certification statement and conditions in the fax emergency application). A telephone emergency application will not be granted unless the solicitor is able to confirm agreement to abide by the conditions which apply.

6.3.3.5.2 A copy of the decision reached will be faxed to the solicitor within the same working day or within the next working day when an application is received near to close of business.

6.4 SUBSEQUENT SUBMISSION OF POSTAL FORMS FOLLOWING THE GRANT OF A TELEPHONE OR FAX APPLICATION

6.4.1 It is a condition of a decision to grant a telephone or faxed emergency application, that:

(a) the full and completed postal forms and supporting documentation must be *received* by the area office within 5 working days of the grant; and

(b) the information provided in the postal forms must be consistent in all material respects with that provided/confirmed in the fax emergency application form/telephone conversation.

6.4.2 If the condition is not met the telephone/fax emergency grant decision will not stand and no emergency certificate will be issued because the solicitor has failed to meet the conditions of the grant. Even where, unusually, the completed postal forms are dated after the date of the grant of an emergency certificate, the certificate will itself be dated with the date of the grant but only provided the condition has been met.

6.4.3. Where it is immediately clear or becomes clear that the forms cannot be submitted within the usual 5 day period an amendment or extension of the period may be sought having regard to the circumstances of the particular case. Extensions must be applied for before the expiry of the time period and amendments/extensions will only be granted for a limited period. In those cases where otherwise completed forms are available but limited information/supporting documents are still awaited from the client it will be preferable to liaise with the area office regarding the immediate submission of the forms so that the assessment process can be put in hand. The area office will have regard to the circumstances of the case leading to the unavailability of information/documents (see para. 6.3.1.4).

6.4.4   If a postal application is submitted which is materially different as against the information provided/confirmed in the fax emergency application form/telephone conversation, the fax/telephone emergency grant decision will not stand because the solicitor has failed to meet the conditions of the grant. In this context "materially" means affecting eligibility as to means or merits (so that the application would not have been granted). Any new but material information received by the solicitor after the fax/telephone grant should be referred to the area office immediately so that the status of the grant can be considered.

6.4.5   Paragraph 6.2.14 (and not this section) deals with upgrades where a full, postal application is pending.

6.5   LIMITATIONS ON THE INITIAL GRANT

6.5.1   SCOPE LIMITATIONS

6.5.1.1   An emergency civil legal aid certificate will not be granted where the applicant is unlikely to fulfil the usual means and merits tests nor unless it is in the interests of justice that the applicant should, as a matter of urgency, be granted legal aid (regulation 20, Civil Legal Aid (General) Regulations 1989). The merits test does not, however, apply to means tested only Children Act applications which must still meet the means and urgency tests.

6.5.1.2   Once a decision has been made that the grant of an emergency certificate is justified the area office will look at the particular steps which need to be taken as a matter of urgency. This is the work which must be undertaken in the very immediate future and the area office will limit the scope of the certificate to the minimum required in the interests of justice.

6.5.1.3   What is necessary and justified will depend on the circumstances of the particular case but the scope limitation imposed will always be specific (*e.g.* as to particular, specified work or a specified hearing on a particular date) rather than open-ended (*e.g.* to be represented on a particular hearing and any adjournment of that hearing). This means that the solicitor may need to seek an amendment to extend scope and at that point the area office will consider all the circumstances of the case again and the extent to which an amendment is justified.

6.5.1.4   The area office may consider that only some of the work anticipated is sufficiently urgent and justifies cover under the certificate. The grant of an emergency certificate does not of itself mean that cover will be given for all future work in the case during the lifetime of the certificate but rather that the minimum steps will be covered. In particular the area office may decide that, for example, a single written document should be prepared or a single step should be taken pending a full means assessment. Where a hearing date has been fixed the area office may, nonetheless, consider that attempts should be made to adjourn that hearing or to deal with the matter in another way *e.g.* by consent or by the applicant in person.

6.5.2   COST LIMITATIONS

6.5.2.1   Every emergency certificate will contain a cost limitation which will limit the costs which can be incurred within the scope of the certificate. This will be for a maximum figure of £1200 outside London and, for cases being dealt with by a solicitor whose office is in the London legal aid area, a maximum of £1500. This sum includes profit costs, counsel's fees and disbursements but not VAT. This is not a ceiling to be worked towards, as in most cases the reasonable costs of the work within the scope of the limitation will be less than the limitation. Costs will fall to be taxed/assessed and the limitation is intended to ensure that, in the minority of cases where the limitation figure is approached, an amendment application must be made to cover future work in excess of the limitation. This is so that the urgency and merits tests as well as the position in relation to means assessment will be reconsidered. Emergency certificates will not contain a costs condition.

6.5.2.2   In those exceptional cases where it is apparent that the urgent steps to be covered by the emergency certificate will involve greater costs than the standard figure, a cost limitation specifically related to the scope limitation will be inserted.

6.5.2.3   The solicitor will put forward a cost estimate as part of the application but it will be for the area office to fix the limitation. There is no right of appeal against the limitation but the solicitor can apply for an amendment to that limitation if the circumstances change or further, fresh information can be made available regarding the likely costs of the work to be covered (*i.e.* to indicate the work cannot be undertaken within the limitation). An amendment to the scope of an emergency certificate or to a cost limitation will not automatically carry with it an amendment to the cost limitation or scope of the certificate respectively. Each must be applied for and the grant of one will not necessarily lead to the grant of the other.

6.5.2.4   When dealing with any request for an increase to the cost limitation or when applying a non-standard cost limitation, careful consideration will be given to the justifiability of such an increase/limitation having regard to all the circumstances of the case. These will include:

— the reason(s) for the request including any change in circumstances in the case directly affecting the likely costs;

— the urgent work to be undertaken and the consequences of not undertaking it;

— the time which it is likely to take for the substantive application to be dealt with;

— the position in relation to the outstanding means assessment, including the applicant's conduct in co-operating in the assessment process and the degree of certainty regarding the applicant's/assisted person's financial eligibility.

6.5.2.5   Where an offer is outstanding, the applicant would, save in the most exceptional circumstances (*e.g.* an apparently clear error in the assessment directly affecting the applicant's contribution) be expected to accept it (and an amendment to the emergency certificate refused) so that further work could then be undertaken under his or her substantive certificate. Where there is an indication that the applicant/assisted person is not co-operating in the means assessment it would not be reasonable to grant further emergency cover. The area office will, if relevant information is not already available to it, seek urgent information regarding the position as to the means assessment.

6.5.2.6   Arrangements will be in place within the area offices to ensure that those minority of exceptional cases involving potential cost limitations significantly in excess of the usual amount are appropriately considered.

6.5.3   TIME LIMITATIONS

6.5.3.1   Every emergency certificate will contain a time limitation. This will be six weeks from the date of issue of the certificate (save in a minority of cases where a shorter period will be applied so as to particularly ensure the applicant's co-operation in the means assessment). This is so that certificates do not run unchecked for a long period of time.

6.5.3.2   The emergency certificate expires when that time period is reached (regulation 22(c)).

6.5.3.3   The area office may, in accordance with regulation 24, only extend the time period and life of the certificate where:

(a) the applicant is offered a full certificate but has not yet accepted the offer or appeals against its terms or

(b)   the application for a full certificate has been refused (*i.e.* out of scope on capital) and either notice of appeal has been given or the time limit for appealing has not expired or

(c)   there are exceptional circumstances.

6.5.3.4   The area office has a discretion whether to extend the duration of the emergency certificate. In accordance with the Regulations it is only where the extension is on the basis of exceptional circumstances that further work can be permitted under the certificate. In all other cases, although the existence of the emergency certificate is preserved (*e.g.* as to costs protection and topping up) by an extension, no further work may be done under it (even if the work would otherwise have fallen within the scope of the certificate). It is for the solicitor to apply for an amendment to extend the life of the certificate—see para. 6.6.2—and an extension based on an outstanding offer/appeal against the terms of an offer or a possible appeal against the refusal of the application for a full certificate only preserves the certificate (but does not allow work under it). (Regulations 24(2) and 23 Civil Legal Aid (General) Regulations 1989.)

6.5.3.5   The area office will consider all the circumstances of the case to decide whether an emergency certificate should be extended and if so on what basis. Its decision is final and there is no right of appeal. The applicant's co-operation in the means assessment process and the urgency of any further work will be relevant. In the event that the area office decides to extend the certificate this will be for a limited time period of days or weeks reflecting the circumstances of the particular case after which the process can, if necessary, be repeated by the solicitor making a further application. The extension would reflect the time it would be likely to take to accept an outstanding offer, to process an outstanding appeal or the particular, exceptional circumstances justifying the extension. In cases involving outstanding offers, regard would be had to when the offer was made and whether acceptance has been delayed for good reason, *e.g.* in the caseworker's view an apparent error has been made in the assessment. It is for the solicitor dealing with the case to be aware of the time limit contained in the certificate and to seek an appropriate amendment in good time. If he fails to do so then the certificate will no longer be in force (regulation 22(c) Civil Legal Aid (General) Regulations 1989).

6.5.3.6   Where the duration of an emergency certificate is extended, further work will only be covered if it is within the scope and limitation of the certificate, *i.e.* there is no automatic amendment to the scope and limitation in the certificate.

6.5.3.7   Where a certificate expires and does not merge with a substantive certificate following continuous existence of the emergency certificate there will be a period between the expiry of the emergency certificate and the issue of the substantive certificate when there will be a break in legal aid cover. This means that, during that period, the assisted person is not protected

109

against a full costs order and that private client funding could be accepted without a breach of regulation 64.

6.5.3.8   Once the time limit including any extension has expired the area office will generally await the outcome of the means assessment to see whether the assisted person would have co-operated/been financially eligible but it is open to the area office to immediately revoke or discharge an emergency certificate on its expiry. This means that it is particularly important that assisted persons and solicitors are aware of the time limitation and that assisted persons co-operate as quickly and as fully as possible in the means assessment process so that it is, as far as possible, concluded within the time specified (or an amendment extending the certificate is sought).

6.6   CONTROL DURING THE LIFE OF THE CERTIFICATE

6.6.1   Subsequent control of emergency certificates is as important as the initial decision to grant. Whilst an emergency certificate is in force there is an element of risk that legal aid may have been provided to a person who is not financially eligible. The continuing emergency certificate, outstanding pending means assessment, may prove to be a debt for the assisted person/loss to the fund. This is relevant both to contributions assessed as payable and the later recovery of costs from a former assisted person.

6.6.2   If an amendment is requested to the description of legal aid, a scope or cost limitation, the area office **must**—

(a) re-apply the initial merits test, especially with regard to the urgency criteria.

(b) check the present position with regards to the means assessment. If there is an outstanding offer, the offer should normally be accepted (*e.g.* in the absence of a clear error in the assessment). If any delay in concluding the means assessment is due to the applicant not fully co-operating (which may lead to an embargo being placed on the certificate), then the amendment should be refused.

(c) consider the particular circumstances of the case.

This guidance will be applied generally including as to limitations in scope, cost and time. There is no right of appeal against the decision of the area office regarding an amendment.

6.6.3   Amendment applications should be made by written postal application, fax or telephone depending on the urgency of the case. Area offices will initially decide whether the urgency of the case justifies the method of application used. Telephone applications will rarely be justified as they will only be necessary where work must be undertaken within the next few hours. Fax applications will only be justified where work must be undertaken within a working day (3 pm to 3 pm for this purpose). Written postal applications should be submitted in all other circumstances.

6.6.4   Where a certificate is embargoed, whether by way of the show cause procedure, an embargo or a restrictive amendment, the area office will, if asked to allow further work, look at all the circumstances of the case. The basis of the request and the urgency of the further work envisaged will be considered to balance whether allowing further work would be justified against the concern which led to the restriction on work. In the absence of good reason (*i.e.* evidence or information) to explain/address the original concern further work is unlikely to be allowed. For example, where an applicant alleges he has co-operated in the means assessment process a bare assertion (as opposed to say the use of an incorrect/incomplete address or a history of lost post to an address occupied by other people as well as the assisted person) will not suffice. Even if the area office agrees to allow further work it will consider the work envisaged and cover only the urgent steps.

6.7   REPRESENTATIONS RECEIVED ABOUT EMERGENCY CERTIFICATES

6.7.1   MERITS REPRESENTATIONS

6.7.1.1   It is for area office to consider the merits of the case as presented. If following representations the area office believes the certificate should continue, then the person making representation should be informed within 5 working days of receipt of the representations.

6.7.1.2   Where reconsideration of the merits including representations leads the area office to change the decision then the certificate should be amended to cover no further work and interested parties advised accordingly—this would not normally be done without first putting the representations to the assisted person's solicitor as a matter of urgency (possibly by fax or telephone) for an urgent response (within a stated time period, again possibly by fax or telephone). There is no direct right of appeal against such an amendment although the ordinary application should be refused (subject to any successful appeal against the substantive refusal) and the emergency certificate discharged/revoked once a means assessment is received.

6.7.2   MEANS REPRESENTATIONS

6.7.2.1   Where representations are made about the means of an assisted person then all information received by the area office must be passed to the assessment office within five working days of

111

receipt. The area office, when forwarding the representations, will consider whether they are sufficiently clear and serious to justify the imposition of an embargo on the certificate, if necessary by way of a restrictive amendment to prevent further work, pending the investigation of the representations or the concluded means assessment.

6.7.2.2   See 6.6.4 above regarding further work.

6.8   BRINGING EMERGENCY CERTIFICATES TO A CLOSE

6.8.1   GENERAL

6.8.1.1   An emergency certificate may be discharged or revoked, be merged in a substantive certificate or expire in accordance with its time limitation including any extension (regulation 22, Civil Legal Aid (General) Regulations 1989). Where a certificate expires it can subsequently be revived by the issue of a full certificate. However, if the emergency certificate does not merge into the full certificate to provide continuous cover then there will be a break in cover (between the expiry of the emergency certificate and the issue of the full, substantive certificate) which will mean that in that period the assisted person is not protected by section 17 Legal Aid Act 1988 against a full costs order and that private client funding could be accepted without a breach of regulation 64.

6.8.2   OFFERS OF FULL LEGAL AID

6.8.2.1   Where an amergency certificate has been issued and a means assessment is obtained requiring the collection of a contribution, an offer of full legal aid will be made in the usual way. Where an offer is outstanding the area office may extend the time limitation contained in the emergency certificate (regulation 24(1)(a)). This is discretionary and where a certificate is extended on this basis no further work may be done unless/until a full certificate is issued.

6.8.2.2   The effect of an extension is to preserve only the existence of the emergency certificate (and not to enable work to be undertaken) with a view to the offer being accepted and the emergency certificate merging in a full, substantive certificate. Any extension granted would be of only sufficient, limited time to enable the outstanding offer to be accepted (this would normally be for a period of days rather than weeks). More than one extension of time would be unlikely to be granted on this basis in view of the opportunity given to the assisted person to consider and accept the offer. Where an emergency certificate is in force it is reasonable to expect the assisted person to react speedily to the making of an offer and the area office may decline to extend the certificate or restrict the scope of the certificate where that is not done.

6.8.2.3 Once an offer of full legal aid has been made it is unlikely that any extension of cover as to scope or costs will be justified until the assisted person accepts the offer of legal aid which has been made to him/her. This means that the solicitor will only be able to work within the existing limitations applicable to the particular certificate.

6.8.3 REVOKING OR DISCHARGING EMERGENCY CERTIFICATES

6.8.3.1 An emergency certificate can be discharged or revoked in accordance with the Civil Legal Aid (General) Regulations 1989, regulations 74 to 86, but see 6.8.3.6 below.

6.8.3.2 An emergency certificate must be revoked where the assisted person is assessed as outside scope on income or where, although in scope on income, he is liable to be refused legal aid having regard to the extent of his disposable capital and the probable costs of the proceedings.

6.8.3.3 An emergency certificate may be revoked or discharged for failure to co-operate or failure to accept an offer of a full certificate. After the show cause procedure has been applied including an embargo on further work (unless specifically authorised by the area office), the area office will normally revoke rather than discharge the certificate unless there are exceptional circumstances justifying discharge. This is because discharging rather than revoking the certificate means that the assisted person retains, despite his non-co-operation or failure to accept an offer, the advantages of being legally aided for the duration of the certificate and means that the legal aid fund bears the costs incurred under the certificate with no possibility of seeking to recover them from the former assisted person. A certificate will not be discharged (rather than revoked) merely because the former assisted person disclosed capital and/or income under a particular sum, was stated to be in receipt of income support or the proceedings were between spouses/co-habitees who are attempting a reconciliation. These are, however, issues which can be considered by the Board's Debt Recovery Unit when deciding what action to take in relation to recovery of the deficiency to the legal aid fund.

6.8.3.4 The area office may revoke or discharge an emergency certificate on the expiry of the time limitation (including any extension). Generally, however, the area office will await the outcome of the means assessment to see whether the assisted person has co-operated and is financially eligible. It is then open to the area office to revoke or discharge the emergency certificate on the basis of its expiry or under any other available power which would be applicable in the circumstances, *e.g.* following

113

in an out of scope income assessment the emergency certificate would be revoked on a mandatory basis.

6.8.3.5 No show cause procedure is required for the discharge or revocation of an emergency certificate based on its expiry. This means that the discharge or revocation can take immediate effect on the expiry of the certificate and without prior notice although this would be exceptional because the area office will normally allow the means assessment to proceed. (See 6.8.3.4, above.)

6.8.3.6 Until the means assessment process has been completed (including by possible non-cooperation by the assisted person) the area office will not discharge an emergency certificate on the merits or by applying any of its general powers (*e.g.* with the assisted person's consent). This is because revocation may ultimately be more appropriate.

6.8.3.7 There is no right of appeal against the discharge or revocation of an emergency certificate. Where a former assisted person submits that the certificate was wrongly discharged/revoked the area office should look at all the circumstances of the case including the basis of discharge/revocation and the reason(s) for the assisted person's view. In the absence of a clear error or good reason (*i.e.* evidence or information) sufficient to make the decision unjustifiable the discharge/revocation should not be withdrawn. For example a bald assertion of co-operation in the means assessment process as opposed to say the use of an incorrect/incomplete address or a history of lost post to an address occupied by other people as well as the former assisted person will not suffice. Where the area office is prepared to withdraw the discharge/revocation it will decide what further work, if any, should be allowed having regard all the circumstances including to the urgency criteria and bearing in mind the absence of a means assessment.

7. CIVIL LEGAL AID MERITS TEST

This guidance sets out the way in which the Legal Aid Board interprets and applies the statutory merits test for civil legal aid. It is not the intention of this guidance to set out rigid or legally binding rules as to how the test must be applied. The statutory tests are widely drawn and each application will be considered on its own merits. The statute provides a wide discretion to consider all the circumstances of the case which make it reasonable or unreasonable to grant legal aid. The intention of the guidance is to ensure that within the context of that wide discretion the Board achieves the best possible degree of consistency of decision-making, whether decisions are made by the Board's area offices, by area committees on appeal or by franchisees acting under powers delegated to them by contract.

THE MERITS TEST GENERALLY   **7–01**

The statutory provisions

A civil legal aid certificate may only be issued where the case has sufficient   **7–01.1**
merit to justify public funding according to certain statutory tests. With the
exception of certain proceedings under the Children Act 1989 and other
limited exceptions, every application for civil legal aid is subject to the
following two statutory tests:

   (a) a person shall not be granted civil legal aid for proceedings unless that
       person satisfies the Board that he or she has reasonable grounds for
       taking, defending or being a party to the proceedings (section 15(2)).
       This is known as the "legal merits test";

   (b) a person may be refused civil legal aid if in the particular circum-
       stances of the case it appears to the Board unreasonable that he or she
       should be granted civil legal aid (section 15(3)(a)). This is known as the
       "reasonableness test".

The legal merits test is a positive hurdle which must be passed before legal aid   **7–01.2**
can be granted. It is further explained in section 7–02 below. The reasonableness test places no onus on the applicant but gives the Board a wide discretion
to refuse legal aid. This is further explained in section 7–03 below.

The legal merits test and reasonableness tests are supplemented by certain   **7–01.3**
other provisions of the Act and Regulations which apply in particular circumstances as explained below. See also *Focus* May 19, 1997 regarding the application of the tests in matrimonial/family cases.

The private client test

The Board will seek to apply both limbs of the merits test in a way that is   **7–01.4**
consistent with the purpose of legal aid, namely that publicly funded representation should be provided with a view to helping persons who might
otherwise be unable to obtain representation on account of their means.
Legal aid does not exist to support cases which the client would not sensibly
bring, even if he or she had the means to do so. The Board therefore applies
what is known as the private client test, namely that in general legal aid will
only be granted in circumstances where a client of moderate means paying
privately would be advised to litigate.

The notional private client being advised must be taken to be a person with   **7–01.5**
adequate means to meet the probable costs of the proceedings, but not with
over-abundant means, so that paying the costs would be possible, although
something of a sacrifice. The private client approach is well established in
practice and case law.

The private client test is a guiding principle, rather than an absolute rule.   **7–01.6**
Sometimes the nature of the case may make it difficult or impossible to com-
pare the position of the applicant to a private client of adequate means, *e.g.*
where the issue is entitlement to a means tested benefit (see para. 7–03.10
below). Where a case does not satisfy the private client test, legal aid will
usually be refused either on the legal merits test or the reasonableness test or
both. Most of the guidance set out below can be seen as applications of the
private client approach.

The Board's approach

7–01.7 When applying the merits test the Board will seek to strike the right balance between the interests of the applicant and those of the taxpayer, bearing in mind that legal aid decisions have important implications also for opponents and the legal system generally. Litigation can be uncertain, so that any attempt to restrict legal aid to certainties or near certainties would be a denial to many applicants of an opportunity to obtain justice. The aim therefore must be not to be over-cautious, but not to grant legal aid for cases unless there is a reasonable prospect of success.

7–01.8 Merits will be kept under review throughout a case and the Board should be informed of any developments which cast doubt upon the initial merit assessment (see regs. 66 and 70 Civil Legal Aid (General) Regulations 1989, NFG 12, and the Bar Council Guidelines at p. 737). A certificate may be discharged if the merits test is no longer satisfied (see reg. 77).

THE LEGAL MERITS TEST

7–02 Nature of the test

7–02.1 Legal aid can only be granted if the Board is satisfied under section 15(2) that there are reasonable grounds for taking, defending or being a party to the proceedings. This test is concerned with the legal merit of the claim, that is whether the claim has a reasonable prospect of success. Factors such as the amount being claimed and the likely costs of the action are not directly relevant to the legal merits test, although they are highly relevant to the reasonableness test (see *R. v. No. 8 Area Committee of the Legal Aid Board, ex p. Megarry* CO 2709/93, July 1, 1994).

7–02.2 The legal merits test can be expressed in a number of ways. Generally the Board must be satisfied that, on the facts put forward and the law which relates to them, there is a case or a defence which is reasonably likely to succeed, assuming the facts are proved. It is not the Board's function to adjudicate on the issues, but there must be an issue of fact or law which it is reasonable to submit to the court for decision. The legal merits test applied by the Board is similar to the test applied by the court in deciding whether there is an arguable case justifying the grant of leave in judicial review proceedings (see *R. v. Legal Aid Board, ex p. Hughes* CA 24 Housing L.R. 693; but see also *R. v. Legal Aid Board, ex p. Owners Abroad* CO/843/96, July 31, 1997).

7–02.3 Before reaching a decision on the merits the Board must consider all the questions of fact or law arising in the action cause or matter to which the application relates and the circumstances in which the application was made (regulation 28). The Board will therefore take into account the availability and strength of evidence to support the facts alleged and should be informed of any likely difficulty in establishing those facts. Estimating the prospects of success can never be an exact science, especially at the outset of litigation. Rather it is a question of applying experience, good sense and judgment to decide whether a claim is likely to succeed.

7–02.4 The Board will give due weight to all relevant material but is not bound to accept the opinion of counsel or others on the merits. When considering legal merits, the Board is entitled to look at the prospects of success of the action as a whole, not just the prospects of success of the next step in the proceedings (*R. v. Area Committee No. 1 (London) Legal Aid Area, ex p. Rondel* [1967] 2 All E.R. 419 at 421).

What percentage prospects of success are needed?

The legal merits test under section 15(2) does not specify any particular percentage figure. However the Board will always seek to obtain the best possible information and advice about estimated prospects of success. When a solicitor completes the application form for legal aid, or when counsel gives advice on the merits of a claim, prospects must be specified in one of the following categories: **7–02.5**

    (a) very good 80 per cent;

    (b) good 60–80 per cent;

    (c) reasonable 50–60 per cent;

    (d) less than evens;

    (e) impossible to say.

If the Board is satisfied that a claim has a better than 50 per cent prospect of success, for practical purposes the legal merits test will be treated as satisfied (although the application may still be refused on the reasonableness test). **7–02.6**

If prospects are below 50 per cent, legal aid is likely to be refused under the legal merits test unless the prospects are nevertheless sufficiently substantial to justify a grant (see generally *R. v. Legal Aid Board, ex p. Owners Abroad,* above). Even then the application is likely to be refused under the reasonableness test unless cost benefit or other factors are overwhelmingly in favour of the applicant.

If prospects are uncertain, limited legal aid will be considered as explained below.

Because the legal merits test is a substantive hurdle, legal aid will not be granted for "nuisance value" claims, that is actions which have no real prospect of success but which are brought on the basis that the defendant is likely to settle rather than pay the costs of a fully contested action. Legal aid will be refused in such cases, even if it could be argued that a private client might take such proceedings in the expectation of such a settlement. **7–02.7**

Estimates of prospects of success will tend to become more reliable as the case progresses. Where a case has been heard at first instance and legal aid is applied for to appeal, the Board will expect prospects of success of at least 50 per cent.

The test for limited legal aid

When legal aid is granted, the Board has wide powers to place limitations on the grant (section 15(4)). Where the legal merits test is only narrowly satisfied because the prospects of success are marginal or uncertain, any grant of legal aid will be subject to strict limitations. Even the most limited possible grant of legal aid, such as a grant limited only to a solicitor's report or counsel's opinion, must still satisfy the legal merits test under section 15(2) before section 15(4) can be applied. There is no separate or different test for "limited legal aid". **7–02.8**

7–02.9   It is not enough for the applicant to show that there are reasonable grounds for seeking the advice of solicitors and counsel as to the prima facie merits of the action. There must be legal grounds for the proceedings themselves in the sense of real merit in the proceedings. (See *Law Society v. Elder* [1956] 2 Q.B. 93, as explained in *R. v. Legal Aid Area No. 8 (Northern) Appeal Committee, ex p. Angell and Others* [1990] 1 Med. L.R. 394 at 406.) In almost any case which is difficult on the merits, an argument can be made that the merits might improve on further investigation. There may be some cases where prospects of success are uncertain and the case plainly merits further investigation. Such cases may justify the grant of a certificate with limited scope. However, if, using its experience and judgment, the Board takes the view at the outset that a case really is unlikely to succeed or that further investigation is unlikely to be of significant help, legal aid will be refused (see also para. 7–03.2 below).

THE REASONABLENESS TEST

7–03   Nature of the test

7–03.1   The reasonableness test in section 15(3) provides that a person may be refused civil legal aid if in the particular circumstances of the case it appears to the Board unreasonable that he or she should be granted legal aid. This is a wide and general test under which the Board can take into account all the factors which would influence a private client considering taking proceedings. Strictly, the reasonableness test is not a test at all, as it places no positive onus on the applicant. However, in practice the Board will always consider the reasonableness of the application before it is granted and must consider all questions of fact or law arising in the action, cause or matter to which the application relates and the circumstances in which the application was made (regulation 28).

7–03.2   The reasonableness test is additional to the legal merits test and an application may therefore be refused under the reasonableness test even if it passes the legal merits test or if no conclusion has been reached on the legal merits test. The Board is not obliged to grant limited legal aid simply in the hope that further investigations might improve the assessment of reasonableness. (See *R. v. Legal Aid Board, ex p. Belcher* CO/2098/92, July 15, 1994.)

7–03.3   The discretion under section 15(3) is wide on its face but there are well recognised circumstances in which the test is particularly relevant, and the most common cases are set out below.

Cost benefit

7–03.4   Legal aid may be refused if the benefits to be obtained in any proceedings do not justify the likely costs. The question for the Board is whether the game is worth the candle (*ex parte Angell*, above). Cost benefit is one of the most important factors for a private client considering litigation. It is therefore a very important factor for the Board to consider, although it is not the sole factor, or necessarily the decisive one. It is something to put into the scales, together with the prospect of success and other relevant information.

There is no absolute right or wrong way to approach cost benefit. In money **7–03.5** claims where costs usually follow the event one approach is as follows:

(a) Estimate costs of taking the claim to a contested first instance trial (costs here, of course, include any counsel's fees, disbursements and VAT).

(b) Estimate amount recoverable if claim succeeds (taking into account any likely reduction due to contributory negligence or otherwise).

(c) Estimate prospects of success and prospects of successfully enforcing any order made against the other side.

If likely recovery is **greater than** likely costs, the application would not be refused solely on cost benefit grounds but these factors would be weighed together with the assessment of the merits. The extent to which the recovery exceeded costs would be a relevant factor if the merits were not particularly strong or if there were other factors casting doubt on the reasonableness of the application, such as uncertainty as to whether any order made could be enforced.

If likely recovery is **less than** likely costs, the   application is likely to be refused unless the Board finds some other reason to outweigh the cost benefit difficulties. Considerations which might do so include the importance of the case to the client (see below) or strong legal merits and consequent good prospect of early settlement.

Most claims settle well before trial, but it is assumed that most private paying **7–03.6** clients would be reluctant to litigate if the cost of taking their claim to trial would exceed the benefit to be obtained, especially bearing in mind the risk of liability in costs to the other side.

Sometimes costs will have been incurred before legal aid is applied for. The **7–03.7** starting point will be to add together costs already incurred to the likely future costs of taking the action to trial for the purposes of the costs benefit assessment. However, the additional incentive of seeking to recover costs already expended might be an important consideration for the private client and therefore might justify the grant of legal aid, especially if the merits are strong and the costs already incurred are substantial compared to the cost of proceeding to trial. By contrast, if the merits are not strong, it is unlikely that a grant of legal aid will be justified, merely in the hope of recovering costs already expended.

The Board will adopt a similar approach when considering the discharge of a certificate and will take into account costs already incurred and the prospects of recovering them, whether the costs were incurred privately or under the certificate.

Solicitors and counsel should report to the Board if the cost benefit position deteriorates after the grant of legal aid. See also *Iverson v. Iverson* [1966] 1 All E.R. 258. The fact that substantial costs have been incurred will not, by itself, be a sufficient reason to justify the continuation of the certificate—see also NFG 12, para. 12–02.

7–03.8   In actions not solely concerned with recovering money or property apply-ing a cost benefit test involves considering the importance of the case to the client, as explained below.

Importance of case to the client and non-money cases

7–03.9   Many cases are not solely about money and, in any case, the importance of the action to the particular client is a relevant consideration. Even where it is impossible to quantify a claim in financial terms, the Board will seek to form a judgment as to whether the benefit justifies the likely costs. The Board will have to consider this issue as objectively as possible, and it is not enough merely for the client to assert that the case is important. Some substantial benefit to the client will be needed to justify the grant of legal aid especially if the case is marginal on the merits or the costs are likely to be high.

7–03.10   An important question is whether the case might result in a real enhance-ment of the quality of life of the applicant. For example, establishing the applicant's entitlement to some welfare benefit may be justifiable if the appli-cant is in serious need of that benefit. Similarly, litigating with a view to pre-serve one's home may be justifiable (especially if there are children involved), even if the property has no, low or negative equity, always providing that the strength of the case and all the other circumstances warrant it. Serious disre-pair cases may fall into the same category. By contrast, litigating over the proceeds of sale of a property with no or negative equity would not be justified.

7–03.11   Legal aid is unlikely to be granted if the only matter at stake is loss of stat-ure, dignity or reputation. However, the Board recognises that discrimination cases may be of considerable importance to the client. When considering the importance of any particular case to a client the Board will take into account any allegations of breach of human rights raised by the case, but legal aid may still be refused if the benefits to be gained from the proceedings do not justify the likely costs or if refusal is justified on any other merits grounds.

7–03.12   In matrimonial cases, protecting a party from violence is of vital import-ance, but granting legal aid to contest injunction or committal proceedings might not be justified if the matter can adequately be dealt with through undertakings. In relation to children, representation of a birth parent in adop-tion proceedings or representation on an application for long-term residence would be far more likely to justify a grant than a temporary dispute as to con-tact. Similarly, in proceedings concerning immigration, a person's long-term right to remain in the country is of far greater weight than a dispute over the right to visit.

7–03.13   However, in proceedings which are clearly of great importance to the cli-ent, it is easy to lose sight of the merits of the claim. For example, in adoption proceedings over a child, or mortgage possession proceedings/other proceed-ings over a home, however important the case may be to the client, legal aid will be refused if the merits of the claim are not sufficient to satisfy the legal merits test under section 15(2).

7–03.14   An application may be refused where it appears to the Board that only a trivial advantage would be gained by the applicant from the proceedings, or where on account of the nature of the proceedings a solicitor would not ordinarily be employed (reg. 29). This will apply to many cases in the Small Claims Court though not all.

Small claims

On January 8, 1996 the jurisdiction of the Small Claims Court was expanded so that the following claims will be referred to arbitration: **7–03.15**

    (a) personal injury claims with a value of up to £1,000;

    (b) all other claims with a value of up to £3,000.

Possession actions are excluded from the small claims jurisdiction, but other non-money claims such as disrepair cases and injunctions, are covered.

The small claims procedure is designed to assist unrepresented parties and only very limited costs are recoverable from the other side. Therefore legal aid will usually be refused under the reasonableness test for claims which would fall within the jurisdiction of the Small Claims Court. Legal aid would only be granted where there were exceptional circumstances justifying the use of a solicitor and where such representation would produce tangible benefit for the client. **7–03.16**

In those cases where the use of a solicitor was justified, the issue of cost benefit would need to be considered very carefully. If civil legal aid were granted for a matter in the Small Claims Court any advantage to the client would often be negated by the legal aid statutory charge. Because of the severe limitations on cost recovery virtually all the costs of representation would eat into any recovery. In money claims the benefit must exceed the costs to the extent that a private client would be advised to proceed. Help for claimants in the Small Claims Court will usually be restricted to advice and assistance. **7–03.17**

The Court now has a wider discretion to remove small claims from the small claims procedure on grounds which include the complexity of the case. Legal aid would not normally be granted for the purpose of arguing complexity and seeking removal of the claim from the small claims procedure, although advice and assistance would be available. If a complex claim involving small damages were removed from the small claims procedure, the Board would then need to consider cost benefit as in any other case. **7–03.18**

Very high cost cases

In exceptionally complex or important litigation, costs can rise to levels far higher than one would expect for more standard litigation. A private client before embarking on very substantial litigation, would be particularly careful to ensure that his claim had sufficient merit and importance to justify the likely costs before instructing his solicitors to proceed. Similarly, whilst the statutory tests for legal aid are the same for very high cost cases as for any other case, before granting legal aid for a potentially very expensive piece of litigation the Board may require far more detailed information than would normally be the case, and is more likely to impose strict limitations on any grant. **7–03.19**

In exceptional cases the Board may decide to obtain further information before making its decision on the merits, either in the form of commissioning its own legal or expert opinion on the case, or through inviting the representations from the proposed opponent or third parties.

Fruitless litigation

7–03.20   Legal aid will not normally be granted where the applicant will gain no real benefit from the proceedings, or where it is unlikely that any judgment obtained could be enforced (see *Wookey v. Wookey, Re S (a minor)* [1991] 3 W.L.R. 135; [1991] 3 All E.R. 365). No difficulty arises if it is known that the defendant has the means to satisfy any judgment and pay costs or is insured for the claim, or if there is a fund available to meet the claim even if the Defendant is not insured (*e.g.* the Motor Insurers Bureau for motor accidents). If there is uncertainty as to whether the defendant is in a position to satisfy any judgment, this will be considered as a ground of refusal together with all other relevant factors and any grant of legal aid might be strictly limited to obtaining better evidence of means of the defendant.

7–03.21   Litigation may also be fruitless if the other party to the proceedings has received or is likely to receive legal aid. In such circumstances the successful party is unlikely to recover costs in full because of the statutory costs protection in favour of legally aided parties and therefore any benefit is likely to be negated by the operation of the legal aid statutory charge. For this reason the Board must be informed whenever an opponent is, or becomes, an assisted person (reg. 70(1)(b)). The Board may be entitled to defer profit costs under regulation 102 if this is not done. Where both sides have legal aid in a non-family damages claim, the Board will usually discharge both certificates unless exceptionally there is real benefit to either party in continuing.

Public interest cases

7–03.22   The purpose of legal aid is to assist individuals who might otherwise be unable to take proceedings on account of their means (Legal Aid Act 1988, s.1). Legal aid is devised to assist those whom it finances in the course of litigation and not directly to assist other parties to the proceedings or other members of the public who are not parties to the proceedings in determining points of general interest (see *UDT v. Bycroft* [1954] 3 All E.R. 455 at 459). Indeed, it would be an abuse of process to pursue proceedings with legal aid which are only of academic interest to lawyers and which no reasonable paying client would fund privately.

7–03.23   There are cases where the existence of other claims can have a bearing on the merits or cost benefit of the applicant, particularly if costs can be shared between claims in a multi-party action or test case (see NFG 17); but public interest in the more general sense will rarely be a significant consideration in legal aid decisions.

Alternative methods of funding

7–03.24   Legal aid may be refused if it appears to the Board that the applicant has available to him rights or facilities which make it unnecessary to obtain legal aid, or if the applicant has a reasonable expectation of obtaining financial or other help from a body of which he is a member, and that he has failed to take all reasonable steps to enforce or obtain such rights, facilities or help. (See reg. 30(1).)

The most common examples are where the applicant could be expected to obtain legal assistance from: **7–03.25**

(a) an estate or trust fund, including any discretionary trust;

(b) a trade union;

(c) the Equal Opportunities Commission;

(d) the Commission for Racial Equality;

(e) the AA or RAC;

(f) a firm of which the applicant is a member;

(g) cover under a policy of insurance (*e.g.* contents insurance) which deals with legal costs;

(h) an employer.

The Board will require the applicant to take all reasonable steps to obtain help from such a body, including taking such steps on its own behalf, but the Board will not necessarily require the applicant to take proceedings against the body (reg. 30). Even if an applicant has taken all reasonable steps to obtain funding which is not forthcoming, legal aid might be refused under the reasonableness test if, say, a trade union or the trustees of a substantial trust fund were refusing to assist in order to place the burden on funding on the Board. **7–03.26**

It will be for the applicant to satisfy the Board that legal aid should be granted, notwithstanding the alternative method of funding available, but the Board will take into account the terms, conditions and adequacy of such funding when reaching a decision. **7–03.27**

Some claims for which legal aid is available may also be funded by conditional fee agreements under section 58 of the Courts and Legal Services Act 1990. The possibility of a conditional fee agreement will not be taken into account by the Board and legal aid will not be refused on the ground, however expressed, that it would be more appropriate for the applicant to enter into a conditional fee agreement. **7–03.28**

Alternative courts and types of legal aid

Legal aid may be refused if there are more effective ways of pursuing a civil claim. Examples include the following: **7–03.29**

(a) Where the proceedings should be taken in a court other than the one specified in the application, *i.e.* where the costs are lower but the proceedings still meet the needs of the applicant. (See also NFG 8, para. 8–23 regarding forum for Children Act proceedings.)

(b) Where it is more appropriate that the applicant be granted ABWOR than civil legal aid (section 15(3)(b)). This can only arise where both ABWOR and civil legal aid are available for the proceedings, which will give the applicant the same remedies, and the applicant is financially eligible under both schemes. Whilst civil legal aid is generally available for most types of proceedings, ABWOR is only available for a limited range of cases. Where both civil legal aid and ABWOR are available, ABWOR will generally be the choice because it is simpler. However, there are different eligibility and contribution regimes for civil legal aid and ABWOR, and the Board will not force a client to apply for ABWOR if that would lead to higher contributions than civil legal aid.

Alternatives to civil litigation

7–03.30 Legal aid may be refused if there are alternatives to civil litigation which a private client would be advised to pursue. Examples include the following:

(a) The applicant is a victim of a crime of violence who could gain compensation from the Criminal Injuries Compensation Authority (CICA) and the circumstances are such that a reasonable fee-paying client would not take civil proceedings as well as, or instead of, applying to the CICA. As from April 1, 1996 the CICA has operated under a tariff system rather than full civil compensation. Even if there is likely to be a sufficiently large difference between the damages likely to be obtained in court proceedings and CICA compensation to justify the proceedings, the Board will consider the likelihood of recovering from the opponent and if this is uncertain the application may be refused.

(b) The applicant is the victim of negligent financial advice or services and is entitled to pursue compensation under the Financial Services Act 1986. The Investors Compensation Scheme (ICS) was set up under that Act to compensate victims of bad advice given by participating firms. Where a firm is concluded to be in default, ICS may compensate the victims of the firm's bad advice in accordance with their rules. Generally statutory remedies will not be identical to the damages which might be obtained through litigation, but the Board would need to be satisfied that any additional benefits of litigation would justify the likely costs, such that a private client would take that course.

(c) The applicant has recourse to an Ombudsman scheme which has remedies that are sufficiently effective that a private client would pursue that option prior to litigating. The Parliamentary Commissioner for Administration has jurisdiction over government and many non-departmental public bodies and there are ombudsman schemes covering areas such as banking, building societies, insurance, social landlords, investments and pensions. Most Ombudsman schemes have far less extensive powers than the courts and generally do not have binding powers to award compensation. However, the Board may require information from applicants as to why such an avenue is not pursued.

7–03.31 Legal aid might be refused where other alternatives exist to litigation such as mediation, or some other form of alternative dispute resolution ("ADR"). However, legal aid would not be refused on this ground if the alternative is not one which in practice is available to the assisted person, for example, because he could not afford the costs of mediation or ADR (for which civil legal aid is not available), or if the applicant was obliged to commence proceedings because of the Limitation Acts. Where there is some alternative to civil litigation the issue for the Board is not whether the alternative offers the same remedies as court proceedings, but rather whether it is reasonable to grant legal aid before that alternative has been considered.

The Board has made special arrangements under Part II, Legal Aid Act 1988 to support some specific mediation initiatives, such as at the Central London County Court. [See also NFG 1, para. 1–12 regarding legally assisted mediation in family matters and section 29 Legal Aid Act 1988.]

Conduct

Legal aid is likely to be refused if the application reveals some illegal motive, or the conduct of the applicant is such as to be unacceptable to the court. However, the general moral character and criminal record of the applicant are not relevant unless in some way they have a bearing on the legal merits of the particular case. Further the Board will not discriminate against applicants on the basis of race, gender, nationality, religion or status.   **7–03.32**

The applicant's legal aid history may be taken into account. For example, failure to co-operate in the means assessment or a revocation of an earlier certificate could lead to the refusal of a subsequent application, but would not be an automatic bar.   **7–03.33**

Civil legal aid might be refused if the applicant's own unlawful act resulted in the need to apply for legal aid, *e.g.* defending a motor claim where the applicant had failed to obtain compulsory insurance. In any event, a grant might not be justified if MIB were defending the claim and had substantially the same interest as the applicant.   **7–03.34**

Over-representation

It may not be reasonable to grant or extend legal aid to a person if another party to the proceedings has substantially the same interest as that person and separate representation is not justified or necessary. This will be particularly true in family matters where several parties are represented and in appeals where the number of issues before the court may be less than at first instance. Solicitors and counsel should notify the area office where such situations may arise and should set out any reasons why separate representation might be justified (see also the Bar Code of Conduct paras. 503A.4 and 503A.5—p. 736 and Bar Council Legal Aid Guidelines paras. 2.9(d) and 4.3—p. 738). If insufficient reasons are advanced the usual approach will be to limit the certificate to prevent separate representation or duplication of work. See also Note 2 to NFG 12, para. 12–02 regarding over-representation.   **7–03.35**

Assignments to obtain legal aid

The circumstances of an application may themselves make a grant unreasonable—for example, where a company has assigned its cause of action to a director so that he may apply for legal aid. Where an application for legal aid relates to a cause of action which has been transferred to the applicant by   **7–03.36** assignment or otherwise from a company or from a person who would not be entitled to legal aid, and it appears to the Board that the assignment was with a view to allowing the action to be brought with the benefit of a legal aid certificate, the application will normally be refused (reg. 33A applying to applications made from June 1, 1996).

7–03.37   Similarly, if a trustee in bankruptcy assigns a cause of action back to the bankrupt, usually reserving a proportion of any proceeds from the action for the benefit of the creditors, a subsequent application for legal aid by the bankrupt will generally be refused if it appears to the Board that the assignment was made with a view to bringing the action with the benefit of legal aid (reg. 33A). In any event, the fact that the trustee or creditors are not prepared to take the risks involved in funding the litigation would be taken into account by the Board on the usual consideration of the merits and cost benefit of the claim.

7–03.38   In any case where legal aid is granted following an assignment of the action to the applicant, in circumstances where the applicant will receive only an agreed proportion of the fruits of the litigation, consideration will be given to Regulation 32 and requiring the other beneficiaries to the litigation to pay the appropriate proportion of the costs of the action.

7–03.39   If a company assigns the benefit of a cause of action to an individual but the company continues to pursue the action, legal aid cannot be granted to the company (see *R. v. Legal aid Board, ex p. Floods of Queensferry Ltd*, CO/3472/97, October 16, 1997, Popplewell J. and December 18, 1997, CA).

7–04   SPECIFIC SUBJECT AREAS

The operation of the civil merits test will vary according to the subject matter of the application. The Board has produced a manual of Guidance on the Exercise of Devolved Powers (the GEDP) by franchised firms. This gives guidance on the merits test in all those areas which can be covered by a franchise contract. The manual is used by franchisees in determining whether to grant emergency certificates and by area offices considering civil applications. The topics covered are:

(a) matrimonial/family (including child care). The guidance in the area of matrimonial/family work was revised with effect from June 1997 and, for domestic violence, October 1997 and was summarised in the Board's *Focus* newsletter (*Focus* 19, May 1997 and *Focus* 21, September 1997);

(b) crime;

(c) housing;

(d) debt;

(e) employment;

(f) personal injury;

(g) welfare benefits;

(h) consumer/general contract;

(i) immigration/nationality;

(j) mental health.

In addition, the following guidance covers specific types of case where application of the merits test requires special consideration.

Neighbour disputes

7–04.1

Legal aid is unlikely to be granted where the dispute can be dealt with by way of undertakings or where the issues and/or the value of the property in dispute do not justify the likely costs involved. Disputes about boundaries in particular often lead to substantial costs out of proportion to the real importance of the case when a private client would not be advised to pursue such a claim. Regard will also be had to the question of the statutory charge, which is often overlooked by advisers and clients.

Possession proceedings

7–04.2

Legal Aid is unlikely to be granted where rent or mortgage arrears are not in dispute, it is unlikely that an immediate order for possession would be made and, in the absence of a defence to the proceedings, the only issue appears to be the terms on which a suspended order would be made. This is particularly so as the case of *Cheltenham & Gloucester Building Society v. Norgan* [1996] 1 All E.R. 449, provides that arrears can be paid over the remaining term of the mortgage. Furthermore, in many cases a solicitor would not need to be employed in proceedings relating only to mortgage or rent arrears or an application to suspend a warrant of possession or execution which raised no significant issue of fact or law.

Housing disrepair cases

7–04.3

Save in cases of real urgency, legal aid will not usually be granted unless the applicant's landlord has been notified of both the defects and the anticipated litigation and been provided with reasonable opportunity to respond and/or carry out the repairs. A private client would investigate the possibility of early repair prior to the issue of proceedings. Generally, where the solicitor is able to obtain details of the disrepair from his client it would not normally be necessary to obtain an expert's report from an Environmental Health Officer or surveyor either prior to writing to the landlord or to support the application for a civil legal aid certificate.

Judicial review

7–04.4

Judicial review is concerned with the decision-making process of a public body rather than the merits of any decision made. Only decisions or failures to act which are unlawful, perverse or procedurally improper can be successfully challenged. For example, in immigration and asylum cases the court will generally not interfere with decisions based on findings of fact by the Special Adjudicator or Immigration Appeal Tribunal. Similarly legal aid will only be granted for judicial review where there are substantial legal grounds to the challenge, regardless of how strongly the applicant objects to the decision he or she is seeking to challenge.

Usually in judicial review the applicant will not be seeking a financial gain. The issue for the Board is primarily whether the tangible advantage to be gained for the applicant justifies the cost of the proceedings, rather than whether there is a general public interest in the decision under review being challenged.

As with almost any litigation, an opponent should be notified of the litigation before issue of proceedings and given an opportunity to respond. Save in cases of real urgency, legal aid will not usually be granted to cover an application for judicial review unless a proper letter before action has been written or the potential respondents have otherwise had a proper opportunity to explain their side of the case. See *R. v. Horsham District Council, ex p. Wenman and Others* (1993), *The Times*, October 12. Letters before action in respect of challenges to legal aid decisions should be copied both to the area office concerned and to Legal Aid Head Office (Legal Department).

In *R. v. Legal Aid Board, ex p. Hughes* the court held that the legal merits test and the test for leave in judicial review were in substance the same. The Board is not bound by the decision as to leave but in general, if a court grants leave and the Board has no additional information casting doubt on the merits of the claim, it is likely that the application will satisfy the legal merits test (though not necessarily the reasonableness test).

Legal aid certificates for judicial review will be limited to the most cost effective way of proceeding, *e.g.* requiring applications for leave to be made on paper in the first instance, rather than applying for leave orally through Counsel. This is particularly so if a number of similar judicial review raise the same issues and duplication should be avoided. Where the applicant considers that there are circumstances making it necessary or reasonable to proceed by way of an oral application for leave, these should be stated in the application form.

Judicial review is not usually appropriate where an applicant has alternative remedies available. For example in proposed judicial review of legal aid decisions, if circumstances have changed or further material information has come to light, it may be more appropriate to make a fresh application for legal aid rather than seeking a judicial review of the earlier decision. In all cases, applications for legal aid to challenge legal aid decisions should be made to an area office other than the one itself under challenge.

The stage of respondents' filing of evidence in opposition to a judicial review is a crucial one and the merits of the action need to be reconsidered at that stage. Limitations on certificates will reflect this and any Counsel's opinion required to be obtained will be expected to comply with the Bar Council's Guidelines (see p. 737. See in particular *R. v. Secretary of State for the Home Department, ex p. Brown* (1984), *The Times*, February 6.

Judicial review in homelessness cases

In housing cases where the applicant may either appeal to the county court on a point of law or judicially review the decision, full reasons will need to be given as to why the right of appeal has not been exercised first.

7–04.5   Medical negligence*

In many potential medical negligence claims it will be difficult for the solicitor, and the Legal Aid Board, to form a clear view of the prospects of success only from the client's understanding of what might have happened. The merits may only start to become clear after the disclosure of the medical records and/or the provision of an explanation by the hospital, trust or medical practitioners.

Uncertainty over the merits at an early stage does not mean that initial applications for legal aid will necessarily be refused, particularly where the claim involves serious injuries or traumatic events, when the grant of limited legal aid to enable preliminary investigations to be carried out may well be justified.

However, the Board will need to be satisfied that there is some prima facie evidence of negligence before granting legal aid limited or otherwise particularly in the case of smaller claims (those to a value of no more than £10,000). The fact that the client has had a less than satisfactory medical result or is suffering in a way which is not anticipated will not normally be sufficient for legal aid to be granted in these cases even in limited form.

In these smaller cases, if there is little prima facie evidence of negligence, legal aid may be refused on the merits and on the basis that the NHS complaints procedure may be a more appropriate avenue for the applicant to pursue. The procedure, which is not available in the private sector and applies only to NHS hospitals and general practitioners, is not designed to resolve allegations of clinical negligence but may provide the complainant with an explanation of what occurred. Complaints are not normally considered more than 12 months after the event, but there is discretion to extend the time limits. If the complaints procedure uncovers information which indicates prima facie negligence, a further application for legal aid may be appropriate.

*At the time of going to print the Board is consulting on revised legal decision making guidance for medical negligence. This comprehensive guidance will cover all aspects of legal decision making in respect of advice, assistance and representation and will apply from January 31, 1999 (when a new medical negligence franchise category is due to be introduced). The guidance will be published in the Boards Guidance: Exercise of Devolved Powers and the Focus *newsletter. See also NFG 1, para. 1–19.*

High Court bail applications 7–04.6

An application for legal aid to cover an application for bail to the High Court is likely to be refused if it appears more appropriate to rely on the Official Solicitor procedure under RSC Ord. 79, *i.e.* where the application is simple without the need for a significant degree of preparation or legal argument. A civil legal aid application for bail to the judge in chambers should include information on the following:

(a) whether the defendant is in the custody of the magistrates' court or Crown Court;

(b) the length of time the defendant would otherwise be likely to remain in custody pending trial;

(c) whether the defendant has already applied for bail to the magistrates' court and/or Crown Court (bail is often granted on a subsequent appearance when difficulties relating to sureties have been sorted out);

(d) whether the defendant has been represented on previous applications for bail;

(e) why bail was refused and whether it is suggested that the reasons given by the court for refusing bail were unreasonable or the grounds for refusing bail have altered;

(f) any special social or other reasons for making an application for bail in the particular case.

7–05 DO PERSONS OTHER THAN THE APPLICANT HAVE AN INTEREST IN THE PROCEEDINGS?
(Civil Legal Aid (General) Regulations 1989, reg. 32)

The rule is that, in addition to the usual legal merits and reasonableness tests, the area office must consider whether there are other persons concerned jointly with, or having the same interest as, the applicant in the outcome of the proceedings. If there are, it is a question of whether, in the circumstances, the applicant needs legal aid at all, and, if he does, whether the other persons involved should pay a contribution towards the costs.

NOTE:

1. *If other persons are already joined as parties to the proceedings by the time the application is submitted, these additional questions will not normally need to be considered. This is because the area office will rely on the normal rules of taxation whereby costs between the non-legally aided parties and the assisted person will automatically be apportioned, so that only those items solely attributable to the assisted person, together with the appropriate proportion of the costs common to all the parties, will be allowed against the assisted person's certificate.*

2. *The solicitor and any counsel should be mindful of the fact that where the assisted person has no conflict of interest with another party sufficient to justify the additional costs of separate represen-tation (by separate solicitors and/or counsel), it may be appropriate for one of the solicitors to represent the assisted persons and/or for there to be a joint instruction of counsel.*

   Failure to consider this at any appropriate point(s) may lead to costs being disallowed on taxation/assessment (in the event of work being unnecessarily duplicated). Should the assisted person decline to accept advice in that regard the show cause procedure may be invoked under regulation 77 of the Civil Legal Aid (General) Regulations 1989 (unjustifiable expense to the Fund).

7–06 The "same" interest

Other persons have the "same" interest as the applicant if each person (including the applicant) is seeking an identical outcome to the proceedings, *e.g.* an order, injunction or declaration which would benefit all equally without the need for them to issue separate proceedings.

Other persons do not have the "same" interest as the applicant if each person has a special interest which might result in different orders for each, such as a claim for damages which must be individual to each person, even if the claims arise from a single event. In such a case, the other persons would have only similar interests not the "same" within the meaning of the regulation.

NOTE: *There may be cases where the persons concerned have both the "same" interest within the meaning of an application, and similar interests. This could happen where there is an application to the court for an order that the common parts of a block of flats be repaired (the "same" interest) and, in the same proceedings, a claim for damages for each person (a similar interest). In such a case whether or not regulation 32 would have to be invoked would depend on which was the main purpose of the proceedings.*

Where there are other persons having the same interest, the application will be:

(a) *Granted* if the applicant would be substantially prejudiced by not being able to take his own proceedings;

(b) *Refused* if the other persons would be likely to proceed without the applicant, and the applicant would get what he wanted as a result of those proceedings.

If the decision is to grant, the other persons having the same interest will be asked to contribute towards the costs of the proceedings if the area office considers it reasonable, bearing in mind the respective benefits to be obtained from the proceedings by the applicant and the others having the same interest. The additional contribution is based, if possible, on an assessment of means but otherwise on a proportional division of the estimated costs of the proceedings. If a contribution from others is sought, payment of the total contribution will be requested in, and be a condition of, the offer of legal aid to the applicant. If the applicant takes all reasonable steps to collect the additional contribution but is unable to do so, the contribution may be varied.

An example would be where six home-owners will benefit from proceedings involving a liability to maintain a road. The area office is satisfied as to the legal merits but only two of the home-owners are parties to proceedings and only one of those has applied for legal aid. There are therefore four home-owners who would benefit from the issue of a legal aid certificate to the applicant while a share of the costs will be attributable to the other named party in accordance with the normal rules of taxation. The area office will estimate the likely costs of a fully contested trial allowable against any legal aid certificate (say £10,000). It will disregard the costs payable by the other named party. This estimate is then divided between those who would benefit from the issue of a legal aid certificate (the applicant for legal aid and the four other home-owners) producing a notional share of costs, £2,000 for each home-owner. If means assessments are available, contributions will be requested in accordance with them (up to £2,000). If no assessment is available, then £2,000 will be sought from each of the four, although it is for the applicant to seek to recover this and arrange its payment.

8. CHILDREN ACT 1989 INCLUDING CARE PROCEEDINGS
(See also *Focus* 19, May 1997)

8–01 WHAT COVER IS AVAILABLE?

Following the implementation of the Children Act 1989 civil legal aid under Part IV Legal Aid Act 1988 is available for all proceedings under the Children Act 1989. The usual civil legal aid means and merits tests apply.

NOTE: *There is special dispensation for certain parties in specified public law proceedings who are entitled to non-means, non-merits tested legal aid (also called "free legal aid") or to means tested only legal aid (see para. 7–01).*

8–02 WHAT ARE THE RELEVANT PROVISIONS?

The relevant provisions are section 15 of the Legal Aid Act 1988 as amended and the Civil Legal Aid (General) Regulations 1989 as amended. The regulations dealing with remuneration are the Legal Aid in Family Proceedings (Remuneration) Regulations 1991 as amended.

8–03 WHAT ARE THE CHILDREN ACT ARRANGEMENTS REGARDING THE MEANS AND MERITS TESTS?

Non-means, non-merits tested legal aid is available to:

    (a) parents (including unmarried fathers);

    (b) children;

    (c) those with parental responsibility

who must be granted civil legal aid on a non-means, non-merits tested basis for proceedings under:

        (i) section 31 (care and supervision orders);
       (ii) section 43 (child assessment orders);
      (iii) section 44 (emergency protection orders); and
      (iv) section 45 (duration and discharge of emergency protection orders).

For the same proceedings:

    (a) parties to the proceedings (*i.e.* required *to be parties* by the Family Proceedings Courts (Children Act 1989) Rules 1991 and the Family Proceedings Rules 1991) and

    (b) those *applying* to be joined

have to satisfy only the civil legal aid means test but no merits test.

In addition non-means, non-merits tested civil legal aid must be granted to the *child only* in applications under section 25 (use of secure accommodation). This will not be necessary where the child is already represented in

132

criminal proceedings to which the section 25 application relates as the criminal legal aid order will cover the section 25 proceedings (Legal Aid Act 1988, s.19(2)).

DO THE SPECIAL ARRANGEMENTS EXTEND TO OTHER PROCEEDINGS?   8–04

The special arrangements do not extend to other proceedings. That is to say education supervision order applications, applications to discharge care orders and other public law proceedings between individuals and the state, as well as private law proceedings between individuals, do not fall within the special arrangements. Means and merits tested civil legal aid is, however, available—see *Focus* 19, May 1997 regarding the application of the merits test.

NOTE:

1. *Civil legal aid including emergency legal aid can be applied for in the usual way to cover proceedings which fall outside the special arrangements.*

2. *Legal aid certificates issued on a non-means, non-merits tested or means tested only basis can cover proceedings relating to an application for an order under sections 31, 43, 44 or 45 (a) from issue, or (b) by subsequent amendment (that is on application by the solicitor). A related matter is one where an order is to be sought at the same time as, and as an alternative to, the order under sections 31, 43, 44 or 45. Applying for a section 8 order in care or supervision proceedings will be sufficiently closely related to the care or supervision proceedings for cover to be available under a non-means, non-merits tested or means tested only certificate BUT specifically stated cover will be necessary (either in the certificate or an amendment) to make (but not to oppose) such an application.*

WHEN WOULD AN AMENDMENT TO A NON-MEANS, NON-MERITS TESTED OR MEANS TESTED ONLY CERTIFICATE BE NECESSARY?   8–05

Normal steps involved in the conduct of the case will be covered, *e.g.* attendance at directions hearings will be covered. As well as the hearing of the application for which the certificate is granted a certificate also covers representation as to:

(a) an interim order;

(b) applying for directions and their variation;

(c) contact and the refusal of contact on the making of an emergency protection or care order;

(d) an application for a search warrant under section 48 in emergency protection order cases;

(e) the extension or discharge of an emergency protection order in emergency protection order cases;

(f) proceedings in relation to an exclusion requirement, *e.g.* in the event of a power of arrest being exercised or a variation or discharge of the order being sought by the excluded person.

A certificate may also cover the proceedings being concluded with a different type of order (*e.g.* where care proceedings are concluded with a section 8 residence order, applied for by another party or made on the court's own motion, or where an application for a child assessment order is treated as an application for an emergency protection order) *but* specifically stated cover (in the certificate or an amendment) will be needed:

(a) to *make* (but not to oppose) an application for a section 8 order in care or supervision proceedings; or

(b) to *appeal* against the making of a care or supervision order.

NOTE:

1. *The proceedings which attract non-means, non-merits tested or means tested only legal aid are governed by the Children (Allocation of Proceedings) Order 1991. Certificates in respect of those proceedings normally cover all steps up to and including the final hearing, reflecting the absence of a merits test. They do not specify the court covered but will, post CIS, contain a costs limitation. They permit representation in all the courts in accordance with the Order, including representation on an application for transfer to a county court following the refusal of the family proceedings court to order a transfer. See para. 8–23 regarding means and merits tested private law cases.*

2. *It remains impossible to amend an existing certificate to appeal from a family proceedings court except in the case of special Children Act proceedings, i.e. proceedings for which free legal aid is available.*

3. *Where proceedings under one of the specified sections are followed by proceedings under another (e.g. emergency protection order proceedings are followed by an application for a care order), an amendment to any existing non-means, non-merits tested or means tested only certificate should be sought (if necessary over the telephone).*

4. *If the client holds any other certificate, i.e. covering private law proceedings, a fresh legal aid application should be made as the public law aspects triggering the special arrangements should, as far as possible, be kept separate.*

8–06 WOULD ANY ADDITIONAL COVER BE MEANS AND/OR MERITS TESTED?

Cover for related proceedings or proceedings under a different section still within the special arrangements will be neither means nor merits tested *but* cover for appeals will be merits tested only.

WHAT IF THE ADDITIONAL PROCEEDINGS ARE NOT SUFFICIENTLY   **8–07**
CLOSELY RELATED TO THE PROCEEDINGS WHICH TRIGGERED THE
NON-MEANS, NON-MERITS OR MEANS TESTED ONLY COVER TO
JUSTIFY BEING COVERED BY THE SAME CERTIFICATE?

Civil legal aid is available subject to the usual means and merits tests and an emergency application could be made for a separate civil legal aid certificate. By way of example, ancillary matters between individuals and applications for injunctions would require a separate application for another certificate.

If the area office does not consider that the additional proceedings attract non-means, non-merits tested or means tested only legal aid it will decline to include the proceedings in the certificate either at the outset or on an application for an amendment. There is a right of appeal to the area committee and a certificate would be issued immediately (or on receipt of a means assessment, where applicable) for the section 31, 43, or 45 proceedings.

WHAT IF A NON-MEANS, NON-MERITS TESTED OR MEANS TESTED   **8–08**
ONLY CERTIFICATE IS FOLLOWED BY PRIVATE LAW PROCEEDINGS?

The existing certificate will not be amended and a separate application will be required because:

(a) both the means and merits tests will be applied; and

(b) the public law proceedings will be kept separate from any operation of the statutory charge.

WHAT APPLICATION FORM MUST BE USED?   **8–09**

The Board has introduced amended application forms during 1997/98 to allow for increased computerisation in its area offices. The appropriate application form for the type of applicant and type of proceedings must be used. In means tested cases the appropriate means form must be submitted.

An emergency application may also need to be made.

IMPORTANT NOTES:

1. *Unless a solicitor is acting for more than one child, only one application form needs to be submitted even where a number of children are involved (including in adoption proceedings), as only one certificate will be issued but if the solicitor is applying for legal aid for a number of children an application must be submitted on behalf of each child. This is because the child is the assisted person and will hold a separate certificate.*

2. *A solicitor can sign and make a civil legal aid application for a child/ minor client but only where the child/minor is entitled to begin, prosecute or defend proceedings without a next friend or guardian ad litem (i.e. in accordance with the Family Proceedings Rules 1991, r. 9.2A). The nominated solicitor must sign the application personally and should insert his own address as the correspondence address*

> *for the application—he is treated as the child/minor's agent includ-*
> *ing for the receipt of notices (Civil Legal Aid (General) Regulations*
> *1989, regs. 16(1) and (4)).*

8–10 WHEN WILL COSTS BE COVERED?

Free legal aid cases
Costs will be covered immediately as, provided a correctly certified application form is *received* at the appropriate area office, at the latest, within
three working days of *receipt of instructions* to act, costs from the time of
receipt of instructions to act in the proceedings will be deemed to be within
the certificate.

There is *no need* for the solicitor to telephone the area office. Previous costs
of legal advice and assistance (green form) (*i.e.* incurred for advice before the
commencement of proceedings) can be claimed (under legal advice and assistance rather than under the certificate) but a solicitor receiving immediate
instructions to act in a free legal aid case where proceedings have been commenced will not need to use legal advice and assistance at all as his legal aid
cover is immediate.

All other cases
In all other cases the deeming provision contained in regulation 103(6) of the
Civil Legal Aid (General) Regulations 1989 applies when the Board's area
office is closed. The solicitor must make a telephone emergency application
and must then submit the written application form to the area office within
the time stipulated if his costs are to be deemed to be within the certificate.

8–11 HOW WILL TIME RUN FOR RECEIPT OF THE SELF-CERTIFICATION FORM?

Time will run in accordance with regulation 7(1) Civil Legal Aid (General)
Regulations 1989. Any day when the appropriate area office is open for business is a working day. If costs are to be covered from the time of instruction
the form must be received as follows:

Instructions to act received on:	Form must be received at the area office on:
Monday	Thursday
Tuesday	Friday
Wednesday	Monday
Thursday	Tuesday
Friday	Wednesday
Saturday	Wednesday
Sunday	Wednesday

8–12 WHAT IF THE SELF-CERTIFICATION FORM IS OUT OF TIME?

Costs will not be deemed to be covered from the time of instruction *but* they
will be covered from the date of issue of the certificate.

CAN TIME BE EXTENDED?   8–13

The area office can on application extend the time for receipt of the form. Extensions will only be granted for good reason (*e.g.* unexpected postal delays). Oversight by the solicitor will not constitute good reason.

WHAT IF THE SELF-CERTIFICATION FORM IS INCORRECTLY   8–14
CERTIFIED?

If the case is not a free legal aid case a free legal aid certificate cannot be issued and costs incurred cannot be recovered. A fresh application (and emergency application) would need to be submitted. Area offices will notify the solicitor where the self-certification form has been used incorrectly.

WILL CHILDREN ACT APPLICATIONS BE DEALT WITH URGENTLY?   8–15

Means tested only cases under sections 31, 43, 44 and 45 may be accepted as urgent enough to be dealt with over the telephone/by fax should the solicitor make an application (see NFG 6 regarding emergency applications) but the appropriate forms would need to be submitted.

Means assessments in all Children Act cases will be prioritised *but* the solicitor should consider whether to submit an emergency application in urgent means and merits tested cases, that is to say in public law cases outside the free legal aid provisions, and in private law cases (see NFG 6 regarding emergency applications).

CAN AN AMENDMENT BE REFUSED TO A NON-MERITS TESTED   8–16
CERTIFICATE?

An amendment can be refused to a non-merits tested certificate if:

(a) the proceedings for which cover is sought are not sufficiently closely related to the proceedings in respect of which free or non-merits tested legal aid is available (in which case a fresh means and merits tested application may be submitted), see para. 8–07; *or*

(b) the amendment sought is for an appeal and the prospects of success do not justify the issue of an amendment or it would be unreasonable in all the circumstances for an amendment to be granted; *or*

(c) the amendment is for a change of solicitor which is not considered to be justified and which is sufficient to trigger the show cause procedure under regulation 77(1)(b) of the Civil Legal Aid (General) Regulations 1989 on the basis that the assisted person is requiring the proceedings to be conducted unreasonably so as to incur an unjustifiable expense to the fund.

IN WHAT CIRCUMSTANCES CAN A NON-MERITS TESTED CERTIFICATE   8–17
BE DISCHARGED?

If the certificate is *means tested only* then it can be:

(a) discharged on financial grounds (reg. 76);

(b) revoked or discharged for abuse of legal aid (reg. 78);

(c) revoked or discharged for failure to provide information (reg. 79).

In addition or if the certificate is non-means, non-merits tested then it could be:

(a) discharged under regulation 80 (except reg. 80(b) in the case of free legal aid);

(b) discharged on the basis that the assisted person has required the proceedings to be conducted unreasonably so as to incur an unjustifiable expense to the legal aid fund within regulation 77(1)(b). The most likely circumstances, but not the only circumstances in which a certificate would be discharged, would be where there had been more than one change of solicitor. (See also note 3 to NFG 12–02.)

The Board does not envisage using the powers contained in regulation 77(1) (a) or (c) of the Civil Legal Aid (General) Regulations 1989 (reasonable grounds/unreasonable in the circumstances) given that any certificate issued would have not been subject to a merits test and bearing in mind the safeguards contained in the Children Act against repeated applications to the court.

See also Note 2 to NFG 12, para. 12–02 regarding over-representation.

8–18 AUTHORITIES (See also NFG 11)

The position in relation to authorities is the same as for any other civil legal aid cases but the solicitor should note that:

(a) under regulation 59(1)(a) Civil Legal Aid (General) Regulations 1989 the authority of the area office is required to instruct counsel in authorised summary proceedings in the family proceedings court (including those under the Children Act 1989), although the costs involved may nonetheless be authorised on assessment. It is preferable for the solicitor to obtain prior authority and factors which may influence the area office are given in NFG 11, para. 11–05. If counsel is instructed without authority and on assessment this is not justified for the proper conduct of the proceedings, costs will be assessed by estimating what would have been allowed to the solicitor had he undertaken the case without counsel. Counsel and the solicitor will then be allowed such reasonable costs as do not together exceed that sum (the maximum fee principle).

(b) if proceedings are transferred up from the family proceedings court no authority for counsel is required save for the instruction of Queen's Counsel or more than one counsel in accordance with regulation 59(1)(b) Civil Legal Aid (General) Regulations 1989;

(c) disbursements must be justified on assessment/taxation in the absence of prior authority and should be appropriately apportioned between parties (whether legally aided or not) where that is reasonable, *e.g.* where only one report is to be obtained for the use of the court (possibly following joint instruction), with or without the leave of the court. This may be equally as between those parties who are legally aided and those who are not (rather than equally as between the number of parties). This is so that the legal aid fund does not bear a disproportionate share;

(d) in Children Act cases where the leave of the court is required for the child to be medically or psychiatrically examined or otherwise assessed, then prior authority for any expert's fees may be applied for but authority will not be given until that leave has been obtained. When applying for prior authority the solicitor should indicate that leave has been obtained and give full details of the expenditure sought, including information as to joint instruction and apportionment between the parties (to avoid any delay arising from the application for authority being refused).

STATUTORY CHARGE

Does the statutory charge apply in Children Act cases?   **8–19**

The statutory charge applies in Children Act cases but Schedule 1 to the Children Act 1989 has been inserted:

(a) in paragraph (viii) of regulation 94 Civil Legal Aid (General) Regulations 1989 applying the £2,500 exemption (the £2,500 exemption applies also in relation to the solicitor's legal advice and assistance (green form) charge); and

(b) in regulation 96(1)(d) Civil Legal Aid (General) Regulations 1989 enabling postponement of enforcement of the charge where the conditions in regulation 96 or 97 are satisfied.

Does the statutory charge apply in respect of public law cases?   **8–20**

The statutory charge applies in respect of public law cases but only if the recovery and the public law aspects arise under the same certificate. As the Board does not consider that financial aspects between the parties are related to the public law sections triggering the special arrangements this does not arise.

WHEN WILL MERITS TESTED CIVIL LEGAL AID BE LIKELY TO BE   **8–21**
GRANTED FOR PROCEEDINGS UNDER THE CHILDREN ACT 1989?

On a merits tested application legal aid/ABWOR is likely to be granted:

(a) unless the court is unlikely to intervene to make an order,

(b) unless the applicant has no reasonable prospects of success in taking/ defending the proceedings (including, where applicable, in the light of the checklist at section 1(3) Children Act 1989);

(c) unless the applicant has an insufficient interest or an insufficiently

separate interest to justify being a party/having separate representation (because his/her interests coincide with those of another party/
parties and/or can be dealt with by way of evidence);

(d) unless there is no indication in the statement or supporting documents of an attempt to compromise the issue(s) between the parties
or such an attempt would be clearly unreasonable in the particular
circumstances;

(e) unless the application is uncontested, although legal aid is likely to be
granted where there are reasons why the court is likely to make an
order and representation is justified in the circumstances of the particular case (*i.e.* it involves a significant point of law or difficult issues
of fact);

(f) unless the issue(s) disputed between the parties are of insufficient
gravity to warrant legal proceedings;

(g) unless the issue(s) could appropriately be dealt with in another way,
e.g. writing a letter, involving the police or social services or by
negotiation;

(h) unless there is insufficient benefit to the applicant to justify the grant
of representation;

(i) unless the court would give significant regard to the child's opposing
wishes (because of his/her age and/or understanding);

(j) unless the issues disputed between the parties do not justify the grant
of representation (although legal aid/ABWOR may be granted if the
applicant is suffering from a material physical or mental disability
such that it would be unreasonable to expect him/her to act in
person).

(k) unless any order obtained is likely to be ineffective or incapable of
successful enforcement.

8–22   Legal aid/ABWOR will only be granted to those applicants and for those
applications to the court which are justified in the particular circumstances
of the case.

(a) An applicant who requires leave to take or to be joined in proceedings
must indicate why he or she is likely to succeed in being joined and
why he or she is the appropriate litigant/applicant for representation.

(b) The fact that a child can make an application to the court will not of
itself justify the grant of legal aid as an application may only be being
made by the child rather than an appropriate adult to secure legal aid
funding (in which case the application is likely to be refused).

(c) An application by a child to apply to the court is likely to be refused in
the absence of information justifying the particular reasons for this
and the likelihood of the leave of the court being granted, as well as in
relation to the apparent failure of relevant adults to take proceedings
(in particular those with whom the child would live in the event of a
residence order being made).

Example: It is unlikely that legal aid would be granted to a child to apply for a residence order (in contrast with say, in appropriate circumstances, a contact order with siblings not in care).

(d) Even where the leave of the court is not required an application is likely to be refused where the interests of the applicant do not justify representation. This includes where any benefit would be to a third party whose interests coincide with those of the applicant (*e.g.* a parent supporting a residence order in favour of grandparents).
Cross-reference: see para. 8–21(c) above.

(e) The requirement on a guardian *ad litem* to appoint a solicitor in certain specified public law cases (for which legal aid is available on a means and merits tested basis) does not of itself mean that the civil legal aid merits test is satisfied on an application for legal aid by the child. If the solicitor is instructed by the guardian *ad litem* legal aid is only likely to be granted where, having regard to the particular circumstances, legal representation under legal aid certificate is justified *e.g.* due to the matter being opposed or involving a significant point of law.

Where more than one order, *e.g.* under section 8, is sought, information sufficient to justify the grant on all aspects must be provided as otherwise legal aid/ABWOR is likely to be refused or partially refused (in respect of those aspects which do not appear justified). A certificate will only cover representation (either taking or defending) on those section 8 orders which are specified (rather than all possible section 8 orders) or which are made by the court of its own motion. Injunction applications are only covered where specified.

In relation to reasonable prospects of success (*i.e.* in terms of achieving the desired outcome), regard should be had to the relevant case law as against the circumstances of the particular case.

Example: the failure to pay maintenance will not of itself lead to the refusal of an application for parental responsibility (as the court's decision will be based on the degree of commitment which the father has shown towards the child, the degree of attachment between the father and the child and the father's reasons for applying for the order).

It must also be remembered that in the case of discharging a care order (including by way of a section 8 application) the applicant would have to show reasonable prospects of succeeding in the particular circumstances of the case, having regard to developments since the court last considered the issue. Equally an application for contact with a child in care will be unlikely to justify the grant of representation unless there has been a relevant and significant change of circumstances since the court last considered the issue.

In cases where the prospects of success are uncertain at the time of the application, but suffice to justify the grant of representation, certificates will be limited so that a final hearing is not covered without a report from the solicitor. Certificates which cover making an application for contact with a child in care, for the discharge of a care order or for a residence order in respect of a child in care will be limited in the first instance to a solicitor's report on the issues and prospects of success (but will not cover issuing proceedings) and, if extended, will be limited thereafter to all steps short of the final hearing.

A legal aid certificate covering proceedings under the Married Women's

Property Act 1882 cannot cover or be amended to cover any family proceedings (including Children Act proceedings) as they are not themselves family proceedings.

8–23 WHAT PROCEEDINGS WOULD BE COVERED AND IN WHICH COURT?

Given the uniformity of procedure and availability of orders under the Children Act 1989, the area office will expect the solicitor to commence proceedings in the family proceedings court where it has jurisdiction and *unless there is a particular and sufficient reason to do otherwise*. If there are insufficient reasons shown for commencing the proceedings in the County Court as opposed to the family proceedings court (or the High Court as opposed to the County Court) then the area office will refuse the application unless, in all the circumstances of the particular case, the grant of legal aid for proceedings in a lower court is available and justified. If so the case will be dealt with as a partial refusal and the application granted to cover proceedings in that lower court (subject to a right of appeal to the Area Committee). ABWOR approvals can only cover proceedings in the family proceedings court in any event.

If no or inadequate information is given regarding jurisdiction then any legal aid certificate issued will bear a condition that the proceedings must be commenced in the family proceedings court, although they may be transferred in accordance with the Children (Allocation or Proceedings) Order 1991.

In the event of a transfer (either horizontal or vertical) in accordance with the Order no specific amendment is required to the legal aid certificate. Applying for the transfer of proceedings is considered to constitute a normal step and therefore be within the scope of the certificate.

Certificates may also be issued containing a condition that proceedings be commenced in the County Court, again subject to transfer in accordance with the Children (Allocation of Proceedings) Order 1991.

If no condition is included in the certificate issued by the area office, the solicitor may commence the proceedings as he considers appropriate and may also continue to act without reference to the area office following a horizontal or vertical transfer.

The insertion of a condition may be appealed to the Area Committee but where a means assessment is available a certificate (or offer) will, despite the possibility of an appeal, be issued immediately (to avoid delay).

Examples of where it would be appropriate to commence proceedings other than in the family proceedings court include those where:

(a) other family proceedings are already pending in another court;

(b) an order made by another court is to be varied, extended or discharged by that court;

(c) the position is covered by a Practice Direction, *e.g.* of February 22, 1993 [1993] 1 All E.R. 820 which makes it clear that applications by children for leave in respect of section 8 orders should be issued in the High Court unless there are other existing related proceedings (including divorce proceedings where a decree absolute has been made), in which case the application should be issued in those proceedings and transferred to the High Court;

(d) an injunction ancillary to Children Act proceedings is sought;

(e) the application to the court relates to a child in care and therefore has to be issued in the court which made the care order;

(f) the anticipated remedy sought is not available in the family proceedings court (*e.g.* a lump sum in excess of £1,000 or a transfer of property);

(g) the proceedings are exceptionally grave or complex;

(h) some novel or difficult point of law is involved.

See also NFG 9, para. 9–11 below, regarding the extent of cover for residence, contact and other section 8 orders generally. Note also that no condition as to forum will normally be applied to applications under Part IV Family Law Act 1996 (domestic violence).

WHAT SHOULD BE APPLIED FOR WHEN ABWOR AS WELL AS CIVIL LEGAL AID IS AVAILABLE?   8–24

Where both ABWOR and civil legal aid are available and an order under the Children Act is to be sought in the proceedings, civil legal aid may be applied for. The area offices will *not* seek to refuse applications for ABWOR on the basis that civil legal aid should be applied for.

HOW WILL CHILDREN ACT CASES BE REMUNERATED?   8–25

In accordance with regulation 104 of the Civil Legal Aid (General) Regulations 1989, family proceedings court costs are assessed rather than taxed. Claims for county court and High Court costs may be assessed if within the assessment limit. Note that the Board will accept claims in respect of the family proceedings court element of transferred cases on the conclusion of that element (*i.e.* before the final conclusion of the case).

The rates are laid down in the Legal Aid in Family Proceedings (Remuneration) Regulations 1991 as amended. The rates applicable in care proceedings (defined as proceedings for an order under Parts IV or V of the Children Act 1989 but including secure accommodation orders and the variation or discharge of an exclusion order under the Children Act 1989) are in Schedules 1 and 1A to the Regulations. They may be enhanced pursuant to regulation 3(4)(c), although there is no separate provision for an uplift for general care and conduct.

The rates applicable to prescribed family proceedings (including matrimonial proceedings and non-care proceedings under the Children Act 1989) are in Schedules 2 and 2A to the Regulations. They may be enhanced although family proceedings court costs in prescribed family proceedings (except under Part IV of the Family Law Act 1996) may not be enhanced.

The costs of other family proceedings (including under Part IV of the Family Law Act 1996) are taxed (or assessed) in accordance with the prescribed hourly rates applicable to Part IV or civil proceedings respectively. The Part IV rate applies irrespective of the venue in which the proceedings are taken and the advocacy rate for all County Court and magistrates' court family proceedings is the same (for certificates issued on or after November 1, 1997). (See *Focus* 22, January 1998.)

NOTE:

1. *The rate(s) applied is (are) the rate(s) applicable to the proceedings for which the certificate was originally issued and where, e.g. a certificate covering a Part IV injunction is amended to cover proceedings within one of the prescribed rates or vice versa the appropriate rates are applied to the work done (i.e. split rates).*

2. *See also Note 2 to NFG 12, para. 12–02 regarding over-representation (as well as NFG 7, para. 7–03.35).*

3. *The Legal Aid Board has issued the following decision in connection with payment of enhanced rates:*

   Care Proceedings: Enhanced rates: Membership of Law Society's Children Panel: *Membership of the Law Society's Children Panel is itself an exceptional circumstance under regulation 3(4)(c)(iii) of the Legal Aid in Family Proceedings (Remuneration) Regulations 1991 which gives a discretion to the assessing officer to allow a larger amount than that specified where it appears to him to be reasonable to do so in any particular part of the bill of costs in question.*

   As a general rule, where a solicitor appeared as an advocate, this is not an exceptional circumstance. Where, however, a Children Panel solicitor appeared as an advocate in care proceedings, this will be an exceptional circumstance. Whether this justifies of itself allowance of a "larger amount" is a question for the exercise of discretion, in consideration of all the circumstances of the case. An uplift in hourly rate for panel membership in cases properly lasting more than two days would normally be justified. (Legal Aid Board reference CLA8 as amended.)

   See also NFG 14–10, p. 192.

9. THE LEGAL AID CERTIFICATE

9–01 HOW IMPORTANT IS THE LEGAL AID CERTIFICATE?

The rule is that the legal aid certificate, and any amendments, are conclusive. On taxation/assessment, save where representation is pursuant to a contract, it is the only authority for the legal aid administration to pay the solicitor and counsel and the solicitor/counsel should check the extent of the legal aid cover (see para. 9–04).

9–02 MATTERS TO BEAR IN MIND ABOUT THE CERTIFICATE

Even where a certificate covers the proceedings up to and including trial it will bear a limitation to that effect. Subsequent work, *e.g.* as to implementation/enforcement, is only covered to the extent specified (see also para. 9–07 below).

The certificate may, however, be limited as to steps in the proceedings, particular parties or to certain work, *e.g.* obtaining an opinion from counsel. If it is so limited, payment will not be made out of the legal aid fund for work done outside the limitation, unless the area office has granted an amendment (see NFG 10).

A certificate limited to counsel's opinion or to preparation of papers for and obtaining counsel's opinion will cover the costs of preparatory work necessary to refer the matter to counsel and a pre-opinion conference with counsel (if necessary) but will only cover one written opinion from counsel and will only cover settling pleadings where this is specified.

The General Council of the Bar has issued guidance on the contents of opinions prepared for legal aid purposes—see p. 737. Where an opinion does not comply with that guidance it will be rejected by the area office.

Even with a full certificate, authority may still be needed to incur certain specific costs, if the solicitor and counsel are to be sure of payment out of the legal aid fund (see NFG 10). Note also that a certificate will generally include a condition or limitation as to costs (see NFG 6, p. 107; regarding emergency certificates and NFG 9–14 and 9–15, p. 154, generally).

The Board's CIS computer system will determine the individual proceedings within each action, cause or matter. Each ABWOR approval or certificate issued will set out for each of the proceedings a scope limitation on the work authorised as well as a costs limitation on the costs to be incurred. This will be a true limitation rather than merely a condition requiring a report once a certain level of costs has been reached. In other words solicitors will only have legal aid cover to carry out work up to the costs limitation imposed.

The certificate will cover only one action, cause or matter apart from the specific exceptions set out in regulation 46. The area office will not cover an application for a grant of representation unless it is required to take proceedings and could not be obtained without legal aid (*i.e.* using the assets of the estate).

The certificate will cover only one assisted person. Joint certificates cannot be issued. In the case of a minor or a person under disability although a next friend or guardian *ad litem* is named in the certificate the assisted person will be the minor or the person under disability.

Any costs limitation or restriction on costs because the nominated solicitor is at a distance from the assisted person (Civil Legal Aid (General) Regulations 1989, reg. 48) will be contained in the certificate.

The certificate will specify both an individual nominated solicitor and a firm of solicitors. If there is a change of firm (although the same individual solicitor continues to be nominated), an amendment of the certificate should be applied for (see NFG 10–03). However, the nominated solicitor can entrust the conduct of the case to a partner of his or to a competent or responsible representative of his who is either employed in his office or otherwise under his immediate supervision (Civil Legal Aid (General) Regulations 1989, reg. 65(2)). The nominated solicitor must hold a valid practising certificate if his (or the firm's) profit costs are to be paid out of the legal aid fund (otherwise only disbursements, including any counsel's fees, will be paid in respect of the uncertificated period).

CAN A CERTIFICATE BE BACKDATED? 9–03

Payment will not be made out of the legal aid fund for any work done in advance of the date of the certificate except:

(a) under legal advice and assistance (green form) or for work done immediately prior to the issue of an emergency certificate at a time when no application for an emergency certificate could be made because the appropriate area office was closed (Civil Legal Aid (General) Regulations 1989, reg. 103(6)); or

(b) under a non-means, non-merits tested, "free", Children Act certificate (Civil Legal Aid (General) Regulations 1989, reg. 12A(3)).

Note that the certificate will not be pre-dated to a date before its issue.

9–04 WHOSE RESPONSIBILITY IS IT TO CHECK THE CERTIFICATE?

It is up to the solicitor and counsel to make sure that the certificate covers all the work that needs to be done for the assisted person. All certificates contain a limitation and it is particularly important to check the effect this has on scope.

Generally if the wording is incorrect or not in accordance with the needs of the assisted person, it will affect:

(a) solicitor and counsel, who will not get paid for work outside scope;

(b) the assisted person who might not be covered by legal aid for all that is necessary and who may become vulnerable to a personal claim for costs by the other party;

(c) a successful opposing party who might not be able to claim costs against the legal aid fund.

See also paras. 9–14 and 9–15 regarding costs conditions/limitations.

9–05 NOTICES OF ISSUE, EXTENSION/AMENDMENT AND DISCHARGE/REVOCATION

A solicitor acting for an assisted person must, without delay and in the approved form, serve:

(a) notice of issue of (emergency) legal aid certificate, in accordance with regulation 50 Civil Legal Aid (General) Regulations 1989;

(b) notice of an extension/amendment of (emergency) legal aid certificate, in accordance with regulations 25 and/or 54 Civil Legal Aid (General) Regulations 1989;

(c) notice of discharge or revocation of (emergency) legal aid certificate, in accordance with regulation 82 Civil Legal Aid (General) Regulations 1989;

when any of these events occurs.

Notices have to be served to ensure that the assisted person's opponent is aware of the assisted person's legal aid status and the proceedings for which legal aid has been granted and (in appeal cases) is aware of all limitations on the legal aid certificate. In appeal cases, the opponent must be given notice of all limitations (except costs limitations) on the certificate—see *Scarth v. Jacobs-Paton* (1978) *The Times*, November 1).

Occasionally, the description of legal aid, on a legal aid certificate, may not fully reveal the scope of the legal aid. For example, the description of legal aid may be "to defend and to counterclaim in proceedings . . ." and the limitation may be "Limited to representation on the counterclaim". In these circumstances, the opponent should, in all cases, be made aware of the true scope of legal aid cover—whether by revealing the limitation or by ensuring that the true scope is specified in the description/scope section of the appropriate notice.

Since the publication of the 1997/98 Legal Aid Handbook, the Board has consulted widely on whether assisted persons should be required to give notice of limitations on legal aid certificates in all cases—not just appeal cases. By a considerable majority, consultees were in favour of making no change to the present requirements. Having noted this and having considered the points made by consultees, the Board will not be changing the disclosure requirements and has not amended the approved forms.

The forms currently approved by the Board for giving:

(a) notice of issue of [emergency] certificate;

(b) notice of extension/amendment of [emergency] certificate; and

(c) notice of discharge or revocation of [emergency] certificate;

are set out in Part Three (see p. 709). They include important information for assisted persons' solicitors and for opponents or opponents' solicitors.

SCOPE OF CERTIFICATES AND COSTS LIMITATIONS

Forum   9–06

Where a certificate specifies the forum for proceedings then that forum must generally be used (but see below). Where a certificate is silent proceedings may be taken either in a family proceedings court (if civil legal aid is available), county court or the High Court. Solicitors must, however, exercise great care in the decisions made as to the forum in view of the possible penalties on taxation (and hardship to the assisted person/prejudice to legal aid fund).

Where a legal aid certificate specifies proceedings in a county court it will not, unless amended, cover proceedings after a transfer to the High Court. If the assisted person wishes to transfer the proceedings to the High Court then an application for an amendment must be made to the area office. If an application for transfer is made by any other party an application for the amendment of the certificate should be made immediately after the order transferring the proceedings. In the absence of an amendment the certificate will not cover any subsequent work.

No amendment is required on a transfer of proceedings from a county court to the High Court where the certificate does not specify a particular court. Nor is an amendment required where the certificate specifies proceedings in the High Court and the proceedings are transferred down to a county court.

Certificates covering private law proceedings under the Children Act 1989 may contain a condition as to the court in which proceedings are to be commenced (see NFG 8, para. 8–23). Certificates covering proceedings under Part IV Family Law Act 1996 do not contain a condition as to forum.

9–07   Conveyancing/implementation work and enforcement

If, unusually, the court order in question is not specific the cost of conveyancing work necessary to give effect to the terms of a court order can be covered by the legal aid certificate (*Copeland v. Houlton* [1955] 3 All E.R. 178). This applies equally to consent orders and work necessary to implement an order (*S v. S* (*Legal Aid Taxation*) [1991] Fam. Law 271) but this will only be the case where the scope, including the limitation applied in the particular case, allows for such conveyancing/implementation work.

In the absence of appropriate cover the solicitor must apply for an amendment to the certificate. This will always be necessary in relation to enforcement work which will not be covered in the absence of an amendment specifying the type of enforcement proceedings which are covered. (See also para. 9–12 below). See also NFG 14, para. 14–25 regarding non-contentious work undertaken as a direct result of a court order in family proceedings.

The solicitor must interpret any relevant court order to ensure that any necessary amendment is obtained.

9–08   Defended divorce/judicial separation proceedings—limitation

Since the Matrimonial Causes Act 1973, the policy is to avoid defended suits unless there are reasons why the suit should be defended in the interests of either party, and to ensure that normally the award of a decree will not compromise decisions over issues relating to children and the other ancillary matters.

Legally aided cases should not be defended without good reason. Certificates, whether to prosecute or defend divorce/judicial separation proceedings, will be limited so as to exclude trial of a defended suit. The effect of this is that an application for an amendment must be made before a case proceeds to trial.

Before a certificate is amended to cover representation in a defended suit the area office must be satisfied that, without detriment to the proper interests of the parties or either of them, the case cannot be dealt with on an undefended basis. The solicitor applying for an amendment should confirm that a defended case cannot be avoided, setting out the reasons and the state of settlement negotiations. Counsel's opinion should also be obtained in accordance with the usual limitation.

9–09   Matrimonial proceedings—scope

These notes equally apply to suits for nullity or judicial separation to the extent that the individual items or their equivalent apply.

The interpretation of the wording of the legal aid certificate, with particular regard to its scope, must always be a matter for decision by the taxing officer concerned in the light of any representations made by the solicitor with the normal remedies by way of objection and review in the event of dissatisfaction. Without in any way fettering his discretion, the following notes (in para. 9–10), which have been agreed with the Senior District Judge of the Family Division, set out for the guidance of solicitors, the Board's views as to the scope of some common forms of certificate.

Certificates to prosecute or defend a suit for divorce 9–10

(1) *Principles*

   (a) Subject to any limitation, restriction or condition expressed, a certificate covers all the steps which are normally necessary for the purpose of prosecuting or defending a suit.

   (b) The certificate will not cover any further steps in the decree proceedings if the cause at any time becomes undefended.

   (c) Unless extended by amendment, the certificate does *not* cover any step after the final decree other than applications for ancillary relief or orders under section 8 of the Children Act 1989 made promptly after the final decree.

(2) *Matters regarded as within the scope of the usual form of certificate*

A certificate covering the prosecution or defence of proceedings for a decree of divorce is regarded as covering:

   (a) filing supplemental pleadings;

   (b) raising or opposing an issue as to domicile;

   (c) making or opposing an application for maintenance pending suit;

   (d) dealing with the court's consideration of the arrangements to be made for a child of the family;

   (e) an application for leave to remove a child of the family from the jurisdiction of the court, provided it is made before the final decree;

   (f) an application for an injunction to prevent molestation of one spouse by the other and/or to require a spouse to leave the matrimonial home, provided it is made any time up to the final decree;

   (g) an application for an order under section 8 of the Children Act 1989 provided it is made before, on or promptly after the final decree;

   (h) an issue as to the status of a child provided it is raised at any time up to the making of an order for ancillary relief in respect of that child which is made before, on or promptly after the final decree;

   (i) an application for an injunction to restrain the other spouse from dealing with property to defeat an order for ancillary relief, provided it is made at any time up to the making of an order for ancillary relief, in respect of a party or a child of the family, which is made before, on or promptly after the final decree;

   (j) an application for rescission of a decree nisi consequent upon the reconciliation of the parties;

   (k) making or opposing an application to expedite the making absolute of a decree nisi;

   (l) making or opposing an application before or promptly after the final decree, for:
      (i) a periodical payments order,
      (ii) a secured periodical payments order,
      (iii) a lump sum order,
      (iv) a transfer of property order,

   (v) a settlement of property order,
   (vi) a variation of settlement order,

in respect of a party or a child of the family but only so far as the court, rather than the Child Support Agency, has jurisdiction;

(m) an application made before the final decree for a variation order;

(n) making or opposing an application for a periodical payments order or a lump sum order in respect of a party or a child of the family when the applicant has been unsuccessful in the main suit but only so far as the court, rather than the Child Support Agency, has jurisdiction;

(o) the registration in a magistrates' court of an order for ancillary relief provided that the application is made not later than six months from the date of the order or the date of the final decree, whichever shall be the later;

(p) steps by a petitioner in connection with an application by the respondent under section 10(2) of the Matrimonial Causes Act 1973;

(q) attendance before a district judge on a summons for directions or pre-trial review;

(r) conveyancing/implementation work necessary to give effect to any order obtained within the scope of the certificate (but not enforcement).

(3) *Matters regarded as outside the scope of the usual form of certificate*
In the absence of a specific amendment a certificate to prosecute or (as a respondent spouse) to defend a suit for divorce will not cover the initiation or opposing, as appropriate, of the following steps in such proceedings:

(a) on the part of the petitioner:
   (i) filing an answer to a separate cross-petition by the respondent;
   (ii) filing a second petition;

(b) on the part of the respondent spouse:
   (i) making cross-charges in an answer, followed by a prayer for divorce or some alternative matrimonial relief;
   (ii) filing a separate cross-petition;

(the cover afforded by such a certificate will be taken to extend to proceedings under a second petition or separate cross-petition which have taken place after an order for consolidation with the previous proceedings, but not otherwise)

(c) an application for a variation order after the final decree;

(d) the enforcement of any final order obtained;

(e) an application under section 7 of the Matrimonial Causes Act 1973;

(f) an application for alteration of a maintenance agreement;

(g) an application for provision to be made out of the estate of a deceased former spouse;

(h) an application for an avoidance of disposition order;

(i) protracted negotiations subsequent to, and to give effect to, an order for contact to a child;

(j) an application by the unsuccessful party for the decree nisi to be made absolute;

(k) proceedings under section 17 of the Married Women's Property Act 1882 (which would require a fresh legal aid application in any event);

(l) opposing an intervention by the Queen's Proctor to show cause against the decree nisi being made absolute;

(m) resisting the respondent's application under section 10(1) of the Matrimonial Causes Act 1973 for rescission of the decree;

(n) an application for committal for breach of an injunction.

(The above list is not exhaustive.)

(4) *Limitations and conditions*

Where a legal aid certificate has been granted to continue to prosecute or to defend a defended suit for divorce, it will provide that the certificate covers the decree proceedings so long as the cause remains defended (see above).

The certificate will also contain the following limitation:

"Limited in defended decree proceedings to all steps up to and including any summons for directions for trial/setting down and thereafter to obtaining Counsel's Opinion on the necessity/merits of the matter continuing as a contested cause."

Certificates relating to undefended decree proceedings and family/matrimonial matters other than prosecuting or defending a suit for divorce

9–11

Legal aid is not available for undefended divorce or judicial separation decree proceedings. It may only be granted for such decree proceedings:

(a) if they become defended (either to the respondent to defend or to the petitioner to continue the proceedings after an answer has been filed); or

(b) if the district judge directs the petition to be heard in open court (for example where he is not satisfied on the merits of the case or on other matters such as domicile); or

(c) if by reason of physical or mental incapacity it is impracticable for the applicant to proceed without legal aid.

Apart from decree proceedings, legal aid may be granted to make or oppose an application for an injunction (but the certificate will not cover the filing of a petition unless the court makes it a condition of the injunction); for a substantive application for ancillary relief; for an order relating to residence, contact or the education of a child (but only where there is reason to believe that the application will be opposed, although see below) and in connection with consideration of the arrangements for children under section 41 of the Matrimonial Causes Act 1973 (but only where there is reason to believe that the application will be opposed—see the Legal Aid Act 1988, para. 5A, Pt. II, Sched. 2).

Legal aid may, however, be granted for the purposes of making or opposing any other application or satisfying the court on any other matter which raises a substantive question for determination by the court. Following the

151

implementation of the Children Act 1989 the Legal Aid Board considers that this provision covers any Children Act section 8 order and that the proceedings need not be opposed. However, if the proceedings are unopposed a legal aid certificate would not normally be granted. See *Focus* 19, May 1997 and *Focus* 21, September 1997 regarding the application of the merits test in matrimonial/family cases and domestic violence/harassment cases respectively.

The following should, also, be noted:

1. All legal aid certificates issued in connection with maintenance or ancillary relief in matrimonial proceedings cover child maintenance only where the court rather than the Child Support Agency has jurisdiction or, in other circumstances, where this is specifically stated. In any event cover only extends to securing one substantive order. This does not prevent applications to the appropriate area office for amendment of the certificate if legal aid is required for any further court hearing. On receipt of such an application for amendment, however, the area office will need to be satisfied about the necessity for the subsequent hearing and be provided with an estimate of the costs to date and an assurance that the effect of the statutory charge has been explained to the assisted person.

2. From June 1, 1997 certificates either to take or to defend proceedings related to finances/property will be limited (other than where they cover only periodical payments and/or transfer of tenancy, or, in the case of the Trusts of Land and Appointment of Trustees Act 1996/Declaration as to Trusts Affecting Property and/or Rights of Occupation, an order for sale). This is to ensure that before a case proceeds to a final contested hearing the solicitor must report as soon as practicable to the area office confirming that this cannot reasonably be avoided and remains justified, having regard to the prospects of success (*i.e.* strength in terms of achieving the desired outcome), value of claim and property in dispute as well as attempts to define the issues between the parties and to settle the matter. In cases which are subject to the Ancillary Relief Pilot Procedure the solicitor will be able to report after any Financial Dispute Resolution (FDR) appointment. Furthermore, in cases relating to finances/property where the issues between the parties are not clear or alternatively appear capable of being minimised or resolved, the certificate will be limited in the first instance to allow the issues to be defined and to cover negotiations as to settlement followed by a solicitor's report.

Proceedings affected are as follows:

(a) section 17 Married Women's Property Act 1882;

(b) Trusts of Land and Appointment of Trustees Act 1996/Declaration as to Trusts Affecting Property/Declaration as to Rights of Occupation;

(c) applications relating to finances/property under the:

   (i) Domestic Proceedings and Magistrates' Courts Act 1978;
   (ii) Children Act 1989; or
   (iii) for financial relief ancillary to divorce, judicial separation or nullity.

3. Only one substantive residence contact or other section 8 order (including any review or further consideration of the matter by the court which, in the particular circumstances of the case, constitutes a restoration of the matter on the court's own motion—but not any fresh application made to the court in that context) is within the scope of a certificate. This is so unless the

certificate is specifically amended to cover a further application to the court. Note also that a certificate will specify what order(s) may be sought or opposed, for example a certificate covering representation on an application for contact (as opposed to residence and/or contact) will not cover applying for a residence order without specific amendment (although the court may make such an order of its own motion).

Proceedings for enforcement 9–12

A certificate (or amendment) granted for the purpose of enforcing an order for ancillary relief or costs will specify the process of enforcement to be adopted and will be regarded as covering one application for enforcement only. Certificates/amendments will not be granted where the Child Support Agency has jurisdiction. (See also para. 9–07 above.)

NOTE:

1. *It should be remembered that legal aid is not available for proceedings for or consequent upon the issue of a judgment summons in the county court.*

2. *Where a maintenance order has been made for payment direct to a child, enforcement proceedings can only be taken by that child acting by next friend or guardian ad litem (Shelley v. Shelley [1952] P. 107; [1952] 1 All E.R. 70). Where the Child Support Agency has jurisdiction legal aid is not available. Where the court, rather than the Child Support Agency, has enforcement jurisdiction the parent's legal aid certificate cannot be amended to include such proceedings, which must be the subject of a separate legal aid application by the child. No separate application by the child is, however, required to register an order in a family proceedings court as registration is regarded as part of the process of obtaining the order and not as procedure for enforcement.*

3. *Legal aid certificates, including those to prosecute or defend a suit for divorce/judicial separation, will cover the registration in a family proceedings court of an order for ancillary relief. Where an application is received relating to proceedings for enforcement of such an order in the original court, the area office will need to be satisfied that there is good reason for not pursuing such proceedings in a family proceedings court following registration.*

Penal notices/power of arrest 9–13

Asking for a penal notice to be endorsed on an order is within the scope of a certificate covering representation in the proceedings and no specific amendment to the certificate is therefore required to cover this step. Equally, no amendment is required to cover representation of the assisted person, whether applicant or respondent, when directions are sought following an arrest in accordance with a power of arrest contained in an order obtained in the proceedings.

An amendment is, however, required to apply for the issue of a warrant of arrest (where a power of arrest has not been attached to the order) and for the representation of either party in contempt of court proceedings.

A respondent's certificate, which covers representation on arrest, either following the exercise of a power of arrest or the execution of a warrant, will also extend to applying for bail and to representation on an adjourned hearing. Likewise, the applicant's certificate, once extended to cover the application for the issue of a warrant or to commit, will cover representation as to bail and at any adjourned hearing.

9–14   Costs conditions* (see also Costs limitations at 9–15)

*Applicable only to pre-CIS certificates

The information supplied in the Board's civil legal aid application form and application for an amendment provide the basis of the Board's control of cases in civil non-matrimonial non-family matters (where certificates are issued on/after September 14, 1992). This means that the Board will not routinely require reports from solicitors under regulation 70(2) of the Civil Legal Aid (General) Regulations 1989.

Using the information provided in these forms, cases are designated to one of three categories on the basis of the actual or expected costs and disbursements in the proceedings exclusive of VAT:

(a) Cases costing less than £2,500;

(b) Cases costing from £2,500 up to £7,500;

(c) Cases where costs are £7,500 or more.

A condition will be attached to all certificates where costs fall within the first or second categories above, namely that the solicitor shall report to the area office using the application for amendment of legal aid certificate form if profit costs, disbursements and Counsel's fees exceed £2,500 or £7,500 as appropriate. Cases in the third category will also include an appropriate condition as to costs and will be allocated to senior staff. Note that the stated costs figure applies to any related or legally linked certificates held by the assisted person or persons covering the proceedings and that the costs figure and costs must be apportioned, *e.g.* where there are two related/legally linked certificates and a costs figure of £2,500, then a total of £2,500 is available between the two certificates.

The condition is a request for a report pursuant to regulation 70(1) of the Civil Legal Aid (General) Regulations 1989 and the sanction for a failure to report is that action may be taken by the Legal Aid Board under regulation 102 to defer the solicitor's profit costs and/or refer the solicitor's conduct to the Solicitors Disciplinary Tribunal. The condition places the legally aided client in the same position as a fee-paying client, in that if the stated costs limit is exceeded and not subsequently extended, then the solicitor may not obtain payment. This is akin to the situation where a fee-paying client authorises a solicitor to incur costs only to a stated amount.

If there has been no report the solicitor's profit costs (excluding disbursements and counsel's fees) may only be deferred where the limit has been exceeded and not extended *and* it is considered that, had there been a report to the area office, the limit would *not* have been increased *and* the certificate would have been discharged. On consideration of any deferment an amended, increased costs condition cannot be imposed—either the costs in excess of the condition are deferred or paid. In the event of a deferment the disbursements and counsel's fees will be paid but the solicitor will only receive his profit costs for the balance of the specified limit.

In a continuing case, if there is a late report (*i.e.* where the limit has been exceeded) rather than no report, then the solicitor is at risk of a regulation 102 deferment if the limit is not increased in respect of future costs. However, costs already incurred in excess of the limit can still be paid either as a result of the limit being extended or no deferment being justified in the particular case.

The condition has no relevance on taxation but on receiving claims for payment the area offices will check the condition and consider whether a regulation 102 deferment would be appropriate.

Any decision to defer may be made by authorised area office staff but their decision can, on the solicitor's request, be reviewed by the Area Committee on whose behalf the delegated decision to defer has been made.

Solicitors will need to check certificates on receipt for any costs condition and to apply for an amendment to the costs figure when the amount in any condition is being approached (although that limit can be increased even though it has been exceeded).

Limitations, including costs limitations, will be used as appropriate. However, in high costs cases (that is where costs and disbursements are expected to be over £2,500) it will be usual for certificates to be limited to obtaining further evidence and counsel's opinion thereafter. If proceedings have already been commenced, certificates will normally require counsel's opinion to be obtained before trial.

Costs limitations

9–15

The Board's CIS computer system no longer imposes costs conditions on the initial grant of legal aid. A costs limitation is imposed for the work authorised under each ABWOR/certificate issued in any case, including all matrimonial and family cases. The limitation is a true limitation rather than merely a condition requiring a report once a certain level of costs has been reached. In other words, solicitors will only have legal aid cover to carry out work up to the costs limitation imposed. The limitation limits the costs to be incurred under the approval/certificate to a figure including disbursements and any counsel's fees, but excluding VAT (on both costs and disbursements). The profit costs element is based on the amount to be claimed on a legal aid basis, *i.e.* prescribed rates with any appropriate mark-up or enhancement in a prescribed rate case.

Solicitors should particularly note the following:

1. *Limitations*

Post CIS the legal aid certificate/ABWOR approval will impose both scope and financial limitations on the work to be done under it. The costs limitation imposed is a single limit for all the work to be done post CIS, rather than stages during the currency of the certificate. The Board's liability where there is a claim on the fund will not exceed the final costs limitation imposed. Payment cannot be made from the fund for either work outside the scope of the certificate or for costs in excess of the costs limit. Solicitors should carefully check the limitations imposed and apply for an amendment where appropriate.

2. Multiple costs limitations

A certificate covering more than one set of proceedings may have more than one costs limitation imposed. It is intended that there should be one effective costs limitation for all the work authorised by the certificate. Accordingly, the costs limit will be the highest of the limitations specified. Solicitors do not need to apportion their costs between the proceedings covered by each limitation and need only apply for an amendment when the total costs for the work to be done under the whole of the certificate are likely to exceed the highest limitation. Solicitors should apply for an amendment on the basis of the total costs under the whole of the certificate to date and should ask for each costs figure to be amended to the new costs limit requested. Any amendment to the costs limitation will not operate retrospectively.

3. Amendments

Amendments to certificates are now issued in the form of a replacement certificate which will show the amended scope, including any new costs limitation imposed. The amended costs limitation will set a new maximum for the costs to be incurred. The costs limitation is a final costs figure and the limitation imposed on the final version of the certificate will be the relevant limitation on taxation/assessment. Solicitors do not need to apportion costs between any costs limitations effective during the life of the certificate in any claim for costs. To exceed a costs limitation is to act outside scope and such costs will be disallowed on taxation/assessment.

4. Transitional cases

Where a certificate was issued prior to CIS, on its first amendment post CIS the amended certificate will, in all cases, replace the costs condition with a costs limitation. The costs condition remains effective for the work done up to the date of the replacement certificate. If no costs condition existed the replacement certificate will impose a costs limitation. The costs limitation is imposed to cover the future work to be undertaken.

For example, if a costs condition of £3,000 was already in force it would be extinguished at the date of the replacement certificate. If a costs limitation of £2,500 was imposed the costs would start to run again from the date of the replacement certificate. In transitional cases solicitors will be required to apportion costs in any costs claim to distinguish between a period where a costs condition was imposed and the period for any subsequent costs limitations.

10. AMENDMENTS AND APPEALS

CAN THE CERTIFICATE BE AMENDED?   10–01
(Civil Legal Aid (General) Regulations 1989, regs. 46, 51, 54, 56, 57 and 58)

The rule is that if the certificate does not cover all the steps needed, or circumstances have changed, application can be made to the area director to amend the certificate (Civil Legal Aid (General) Regulations 1989). An amendment may also be needed to increase the costs figure in a costs condition or limitation (see NFG 9, paras 9–14 and 9–15, p. 154)—an amendment which increases the scope of a certificate does not automatically increase the costs figure.

WILL THE AMENDMENT BE GRANTED?   10–02

The amendment will not be granted unless the area office has all the information needed. An application for an amendment is subject to the same requirements as an initial application for legal aid and the amendment must be within the categories set out in regulations 46 or 51. An amendment must not, however, be granted to take enforcement proceedings outside England and Wales even though the judgment was obtained in the jurisdiction.

The General Council of the Bar has issued guidance on the contents of counsel's opinions prepared for legal aid purposes (see p. 737) and the area office will reject the opinion or refuse an amendment where the guidance is not complied with.

Certificates, other than non-means, non-merits tested Children Act certificates, cannot be amended to cover proceedings in the House of Lords or on appeal from a magistrates' court.

There is an appeal against a refusal of an amendment by the area office to the area committee, as in the case of the initial application for legal aid. There is no right to attend or be represented at the hearing of the appeal. Area committees will not permit such attendance or representation if they consider it unnecessary.

The area office has power to amend the certificate without an application from the solicitor, including in the case of a reassessment of the assisted person's means.

Notice of the fact of an amendment must be given immediately to all other parties to the proceedings, as well as to those who become parties. This does not apply to financial amendments altering an assisted person's contribution. See also NFG 9–05 regarding notices. The Board's approved form appears in Part Three (see p. 711).

WHAT HAPPENS ON A CHANGE OF SOLICITOR?   10–03

No application for an amendment is necessary if the change is within the same firm as this is treated as a delegation of the case (Civil Legal Aid (General) Regulations 1989, reg. 65(2)), provided the nominated solicitor holds a valid practising certificate *and* remains with the firm. If there is to be a change of firm, even if the nominated solicitor stays the same, an application should be made to the area office for amendment so that the Board's records and certificate can be updated. The application will be made by the new solicitor and the Board's standard form of application for an amendment which includes information as to the costs and merits of the case must be used. The reason(s) for the proposed change should be made clear in the application.

In dealing with the amendment request, whether to an emergency or a substantive certificate, the area office will consider the reason(s) for the change as well as all the circumstances of the particular case. The civil legal aid merits test is reapplied and the reasonableness of the proposed change considered. Factors relevant to the application are the work which has been done, the scope of the certificate and the work remaining to be done, so as to balance the reason(s) put forward for the change and the likely increase in costs.

Where an amendment to an emergency certificate is sought, the assisted person's co-operation in the means assessment process will also be a relevant factor.

In any event an application will not be granted only because the matter is urgent and applications should therefore be made without delay as soon as they become appropriate.

An amendment is likely to be granted where:

    (a) no or only minimal costs have been incurred under the certificate, or the application is made before a certificate has been issued;

    (b) the change request follows a change of address by the assisted person such that it would no longer be reasonable for him to continue to instruct the existing solicitor (having regard to necessary personal attendances);

    (c) the change is based on a conflict of interest, between the existing solicitor and client or between clients, or the absence of a conflict of interest sufficient to justify separate representation by the existing solicitor;

    (d) the change is based on a change of firm by the existing solicitor; or

    (e) the amendment applied for is by a child to their own certificate in a public law Children Act case involving a guardian *ad litem* and the court has sanctioned the proposed change. If it is not clear that the court has sanctioned the change, the amendment will be refused (rather than granted with more restrictive scope). This is because it is appropriate for the court to consider the position, having a regard to the involvement of a guardian *ad litem* to protect the child's interests.

An amendment is likely to be refused where:

    (a) the current scope of the certificate is narrowly limited (*e.g.* to obtain an expert's report, solicitor's report and/or counsel's opinion on the merits). This is because where only limited, preliminary work is covered, the increase in costs arising from a change is unlikely to be justified until that work has been done;

    (b) there has been a previous change of solicitor amendment. The greater the number of requests, the less likely the amendment is to be granted;

(c) the stage reached in the proceedings is such that most of the necessary work has been undertaken and the likely increase in costs would be significant, *e.g.* the remaining work is to deal with a fully contested final hearing (even where the application is made shortly before trial); or

(d) in cases of client dissatisfaction with the conduct of the case and/or of the solicitor, no complaint has been made under the solicitor's complaints procedure under Practice Rule 15.

If the existing solicitor is no longer prepared to represent the assisted person the reason(s) for that are relevant and where appropriate the area office will institute the show cause procedure, rather than amend the certificate. The solicitor/client relationship is one requiring mutual trust. When that relationship has broken down, the costs involved in conducting even straightforward cases could rise sharply as each step along the way becomes fraught with difficulties. On the other hand, the costs of duplicating work which are likely to arise from a change of solicitor should only be incurred where this is justified. The request for a transfer may arise where the client does not want to accept the solicitor's advice. The nominated solicitor has a duty to consider whether unreasonable use is being made of the certificate. Where circumstances suggest this to be the case, an amendment will be refused.

If the amendment is refused, the show cause procedure may be instituted, having regard to the merits test and/or the change of solicitor amendment request itself. This would be where it appeared from the making of the amendment request itself that the assisted person had required the proceedings to be conducted unreasonably so as to incur an unjustifiable expense to the fund, or it was unreasonable in the particular circumstances that the assisted person should continue to receive legal aid.

Even where the amendment is granted, it may be appropriate to restrict the scope of the certificate more tightly than was previously the case. This may reflect the current costs and/or merits of the case or may be to obtain a report from the new, incoming solicitor on costs and/or merits or particular aspects of the case, so that the continuation of the certificate can be further considered. In the event of a report being required from the incoming solicitor under the amended certificate, the area office will then specify an appropriate time period for its provision, usually two months. If a report is not received the area office will reconsider the continuation of the certificate.

As to the release of papers and solicitor's lien, see Legal Aid and Solicitors' Professional Conduct at p. 740 below. Any lien for pre-certificate costs and disbursements (apart from those covered by an application for legal advice and assistance) is protected by regulation 103 of the Civil Legal Aid (General) Regulations 1989.

LEGAL AID FOR APPEALS TO A HIGHER COURT   10–04

Generally, if a litigant is unsuccessful, he/she can apply for legal aid to appeal to a higher court. The rules in NFG 7 still apply to such appeals (see NFG 7) although it may be possible for an existing certificate to be amended to cover an appeal. Note for Guidance 9–05 deals with notice of issue/amendment of certificates covering appeals.

Appeals to the House of Lords or appeals from magistrates' courts

Even where the proceedings in the court below were legally aided, a fresh application for a new certificate must be submitted to make or defend an appeal to the House of Lords or an appeal from a magistrates' court, unless the existing certificate covered special Children Act proceedings (*i.e.* proceedings for which "free", non-means, non-merits tested legal aid is available (Civil Legal Aid (General) Regulations 1989, reg. 46(2)). A new means assessment does not have to be carried out.

When considering applications for appeals to the House of Lords, area offices will:

(a) Refuse the application where it appears that there are no reasonable grounds for appeal (or the reasonableness test is not satisfied); or

(b) Grant the application where it considers there are reasonable grounds and the reasonableness test is satisfied; or

(c) Grant the application for the purposes of obtaining an opinion from counsel who conducted the case in the Court of Appeal (whether leading counsel or not).

To ensure consistency and to reflect the House of Lords Practice Directions the following standard wordings will be used as far as possible:

(1) To petition the House of Lords for leave to appeal the judgment of the Court of Appeal and, if successful, thereafter to prosecute the appeal in the case between the assisted person and _____ .

(2) To obtain for consideration by the area office counsel's written opinion on the merits of an appeal to the House of Lords against the judgment of the Court of Appeal; if junior counsel so advises he may settle the petition for leave to appeal; leading counsel may not settle the petition and may only be instructed to advise where he conducted the appeal hearing in the Court of Appeal in the case between the assisted person and _____ .

Wording 1 is to be used where the area office is satisfied as to the merits of the appeal without the need for counsel's opinion to be obtained and wording 2 is to be used where counsel's opinion is to be obtained to satisfy the area office as to the merits of proceeding.

Wording 2 permits junior counsel to settle the petition but only allows leading counsel to be instructed (to advise on the merits but not settle the petition) where he conducted the appeal hearing in the Court of Appeal. Wordings in the same terms will be used for appeals from the Divisional Court.

Where a positive opinion is obtained following the use of wording 2 then the certificate may be amended to delete that wording and substitute wording 1. Wording 2 may cover a conference or consultation but this will need to be justified on taxation. In the House of Lords such costs are only exceptionally considered to be justified *at the leave stage*.

See also NFG 11, para. 11–04, pp. 163–164 *as to authorities for counsel*.

Other appeals

Where the proceedings in the court below have been legally aided, the certificate may be amended to include making or defending an appeal or making an interlocutory appeal. An application for an amendment should be made to the area office as soon as possible in the light of the time limits for appealing and the general principle that appeals should be heard as quickly as possible. Any amendment will not operate retrospectively.

The Court of Appeal has indicated that, where the liberty of the subject is involved and the solicitor considers that there are grounds for appeal, he should lodge the notice of appeal in accordance with the time limits despite the absence of legal aid (*Jordan v. Jordan* (1992) *The Times*, June 22). It is the Board's view that the solicitor should apply promptly for an amendment or certificate and, if the merits justify it, an urgent amendment or certificate can be granted, limited, if appropriate, to putting in the notice of appeal, applying for any necessary stay of execution and obtaining counsel's opinion on the merits.

In any event, prompt notification should be given to the opposite side of the intention to appeal and of the fact that application is being made immediately, either for a legal aid certificate or for an amendment to an existing certificate. In giving such notification the other party or parties should be asked if they will consent to an extension of time (but see also *Jordan v. Jordan* above).

Defending of an interlocutory appeal is regarded as being included within the scope of the original certificate and no application to amend the certificate is necessary. Note, however, that an order for ancillary relief including in the Family Division is no longer interlocutory and therefore a specific amendment is required both to prosecute or defend such an appeal.

If there is no existing certificate covering proceedings in the court below, a full application must be made in the usual way.

Appeals to the Employment Appeal Tribunal

The procedure for making appeals to the Employment Appeal Tribunal is contained in the Employment Appeal Tribunal Rules 1993 (S.I. 1993 No. 2854) as amended by the Employment Appeal Tribunal (Amendment) Rules 1996 (S.I. 1996 No. 3216) and a Practice Direction dated March 29, 1996 ([1996] I.C.R. 422; [1996] I.R.L.R. 430).

The time for appeal is 42 days from the date when the extended written reasons for the decision or order of the Industrial Tribunal were sent to the appellant, or, in the case of an appeal from a decision of the certification officer, 42 days from the date on which the written record of the decision was sent. Every notice of appeal sent out of time must be accompanied by a written application for an extension of time setting out the reason for the delay. An application for an extension of time cannot be considered until a notice of appeal has been presented.

It is not necessarily a good reason for delay in appealing that legal aid has been applied for, but not yet determined. In any case of doubt or difficulty, a notice of appeal should be served in time and an application made to the registrar for directions.

11. AUTHORITIES

11–01 IS ANY AUTHORITY REQUIRED FOR WORK UNDER THE CERTIFICATE?
(Civil Legal Aid (General) Regulations 1989, regs. 59–65)

The rule is that no question as to the propriety of any step or act in relation to which prior authority has been obtained shall be raised on any taxation of costs, but where a limit has been imposed the amount can only be disallowed on taxation if the solicitor or assisted person knew or ought reasonably to have known that the purpose for which such authority was given had failed or become irrelevant or unnecessary before the costs were incurred (Civil Legal Aid (General) Regulations 1989, reg. 63(1) and (2)).

An authority may currently be given in the certificate itself, in an amendment or in a separate letter. Following increased computerisation in the Board's area offices all authorities will be given by letter.

NOTE:

1. *The area office cannot give retrospective authorities. In* Wallace v. Freeman Heating Co. Ltd *[1955] 1 W.L.R. 172, Pearson J., having adjourned a summons to review a taxation into open court, agreed with the decision of the taxing master that he could disallow a sum in the solicitor's bill for the legally aided appellant of the costs of bespeaking a shorthand transcript of the proceedings in the court of first instance because the legal aid committee had not, when granting the legal aid certificate for the appeal, authorised the bespeaking of a transcript. Their retrospective approval, after the master had first disallowed the amount, was insufficient to bind the taxing master.*

2. *When obtaining authority to instruct leading counsel (or to incur unusual or unusually large expenditure) the solicitor should also obtain the client's consent after advising him of the probable additional costs and the effect of the statutory charge (*Re Solicitors (Taxation of Costs) *[1982] 2 All E.R. 683).*

11–02 THE MAIN AREAS OF WORK CONCERNED

The main areas of work concerned are:

(a) the instruction of counsel;

(b) the employment of experts and the incurring of unusual expenditure.

11–03 AUTHORITIES FOR INSTRUCTING COUNSEL AND LEADING COUNSEL

Under regulation 59 of the Civil Legal Aid (General) Regulations 1989, a solicitor acting for an assisted person may instruct counsel where it appears necessary for the proper conduct of proceedings. When counsel entrusts a case to another counsel under section 32(1)(b) of the Legal Aid Act 1988 the leave of the area office is not required.

However, unless authority has been given in the certificate or subsequently, counsel should not be instructed in authorised summary proceedings nor should leading counsel or more than one counsel be instructed. Notwithstanding this, in the case of summary proceedings, unauthorised costs involved in instructing counsel may be allowed on assessment or may be assessed on the basis that the solicitor undertook all the work with the amount allowed being shared between the solicitor and counsel (the maximum fee principle).

Where there is no *inter partes* taxation there is no discretion to allow unauthorised costs incurred in instructing counsel (*Din v. Wandsworth London Borough Council (No. 3)* [1983] 1 W.L.R. 1171; *Robyn Hayley Hunt v. East Dorset Health Authority* [1992] 2 All E.R. 539 and Civil Legal Aid (General) Regulations 1989, reg. 63(3)).

Types of authority

11–04

On receiving instructions, counsel should satisfy him or herself that any necessary authority has been obtained and that a copy of the certificate together with any amendments and or authorities are included with the instructions (Civil Legal Aid (General) Regulations 1989, reg. 59(2), see also *Robyn Hayley Hunt v. East Dorset Health Authority*).

When applying for authority for counsel the solicitor should make it entirely clear whether authority is sought to:

(a) brief leading counsel alone;

(b) brief leading and junior counsel;

(c) instruct leading counsel alone; or

(d) instruct leading and junior counsel

and should submit the application in good time with sufficient information for the decision to be made. There is no right of appeal against a refusal of authority but the area office must give reasons for the refusal and the application may be renewed at any time.

An authority for *"briefing counsel"* in respect of a hearing only covers the brief to appear itself, any necessary conference/consultation on the brief *after* its delivery and, in Court of Appeal cases, preparation of the skeleton argument. It does not cover any conference/consultations or other work done on instructions before the delivery of the brief (*Din v. Wandsworth London Borough Council (No. 3)*).

An authority for *"instructing counsel"* is wider than one for "briefing counsel." It covers the involvement of counsel generally in the further conduct of the proceedings *including* being briefed to appear, subject only to assessment/taxation.

An authority for *"instructing leading counsel alone"* permits him to settle pleadings or draft such other documents as are normally drafted by junior counsel where he has agreed to appear as an advocate without a junior.

If an authority is given to instruct leading counsel it should be made quite clear whether this includes the continued employment of junior counsel in addition to leading counsel or whether leading counsel alone should be employed. Fees outside the authority will be disallowed (but see above). Leading counsel may not settle an application for leave to appeal to the House of

Lords, although authority may be granted for him to advise on the merits of such an appeal but only where he conducted the appeal hearing in the Court of Appeal.

In House of Lords cases the following authority wordings will normally be used:

(a) Authority is included to instruct leading and junior counsel but only after leave to appeal has been obtained.

(b) Authority is included to instruct leading counsel alone but only after leave to appeal has been obtained.

These authority wordings reflect the following considerations:

(a) The House of Lords will not authorise payment of leading counsel's fees for settling the petition for leave (Practice Direction (HL) 1.9 [1996]).

(b) Applications for leave are generally dealt with without an oral hearing. If there is an oral hearing the House of Lords directions only provide for the payment of junior counsel's fee (Practice Direction (HL) 4.13 [1996]).

(c) A conference (or consultation with leading counsel) before leave is obtained would not be considered to be justified on taxation and if specific authority from the area office is sought in that regard it would be likely to be refused.

See also NFG 10, para. 10–04, p. 160 as to House of Lords cases.

11–05 Factors taken into account

Factors taken into consideration by the area office will include:

(a) the reason for the application. If it is merely that the case is of great importance to the assisted person (*e.g.* a parent in opposed care or adoption proceedings) or because the other side has instructed counsel (in summary proceedings), leading counsel or more than one counsel (in other proceedings), it is likely that this will not be sufficient on its own to persuade the area office to grant;

(b) if a junior counsel already instructed has been appointed leading counsel, the decision may depend on the date of the appointment and whether the leading counsel is prepared to continue to act as a junior and, if so, for how long (see below);

(c) the relevance of the abolition of the two counsel rule which will make authority for leading and junior counsel inappropriate, unless the particular circumstances are such that leading counsel is not prepared to act without a junior (see below);

(d) whether or not the client has agreed to the instruction of leading or additional counsel where the additional cost may affect the amount of the statutory charge. If the client has not been informed of the position the propriety of any authority may be queried on taxation (see *Re Solicitors (Taxation of Costs)* [1982] 2 All E.R. 683);

(e) in the case of summary proceedings, authority is likely to be granted where the case poses:

    (i) unusually complex evidential problems; or

    (ii) novel or difficult points of law

but not if the reason for instructing counsel is:

    (i) that the case is contested, protracted or involves the cross examination of witnesses or arguments on points of law;

    (ii) the personal circumstances or convenience of the solicitor; or

    (iii) it would be more appropriate to instruct a solicitor agent.

Authority to instruct Queen's Counsel is only needed where Queen's Counsel will be acting as such. When a junior who has been instructed takes silk, the area office will, on an application for authority for him to continue as a leader, take the following into account:

(a) Queen's Counsel is permitted, and should normally be willing at any time before the first anniversary of his appointment as Queen's Counsel, to do any ordinary work of a junior in any proceedings he was instructed to settle before his appointment;

(b) he may, at his discretion, continue to act as a junior for an unlimited time, *inter alia*, in a civil suit in which he was instructed before his appointment as Queen's Counsel and appeared as a junior at the trial or on an appeal before the first anniversary of his appointment;

(c) except as above he should refuse to act as a junior after the first anniversary of his appointment as Queen's Counsel unless, in his opinion, such a refusal would cause harm to the client. In that event he may, at his discretion, continue to act until the second anniversary of his appointment;

(d) in the event of Queen's Counsel not electing or being able to continue as a junior it is open to a solicitor to instruct a fresh junior.

If, however, authority is sought for leading and junior counsel (as opposed to leading counsel alone), the area office will bear in mind that, in view of the abolition of the two counsel rule, leading counsel may accept instructions to appear as an advocate without a junior. Where the area office grants authority for leading counsel this will be restricted to leading counsel alone, unless the area office is satisfied that leading counsel would be unable to conduct the case properly unless a junior was also involved. A further application for a wider authority can of course be made if it becomes clear that this is leading counsel's view in the particular case.

EMPLOYMENT OF EXPERTS, INCURRING UNUSUAL EXPENDITURE AND OBTAINING TRANSCRIPTS OF PROCEEDINGS   11–06

Authority is not needed if the solicitor is prepared to take his chance of being allowed the costs on assessment or taxation, but it is required if the solicitor wishes to safeguard himself on assessment or taxation. See also Legal Aid and Solicitors' Professional Conduct, p. 740 below as to the payment of witnesses.

Authority will be granted if the area office is satisfied that the steps are necessary for the proper conduct of the proceedings. Applications must be made in good time and with sufficient information to make the decision.

There is no right of appeal against a refusal of authority but the area director must give reasons for any refusal and the application can be renewed. The area director must either grant or refuse any application which is made.

NOTE:

1. *If authority is granted, it will specify the maximum fee payable for any report, opinion, expert advice (or transcript). If the ultimate fee is difficult to predict, an initial sum may be authorised to establish the benefit and costs involved in undertaking further work.*

2. *Solicitors are expected to identify and instruct appropriate experts direct (rather than through any agency or third party whose involvement is considered to be an unjustifiable expense).*

3. *Where a partner or employee (including a solicitor employee) of a firm advising or acting for a client is involved in the provision of non-legal services then authority will be refused unless the area office is satisfied as to the following:*

   (a) *The business providing the service (e.g. photography) has been legitimately set up and does exist as a separate entity.*

   (b) *Those involved appear to have the necessary expertise to undertake the work involved.*

   (c) *It appears unlikely that those involved would have to give evidence—other than formal evidence.*

   (d) *The expenditure is justified in terms of the work to be undertaken and the amount involved, at least one other estimate being available.*

   (e) *The client has been informed of the position and agrees that the disbursement should be incurred using the business connected with the solicitor. Principle 15–04 of the "Guide to Professional Conduct of Solicitors" refers.*

   This reflects the private client position and is to ensure that the client's interests are protected, having particular regard to any contribution payable by the client and the possible operation of the solicitor's/statutory charge.

   These principles apply equally to claims for payment/payments on account as well as to legal advice and assistance and criminal legal aid.

4. *The area office will not grant an authority for an item which would not be recoverable applying the normal principles of assessment/taxation.*

5. *See para. 11–09 below regarding assisted persons' expenses.*

11–07 Factors which may influence the area office

These will be:

(a) the total financial commitment as far as an expert is concerned, including the cost of obtaining a report and tendering evidence;

(b) whether the assisted person has agreed to costs which may increase the amount of any statutory charge.

Costs

Payment may still be allowed on taxation even if the solicitor fails to apply for or to obtain authority. Note, also that costs in excess of the authority obtained can be claimed (see NFG 14, para. 14–33, Costs Appeals Committee decision CLA 19).

ASSISTED PERSONS' TRAVEL COSTS AND OTHER EXPENSES

Basic principle and background

The basic principle is that costs, whether paid by the client or the legal aid fund, are in reimbursement of the solicitor's profit costs, counsel's fees and disbursements properly and reasonably incurred.

Since the solicitor is instructed by the client, it is only in limited circumstances that the solicitor could properly incur a disbursement in relation to his client's own expenses, *e.g.* travel costs.

R. v. Legal Aid Board, ex p. Eccleston

The case of *R. v. Legal Aid Board, ex p. Eccleston* (QBD April 3, 1998, *Law Society's Gazette* May 20, 1998, *The Times*, May 5, 1998) is important as the law has now been clarified.

The area office refused to grant prior authority for the assisted person (who lived in Liverpool) to incur the assisted person's travelling costs to see a consultant psychiatrist in Harley Street, London, in connection with his proposed action for damages against the local authority.

One of the area office's grounds for refusal was that authority under regulation 61 of the Civil Legal Aid (General) Regulations 1989 could not be given in respect of an assisted person's own expenses in attending his own legal or medical advisers, as such expenses would not be allowed on taxation. The area office considered that the Board did not have power to authorise such expenditure.

The assisted person challenged the area office decision by way of judicial review proceedings. Mr Justice Sedley concluded that the assisted person's travel expenses could amount to a proper solicitor's disbursement for which the Board could grant prior authority if the assisted person needed to see an expert whose report was essential for the proper conduct of the proceedings, and the assisted person could not otherwise afford the expenses involved in travelling to see that expert.

Implications of the judgment

The implications of this judgment are potentially wide-ranging and will affect both costs assessments and applications for prior authority made under regulation 61 of the Civil Legal Aid (General) Regulations 1989. Such applications will normally be made under regulation 61(2)(d), *i.e.* performing an act which is either unusual in its nature or involves unusually large expenditure.

Whilst the amount requested is unlikely to be unusually large, the fact that the request concerns a personal expense of the assisted person may arguably make the expense unusual in its nature.

The solicitor is not, of course, obliged to seek a prior authority. In future, such expenses may be recoverable on taxation or assessment as a disbursement provided that they have been reasonably incurred and are reasonable in amount. If the expense is allowed as a disbursement on taxation or assessment and the client recovers or preserves money or property as a result of the proceedings, then it will serve to increase the assisted person's statutory charge liability. This type of expenses will generally not be recoverable *inter partes* (as an item of costs as opposed to part of a special damages claim), but may, in future, be recoverable on a legal aid taxation. Similar principles apply where the bill is assessed by the Board.

GUIDANCE

1.   Assisted persons' travel costs to attend court

1.1   The position has not been affected by the judgment in *R. v. Legal Aid Board, ex p. Eccleston.*

1.2   Any person attending court, whether as a party, or as a witness called or reasonably intended to be called to give evidence, is entitled to recover their expenses as to:

    (a)   loss of income;

    (b)   travel;

    (c)   hotel expenses;

    (d)   subsistence.

1.3   A solicitor may pay these expenses on behalf of his or her client and then include the payments in the solicitor's bill of costs as they would generally be recoverable as a disbursement. Receipts should be produced where relevant.

1.4   The usual principles as to reasonableness apply. If it was unreasonable for the client to attend the hearing in furtherance of his or her case, *e.g.* because there was no intention that the client would give evidence, or the hearing was an interlocutory hearing where the client's presence was not strictly necessary, then the disbursements would not normally be allowed.

1.5   The expenses must also be reasonable as to amount and could be expected to fall within the following categories:

    (a) *Loss of income:* only actual losses are claimable, therefore if the client is still paid while attending court, no notional loss of income is claimable.

    (b) *Travel costs:*
        (i)   travel by car at the mileage rate (currently 36 pence per mile);
        (ii) reasonable public transport costs: this will cover travel by the most economical and direct method. It would not generally be reasonable to allow a first class fare.

Travel by coach may often be more economical than travel by rail;

(iii) hotel expenses: accommodation charges vary considerably across the country and it is difficult to give guidelines on specific amounts. It would be reasonable for accommodation to be of an adequate, but not luxurious standard;

(iv) subsistence: this would include reasonable expenditure on meals and non-alcoholic beverages, but not items such as cigarettes, newspapers etc.

1.1 Note also the existing guidance in point of principle CLA14 (NFG14, para. 14–29).

2. Assisted persons' travel costs to attend experts

2.1 Following the *Eccleston* judgment, an assisted person may be entitled to recover his or her travel expenses in connection with attending a medical or other expert. In his judgment, Mr Justice Sedley determined that the client must be "impecunious" and that the expense must be necessary "in order to make or keep the case viable". When considering an application for prior authority in connection with such expenses the following criteria should be applied.

(a) It must be demonstrated that the expenditure is necessary to keep the proceedings viable. In other words the test is that the litigation would not be able to continue or would fail unless this expense is met.

(b) The assisted person must establish that he or she does not have the resources to meet the expense. The fact that a litigant is in receipt of social security benefits or legal aid does not automatically satisfy the test of "impecuniosity". The assisted person should provide a full breakdown of weekly income and outgoings, together with capital resources, to demonstrate that he cannot afford to meet the particular expense. A relatively small expense is unlikely to justify the grant of a prior authority and should not generally be allowed on assessment unless the client is impecunious. This test will be more difficult to satisfy where the amount is small, although each case should be determined according to its individual circumstances.

(c) If the expert is based locally, then it would not generally be reasonable for the assisted person to seek financial assistance from the Board to attend the appointment. This is akin to a visit to the assisted person's own solicitor's office. An application for prior authority or payment should generally be refused in these circumstances, unless the assisted person can demonstrate that he or she is impecunious and that the proceedings would otherwise fail.

(d) If the expert is based some distance from the client's home

169

and the court where the case would be dealt with, justification should be provided as to why a local expert should not or could not be instructed. The solicitor should set out the steps which had been taken to identify an appropriate local expert, *e.g.* by reference to the Law Society Directory of Experts. It would not generally be reasonable to instruct a distant expert simply to avoid delay if adequate expertise is available locally.

The test should be based on the nature of the expertise available. It may be appropriate to instruct an expert outside of the local area if he or she has specific expertise which is unavailable locally or a limitation period is approaching and the assisted person could not be seen promptly locally (provided that the assisted person and his or her solicitors were not responsible for the delay in instructing an expert). The nearest expert with appropriate expertise should be used, *e.g.* it is not necessarily justified to use a London expert in a Manchester case if an appropriate expert is available in Liverpool.

(e) The assisted person must justify why he or she needs to attend the meeting with the expert, *e.g.* if a physical examination is necessary, then clearly it would be reasonable to do so.

(f) The applicant must provide a full breakdown of the proposed expense.

(g) Any available alternative sources of funding should be considered (see also paragraph 5 below).

2.2 Before granting an application for prior authority the area office should take into account all the above criteria when determining whether it is necessary for the proper conduct of the proceedings to incur the expense. If the authority is refused written reasons must be provided for the decision (regulation 62 of the Civil Legal Aid (General) Regulations 1989).

2.3 When considering applications area offices should also consider whether a private client of moderate means would incur the expenditure in all the circumstances of the particular case.

2.4 Where an assisted person is required to submit to a medical examination at the request of the other side, it is normal for those expenses to be borne by the party requesting the examination. In those circumstances, the expense is generally settled in advance and would not usually form part of the assisted person's costs. If the expense had not already been paid by the opposing party, it should be claimed as an inter partes item in the bill. Prior authority should be refused.

2.5 Note also the existing guidance in point of principle CLA 19 (NFG 14, para. 14–34) to the effect that costs in excess of any prior authority may nonetheless be allowed on costs assessment/taxation.

3.   Assisted persons' travel costs to attend legal advisers (*e.g.* conference with counsel)

3.1   The same criteria as above should be applied. It would generally not be reasonable for the assisted person to seek prior authority to cover such expenses unless the above criteria can be met, *e.g.* where attendance in conference with a specialist counsel in London was essential before counsel could review the merits of the case.

4.   The costs of an expert attending on the assisted person

4.1   The general principle is that litigants are expected to visit their professional advisers unless they are unable to do so.

4.2   It is generally more economical for the assisted person to visit the expert rather than vice versa as the attendance of an expert on the assisted person would involve a claim for both travel and incidental expenses *and* the time spent in both travelling and the attendance.

4.3   Prior authority for an expert's costs of visiting the litigant should only be granted in exceptional circumstances, *e.g.* where the assisted person is unable to visit the expert due to physical incapacity or the visit itself is the purpose, *e.g.* assessing the litigant at home.

5.   Assisted person's travel costs to hospital

5.1   Hospitals will pay the fares of patients attending for NHS treatment if they are in receipt of income-based Jobseeker's Allowance, disability working allowance, income support or family credit, or they are covered by a low income exemption certificate issued by the Benefits Agency's Benefits Unit.

6.   Other travel and related expenses

6.1   The above covers the most common scenarios; however, other types of application of a similar nature may be made, *e.g.* the costs of travel pursuant to a court order for interim contact with a child, attendance at a social services case conference/assessment centre/family mediation appointment, etc. If the expense would have arisen even if the person was not legally aided i.e. because it arose due to the circumstances generally rather than directly and solely as a consequence of the proceedings or proposed proceedings, then it does not constitute a disbursement and must be refused. If the expenses arise as part of the implementation of a court order or agreement, then they do not form part of the assisted person's costs (but are rather the consequences of implementation) and applications for prior authority/payment should be refused.

6.2   Each application should be considered on its own merits applying the criteria set out in paragraph 2.

12. SPECIAL DUTIES AND RESPONSIBILITIES OF SOLICITORS AND COUNSEL

12–01 **ARE THERE SPECIAL DUTIES AND RESPONSIBILITIES IMPOSED ON SOLICITORS AND COUNSEL WORKING UNDER A LEGAL AID CERTIFICATE?**

The rule is that the area office needs to be satisfied that legal aid money is being used for proper purposes. It is entitled to receive reports from solicitors and counsel in various circumstances, so that it can decide whether or not legal aid should continue.

The General Council of the Bar has also issued guidance on the contents of opinions prepared for the purposes of legal aid (see p. 737). If the guidelines are not followed and the area office does not have the necessary information to enable it to decide whether to extend or continue legal aid, the opinion will be returned to the solicitor for clarification or amendment. It is unlikely that further costs would be allowed on taxation/assessment for any such clarification or amendment.

Note that professional privilege does not prevent disclosure of information (Civil Legal Aid (General) Regulations 1989, reg. 73).

12–02 The main circumstances in which reports are necessary are:

(a) suspected abuse of legal aid by the assisted person (reg. 67);

(b) reasons for a solicitor or counsel refusing to act or giving up a case or having doubts about whether he should continue to act (regs. 67 and 69);

(c) where the assisted person no longer has reasonable grounds for being involved in the proceedings, has required the proceedings to be conducted unreasonably (so as to incur an unjustifiable expense to the fund) or it is unreasonable in the particular circumstances that he should continue to receive legal aid. Regulation 77 imposes an obligation to discharge the certificate in any of these circumstances;

(d) when the area office calls for information about the conduct of proceedings (reg. 70) (see NFG 14, para. 14–15 and also NFG 9, para. 9–14 regarding costs conditions);

(e) an assisted person declines to accept a reasonable offer of settlement or a payment into court (reg. 70);

(f) a legal aid certificate is issued to another party to the proceedings (as it may no longer be worthwhile to pursue the matter (reg. 70, see also NFG 7);

(g) an assisted person has died or become bankrupt (reg. 71);

(h) work under the certificate has been completed or cannot be completed for some reason (reg. 72);

(i) where property is recovered or preserved by someone who has or had a legal aid certificate in the proceedings (reg. 90(1) and reg. 3). See also NFG 16, para. 16–23(d).

NOTE:

1. *There is a general duty on assisted persons to co-operate and provide information or documents when required to do so by the area office (reg. 66A). Failure to do so can lead to discharge or revocation of the assisted person's certificate.*

2. *The solicitor and any counsel instructed are under an obligation to report to the area office under regulation 67 where they have reason to believe that the assisted person has required his case to be conducted unreasonably so as to incur an unjustifiable expense to the fund, has required unreasonably that the case be continued or has intentionally failed to supply information or knowingly made a false statement or representation (whether as to means or merits). Regulation 67(2) imposes an obligation to report where the solicitor or counsel is uncertain whether it would be reasonable for him to continue acting for the assisted person. On this basis, if at any stage the assisted person's solicitor or counsel consider that there is no longer a reasonable prospect of success, that nothing worthwhile is to be gained from continuing with the case or that for any other reason it seems unreasonable for the assisted person to receive legal aid, then it is their duty to report to the area office. A report should also be made in such circumstances, even where the solicitor and counsel do not consider it necessary to give up the case (Iverson v. Iverson* [1966] 1 All E.R. 258). The duty to make a report may arise in a number of circumstances including: where it becomes apparent that an action, although properly begun, has little prospect of success (*Neill v. Glacier Metal Co. Ltd* [1985] 1 Q.B. 16); where it becomes obvious on discovery that a case is bound to fail (*Edwards v. Edwards* [1958] P.235); where, in connection with an appeal, the circumstances have radically changed since the hearing in the court below (*Minkley v. Minkley* [1953] 1 All E.R. 1176, DC); where there is a good cause of action but any judgment is likely to prove fruitless, particularly bearing in mind the Board's statutory charge on any damages or other property which is recovered; where there will be no advantage to either party (*Morris v. Zbytniewska* (1967) 111 S.J. 520); where the assisted person unreasonably refuses to accept the advice of his solicitor and counsel that he should accept on offer of settlement (*R. v. Area Committee No. 14 (London West) Legal Aid Area, ex p. Dhargalkar* [1968] 1 All E.R. 225, CA). An offer should be reported if it appears to be a reasonable offer by the other side in the light of the merits of the case, even if (because of the statutory charge) the client would personally have little to gain from the offer.

   The duty to report also arises where it is thought to be unreasonable to continue with part only of the proceedings covered by the certificate (*McGregor v. McGregor* (1964) 108 S.J. 303) and in the specific circumstances of regulation 70 which includes a duty to report in relation to any payment into court (see Note 5 below).

   It should also be noted that the solicitor should not blindly follow counsel's advice but must exercise his own judgment (see *Davey Chiesman v. Davey Chiesman* [1984] 1 All E.R. 321, CA).

3. On longstanding certificates reports may be called for by the area office. If so, the solicitor will be required to certify that it is reasonable for legal aid to continue. Failure to report may lead to discharge of the certificate. See also NFG 9, para. 9–14 and NFG 14, para. 14–15.

4. The solicitor and any counsel should be mindful of the fact that where the assisted person has no conflict of interest with another party sufficient to justify the additional costs of separate representation (by separate solicitors and/or counsel), it may be appropriate for one of the solicitors to represent the assisted persons and/or for there to be a joint instruction of counsel. This applies to all cases, but may be of particular relevance in cases concerning child care.

   Failure to consider this at any appropriate point(s) may lead to costs being disallowed on taxation/assessment (in the event of work being unnecessarily duplicated). Should the assisted person decline to accept advice in that regard this must be reported to the area office under regulation 67(1)(a) of the Civil Legal Aid (General) Regulations 1989 and the show cause procedure may be invoked under regulation 77 (on the basis of unjustifiable expense to the fund).

5. Solicitors should be mindful that, whilst their duty to report on offers of settlement only arises when an offer is unreasonably refused by the assisted person, the duty arises in respect of **any** payment into court that is declined. The regulations make the distinction because of the costs consequences of a refusal of a payment into court. A solicitor reporting on a refused payment into court should provide an up to date report on the case, its estimated value, the costs incurred to date, the costs to be incurred and the solicitor's view on the payment made.

12–03 The court has power to refer suspected abuse of the legal aid scheme direct to the area office (reg. 68).

13. DISCHARGE AND REVOCATION OF CERTIFICATES INCLUDING REPRESENTATIONS

13–01 IN WHAT CIRCUMSTANCES WILL A LEGAL AID CERTIFICATE BE TERMINATED BY DISCHARGE OR REVOCATION?

The rule is that in certain circumstances the area office must revoke or discharge the certificate. In other circumstances there is an obligation to take action, but an option as to whether to revoke or discharge. In other circumstances there is an option as to whether to revoke or discharge at all (Civil Legal Aid (General) Regulations 1989, regs. 74 to 86).

WHAT IS THE DIFFERENCE BETWEEN REVOCATION AND DISCHARGE?   13–02

Solicitors and counsel will be paid out of the legal aid fund in either event. The difference lies in the effect on the assisted person who, on revocation, will (except when considering the rights of unassisted parties to claim costs out of the legal aid fund) be regarded as never having been legally aided. He or she will have a legal liability to reimburse the legal aid fund for any costs paid out on his or her behalf. On discharge, the assisted person will stay legally aided to the date of discharge.

WHAT ARE THE CIRCUMSTANCES IN WHICH A CERTIFICATE WILL BE   13–03
REVOKED OR DISCHARGED?

(See para. 13.08 below for guidance on revocation or discharge under regulation 78 or 79.)

(a) Assisted person over income limit (emergency certificate—revocation obligatory; substantive certificate—discharge obligatory).

(b) Assisted person over capital limit (emergency certificate, if contribution would exceed costs—revocation obligatory; substantive certificate—in some circumstances, discharge obligatory).

(c) Assisted person no longer having reasonable grounds for the proceedings (discharge obligatory).

(d) Assisted person having required proceedings to be conducted unreasonably so as to incur unjustifiable expenses to legal aid fund (discharge obligatory).

(e) It being unreasonable for assisted person to continue to receive legal aid (discharge obligatory).

(f) Assisted person having failed either to attend for interview or to provide documents to the area office or (in the case of an emergency certificate) to accept offer of a substantive certificate (revocation or discharge option).

(g) There having been an abuse of legal aid in the form of untrue statements by the assisted person or a failure to provide material information (revocation or discharge option). Note that conduct in relation to one certificate can be used as a ground for the discharge or revocation of another certificate or certificates.

(h) Assisted person having consented to discharge or having died or having been made bankrupt or in arrears with contribution (discharge option). The assisted person remains liable for his contribution until discharge and for any accrued arrears after discharge (see NFG 5, para. 5–04(a)).

(i) The proceedings having been disposed of or work under the certificate having been completed (discharge option). Note that wardship certificates are discharged on the conclusion of the (initial) application for which they were granted.

(j) The period allowed for the duration of the certificate having expired (emergency certificates only—revocation or discharge option).

13–04 WHAT IS THE EFFECT OF APPEALING AGAINST REVOCATION OR DISCHARGE?

While an appeal is pending to the area committee the status of an assisted person remains at large, but the retainer of the assisted person's solicitor does not determine unless and until the appeal has been heard and dismissed and any required notice has been served at court (see Civil Legal Aid (General) Regulations 1989, regs. 82 and 83).

Where an appeal against discharge or revocation is dismissed, the discharge or revocation will be upheld and effective from the date of the area office decision.

The area committee on appeal has wide powers to determine any appeal in such manner as appears to it to be just. For example, an appeal against a revocation could reinstate the certificate, uphold the revocation, or convert the revocation into a discharge. Where a certificate is reinstated on appeal, unless the area committee decides otherwise, the effect will be that:

(a) The decision of the area office will be treated as set aside and the assisted person will (subject to the points below) be treated as assisted throughout.

(b) In principle solicitors may ultimately claim payment from the legal aid fund for work done whilst the appeal is pending. This will only be in cases of real urgency as it will usually be unreasonable to carry out such work until the area committee decision is known, especially as the normal practice of the Board is for solicitors to be instructed to cease work when a show cause letter is issued.

(c) Where the area office has placed a formal limitation or condition on the certificate prior to discharge or revocation, the scope of the certificate may not be increased retrospectively so any work done pending appeal must either be within the scope of the certificate or else carried out on a private basis.

(d) Contributions cease from the date of discharge or revocation, and will not be reclaimed retrospectively, but will restart from the date of reinstatement.

(e) The assisted person will be treated as protected against costs orders prior to reinstatement save where the certificate is or becomes spent (see NFG 15, para. 15–02). Any costs order made between withdrawal of legal aid and reinstatement may need to be amended to ensure that such costs cannot be enforced until there has been a determination under section 17.

13–05 REPRESENTATIONS AGAINST THE GRANT OF A LEGAL AID APPLICATION OR THE CONTINUATION OF A CERTIFICATE

Anyone can make representations against the granting of an application for legal aid or the continuation of a legal aid certificate, but it is usually the opponent, their solicitors or another party in the proceedings who does so.

Anonymous representations are sometimes received. It may or may not be possible to action these, depending on the *nature, clarity and the amount of detail provided* of the allegations made but where, in the case of merits representations, sufficient information is provided to justify it, the assisted person's solicitor will be asked to provide a report to the area office.

Representations can be on either legal merit/reasonableness (merits) or financial eligibility (means), or both; and can be against the granting or the continuation of a certificate.

Representations should be made in writing to the relevant area office, with the assisted person's name and reference number, if known, clearly stated at the top of the letter. The letter should be boldly marked "Representations".

Those making representations will receive a leaflet from the Board which explains the process for handling representations.

Representations against the continuation of a certificate

(a) Merits representations

Merits representations are dealt with by the area office which issued the certificate. Area offices will aim to ensure that resources are diverted towards dealing with those representations which reasonably appear to be capable, within the time frame available, of affecting the continuation of legal aid. Criteria have therefore been adopted to allow those representations which are unlikely to make any difference to the continuation of legal aid to be rejected at the outset.

Representations are likely to be rejected in the following circumstances:

(i) The representations cover matters that have already been taken into account and no information has come to light subsequently to change the view taken at that time.

(ii) Insufficient time remains before trial to investigate the representations. As a general rule, representations received less than 14 days before the trial date will be rejected, although before doing so the area office will carefully consider the seriousness of the representations and the possibility of investigating them, perhaps with a shorter, faxed show cause procedure or at least by a telephone call to the assisted person's solicitor to discuss the matter before deciding on any action. An example of a serious representation which would warrant investigation at a late stage would be a non-reported payment into court which seems to equal or exceed the estimate of quantum in the case.

(iii) The representations relate to a question of fact which should be left to the court to decide, unless the person making the representations provides independent evidence (such as independent witness statements) which cast serious doubt on the assisted person's version of events.

(iv) The representations, even if established, would not affect the continuation of the assisted person's certificate, *e.g.* they are on irrelevant matters or relate only to a small part of the assisted person's claim and the cost/benefit of proceeding with the remainder of the case would be sufficient to justify continuation.

(v) The representations relate to an offer of compromise which, on the information available, is not reasonably capable of settling the matter, *e.g.* because it falls well below the estimate of quantum supplied by counsel or the solicitor for the assisted person.

(vi) The proceedings have already concluded and legal aid has not been extended to cover any appeal, unless the representations relate to a material non disclosure which may lead to revocation of the certificate under regulation 78 of the Civil Legal Aid (General) Regulations 1989 and/or raise issues of fraud.

If the area office decides that the representations merit investigation, the assisted person and their solicitor will be given the opportunity to comment on the representations. This is because a legal aid certificate cannot be discharged or revoked in these circumstances without giving the assisted person the opportunity to show cause why the certificate should not remain in force. To do this the area office will normally have to disclose the representations themselves.

Solicitors making representations on their clients' behalf should, therefore, be aware that the area office will normally disclose such representations to the assisted person and his legal representatives without first seeking consent to do so. This represents a change from the Board's previous practice and is on the basis that solicitors making representations should be aware of the relevant regulations and the Board's duty to disclose matters to the assisted person before taking any decision.

Representations will not automatically be disclosed if they are made by the opponent in person unless consent to disclose is contained in the representations or is obviously unnecessary (*e.g.* because the letter has already been copied to the assisted person). Instead, the area office will write to the person making the representations to ask for their consent.

If the representations are made explicitly on the basis that they cannot be disclosed to the assisted person then the area office will, for the reasons already outlined, usually not be able to take any further action on them.

The assisted person and their solicitors will be given sufficient but limited time to respond fully to the representations and then the matter will be considered by the area office. It should be noted that investigations of this nature do take some time because avenues of enquiry have to be followed, the area office may have to engage in correspondence and, in many cases, the area office requires appropriate documents to be produced for its consideration. The area office will monitor progress to ensure that the representations are considered as quickly as possible.

The result of the representations will *normally* be disclosed to the representor *i.e.* whether the certificate has been discharged or revoked, or allowed to continue although there may subsequently be an appeal (see below). However, the Board's general duty of confidentiality and the confidentiality provisions of section 38 of the Legal Aid Act 1988 prevent the disclosure of any information supplied by or on behalf of the assisted person, without their consent. This means that the reasons behind the decision cannot be elaborated upon.

(b) Means representations

Means representations should be addressed to the relevant area office. Again, the aim will be to devote resources to dealing with those representations which are reasonably capable of proof and which will, if proved, affect continuing entitlement to legal aid.

The following should be borne in mind:

(i) Where an assisted person's annual disposable income or disposable capital increases by less than £750 there is no reassessment required.

(ii) Some assets are not taken into account in means assessment in any event, *e.g.* the subject matter of dispute, or motor vehicles of low value which are in regular use.

(iii) Allegations can only be properly investigated if they relate to a specific source of income or capital asset and are not merely observations on ordinary lifestyle which could be funded within the disposable income or capital limits in any event. Further, in order for allegations to be pursued, sufficient detail must be given to the area office to enable them to investigate the matter. For example, representations to the effect that the applicant is working cannot be effectively pursued unless the name and address of the alleged employer are supplied. It should also be borne in mind that the fact that somebody is working or is self-employed does not necessarily mean that they are not entitled to legal aid. Eligibility takes account of income but also makes allowances for some outgoings.

(vi) Where the assisted person or their partner is in receipt of income support or income-based Jobseeker's Allowance, which acts as a passport to civil legal aid, the Board has only limited powers to investigate the matter. Eligibility for these benefits is a matter for the Department of Social Security (DSS) and not the Board, and a person who wishes to make means representations in these cases can approach the DSS directly with information. The DSS will then inform the Board if the assisted person ceases to receive the benefits and therefore loses their automatic entitlement to civil legal aid.

The action taken by the area office may include issuing forms to the assisted person for them to provide their current financial circumstances, contacting the local benefit payment office where relevant or obtaining written confirmation from third parties, such as banks to support the applicant's/assisted person's statement of means. (See NFG 5, para. 5–01 regarding the resources of those other than the assisted person.)

The area office will take the appropriate action following the conclusion of the investigation. The assisted person will be given sufficient but limited time to respond/provide information and the area office will monitor progress to ensure that the representations are considered as quickly as possible. *Normal procedures will be followed to discharge or revoke the certificate, if appropriate.* No certificate will be discharged or revoked until after the show cause procedure has been followed (if that is required by the regulations). Again, the representor will *normally* be notified whether the certificate has been discharged or revoked, or allowed to continue although there may subsequently be an appeal (see below). (See paras. 13–03 and 13–06 regarding discharge, revocation and the show cause procedure.)

Representations against the grant of a legal aid application

The Board is unable to deal with representations unless an application for legal aid has already been submitted and a reference number allocated.

The same considerations will apply as for representations against the continuation of a certificate.

The applicant's/assisted person's right of appeal

The applicant/assisted person will have all normal rights of appeal against the refusal, discharge or revocation of their application/certificate. The originator of representations will be notified of the outcome of the appeal.

13–06   WILL THERE BE A "SHOW CAUSE" PROCEDURE AND IS THERE A RIGHT OF APPEAL AGAINST THE AREA OFFICE'S DECISION?

There will be a "show cause" procedure in all cases of revocation of a substantive (as opposed to an emergency) certificate, but for discharge it depends on the circumstances (Civil Legal Aid (General) Regulations 1989, reg. 81). The area office has to serve notice of revocation or discharge and, in those cases where the "show cause" procedure must be followed (see above), there is a right of appeal to the area committee on the same conditions as a right of appeal against a refusal of legal aid (see NFG 4, para. 4–12). The area committee will give reasons for its decision.

13–07   GUIDANCE ON THE DECISION-MAKING PROCESS—REGULATIONS 78 AND 79

Before reaching decisions on revoking or discharging a certificate for non-disclosure, area offices must make sure that they go through the necessary steps required by the regulations. A failure to address each of these steps both in the decision making process and in the reasons is likely to lead to a successful challenge. The steps to consider before revoking or discharging under regulation 78 or 79 are as follows.

13–07/1   Regulation 78—false or non-disclosure of means

There are four questions which the area office or area committee should ask:

1. Has the assisted person made an untrue statement or failed to disclose a material fact?
   NOTE: *In the light of* R. v. Legal Aid Board ex p. Doran (The Times, *July 22, 1996) a fact may be material even if ultimately it would not*

have affected the eventual assessment. For example, it is not enough for an assisted person who has failed to disclose a fact to say that the asset would have been treated as subject matter of the dispute. Material means something significant and capable of influencing the reasoning of a reasonable Legal Aid official. However, the issue of whether or not the fact would have affected the assessment may be relevant to question 2 below.

2. If so, has the assisted person used due care or diligence to avoid the untrue statement or non-disclosure?
   NOTE: *The onus is on the assisted person to satisfy the area office that he or she has used due care and diligence. The defence will not apply if the area office feels the assisted person is dishonest or has failed to be sufficiently careful when filling out the forms. The more significant and substantial the non-disclosure the harder it will be for the assisted person to satisfy the area office that due care and diligence was used. If the area office is satisfied that due care and diligence was used, the certificate can neither be discharged nor revoked.*

3. If the assisted person has not used due care or diligence, should the legal aid certificate continue in force?
   NOTE: *The power to revoke or discharge is discretionary so there may be cases where there has been non-disclosure and a lack of due diligence but nevertheless it is decided to let the certificate continue. The main factors here are the size and extent of the non-disclosure its effect on the assessment, and whether it was deliberate. If the non-disclosure was significant and was more than a mere oversight by the assisted person, the certificate should not normally continue in force.*
   However, if the area office are satisfied that the assisted person reasonably and genuinely believed that the asset in question was not material, the certificate should normally continue.

4. If the certificate will not continue should it be revoked or discharged?
   NOTE: *In deciding whether to revoke or discharge the seriousness of the non-disclosure is again the key factor. Revocation is a draconian sanction leading to the loss of costs protection and the obligation to repay all legal aid costs incurred. By contrast, discharge may be no sanction at all since even if the proceedings are continuing the assisted person may be able to apply again. The importance of the case to the individual is also relevant. Where there has been either dishonesty or serious and substantial non-disclosure, revocation should be the normal result. In cases where the non-disclosure would not have made any difference to the assessment, revocation will not usually be appropriate except in the most serious cases.*

Regulation 78—false or non-disclosure on merits   **13–07/2**

Revocation or discharge for non-disclosure not connected with means is uncommon. It is governed by regulation 78(1)(b) and (c). The fact that an assisted person's case or version of events is not accepted by the court should not normally lead to revocation or discharge under this regulation. The approach to the regulation should be the same as in means cases above, but note that there is no separate due care and diligence defence. Also the regulation requires that the act or omission must be deliberate, hence the reference to knowingly or intentionally failing. The three questions to be considered are as follows:

1. Has the assisted person either:
   (i) knowingly made an untrue statement (regulation 78(1)(b)); or
   (ii) intentionally failed to furnish material information to the area office or the solicitor when required to do so under the Regulations (regulation 78(1)(c))?

   NOTE: *The second limb of this obligation largely overlaps with the obligation to provide information and documentation required to do so under regulation 79. The main difference is that regulation 78(1)(b) is a general sanction applied where material information is withheld. It can be applied when the assisted person has failed to give information to his solicitor. The assisted person has an obligation under regulation 66 to inform his solicitor at any time of any change in his circumstances or the circumstances of the case which he has reason to believe might affect the continuation of his certificate. The assisted person's main obligation to the Board is to provide information when requested to do so. At the time of the initial application this is governed by regulation 12(3). Subsequently it is governed by the general obligation under regulation 66A. See above for the meaning of "material".*

2. If so, should the legal aid certificate continue? See 13–07/1 above.

3. If the certificate will not continue, should it be discharged or revoked? See 13–07/1 above.

13–07/3 | **Regulation 79—failure to co-operate**

The power under regulation 79 to revoke or discharge for non co-operation is a wide and general power. An assisted person has a general obligation under the regulations to attend for an interview or to provide information and documents when requested to do so by the area office. At the time of the application for legal aid this obligation is set out in regulation 12(3). Subsequently the obligation is set out in regulation 66A. Requests for information can relate to either means or merits. The three questions to consider are:

1. Has the assisted person failed to attend for interview or provide information or documents when required to do so?

2. If so, should the legal aid certificate continue?

   NOTE: *Any excuse given by the assisted person for failing to provide information should be considered. If through no fault of his/her own the assisted person did not receive the request for information, the certificate should continue. Although there is no express "due care and diligence" defence, the extent to which the assisted person has used due care to comply with the request is relevant to the discretion on whether or not to withdraw legal aid. If the assisted person receives the request for information, understands what is needed but fails to provide the information within the time specified or a reason-*

able time (say 28 days—14 days before show cause and 14 days after—or a shorter period in urgent cases), legal aid should not generally continue.

3. If the certificate will not continue should it be revoked or discharged? NOTE: *As for non-disclosure under regulation 78, the nature of the sanction and the importance of the case to the client need to be considered. It is again a question of degree, revocation being appropriate in the most serious cases or where the assisted person fails to give any reasonable excuse for the non-compliance.*

SHOW CAUSE LETTERS   13–07/4

Show cause letters must specify the act or omission which is causing the area office to consider revoking or discharging in the circumstances of the particular case.

REASONS   13–07/5

The nature and extent of reasons necessary on revocation or discharge will depend on the circumstances of the case. In the light of *ex p. Doran* it will seldom be sufficient for purely standard reasons to be given.

WHAT ARE THE INCIDENTAL EFFECTS OF REVOCATION OR   13–08
DISCHARGE?

(a) Notice has to be served by the solicitor on the court and other parties.

(b) The solicitor's retainer is determined so that costs can be taxed or assessed.

(c) The statutory charge still operates in respect of costs incurred under the certificate.

(d) The operative date of discharge/revocation is at the discretion of the area office.

14. COSTS OF ASSISTED PARTIES AND THEIR LEGAL REPRESENTATIVES (INCLUDING PRESCRIBED CIVIL HOURLY RATES)

WHAT IS THE GENERAL PRINCIPLE ON WHICH THE LEGAL AID FUND   14–01
OPERATES?

After the issue of a legal aid certificate, all legal aid moneys in that case collected or paid must go through the legal aid fund, which keeps a balance sheet in respect of each assisted person and each certificate.

The solicitor can only look elsewhere for payments in the very limited circumstances described in *Littaur v. Steggles Palmer* [1986] 1 All E.R. 780 and as permitted by regulation 107B of the Civil Legal Aid (General) Regulations 1989.

14–02 REGULATION 64 OF THE CIVIL LEGAL AID (GENERAL) REGULATIONS 1989—TOPPING UP

The case of *Littaur v. Steggles Palmer* is the first decision on the meaning of what is now regulation 64 of the Civil Legal Aid (General) Regulations 1989, which restricts payments otherwise than from the legal aid fund where a legal aid certificate has been issued. The Court of Appeal confirmed that the purpose of the regulation is to prevent an abuse of legal aid.

Save as permitted by regulation 107B of the Civil Legal Aid (General) Regulation 1989 (which applies to certificates to which prescribed hourly rates apply), solicitors and counsel may not take their taxed or assessed legal aid costs or fees and take, in addition, a "topping-up" from the assisted person, or indeed from anyone else. Neither may solicitors nor counsel avoid legal aid taxation or assessment once work has been carried out under a legal aid certificate.

Solicitors and counsel may, of course, charge privately for work carried out *before* the issue and/or *after* the discharge of a legal aid certificate.

Generally, the proceedings covered by an assisted person's legal aid certificate will be the whole action but a certificate may have a limitation restricting the steps in the action which may be taken without an amendment, for example, a certificate may cover defending proceedings and counterclaiming but be limited to all steps up to close of pleadings.

However, certificates are sometimes issued:

(a) to cover a specific step or steps in an action, and

(b) applications for legal aid are sometimes not granted in full.

For example, an application for legal aid to defend and counterclaim might be granted only to defend and the application in respect of the counterclaim might be refused. In *Littaur*, the Court of Appeal found that "proceedings" in what is now regulation 64 does not necessarily refer to the whole of an action but may refer only to a specific step in an action.

Certificates for a specific step

If a certificate is issued to cover only a specific step in an action, for example, to purge the assisted person's contempt, and on completion of that specific step, no further steps in the action are expected, the assisted person's solicitor should apply promptly, with his client's agreement, for discharge of the certificate and serve the appropriate notices of discharge.

If further steps in the action are contemplated, the assisted person's solicitor should apply promptly for an amendment of the certificate. If the amendment is refused, but discharge of the certificate has not been effected or is not yet appropriate, regulation 64 does not then prevent the solicitor from acting privately for his client in the steps for which an amendment was sought and refused.

Certificates not granted in full

If an application for legal aid is only partially granted, for example, an application for legal aid to cover a defence and counterclaim is made but a certificate is granted only to defend, then regulation 64 does not prevent the solicitor from acting privately for his client in that part of the action (the counterclaim) which is not covered by the legal aid certificate. This applies also where an application for legal aid is made to cover defending divorce decree proceedings and representation as to ancillary relief, but legal aid is granted only to cover ancillary relief. Regulation 64 does not prevent the solicitor from acting privately in defending the decree proceedings.

Before acting privately for a client in any steps in an action in which the client is legally aided, his solicitor should first either:

(a) ensure that an appropriate application for legal aid or for an amendment has been made and refused; or

(b) have his client's consent either:

(i) not to apply for legal aid for an amendment to cover the step or steps; or

(ii) to act prior to the application being determined

and in either case should ensure that he:

(a) has his client's instructions to act privately;

(b) explains what this means; and

(c) advises his client that the legal aid area office will have to be informed.

Whenever a solicitor is instructed to act privately for a client in an action in which the client is legally aided, he should inform the appropriate area office in writing, as soon as possible, explaining the reason. The very fact that an assisted person is also instructing his solicitor privately may be a matter which the area office should take into account when considering whether it is reasonable for the assisted person to continue to receive legal aid. See p. 740 for the solicitors' professional conduct requirements concerning advice to clients on the availability of legal aid.

MONEYS PAID INTO THE FUND (DAMAGES, INTER PARTES COSTS, CONTRIBUTION)—WHAT ARE THE RULES? 14–03

Moneys in (*i.e.* costs from the other party, damages and interest) have to be paid to the solicitor for the assisted party, who has to pay them to the legal aid office. When monies are paid to the Board the solicitor must state if they are costs or damages as otherwise they will be returned with a request for identification (Civil Legal Aid (General) Regulations 1989, regs. 87 and 90). Only the solicitor or the Board can give a good receipt for moneys in. It is the view of the Board that it is the duty of the solicitor to bring to the notice of the paying party the express provisions of regulation 87 and to emphasise that only the solicitor for the assisted person or, as the case may be, the Board can give a good discharge for moneys payable to an assisted person (see also NFG 12, para. 12–02(i)).

An assisted person has no personal entitlement to costs though they may be awarded in his name (*The Debtor v. The Law Society (No. 5883 of 1979)* (1981) *The Times*, February 21, CA). It is the duty of an assisted person to pursue a claim for costs if, in the same circumstances, a paying client would do so in his own interests. Ultimately regard must be had to the amount involved and the prospects of successful recovery.

Interest on costs

Interest is payable on *inter partes* orders for costs in the High Court and on most county court orders over £5,000 (see County Court (Interest on Judgment Debts) Order 1991). Interest on costs runs from the date of the order to pay costs, not the date the costs are quantified (*Hunt v. R.M. Douglas Roofing Ltd* [1988] 3 W.L.R. 975, see also *Nykredit Mortgage Bank Plc v. Edward Erdman Group (No. 2)* [1998] 1 All E.R. 305, HL). Interest on costs in respect of any period while a legal aid certificate is in force, like any other sum recovered by virtue of an order or agreement for costs, must be paid to the Board (Legal Aid Act 1988, s. 16(5)).

Where costs and interest on costs are recovered in a prescribed rates case (see below, para. 14–08 *et seq.*) the Board will retain any interest on costs as calculated at prescribed rates, but the solicitor may retain any excess interest recovered (regulations 92(1)(b) and 107B(4)). In all other circumstances interest on costs will be retained by the Board but will count as a credit on the account of the assisted person for the purposes of the statutory charge or any refund of contribution.

The area office has power to allow the solicitor to release all or part of the damages to the assisted person on condition that the solicitor retains sufficient money to safeguard the fund and pays that money to the legal aid office with an undertaking that the solicitor's claim against the legal aid fund will not exceed that amount (Civil Legal Aid (General) Regulations, reg. 90(2)).

The Board can take proceedings in its own name to enforce any order made in favour of the assisted person (reg. 91(1)(a)). The assisted person can take such proceedings in his own name *provided* he has the Board's consent (reg. 91(2)). This consent can be either by way of amendment to the certificate or in some other way, *e.g.* by letter from the area office or Debt Recovery Unit. Clearly consent should not be granted where the Board itself is taking enforcement proceedings. For the special position in relation to the recovery of costs where regulation 107(3) Civil Legal Aid (General) Regulations 1989 applies, see para. 14–14.

Post CIS

As the Board's CIS computer system is designed to automate refunds, all moneys recovered for the assisted person are still required to be paid into the fund, but subject to limited exceptions. When solicitors pay moneys into the fund they must use CIS form ADMIN4 to identify what the moneys relate to. The exceptions are:

(a) Pre-prescribed rates cases where all costs have been agreed and there is no claim on the fund; in such cases solicitors should use form CLAIM2.

(b) Prescribed rates cases where *inter partes* costs have been agreed and paid and the legal aid only costs are to be taxed or assessed. Solicitors should use form CLAIM2 and ADMIN3 following NFG 14–13, headed "Procedures post CIS".

(c) Those cases where the costs under the certificate have been paid out of the fund, recovery subsequently takes place which includes pre-certificate non-green form costs, and the solicitor is able to pay into the fund sufficient moneys to discharge the deficit on the assisted person's account. CIS form ADMIN4 must be used to notify the Board that authority is sought to retain the pre-certificate non-green form costs and to identify the amount retained. Authority will be given provided the following conditions are met:

   (i) there has been full recovery of all legal aid and pre-certificate costs from the other party;
   (ii) the amount paid in is sufficient to cover the net deficit on the assisted person's account, including any green form costs and the costs of any *inter partes* taxation; and
   (iii) the solicitor informs the Board of the amount retained.

MONEYS PAID OUT OF THE FUND (COSTS)—WHAT ARE THE RULES? 14–04

Moneys out (*i.e.* costs of the solicitor [including charges of solicitor agents which are profit costs and not disbursements], counsel's fees and disbursements) are paid out of the fund only on the basis of certification proved by either taxation by the court or assessment by the area office (Civil Legal Aid (General) Regulations 1989, regs. 100 to 122). This may include expenses payable to third parties pursuant to (implied) undertakings given by assisted persons (see *Z Limited v. A and Others* [1982] Q.B. 558; [1982] 1 All E.R. 556) but note that damages payable pursuant to (implied) undertakings given by an assisted party (*e.g.* on a Mareva injunction) are a personal liability and cannot be paid out of the legal aid fund. Note also that in some exceptional circumstances assisted persons' travel costs and other expenses can be treated as a solicitor's disbursement (see NFG 11, para. 11–09 and *R. v. Legal Aid Board, ex p. Eccleston*).

There are provisions for payments on account (see para. 14–15) but otherwise payment will only be made at the end of the case (or on termination of the solicitor's retainer) when any adjustment relating to payments on account will be made.

The regulations set out the detailed procedures for taxation, and the series of appeals which is available if costs are reduced (regs. 107 *et seq.*). Permission from the area committee is obligatory to carry in objections to taxation (reg. 113) and from the Board (*i.e.* a committee of the Board called the Costs Appeals Committee, not the area committee) to apply to the judge for review of taxation (reg. 114) or to appeal against that review (reg. 115). Applications for Regulation 114/115 authority should be forwarded to the Policy and Legal Department at Legal Aid Head Office with copies of the relevant documents which will include the Regulation 113 authority granted and the District Judge's written reasons on the objections.

The regulations also set out the detailed procedures for assessment by the area office, and appeals from its decisions (regs. 104 and 105). Costs must be assessed (rather than taxed) in the case of:

(a) all authorised summary proceedings (including care proceedings);

(b) in other cases where the retainer of the assisted person's solicitor or counsel is determined before proceedings are begun and there has been no change of solicitor or counsel under the certificate and;

(c) where proceedings have begun and the solicitor is of the opinion the total amount allowed on taxation on the standard basis for his costs and disbursements and counsel's fees (exclusive of VAT) would not be more than £500.

The solicitor can *choose* whether to have the bill taxed or assessed where proceedings have begun and he considers the amount allowed on taxation would be more than £500 but no more than £1,000 (Civil Legal Aid (General) Regulations 1989, reg. 105(3)(b)). All VAT is disregarded in deciding whether a claim falls within the assessment limit. Where the claim is in respect of legal aid only costs in a prescribed civil hourly rates case, the limits apply to the legal aid only costs, regardless of the amount of *inter partes* costs agreed and paid.

Counsel's fees are assessed or taxed with the solicitor's bill, even though counsel has a separate right of appeal against assessment or taxation (regs. 105 and 116) and is paid separately by the legal aid fund. The solicitor must keep counsel informed (reg. 112).

The instructing solicitor should use his best endeavours to secure the allowance on the taxation of a proper fee for counsel and must inform counsel's clerk of any reduction in time to give an opportunity to apply for authority for the lodging of objections within the terms of regulation 113 of the Civil Legal Aid (General) Regulations 1989. If the instructing solicitor feels unable to support before the taxing master the amount of the fees for which counsel asks, the instructing solicitor should inform counsel beforehand.

The solicitor also has responsibilities to the assisted person whether the assisted person has (reg. 119) or has no (reg. 118) interest in the outcome of taxation, as well as a duty to safeguard the legal aid fund on a taxation of *inter partes* costs. See para. 14–07 below regarding assisted persons with a financial interest in an area office assessment and the *Practice Direction: (Sup. Ct. Taxing Office) (Taxation; Practice) (No. 2 of 1992)* dated November 11, 1992: [1993] 1 All E.R. 263, where the assisted person has a financial interest in a taxation. The solicitor must, before lodging the bill for taxation, send the assisted person a copy, explain the implications and, if requested by the assisted person, give notice to the court of the assisted person's interest. The bill must be appropriately endorsed and the costs of taxation (including any taxing fee) must be separately shown as they will be borne by the legal aid fund (and not the assisted person—Civil Legal Aid (General) Regulations 1989, reg. 119(2)). The procedures are modified in respect of prescribed civil hourly rates bills (see para. 14–08, and *Practice Direction: (Sup. Ct. Taxing Office) (No. 3 of 1994) (Legal Aid Taxations)*. If the solicitor causes a loss to the legal aid fund, payment of his profit costs can be deferred (reg. 102, see NFG 16, para. 16–19).

APPEALS AGAINST AREA OFFICE ASSESSMENTS OF COSTS   14–05

Where a solicitor or counsel is dissatisfied with an assessment of costs carried out by area office staff there is a right to make written representations to the area committee—the computer system produces an appropriate notice. The committee then reviews the assessment and has power to confirm, increase or reduce it.

An appeal from the area committee to the Board's Costs Appeals Committee only lies where the area committee has certified a point of *principle* of *general* importance.

The Legal Aid Board considers that the solicitor and/or counsel should be permitted to attend before the area committee to support written representations on reviews of area office assessments. Therefore, the Legal Aid Board is recommending area committees to allow attendances by solicitors and/or counsel, at their own expense, where the attendance has been requested.

Practitioners wishing to attend before the area committee on a review must:

(a) request that their attendance be permitted when they apply for the review; and

(b) submit written representations in the usual way so that they can be made available to the committee members before the hearing.

Practitioners should note that where the solicitor and/or counsel are to be permitted to attend on a review and the assisted person has a financial interest in a civil legal aid case he/she will also be given the opportunity to attend.

Attendances will not be permitted on requests to certify points of principle of general importance nor in relation to the consideration of appeals by the Costs Appeals Committee.

WHAT HAPPENS AFTER ALL PAYMENTS IN AND OUT HAVE BEEN   14–06
MADE?

The Board will retain against what is paid out, *inter partes* costs, including any interest on post certificate costs in High Court cases (both in the original and any enforcement proceedings) and the amount of the statutory charge, and pay the balance to the assisted person (reg. 92).

RIGHTS OF AN ASSISTED PERSON WITH A FINANCIAL INTEREST ON   14–07
THE ASSESSMENT OF CIVIL BILLS

Where an assisted person has a financial interest in an assessment, review or appeal of a civil costs claim (including a claim relating to magistrates' court or family proceedings) he is entitled to make written representations to the area office, area committee or to the Board's Costs Appeals Committee within 21 days of being notified of this right (Civil Legal Aid (General) Regulations 1989, reg. 105A). An assisted person has a financial interest where he has a contribution or the statutory charge will apply. An interest should also be assumed where there is a contribution reassessment pending, the statutory charge may apply or there has been a revocation.

Where the solicitor's retainer has determined but the assisted person is likely to have a financial interest on the future conclusion of the matter, it would be prudent for the solicitor to provide the assisted person with a copy of the bill (to minimise the possibility of a subsequent complaint regarding costs).

Where an assisted person has a financial interest the solicitor has a duty to:

(a) supply the assisted person with a copy of this bill;

(b) inform the assisted person of the extent of his financial interest and his right to make written representations;

(c) endorse on the bill that the assisted person has a financial interest and that (a) and (b) above have been complied with.

This accords with the solicitor's duty in cases where the bill is to be taxed rather than assessed. The Board's claim form now includes an appropriate endorsement dealing with regulation 105A. See below* for non-CIS offices.

Where a legal representative (or counsel) applies for a review of the area office assessment by the area committee or appeals to the Board's Costs Appeals Committee on a point of principle of general importance *and* the assisted person has made representations prior to the assessment, then the legal representative must notify the assisted person of the decision to be reviewed or appealed, the grounds of appeal and the assisted person's right to make further written representations. Practitioners should note that the assisted person has no right to make representations on a review or appeal where he has not made representations prior to the assessment but that the assisted person's rights on review or appeal are not limited to those cases where the representation actually affected the amount of the assessment.

Area offices will inform assisted persons who make representations of the outcome of the assessment and will provide the legal representative with a copy of the representations where they affect the amount allowed.

Practitioners should note that if the legal representative wishes to attend the area committee meeting on a review of an assessment, then the assisted person will be informed of this and also given the opportunity to attend (see para. 14–05).

Non-CI5 offices will accept regulation 105A endorsements on the reverse of the report on case or in the form of a letter or a separate sheet attached to the bill.

A suggested form of endorsement is shown below:

> **Suggested Certification pursuant to Regulation 105A Civil Legal Aid (General) Regulations 1989**
>
> I certify that a copy of the attached bill has been provided to the assisted person, pursuant to Regulation 105A of the Civil Legal Aid (General) Regulations 1989, with an explanation of his/her financial interest in the assessment of the bill and his/her right to make written representations on the bill and thereafter on any subsequent review to the area committee or appeal to the Legal Aid Board's Costs Appeals Committee.
> I confirm that 21 days have passed since the copy bill was provided to the assisted person.
>
> (signed) ....
> solicitor
>
> (dated) ....

Where regulation 105A has not been complied with, area offices will reject the costs claim so that the Regulation can be complied with and the claim resubmitted. To minimise delay and avoid any unnecessary rejections, practitioners should forward any representations received by them to the area office with the costs claim or mark the report on case form in cases where there is no financial interest. This should be done by writing **"NO FINANCIAL INTEREST"** in bold in the top left hand corner of the form.

PRESCRIBED CIVIL HOURLY RATES

Regulatory framework

14–08

The relevant regulations are the Civil Legal Aid (General) (Amendment) Regulations 1994, the Legal Aid in Civil Proceedings (Remuneration) Regulations 1994 and the Legal Aid in Family Proceedings (Remuneration) (Amendment) Regulations 1994 (as amended). These regulations came into force on February 25, 1994 and apply in respect of civil legal aid certificates (emergency or full) issued on or after that date.

The previous remuneration arrangements continue to apply in respect of certificates issued before February 25, 1994, even if an amendment is made to the certificate after that date. If two or more legal aid certificates are issued to two or more assisted persons represented by the same solicitor for the same proceedings, and at least one was issued prior to February 25, all claims will be taxed or assessed under the old regime.

When do prescribed rates apply?

14–09

If the legal aid fund will be paying the bill, the legal representatives will be paid in accordance with the prescribed rates (unless payment at enhanced rates is justified). If the opponent is paying the bill, the solicitor may claim from the opponent the "private" rate. The prescribed hourly and item rates are set out in full in the schedule to the Legal Aid in Civil Proceedings (Remuneration) Regulations 1994 as amended (and see p. 458).

14–10   When and how can enhanced rates be claimed?

In respect of civil cases, fees at more than the prescribed rate may be allowed where, taking into account all the relevant circumstances of the case:

    (a) the work was done with exceptional competence, skill or expertise;

    (b) the work was done with exceptional dispatch; or

    (c) the case involved exceptional circumstances or complexity.

Any enhancement will be calculated as a percentage proportion of the prescribed rate. Claims on the basis of the Broad Average Direct Cost of the work plus uplift are not allowed.

In determining the percentage by which fees may be claimed regard must be given to:

    (a) the degree of responsibility accepted by the solicitor

    (b) the care, speed and economy with which the case was prepared

    (c) the novelty, weight and complexity of the case.

Generally the amount of enhancement that may be claimed is limited to 100 per cent, but in certain High Court cases the limit is 200 per cent.

In family cases fees at more than prescribed rates may be allowed where it is reasonable to do so, having regard to:

    (a) the exceptional competence with which the work was done; or

    (b) the exceptional expedition with which the work was done; or

    (c) any other exceptional circumstances of the case including, in the case of care proceedings, the fact that the solicitor was a member of the Law Society's Children Panel. (See NFG 14, paras. 14–24 and 14–26).

Practitioners may wish to refer to the case of *Re Children Act 1989 (Taxation of Costs)* [1994] 2 F.L.R. 934, otherwise known as *London Borough of A.*

14–11   Claiming costs in prescribed rates cases

If the assisted person loses
Where there is no *inter partes* costs order, the costs will be either taxed or assessed, having regard to the assessment limits. The costs will be taxed or assessed at the prescribed rates and paid by the Board in the usual way.

If the assisted person wins
    (a) *Inter partes costs agreed and paid—no legal aid only costs claim*: Where all the costs are agreed with the opponent in full and final settlement there is no change to the existing system. Solicitors must complete and submit form CLAIM 2 (Report in civil cases—costs met in part or in full by other party) to the area office.

    (b) *Inter partes costs cannot be agreed (or are agreed but not paid)*: In these cases the costs must be taxed. The taxation will be of the *inter partes* costs at the private rate and at the prescribed rate of the legal aid only costs. *Supreme Court Taxing Office Practice Direction* (No. 3 of 1994) sets out the procedures to be followed on taxation.

If the *inter partes* costs are not paid after taxation then the Board will pay from the fund (a) the *inter partes* costs taxed on the legal aid basis, and (b) the legal aid only costs. If any *inter partes* costs are recovered they reduce the deficiency to the fund.

When sufficient money has been paid in to the fund by way of *inter partes* costs to cover the amount *paid out of the fund as inter partes costs* (*i.e.* not including the legal aid only costs), then any additional *inter partes* costs recovered can be paid out.

(c) *Solicitor agrees inter partes costs and these are paid, but also wishes to claim the legal aid only costs*: Provided that the *inter partes* costs are agreed and paid, the solicitor may submit a claim for the legal aid only costs for taxation or assessment. The procedures set out below should be followed.

Agreeing inter partes costs and claiming the legal aid only costs 14–12

In prescribed rate cases, solicitors may claim for legal aid only costs where *inter partes* costs have been agreed and paid. The Board's appropriate form must be used to claim for legal aid only costs where the claim is to be assessed by the legal aid area office. It may also be used, if appropriate, where the claim is to be taxed by the court. Solicitors may seek assessment of the legal aid only costs where these do not exceed the assessment limit (regardless of the amount of the agreed and paid *inter partes* costs).

There will be two types of legal aid only costs to be claimed:

(a) items in respect of which there is no *inter partes* order;

(b) items which are covered by an *inter partes* order, but for which the paying party will not accept (full) responsibility.

When claiming the second type of costs solicitors should state:

(i) the amount claimed from the paying party in respect of each item concerned;

(ii) the amount agreed and paid;

(iii) the amount of the shortfall, calculated at prescribed rates;

(iv) solicitors, will also need to satisfy the Board/Taxing Officer, by reference to correspondence or otherwise, that the paying party refused to accept the particular item wholly or in part and justify the reasonableness of making a claim against the Board for these costs.

What are the procedures for claiming legal aid only costs? 14–13

Procedures post CIS

It will not be necessary for any money relating to the agreed costs to be paid into the legal aid fund.

If the legal aid only claim is to be assessed it will be dealt with in the normal way by the area office and if any reduction is made to the claim, the normal appeals procedure will apply.

If the legal aid only claim is to be taxed, the solicitor should send the form CLAIM 2 to the court (or the full bill) for provisional taxation. The usual taxation procedures will apply. When the taxation certificate has been received from the court, the solicitor should send the taxation certificate and the form CLAIM 2 to the area office and the Board will pay the legal aid only costs as taxed.

The solicitor should:

(a) retain the agreed and paid *inter partes* costs and sufficient damages to cover the claim for legal aid only costs. The balance of the damages can be released to the client provided the solicitor gives an undertaking for the amount of the legal aid only costs. This undertaking should be given of a form ADMIN 3;

(b) send to the area office a completed form CLAIM 2 and sufficient monies from the client's damages to cover the legal aid only costs.

Procedures pre CIS

(1) Where chargeable monetary damages have been recovered which exceed the claim for legal aid only costs and the claim for legal aid only costs is to be assessed:

Where the agreed *inter partes* costs and chargeable damages have been paid, the solicitor should retain the agreed and paid *inter partes* costs and sufficient of the damages to cover the claim for legal aid only costs. *The Board does not want solicitors to pay these damages into the fund but to retain them on behalf of the fund.* If the solicitor wishes to release a proportion of the damages to the assisted person, the solicitor may do so provided that an undertaking is provided to the area office. The amount to be entered on the undertaking should be the amount of the claim for legal aid only costs.

The figures for profit costs, disbursements and counsel's fees to be entered on the report on case form are the totals of the relevant agreed and paid *inter partes* amounts PLUS the corresponding legal aid only amounts claimed.

The area office will assess the claim and inform the solicitor of the outcome of the assessment by standard letter. If the claim for legal aid only costs has been assessed at a reduced amount the amounts allowed will be notified to the solicitor. If dissatisfied with the assessment the solicitor may seek a review by the Area Committee in the usual way.

On receipt of the notification of the assessment (or after review by the Area Committee), the solicitor may release to him/herself the legal aid only costs retained and allowed on assessment (if the claim for legal aid only costs has been reduced on assessment the balance must be refunded to the assisted person).

(2) Where the claim for legal aid only costs is to be assessed and

(a) **the chargeable monetary damages recovered do not exceed the claim for legal aid only costs; or**

(b) **no damages have been recovered; or**

(c) **damages other than money have been recovered (for example, a house),**

or where the claim for legal aid only costs is to be taxed:

In such cases the agreed and paid *inter partes* costs MUST be paid in to the fund (together, if appropriate, with any damages recovered).

In assessment cases

The solicitor should submit two copies of form CLA32 together with two copies of form CLA16 (Report on Case and Claim for Costs) to the area office along with any other relevant documents (for example, counsel's fee notes). The amounts to be entered in boxes 1, 2, 3 and 4 of the section headed "Claim for Costs" on form CLA16 are the totals of the agreed and paid *inter partes* costs PLUS the relevant amounts claimed on form CLA32. The claim will then follow the usual assessment procedure and the solicitor will be paid the total of the agreed and paid *inter partes* costs plus the legal aid only costs allowed on assessment. If the claim for legal aid only costs is reduced on assessment, a Notice of Assessment (form CLA18) will be sent showing the total of the agreed and paid *inter partes* costs and the legal aid only costs allowed on assessment. (If dissatisfied with the assessment the solicitor may seek a review by the Area Committee in the usual way).

In taxation cases

The solicitor should send the claim on form CLA32 (or the full bill) to the court for provisional taxation. The usual taxation procedures will apply. At the end of the taxation the court will send a legal aid taxation certificate (formerly called the allocatur) to the solicitor.

After the taxation, the solicitor should send two copies of form CLA16 (Report on Case and Claim for Costs) to the area office, together with the legal aid taxation certificate. The claim will then follow the usual procedure for payment of taxed bills and the Board will pay the total of the agreed and paid *inter partes* costs and the legal aid only costs allowed on taxation.

Recovering costs in prescribed rates cases   14–14

Where *inter partes* costs are taxed but remain unpaid, the Board will pay the *inter partes* costs at the prescribed rates. The Board will seek to recover any deficiency to the fund.

Whilst there is any deficiency to the fund, any costs recovered will be used to reduce that deficiency. If costs are incurred in seeking to collect unpaid costs or damages then those costs will form part of the deficiency to the fund.

When *inter partes* costs at prescribed rates have been paid out by the Board, solicitors must obtain the consent of the Area Director before beginning any recovery proceedings. Once the deficiency to the fund has been paid the solicitor will be notified that he/she may collect the additional element. This will be at his/her own expense.

If solicitors do happen to recover any *inter partes* costs whilst there is still a deficiency to the fund, these costs must be paid to the Board.

PAYMENTS ON ACCOUNT   14–15

Provisions for payment on account in civil legal aid cases are contained in regulations 100 and 101. All payments on account should be requested on form CLAIM 4. Regulation 101 provides for payment on account of disbursements, profit costs and counsel's fees in certain specified circumstances and supplements the permanent payment on account provisions in regulation 100. Regulation 101(3) contains a provision for solicitors who have had to wait six months or longer since submitting their bill for taxation and have not yet been paid.

Under regulation 100 a solicitor or counsel may claim a maximum percentage of profit costs incurred or fees for work done provided the certificate has been issued for *12 months* with further claims being possible after a period of *12 or 24 months* from the date on which a claim could first be made. The solicitor remains obliged to submit his costs and counsel's fees for taxation or assessment on conclusion of the case when any excess must be repaid on demand by the solicitor or counsel or the balance due will be paid out of the legal aid fund.

Regulation 100(6) allows a payment on account where there has been a change of solicitor (to another firm) and it appears unlikely that the costs will be taxed within six months of the determination of the original solicitor's retainer.

Regulation 101(2) allows counsel to apply for payment of 75 per cent of the amount claimed on account of his fees where six months have passed since the proceedings were concluded or the solicitor was otherwise entitled to have his costs taxed. Counsel should apply direct by completing the appropriate part of the payment application form and attaching the fee note. The aim of this regulation is to ensure that counsel is not penalised by delays in the taxation process. Generally costs are only taxed when proceedings are concluded (see R.S.C., Ord. 62, r. 8), but entitlement under regulation 101(2) can also be triggered where the Court orders taxation forthwith or where there is to be a taxation following the conclusion of a particular aspect of ongoing family proceedings.

The provision for solicitors under regulation 101(3) gives them similar rights to counsel under regulation 101(2), although it only applies to certificates issued on or after April 1, 1996.

Solicitors may apply for payment on account under regulation 101(3) where:

(a) the proceedings have concluded or the solicitor is otherwise entitled to have his costs taxed, and

(b) the solicitor commenced proceedings for taxation in accordance with the time limits laid down by rules of court, and

(c) the solicitor has not received payment in respect of those costs for at least six months since he submitted his bill.

Where the requirements are satisfied the solicitor may apply for payment of 75 per cent of profit costs. This power may be of use to solicitors who are unable to claim the sums in question under the permanent payment on account scheme in regulation 100 because the appropriate window for applying has been missed, and those who are unable to apply for hardship payments on account under regulation 101(1) because application can only be made under that regulation where it appears unlikely that an order for taxation will be made in the next 12 months.

A provision also allows franchised solicitors to claim 75 per cent of profit costs incurred to date for legal aid certificates issued in categories for which they hold a franchise contract, every six months, instead of every nine months. This is in comparison to non-franchisees, who can only claim every 12 months. The six-monthly cycle is calculated from the date of the certificate, including certificates issued prior to April 1, 1996. All claims for payment must be submitted for payment within two months after the due date, and any payments made will be net of any previous payments on account. Franchisees also receive an automatic payment on account of £250 on the issue of a certificate.

The following paragraphs apply to payments under regulation 101 which must be applied for using the Board's CLAIM 4 form:

Disbursements

(a) Can solicitors seek a payment on account of disbursements incurred under a legal aid certificate?

(a) YES—but see (b) below (reg. 101(1)(a)). Note that a payment can be sought where the certificate has been discharged or revoked (reg. 101(1A)) and also that solicitor agent's charges are profit costs, not disbursements.

(b) Can solicitors seek a payment on account of disbursements which have not yet been incurred?

(b) YES—provided that the payment is about to be incurred. Area offices should only raise queries if it is clear that the disbursement will not have to be paid within the next three months.

(c) Is there any financial limit on the amount which can be claimed?

(c) NO—but claims of under £30 must be rejected on the basis that payment would involve disproportionate administrative expense. It is open to the solicitor to make a composite application including other disbursements which will be necessary within the near future.

Profit Costs/Counsel's Fees

(a) Can an application be made for a payment on account of profit costs or counsel's fees?

(a) YES—provided that the proceedings (including an application for pre-action discovery) to which the certificate relates have continued for more than 12 months, *and* it appears unlikely that an order for taxation will be made within the next 12 months, *and* delay in the taxation of those costs or fees will cause hardship to the solicitor or counsel (reg. 101(1)(b)). The solicitor can also apply for 75 per cent of his profit

Profit Costs/Counsel's Fees—cont.

(a) Can an application be made for a payment on account of profit costs or counsel's fees?—*cont.*

costs if the relevant certificate was issued on or after April 1, 1996 where the proceedings have concluded or the solicitor is otherwise entitled to have his costs taxed and he commenced proceedings for taxation in accordance with the time limits laid down by rules of court and he has not received payment in respect of those costs for at least six months since he submitted his bill for taxation (reg. 101(3)).

(b) Must the legal aid certificate have been in force for more than 12 months before an application under reg. 101(1)(b) can be made?

(b) NO—where proceedings were commenced before the legal aid certificate was issued the solicitors acting under the certificate may seek a payment on account as soon as the proceedings have been in force for 12 months.

BUT if the certificate has only been in force for a short period it is less likely that the solicitors will be able to show hardship as the claim can only relate to costs incurred under the certificate.

(c) In a multi-party action is it necessary for the proceedings to have been in force for more than 12 months under each certificate for claims to be made under those certificates?

(c) NO—provided that proceedings have been in force for more than 12 months under a lead or test case relating to the same multi-party action.

(d) Can a claim be made where it is likely to be more than 12 months before the solicitor's bill is taxed?

(d) NO—the relevant date is the date when the *order for taxation* is likely to be made, not when taxation might be undertaken or payment made. Some claims will not qualify because, although it is unlikely that *taxation* or *payment* will take place within 12 months, the *order for taxation* is likely to be made within that period. The reg. 101(3) provision may be available for certificates issued on or after April 1, 1996 where payment is delayed at least six months from submission of the bill for taxation.

(e) Is it sufficient for the solicitor to show that delay in taxation *may* cause hardship?

(e) NO—the regulation places an onus on the solicitor to show that the delay *will* cause hardship.

(f) To establish hardship is it sufficient for the solicitor to show that non-payment under this scheme would have some effect on the firm's practice?

(f) NO—the solicitor must be able to satisfy the area office that non-payment would have a *serious* effect on the practice. The area office will require sight of the following to enable it to determine whether hardship will be caused:

— bankers' letters or other information about the firm's overdraft including the limit;
— details of steps taken to seek an increase to that limit;
— copies of bank statements for the last six months; and
— details of usual monthly income and expenditure.

The following information may also be requested if it is considered necessary to determine whether hardship will be caused in a particular case:

— details of any anticipated private client income; and/or
— details of any loans; and/or
— projected cashflow for the next six months.

(g) Is it sufficient for solicitors to point to high interest rates or the general economic climate at the relevant time?

(g) NO—the solicitor must specify the reasons why delay in the taxation in the case in question will cause them hardship. But a large bank overdraft coupled with high interest rates will be relevant in deciding whether hardship has been established.

(h) Is the size of the firm seeking the payment on account a relevant factor?

(h) YES—the ability of the firm to bear the outstanding costs must be taken into account and it will generally be easier for a small firm to establish hardship.

(i) Is the amount claimed a relevant factor?

(i) YES—if the outstanding costs are substantial it will be easier to establish hardship particularly where a small firm is concerned.

(j) Is there any limit to the amount which can be claimed?

(j) NO—there is no upper limit but if the amount claimed is less than £1,000 it is unlikely that hardship will be established. Where a number of claims are submitted at the same time, however, area offices are entitled to take into account the cumulative effect, particularly where a small firm is concerned.

(k) If hardship is established should the full amount claimed be paid?

(k) Not necessarily. The proportion allowed will depend on the particular circumstances. There may also be a deduction, to protect the fund against overpayment, where the area office considers that the solicitors may be unable to justify the amount claimed on taxation.

(l) Must the hardship result from the delay in taxation rather than from some other cause?

(l) YES—for example if costs have been agreed with the other side and fall to be assessed in the area office under reg. 105(3)(b) or reg. 106 a payment on account pending payment of those costs cannot be made as any hardship would not be as a result of delay in taxation.

(m) Where solicitors are acting for both legally aided and unassisted clients in a multi-party action can they establish hardship where no payments on account have been sought from any of the private clients?

(m) NO—in those circumstances any hardship is not at that stage as a result of delay in taxation.
BUT once pro rata payments on account have been obtained from the private clients it may then be possible for the solicitors to establish hardship.

(n) If the requirements of reg. 101(1)(b) are met at the time the application is made, can a payment on account be made even though one or more of the requirements are no longer met when the application is considered in the area office?

(n) NO—for example where proceedings are settled after an application has been made but before it has been considered, it will not be possible for the solicitors to show that it is unlikely that an order for taxation will be made within the next 12 months.

See also NFG 11, para. 11–06 for the position regarding disbursements where a solicitor, his partner or employee is involved in the provision of non legal services.

COSTS ASSESSED BY THE LEGAL AID BOARD—POINTS OF PRINCIPLE OF GENERAL IMPORTANCE

The Legal Aid Board has issued the following decisions on points of principle of general importance in connection with civil legal aid costs assessments:

14–16 **Meaning of the limitation "Limited to obtaining counsel's opinion"**

A certificate bearing a limitation containing the words "Limited to obtaining counsel's opinion" covers the obtaining of *one* opinion only (which may follow a conference). Work undertaken by a solicitor to clarify a genuine ambiguity in the opinion itself could, however, be allowed.

If, at the time of receipt of counsel's written opinion, counsel is not in a position to advise on the settling of proceedings, no further work can be carried out until the limitation is removed or amended to allow either a further written opinion from counsel or further work by the solicitor. (Legal Aid Board Reference CLA1 as amended.)

Allowance for checking the bill, signing the report on case and complying with other formalities in assessment cases

14–17

Practice Direction No. 2 of 1992 (Direction 2, paragraph 1.17) states that the drawing of a bill of costs is not fee earner work and, save in exceptional circumstances, no charge should be sought for such work. However, on an assessment to which regulation 105 of the Civil Legal Aid (General) Regulations 1989 relates, where a claim is made for preparing the bill (and the case is not exceptional justifying such a payment), consideration should be given to making a small allowance which is for the solicitor's time in checking the bill, signing the Report on Case and complying with the other requirements of the Civil Legal Aid (General) Regulations 1989 and the Legal Aid Board generally. Normally an allowance of 10–20 minutes would be appropriate for cases within regulation 105(3)(a) of the Civil Legal Aid (General) Regulations 1989 although a higher allowance may be appropriate for more complex cases. (Legal Aid Board reference CLA2 as amended.)

Failure to report a significant change

14–18

If a solicitor fails to report a significant change, which is known to him, in either the circumstances of the assisted person or the case, costs subsequently incurred may be considered not to have been reasonably incurred and may be disallowed. (Legal Aid Board reference CLA3.)

Inspection of original documents in medical negligence cases

14–19

When assessing the merits of possible medical negligence proceedings, it would not be reasonable for a solicitor to inspect the original records as a matter of course but where a solicitor has reason to believe that the copy records supplied are incomplete or inaccurate it would be reasonable for him to inspect the originals. Where cases fall within this principle, a certificate limited to obtaining or perusing medical records will cover inspection of original records. (Legal Aid Board reference CLA4.)

Rates to be allowed on assessments under regulation 105 of the Civil Legal Aid (General) Regulations 1989

14–20

Costs assessed under regulation 105 of the Civil Legal Aid (General) Regulations 1989 should be assessed to ensure that the costs allowed are those which would, not should, be allowed on a taxation on the standard basis under rules of court. The rates which would be allowed are those which are being allowed in the court where the litigation was or most likely would have been issued and conducted. The expense rate chargeable will be the broad average direct cost of doing the work as allowed by the local taxing officer or District Judge. Regard may be had to the local Law Society survey on expense rates to determine the broad average direct cost. In areas where the survey expresses an hourly rate by one single composite figure, this is only an average figure. The seniority and expertise required by the particular case will be relevant to the hourly rate allowed to reflect the true broad average direct cost of the case. (Legal Aid Board Reference CLA5 as amended.)

14–21 Consideration of unusual or substantial papers

Where claims for costs are made for perusal of unusual or substantial papers and the assessor/area committee is minded to disallow those costs in whole or in part it will normally be necessary for the papers in question to be considered. (Legal Aid Board reference CLA6.)

14–22 Consideration of medical records by solicitors in medical negligence cases

It is reasonable in medical negligence cases for the assisted person's solicitor to consider in detail copies of the medical records relevant to the issues in the case. (Legal Aid Board reference CLA7.)

14–23 Prescribed rates: enhancement: membership of Law Society's Children Panel

Membership of the Law Society's Children Panel is itself an exceptional circumstance under regulation 3(4)(c)(iii) of the Legal Aid in Family Proceedings (Remuneration) Regulations 1991 which gives a discretion to the assessing officer to allow a larger amount than that specified where it appears to him to be reasonable to do so in any particular part of the bill of costs in question.

As a general rule, where a solicitor appeared as an advocate, this is not an exceptional circumstance. Where, however, a Children Panel solicitor appeared as an advocate in care proceedings, this will be an exceptional circumstance. Whether this justifies of itself allowance of a "larger amount" is a question for the exercise of discretion, in consideration of all the circumstances of the case. An uplift in hourly rate for panel membership in cases properly lasting more than two days would normally be justified. (Legal Aid Board reference CLA8 as amended.)

14–24 Care proceedings: Enhanced rates: Possible "exceptional circumstances"

When considering a claim for enhanced rates on the basis of regulation 3(4)(c)(iii) of the Legal Aid in Family Proceedings (Remuneration) Regulations 1991 consideration should, when deciding if there are "any other exceptional circumstances" of the case, be given to whether any of the following exist:

(A) Factors which might raise an exceptional circumstance:

(i) innate difficulties of communication with the client *e.g.* mental health problems, deaf, speech-impaired, or autistic clients, or clients requiring an interpreter (although attention should first be given as to whether this has been covered by longer than normal hours of attendance being claimed);

(ii) a *conflict* of detailed expert evidence (as opposed to merely contested expert evidence, and/or a proliferation of expert witnesses);

(iii) a hearing in excess of two days without counsel;

(iv) conflict between the guardian *ad litem* and the child, where the child instructs his own solicitor;

(B) Factors which might but not necessarily would raise exceptional circumstances:

(i) detailed contested allegations of sexual or serious abuse;

(ii) a large number of parties with competing applications;

(iii) involvement of children with different needs.

The transfer of the case to a care centre or from a care centre to the High Court is indicative of complexity and weight only and is not conclusive of exceptional circumstances. Where exceptional circumstances are said to arise there must be a factor, or combination of factors in the particular case which is exceptional or are unusual in care proceedings.

The factors set out above are a non-exhaustive list. They relate to the circumstances of the case itself and not to claims for enhanced rates based on regulations 3(4)(c)(i) and (ii) of the Legal Aid in Family Proceedings (Remuneration) Regulations 1991 which have regard to the manner in which the work was done.

Where exceptional circumstances are sought to be established and solicitors seek remuneration on the basis of the exercise of the assessing officer's discretion pursuant to regulation 3(4)(c), the solicitor must precisely identify the exceptional circumstances and those specific items of work in respect of which enhancement is sought. See *Re Children Act 1989 (Taxation of Costs)* [1994] 2 F.L.R. 934. (Legal Aid Board reference CLA9 as amended.)

Non-contentious work undertaken as a direct result of a court order in family proceedings   14–25

The rates of remuneration in the Legal Aid in Family Proceedings (Remuneration) Regulations 1991 do not apply to non-contentious work undertaken on behalf of an assisted person as a direct result of a court order. The rates allowed should be those which are reasonable in all the circumstances of the case for privately funded non-contentious work. (Legal Aid Board reference CLA10.)

Enhanced rates in family proceedings   14–26

Where the criteria for paying enhanced rates set out in regulation 3(4)(c) of the Legal Aid in Family Proceedings (Remuneration) Regulations 1991 are met, the relevant authority may exercise their discretion in determining the amount of costs to be allowed in accordance with regulation 3(7) of the Legal Aid in Family Proceedings (Remuneration) Regulations 1991.

Following the decision of *Freeman v. Freeman*, February 21, 1992 (reported in Butterworths Costs Service) such claims will be assessed on the basis of the broad average direct cost of the work (the '*A*' figure) to which is added a percentage uplift (the '*B*' figure) to take into account all the relevant circumstances of the case. (Legal Aid Board reference CLA11.)

14–27   Status of medico-legal assistants as fee-earners

Work carried out by an in-house medico-legal assistant will generally be fee earning work. The hourly rate and mark up applicable will be what is appropriate in all the circumstances having regard to the nature of the work carried out and the special skills and qualifications possessed by the person concerned. (Legal Aid Board reference CLA12.)

14–28   Preparation of attendance notes

In principle, the time taken in recording and preserving information necessary to be recorded and preserved for the proper conduct of a client's affairs is allowable on assessment. (Legal Aid Board reference CLA13.)

14–29   Assisted person's and other witnesses' travelling (and similar) expenses

On the assessment of a bill, in respect of which, if it had been taxed, the County Court Rules would have applied, when considering a claim for travel or other expenses, the appropriate authority shall allow, on the assessment, such expenses as would have been allowed under Order 38 rule 15 County Court Rules on taxation.

On the assessment of a bill, in respect of which, if it had been taxed, the Matrimonial Causes (Costs) Rules 1988 would have applied, when considering a claim for travel or other expenses, the appropriate authority shall allow, on the assessment, such expenses as would have been allowed under rule 17 Matrimonial Causes (Costs) Rules 1988. (Legal Aid Board reference CLA14.)

14–30   Preparation of Annual Report on Case

Practice Direction No. 2 of 1992 (Direction 2, paragraph 1.17) states that the drawing of a Bill of Costs is not fee earner work and, save in exceptional circumstances, no charge should be sought for such work.

However, where a claim is made for preparing the Board's Annual Report on Case and claim for costs form (and the case does not itself present exceptional circumstances), consideration should be given to making a small allowance which is for the solicitor's time in preparing and submitting the Annual Report on Case. Normally an allowance of 6 to 12 minutes would be appropriate although a higher allowance may be appropriate for more complex cases. (Legal Aid Board reference CLA15.)

Applications to the European Commission 14–31

Where an application to the European Commission is an essential preliminary step in court proceedings in England and Wales, such an application would be within the scope of a certificate granted to cover such court proceedings. (Legal Aid Board reference CLA16.) (See NFG 20, para. 20–02 and note that this decision does not relate to the European Commission of Human Rights but to the European Commission of the European Union.)

Routine Letters in the Legal Aid in Civil Proceedings (Remuneration) 14–32
Regulations 1989

In Item 3 column 1 of Schedule 1 of the Legal Aid in Civil Proceedings (Remuneration) Regulations the words "which are not routine" relate to each of: (1) Letters written; (2) Letters received; (3) Telephone calls. (Legal Aid Board reference CLA17.)

Prescribed rates and non-contentious business 14–33

Remuneration under the Legal Aid in Civil Proceedings (Remuneration) Regulations 1994 or the Legal Aid in Family Proceedings Regulations 1991 includes all work undertaken in respect of anticipated or contemplated proceedings notwithstanding that no proceedings were actually issued. (Legal Aid Board reference CLA18.)

Assessment of authorised disbursements 14–34

An authority given under regulations 59, 60 or 61 of the Civil Legal Aid (General) Regulations 1989 does not place a ceiling on the fees that can be claimed in respect of the disbursement so authorised. On assessment further consideration may be given to any additional sums claimed. (Legal Aid Board reference CLA19.)

Reasons for reductions in experts' fees 14–35

Where experts' fees are reduced on an assessment and the reduction is not accepted, reasons for the reduction must be given on application. (Legal Aid Board reference CLA20.)

Prescribed rates: enhancement: membership of the Law Society's 14–36
Medical Negligence Panel

Membership of the Law Society's Medical Negligence Panel is not in itself an exceptional circumstance justifying payment of an enhanced rate under regulation 5(1)(2) of the Legal Aid in Civil Proceedings (Remuneration) Regulations 1994, but membership of the Panel may be a factor which contributes to a decision that enhanced rates are justified. (Legal Aid Board reference CLA21.)

14–37 Review and supervision on a franchised file

Time properly spent by a franchised firm reviewing and supervising files to meet the franchising criteria is time properly chargeable provided that it coincides with the stage in the proceedings at which the file would normally be reviewed and work done would be recoverable on taxation as work reasonably done having regard to the needs of the case. (Legal Aid Board reference CLA22; applies to legal aid certificates granted on or after December 1, 1998.)

15. COSTS AGAINST ASSISTED PERSONS AND THE LEGAL AID BOARD

15–01 IF THE ASSISTED PERSON LOSES, CAN THERE BE ANY PERSONAL LIABILITY FOR COSTS AGAINST THE ASSISTED PERSON OR THE LEGAL AID BOARD, OR BOTH?

The assisted person and/or the Legal Aid Board can have orders for costs made against them, but only subject to a number of restrictions and limits (Legal Aid Act 1988, ss.17 and 18).

15–02 WHAT ARE THE LIMITS ON AN ASSISTED PERSON'S LIABILITY?

The assisted person can only be ordered to pay what is reasonable having regard to all the circumstances, including:

(a) the financial resources of all the parties; and

(b) their conduct in connection with the dispute.

In assessing the resources of the assisted person for this purpose as well as on enforcement, the assisted person's house, its contents and the tools of his or her trade will be exempt. (Legal Aid Act 1988, s.17 contains the general principles; Civil Legal Aid (General) Regulations 1989, regs. 123 to 133 contain the detailed procedures.)

Section 17 Legal Aid Act 1988 is sometimes wrongly regarded as giving almost complete protection to an assisted person from costs orders. This is not so, and opponents of assisted persons could apply for determinations of an assisted person's liability under section 17 far more often than they do in practice.

Costs against an assisted person are commonly ordered "not to be enforced without leave of the court". The effect of such an order is to determine the assisted person's liability at nil under regulation 129(b) Civil Legal Aid (General) Regulations 1989. At any time in the following six years the opponent can then apply to vary the order under regulation 130 of the General Regulations if either new information has come to light about the assisted person's means which could not have been obtained with reasonable diligence at the time the order was made, or if there has been a change in the assisted person's circumstances since the date of the order.

Alternatively, an opponent may ask the court which heard the proceedings to determine the assisted person's liability (regulations 124 and 129 of the General Regulations) or may simply ask that the determination be adjourned (regulation 127 of the General Regulations).

See generally *Parr v. Smith* [1995] 2 All E.R. 1031 at 1037 and 1041 and *Chaggar v. Chaggar* [1995] 1 All E.R. 104, CA and *Ager v. Ager*, [1998] 1 All E.R. 703, CA, which held that a court of first instance has power to enforce a section 17 order made in the Court of Appeal.

Regard should be had to the fact that failure to serve notice of issue of a legal aid certificate may not affect the assisted person's costs protection (*King v. Farmeloe* 1953 1 All E.R. 614).

Note also that following the case of *Turner v. Plasplugs Ltd, The Times,* February 1, 1996, if a certificate is spent, *i.e.* everything authorised under the certificate has been done and the solicitor is acting outside its scope, then the assisted person does not receive costs protection. However, if a certificate is not spent because some of the authorised work has not yet been completed, then the assisted person does receive costs protection even for steps which are outside the measures authorised. For example, if a certificate is limited to obtaining counsel's opinion then while that is being done the assisted person counts, for the purposes of costs protection, as an assisted person for other steps in the proceedings (see *Dugon v. Williamson* (1964) Ch. 59 and *Boorman v. Godfrey* (1981) 2 All E.R. 1012).

WHAT ARE THE RESTRICTIONS ON AN ORDER FOR COSTS AGAINST THE LEGAL AID BOARD? 15–03

(a) The party claiming costs against the Board must be unassisted. He need not be unassisted at the time the order is made, but the order for costs can only be made in respect of periods when he was unassisted and was facing an assisted party (see *Re H* [1992] 3 All E.R. 380 and Legal Aid Act 1988, s.18(6)). Note that the statutory charge will apply to any section 18 order made in favour of a person who was assisted for part of the proceedings, and the fact that the charge might absorb much of the costs ordered may influence the court's decision as to whether it is just and equitable to make an order, or as to whether the unassisted party can demonstrate severe financial hardship.

(b) The proceedings must have finally been decided in favour of the unassisted party (*i.e.* there is no right of appeal or the appeal is time barred).

(c) It must be a case in which, apart from legal aid, there would be an order for costs against the assisted person.

(d) It must be just and equitable for costs to be paid out of public moneys (*i.e.* the legal aid fund).

(e) The proceedings must have been commenced by the assisted person (courts of first instance only)—see *Thew (R. & T.) v. Reeves* [1981] 3 W.L.R. 190.

(f) The court must be satisfied that the unassisted party would suffer severe financial hardship if an order were not made (courts of first instance only)—see *Hanning v. Maitland (No. 2)* [1970] 1 Q.B. 580.

(g) The court must first have considered and disposed of the liability of the assisted person for costs (see para. 15–02, above).

(h) The Legal Aid Act 1988, s.18 contains the general principles and the Civil Legal Aid (General) Regulations 1989, regs. 134 to 147 contain the detailed procedures which differ from court to court. There are a number of reported cases relating to the general principles, see those above as well as *Gayway Linings Ltd v. The Law Society* and *Megarity v. Ryan & Sons Ltd* [1982] A.C. 81. Where severe financial hardship must be shown, the unassisted party must file an affidavit of costs and resources in accordance with Schedule 2 to the Regulations. An order for costs may be refused if the affidavit does not comply fully with the Regulations (*Jones v. Zahedi* [1993] 1 W.L.R. 1445. The time limits contained in the Regulations must be strictly complied with as the Court has no general power to extend certain time limits (*Middleton v. Middleton* (1993) *The Times*, December 30, CA).

16.   THE STATUTORY CHARGE

(See para. 16–17 for the Board's standards to promote consistency of decision making and p. 698 for the leaflet "Paying Back the Legal Aid Board".)

16–01   STATUTORY AUTHORITY AND FRAMEWORK

The statutory provisions relating to the charge are contained in section 16 of the Legal Aid Act 1988 (see p. 294) and Part XI of the Civil Legal Aid (General) Regulations 1989 (see p. 402).

The underlying principle of the charge is to put the legally assisted person as far as possible in the same position in relation to proceedings as an unassisted person, whose first responsibility at the end of the proceedings is to pay whatever legal costs are not being paid by the other side. It prevents an assisted person from making a profit at the expense of legal aid and is a deterrent to running up costs unreasonably.

It is one of three financial obligations imposed on assisted persons *i.e.*:

(a) to pay any assessed contribution out of income or capital;

(b) to pay what the court considers reasonable towards the other side's costs; and

(c) to pay his/her own legal costs out of any money or property recovered or preserved (the charge). Money or property treated as subject matter of the dispute and therefore disregarded for means assessment purposes is liable to be subject to the statutory charge.

The application forms contain warnings about the effect of the charge, but the Board is firmly of the view that it is the solicitor's responsibility to ensure that the client is kept fully informed about its implications throughout the case. The Board's leaflet "Paying Back the Legal Aid Board" is reproduced at p. 698.

As with all legal aid payments the solicitor's costs and counsel's fees are paid out of the legal aid fund, not out of the charge. The solicitor and counsel must, therefore, still look to the legal aid fund for payment even though the client may bear the ultimate responsibility.

HAS THE ASSISTED PERSON BEEN SUCCESSFUL WHOLLY OR IN PART IN THE PROCEEDINGS OR OBTAINED AN OUT OF COURT SETTLEMENT WITH THE BENEFIT OF LEGAL AID? 16–02

(a) If not, the statutory charge cannot arise.

(b) If so, the charge may arise so the following questions need to be considered. The discharge of the certificate does not affect the charge liability for costs incurred during the life of the certificate and where the assisted person is no longer represented by a solicitor only the Legal Aid Board can give a good discharge for moneys payable to the assisted person connected with the action, cause or matter to which his certificate related (see also paras 16–21 and 16–23 below).

IS THERE A NET LIABILITY OF THE LEGAL AID BOARD ON THE ASSISTED PERSON'S ACCOUNT IN RESPECT OF ANY PROCEEDINGS? 16–03

First calculate the total costs paid or payable to solicitors and counsel on behalf of the assisted person, including green form costs for advice and assistance given in the same matter.

NOTE: *When considering what sums are payable by the Board "in respect of any proceedings" remember:*

1. *Proceedings means the whole proceedings, i.e. action, cause or matter (Hanlon v. The Law Society [1980] 2 All E.R. 199). So, if there is a transfer of property in one part of the proceedings, the charge on that property will cover the costs of any other part of the proceedings for which legal aid was granted.*

2. *A legal aid certificate usually covers only one set of proceedings (regulation 46 of the Civil Legal Aid (General) Regulations 1989). If a certificate covers more than one set of proceedings, the costs incurred under the certificate must be apportioned for the purpose of calculating the amount of the charge.*

3. *Proceedings do not have to have been commenced. If a settlement is reached either before or during proceedings the charge will affect all property received by the assisted person as a result of the settlement whether or not it was claimed in the potential or actual proceedings (Van Hoorn v. The Law Society [1985] Q.B. 106).*

4. *The statutory charge applies where property is recovered or pre-*

served following the discharge or revocation of the assisted person's certificate.

Having reached a decision on the total amount payable out of the legal aid fund, calculate the amount of costs (if any) paid by the other side.

NOTE: *Does the amount of costs paid by the other side exceed or equal the total costs paid or payable out of the legal aid fund? If so, there is no net liability and no charge.*

If the total costs paid or payable out of the fund exceed the amount paid by the other side, then calculate the amount of the assisted person's legal aid contribution paid.

NOTE: *Does the total of the costs paid by the other side and the contribution paid by the assisted person exceed or equal the total costs paid or payable out of the fund? If so, there is no net liability and no charge. If the total costs paid or payable out of the fund still exceed the total of the costs paid by the other side and the contribution paid by the assisted person, there is a net liability and the statutory charge may arise in respect of the balance.*

16–04   This can be shown as:

Costs paid by other side	equal to or greater than	costs paid or payable out of fund	no charge
Costs paid by other side	less than	costs paid or payable out of fund	calculate assisted person's contribution
Costs paid by other side plus assisted person's contribution	equal to or greater than	costs paid or payable out of fund	no charge
Costs paid by other side plus assisted person's contribution	less than	costs paid or payable out of fund	possible charge in respect of balance
No costs paid by the other side	nil contribution and exemption from charge or nil contribution and no recovery or preservation		legal aid fund bears all the assisted person's costs

Setting off costs

An order for costs nominally in favour of an assisted person "belongs to the Legal Aid Board" (see *The Debtor 1988 v. The Law Society (No. 5883 of 1979)* (1981) *The Times*, February 21, section 16(5) Legal Aid Act 1988 and NFG 14–03). However, the court can still order such costs to be set off against costs or damages ordered in favour of the unassisted party and the costs awarded in favour of the assisted party may not be recovered in full or at all. Where the court has not ordered the set-off of costs but it is contended that a set-off should apply, the area offices and the Debt Recovery Unit should bear in mind the approach which the courts take towards the set-off of legal costs, which can be summarised as follows:

(a) There is a general rule that it is just and equitable for mutual orders for costs to be set-off against each other so that parties only bear the net result of orders (see *Lockley v. National Blood Transfusion Service* [1992] 2 All E.R. 589).

(b) The courts will endeavour to make orders which do not unduly penalise an unassisted party and will normally allow an unassisted party to have the benefit of set-off so he is only liable for any net liability (see *Cooke v. S* [1967] 1 All E.R. 299 and *Brookes v. Harris* [1995] 1 W.L.R. 918).

(c) There may be particular circumstances where the unassisted party ought not have the benefit of the set-off and the unassisted party should pay costs ordered in favour of the assisted party in full. An example is where a wasted costs order is made against solicitors (see *Currie & Co v. Law Society* [1976] 3 All E.R. 832).

CAN MORE THAN ONE CERTIFICATE COUNT TOWARDS THE STATUTORY CHARGE?

Yes. In most cases where property is recovered or preserved under a certificate, only the costs under that certificate will be charged against the property. However, if a person has been issued with more than one legal aid certificate relating to the same proceedings, either simultaneously or subsequently, costs under the additional certificates may count towards the charge in the following situations:

(a) The charge applies where property is recovered or preserved after a certificate has been discharged (regulation 85 of the Civil Legal Aid (General) Regulations 1989). Therefore, if certificate A is issued and discharged and later certificate B is issued in the same proceedings and leads to a recovery or preservation of property, the costs under both certificates A and B will form part of the charge. But note that if recovery or preservation had taken place under certificate A, the subsequent costs under certificate B would not usually form part of the charge.

(b) There are cases where a single certificate does not represent the true account of the assisted person with the Board. Examples of this are where there happen to be simultaneous certificates in force in relation to the same proceedings, or where work is carried out on behalf of an assisted person in a multi-party action both under his own certificate and under a certificate covering generic work.

(c) The charge would always be applied where certificates have been manipulated with the intention of avoiding the charge, under the principles of *Manley v. The Law Society* (para. 16–09).

16–07 HAS MONEY OR PROPERTY BEEN "RECOVERED" OR "PRESERVED" OUT OF WHICH THE NET LIABILITY CAN BE MET IN WHOLE OR IN PART?

(a) If not, the charge does not arise.

(b) If it has, the charge does arise.

16–08 What is "recovery"?

It is where the assisted person succeeds in claiming ownership of someone else's property or possession of property to which the title was not in issue (or in compelling the sale and distribution of proceeds of sale), *i.e.* at the end of the day there is a gain for the assisted person.

16–09 What is "preservation"?

It is where the assisted person succeeds in fending off a claim by someone else to his (the assisted person's) property or to possession of his property, *i.e.* at the end of the day the assisted person keeps all or part of what he regards as his own. If he keeps only part, he may be worse off than at the start, but the charge will still arise on what he has kept (*Till v. Till* [1974] Q.B. 558; [1974] 1 All E.R. 1094). Even where there is no issue as to the title to property there may be a preservation where someone else's claim to possession is defeated (*Curling v. The Law Society* [1985] 1 W.L.R. 470; [1985] 1 All E.R. 705) or where the assisted person avoids an order for sale of the property (*Parkes v. Legal Aid Board* [1996] 4 All E.R. 271, CA).

NOTE: *In either case:*

1. *Subject to 2. below, the property or money must have been in issue in the proceedings. What is in issue is a question of fact to be determined from the pleadings evidence, judgment and/or order (*Hanlon v. The Law Society *[1980] 2 All E.R. 199).*

2. *If a settlement is reached either before or during proceedings the charge will affect all property received by the assisted person as a result of the settlement whether or not it was claimed in the actual or potential proceedings (*Van Hoorn v. The Law Society *[1985] Q.B. 106). This can include property received in other proceedings if those proceedings have been brought to an end as a result of an agreement which also effectively resolves the proceedings in which the assisted person is legally aided.*

3. *The words mean the same as in the Solicitors' Acts 1934–1974 under which a solicitor may be able to obtain a charging order on property which he recovered or preserved for his client.*

4. *In the case of* Manley v. The Law Society *[1981] 1 W.L.R. 335 the court considered the responsibility of legal advisers conducting litigation for assisted persons. The court ruled that if parties reach a settlement the legal advisers have a responsibility to the legal aid fund and should not try to manipulate the destination of the money or property so as to avoid the statutory charge. Payment to creditors was in effect payment to the assisted person and a proposed settlement for payment to creditors direct, bypassing the assisted person, failed in its intention of avoiding the statutory charge.*

5. *Solicitors are, however, perfectly entitled to—and indeed should— endeavour to minimise the areas of disagreement at an early stage and this may have the effect of reducing the property that is in issue and which can be recovered or preserved.*

DOES THE CASE COME WITHIN ANY OF THE EXEMPTIONS? 16–10

There is no short cut to looking at the detailed exemptions set out in regulation 94 of the Civil Legal Aid (General) Regulations 1989 (see p. 363). They must be considered in each case.

NOTE:

1. *The exemption of interim payments only applies while the payments remain interim. Once the final award of damages is made, interim damages are included in the calculation for the statutory charge. If at that time damages and costs recovered are insufficient to meet the charge the assisted person may be liable to reimburse the balance to the fund out of what was originally an interim payment.*

2. *Some of the exemptions in matrimonial proceedings relate solely to awards between spouses, so will not apply to awards made to intervening parties.*

3. *Arrears of periodical payments of maintenance (as opposed to the payment of a lump sum in satisfaction of liability for future maintenance) are exempt (*Stewart v. The Law Society *(1986) The Times, July 19).*

4. *Regulation 94(g) of the Civil Legal Aid (General) Regulations 1989 creates an exemption from the statutory charge in respect of any sum or benefit which, by virtue of any provision of or made under an Act of Parliament, cannot be assigned or charged. The trigger to bring the exemption into play is that provision of or made under an Act of Parliament must prevent the moneys in question from being assigned or charged. These exclusions cover various matters including state benefits, forces pay/pensions, civil service pensions and some local authority pensions. Such provisions may have consequences beyond the statutory charge as it may be that no benefit can be obtained from proceedings as the at all relevant statutory provision may con-*

213

stitute a bar on court orders, assignments, charges or agreements to assign or charge pay or pensions. However, an "earmarking" order for a lump sum payable from a pension will attract the statutory charge in the hands of the recipient as what has been recovered is a lump sum and not the pension rights themselves.

16–11 Enforcement—property

Will the property have to be sold to pay the charge immediately?

As from August 1, 1994 the Board has had power to agree to defer enforcement of the statutory charge over a home regardless of the proceedings in which the home was recovered or preserved, providing certain conditions are met. Application to postpone enforcement should be made by completing the form ADMIN 1. Note that:

(i) The order or agreement under which the property was recovered or preserved must provide that it is to be used as a home for the assisted person or his/her dependants (but see the transitional provisions of the amended regulations at p. 437).

(ii) The assisted person must agree to the charge carrying simple interest at rates laid down in the regulations (currently 8 per cent per annum).

(iii) Payment of interest and capital need only be made when the property is sold or transferred, but payments towards the charge can be made at any time.

(iv) The Board can only agree to postponement if the property provides adequate security for the charge and the charge is duly protected by registration.

(v) Interest runs from the date of registration but provided an interest agreement is signed after August 1, 1994 no interest is payable in respect of chargeable costs until the solicitor's bill is actually paid.

(vi) If the assisted person does not complete the appropriate form or the other conditions of postponement are not met, the Board has no discretion and must enforce the charge immediately which may involve taking proceedings to obtain possession and sale of the property.

See *Practice Direction* [1991] 3 All E.R. 896.

16–12 Enforcement—money

Will any money recovered or preserved have to be paid to the Legal Aid Board?

(a) If the case comes within regulation 96 of the Civil Legal Aid (General) Regulations 1989 (see p. 409) *i.e.* the proceedings are under the Married Women's Property Act 1882, Matrimonial Causes Act 1973, Inheritance (Provision for Family and Dependants) Act 1975, Schedule 1 to the Children Act 1989, section 30 of the Law of Property Act 1925 (now section 14 Trusts of Land and Appointment of Trustees Act 1996) or the Matrimonial and Family Proceedings Act 1984, Part III, and the money is by virtue of an order of the court or an agreement, to be used to purchase a home for the assisted person or his/her dependants, the charge can be registered against the new home, with payment of simple interest. The assisted person must execute the charge contained in the Board's form ADMIN 1 and agree to the charge being registered on the property and bearing simple interest. The area office must be satisfied that the property to be purchased will provide adequate security for the amount of the charge.

The assisted person's solicitor may, provided that the Board has agreed to deferment, release the money in question to the vendor on completion of the purchase of the property or release the money to another solicitor or person providing conveyancing services. That person taking over the conduct of the conveyancing must give an undertaking to fulfil the obligations imposed on the assisted person's solicitor.

Subject to an overriding discretion in the area office to grant an extension of time, money which has not been used for the purchase of a home within one year from the date of the order or agreement must be paid to the Board. Any interest earned on the money in the meantime will be payable to the assisted person. In dealing with an application for an extension of time the area office will look at all the circumstances of the case, although delays in payment pursuant to the order/agreement, the state of the local housing market and the efforts made by the assisted person to purchase a property will be of particular relevance. Note that an extended time period may be extended again and extensions will be stated in weeks from the expiry of the one year period. See *Practice Direction* [1991] 3 All E.R. 896.

(b) In any other cases, all the money must be paid to the area office forthwith unless it is obvious that the money recovered or preserved will be more than the likely amount of the costs. In that case, the solicitor can estimate the amount of costs and pay that amount to the area office with an *undertaking* that his/her bill will not exceed that amount. If the area office is satisfied that the fund will be safeguarded, the balance can be released to the assisted person, but the solicitor will not be paid more than the amount in the undertaking (Civil Legal Aid (General) Regulations 1989, reg. 90, p. 403).

When does the duty to report arise? 16–13

In the case of either property or money, the solicitor has a duty to inform the area office *immediately* an order is made or agreement is reached under which money or property is to be recovered or preserved so that the office can take adequate steps to enforce the charge and safeguard the fund. The Board's form ADMIN 1 should be used to report to the area office.

Does the Board have power to transfer the charge to a substituted property? (Civil Legal Aid (General) Regulations 1989, reg. 98) 16–14

The Board has a discretion which will only be exercised if it is reasonable to do so and in the following circumstances:

(a) there must be an existing charge registered in favour of the Board against the original property;

(b) the assisted person must satisfy the Board that the new property is in England, Wales or Scotland and will provide adequate security to meet the amount of the charge and payable interest;

(c) all the sale proceeds will be utilised in the purchase and the purchase is as a home for the former assisted person, co-owner and any dependants;

(d) all beneficial owners must agree in writing and execute the contractual charge on the Board's appropriate form to be registered on the new property.

NOTE: *The payment of interest will continue if the charge was originally registered in respect of an order made after December 1988.*

16–14/1 | **Further advances**

The following information will be required to consider a request for postponement of the statutory charge where a further advance is to be made:

(a) the full name and address of the assisted person and their legal aid certificate reference(s);

(b) the amount of the proposed advance;

(c) the current market value of the property;

(d) the amount of the outstanding mortgage;

(e) the reason for the proposed further advance;

(f) details of the assisted person's income (and where remarriage/cohabitation has taken place, their partner's income);

(g) whether any part of the advance could be used to repay the statutory charge.

The Board has a discretion which will only be exercised if it is reasonable to do so. The following is a guide:

(a) Postponement will generally be agreed where the advance is sought for effecting essential repairs to the property.

(b) Postponement is unlikely to be agreed where the purpose of the advance is to reschedule debts, purchase a car/holiday/other luxury item or to purchase a second property.

(c) Postponement is unlikely to be agreed in any case where the statutory charge could realistically be redeemed, where the postponement would diminish the charge or where the property would no longer be adequate security for the amount owed under the statutory charge.

(d) Postponement will generally be agreed where there is a "buyout" of a co-owner's share, but only after consideration of whether sufficient funds could be raised to redeem the charge.

(e) Where the charge is non-interest-bearing and made in relation to a costs or contribution debt, postponement will not be agreed.

NOTE:

1. *There can also be a subsequent substitution if similar conditions are satisfied.*
2. *The Land Charge Section at the Finance Department (not the area office) handles all dealings with the statutory charge after registration (including substitutions, further advances and redemptions). If the legal aid reference number is not known, contact the Land Charge Section with the full name (including any change of name) and address of the assisted person and the title number or land charge reference number, as well as the assisted person's CIS reference; if known. The certificate reference can then be ascertained.*

Does the Board have power to waive the charge altogether? 16–15

There is no power to waive the legal aid charge (as compared with the solicitor's advice and assistance charge which can be waived on the grounds of grave hardship or distress).

Proceedings about the statutory charge 16–16

If there is a genuine dispute about the operation of the charge (*i.e.* after the case has been referred by the area office or by the solicitor to Legal Aid Head Office for consideration in detail) the only way of testing the matter will be by proceedings. If so, proceedings should be taken against the Board for a declaration that the charge does not arise. It is not appropriate to extend the original certificate as separate proceedings will be involved. Legal aid is available and if the assisted person is successful the original statutory charge will not apply. He will, however, have preserved his interest in the amount of the charge and therefore the charge will operate in respect of the costs of the declaration proceedings if he is successful in them.

STANDARDS ON CONSISTENCY OF DECISION-MAKING IN 16–17
CONNECTION WITH THE STATUTORY CHARGE

(See NFG 1, para. 1–26.)

Does the statutory charge arise and to what does it relate?

Principle
There is always a right and wrong decision as to whether or not the charge arises. It is not a matter of exercise of discretion. If incorrect decisions are made about whether or not the statutory charge arises they will not be justifiable to the stakeholders of legal aid. If the charge is said to arise when it does not, it is not justifiable to the assisted person and may lead to unnecessary costs in court proceedings to challenge the decision. If the charge is said not to arise when it does, it is not justifiable to the taxpayer, since there will be a loss to public funds.

Standard

A decision that the statutory charge arises should only be made where:

(a) **in a judgment or settlement an assisted person has, wholly or in part, recovered or preserved property or money which does not come within any of the exemptions in regulation 94 of the Civil Legal Aid (General) Regulations 1989; and**

(b) **there is a net deficiency on the assisted person's account with the legal aid fund.**

Basic principles

1. Has there been a judgment or settlement in which the assisted person wholly or in part recovered or preserved property or money?

   1. If YES go to next question.
   If NO the standard is not satisfied and the charge will not arise.

Is there a net deficiency?

2. Is it part of the judgment or settlement that costs will be paid by the other side?

   2. If YES go to next question.
   If NO go to question 5.

3. Have the costs been paid by the other side?

   3. If YES go to next question.
   If NO go to question 5.

4. Do the costs paid by the other side cover *all* the costs including legal aid costs and any related green form costs?

   4. If YES there is no net deficiency and the charge will not arise.
   If NO go to next question.

5. Has the assisted person paid a contribution?

   5. If YES go to next question.
   If NO go to question 8.

6. Does the total amount of the contribution and the costs paid by the other side cover *all* the costs including legal aid and green form?

   6. If YES there is no net deficiency and the charge will not arise.
   If NO go to next question.

7. Are there any legal aid or green form costs which are not covered by the contribution and the costs paid by the other side?

   7. If YES there is a net deficiency in the fund and the standard is satisfied on this aspect.
   If NO there is no net deficiency and the charge will not arise.

(NOTE: If the solicitor's profit costs have been deferred under reg. 102(a) because of failure to comply with the regulation there is still a net deficiency because there is an obligation to pay as soon as the failure has been corrected.)

Recovery and preservation

8. Was the property the subject of a claim in the proceedings or potential proceedings, whether by the assisted person or the other party, or recovered or preserved by way of settlement of a claim relating to other property (*Van Hoorn v. The Law Society*)?

8. If YES go to next question. If NO the standard is not satisfied and the charge does not arise.

9. Was the claim, wholly or in part, either disputed or not conceded (so that proceedings were necessary to try to establish it)?

9. If YES go to next question. If NO the standard is not satisfied and the charge does not arise.

10. Was the claim the subject of a judgment?

10. If YES go to next question. If NO go to question 12.

11. Was the judgment by consent?

11. If YES treat as if it were a settlement and go to next question. If NO go to question 14.

12. If the claim was, wholly or in part, disputed or not conceded was it settled by an offer (*i.e.* I give you the property in settlement of your claim)?

12. If YES go to question 14. If NO go to next question.

13. If the claim was not settled by an offer was it settled by concession before the certificate was issued (*i.e.* I agree your claim because I have always regarded the property as yours)?

13. If YES the standard is not satisfied and the charge does not arise. If NO go to next question.

14. Was the claim made by the assisted person?

14. If YES go to next question. If NO go to question 16.

15. Has the assisted person gained property as a result of pursuing the claim (recovery)?

15. If YES go to question 18. If NO go to next question.

16. Was the claim made by the other party?

16. If YES go to next question. If NO go to question 18.

17. Has the assisted person successfully resisted that claim either wholly or in part (preservation)?

17. If YES go to next question. If NO the standard is not satisfied and the charge does not arise.

219

Exemptions—regulation 94

18. Does the case come within any of the following:

    (a) an interim payment under Rules of Court;

    (b) a payment under Inheritance (Provision for Family and Dependants) Act 1975, s.5;

    (c) periodical payments of maintenance;

    (d) the first £2,500 recovered or preserved under certain Acts of Parliament specified in para. (d) of reg. 94;

    (e) omitted-transitional provision for certificates issued before May 3, 1976;

    (f) a payment in accordance with an order of the Employment Appeal Tribunal;

    (g) payments which by statute cannot be assigned or charged;

    (h) tools of the assisted person's trade; or

    (i) any payment made under the Earnings Top-up Scheme 1996.

18. If the answer is YES to any of these questions (after checking the exact wording of reg. 94), insofar as the exempt property is concerned, the standard is not satisfied and the charge will not arise.
    If NO to all the questions go to next question.

What are the proceedings in respect of which the charge arises?

19. Is the case divorce/nullity/judicial separation?

19. If YES go to next question.
    If NO go to question 21.

20. Is the assisted person legally aided for:

    (a) the main suit; and/or

    (b) claims for financial relief; and/or

    (c) claims relating to children; and/or

    (d) other claims in the proceedings?

20. If YES to all or any of these questions the proceedings are all part of one action, cause or matter and the total costs will be subject to the charge.

21. Does the legal aid certificate cover more than one action, cause or matter?

21. If YES consider each action, cause or matter separately and go to next question.
If NO consider whether enforcement can be deferred.

22. Can the costs of the actions, causes or matters be separated?

22. If YES the charge should be set against only the costs of the action, cause or matter in which the property was recovered or preserved.
If NO consider all costs together and consider whether enforcement can be deferred.

Can enforcement of the statutory charge be deferred?

Principle
If incorrect decisions are made to defer enforcement of the charge where there is no power to do so, this is not justifiable to the taxpayer since the legal aid fund will be deprived of settlement for perhaps a considerable period.

Standard
A decision to defer enforcement of the statutory charge should only be made where the regulations specifically allow such deferment, and on the terms provided by the regulations.

Enforcement

Money

1. Is the money to be used by order of the court or under the terms of any agreement to purchase a home for the assisted person or his or her dependants?

1. If YES go to next question.
If NO the standard is not satisfied and enforcement cannot be deferred—go to question 4.

2. Has the money been recovered or preserved in proceedings under the Married Women's Property Act 1882, the Matrimonial Causes Act 1973, the Inheritance (Provision for Family and Dependants) Act 1975 Schedule 1 to the Children Act 1989, section 30 of the Law of Property Act 1925 (now section 14 Trusts of Land and Appointment of Trustees Act 1996) or Part III Matrimonial and Family Proceedings Act 1984?

2. If YES to any of these go to next question.
If NO the standard is not satisfied and enforcement cannot be deferred—go to question 4.

3. Has the assisted person agreed to the property to be purchased being subject to a registered charge and to pay interest on that charge?

3. If YES and the property will provide adequate security for the charge, the standard is satisfied and the money may be dealt with in accordance with reg. 96(4), (5), (6) and (7).
If NO the standard is not satisfied and enforcement cannot be deferred—go to next question.

4. Will the rights of the legal aid fund be safeguarded by allowing payment into the fund of part only of the money (reg. 90)?

4. If YES accept solicitor's undertaking and payment in of maximum sum specified in undertaking and release remainder of money to assisted person.
If NO go to next question.

5. Has the money been paid into the legal aid fund?

5. If YES retain, on deposit where appropriate, until bills are taxed and assessed and payment can be made in accordance with reg. 92.
If NO call for money to be paid in.

Property

6. Is the property to be used by order of the court or under the terms of any agreement as a home for the assisted person or his or her dependants?

6. If YES go to next question.
If NO the standard is not satisfied and enforcement cannot be deferred—go to question 10.

7. Has the assisted person agreed to stay in the property and pay interest on the charge?

7. If YES and the property will provide adequate security for the charge enforcement may be deferred.
If NO the standard is not satisfied and enforcement cannot be deferred—go to question 10.

8. Does the assisted person wish to purchase a different property in substitution for the original property whether before or after registration of the charge?

8. If YES go to next question.
If NO go to question 10.

9. Does the assisted person agree to registration of a charge on the substituted property and payment of interest?

9. If YES and the property will provide adequate security for the charge the standard is satisfied and deferment may be authorised.
If NO go to next question.

Money and property

10. Does the recovery or preservation come outside any of the circumstances permitting deferment of enforcement?

10. If YES immediate enforcement may be necessary by whatever means are appropriate. Area office refers to the Debt Recovery Unit at Head Office. Go to question 11.
If NO reconsider which category the case comes into and the appropriate question.

11. If both money and property are recovered or preserved will the charge be enforced against the money first?

11. YES but the assisted person will be permitted to apply the £2,500 exemption (reg. 94(d)) to the first £2,500 of any money which is recovered or preserved.

HOW TO REDEEM THE STATUTORY CHARGE — 16–18

The Finance Department (not the area office) deals with requests for redemption figures, vacation of land charges and redemption of the statutory charge. Requests for redemption figures and vacations should be addressed to the Land Charge Section, Legal Aid Finance Department, 85 Gray's Inn Road, London WC1X 8AA (tel: 0171–813 1000). The Finance Department (not the area office) also deals with substitutions and further advances.

Ideally the civil legal aid certificate reference number or numbers should be quoted as well as the full name (including any changes since the charge was registered), the assisted person reference, under CIS, and address of the assisted person and the title number or land charge reference number. The minimum information required is the assisted person's full name at the time of registration of the charge and the title number or land charge reference. Quoting the civil legal aid certificate reference number or numbers is not essential but should enable a redemption figure to be supplied without delay. The civil legal aid certificate reference number can be taken from the top of the certificate, any amendments to it or the notice of its discharge, all of which will have been sent to the assisted person.

DOES THE BOARD HAVE POWER TO REFUSE TO PAY SOLICITOR'S COSTS? — 16–19

Where a solicitor has been practising without a current practising certificate the Board will only pay disbursements and any counsel's fees in respect of the relevant period. In addition, the Board has power to defer payment of the solicitor's costs if there has been a loss to the fund because the solicitor has failed to comply with regulations.

(a) Regulation 102 of the Civil Legal Aid (General) Regulations 1989 provides that where an assisted person's solicitor has failed to comply with any provision of these regulations and as a result of his default or omission the fund incurs a loss:

(i) the appropriate area committee may defer payment of all or part of the solicitor's profit costs in connection with the proceedings to which the certificate relates until he has complied with such provisions; and

(ii) if the Board refers the conduct of the solicitor to the Solicitors' Disciplinary Tribunal and the solicitor is disciplined, the Board may retain any sum, payment of which has been deferred under sub-paragraph (a), in accordance with the finding of the Tribunal.

(b) The only profit costs, payment of which may be deferred, are those arising under the legal aid certificate in connection with which the solicitor's default or omission has occurred.

(c) Payment of a solicitor's profit costs may be deferred if he has failed to comply with any of the provisions in Part XI of the Civil Legal Aid (General) Regulations 1989—this includes the solicitor's obligations as to the conduct of the proceedings in Part IX and the obligations to report the recovery or preservation of property (including moneys and costs) and to pay moneys received to the Board in accordance with regulation 90(1) of the Civil Legal Aid (General) Regulations 1989.

(d) As regulation 102 is compensatory, not punitive, deferment will not be of an amount in excess of the loss to the fund. The loss to the fund may comprise:

(i) the net liability of the fund as defined in section 16(9) of the Legal Aid Act 1988;

(ii) any additional costs incurred by the legal aid fund, *e.g.* under regulation 91(1) of the Civil Legal Aid (General) Regulations 1989; and

(iii) the amount of any costs caught by section 16(5) of the Legal Aid Act 1988.

Note also that costs incurred in excess of any costs condition may be deferred (see NFG 9, para. 9–14, p. 154).

16–20 Special cases

In some cases, where the solicitor has been in breach of statutory duty or negligent, proceedings may have to be taken against him. Even in such cases:

(a) counsel's fees will be paid; but

(b) payment of disbursements may be withheld as credit against the claim for damages (witholding payment of disbursements in this way is not, however, deferring payment under regulation 102 of the Civil Legal Aid (General) Regulations 1989).

16–21 Failure to comply with regulation 90 of the Civil Legal Aid (General) Regulations 1989—notification to the Board

The most common default or omission giving rise to the application of regulation 102 is failure to comply with regulation 90. When considering regulation 90 it should be borne in mind that:

(a) property (which includes moneys and costs) is recovered or preserved at the moment any action is disposed of either by compromise or judgment. It is at that moment that the statutory charge attaches. It continues to attach unless and until the judgment is reversed on appeal; and

(b) regulation 90(1)(a) requires an assisted person's solicitor to inform the area director forthwith of any property (including moneys and costs) recovered or preserved. This obligation to report arises immediately there is a compromise or judgment which gives rise to recovery or preservation.

Has there been a loss to the fund?   16–22

Payment of profit costs will not be deferred under regulation 102 unless there has been a loss to the fund. This may depend upon whether (a) money or (b) other property was originally subject to the charge and whether the discretion to transfer the charge to substituted property would have arisen and been exercised.

Moneys (including costs) subject to the statutory charge and costs   16–23
payable to the Legal Aid Fund under section 16(5) of the Legal Aid Act
1988

(a) Where a solicitor does not report forthwith that moneys were recovered or preserved under a compromise or order and, as a result of the delay, the compromise or order is rendered worthless, there has been a loss to the fund.

(b) Where moneys are recovered or preserved and paid to the assisted person or a third party who dissipates them, there has been a loss to the fund.

(c) As a result of a case in which a solicitor paid a sum awarded by way of damages direct to his assisted client, contrary to the provisions of what is now regulation 90 of the Civil Legal Aid (General) Regulations 1989, the Council of the Law Society sought an opinion of leading counsel upon the question of liability. Leading counsel advised that a solicitor acting for an assisted person was under a clear statutory duty to pay over the moneys recovered in an action to the Law Society (now to the Board) and that, if he committed a breach of that duty, he would, in counsel's view, be ordered by the court to make good the resulting loss suffered by the legal aid fund. Subject to the provisions of regulation 90, the Board is of the same view.

(d) The duties in regulation 90(1) to report on property recovered or preserved and to pay over to the Board all moneys received apply to any solicitor acting for a person who is or has been legally aided in the proceedings. It makes no difference whether the solicitor is nominated on an existing legal aid certificate, was nominated on a certificate which has been discharged or revoked, or has taken over (on a private client basis) a case which was previously covered by legal aid.

17. MULTI-PARTY ACTIONS

NOTE: *In June 1997 the Board published a report, "When the Price is High", which recommended radical changes to the way in which legal aid for multi-party actions is administered. The proposals included setting up a specialist multi-party action panel of experienced firms who would be given preference in awarding contracts, and implementing new multi-party arrangements which would provide for price tendering and other changes. The Lord Chancellor has asked the Board to implement these changes. New arrangements and guidance are therefore likely in 1999. The changes will be publicised when finalised. The following Notes for Guidance are based upon the existing arrangements and procedures.*

17–01 WHAT IS A MULTI-PARTY ACTION?

For the purposes described below, a multi-party action is defined as any action or actions in which 10 or more assisted persons have causes of action which involve common issues of fact or law arising out of the same cause or event (see Legal Aid Board Multi-Party Action Arrangements 1992 at p. 639).

A multi-party action normally comprises several sets of proceedings, which may be brought against different defendants and may even be commenced in different courts. The requirement is that there must be causes of action with common features and these generally fall into two categories:

(a) claims arising out of a specific event, such as a disaster;

(b) claims based upon a common cause, such as a harmful drug or method of treatment.

17–02 WHAT SPECIAL RULES APPLY TO MULTI-PARTY ACTIONS?

In most respects legal aid as regards a multi-party action operates in the same way as in any other case. Any person applying for civil legal aid in a multi-party action must still satisfy the usual means and merits tests.

The private client test, namely the principle that legal aid will normally only be granted in circumstances where a client of sufficient but not superabundant means would be prepared to litigate, applies to a multi-party action just as to any other action.

However, actions involving large numbers of claimants with common issues may only be viable if a sufficient number of claimants come together and coordinate their claims. Therefore, the strength and viability of the action must be considered globally. An action can only be supported if a sufficient pool of prima facie viable claimants exists to justify the estimated expenditure of the generic trial. To ensure that the action remains efficient, the Board will not permit generic work to be duplicated and will seek to ensure that the costs of such work are shared fairly between claimants.

Experience of multi-party litigation has shown how total costs can escalate to very high levels without bringing significant benefits to the claimants. The Board will therefore monitor the costs of multi-party actions carefully and in particular consideration will be given to whether and to what extent it is reasonable to investigate and progress each individual claim pending trial of the generic issues.

For potentially very large actions the Board is likely to expect more detailed information about the claims to be available before legal aid is granted than would be the case for a standard claim. For a major multi-party action the Board would wish to know:

(a) the number of potential plaintiffs who would be parties to the multi-party action;

(b) the generic issues that would arise;

(c) the costs of the generic issues;

(d) the costs of the litigation generally.

(See *R. v. Legal Aid Board, ex p. Belcher*, CO/2098/92, July 15, 1994).

The principal legal difference of multi-party actions is that the Legal Aid Board has the power to secure representation by means of contracts with solicitors in any multi-party action (see Legal Aid Act 1988, s.4(5) and Part XVI of the Civil Legal Aid (General) Regulations 1989). The Board may enter into a contract under which the solicitors will provide some or all of the representation in the action. When a contract is in place, only the contracting solicitors will be allowed to carry out the work covered by the contract. Most contracts will cover generic work only. Contracting solicitors will, however, be subject to a number of special obligations under the contract to ensure that the action is properly managed on behalf of claimants.

WILL THE CONTRACTING POWERS BE APPLIED TO ALL MULTI-PARTY ACTIONS?

17–03

No. The Board has a discretion and will only contract in appropriate cases. The Board will only consider a contract if the action involves significant complexity in terms of assembling statements, undertaking research, obtaining expert evidence, examining and processing large volumes of documentation, or otherwise. Further:

(a) contracts are more likely to be awarded in newly emerging actions rather than those which are well established under existing procedures;

(b) only an action which requires a high degree of co-ordination and management by one firm or steering committee is likely to be chosen;

(c) contracts will be more appropriate where the complexity of the case stems primarily from the common or generic issues, rather than the individual claims. Once the main generic issues in a case have been decided a contract may no longer be appropriate;

(d) contracts will be intended to cover substantial and effective litigation. This would not be the case where, for example, liability was not in dispute and the action raised no difficult issues of causation;

(e) a contract is unlikely to be awarded if only a minority or a small proportion of the plaintiffs have legal aid.

Even where there is no contract the Board would wish to see the spirit of the

Multi-Party Action Arrangements (see para. 17–04 and p. 639) applied, particularly in the areas of monitoring the action and keeping claimants informed.

17–04   HOW DO THE CONTRACTING PROCEDURES WORK?

The Board has produced Multi-Party Action Arrangements (see p. 639). These set out the procedures which apply up to and after a contract is entered into. The procedures will not be repeated in these notes, but some of the important features are that:

(a) a special committee appointed by the Board will decide whether to invoke the contract procedures for an action;

(b) tenders will be invited in accordance with Part III of the Arrangements and may be submitted either by one firm or by a group of firms forming a consortium or steering committee;

(c) the Committee will make a selection based upon the criteria set out in the Arrangements and enter into a short standard contract with the chosen firm or firms. This contract will incorporate the provisions of Part V of the Arrangements which are standard terms setting out the procedures which will apply once a contract is in force;

(d) legal aid certificates will be amended or transferred as necessary to provide that contract work may only be undertaken by contracting firms. Contracting firms undertaking generic work do not need to have any certificates or clients of their own;

(e) firms may be added to or removed from the group to meet the needs of the action as it progresses. Solicitors should not put forward very large groups of firms at the outset, merely because there is a prospect that the action will expand.

NOTE: *Although the Board has power to contract on other terms, the provisions of the standard contract and the Arrangements are not negotiable. The Board may amend the Arrangements from time to time which will take effect on both existing and new contracts.*

17–05   HOW DOES THE CONTRACT RELATE TO EXISTING REGULATIONS AND PROCEDURES?

The contract is to provide representation under Part IV of the Act. Therefore the general rule is that all regulations which apply to civil legal aid also apply to representation pursuant to a contract and contractual obligations are additional to obligations under regulations. The exception is that remuneration of solicitors and counsel is determined by the contract and not by regulations (see s.15(7) of the Legal Aid Act 1988). The remuneration provisions of the Arrangements which form part of the contract set out special rules, particularly as regards payments on account, but provide that fees are still subject to taxation and that in other respects remuneration is determined in accordance with the provisions of the regulations.

The prospect of a contract should not prevent solicitors from undertaking generic work which is authorised under a legal aid certificate. There is no moratorium on representation awaiting a possible contract. In a disaster case, the Board will not rush into awarding a contract and in emergencies solicitors should rely on existing procedures of emergency certificates and authorities. However, solicitors should take steps to co-ordinate pre-contract work and may not be permitted to duplicate such work. The Board may impose conditions on certificates and authorities to ensure that experts' reports and other items of generic work is available for the benefit of all assisted claimants within the action, subject to any conflict of interest.

WHAT WORK WILL BE COVERED BY THE CONTRACT?   17–06

The contract may cover some or all legal aid representation in the action. However, most contracts will cover "generic work" only. In such cases contracting firms will carry out generic work pursuant to the contract while each claimant may select and be represented by a local solicitor in respect of non-generic work in accordance with the legal aid certificate.

"Generic work" is defined as representation in respect of the issues common to all claimants or to a particular group of claimants and includes the selection, preparation and trial of preliminary issues and lead cases. In doubtful cases the Board can determine work to be generic. In doing so, the Board will have regard to any directions given by the Court and will consider what steps can most efficiently be carried out by contracting firms and what is best left to local firms.

Representation in a large action includes co-ordination of the action on behalf of claimants generally, but does not cover steps which do not progress the litigation for claimants. For example, dealing with inquiries from the public or setting up telephone information lines would not be covered by the contract.

Contracting firms must comply with any conditions or limitations imposed by the Board. Formal and sequential authorities will be issued on forms approved by the Board setting out the limits of contract work in the same way that successive limitations are placed upon a certificate. These forms must be produced on taxation. They will also be used for granting authority to incur costs pursuant to regulation 61 of the Civil Legal Aid (General) Regulations 1989.

Subject to any directions from the Board, contracting firms may divide the contract work between them as they see fit. However, the tender report before the contract is made must set out the proposed responsibilities of the firms within the group and the Board must be notified of any major change in the division of contract work.

WHAT ARE THE MAIN CONTRACT RIGHTS AND OBLIGATIONS?   17–07

The special contractual obligations are set out in Part V of the Arrangements. Some of the main provisions are the following, the numbers given in parenthesis being the relevant paragraphs of the Arrangements:

    (a) the Board will play a greater role in monitoring the progress of contract actions and contracting firms must provide a detailed report on the action to the Board every six months (29–33);

(b) claimants will be kept properly informed of the progress of the action and contracting firms must send a report to each claimant every three months (34–37);

(c) contracting firms and counsel may claim payments on account in respect of contract work on behalf of legally aided claimants and will be paid 75 per cent of their reasonable fees as soon as practicable after the work is done. The restrictions of regulations 100 and 101 of the Civil Legal Aid (General) Regulations 1989 shall not apply (39);

(d) contracting firms will operate a proper complaints procedure and should notify the Board of complaints about the conduct of local firms. Complaints procedures should comply with Law Society guidance on Client Care (44);

(e) the Board will terminate a contract in appropriate circumstances (49–50 and Schedule to the Arrangements);

(f) the Board has wide powers to apportion costs paid under a contract (53–55).

The following areas require particular attention:

Taxation of costs

Costs incurred pursuant to a contract will still be subject to taxation or assessment and the normal tests of reasonableness will be applied on taxation. Prima facie it will be reasonable to take any steps which are required and authorised under the contract but note that:

(a) steps taken pursuant to the contract may still be unreasonable, particularly if the contracting firm knew or ought reasonably to have known that the purpose of the work had failed or become irrelevant or unreasonable before costs were incurred. For example, preparing a detailed six-monthly report might be pointless if the trial was in progress;

(b) any unnecessary duplication of contract work will be disallowed on taxation;

(c) copies of any bills lodged for taxation should also be served on the Board as the Board may wish in some cases to be represented on taxation.

Private clients

The purpose of the contract is to provide representation to assisted claimants. However, generic work will also be for the benefit of any private clients in the action and it is, therefore, important that they make a proper contribution to the generic costs at all stages. To this end:

(a) contracting firms must state in their tender reports how they propose private clients will contribute to the costs of the action. This could involve arranging through local firms for private clients to make payments initially and at intervals to contracting firms, or requiring private clients to make such payments into interest-bearing accounts to be held pending the outcome of the action;

(b) payments on account by the Board will normally be reduced to take account of the proportion of private clients in the action. Only in very exceptional circumstances will payments be made at a higher rate (see paras. 40 and 41 of the Arrangements);

(c) if, at the end of the action, payments on account by the Board exceed the taxed legal aid share of the costs of the action, the excess will immediately be recouped from contracting firms.

Claimant meetings

The Board recognises that claimant meetings and committees may in exceptional circumstances be an important and necessary means of progressing a multi-party action. If the requirements of para. 42 of the Arrangements are satisfied, the Board will pay the reasonable travelling costs within the United Kingdom, equivalent to second class return rail fare, of those claimants who attend. The logistics in making such payments will be primarily the responsibility of a contracting firm ("the firm"). The following procedure is recommended:

(a) the firm will issue details of the meeting to claimants informing them of the right to payment of their reasonable travelling costs, but also warning of the operation of the statutory charge should such costs not be recovered *inter partes*. Claimants who need payment in advance of the meeting will be asked to send details to the firm;

(b) the firm will arrange rail warrants for those claimants who need them in advance or send payment to such claimants in some other form. If necessary the Board will assist the firm with a payment on account;

(c) claimants who attend the meeting should register and fill in details of the amount they are claiming. The firm will draw up a schedule of sums claimed;

(d) the Board will make a payment to the firm of the total of reasonable travelling costs as defined which can then be distributed to the claimants.

Keeping records

It is particularly important for contracting firms in a multi-party action to keep detailed and accurate records of clients and of work done and specifically:

(a) separate records must be maintained of work done under the contract as against non-contract work done for individuals;

(b) proper details must be sent with any application for a payment on account under the contract to enable the Board to assess the claim. Note that each contracting firm is paid individually for the work it does;

231

(c) numbers of assisted and private clients need to be recorded to enable the Board to make payments on account at the appropriate level.

(d) sufficient details must be sent to the Board to enable it to carry out any apportionment of costs.

Early leavers

The Board may use its powers to apportion contract costs under section 16(10) of the Legal Aid Act to specify and fix the generic costs liability of a claimant who accepts an offer of settlement or otherwise leaves the action before its conclusion. This may permit damages to be released or large contributions to be refunded before the final taxation of the action. Where costs are specified in this way for an early leaver the balance of the contract costs will fall to be apportioned among those who remain in the action. Solicitors should advise clients that in this, as in many other aspects of multi-party actions, the acts of one claimant can have an influence, for benefit or detriment, on all others in the action.

The Board may specify costs for an early leaver where it considers that the following apply:

(a) failure to specify costs would cause the early leaver hardship;

(b) it is possible at the relevant time to make a fair estimate of the costs liability of the early leaver;

(c) it is unlikely that specifying costs for early leavers would have a substantial effect on the costs liability of those who remain in the action.

18. CRIMINAL LEGAL AID

18–01 CRIMINAL LEGAL AID

If a person has been summonsed/charged with a criminal offence, he/she can apply for criminal legal aid.

18–02 DUTY SOLICITOR SCHEMES

A person who is questioned by the police about an offence—whether or not he/she has been arrested—has a right to free legal advice. There is no means test for such advice. (The questioning may be at the police station or elsewhere.) The person may ask for a solicitor he/she knows, the 24-hour duty solicitor, or may choose a solicitor from the list kept by the police.

If a person has to go to the magistrates' court on a criminal case there will often be a duty solicitor available either at the court or on call to give free advice and representation on the first appearance. Again, there is no means test.

18–03 ADVICE

If a person needs legal advice about a criminal matter, he/she can see a solicitor under the legal advice and assistance scheme (see para. 2–01). The solicitor can also give the client advice and assistance in preparing the case for court under that scheme but criminal legal aid may be available as may assistance from a duty solicitor.

WHAT DOES CRIMINAL LEGAL AID COVER?   18–04

Criminal legal aid covers the cost of a solicitor to prepare the client's defence before he/she goes to court and to represent the client there. If the case requires counsel, particularly if it is to be heard in the Crown Court, that may also be covered.

Criminal legal aid can also cover advice on appeal/preparing the notice of appeal against a verdict or sentence of the magistrates' court, the Crown Court or the Court of Appeal, and preparing the appeal itself (including where an appeal is made to the Court of Appeal by the personal representative of a convicted defendant who has died).

Criminal legal aid also covers an application for bail (including to the Crown Court in the case of magistrates' court proceedings).

Legal aid is not available to bring a private prosecution.

APPLICATION FOR CRIMINAL LEGAL AID   18–05

An application should be made to the court that is dealing with the case as soon as possible after the applicant has been summoned/charged with a criminal offence. The court will supply the necessary forms. The applicant will be asked to give details of income and savings. If he/she is under 17, the parents or guardian can apply for him/her. If the court refuses criminal legal aid, he/she can apply again. There is no limit to the number of applications which can be made to the court, and these can be made at any time up to the trial itself.

CRITERIA FOR THE GRANT OF CRIMINAL LEGAL AID   18–06

The court will grant criminal legal aid if it decides that it is in the "interests of justice" that the defendant should have legal representation, and that he/she needs help to pay the costs of the case. The court's decision will be based on the information given in the criminal legal aid application form and statement of means form.

APPLICATION FOR REVIEW OF REFUSAL   18–07

If legal aid is refused, the court will write to the applicant giving the reason for refusing criminal legal aid. In some more serious cases, if the court has decided that the grant of criminal legal aid is not in the interests of justice, the defendant may be able to make another application to an area committee of the Board to review his/her case. The court notice will indicate whether such a right exists.

For less serious (summary only) offences (including criminal damage up to £5,000 and aggravated vehicle taking offences which are required to be dealt with as if they were summary offences) or where the court has refused criminal legal aid on financial grounds, the defendant can also apply again but only to the court. If he/she is refused criminal legal aid by the magistrates' court and has to go to the Crown Court, an application can be made to that court for criminal legal aid. A solicitor may be able to give help under legal advice and assistance to assist a defendant in preparing a case for court.

18–08   PAYMENT OF CONTRIBUTIONS

A defendant may be asked to pay towards his/her costs as a condition of criminal legal aid. A defendant who is in receipt of income support, income-based Jobseeker's Allowance, family credit or disability working allowance is financially eligible without a contribution. A defendant will not be asked for a contribution from income if his/her disposable income (which is the amount left after allowances for tax, National Insurance contributions, housing, travel to and from work, dependants such as children, and any other reasonable living expenses) is £51 per week or less.

If his/her weekly disposable income is more than £50, the defendant will be asked to make a contribution of £1 for every £3 or part of £3 by which his/her weekly disposable income exceeds £50, payable weekly from the date of the grant of criminal legal aid to the final conclusion of the proceedings or the date when the legal aid order is withdrawn or revoked (whichever is the sooner). For example, if the weekly disposable income is £80 the contribution will be £10 per week for the lifetime of the order or proceedings whichever is the shorter. If the defendant's capital, which includes savings and the value of any luxury goods such as expensive jewellery or a yacht, is assessed as £3,000 or less, no contribution will be required from capital. If it is above £3,000 he/she will be asked to pay the excess as assessed over £3,000 towards the cost of the case.

For applications from June 1, 1996 (with the exception of those made by applicants in receipt of passported benefits, which are unaffected) the treatment of an applicant's dwelling house, which was previously wholly exempt for eligibility purposes, was amended so that:

(a) the capital value of the property (that is market value less amount outstanding on any mortgage debt or charge) will be taken into account in so far as it exceeds £100,000;

(b) the capital amount allowed in respect of a mortgage debt or charge over the property cannot exceed £100,000;

(c) as regards allowances against income for mortgage payments, if the mortgage debt exceeds £100,000 the amount allowed will be reduced in proportion (for example, if mortgage debt is £200,000, only half the amount actually paid will be taken into account);

(d) there are also provisions for second and subsequent dwellings, which provide that the total amount of mortgage debt to be allowed for all the properties cannot exceed £100,000.

This means that for capital assessment, the value of an applicant's home, is reduced by the amount of the mortgage or by £100,000, whichever is the less, to produce a net equity figure. If this net equity figure exceeds £100,000, the excess over £100,000 is taken into account as the capital of the assisted person.

An additional discretionary power was also introduced for applications made on or after June 1, 1996 which allows the assets of persons other than the applicant for legal aid to be taken into account. The regulation may be applied where the other person has transferred resources to the applicant, has been maintaining the applicant in the proceedings, or where any of the resources of the other person have been made available to the applicant. If this happens, the resources of the other person can be treated as those of the applicant. Note also that applications in respect of an appeal to the Court of Appeal made by a personal representative on behalf of a convicted person who has died are assessed on the deceased's estate and that assets subject to a *Mareva* injunction or other freezing order are still treated as the applicant's unless he has applied for assets to be released for the purposes of the case and been refused.

The court will send the defendant a notice indicating how much he/she will have to pay. The defendant can ask for criminal legal aid to be withdrawn because he/she does not want to pay the contribution, but must tell the court and the solicitor immediately.

CHANGE OF FINANCIAL CIRCUMSTANCES 18–09

The defendant must tell the court if his/her income or capital change.

REFUND OF CONTRIBUTIONS 18–10

At the end of the case, the court will decide what should happen to any instalments, paid or unpaid. The court may cancel any outstanding instalments or it may order the repayment of any sum due or paid where the assisted person is acquitted or the case is discontinued or withdrawn. If, at the end, the contribution paid is more than the actual costs of the case, the court will refund the difference to the defendant. If he/she is acquitted or the case is discontinued or withdrawn it is likely that all the contribution will be returned, unless the court decides that the defendant brought the prosecution on himself/herself.

CHOICE OF SOLICITOR 18–11

In general a defendant has the right to choose any solicitor who is willing to act. If he/she has been granted criminal legal aid and has not chosen a solicitor, the court can assign one to act. If he/she is being tried with others, the court may assign one solicitor to cover representation of all the defendants unless there is a conflict of interest or other good reason not to do so.

If the defendant wants to change solicitors, he/she will have to give the court a good reason. If the court does not think the request is reasonable its decision can in some circumstances be renewed to one of the area committees of the Legal Aid Board.

18–12   STATUTORY FRAMEWORK AND CONDITIONS

The statutory framework for criminal legal aid is contained in Part V of the Legal Aid Act 1988, ss. 19–26 (see pp. 296 *et seq.*).

Details of the system are set out in the Legal Aid in Criminal and Care Proceedings (General) Regulations 1989 (see pp. 476 *et seq.*).

The general principle of Part V is that representation for criminal proceedings may be granted where it appears desirable in the interests of justice. The factors to be taken into account are defined in section 22(2) (see p. 300—by which the former Widgery criteria are given statutory authority).

Legal aid can only be granted by a competent authority, which is normally the court trying the proceedings. The Legal Aid Board has a limited role in criminal legal aid, dealing only with reviews of refusals by the magistrates' courts to grant legal aid, amend orders or to assign counsel, as well as with authorities for certain work in magistrates' courts and the Crown Court, and payment of costs in the magistrates' courts. The Board's application form should be used to make an application to an area office.

In addition, since April 1998 a small selection of magistrates' courts and Crown Court centres have been able to refer cases to the Board's Special Investigations Unit who investigate and report to the court on the applicant's finances. In such cases it is still the courts who determine whether to grant a legal aid order. It is planned that the role of the Unit will be extended to cover all criminal courts as soon as possible.

The Notes for Guidance below deal only with the exercise of powers by the Board and not by the courts.

18–13   MATTERS FOR CONSIDERATION BY AREA COMMITTEE ON RECEIPT OF APPLICATIONS FOR REVIEW OF A REFUSAL OF LEGAL AID IN A MAGISTRATES' COURT

(a) *Has the application for review been made to the appropriate area committee?* It has if the committee is the one in whose area is situated the court to which the application for or concerning the legal aid order was made. Otherwise the application may be transferred to the appropriate office or returned.

(b) *Was the applicant charged with an indictable offence or one triable either way, or is he/she to be brought before the court in connection with such offence?* For the purpose of a right of review, yes—even if summary offences are also alleged. Note that the committee may then grant an order covering all the offences to which the original refusal related.

(c) *Was the original application for legal aid refused in the interests of justice?*

    (i) If it was, there is a right of review.

    (ii) If not (*i.e.* the original application was refused on means, whether or not it was also refused on the interests of justice ground), the review cannot be accepted.

(d) *Was there a date fixed for trial or committal at the time the original application was submitted? If so, was the original application made less than 21 days before such date?* If the answer to both questions is in the affirmative, the application for a review cannot be accepted.

(e) *Was the application for review submitted within 14 days from the date* of refusal of the original application? If not, is there "good reason" for the delay? If the answer to both questions is negative, the application for review will not be accepted. "Good reason" will usually mean matters outside the control of the applicant or the solicitor, such as postal delays. It is unlikely to be accepted as a good reason that there has been an unsuccessful reapplication to the court by the applicant, resulting in the application for review being made outside the 14 day period.

(f) *Was the refusal made after the application had been considered for the first time by a magistrates' court or justices' clerk?* If not (*i.e.* that when the application for review was submitted there had been more than one unsuccessful application to the court) the application for review will not be accepted. If, however, at the time the application was made there was only one refusal and subsequently a renewed application to the court is made and determined prior to the review decision, no point will be taken about the second application to the court. If the second application is successful, there will be no need for the review decision. If it is unsuccessful, the review application will still proceed on the first refusal.

Substantive decision 18–14

(a) *Has sufficient information been supplied to enable the substantive decision to be made?* The notification of refusal of legal aid must be submitted with the application for review. A copy of the original legal aid application to the court under regulations 12(2) and (16) should also be submitted.

The charge sheet will only be needed if the other documents do not make the charges clear or there is some doubt as to whether the offences are summary only. Fuller information can be given to the area office rather than to the court because there is no possibility of prejudicing the proceedings.

(b) *The review should be allowed on the merits if one or more of the factors set out in section 22(2) of the Legal Aid Act 1988 are met.*

NOTE:

1. *Any decision to refuse criminal legal aid is made by the area committee, not the area director.*

2. *The factors on which the area committee reach its conclusions are the same as those a court would consider.*

3. *Doubts as to compliance with the factors are resolved in favour of the applicant.*

4. *There is no right of appeal from the decision of the area committee. The function of the area committee is an appellate one. There is no bar to reapplication to the court.*

IS ANY AUTHORITY REQUIRED FROM THE AREA COMMITTEE FOR 18–15 PARTICULAR EXPENDITURE UNDER A LEGAL AID ORDER? (Legal Aid in Criminal and Care Proceedings (General) Regulations 1989, regs. 54 and 55)

The rule is that where a solicitor acting under a legal aid order considers it necessary for the proper conduct of proceedings in a magistrates' court or in the Crown Court for costs to be incurred in taking certain steps, he *may* apply to the appropriate area committee for prior authority to do so. The Board's appropriate application form must be used to apply.

The effect of obtaining an authority is that no question as to the propriety of the step taken or the amount authorised will be raised on the eventual determination of costs, unless the solicitor knew or ought reasonably to have known, before incurring the costs, that the purpose of the authority had failed or become irrelevant or unnecessary.

NOTE:

1. *Applying for authority is not mandatory in criminal cases.*

2. *A decision to refuse (rather than to grant as asked or for a reduced amount/rate) will be that of the area committee not the area office. There is no right of appeal against a refusal but a further application can be made at any time before the actual expenditure is incurred.*

3. *Amounts authorised will usually be in accordance with guideline rates issued from time to time by the Lord Chancellor's Department.*

4. *Only the area committee and not the court can grant authority under this provision, but the Crown Court can grant authority for travelling and accommodation expenses within regulation 54A.*

5. *In Crown Court cases where authority is granted for individual (rather than aggregated) expenditure of £100 or more and actual expenditure of £100 or more is incurred, the solicitor may apply to the Crown Court for a payment on account of the disbursement.*

The main areas of work concerned are:

(a) instructing a Queen's Counsel alone without junior counsel;

(b) the employment of experts and incurring unusual or unusually large expenditure.

NOTE: *There is no power to authorise the tendering of expert evidence as opposed to the obtaining of written opinions or reports.*

18–16 The instruction of a Q.C. to act alone

Authority will be granted if the legal aid order provides for the services of solicitor and counsel and the area committee is satisfied that the proper conduct of the proceedings so requires. The Board's appropriate application form must be used to apply.

18–17 Obtaining written reports from experts and others, bespeaking transcripts and performing acts which are unusual in their nature or involve unusually large expenditure

The authority must specify a maximum amount and will usually specify a maximum rate. The Board's appropriate application form must be used to

238

apply. Solicitors should note that applications before the area committee that are poorly prepared or incomplete are likely to be refused because the area committee is unable to establish whether it is reasonable to incur the expenditure requested. This is particularly important in cases where the application is made close to trial and where refusal may cause an adjournment. In particular cases the area committee may consider writing to the court explaining the Board's reasons for refusal. Further guidance will be issued on this point.

Authority will be:

(a) *Granted* if the area committee is satisfied that the proper conduct of the proceedings so requires and it is reasonable in the circumstances.

(b) *Refused* where the application is for tendering expert evidence or the reports in question have been/could be ordered by the court in its consideration of a disposal under the Mental Health Act/probation order with treatment and would thus be payable out of Central Funds. *See below for further guidance.*

(c) *Refused* where the application is in respect of a medical assessment for which it would be reasonable to expect alternative funding (*e.g.* through the National Health Service or Secretary of State for the Home Office) to be used.

(d) *Refused* for photocopying done in-house which is an office overhead (*R. v. Zemb*, 1985), unless the circumstances are unusual, or the documents to be copied unusually numerous in relation to the nature of the case (see para. 18–26).

(e) *Refused* where the application is for a conference with counsel or to obtain counsel's written opinion (unless counsel is instructed *qua* expert rather than *qua* counsel).

(f) *Refused* where the application is for travelling expenses to attend at a distant court. That is a matter for the determination of costs.

See also NFG 11, para. 11–06 for the position where a solicitor, or his partner or employee are involved in the provision of non legal services.

Also note the following regarding medical reports. This guidance is written in order to clarify the circumstances in which applications for prior authority in criminal cases for the commissioning of medical reports may be considered. Such requests have been refused previously on the basis of point of principle CRIMLA 3 (see para. 18–28 below), on the assumption that the court may order the report and the costs would be met from Central Funds. The courts have given guidance which shows that the courts will only pay for written medical reports out of Central Funds in very limited circumstances.

Essentially, the Board's basic starting point in respect of medical reports is that if the court would normally pay the costs of the report out of Central Funds, then it should do so, notwithstanding the existence of a legal aid order. The court will only pay for reports in certain very limited circumstances. These are where:

(a) the court has ordered the report to be prepared; *and*

(b) the report is required for the purposes of determining whether to make a hospital or guardianship order, or a probation order requiring medical treatment for a mental or other condition.

If both these conditions apply, then an application for prior authority should be refused. If they do not, then an application for prior authority may be granted, subject to the usual principles.

If a request has been made of the court but the court has refused to order the report, then the application may be considered in the normal way. If the court has ordered the report and the solicitors submit an application for prior authority to support the same, area offices should first clarify the basis on which the court has ordered the report. Once the purpose is known, the area office will be in a position to judge whether it is one which will attract payment out of Central Funds, and hence whether to grant a prior authority. Sometimes the court will be persuaded to "order" a report in circumstances in which the report would not be payable out of Central Funds. This should not affect the decision to grant a prior authority.

The circumstances in which a medical report may be requested by the court are set out in regulation 25 of the Costs in Criminal Cases (General) Regulations 1986 and section 19(3) of the Prosecution of Offences Act 1985. A written report may only be ordered in cases to which section 32(2) of the Criminal Justice Act 1967 applies.

This covers the following:

(a) section 3 and Schedule 1A of the Powers of the Criminal Courts Act 1973 (as amended by section 9 of the Criminal Justice Act 1991) (probation orders with additional requirements *i.e.* treatment for a mental condition, treatment for drug or alcohol dependency and extension of requirements for sexual offenders), or otherwise for the purpose of determining the most suitable method of dealing with an offender; or

(b) section 37 of the Mental Health Act 1983 (hospital orders and guardianship orders); or

(c) section 12(4) of the Children and Young Persons Act 1969 (supervision orders requiring treatment for a mental condition); or

(d) the exercise of the powers conferred by section 30 of the Magistrates' Courts Act 1980 (remanding a defendant for medical examination before disposal after a summary trial).

There is also provision under section 34(5) of the Mental Health (Amendment) Act 1982 which permits a Crown Court to order the payment out of Central Funds of such sums as appear to it reasonably sufficient to compensation any medical practitioner for the expense, trouble, or loss of time properly incurred in preparing and making a report to the court on the mental condition of a person accused of murder.

Whilst section 32(2) does theoretically allow the court to order a medical report for the purposes of determining a suitable method of dealing with an offender, it is clear from guidance issued to Crown Court judges that court orders should only be made for medical reports where the report is required because the judge is considering a hospital/guardianship order or probation order requiring medical treatment for a mental condition.

A medical report will not therefore be ordered or paid for from Central Funds if it is required to assist a solicitor to advise on the appropriate plea or to mitigate the seriousness of the offence on sentencing.

Point of principle decision CRIMLA 3 as amended is intended to mean that if the court is considering a disposal under the Mental Health Act and the solicitor makes a request for prior authority to the Board for the cost of the medical report, the application would only be allowed in exceptional cases if no request has been made of the court. The Board's first position would be to say that the court should order the cost of the report and an application should be made to the court. If in an exceptional case the application has been refused a prior authority may be considered by the Board. If it has never been made then it will be exceptional for the Board to consider granting a prior authority.

In considering any application by a solicitor for prior authority to cover the commissioning of a medical report, area offices should assume judges will not normally order medical or psychiatric reports except where there is likely to be a Mental Health Act disposal or a probation order requiring medical treatment for a mental or other condition. On occasion, in granting an adjournment to allow a report to be prepared for sentence, a judge will agree that a report would assist the court and may be persuaded to "order" it. Area offices should treat any suggestion by solicitors that the court has "ordered" the report with caution and must enquire whether the court ordered it for a likely disposal for a mental or other condition.

The courts have revised guidance so that orders made by the courts should state the section/Act under which the order is made. Only if the court has ordered it and the purpose is to enable disposal under the Mental Health Act or a probation order requiring medical treatment will a prior authority be refused as the cost of the report would be payable out of Central Funds. In all other circumstances the commissioning of a medical report, whether before or after conviction, may be considered by way of an application for prior authority.

Solicitors will always need to illustrate that it is a reasonable and necessary disbursement for the proper conduct of the proceedings. Area offices and area committees may then assess whether it is reasonable and justified for the authority to be granted.

WHAT IS THE EFFECT OF FAILURE TO OBTAIN OR REFUSAL OF AUTHORITY FOR EXPENDITURE?   18–18

(a) The solicitor's costs may still be allowed on the determination of costs. This is also the case if the amount of an authority is exceeded.

(b) The solicitor can obtain payment other than out of the legal aid fund for experts' fees or bespeaking transcripts where an application for authority has been refused.

WHERE THE ORIGINAL LEGAL AID ORDER DID NOT ASSIGN COUNSEL, CAN IT BE AMENDED TO PROVIDE FOR REPRESENTATION BY COUNSEL?   18–19
(Legal Aid in Criminal and Care Proceedings (General) Regulations 1989, regs. 51, 52 and 53)

Yes, if the circumstances are those set out in regulation 44(3) (*i.e.* unusually grave or difficult circumstances where the proceedings are for an indictable offence) but application must be made first to the proper officer of the court. If he refuses the application, it may be renewed either to the court or, subject to certain exceptions, to the appropriate area committee. Solicitors should use the Board's appropriate application form to apply to the area committee.

There is no power for the proper officer to refer the matter to the court or for the court to deal with it in the first instance—such decisions would be *ultra vires*.

Where counsel is assigned authority may be obtained from the area committee to instruct a Q.C. alone but otherwise it is *not* possible to instruct a Q.C. under a legal aid order covering proceedings in the magistrates' court. The magistrates' court can *only* make an order providing for a Q.C. and junior counsel for the Crown Court trial on a charge of murder (and the order is made upon committal/transfer for trial) or where the prosecution is brought by the Serious Fraud Office and the order is made upon receiving a notice of transfer under section 4 of the Criminal Justice Act 1987. As for civil legal aid, authority for a Q.C. cannot be granted retrospectively (*R. v. Welsby*, Swansea Crown Court, July 30, 1997).

NOTE: *The appropriate area committee cannot consider an application for renewal if:*

1. *a previous application for renewal in the same circumstances has already been refused by the court or the area committee; or*

2. *the application is made outside the time limit specified in regulation 51(b); or*

3. *the application is in respect of proceedings in the Court of Appeal, the Courts Martial Appeal Court or the House of Lords.*

These exceptions do not apply to renewal to the court.

18–20 APPLICATION FOR A LEGAL AID ORDER TO BE AMENDED GENERALLY OR WITHDRAWN
(regs. 50, 51, 52 and 53)

Such an application must be made to the proper officer of the court and, after refusal by the proper officer, by renewal to the court or, subject to certain exceptions, to the appropriate area committee. There is no power for the proper officer to refer the matter to the court or for the court to deal with it in the first instance—such decisions would be *ultra vires*. Solicitors should use the Board's appropriate application form to apply to the area committee.

NOTE: *The exceptions to the area committee's powers to consider applications for renewal are set out in para. 18–19.*

18–21 HOW IS AN APPLICATION MADE TO THE APPROPRIATE COMMITTEE FOR THE ASSIGNMENT OF COUNSEL, AMENDMENT OR WITHDRAWAL OF A LEGAL AID ORDER?

The application is made by sending to the area office the legal aid order, notice of refusal, supporting papers and any necessary additional documents. The Board's appropriate application form must be used.

The area committee may grant or refuse the application and amend or withdraw the order accordingly, giving notice of its decision to the court, the solicitor and the legally assisted person.

COSTS 18–22

The detailed provisions for assessment of costs of both solicitors and counsel are contained in the Legal Aid in Criminal and Care Proceedings (Costs) Regulations 1989.

Costs are assessed by the appropriate authority which is the registrar in the case of proceedings in the Court of Appeal, an officer appointed by the Lord Chancellor for proceedings in the Crown Court, and the Legal Aid Board for criminal proceedings in a magistrates' court.

The basis on which costs are assessed is that all the relevant circumstances of the case including the nature, importance, complexity or difficulty of the work and time involved are considered and a reasonable amount is allowed in respect of all work actually and reasonably done. Interim payments may be made in Crown Court cases where a previously authorised disbursement in excess of £100 is incurred or solicitor's costs (including disbursements) or Counsel's fees of £4,000 or more (excluding VAT) are outstanding three months after the relevant bill is ready to tax or six months after that case concludes if sooner. In the latter case 40 per cent of the total claim (less any sum already paid) is payable. Prior approval from a Crown Court determining officer may be obtained for travelling and/or accommodation expenses incurred in attending a Crown Court trial or other main hearing. If the case occupies 20 days or more such expenses (if given prior approval) may be included in a claim for interim payment. The prior approval will be binding in principle on any application for iterim payment or costs assessment. The amount claimed remains subject to assessment in any event.

The Lord Chancellor has introduced standard fees for most legally aided magistrates' court proceedings by virtue of Part III, Schedule 1 of the Legal Aid in Criminal and Care Proceedings (Costs) Regulations 1989 as well as graduated fees for advocates in Crown Court cases, where staged payments, interim payments, advance payments, hardship payments and deductions in the event of adverse observations by the trial judge may also be allowed/made.

Provision is made for three defined categories of magistrates' proceedings with a lower or higher standard fee or non-standard fee being payable, dependent upon which monetary band the claim is determined to fall within. Details of the fees are at pp. 565 and 678.

Note that standard fees do not apply to proceedings in which counsel has been assigned, to extradition proceedings or to cases where an enhanced rate of payment is allowed.

The Legal Aid Board continues to assess claims for a higher standard fee or for a non-standard fee on an *ex post facto* basis to determine whether a higher standard fee is appropriate (as opposed to a lower standard fee) and to determine whether a non-standard fee is appropriate (as opposed to a standard fee).

The regulations require the conducting solicitor to agree an unassigned counsel's fee prior to submission of the bill. The agreed fee will be paid direct to counsel by the Legal Aid Board. The solicitor will submit his claim on the basis of the work undertaken by the solicitor and unassigned counsel, the value of whose work will be calculated at the rates applicable to solicitors (for the purpose of determining the core costs which fix the level of standard fee). The Board's appropriate claim forms must be used.

The charges of solicitor agents should be claimed as profit costs (and not as a disbursement) and NFG 11, para. 11–06 (p. 166) deals with the position where the solicitor, his partner or employee are involved in the provision of non-legal services.

Magistrates' court assessments are carried out by the Board's area office staff. They can be reviewed by the relevant area committee which has the power to confirm, increase or reduce the assessment. Reviews are considered by area committees *de novo* and the amount allowed by the area committee may be the same as, more than or less than the amount allowed by the area office. Reviews are by way of written representations but see NFG 14, para. 14–05.

Dissatisfied solicitors and assigned counsel can appeal to a committee appointed by the Board (the Costs Appeals Committee) but only where the Area Committee certifies a point of principle of general importance (see paras. 18–26 *et seq.*).

The following should be noted in relation to the instruction of interpreters. The Royal Commission on Criminal Procedure (Chapter 3 para. 43) recommended that "a fully qualified interpreter, independently employed by or on behalf of the suspect, is used wherever practicable when the suspect is giving instructions to a solicitor". The Government accepted this recommendation.

The Institute of Linguists maintains the National Register of Public Service Interpreters (NRPSI). In order to be entered on the Register, interpreters must undergo training and demonstrate competence. They should, therefore be "fully qualified" within the meaning of the Royal Commission's recommendation—that is not to say that there are not competent interpreters who are not on the National Register. Criminal justice agencies have agreed to secure all their interpreters, wherever possible, from an approved national register by the year 2002. Police, courts and other legal agencies will aim to use the NRPSI for criminal cases in England and Wales.

The fees charged by interpreters vary; they depend on market forces and, in general, the fees charged for interpreting in more obscure languages are higher than in more common languages. In a legal aid case, just as in a privately funded case, a solicitor should aim to secure value for money when instructing any third party. This may, sometimes, involve obtaining competitive quotes. The fees charged by the competent interpreter should not be any higher merely because they are on the National Register.

A CASE—MAGISTRATES' COURT PROCEEDINGS

A standard fee is payable for "a case" which may comprise one or more of the types of proceedings listed in the Table in paragraph 2(2) of Schedule 1 Part III of the Legal Aid in Criminal and Care Proceedings (Costs) Regulations 1989. Paragraph 1 of the Schedule states that:

> "a 'case' (except where the context otherwise requires) comprises proceedings relating to one or more charges or informations which are preferred or laid at the same time or which are founded on the same facts or which form or are part of a series of offences."

The definition is modelled on rule 9 of the Indictment Rules but omits the words "of the same or a similar character" in relation to a "series of offences."

The definition consists of three independent elements or tests. One or more of the three tests will need to be satisfied to form a case in respect of which a claim for a standard fee can be made. They are:

(a) where the charges or informations are preferred or laid at the same time;

(b) where the charges or informations are founded on the same facts;

(c) where the charges or informations form part of a series of offences.

Preferred or laid at the same time

This element of the definition is self-explanatory. Where a solicitor represents a defendant suspected of burglary who is also found in possession of proscribed drugs, only one standard fee will be payable if the two charges are preferred together. If, however, the defendant was bailed back to await a drugs analysis, the terms of this first test would not have been satisfied, and the other elements should be tested.

Same facts

The test here is whether the charges have a common factual origin. It would cover substituted and alternative charges such as theft and handling. For example, where a charge such as section 47 assault is withdrawn and a section 39 offence is substituted the test would be satisfied and only one standard fee would be payable.

Series of offences

The test here is whether the offences exhibit some similar feature which would allow them to be described as a series of offences. Questions which might help are "would these allegations have been tried together on a single indictment" or "could the defendants properly be placed in the dock together". A sufficient nexus *may* be demonstrated by the following facts:

(a) that the charges are based on a system of conduct;

(b) that the charges are similar in their nature and could have been tried together (*e.g.* burglaries and thefts);

(c) that the evidence of one offence would be admissible at the trial of another.

But the test is *not* restricted to these possibilities.

The following factors would not in themselves prevent a series of offences being established:

(a) some separate hearings, possibly in different magistrates' courts;

(b) the fact that the offences were committed some years apart;

(c) evidence of one offence was not admissible at the trial of one of the other offences;

245

(d) the fact that the offences were committed in different places or on different days;

(e) the fact that there was more than one legal aid order for the offences;

(f) the fact that the offences are tried separately by magistrates;

(g) the fact that the offences appear on separate indictments at the Crown Court.

The following factors would not in themselves make two or more charges part of a series:

(a) that all hearings were at the same court;

(b) that only one legal aid order exists;

(c) that offences were committed on the same day or dates close to each other.

See also para. 18–74 below (CRIMLA 50—as amended).

Completion of a series of offences

A series of offences can be regarded has having ended when all outstanding charges or informations in respect of a defendant, or co-defendants, have been disposed of in some way by the court.

Legal aid orders

The practice as to the granting of legal aid orders has varied between different magistrates' courts. Some courts issued orders for each charge whereas others granted orders for a number of charges even though they might constitute more than one case. This definition is *not* currently tied to the charges contained in a legal aid order although it is hoped in due course that the two should be brought together, and the legal aid order will be the "trigger" for a standard fee. With the current definition it will therefore be possible to have more than one legal aid order attached to a case, or for a legal aid order to cover more than one case.

The onus will be on the solicitor claiming the costs to satisfy the appropriate authority that charges against a defendant or co-defendants constitute more than one case.

Enhanced rates for legal aid orders granted on or after October, 1994

The following should be noted:

1. When determining a claim for enhancement under paragraph 3 of Part I, Schedule 1 to the Legal Aid in Criminal and Care Proceedings (Costs) Regulations 1989, the assessing officer must first consider whether or not the case is "exceptional" and justifies enhancement. The Regulations provide that it may be appropriate to allow an enhancement for any item or class of work where, taking into account all the circumstances of the case, it can be established that:

    (a) the work was done with exceptional competence, skill or expertise;

    (b) the work was done with exceptional dispatch; or

    (c) the case involved exceptional circumstances or complexity.

2. The proper test of "exceptional" within the phrase "exceptional circumstances" is the ordinary and actual meaning of the word "exceptional", *i.e.* "out of the ordinary" (*R. v. Legal Aid Board, ex. p. R M Broudie & Co* [1994] 138 S.J. 94).

3. If an assessing officer decides that enhancement should be applied to a case he may apply the percentage to particular items of work. If an enhancement is allowed for one item of work it does not have to be allowed for other items. It will depend on the circumstances of the case. Enhancement may be applied to any item of work including travel and waiting.

4. If an assessing officer receives a claim for enhancement but decides not to allow an enhancement the solicitor should be notified of the reasons why the case was not considered to fall within the criteria set out in the Regulations.

5.1 If the assessing officer considers that an enhancement should be applied to any item of work he must apply what he considers to be the appropriate percentage uplift to the prescribed legal aid rate applicable to that item of work. In determining the percentage, regard should be had to:

    (a) the degree of responsibility accepted by the solicitor and his staff;

    (b) the care, speed and economy with which the case was prepared;

    (c) the novelty, weight and complexity of the case.

5.2 However, the assessing office must in each case then go on to consider what hourly rate and percentage uplift would have been applied if the legal aid order had been granted before October 1, 1994 when the "Backhouse" principle applied. This principle is set out in CRIMLA 13 (see para. 18–37 below). A "Backhouse" calculation must be carried out. Once that composite figure is known (the hourly broad average direct cost rate plus appropriate uplift), the assessing officer should then ensure that the relevant percentage applied in the assessment of that item of work provides a figure not lower than that composite rate, subject always to the maxima provided by the regulations.

6. The percentage by which the prescribed rate may be enhanced shall not exceed 100 per cent except for where the proceedings relate to serious or complex fraud, where the percentage may not exceed 200 per cent. Such cases are, for example, those conducted by the Serious Fraud Office or those transferred under section 4 of the Criminal Justice Act 1987.

LATE CLAIMS AND CLAIMS QUERIES   18–23

There are strict time limits on submission of bills: three months from conclusion of the proceedings, unless extended by the appropriate authority for good reason (although where an arrest warrant is issued the claim must be submitted between 6 and 19 weeks after the issue of the warrant).

The legal provisions regarding late submission of bills for Court Duty Solicitor and Advice at Police Station claims are the same as for criminal legal aid, and this guidance applies equally to them.

Although claims may be submitted out of time, a fair balance has to be achieved between the interests of the legal aid administration in securing prompt submission of bills and those of the profession in not being deprived, merely due to late submission, of costs for work properly carried out. It will, however, generally be reasonable to expect solicitors to be aware of and to comply with the time limits, particularly as firms will wish to obtain payment as soon as possible and will have access to appropriate support systems to monitor their cashflow. The vast majority of claims processed by the Board meet the time limits. However, there is a small (and diminishing) minority of claims which are submitted late. It is clear that these late claims require a disproportionate amount of time to process—to the detriment of the majority of claims received in time.

The three-month time limit for the submission of claims may be extended for "good reason". A common example may, however, be where a co-defendant's case is still awaiting disposal. What constitutes "good reason" is a question of fact in every case, although regard can be had to the particular firm's history of late claims, particularly where the "good reason" put forward relates to the firm's own conduct.

To avoid any difficulties on assessment, the solicitor should apply to the area office for an extension to the time limit *before* it expires. However, the area office may still extend the time limit, on receipt of a costs claim after a three-month period, provided the solicitor can show "good reason". Where "good reason" has been shown, the solicitor's claim for costs should not be reduced only because of late submission.

Where the solicitor is unable to show "good reason", the area office must then go on to consider whether there are "exceptional circumstances" which would justify extending the time limit in the particular case. Each case will be judged on its own merits, although regard can be had to the particular firm's history of late claims.

Where the area office decides that there were "exceptional circumstances", it must then go on to consider whether to impose a penalty for late submission. Deductions will be imposed to a maximum of:

— 5 per cent for bills submitted up to three months out of time;

— 10 per cent for bills submitted up to six months out of time (*i.e.* up to nine months after the conclusion of the matter).

Generally, it should be possible for late claims to be submitted within nine months of the conclusion of the matter (*i.e.* up to six months out of time) but there may be truly exceptional cases where the claim is submitted so late that higher deductions may be warranted.

Where a solicitor has failed to show either "good reason" or "exceptional circumstances", his claim for costs will be disallowed in full. He may then appeal to the area committee.

Deductions are based on the global bill (including any counsel's fees and disbursements) and not just the solicitor's profit costs but are made from the payment which would otherwise be made to the solicitor unless counsel has been responsible for the delay. Counsel's fees (*i.e.* the amount the solicitor agreed to pay him in standard fee cases) are preserved for payment provided he/she has not caused or contributed to the delay.

Where, however, costs are disallowed in full it is the view of the Board that a payment from the solicitor to counsel in these circumstances would not be in breach of regulation 55 of the Legal Aid in Criminal and Care Proceedings (General) Regulations 1989.

Many queries over apparent non-payment of claims which are raised with the Board's area offices arise from cases where payment has in fact been made but solicitors have not posted the payment. It is a particular problem where matters are followed up only after a delay. It is reasonable to expect solicitors to monitor the receipt of payments on a regular basis and therefore to be in a position to raise such queries promptly after having posted payments and checked remittance advices. Except in a small minority of cases non-civil bills are paid by the Board within a maximum of 8 to 10 weeks of receipt of the claim for costs. The solicitor should therefore make an enquiry of the area office if payment is not received within three months of submission of the claim.

Before raising a query with the relevant area office the solicitor should specifically check for payment and if an enquiry of the area office is appropriate should confirm that all remittance advices since the submission of the original claim have been checked for the appropriate payment and a copy of the claim previously submitted, as well as any proof of receipt by the area office, should be forwarded. The process of the solicitor checking for payment and the inclusion of a copy of the claim (and any supporting documents available) will reduce unnecessary queries and assist the area offices in dealing with such queries as are received. Where the solicitor cannot provide proof of receipt of the claim by the area office, the matter may be treated as a late claim (see above).

PRE-LEGAL AID ORDER WORK   18–24

Criminal legal aid orders do not operate retrospectively but regulation 44(7) of the Legal Aid in Criminal and Care Proceedings (General) Regulations 1989 allows work done before a legal aid order is made to be deemed as within the order (and therefore capable of being claimed and paid under the order) where:

(a) the interests of justice required that the representation or advice be provided as a matter of urgency;

(b) there was no undue delay in making an application for legal aid; and

(c) the representation or advice was given by the solicitor who was subsequently assigned under the legal aid order.

The Costs Appeals Committee of the Legal Aid Board has considered regulation 44(7) (see para. 18–79, decision CRIMLA 55) and is of the view that, although each case must be considered on the basis of its particular circumstances, the criteria in regulation 44(7)(a) and (b) above are likely to be satisfied where there is a court hearing within 10 days or less of the date when initial instructions were taken and an application for legal aid was made no more than seven days after initial instruction. Circumstances other than a court hearing fixed for within 10 days of initial instruction may justify the provision of representation or advice as a matter of urgency and the particular circumstances of a case may be such that an application made more than seven days after initial instruction would be not considered to have been unduly delayed.

The time periods mentioned are computed on the basis that time starts to run on the day following initial instruction and that Saturdays, Sundays and bank holidays are counted.

In order to decide whether regulation 44(7) applies solicitors will need to provide the date of initial instruction, the date the application for legal aid was lodged with the court, the date of the court hearing and the circumstances that it is claimed made provision of the representation or advice necessary as a matter of urgency. See also paras. 18–33, 18–53 and 18–79.

18–25   **SECTION 6(2) COMMITTALS**

The Home Office issued guidance (Circular No. 71/1986) to magistrates' courts and prosecuting agencies suggesting steps whereby defence solicitors can take advantage of section 6(2) of the Magistrates' Courts Act 1980 not to attend committal proceedings involving only written statements.

The Home Office Circular points out that where an accused person has a solicitor acting for him, examining justices may commit him for trial on written statements alone. The solicitor does not need to be present in court unless he or she disputes the sufficiency of the evidence disclosed in the written statements or there are other circumstances in which the defendant may need to be represented.

The Circular emphasises that to enable the procedure to work it is essential for the prosecution to provide written statements in good time before the date of hearing to enable the solicitor to take instructions from the accused person on the written statements and to decide whether or not an attendance is necessary.

The Legal Aid Board is of the opinion that, subject to the correct procedure being followed, solicitors should be expected to exercise the option not to attend court in appropriate cases. Accordingly payment will not be made out of the legal aid fund for attendances at committal proceedings by either solicitors or counsel *except* in any of the following circumstances:

(a) where a submission is to be made of no case to answer;

(b) where there is to be an application for bail or for variation of bail conditions;

(c) where there is to be an application to lift reporting restrictions;

(d) where there is to be an application in relation to the venue of the trial;

(e) where the written statements on which the committal will be based have been served less than 14 days before the date fixed for the committal proceedings;

(f) where the solicitor has to attend to make an oral legal aid application to the magistrates' court or to make representations about the grant of legal aid for the Crown Court proceedings; or

(g) where there is any other matter requiring the solicitor's (or counsel's) attendance at the hearing which may be reasonable in the particular circumstances of the case.

Solicitors will be expected to state precisely why their attendance was necessary on each occasion and in the absence of a sufficient justification costs of attendance will be disallowed on assessment. The Board recognises that following the introduction of the amended committal procedure from April 1997, solicitors will continue to be required to attend section 6(1) committals. The fact that a case proceeded as a section 6(1) committal will therefore be an acceptable reason for attendance.

Attached to the Home Office Circular is a copy of a form of notice of non-attendance for use by defence solicitors wishing to inform the court that they will not be present at committal proceedings based on written statements alone. This form was prepared by the Home Office in consultation with the Law Society and issued to courts with the request that, in cases where the defence solicitor has applied for legal aid, the clerk to the justices should enclose a copy of the form with the court's response to the legal aid application.

POINTS OF PRINCIPLE OF GENERAL IMPORTANCE

The Board has issued the following decisions on points of principle of general importance in connection with criminal legal aid assessment of costs:

Photocopying   18–26

The making of copies of documents is part of the solicitor's normal overhead expense, and thus would not normally be remunerated separately. However an allowance may be made for copying in unusual circumstances or where the documents copied are unusually numerous in relation to the nature of the case. The cost should be claimed as a disbursement. If copies have been made out of the office the actual cost should be claimed. If made in the office a charge equivalent to the commercial cost should be claimed. A charge based on the time expended by a member of the solicitor's staff will not be allowed. (Legal Aid Board reference CRIMLA 1 as amended.)

Confirmation to clients of next hearing date and final outcome   18–27

The solicitor may, if he considers it appropriate, write to his client and, in the case of a youth, his parent or other carer after each court appearance giving details of the decision of the court and the client's next appearance before the court. The solicitor may also write to his client and, in the case of a youth, his parent or other carer at the conclusion of the matter giving the decision of the court. (Legal Aid Board reference CRIMLA 2 as amended.)

Medical or psychiatric reports in mitigation   18–28

Where it appears a court may be considering a disposal under the Mental Health Act, only in exceptional cases will the cost of medical or psychiatric reports be allowed for use in mitigation on conviction where no request has been made by the court. (Legal Aid Board reference CRIMLA 3 as amended.) (See also para. 18–17 above.)

18–29 Enhanced rates: foreign language spoken by solicitor

When a solicitor who is able to speak a foreign language is able to deal with a case without an interpreter, enhanced rates may be allowed. (Legal Aid Board reference CRIMLA 4.)

18–30 Substantiation of claims

In the absence of evidence to substantiate claims for work done, the Board will not normally allow these claims. Items claimed should be supported by proper records. (Legal Aid Board reference CRIMLA 5.)

18–31 Work done after amendment showing change of solicitor

The Legal Aid in Criminal and Care Proceedings (Costs) Regulations 1989 do not permit payment for work after the amendment of a criminal legal aid order to the solicitor no longer assigned under that order. (Legal Aid Board reference CRIMLA 6.)

18–32 Attendance at formal remand hearings

Attendance at formal remand hearings should not be necessary unless the solicitor is aware that he has an application to make or oppose, or the court appearance presents a convenient and economical opportunity for the solicitor to obtain further instructions from a client who is in custody. (Legal Aid Board reference CRIMLA 7.)

18–33 Work done before issue of legal aid order: regulation 44(7) of the Legal Aid in Criminal and Care Proceedings (General) Regulations 1989

The provisions of regulation 44(7) of the Legal Aid in Criminal and Care Proceedings (General) Regulations 1989 apply to any legal aid order, including orders following a renewal to court or a review by the area committee. Further, the provisions of regulation 44(7)(b) of the Regulations refer only to the original legal aid application. (Legal Aid Board reference CRIMLA 8.)

18–34 Attendances on clients remanded in custody at a distance (local court)

Where a solicitor is representing a client in a local court where that solicitor normally practises and the client is remanded in custody at a distance, then the solicitor will normally be permitted to attend this client in custody to take instructions, although in all cases all the circumstances should be taken into account, including, by way of example, the nature and seriousness of the charge, whether the client is under a disability, the relationship, if any, between the solicitor and client, the practicability of taking instructions at court and the likelihood of the client being granted bail or being moved to a place of detention closer to the solicitor's office. (Legal Aid Board reference CRIMLA 9.)

Separate representation

18–35

Where the interests of justice require it, two or more legally aided defendants represented by the same firm of solicitors can be represented by separate advocates in court. It is for the solicitor to justify both the separate represen- tation and the number of advocates used. Where separate representation is justified, the firm of solicitors may appear by in-house solicitor, solicitor agent or counsel, but where non-assigned counsel is briefed, the assessment will be on the maximum fee basis. Where it is sought to justify separate rep- resentation on the basis of interests of justice and it appears that there is a conflict which is such that the solicitor should withdraw from acting for one or more defendants, the Board should, in determining the solicitor's fees, con- sider whether it was reasonable for the solicitor to continue to act in those circumstances. (Legal Aid Board reference CRIMLA 11.)

Determination of costs

18–36

Where the Board disallows a specific item for a specific reason, the item should be identified and the reason given but the Board is not precluded from reducing claims for classes of work without specifically identifying particular items of work. An area committee may determine a review of an assessment without considering the solicitor's file of papers provided that it otherwise has sufficient information to determine the appeal or the solicitor has failed to provide that information after having been given an opportunity to do so. Where, in determining costs, the Board has taken into account some specific factor or factors other than the nature, importance, complexity, or difficulty of the work and time involved it should indicate that factor or factors. (Legal Aid Board reference CRIMLA 12.)

Enhanced rates in criminal cases

18–37

Where the criteria for paying enhanced rates in criminal proceedings under the Legal Aid in Criminal and Care Proceedings (Costs) Regulations 1989 are met, such claims will be assessed on the basis of the broad average direct cost of the work (the A figure), to which is added a percentage uplift (the B figure) to take into account all the relevant circumstances of the case.

The A figure will represent the broad average direct cost of undertaking the work. Factors to be taken into account in identifying this figure may include the rate likely to be allowed in an enhanced rates case by the appropriate Crown Court for the relevant level of fee earner at the time to which the costs claim relates, and evidence of the results of surveys of local solicitors' expense rates for the locality in which the solicitor's office is situated.

As to the B figure, 35 per cent should be considered as a starting point in respect of preparation. Solicitor advocacy would normally be expected to carry an uplift of 40–60 per cent, and attendances with counsel 20 per cent.

In the majority of cases where enhancement is claimed and allowed it will, nonetheless, be usual to pay travel and waiting without enhancement at the prescribed legal aid rate. Each case must be considered on its own particular merits having regard to all the relevant circumstances of the case. A claim for travel and waiting at the A figure may be allowed in exceptional cases. Even then, travel and waiting would not be expected to attract an uplift on the A figure.

When enhanced rates apply to routine letters written and to telephone calls made or received and they are not timed, the method of assessment is to allow them at one-tenth of the hourly rate plus, in appropriate cases, an uplift for preparation.

Save for the purpose of CRIMLA 59, this decision only applies to cases where the legal aid order was granted prior to October 1, 1994. (Legal Aid Board reference CRIMLA 13 as amended.)

18–38 Delay in submitting costs claim

The fact that a particular solicitor or firm submits a large number of criminal bills in time and only rarely submits bills out of time does not constitute good reason for delay in submitting the bill in any particular case. (Legal Aid Board reference CRIMLA 14.)

18–39 Payment of witness expenses

The effect of the provisions of section 25(3) of the Legal Aid Act 1988 and regulations 15 and 16 of the Costs in Criminal Cases (General) Regulations 1986 made under the Prosecution of Offences Act 1985 is that witness expenses, defined as including compensation for trouble or loss of time and out of pocket expenses, are not payable under a criminal legal aid order unless the court directs that they may not be paid from central funds. If the court does so direct then they may be paid under the legal aid order where they were reasonably incurred in accordance with regulation 7 of the Legal Aid in Criminal and Care Proceedings (Costs) Regulations 1989. (Legal Aid Board reference CRIMLA 15.)

18–40 Correction of prosecution papers

The primary responsibility for the accuracy and admissibility of prosecution papers lies with the Crown Prosecution Service and in the event of inaccuracies or objections to admissibility these should, in the first instance, be drawn to the attention of the Crown Prosecution Service who should be invited to correct them. There may, however, be rare cases where it is justified for the defence solicitors to correct the prosecution papers. (Legal Aid Board reference CRIMLA 16.)

18–41 Enhanced rates: representation of several defendants does not of itself justify

The fact that a solicitor is representing several defendants does not of itself justify the payment of an enhanced rate within paragraph 3 of Part I, Schedule 1 of the Legal Aid in Criminal and Care Proceedings (Costs) Regulations 1989. (Legal Aid Board reference CRIMLA 17.)

Enhanced rates: imminent hearing: exceptional competence cannot be inferred

18–42

Where a solicitor takes over a case from previously instructed solicitors which requires work at short notice for an imminent hearing, this will usually constitute exceptional despatch within paragraph 3(a) of Part I, Schedule 1 of the Legal Aid in Criminal and Care Proceedings (Costs) Regulations 1989, but whether exceptional competence is involved will depend on the circumstances of the case and cannot be inferred. (Legal Aid Board reference CRIMLA 18.)

Transcription of taped interviews

18–43

Where a solicitor applies for prior authority to transcribe a tape whether audio or video using an outside agency and satisfies the area committee that such a transcript is necessary, then authority should normally be granted. Where a solicitor chooses to transcribe a tape in-house, the work of transcription would not normally be regarded as fee-earner's work and will not therefore be remunerated under the legal aid order. Consideration of the tapes to decide whether any part of them should be transcribed and the checking of the accuracy of any transcripts obtained constitute fee earner's work which may be remunerated as such. (Legal Aid Board reference CRIMLA 19, as amended. This decision incorporates and replaces decision CRIMLA 10.)

Enhanced rates in murder cases

18–44

Murder cases are extremely serious and often fall within the exceptional circumstances limb of paragraph 3 of Part I, Schedule 1 of the Legal Aid in Criminal and Care Proceedings (Costs) Regulations 1989. (Legal Aid Board reference CRIMLA 20.)

Attendance on clients remanded in custody at a distance (non local court)

18–45

Where a solicitor is representing a client in a court where that solicitor does not normally practise and the client is remanded in custody at a distance from the solicitor's office, then the solicitor may be permitted to attend the client in custody to take instructions if the circumstances of the case make this appropriate. Circumstances to be taken into account when reaching this decision include, by way of example, the nature and seriousness of the charge; whether the client is under a disability; the relationship, if any, between the solicitor and the client; the practicability of taking instructions at court and the likelihood of the client being granted bail or being moved to a place of detention closer to the solicitor's office. (Legal Aid Board reference CRIMLA 21.)

18–46   Enhanced rates in care proceedings

The circumstances of each case have to be examined to determine whether they are exceptional or whether the work has been done with exceptional competence and despatch. No one factor can be identified as inevitably justifying an enhanced rate. Substantial contested expert evidence is capable of constituting an exceptional circumstance so as to justify the allowing of an enhanced rate. (Legal Aid Board reference CRIMLA 22.)

18–47   Work covered after service of a notice of transfer in serious fraud cases

In serious fraud cases where a notice of transfer is served a legal aid order covering only proceedings in the magistrates' court continues in full force until the magistrates' court has discharged all its functions in relation to the proceedings.

Although after service of a notice of transfer the functions of the magistrates' court are limited to dealing with bail, witness orders and the grant of legal aid for the Crown Court, the work which may be carried out by the solicitor under the order until the magistrates have discharged all their functions is not limited to these matters. Work actually and reasonably done up until the last hearing in the magistrates' court may be incorporated in a bill to be assessed by the Board's area office and may be remunerated as being work preliminary in proceedings in the Crown Court in accordance with section 19(2) of the Legal Aid Act 1988.

It therefore follows that where a through order is granted by the magistrates' court all work actually and reasonably done by the solicitor up until the last hearing in the magistrates' court should be incorporated in the bill to be assessed by the Board's area office. (Legal Aid Board reference CRIMLA 23.)

18–48   Enhanced rates: length of hearing

The unusual length of a hearing is a factor which may justify payment of an enhanced rate on the basis of either paragraph 3(a) or (b) of Part I, Schedule 1 to the Legal Aid in Criminal and Care Proceedings (Costs) Regulations 1989. (Legal Aid Board reference CRIMLA 24.)

18–49   Factual enquiries: use of enquiry agent

Whether it is reasonable for a solicitor to undertake factual enquiries himself or instruct an enquiry agent will depend on all the circumstances of the case including the nature of the case, the nature and number of enquiries to be undertaken, the travel involved and any unusual aspects of the case or the evidence.

Where a claim for profit costs for making enquiries is disallowed the Board may allow a notional amount, as part of the profit costs, for the instruction of an enquiry agent. (Legal Aid Board reference CRIMLA 25.)

18–50   Error in notification of assessment: normal rules of estoppel apply

Where an error occurs in the notification of the assessment of a criminal costs claim as a result of which the solicitor was misled the normal rules of estoppel apply. (Legal Aid Board reference CRIMLA 26.)

The costs/disbursements of complying with a court order or undertaking   **18–51**
must be assessed in accordance with the Legal Aid in Criminal and Care
Proceedings (Costs) Regulations 1989 (as amended)

In the magistrates' court, even where a solicitor is acting under an order of the court or pursuant to an undertaking given to the court, the costs and/or disbursements of complying with the order or undertaking must be assessed in accordance with the Legal Aid in Criminal and Care Proceedings (Costs) Regulations 1989 (as amended). (Legal Aid Board reference CRIMLA 27.)

Review of assessment of claims for costs by area committee   **18–52**

An area committee dealing with a review of an assessment deals with it *de novo*. (Legal Aid Board reference CRIMLA 28.)

Transfer of magistrates' court legal aid order: work done by new solicitor   **18–53**
prior to transfer

Regulation 44(7) of the Legal Aid in Criminal and Care Proceedings (General) Regulations 1989 does not apply to a situation where there is already a legal aid order in force and therefore there is no authority for paying a second solicitor for work done by him or her before the date of transfer of the legal aid order into that solicitor's name. (Legal Aid Board reference CRIMLA 29.)

Work undertaken prior to committal: scope of magistrates' court order   **18–54**

Where a legal aid order is made to defend criminal proceedings in the magistrates' court and the case proceeds by way of committal to the Crown Court, the costs payable under the order will be limited to items of work relating to proceedings in the magistrates' court. It is for the solicitor to justify work undertaken while the proceedings are in the magistrates' court, taking into account the nature of the case and the issues involved, the time when the work was undertaken, the then state of proceedings, the nature of any evidence obtained and the effect of delaying the work to a date subsequent to committal. (Legal Aid Board reference CRIMLA 30.)

Use of local solicitor agents   **18–55**

In evaluating whether it is appropriate to employ a solicitor agent for any particular hearing, the assigned solicitor should take into consideration all the circumstances of the case, including by way of example:

   (a) the nature and purpose of the hearing, and/or what could be achieved in furthering the preparation of the case by personal attendance;

   (b) the nature, gravity and complexity of the proceedings;

(c) the relationship between client and solicitor;

(d) whether the client suffers from any disability; and

(e) the availability of local agents.

In the absence of any factors justifying the assigned solicitor's attendance, the assigned solicitor will be expected to have regard to the cost effectiveness of employing a local solicitor agent, having regard to the time that will be spent by the assigned solicitor in briefing the agent and the agent in preparing for the hearing, compared with the likely cost of attending in person, including the time that would be spent in travel and waiting. (Legal Aid Board reference CRIMLA 31 as amended.)

18–56   Enhanced rates: assignment of counsel

A finding by magistrates under regulation 44(3)(a) of the Legal Aid in Criminal and Care Proceedings (General) Regulations 1989 that a case is unusually grave or difficult justifying the assignment of counsel under a legal aid order does not override the discretion vested in the appropriate authority to consider whether the circumstances of paragraph 3 of Part I, Schedule 1 of the Legal Aid in Criminal and Care Proceedings (Costs) Regulations 1989 apply, and whether the case attracts fees at more than the relevant basic rate (enhanced rates). (Legal Aid Board reference CRIMLA 32.)

18–57   Travel: time spent and costs incurred

In determining the amount to be allowed in respect of travel:

(a) Prima facie the amount to be allowed is the cost of the time expended on and the expenses incurred in making the journey by public transport, provided that public transport is available and is reasonably convenient, having regard to the relevant circumstances in each case; and

(b) Allowances made should include the time spent and expense incurred in getting from the starting point to the railhead or coach station and also the time spent and expense in getting from the terminus to the destination. (Legal Aid Board reference CRIMLA 33 as amended.)

18–58   Assessment of costs: location of solicitors' offices

The fact that the firm of solicitors assigned under a legal aid order is not local to the court does not in itself mean that their costs must be assessed as if they were a firm local to the court. Guidance has already been given on the correct approach in decisions CRIMLA 21 and 31. (Legal Aid Board reference CRIMLA 34.)

18–59   Time spent listening to tape recordings of police interviews

It is reasonable in principle for solicitors to listen to tape recordings of police interviews where the client cannot confirm that the summary is correct. (Legal Aid Board reference CRIMLA 35.)

**The relationship between decisions of taxing masters, the Costs Appeals   18–60
Committee, area committees and area offices**

(a) Decisions of the Costs Appeals Committee are binding on area committees and area offices.

(b) Decisions of taxing masters are not automatically binding on the Costs Appeals Committee, area committees and area offices.

(c) If a conflict arises between a taxing master's decision and existing Board practice or a Costs Appeals Committee decision, then the existing Board practice or Costs Appeals Committee decision should be followed. In such circumstances, however, an area committee should give consideration to certification of a point of principle of general importance. (Legal Aid Board reference CRIMLA 37 as amended.)

Reasonableness of undertaking work: solicitor's then knowledge   18–61

When considering whether or not an item in a bill is reasonable, the correct approach is to consider whether it was reasonable for the solicitor, in the light of his then knowledge, to undertake the work. (Legal Aid Board reference CRIMLA 38.)

Use of more than one fee-earner at interviews or conference   18–62

Where the circumstances of the case justify it, a charge may be made for the attendance of more than one fee-earner at the same interview or conference. (Legal Aid Board reference CRIMLA 39.)

Magistrates' court standard fees: definition of a case: series of offences   18–63

For the purposes of interpreting the definition of a case as set out in Part III, Schedule 1 to the Legal Aid in Criminal and Care Proceedings (Costs) Regulations 1989, the following factors:

(a) that all the offences are ones of dishonesty; or

(b) that all the offences are finally disposed of at the same hearing

would not of themselves establish that two or more charges or informations form or are part of a series of offences. (Legal Aid Board reference CRIMLA 40.)

**Magistrates' court standard fees: cracked trials: time of discontinuance: 18–64
category of case**

For the purposes of magistrates' court standard fees (set out in the table annexed to paragraph 2 of Part III, Schedule 1 to the Legal Aid in Criminal and Care Proceedings (Costs) Regulations 1989):

(a) *Category 2.2*—it is not essential for the change of plea to be notified on the day of trial provided that the proceedings were listed and fully prepared for trial.

(b) *Category 2.3*—it is not essential for the proceedings to be discontinued on the day of trial provided that proceedings were listed and fully prepared for trial.

(Legal Aid Board reference CRIMLA 41 as amended.)

18–65 Magistrates' court standard fees: Bail Act offences

Proceedings under section 6 of the Bail Act 1976 for failure to surrender to custody are not incidental to the original proceedings for which bail was granted and do constitute a separate case. (Legal Aid Board reference CRIMLA 42 as amended.)

18–66 Use of enquiry agents for tracing witnesses

If it is necessary to employ an enquiry agent to trace a potential witness, then the fee for doing so, together with the fee for obtaining a statement from the witness when traced, may be allowable as a disbursement. (Legal Aid Board reference CRIMLA 43.)

18–67 Enhanced rates: meaning of exceptional

The proper test of "exceptional" within the phrase "exceptional circumstances of the case" in paragraph 3(b) of Part I, Schedule 1 to the Legal Aid in Criminal and Care Proceedings (Costs) Regulations 1989 is the ordinary and actual meaning of the word "exceptional", *i.e.* "unusual or out of the ordinary".

(Legal Aid Board reference CRIMLA 36 as amended.) This decision replaces the previous decision CRIMLA 36 which was quashed by the Divisional Court in proceedings *R. v. Legal Aid Board, ex p. R.M. Broudie & Co. (A Firm)* (1994) 138 S.J. (LB) 94. The Divisional Court determined that "exceptional" means exceptional when compared with an ordinary criminal case, not exceptional when compared with other cases of the same type.

18–68 Magistrates' court standard fees: either-way offences discontinued prior to mode of trial

A charge or summons for an offence which is triable either way which is discontinued or withdrawn before mode of trial is determined in accordance with the procedures set out in sections 19–23 of the Magistrates' Courts Act 1980 attracts a category 1 standard fee. (Legal Aid Board reference CRIMLA 44.)

18–69 Magistrates' court standard fees: claims which attract a standard fee

A claim for costs is only to be dealt with in accordance with the standard fee regime if the claim falls within one of the categories specified in the table set out in paragraph 2(2) of Part III, Schedule 1 to the Legal Aid in Criminal and Care Proceedings (Costs) Regulations 1989. Claims which do not fall into any of those categories attract a non-standard fee. (Legal Aid Board reference CRIMLA 45.)

Magistrates' court standard fees: Newton hearings   18–70

The fact that in a case to which magistrates' court standard fees regime applies there is a hearing in accordance with the principles in *R. v. Newton* [1982] 77 Cr.App.R. 13 does not mean the case attracts a category 2 standard fee. (Legal Aid Board reference CRIMLA 46.)

Magistrates' court standard fees: enhanced rates: use of unassigned   18–71
counsel

A solicitor acting under a legal aid order granted on or after June 1, 1993 is entitled to claim for work done by unassigned counsel at an enhanced rate if the criteria set out in paragraph 3 of Part 1, Schedule 1 to the Legal Aid in Criminal and Care Proceedings (Costs) Regulations 1989 apply to such work. (Legal Aid Board reference CRIMLA 47.)

Magistrates' court standard fees: special reasons hearings   18–72

In a case to which the magistrates' court standard fee regime applies, the fact that there is a "special reasons" hearing does not of itself mean that the case attracts a category 2 standard fee. (Legal Aid Board reference CRIMLA 48.)

Attendance on the editing of interview tapes   18–73

Where there is only one interview tape in existence (without any copies) it is reasonable for a solicitor to attend and be present when the tape is opened and either edited or copied by the police. (Legal Aid Board reference CRIMLA 49.)

Magistrates' court standard fees: series of offences: offences separately   18–74
committed

Whilst offences may, subsequent to committal, appear on separate indictments, that does not of itself mean that they cannot form a series of offences and be classed as one case, although it is a strong indication that they are separate cases. A similar approach should be adopted for offences triable either way that are committed.

In summary only matters or either way offences tried by magistrates, where the magistrates have determined that the offences are incapable of being tried together, although it is a strong indication they are separate cases, it is possible for a series of offences to be established. (Legal Aid Board reference CRIMLA 50 as amended.)

18–75 Travel and waiting: enhancement

Where paragraph 3 of Part I, Schedule 1 to the Legal Aid in Criminal and Care Proceedings (Costs) Regulations 1989 applies, items or classes of work allowed at more than the prescribed rates can include travel and waiting time. (Legal Aid Board reference CRIMLA 51.)

18–76 Work reasonably undertaken when the legal aid order covers both solicitor and counsel

Where a legal aid order is granted to cover both solicitor and counsel the solicitor is entitled to proper remuneration for considering such papers and other materials to the extent reasonably necessary to enable the solicitor to understand the case and properly instruct and attend on counsel. (Legal Aid Board reference CRIMLA 52.)

18–77 An area committee's decision to proceed with an appeal

In looking afresh at a costs assessment the area committee has an unfettered discretion. The solicitor has a duty to place all relevant matters before the committee. There is no breach of natural justice in refusing to allow an adjournment at the solicitor's request nor to give reasons for the refusal to adjourn. (Legal Aid Board reference CRIMLA 53.)

18–78 Review and supervision on franchised file

Time properly spent by franchised firms reviewing and supervising files to meet the franchising criteria is time properly chargeable provided that it coincides with the stage in the proceedings at which the file would normally be reviewed and the work done would be recoverable on taxation as work reasonably done having regard to the needs of the case. (Legal Aid Board reference CRIMLA 54 as amended; applies to legal aid orders granted on or after December 1, 1998.)

18–79 Regulation 44(7) of the Legal Aid in Criminal and Care Proceedings (General) Regulations 1989

In considering the deeming provisions under regulation 44(7) of the Legal Aid in Criminal and Care Proceedings (General) Regulations 1989, although each case must be considered on the basis of its particular circumstances, the criteria in regulation 44(7)(a) and (b) are likely to be satisfied where there is a court hearing within 10 days or less of the date when initial instructions were taken and an application for legal aid was made no more than seven days after initial instruction. Circumstances other than a court hearing fixed for within 10 days of initial instructions may justify the provision of representation or advice as a matter of urgency and the particular circumstances of the case may be such that an application made more than seven days after initial instructions would not be considered to have been unduly delayed.

The time periods mentioned are computed on the basis that time starts to run on the day following initial instruction, and that Saturdays, Sundays and Bank Holidays are counted.

In order to decide whether regulation 44(7) applies, solicitors will need to provide the date of initial instruction, the date the application for legal aid was lodged with the court, the date of the court hearing and the circumstances that it is claimed made provision of the representation or advice necessary as a matter of urgency. (Legal Aid Board reference CRIMLA 55.)

Magistrates' court standard fees: claim for enhanced rates (pre-October 1, 1994)   18–80

When a claim for enhancement is made under paragraph 3 of Part I, Schedule 1 to the Legal Aid in Criminal and Care Proceedings (Costs) Regulations 1989, the determining officer should first consider whether the case is "exceptional" and justifies enhancement. If the claim for enhancement is refused, the solicitor should be notified that the case is not exceptional and given reasons. If the determining office considers the claim for enhancement to be justified, the costs should be assessed on the broad average direct cost of the work, with an appropriate percentage uplift. (Legal Aid Board reference CRIMLA 56.)

Magistrates' court standard fees: definition of a case   18–81

Having regard to Part III, Schedule 1 of the Legal Aid Criminal and Care Proceedings (Costs) Regulations 1989, a charge of escape from lawful custody can be a separate case. (Legal Aid Board reference CRIMLA 57.)

Magistrates' court standard fees: change of solicitor   18–82

Where a defendant is charged with an indictable only offence and the legal aid order is transferred to another solicitor before the committal takes place the work undertaken by the solicitor falls within a category 3 fee (Legal Aid Board reference CRIMLA 58.)

Enhanced rates for legal aid orders granted on or after October, 1994   18–83

In determining the percentage due under paragraph 3 of Part I of Schedule 1 to the Legal Aid in Criminal and Care Proceedings (Costs) Regulations 1989, regard should be had to the Lord Chancellor's Directions for Determining Officers. Area offices and area committees must undertake the calculation set out in the guidance (see para. 18–22, p. 246) which must include a full

"Backhouse" calculation for comparative purposes. (Legal Aid Board reference CRIMLA 59 as amended.)

18–84 Magistrates' court standard fees enhanced rates: serious or complex frauds

When a claim for enhancement is made under paragraph 3 of Part I, Schedule 1 to the Legal Aid in Criminal and Care Proceedings (Costs) Regulations 1989, the fact that the case was transferred to the Crown Court under section 4 of the Criminal Justice Act 1987 is a relevant factor in the determining officer's decision on whether the case involved exceptional circumstances. (Legal Aid Board reference CRIMLA 60.)

18–85 Breach proceedings: separate case

Having regard to Part III, Schedule 1 to the Legal Aid in Criminal and Care Proceedings (Costs) Regulations, a legal aid order granted for breach proceedings which are uncontested can be a separate case. (Legal Aid Board reference CRIMLA 61.)

18–86 Work undertaken in a foreign country under a criminal legal aid order

When a solicitor undertakes work in a foreign country he may be remunerated for what is reasonable waiting time depending on the facts and circumstances of the case, including whether, prior to leaving the United Kingdom, the solicitor made all reasonable efforts to contact witnesses and, where possible, make convenient appointments.

In respect of enhancement on travelling and waiting times, the solicitor may be allowed an enhancement in accordance with point of principle CRIMLA 51.

Where an authority has been granted for reasonable travel and accommodation costs, the authority may include the directly consequential costs of the journey, *e.g.* entry visa charges and inoculation costs. (Legal Aid Board reference CRIMLA 62.)

18–87 Magistrates' court standard fees: driving whilst disqualified: series of offences

Whether two or more offences of driving whilst disqualified constitute a series of offences will depend on the circumstances of each case and whether there is sufficient evidential or factual nexus between them. The fact that the offences are tried or listed for trial separately may be a relevant factor in the determining officer's decision whether there is one or more cases. (Legal Aid Board reference CRIMLA 63.)

18–88 Magistrates' court standard fees: Bail Act offences: series of offences

Two or more offences under either section 6(1) or section 6(2) of the Bail Act

1976 may constitute a series of offences, depending on the circumstances of each case and whether there is an evidential or factual nexus between them. (Legal Aid Board reference CRIMLA 65).

Magistrates' court standard fees: serious or complex fraud 18–89

A criminal case may be serious or complex under paragraph 3(5) of Part I to Schedule 1 to the Legal Aid in Criminal and Care Proceedings (Costs) Regulations 1989 even if not conducted by the Serious Fraud Office. (Legal Aid Board reference CRIMLA 69.)

Enhanced rates: assignment of leading counsel 18–90

Where a legal aid order provides for the services of Queen's Counsel in the Crown Court, this may be a relevant factor in considering whether the criteria set out in paragraph 3, Part I, Schedule 1 to the Legal Aid in Criminal and Care Proceedings (Costs) Regulations 1989 have been met. (Legal Aid Board reference CRIMLA 66.)

Allowance for completing application for prior authority under 18–91
Regulation 54 of the Legal Aid in Criminal and Care Proceedings
(General) Regulations 1989

Work reasonably undertaken in making an application for the grant of prior authority should be remunerated as part of the solicitor's claim for preparation. (Legal Aid Board reference CRIMLA 67.)

Use of unassigned counsel in non-standard fee cases 18–92

Regulation 7A of the Legal Aid in Criminal and Care proceedings (Costs) Regulations 1989 (as amended) does not provide for payment from the legal aid fund of unassigned counsel's travelling and waiting time and/or travelling expenses in cases which attract a non-standard fee by virtue of the fact that they are excluded from the table in paragraph 2 of Part III, Schedule 1 to the Legal Aid in Criminal and Care Proceedings (Costs) Regulations 1989. (Legal Aid Board reference CRIMLA 68.)

Magistrates' court standard fees: Bail Act offences: fee category 18–93

Where a defendant is charged with offences both under sections 6(1) and 6(2) of the Bail Act 1976, and has legal aid for both matters, and pleads guilty to one, and pleads not guilty to the other, the whole matter should be treated as a category 2 mixed plea for standard fee purposes. (Legal Aid Board reference CRIMLA 69).

Magistrates' court standard fees: deferred sentence 18–94

Where sentence is deferred, two separate standard fee claims may be submitted. The first claim should be made on deferment of sentence. A subsequent claim may be made in category 1 once the final deferred sentence hearing has taken place.

If there are multiple cases where the sentence is deferred and the original claim(s) for costs were assessed as consisting of more than one case for standard fee purposes, the later claims for the work relating to the deferred sentence hearing should be assessed at the same number of cases. (Legal Aid Board reference CRIMLA 70.)

18–95 | Enhanced rates: separate representation

If co-defendants are separately represented in the same proceedings and enhanced rates are allowed on assessment in relation to work undertaken on behalf of one or more co-defendants, that may be a relevant factor in considering whether the criteria set out in paragraph 3 of Part I, Schedule 1 to the Legal Aid in Criminal and Care Proceedings (Costs) Regulations 1989 have been met.

It will be for the solicitor seeking the enhanced rates to identify for the determining officer the issues which are common to the work undertaken by them and by other solicitors on behalf of any co-defendant. (Legal Aid Board reference CRIMLA 71.)

18–96 | Magistrates' court standard fees: breach of bail conditions

A breach of bail conditions leading to an arrest under section 7 of the Bail Act 1976 does not constitute a separate case for standard fee purposes when no section 6 offence is charged. Section 7 does not create an offence. Work undertaken in relation to a breach of bail is therefore incidental to the main proceedings. (Legal Aid Board reference CRIMLA 72.)

19. REPRESENTATION IN CONTEMPT PROCEEDINGS

19–01 AVAILABILITY

Non-means tested representation is available to people liable to be committed or fined:

    (a) by a magistrates' court under section 12 of the Contempt of Court Act 1981 (wilfully insulting the justice(s), any witness or court officer, solicitor or barrister in court or going to/returning from court or wilfully interrupting or otherwise misbehaving in court);

    (b) by a county court under sections 14, 92 or 118 of the County Courts Act 1984 (assaulting an officer of the court in the execution of his duty; rescuing or attempting to rescue goods seized by the bailiff; wilfully insulting the judge, any juror or witness or court officer in court or going to/returning from court or wilfully interrupting the proceedings or otherwise misbehaving in court);

(c) by a superior court for contempt in the face of that or any other court.

The relevant provisions are sections 29 and 30(3) of the Legal Aid Act 1988, the Legal Aid Act 1988 (Commencement No. 4) Order 1991 and the Legal Aid in Contempt Proceedings (Remuneration) Regulations 1991 as amended. Note that this representation is for *contempt in the face of the court* and *not for breaches of civil court orders/applications for committal*, for which civil legal aid may be granted, subject to the usual means and merits tests.

There is *no means test* for this representation which is granted by the court where it appears "to be desirable to do so in the interests of justice." Representation can be granted in *any* proceedings where a person may be dealt with within the provisions of section 29 of the Legal Aid Act 1988. Representation may be either by a solicitor *or* barrister.

PAYMENT   19–02

Payment is by way of a *standard fee*, currently £72.75 plus VAT, for each day of appearance although the paying authority may, where it is of the opinion that there are exceptional circumstances, allow an assessed reasonable fee having regard to the amount of the standard fee. Where the assisted person is represented by two legal representatives, the standard fee is required to be divided as to £46.50 for the advocate and £26.25 for the other legal representative (solicitor).

The Board is paying authority for all the courts *except* the Court of Appeal, Criminal Division, and the Crown Court exercising its criminal jurisdiction. In those courts where the Board is the paying authority grants of representation will be confirmed by the court by the issue and completion of the Board's appropriate form (CLA35/claim 11). The solicitor or barrister will submit the form including his claim for payment direct to the Board's London area office—only that office processes claims for payment. The order and claim form includes full instructions as to its completion and will be rejected for resubmission if incorrectly completed.

If the representative seeks an assessed fee the form allows him/her to:

(a) indicate that he/she wishes to apply for a non-standard fee;

(b) give details of the exceptional circumstances of the case to justify the payment of a non-standard fee (*e.g.* work required to be undertaken by the court after the court hearing and before a further court hearing in the case);

(c) give full details of the work done and time spent.

Only the standard fee will be authorised where it is *not* considered that there are exceptional circumstances.

Claims must be made within three months of completion of the work and, although this period may be extended for good reason, oversight on the part of the solicitor or barrister would be unlikely to be considered to constitute good reason. The same rights of review/appeal are available as in relation to other area office costs assessments (see NFG 18, para. 18–22) and there is a right of appeal against a refusal to extend the time for claiming and against the payment of a standard fee where a non standard fee is claimed.

20. LEGAL AID ABROAD

20–01 **FORUM NON CONVENIENS**

Where a court is deciding whether an action may be brought in England and Wales under the doctrine of forum non conveniens, the availability of legal aid in England and Wales or the lack of it in another jurisdiction may be taken into account, notwithstanding the wording of Section 31 Legal Aid Act 1988 (see *Connelly v. RTZ Corporation Plc and Another*, HL, July 24, 1997).

20–02 **LEGAL AID FOR REFERENCES TO THE EUROPEAN COURT AT LUXEMBOURG**

Civil and criminal legal aid are available for a reference to the European Court at Luxembourg. A civil legal aid certificate will require amendment and, where there is no certificate, a legal aid application may be made for representation in the proceedings in England and Wales (which can then include representation on the reference to the European Court). See also NFG 14, para. 14–31 regarding an application to the European Commission of the European Union.

Representation will cover the oral hearing and, subject to taxation/assessment, the solicitor would be paid his costs and disbursements for supporting counsel at the oral hearing.

Legal aid under the system for England and Wales does not cover the European Court of Human Rights at Strasbourg (which has its own system of legal aid).

20–03 **LEGAL AID FOR THE EUROPEAN COMMISSION FOR HUMAN RIGHTS (ECHR)**

Legal aid under the system for England and Wales does not cover the European Commission/Court of Human Rights at Strasbourg, which has its own system of legal aid. Applications for legal aid for cases connected with the ECHR are considered by the European Commission and not the Legal Aid Board.

The European Commission will, however, ask the applicant to obtain a certificate of indigence from the Board confirming whether they would be financially eligible for civil legal aid in England and Wales. An application for that certificate should be made using the relevant civil legal aid financial application form, *e.g.* MEANS 1, MEANS 2 etc.

No civil legal aid merits form is required—a covering letter will suffice. All such applications are dealt with by the Board's London area office. The area office will undertake a normal assessment of means and notify the relevant solicitor of the result. The applicant or solicitor is then responsible for forwarding that notification to the ECHR who will then make their determination of the application for legal aid.

20–04 **EUROPEAN AGREEMENT ON THE TRANSMISSION OF APPLICATIONS FOR LEGAL AID—STRASBOURG, JANUARY 27, 1977**

Legal aid area offices receive a number of enquiries about legal aid abroad and practitioners are reminded of the provisions of the European Agreement on the Transmission of Applications for Legal Aid which was ratified by the United Kingdom on January 17, 1978.

Ratification by other parties

20–05

Other countries to have ratified the Strasbourg Agreement are:

(a) Austria;

(b) Belgium;

(c) Bulgaria;

(d) Denmark;

(e) Republic of Ireland (Eire);

(f) Finland;

(g) France;

(h) Greece;

(i) Italy;

(j) Luxembourg;

(k) Norway;

(l) Poland;

(m) Portugal;

(n) Spain;

(o) Sweden;

(p) Switzerland; and

(q) Turkey.

Transmission of applications

20–06

Under the Agreement, the Legal Aid Board is the Transmitting and Receiving Authority for England and Wales. This means that where a person requires legal aid for civil, commercial or administrative (but not criminal) proceedings in one of the above countries, he/she may send his/her application to the Legal Aid Board which will transmit it to the appropriate authority in that country. Applications for transmission should be sent to Policy and Legal Department, Legal Aid Head Office, 85 Gray's Inn Road, London WC1X 8AA. Similarly, as the Receiving Authority, the Legal Aid Board accepts applications transmitted under the Agreement and passes them to the appropriate legal aid area office (at present No. 1 legal aid area, London).

Format of applications for transmission

20–07

Applications for transmission to foreign authorities should be made using a standard combined application and means form which is available from Legal

Aid Head Office. In the case of applications for Legal Aid in Spain the Board's appropriate means form must also be completed as a means assessment will be carried out.

Most countries will accept applications in English but it is helpful if applications and relevant supporting documents can be made available in the official language of the country involved. In any event France requires a narrative statement of means in French as well as statements, medical reports (if submitted) and other documents to be accompanied by translations in French. Austria requires applications to be accompanied by translations in German.

20–08 Legal advice and assistance

Advice and assistance under the legal advice and assistance (green form) scheme is available (subject to financial eligibility) for the preparation of applications for transmission under the Agreement including obtaining any necessary translations. Any application for an extension to the financial limit should be made to the area office in the usual way.

Part Two

Part Two

Legal Aid (Functions) Order 1989*

Came into force April 1, 1989

Citation and commencement

1. This Order may be cited as the Legal Aid (Functions) Order 1989 and shall come into force on April 1, 1989

Functions under Part V of the Legal Aid Act 1988

2. The general function conferred on the Legal Aid Board by section 3(2) of the Legal Aid Act 1988 shall include all such functions mentioned in subsection (4)(b) of that section as are required to be exercised by the Board to enable it—

    (a) to determine under the Legal Aid in Criminal and Care Proceedings (General) Regulations 1989 as respects representation under Part V of that Act:

        (i) an application for review of a refusal by a magistrates' court to grant representation;

        (ii) a renewed application for amendment or withdrawal of a grant of representation, or for representation by counsel; and

        (iii) an application for prior authority to incur expenditure; and

    (b) to promote or assist in the promotion of publicity relating to the functions mentioned in that subsection.

Functions under Part VI of the Legal Aid Act 1988

3. The general function conferred on the Legal Aid Board by section 3(2) of the Legal Aid Act 1988 shall include all such functions mentioned in subsection (4)(c) of that section as are required to be exercised by the Board to enable it to determine under the Legal Aid in Criminal and Care Proceedings (General) Regulations 1989 as respects representations under Part VI of that Act—

    (a) a renewed application for amendment or withdrawal of a grant of representation; and

    (b) an application for prior authority to incur expenditure.

EXPLANATORY NOTE

(*This note is not part of the Order*)

This Order confers on the Legal Aid Board the functions required to enable area committees under the Legal Aid in Criminal and Care Proceedings Regulations 1989 (S.I. 1989 No. 344) to determine the applications mentioned in articles 2 and 3.

In criminal proceedings the relevant applications are applications for review of refusals of representation by magistrates' courts, renewed applications for amendment or withdrawal of representation (or for representation by counsel), and applications for prior authority to incur expenditure.

* S.I. No. 551.

In care proceedings the relevant applications are renewed applications for amendment or withdrawal of representation, and applications for prior authority to incur expenditure.

Article 2 also confers on the Board the functions required to enable it to promote publicity about Criminal Legal Aid.

Legal Aid (Functions) Order 1997*

Came into force

Citation and commencement

1. This Order may be cited as the Legal Aid (Functions) Order 1997 and shall come into force:

(a) as to article 4, on April 1, 1997;

(b) as to the rest of the Order, on the day following the day on which it was made.

Interpretation

2. Any reference in this Order to a section or Part by number alone means a section or Part so numbered in the Legal Aid Act 1988.

Functions of assessing costs in civil cases

3. The general function conferred on the Legal Aid Board by section 3(2) shall include the function mentioned in section 3(4)(a) to the extent required to enable the Board to conduct any assessment of the costs of representation under Part IV which regulations made under section 34(2)(e) provide for it to conduct, and any review or appeal arising from such an assessment.

Functions of determining financial resources

4. The general function conferred on the Legal Aid Board by section 3(2) shall include the function mentioned in section 3(4)(d) to the extent required to enable the Board to determine the financial resources of any person where regulations made under section 34(2)(c) provide for it to do so.

EXPLANATORY NOTE

(*This note is not part of the Order*)

This Order confers on the Legal Aid Board the functions of assessing:

(a) costs in civil proceedings, and

(b) the resources of any person, for any of the purposes of the Legal Aid Act 1988;

when required to do so by regulations.

* S.I. No. 998.

Legal Aid Act 1988*

CHAPTER 34

ARRANGEMENT OF SECTIONS

Part I

Preliminary

---

* As amended by the Children Act 1989, the Civil Legal Aid (Matrimonial Proceedings) Regulations 1989 (S.I. 1989 No. 549), the Courts and Legal Services Act 1990, the Legal Aid Act 1988 (Children Act 1989) Order 1991 (S.I. 1991 No. 1924), The Civil Legal Aid (General) (Amendment) (No. 2) Regulations 1991 (S.I. 1991 No. 2036), the War Crimes Act 1991, the Criminal Justice Act 1991, the Civil Legal Aid (Scope) Regulations 1993 (S.I. 1993 No. 1354), the Trade Union Reform and Employment Rights Acts 1993, the Criminal Procedure and Investigations Act 1996, the Family Law Act 1996 and the Crime and Disorder Act 1998.

Part VII

General and Supplementary

Part VIII

Miscellaneous

Scottish provisions

Supplementary

An Act to make new provision for the administration of, and to revise the law relating to, legal aid, advice and assistance.

[July 29, 1988]

Part I

Preliminary

Purpose of this Act

1. The purpose of this Act is to establish a framework for the provision under Parts II, III, IIIA, IV, V and VI of advice, assistance, mediation and representation which is publicly funded with a view to helping persons who might otherwise be unable to obtain advice, assistance, mediation or representation on account of their means.

Interpretation

2.—(1) This section has effect for the interpretation of this Act.

(2) "Advice" means oral or written advice on the application of English law to any particular circumstances that have arisen in relation to the person seeking the advice and as to the steps which that person might appropriately take having regard to the application of English law to those circumstances.

(3) "Assistance" means assistance in taking any of the steps which a person might take, including steps with respect to proceedings, having regard to the application of English law to any particular circumstances that have arisen in relation to him, whether by taking such steps on his behalf (including assistance by way of representation) or by assisting him in taking them on his own behalf.

(3A) "Mediation" means mediation to which Part IIIA of this Act applies; and includes steps taken by a mediator in any case—

(a) in determining whether to embark on mediation;

(b) in preparing for mediation; and

(c) in making any assessment under that Part.

(4) "Representation" means representation for the purposes of proceedings and it includes—

(a) all such assistance as is usually given by a legal representative in the steps preliminary or incidental to any proceedings;

(b) all such assistance as is usually so given in civil proceedings in arriving at or giving effect to a compromise to avoid or bring to an end any proceedings; and

(c) in the case of criminal proceedings, advice and assistance as to any appeal;

and related expressions have corresponding meanings.

(5) Regulations may specify what is, or is not, to be included in advice or assistance of any description, or representation for the purposes of proceedings of any description, to which any Part or provision of a Part of this Act applies and the regulations may provide for the inclusion, in prescribed circumstances, of advice or assistance given otherwise than under this Act.

(6) Advice, assistance and representation under this Act, except when made available under Part II, shall only be by legal representative, but in the case of Part II, may be by other persons.

(7) Subject to section 59 of the Courts and Legal Services Act 1990, regulations—

(a) may prescribe the circumstances in which representation shall be only by one legal representative and may require him to be from a prescribed category;

(b) may regulate representation by more than one legal representative from any one or more prescribed categories.

(7A) If it is satisfied that the circumstances of a particular case in the

Supreme Court or the House of Lords warrant a direction under this subsection, the Board or, in the case of criminal proceedings the competent authority, may direct that representation in that case shall be by one legal representative.

(7B) In subsection (7A), "competent authority" shall be construed in accordance with section 20.

(8) The Lord Chancellor may, if it appears to him to be necessary to do so for the purpose of fulfilling any obligation imposed on the United Kingdom or Her Majesty's Government in the United Kingdom by any international agreement, by order direct that such advice or assistance relating to the application of other laws than English law as is specified in the order shall be advice or assistance for any of the purposes of this Act.

(9) For the purposes of the application of subsection (8) above in the case of an obligation to provide for the transmission to other countries of applications for legal aid under their laws, the reference to advice or assistance relating to the application of other laws includes a reference to advice or assistance for the purposes of making and transmitting such an application.

(10) In this Act "person" does not include a body of persons corporate or unincorporate which is not concerned in a representative, fiduciary or official capacity so as to authorise advice, assistance or representation to be granted to such a body.

(11) In this Act "legally assisted person" means any person who receives, under this Act, advice, assistance, mediation or representation and, in relation to proceedings, any reference to an assisted party or an unassisted party is to be construed accordingly.

PART II

LEGAL AID BOARD AND LEGAL AID

The Legal Aid Board

3.—(1) There shall be established a body to be known as the Legal Aid Board (in this Act referred to as "the Board").

(2) Subject to subsections (3) and (4) below, the Board shall have the general function of securing that advice, assistance, mediation and representation are available in accordance with this Act and of administering this Act.

(3) Subsection (2) above does not confer on the Board any functions with respect to the grant of representation under Part VI for the purposes of proceedings for contempt.

(4) Subsection (2) above does not confer on the Board any of the following functions unless the Lord Chancellor so directs by order and then only to the extent specified in the order.

The functions referred to are—

(a) determination of the costs of representation under Part IV;

(b) functions as respects representation under Part V other than determination of the costs of representation for the purposes of proceedings in magistrates' courts;

(c) [repealed by the Children Act 1989];

(d) determination of the financial resources of persons for the purposes of this Act.

(5) Subject to subsection (6) below, the Board shall consist of no fewer than

11 and no more than 17 members appointed by the Lord Chancellor; and the Lord Chancellor shall appoint one of the members to be chairman.

(6) The Lord Chancellor may, by order, substitute, for the number for the time being specified in subsection (5) above as the maximum or minimum membership of the Board, such other number as he thinks appropriate.

(7) The Board shall include at least two solicitors appointed after consultation with the Law Society.

(8) The Lord Chancellor shall consult the General Council of the Bar with a view to the inclusion on the Board of at least two barristers.

(9) In appointing persons to be members of the Board the Lord Chancellor shall have regard to the desirability of securing that the Board includes persons having expertise in or knowledge of—

(a) the provision of legal services;

(aa) the provision of mediation;

(b) the work of the courts and social conditions; and

(c) management.

(10) Schedule 1 to this Act shall have effect with respect to the Board.

Powers of the Board

4.—(1) Subject to the provisions of this Act, the Board may do anything—

(a) which it considers necessary or desirable to provide or secure the provision of advice, assistance, mediation and representation under this Act; or

(b) which is calculated to facilitate or is incidental or conducive to the discharge of its functions;

and advice, assistance, mediation and representation may be provided in different ways in different areas in England and Wales and in different ways in different fields of law.

(2) Without prejudice to the generality of subsection (1) above, the Board shall have power—

(a) to enter into any contract including, subject to subsection (7) below, any contract to acquire or dispose of land;

(b) to make grants (with or without conditions, including conditions as to repayment);

(c) to make loans;

(d) to invest money;

(e) to promote or assist in the promotion of publicity relating to the functions of the Board;

(f) to undertake any inquiry or investigation which the Board considers necessary or expedient in relation to the discharge of its functions; and

(g) to give the Lord Chancellor such advice as it may consider appropriate in relation to the provision of advice, assistance, mediation and representation under this Act.

(3) Subsection (1) above does not confer on the Board power to borrow

money or to acquire and hold shares in bodies corporate or take part in forming bodies corporate.

(4) The powers to provide advice, assistance, mediation or representation under this Part and to secure its provision under this Part by means of contracts with, or grants or loans to, other persons or bodies—

    (a) shall not be exercisable unless the Lord Chancellor so directs and then only to the extent specified in the direction; and

    (b) if exercisable, shall be exercised in accordance with any directions given by him.

(5) The power to secure the provision of representation under Part IV by means of contracts with other persons shall only be exercisable in the classes of case prescribed in regulations.

(6) Advice, assistance and representation provided by the Board under this Part may be granted with or without limitations and may be amended, withdrawn or revoked.

(7) The power under subsection (2) above to enter into contracts to acquire or dispose of land shall not be exercised without the approval in writing of the Lord Chancellor.

(8) The Board may, from time to time, prepare and submit to the Lord Chancellor proposals for the assumption by it of any functions in relation to the provision of advice, assistance or representation under this Act.

Duties of the Board

5.—(1) The Board shall, from time to time, publish information as to the discharge of its functions in relation to advice, assistance, mediation and representation including the forms and procedures and other matters connected therewith.

(2) The Board shall, from time to time, furnish to the Lord Chancellor such information as he may require relating to its property and to the discharge or proposed discharge of its functions.

(3) It shall be the duty of the Board to provide to the Lord Chancellor, as soon as possible after 31st March in each year, a report on the discharge of its functions during the preceding twelve months.

(4) The Board shall deal in any report under subsection (3) above with such matters as the Lord Chancellor may from time to time direct.

(5) The Board shall have regard, in discharging its functions, to such guidance as may from time to time be given by the Lord Chancellor.

(6) Guidance under subsection (5) above shall not relate to the consideration or disposal, in particular cases, of—

    (a) applications for advice, assistance or representation;

    (b) supplementary or incidental applications or requests to the Board in connection with any case where advice, assistance, mediation or representation has been made available.

(7) For the purposes of subsection (2) above the Board shall permit any person authorised by the Lord Chancellor for the purpose to inspect and make copies of any accounts or documents of the Board and shall furnish such explanations of them as that person or the Lord Chancellor may require.

Board to have separate legal aid fund

6.—(1) The Board shall establish and maintain a separate legal aid fund.

(2) Subject to regulations, there shall be paid out of the fund—

(a) such sums as are, by virtue of any provision of or made under this Act, due from the Board in respect of remuneration and expenses properly incurred in connection with the provision, under this Act, of advice, assistance, mediation or representation;

(b) costs awarded to any unassisted party under section 13 or 18;

(c) any part of a contribution repayable by the Board under section 16(4) or 23(7); and

(d) such other payments for the purposes of this Act as the Lord Chancellor may, with the concurrence of the Treasury, determine.

(3) Subject to regulations, there shall be paid into the fund—

(a) any contribution payable to the Board by any person in respect of advice, assistance, mediation or representation under this Act;

(b) any sum awarded under an order of a court or agreement as to costs in any proceedings in favour of any legally assisted party which is payable to the Board;

(c) any sum which is to be paid out of property recovered or preserved for any legally assisted party to any proceedings;

(ca) any sum which is to be paid out of property on which it is charged under regulations under section 13C(5) below;

(d) any sum in respect of the costs of an unassisted party awarded under section 13 or 18 which is repaid to the Board under that section;

(e) the sums to be paid by the Lord Chancellor in pursuance of section 42(1)(a); and

(f) such other receipts of the Board as the Lord Chancellor may, with the concurrence of the Treasury, determine.

Paragraph (ca) inserted by Schedule 8 to the Family Law Act 1996.

Accounts and audit

7.—(1) The Board shall keep separate accounts with respect to—

(a) its legal aid fund; and

(b) the receipts and expenditure of the Board which do not relate to that fund;

and shall prepare in respect of each financial year a statement of accounts.

(2) The accounts shall be kept and the statement of accounts shall be prepared in such form as the Lord Chancellor may, with the approval of the Treasury, direct.

(3) The accounts shall be audited by persons to be appointed in respect of each financial year by the Lord Chancellor in accordance with a scheme of audit approved by him, and the auditors shall be furnished by the Board with copies of the statement and shall prepare a report to the Lord Chancellor on the accounts and statement.

(4) No person shall be appointed auditor under subsection (3) above unless he is—

(a) eligible for appointment as a company auditor under section 25 of the Companies Act 1989; or

(b) a member of the Chartered Institute of Public Finance and Accountancy.

(5) Upon completion of the audit of the accounts, the auditors shall send to the Lord Chancellor a copy of the statement of accounts and of their report, and the Lord Chancellor shall send a copy of the statement and of the report to the Comptroller and Auditor General.

(6) The Lord Chancellor and the Comptroller and Auditor General may inspect the accounts and any records relating to them.

(7) The Lord Chancellor shall lay before each House of Parliament a copy of every statement of accounts and reports of the auditors sent to him under subsection (5) above.

(8) In this section "financial year" means the period beginning with the day on which the Board is established and ending with 31st March next following and each subsequent period of 12 months ending with 31st March in each year.

PART III

ADVICE AND ASSISTANCE

Scope of this part

8.—(1) Subject to the provisions of this section, this Part applies to any advice or assistance and advice and assistance under this Part shall be available to any person subject to and in accordance with the provisions of this section and sections 9, 10 and 11.

(2) This Part only applies to assistance by way of representation if, and to the extent that, regulations so provide; and regulations may make such provision in relation to representation for the purposes of any proceedings before a court or tribunal or at a statutory inquiry.

(3) Advice or assistance of all descriptions or advice or assistance of any prescribed description is excluded from this Part, or is so excluded as regards any area, if regulations so provide; and if regulations provide for all descriptions to be excluded as regards all areas then, so long as the regulations so provide, this Part (other than this subsection) shall not have effect.

(4) Advice or assistance of any prescribed description is restricted to its provision to prescribed descriptions of persons if regulations so provide.

(5) This Part does not apply to advice or assistance given to a person in connection with proceedings before a court or tribunal or at a statutory inquiry at a time when he is being represented in those proceedings under any other Part of this Act.

Availability of, and payment for, advice and assistance

9.—(1) Advice and assistance to which this Part applies shall be available to any person whose financial resources are such as, under regulations, make him eligible for advice or assistance under this Part.

(2) If regulations so provide, advice or assistance to which this Part applies shall be available, in prescribed circumstances and subject to any prescribed conditions, to persons without reference to their financial resources.

(3) Subject to any prescribed exceptions, assistance by way of representation under this Part shall not be given without the approval of the Board.

(4) Approval under subsection (3) above may be given with or without limitations and may be amended, withdrawn or revoked.

(5) Except as provided by subsection (6) or (7) below, the legally assisted person shall not be required to pay to his legal representative any charge or fee.

(6) Except as provided by subsection (7) below, a legally assisted person shall, if his financial resources are such as, under regulations, make him liable to make a contribution, be liable to pay to his legal representative, in respect of the advice or assistance, charges or fees of such amount as is determined or fixed by or under the regulations.

(7) A legally assisted person to whom advice or assistance is made available by virtue of regulations under subsection (2) above shall, in circumstances prescribed by the regulations and, if the regulations apply only to persons of a prescribed description, he is a person of that description, be liable to pay to his legal representative, in respect of the advice or assistance, a fee of such amount as is fixed by or under the regulations (in lieu of a contribution under subsection (6) above).

Financial limit on prospective costs of advice or assistance

10.—(1) Where at any time (whether before or after the advice or assistance has begun to be given) it appears to a legal representative that the cost of giving advice or assistance to a person under this Part is likely to exceed the prescribed limit—

(a) the legal representative shall determine to what extent that advice or assistance can be given without exceeding that limit; and

(b) shall not give it (nor, as the case may be, instruct an additional legal representative to give it) so as to exceed that limit except with the approval of the Board.

(2) Approval under subsection (1)(b) above may be given with or without limitations and may be amended, withdrawn or revoked.

(3) For the purposes of this section the cost of giving advice or assistance shall be taken to consist of such of the following as are applicable in the circumstances, namely—

(a) any disbursements, that is to say, expenses (including fees payable to an additional legal representative) which may be incurred by the legal representative in, or in connection with, the giving of the advice or assistance; and

(b) any charges or fees (other than charges for disbursements) which would be properly chargeable by the legal representative in respect of the advice or assistance.

Payment for advice or assistance otherwise than through legally assisted person's contribution

11.—(1) This section applies to any charges or fees which, apart from section 9, would be properly chargeable in respect of advice or assistance given under this Part, in so far as those charges or fees are not payable by the legally assisted person in accordance with that section.

(2) Except in so far as regulations otherwise provide, charges or fees to which this section applies shall constitute a first charge for the benefit of the legal representative—

(a) on any costs which are payable to the legally assisted person by any other person in respect of the matter in connection with which the advice or assistance is given; and

(b) on any property which is recovered or preserved for the legally assisted person in connection with that matter.

(3) In so far as the charge created by subsection (2) above in respect of any charges or fees to which this section applies is insufficient to meet them, the deficiency shall, subject to subsection (5) below, be payable to the legal representative by the Board.

(4) For the purposes of subsection (2) above, it is immaterial, in the case of costs, whether the costs are payable by virtue of a judgment, order of a court or otherwise and, in the case of property, what its nature is and where it is situated and the property within the charge includes the legally assisted person's rights under any compromise or settlement arrived at to avoid proceedings or bring them to an end.

(5) For the purpose of determining what charges or fees would be properly chargeable, and whether there is a deficiency to be paid by the Board, charges or fees in respect of advice or assistance under this Part shall, in prescribed circumstances, be determined in such manner as may be prescribed.

Limit on costs against person receiving assistance by way of representation

12.—(1) Where a person receives any assistance by way of representation in any proceedings before a court or tribunal or at a statutory inquiry, then, except in so far as regulations otherwise provide, his liability by virtue of an order for costs made against him with respect to the proceedings shall not exceed the amount (if any) which is a reasonable one for him to pay having regard to all the circumstances, including the financial resources of all the parties and their conduct in connection with the dispute.

(2) Regulations shall make provision as to the court, tribunal or person by whom that amount is to be determined and the extent to which any determination of that amount is to be final.

(3) None of the following, namely, a legally assisted person's dwelling house, clothes, household furniture and the tools and implements of his trade shall—

(a) be taken into account in assessing his financial resources for the purposes of this section, or

(b) be subject to execution or any corresponding process in any part of the United Kingdom to enforce the order,

except so far as regulations may prescribe.

Costs of successful unassisted parties

13.—(1) This section applies to proceedings in which a person who receives assistance by way of representation is a party and which are finally decided in favour of an unassisted party.

(2) In any proceedings to which this section applies the court by which the proceedings are so decided may, subject to subsections (3) and (4) below, make an order for the payment by the Board to the unassisted party of the whole or any part of the costs incurred by him in the proceedings.

(3) Before making an order under this section, the court shall consider what order for costs should be made against the assisted party and for determining his liability in respect of such costs.

(4) An order under this section in respect of any costs may only be made if—

(a) an order for costs would be made in the proceedings apart from this Act;

(b) as respects the costs incurred in a court of first instance, those proceedings were instituted by the assisted party and the court is satisfied that the unassisted party will suffer severe financial hardship unless the order is made; and

(c) in any case, the court is satisfied that it is just and equitable in all the circumstances of the case that provision for the costs should be made out of public funds.

(5) Without prejudice to any other provision restricting appeals from any court, no appeal shall lie against an order under this section, or against a refusal to make such an order, except on a point of law.

(6) In this section "costs" means costs as between party and party, and includes the costs of applying for an order under this section; and where a party begins to receive the assistance after the proceedings have been instituted, or ceases to receive the assistance before they are finally decided or otherwise receives the assistance in connection with part only of the proceedings, the reference in subsection (2) above to the costs incurred by the unassisted party in the proceedings shall be construed as a reference to so much of those costs as is attributable to that part.

(7) For the purposes of this section proceedings shall be treated as finally decided in favour of the unassisted party—

(a) if no appeal lies against the decision in his favour;

(b) if an appeal lies against the decision with leave, and the time limited for application for leave expires without leave being granted; or

(c) if leave to appeal against the decision is granted or is not required, and no appeal is brought within the time limited for appeal;

and where an appeal against the decision is brought out of time the court by which the appeal (or any further appeal in those proceedings) is determined may make an order for the repayment by the unassisted party to the Board of the whole or any part of any sum previously paid to him under this section in respect of those proceedings.

(8) Where a court decides any proceedings in favour of the unassisted party and an appeal lies (with or without leave) against that decision, the court may, if it thinks fit, make or refuse to make an order under this section forthwith, but if an order is made forthwith it shall not take effect—

(a) where leave to appeal is required, unless the time limited for applications for leave to appeal expires without leave being granted;

(b) where leave to appeal is granted or is not required, unless the time limited for appeal expires without an appeal being brought.

(9) For the purposes of this section "court" includes a tribunal.

Part IIIA

Mediation

13A.—(1) This Part applies to mediation in disputes relating to family matters.

(2) "Family matters" means matters which are governed by English law and in relation to which any question has arisen, or may arise—

(a) under any provision of—

    (i) the 1973 Act;

    (ii) the Domestic Proceedings and Magistrates' Courts Act 1978;

    (iii) Parts I to V of the Children Act 1989;

    (iv) Parts II and IV of the Family Law Act 1996; or

    (v) any other enactment prescribed;

  (b) under any prescribed jurisdiction of a prescribed court or tribunal; or

  (c) under any prescribed rule of law.

(3) Regulations may restrict this Part to mediation in disputes of any prescribed description.

(4) The power to—

  (a) make regulations under subsection (2), or

  (b) revoke any regulations made under subsection (3),

is exercisable only with the consent of the Treasury.

13B.—(1) The Board may secure the provision of mediation under this Part.

(2) If mediation is provided under this Part, it is to be available to any person whose financial resources are such as, under regulations, make him eligible for mediation.

(3) A person is not to be granted mediation in relation to any dispute unless mediation appears to the mediator suitable to the dispute and the parties and all the circumstances.

(4) A grant of mediation under this Part may be amended, withdrawn or revoked.

(5) The power conferred by subsection (1) shall be exercised in accordance with any directions given by the Lord Chancellor.

(6) Any contract entered into by the Board for the provision of mediation under this Part must require the mediator to comply with a code of practice.

(7) The code must require the mediator to have arrangements designed to ensure—

  (a) that parties participate in mediation only if willing and not influenced by fear of violence or other harm;

  (b) that cases where either party may be influenced by fear of violence or other harm are identified as soon as possible;

  (c) that the possibility of reconciliation is kept under review throughout mediation; and

  (d) that each party is informed about the availability of independent legal advice.

(8) Where there are one or more children of the family, the code must also require the mediator to have arrangements designed to ensure that the parties are encouraged to consider—

  (a) the welfare, wishes and feelings of each child; and

  (b) whether and to what extent each child should be given the opportunity to express his or her wishes and feelings in the mediation.

(9) A contract entered into by the Board for the provision of mediation under this Part must also include such other provision as the Lord Chancellor may direct the Board to include.

(10) Directions under this section may apply generally to contracts, or to

contracts of any description, entered into by the Board, but shall not be made with respect to any particular contract.

13C.—(1) Except as provided by this section, the legally assisted person is not to be required to pay for mediation provided under this Part.

(2) Subsection (3) applies if the financial resources of a legally assisted person are such as, under regulations, make him liable to make a contribution.

(3) The legally assisted person is to pay to the Board in respect of the costs of provding the mediation, a contribution of such amount as is determined or fixed by or under the regulations.

(4) If the total contribution made by a person in respect of any mediation exceeds the Board's liability on his account, the excess shall be repaid to him.

(5) Regulations may provide that, where—

(a) mediation under this Part is made available to a legally assisted person, and

(b) property is recovered or preserved for the legally assisted person as a result of the mediation,

a sum equal to the Board's liability on the legally assisted person's account is, except so far as the regulations otherwise provide, to be a first charge on the property in favour of the Board.

(6) Regulations under subsection (5) may, in particular, make provision—

(a) as to circumstances in which property is to be taken to have been, or not to have been, recovered or preserved; and

(b) as to circumstances in which the recovery or preservation of property is to be taken to be, or not to be, the result of any mediation.

(7) For the purposes of subsection (5), the nature of the property and where it is situated is immaterial.

(8) The power to make regulations under section 34(2)(f) and (8) is exercisable in relation to any charge created under subsection (5) as it is exercisable in relation to the charge created by section 16.

(9) For the purposes of subsections (4) and (5), the Board's liability on any person's account in relation to any mediation is the aggregate amount of—

(a) the sums paid or payable by the Board on his account for the mediation, determined in accordance with subsection (10);

(b) any sums paid or payable in respect of its net liability on his account, determined in accordance with subsection (11) and the regulations—
 (i) in respect of any proceedings, and
 (ii) for any advice or assistance under Part III in connection with the proceedings or any matter to which the proceedings relate,
 so far as the proceedings relate to any matter to which the mediation relates; and

(c) any sums paid or payable in respect of its net liability on his account, determined in accordance with the regulations, for any other advice or assistance under Part III in connection with the mediation or any matter to which the mediation relates.

(10) For the purposes of subsection (9)(a), the sums paid or payable by the Board on any person's account for any mediation are—

(a) sums determined under the contract between the Board and the mediator as payable by the Board on that person's account for the mediation; or

(b) if the contract does not differentiate between such sums and sums payable on any other person's account or for any other mediation, such part of the remuneration payable under the contract as may be specified in writing by the Board.

(11) For the purposes of subsection (9)(b), the Board's net liability on any person's account in relation to any proceedings is its net liability on his account under section 16(9)(a) and (b) in relation to the proceedings.

Inserted by the Family Law Act 1996 pursuant to Commencement (No. 1) Order 1997—S.I. 1997 No. 1077 (c. 38).

PART IV

CIVIL LEGAL AID

Scope of this part

14.—(1) This Part applies to such proceedings before courts or tribunals or at statutory inquiries in England and Wales as—

(a) are proceedings of a description for the time being specified in Part I of Schedule 2 to this Act, except proceedings for the time being specified in Part II of that Schedule; and

(b) are not proceedings for which representation may be granted under Part V,

and representation under this Part shall be available to any person subject to and in accordance with sections 15 and 16.

(2) Subject to subsection (3) below, Schedule 2 may be varied by regulations so as to extend or restrict the categories of proceedings for the purposes of which representation is available under this Part, by reference to the court, tribunal or statutory inquiry, to the issues involved, to the capacity in which the person seeking representation is concerned or otherwise.

(3) Regulations under subsection (2) above may not have the effect of adding any proceedings before any court or tribunal or at any statutory inquiry before or at which persons have no right, and are not normally allowed, to be represented by a legal representative.

(4) Regulations under subsection (2) above which extend the categories of proceedings for the purposes of which representation is available under this Part shall not be made without the consent of the Treasury.

Availability of, and payment for, representation under this Part

15.—(1) Subject to subsections (2) to (3D) and (3F) below, representation under this Part for the purposes of proceedings to which this Part applies shall be available to any person whose financial resources are such as, under regulations, make him eligible for representation under this Part.

(2) A person shall not be granted representation for the purposes of any proceedings unless he satisfies the Board that he has reasonable grounds for taking, defending or being a party to the proceedings.

(3) A person may be refused representation for the purposes of any proceedings if, in the particular circumstances of the case it appears to the Board—

    (a) unreasonable that he should be granted representation under this Part, or

    (b) more appropriate that he should be given assistance by way of representation under Part III;

and regulations may prescribe the criteria for determining any questions arising under paragraph (b) above.

    (3A) Representation under this Part shall not be available—

    (a) to any local authority; or

    (b) to any other body which falls within a prescribed description, or

    (c) to a guardian *ad litem,*

for the purposes of any proceedings under the Children Act 1989.

    (3B) Regardless of subsection (2) or (3), representation under this Part must be granted where a child who is brought before a court under section 25 of the 1989 Act (use of accommodation for restricting liberty) is not, but wishes to be, legally represented before the court.

    (3C) Subject to subsection (3A) but regardless of subsections (2) or (3), representation under this Part must be granted to the child in respect of whom the application is made, to any parent of such a child and to any person with parental responsibility for him within the meaning of the 1989 Act to cover proceedings relating to an application for the following orders under that Act—

    (a) an order under section 31 (a care or supervision order);

    (b) an order under section 43 (a child assessment order);

    (c) an order under section 44 (an emergency protection order); or

    (d) an order under section 45 (extension or discharge of an emergency protection order).

    (3D) Subject to subsections (2), (3) and (3F), representation must be granted to cover proceedings relating to an appeal against an order made under section 31 of the 1989 Act to a person who has been granted representation by virtue of subsection (3C).

    (3E) Subject to subsections (1) and (3A) but regardless of subsections (2) or (3), representation under this Part must be granted where a person applies to be or has been joined as a party to any of the proceedings mentioned in subsection (3C).

    (3F) A person shall not be granted representation for the purposes of proceedings relating to family matters, unless he has attended a meeting with a mediator—

    (a) to determine—

      (i) whether mediation appears suitable to the dispute and the parties and all the circumstances, and

      (ii) in particular, whether mediation could take place without either party being influenced by fear of violence or other harm; and

    (b) if mediation does appear suitable, to help the person applying for representation to decide whether instead to apply for mediation.

    (3G) Subsection (3F) does not apply—

    (a) in relation to proceedings under—

(i) Part IV of the Family Law Act 1996;

(ii) section 37 of the Matrimonial Causes Act 1973;

(iii) Part IV or V of the Children Act 1989;

(b) in relation to proceedings of any other description that may be pre-scribed; or

(c) in such circumstances as may be prescribed.

(3H) So far as proceedings relate to family matters, the Board, in determin-ing under subsection (3)(a) whether, in relation to the proceedings, it is reasonable that a person should be granted representation under this Part—

(a) must have regard to whether and to what extent recourse to mediation would be a suitable alternative to taking the proceedings; and

(b) must for that purpose have regard to the outcome of the meeting held under subsection (3F) and to any assessment made for the purposes of section 13B(3).

(3I) A person may be refused representation for the purposes of any proceed-ings if—

(a) the proceedings are marital proceedings within the meaning of Part II of the Family Law Act 1996; and

(b) he is being provided with marriage counselling under section 23 of that Act in relation to the marriage.

(4) Representation under this Part may be granted by the Board with or without limitations and may be amended, withdrawn or revoked.

(4A) A person may not be refused representation for the purposes of any proceedings on the ground (however expressed) that it would be more appro-priate for him and a legal representative of his to enter into a conditional fee agreement (as defined by section 58 of the Courts and Legal Services Act 1990).

(5) Where the case is one in which the Board has power to secure the pro-vision of representation under this Part by means of contracts with other per-sons, the grant of representation under this Part may be limited under subsection (4) above as regards the persons who may represent the legally assisted person to representation only in pursuance of a contract made with the Board.

(6) Except in so far as he is required under section 16 to make a contribution, a legally assisted person shall not be required to make any payment in respect of representation under this Part and it shall be for the Board to pay his legal representative.

(7) The Board's obligation under subsection (6) above is—

(a) in the case of representation provided in pursuance of a contract between the Board and the legally assisted person's legal representa-tive, to make such payments as are due under the contract; and

(b) in the case of representation provided otherwise than in pursuance of such a contract, to make such payments as are authorised by regulations.

(8) Nothing in subsection (6) above affects the duty of the legal representa-tive to pay in the first instance expenses incurred in connection with the pro-

ceedings that would ordinarily be paid in the first instance by a person's legal representative.

Amended by Schedule 8 to the Family Law Act 1996.
Section 15(4A) is not yet in force.

Reimbursement of Board by contributions and out of costs or property recovered

16.—(1) A legally assisted person shall, if his financial resources are such as, under regulations, make him liable to make such a contribution, pay to the Board a contribution in respect of the costs of his being represented under this Part.

(2) The contribution to be required of him by the Board shall be determined by the Board in accordance with the regulations and may take the form of periodical payments or one or more capital sums or both.

(3) The contribution required of a person may, in the case of periodical payments, be made payable by reference to the period during which he is represented under this Part or any shorter period and, in the case of a capital sum, be made payable by instalments.

(4) If the total contribution made by a person in respect of any proceedings exceeds the net liability of the Board on his account, the excess shall be repaid to him.

(5) Any sums recovered by virtue of an order or agreement for costs made in favour of a legally assisted person with respect to the proceedings shall be paid to the Board.

(6) Except so far as regulations otherwise provide—

> (a) any sums remaining unpaid on account of a person's contribution in respect of the sums payable by the Board in respect of any proceedings; and

> (b) a sum equal to any deficiency by reason of his total contribution being less than the net liability of the Board on his account,

shall be a first charge for the benefit of the Board on any property which is recovered or preserved for him in the proceedings.

(7) For the purposes of subsection (6) above it is immaterial what the nature of the property is and where it is situated and the property within the charge includes the rights of a person under any compromise or settlement arrived at to avoid the proceedings or bring them to an end and any sums recovered by virtue of an order for costs made in his favour in the proceedings (not being sums payable to the Board under subsection (5) above).

(8) The charge created by subsection (6) above on any damages or costs shall not prevent a court allowing them to be set off against other damages or costs in any case where a legal representative's lien for costs would not prevent it.

(9) In this section references to the net liability of the Board on a legally assisted person's account in relation to any proceedings are references to the aggregate amount of—

> (a) the sums paid or payable by the Board on his account in respect of those proceedings to any legal representative; and

> (b) any sums so paid or payable for any advice or assistance under Part III in connection with those proceedings or any matter to which those proceedings relate; and

> (c) if and to the extent that regulations so provide, any sums paid or pay-

able in respect of the Board's liability on the legally assisted person's account in relation to any mediation in connection with any matter to which those proceedings relate.

being sums not recouped by the Board by sums which are recoverable by virtue of an order or agreement for costs made in his favour with respect to those proceedings or by virtue of any right of his to be indemnified against expenses incurred by him in connection with those proceedings.

(10) Where a legally assisted person has been represented in any proceedings in pursuance of a contract made with the Board on terms which do not differentiate between the remuneration for his and other cases, the reference in subsection (9)(a) above to the sums paid or payable by the Board on his account in respect of the proceedings shall be construed as a reference to such part of the remuneration payable under the contract as may be specified in writing by the Board.

(11) For the purposes of subsection (9)(c) above, the Board's liability on any person's account in relation to any mediation is its liability on his account under section 13C(9)(a) and (c) above in relation to the mediation.

Amended by Schedule 8 to the Family Law Act 1996.

Limit on costs against assisted party

17.—(1) The liability of a legally assisted party under an order for costs made against him with respect to any proceedings shall not exceed the amount (if any) which is a reasonable one for him to pay having regard to all the circumstances, including the financial resources of all the parties and their conduct in connection with the dispute.

(2) Regulations shall make provision as to the court, tribunal or person by whom that amount is to be determined and the extent to which any determination of that amount is to be final.

(3) None of the following, namely, a legally assisted person's dwelling house, clothes, household furniture and the tools and implements of his trade shall—

(a) be taken into account in assessing his financial resources for the purposes of this section, or

(b) be subject to execution or any corresponding process in any part of the United Kingdom to enforce the order,

except so far as regulations may prescribe.

Costs of successful unassisted parties

18.—(1) This section applies to proceedings to which a legally assisted person is a party and which are finally decided in favour of an unassisted party.

(2) In any proceedings to which this section applies the court by which the proceedings were so decided may, subject to subsections (3) and (4) below, make an order for the payment by the Board to the unassisted party of the whole or any part of the costs incurred by him in the proceedings.

(3) Before making an order under this section, the court shall consider what order for costs should be made against the assisted party and for determining his liability in respect of such costs.

(4) An order under this section in respect of any costs may only be made if—

(a) an order for costs would be made in the proceedings apart from this Act;

(b) as respects the costs incurred in a court of first instance, those proceedings were instituted by the assisted party and the court is satisfied that the unassisted party will suffer severe financial hardship unless the order is made; and

(c) in any case, the court is satisfied that it is just and equitable in all the circumstances of the case that provision for the costs should be made out of public funds.

(5) Without prejudice to any other provision restricting appeals from any court, no appeal shall lie against an order under this section, or against a refusal to make such an order, except on a point of law.

(6) In this section "costs" means costs as between party and party, and includes the costs of applying for an order under this section; and where a party begins to receive representation after the proceedings have been instituted, or ceases to receive representation before they are finally decided or otherwise receives representation in connection with part only of the proceedings, the reference in subsection (2) above to the costs incurred by the unassisted party in the proceedings shall be construed as a reference to so much of those costs as is attributable to that part.

(7) For the purposes of this section proceedings shall be treated as finally decided in favour of the unassisted party—

(a) if no appeal lies against the decision in his favour;

(b) if an appeal lies against the decision with leave, and the time limited for applications for leave expires without leave being granted; or

(c) if leave to appeal against the decision is granted or is not required, and no appeal is brought within the time limited for appeal;

and where an appeal against the decision is brought out of time the court by which the appeal (or any further appeal in those proceedings) is determined may make an order for the repayment by the unassisted party to the Board of the whole or any part of any sum previously paid to him under this section in respect of those proceedings.

(8) Where a court decides any proceedings in favour of the unassisted party and an appeal lies (with or without leave) against that decision, the court may, if it thinks fit, make or refuse to make an order under this section forthwith, but if an order is made forthwith it shall not take effect—

(a) where leave to appeal is required, unless the time limited for applications for leave to appeal expires without leave being granted;

(b) where leave to appeal is granted or is not required, unless the time limited for appeal expires without an appeal being brought.

(9) For the purposes of this section "court" includes a tribunal.

PART V

CRIMINAL LEGAL AID

Scope of this part

19.—(1) This Part applies to criminal proceedings before any of the following—

(a) a magistrates' court;

(b) the Crown Court;

(c) the criminal division of the Court of Appeal or the Courts-Martial Appeal Court; and

(d) the House of Lords in the exercise of its jurisdiction in relation to appeals from either of those courts;

and representation under this Part shall be available to any person subject to and in accordance with sections 21, 22, 23, 24 and 25.

(2) Representation under this Part for the purposes of the proceedings before any court extends to any proceedings preliminary or incidental to the proceedings, including bail proceedings, whether before that or another court.

(3) Representation under this Part for the purposes of the proceedings before a magistrates' court extends to any proceedings before a youth court or other magistrates' court to which the case is remitted.

(4) In subsection (2) above in its application to bail proceedings, "court" has the same meaning as in the Bail Act 1976, but that subsection does not extend representation to bail proceedings before a judge of the High Court exercising the jurisdiction of that Court.

(5) In this Part—

"competent authority" is to be construed in accordance with section 20;

"Court of Appeal" means the criminal division of that Court;

"criminal proceedings" includes proceedings for dealing with an offender for an offence or in respect of a sentence or as a fugitive offender and also includes proceedings instituted under section 115 of the Magistrates' Courts Act 1980 (binding over) in respect of an actual or apprehended breach of the peace or other misbehaviour and proceedings for dealing with a person for a failure to comply with a condition of a recognizance to keep the peace or be of good behaviour and also includes proceedings under section 15 of the Children and Young Persons Act 1969 (variation and discharge of supervision orders) and section 16(8) of that Act (appeals in such proceedings);

"proceedings for dealing with an offender as a fugitive offender" means proceedings before a metropolitan stipendiary magistrate under section 9 of the Extradition Act 1870, section 7 of the Fugitive Offenders Act 1967 or section 6 of the Criminal Justice Act 1988; and

"remitted," in relation to a youth court, means remitted under section 56(1) of the Children and Young Persons Act 1933;

and any reference, in relation to representation for the purposes of any proceedings, to be proceedings before a court includes a reference to any proceedings to which representation under this Part extends by virtue of subsection (2) or (3) above.

Competent authorities to grant representation under this Part

20.—(1) Subject to any provision made by virtue of subsection (10) below, the following courts are competent to grant representation under this Part for the purposes of the following proceedings, on an application made for the purpose.

(2) The court before which any proceedings take place, or are to take place, is always competent as respects those proceedings, except that this does not apply to the House of Lords; and, in the case of the Court of Appeal and the Courts-Martial Appeal Court, the reference to proceedings which are to take

place includes proceedings which may take place if notice of appeal is given or an application for leave to appeal is made.

(3) The Court of Appeal or, as the case may be, the Courts-Martial Appeal Court is also competent as respects proceedings on appeal from decisions of theirs to the House of Lords.

(4) The magistrates' court—

(a) which commits a person for trial or sentence or to be dealt with in respect of a sentence;

(aa) which sends a person for trial under section 51 of the Crime and Disorder Act 1998 (no committal proceedings for indictable-only offences);

(b) which has been given a notice of transfer under section 4 of the Criminal Justice Act 1987 (transfer of serious fraud cases) or section 53 of the Criminal Justice Act 1991 (transfer of certain cases involving children);

(bb) *[Repealed by the Criminal Procedure and Investigations Act 1996.]*

(c) from which a person appeals against his conviction or sentence,

is also competent as respects the proceedings before the Crown Court.

(5) The magistrates' court inquiring into an offence as examining justices is also competent, before it decides whether or not to commit the person for trial, as respects any proceedings before the Crown Court on his trial.

(5A) A magistrates' court which has a duty or a power to send a person for trial under section 51 of the Crime and Disorder Act 1998 is also competent, before discharging that duty or (as the case may be) deciding whether to exercise that power, as respects any proceedings before the Crown Court on the persons' trial.

(6) The Crown Court is also competent as respects applications for leave to appeal and proceedings on any appeal to the Court of Appeal under section 9(11) of the Criminal Justice Act 1987 (appeals against orders or rulings at preparatory hearings).

(7) On ordering a retrial under section 7 of the Criminal Appeal Act 1968 (new trials ordered by Court of Appeal or House of Lords on fresh evidence) the court ordering the retrial is also competent as respects the proceedings before the Crown Court.

(8) Any magistrates' court to which, in accordance with regulations, a person applies for representation when he has been arrested for an offence but has not appeared or been brought before a court is competent as respects the proceedings in relation to the offence in any magistrates' court.

(9) In the event of the Lord Chancellor making an order under section 3(4) as respects the function of granting representation under this Part for the purposes of proceedings before any court, the Board shall be competent as respects those proceedings, on an application made for the purpose.

(10) An order under section 3(4) may make provision restricting or excluding the competence of any court mentioned in any of subsections (2) to (8) above and may contain such transitional provisions as appear to the Lord Chancellor necessary or expedient.

Amended by the Crime and Disorder Act 1998.

Availability of representation under this Part

21.—(1) Representation under this Part for the purposes of any criminal proceedings shall be available in accordance with this section to the accused or convicted person but shall not be available to the prosecution except in the case of an appeal to the Crown Court against conviction or sentence, for the purpose of enabling an individual who is not acting in an official capacity to resist the appeal.

(2) Subject to subsection (5) below, representation may be granted where it appears to the competent authority to be desirable to do so in the interests of justice; and section 22 applies for the interpretation of this subsection in relation to the proceedings to which that section applies.

(3) Subject to subsection (5) below, representation must be granted—

    (a) where a person is committed or sent for trial on a charge of murder, for his trial;

    (b) where the prosecutor appeals or applies for leave to appeal to the House of Lords, for the proceedings on the appeal;

    (c) where a person charged with an offence before a magistrates' court—

        (i) is brought before the court in pursuance of a remand in custody when he may be again remanded or committed in custody, and

        (ii) is not, but wishes to be, legally represented before the court (not having been legally represented when he was so remanded),

    for so much of the proceedings as relates to the grant of bail; and

    (d) where a person:

        (i) is to be sentenced or otherwise dealt with for an offence by a magistrates' court or the Crown Court, and

        (ii) is to be kept in custody to enable enquiries or a report to be made to assist the court,

    for the proceedings on sentencing or otherwise dealing with him.

(4) Subject to any provision made under section 3(4) by virtue of section 20(10), in a case falling within subsection (3)(a) above, it shall be for the magistrates' court which commits or sends the person for trial, and not for the Crown Court, to make the grant of representation for his trial.

(5) Representation shall not be granted to any person unless it appears to the competent authority that his financial resources are such as, under regulations, make him eligible for representation under this Part.

(6) Before making a determination for the purposes of subsection (5) above in the case of any person, the competent authority shall, except in prescribed cases, require a statement of his financial resources in the prescribed form to be furnished to the authority.

(7) Where a doubt arises whether representation under this Part should be granted to any person, the doubt shall be resolved in that person's favour.

(8) Where an application for representation for the purposes of an appeal to the Court of Appeal or the Courts-Martial Appeal Court is made to a competent authority before the giving of notice of appeal or the making of an application for leave to appeal, the authority may, in the first instance, exercise its power to grant representation by making a grant consisting of advice on the question whether there appear to be reasonable grounds of appeal and assistance in the preparation of an application for leave to appeal or in the giving of a notice of appeal.

(9) Representation granted by a competent authority may be amended or withdrawn, whether by that or another authority competent to grant representation under this Part.

(10) Regulations may provide for an appeal to lie to a specified court or body against any refusal by a magistrates' court to grant representation under this

Part and for that other court or body to make any grant of representation that could have been made by the magistrates' court.

(10A) Where section 44A of the Criminal Appeal Act 1968 (death of convicted person) applies, the reference in subsection (1) above to the convicted person shall be construed as a reference to the person approved under that section.

(11) Subsection (3) above shall have effect in its application to a person who has not attained the age of eighteen as if the references in paragraphs (c) and (d) to remand in custody and to being remanded or kept in custody included references to being committed under section 23 of the Children and Young Persons Act 1969 to the care of a local authority or a remand centre.

Amended by the Criminal Appeal Act 1995 and the Crime and Disorder Act 1998.

Criteria for grant of representation for trial proceedings

22.—(1) This section applies to proceedings by way of a trial by or before a magistrates' court or the Crown Court or on an appeal to the Crown Court against a person's conviction.

(2) The factors to be taken into account by a competent authority in determining whether it is in the interests of justice that representation be granted for the purposes of proceedings to which this section applies to an accused shall include the following—

(a) the offence is such that if proved it is likely that the court would impose a sentence which would deprive the accused of his liberty or lead to loss of his livelihood or serious damage to his reputation;

(b) the determination of the case may involve consideration of a substantial question of law;

(c) the accused may be unable to understand the proceedings or to state his own case because of his inadequate knowledge of English, mental illness or other mental or physical disability;

(d) the nature of the defence is such as to involve the tracing and interviewing of witnesses or expert cross-examination of a witness for the prosecution;

(e) it is in the interests of someone other than the accused that the accused be represented.

(3) The Lord Chancellor may, by order, vary the factors listed in subsection (2) above by amending factors in the list or by adding new factors to the list.

Reimbursement of public funds by contributions

23.—(1) When representation under this Part is granted to any person whose financial resources are such as, under regulations, make him liable to make a contribution, the competent authority shall order him to pay a contribution in respect of the costs of his being represented under this Part.

(2) Where the legally assisted person has not attained the age of sixteen, the competent authority may, instead of or in addition to ordering him to make a contribution, order any person—

(a) who is an appropriate contributor in relation to him; and

(b) whose financial resources are such as, under regulations, make him liable to make a contribution,

to pay a contribution in respect of the costs of the representation granted to the legally assisted person.

(3) Regulations may authorise the making of a contribution order under subsection (1) or (2) above after the grant of representation in prescribed circumstances.

(4) The amount of the contribution to be required under subsection (1) or (2) above by the competent authority shall be such as is determined in accordance with the regulations.

(5) A legally assisted person or appropriate contributor may be required to make his contribution in one sum or by instalments as may be prescribed.

(6) Regulations may provide that no contribution order shall be made in connection with a grant of representation under this Part for the purposes of proceedings in the Crown Court, the Court of Appeal or the House of Lords in a case where a contribution order was made in connection with a grant of such representation to the person in question in respect of proceedings in a lower court.

(7) Subject to subsection (8) below, if the total contribution made in respect of the costs of representing any person under this Part exceeds those costs, the excess shall be repaid—

(a) where the contribution was made by one person only, to him; and

(b) where the contribution was made by two or more persons to them in proportion to the amounts contributed by them.

(8) Where a contribution has been made in respect of the costs of representing any person under this Part in any proceedings and an order for costs is made in favour of that person in respect of those proceedings, then, where sums due under the order for costs are paid to the Board or the Lord Chancellor under section 20(2) of the Prosecution of Offences Act 1985 (recovery regulations)—

(a) if the costs of the representation do not exceed the sums so paid, subsection (7) above shall not apply and the contribution shall be repaid;

(b) if the costs of the representation do exceed the sums so paid, subsection (7) above shall apply as if the costs of the representation were equal to the excess.

(9) References in subsection (8) above to the costs of representation include any charge or fee treated as part of those costs by section 26(2).

(10) In this Part—

"appropriate contributor" means a person of a description prescribed under section 34(2)(c); and

"contribution order" means an order under subsection (1) or (2) above.

Contribution orders: supplementary

24.—(1) Where a competent authority grants representation under this Part and in connection with the grant makes a contribution order under which any sum is required to be paid on the making of the order, it may direct that the grant of representation shall not take effect until that sum is paid.

(2) Where a legally assisted person fails to pay any relevant contribution when it is due, the court in which the proceedings for the purposes of which he has been granted representation are being heard may, subject to subsection (3) below, revoke the grant.

(3) A court shall not exercise the power conferred by subsection (2) above unless, after affording the legally assisted person an opportunity of making representations in such manner as may be prescribed, it is satisfied—

(a) that he was able to pay the relevant contribution when it was due; and

(b) that he is able to pay the whole or part of it but has failed or refused to do so.

(4) In subsection (2) above "relevant contribution," in relation to a legally assisted person, means any sum—

(a) which he is required to pay by a contribution order made in connection with the grant to him of representation under this Part; and

(b) which falls due after the making of the order and before the conclusion of the proceedings for the purposes of which he has been granted such representation.

(5) Regulations with respect to contribution orders may—

(a) provide for their variation or revocation in prescribed circumstances;

(b) provide for their making in default of the prescribed evidence of a person's financial resources;

(c) regulate their making after the grant of representation;

(d) authorise the remission or authorise or require the repayment in prescribed circumstances of sums due or paid under such orders; and

(e) prescribe the court or body by which any function under the regulations is to be exercisable.

(6) Schedule 3 to this Act shall have effect with respect to the enforcement of contribution orders.

Payment of costs of representation under this Part

25.—(1) Where representation under this Part has been granted to any person the costs of representing him shall be paid—

(a) by the Lord Chancellor; or

(b) by the Board,

as the Lord Chancellor may direct.

(2) Subject to regulations, the costs of representing any person under this Part shall include sums on account of the fees payable to his legal representative and disbursements reasonably incurred by his legal representative for or in connection with his representation.

(3) The costs required by this section to be paid in respect of representing him shall not include any sum in respect of allowances to witnesses attending to give evidence in the proceedings for the purposes of which he is represented in any case where such allowances are payable under any other enactment.

Payment for advice or assistance where representation under this Part is subsequently granted

26.—(1) This section has effect where—

(a) advice or assistance under Part III is given to a person in respect of any matter which is or becomes the subject of criminal proceedings against him; and

(b) he is subsequently granted representation under this Part for the purposes of those proceedings.

(2) If the legal representative acting for the person under the grant of representation is the one who gave him the advice or assistance, any charge or fee

in respect of the advice or assistance which, apart from this section, would fall to be secured, recovered or paid as provided by section 11 shall instead be paid under section 25 as if it were part of the costs of the representation.

(3) If a contribution order is made in connection with the grant of representation under this Part to him—

(a) any sum which he is required by virtue of section 9(6) or (7) to pay in respect of the advice or assistance (whether or not already paid) shall be credited against the contribution to be made by him under the contribution order; and

(b) section 25 shall have effect in a case to which subsection (2) above applies as if the charges and fees properly chargeable in respect of the advice or assistance were part of the costs of the representation under this Part and as if any such sum as is mentioned in paragraph (a) above which he has paid were part of the contribution made under the contribution order.

PART VI

LEGAL AID IN SPECIAL CASES

Care proceedings

Representation in care proceedings: scope and competent authorities

27.—(1) This section and section 28 apply, subject to subsection (2) below, to the following proceedings (referred to as "care proceedings"), that is to say—

(a) proceedings under section 1 of the 1969 Act or under section 21A of the 1980 Act (care proceedings);

(b) proceedings under section 15 or 21 of the 1969 Act (variation and discharge of supervision or care orders);

(c) proceedings under section 2(12), 3(8), 16(8) or 21(4) of the 1969 Act or section 21A of the 1980 Act (appeals in such proceedings);

(d) proceedings under section 3 of the Children and Young Persons Act 1963 (application by parent or guardian for an order directing a local authority to take proceedings under section 1 of the 1969 Act);

(e) proceedings under section 3, 5 or 67(2) of the 1980 Act (proceedings in connection with resolutions by local authorities with respect to the assumption of parental rights and duties); and

(f) proceedings under Part 1A of the 1980 Act (access orders);

and representation for the purposes of care proceedings to which this section applies shall be available to any person subject to and in accordance with section 28.

(2) Subsection (1) above may be varied by regulations so as to restrict the categories of proceedings for the purposes of which representation is available under this section and section 28.

(3) Representation for the purposes of care proceedings before a youth court extends to the proceedings before any youth court to which the case is remitted.

(4) Subject to any provision made by virtue of subsection (6) below, the authorities competent, on an application made for the purpose, to grant representation for the purposes of care proceedings are—

   (a) as respects proceedings before a youth court, the court;

   (b) as respects appeals from decisions of youth courts to the Crown Court, the Crown Court or the youth court from which the appeal is brought;

   (c) as respects appeals from decisions of youth courts to the High Court, the Board;

   (d) as respects proceedings before a justice of the peace under section 12E of the 1980 Act (applications for emergency orders), the justice of the peace.

(5) In the event of the Lord Chancellor making an order under section 3(4) as respects the function of granting representation for the purposes of any care proceedings, the Board shall be competent as respects those proceedings, on an application made for the purpose.

(6) An order under section 3(4) may make provision restricting or excluding the competence of any authority mentioned in subsection (4) above and may contain such transitional provisions as appear to the Lord Chancellor necessary or expedient.

(7) In this section and section 28—

   "the 1969 Act" means the Children and Young Persons Act 1969;

   "the 1980 Act" means the Child Care Act 1980; and

   "remitted" in relation to a youth court, means remitted under section 2(11) of the 1969 Act.

[By virtue of the Children Act 1989 and the Legal Aid Act 1988 (Children Act 1989) Order 1991 (S.I. 1991 No. 1924) section 27 was repealed in respect of applications for legal aid for proceedings commenced on or after October 14, 1991.]

Care proceedings: availability

28.—(1) Representation for the purposes of care proceedings to which this section applies shall be available to any person, other than a local authority, who is a party to the proceedings.

(2) Subject to subsection (4) below, representation may be granted where it appears to the competent authority to be desirable to do so in the interests of justice.

(3) Subject to subsection (4) below, representation must be granted where a child—

   (a) is brought before a youth court under section 21A of the 1980 Act; and

   (b) is not legally represented before the court but wishes to be.

(4) Representation shall not be granted to any person unless it appears to the competent authority that his financial resources are such as, under regulations, make him eligible for representation.

(5) Where a doubt arises whether representation should be granted to any person, the doubt shall be resolved in that person's favour.

(6) Representation granted by a competent authority may be amended or withdrawn, whether by that or another authority competent to grant representation.

(7) Regulations may provide for an appeal to lie to a specified court or body against any refusal by a youth court to grant representation for the purposes of care proceedings and for that other court or body to make any grant of representation that could have been made by the youth court.

[By virtue of the Children Act 1989 and the Legal Aid Act 1988 (Children Act 1989) Order 1991 (S.I. 1991 No. 1924) Section 28 was repealed in respect of applications for legal aid for proceedings commenced on or after October 14, 1991.]

Contempt proceedings

Representation in contempt proceedings

29.—(1) This section applies to any proceedings where a person is liable to be committed or fined—

(a) by a magistrates' court under section 12 of the Contempt of Court Act 1981;

(b) by a county court under section 14, 92 or 118 of the County Courts Act 1984;

(c) by any superior court for contempt in the face of that or any other court;

and in this Act "proceedings for contempt" means so much of any proceedings as relates to dealing with a person as mentioned in paragraph (a), (b) or (c) above.

(2) In any proceedings for contempt against a person the court may order that he be granted representation under this section for the purposes of the proceedings if it appears to the court to be desirable to do so in the interests of justice.

(3) In this section, "superior court" means the Court of Appeal, the High Court, the Crown Court, the Courts-Martial Appeal Court, the Restrictive Practices Court, the Employment Appeal Tribunal and any other court exercising in relation to its proceedings powers equivalent to those of the High Court, and includes the House of Lords in the exercise of its jurisdiction in relation to appeals from courts in England and Wales.

[Section 29 came into force on May 1, 1991 by virtue of the Legal Aid Act 1988 (Commencement No. 4) Order 1991 (S.I. 1991 No. 790).]

Supplementary

Supplementary

30.—(1) *[Repealed by the Children Act 1989.]*

(2) *[Repealed by the Children Act 1989.]*

(3) In Part V, section 25 shall apply for the purposes of representation in

proceedings for contempt as it applies for the purposes of representation under that Part in criminal proceedings.

[By virtue of the Children Act 1989 and the Legal Aid Act 1988 (Children Act 1989) Order 1991 (S.I. 1991 No. 1924) sections 30(1) and (2) have been repealed in respect of applications for legal aid for proceedings commenced on or after October 14, 1991. Section 30(3) came into force on May 1, 1991 by virtue of the Legal Aid Act 1988 (Commencement No. 4) Order 1991 (S.I. 1991 No. 790).]

PART VII

GENERAL AND SUPPLEMENTARY

Act not generally to affect position of legal representatives or other parties

31.—(1) Except as expressly provided by this Act or regulations under it—

(a) the fact that the services of the legal representative are given under this Act shall not affect the relationship between or rights of a legal representative and client or any privilege arising out of such relationship; and

(b) the rights conferred by this Act on a person receiving advice, assistance or representation under it shall not affect the rights or liabilities of other parties to the proceedings or the principles on which the discretion of any court or tribunal is normally exercised.

(2) Without prejudice to the generality of subsection (1)(b) above, for the purpose of determining the costs of a legally assisted person in pursuance of an order for costs or an agreement for costs in his favour (other than an order under Part II of the Prosecution of Offences Act 1985) the services of his legal representative shall be treated as having been provided otherwise than under this Act and his legal representative shall be treated as having paid the fees of any additional legal representative instructed by him.

(3) A person who provides advice, assistance or representation under this Act shall not take any payment in respect of the advice, assistance or representation except such payment as is made by the Board or authorised by, or by regulations under, this Act.

(4) The revocation under this Act of a grant (or, in the case of Part III, of approval for a grant) of advice, assistance or representation to a legally assisted person shall not affect the right of any legal representative of his, arising otherwise than under a contract, to remuneration for work done before the date of the revocation.

Selection and assignment of legal representatives

32.—(1) Subject to the provisions of this section, a person entitled to receive advice or assistance or representation may select the legal representative to advise, assist or act for him from among the legal representatives willing to provide advice, assistance or representation under this Act.

(2) Where the Board limits a grant of representation under Part IV to representation in pursuance of a contract made by the Board, it may, as it thinks fit, assign to the legally assisted person one or more legal representatives or direct that he may only select a legal representative from among those with whom such a contract subsists.

(3) A person's right to select his legal representative is subject, in the case of representation under Part V, to regulations under subsection (8) below.

(4) Subsection (1) above does not confer any right of selection in relation to proceedings under section 29 for the purposes of proceedings for contempt.

(5) Where a court grants representation to a person for the purposes of proceedings for contempt, it may assign to him for the purposes of the proceedings any legal representative who is within the precincts of the court at the time.

(6) The selection by or assignment to a person of a legal representative shall not prejudice the law and practice relating to the conduct of proceedings by a solicitor or counsel or the circumstances in which a solicitor or counsel may refuse or give up a case or entrust it to another.

(7) Regulations may provide that the right conferred by subsection (1) above shall be exercisable only in relation to legal representatives who are for the time being members of a prescribed panel.

(8) Regulations may provide as respects representation under Part V that subsection (1) above shall not apply in cases of any prescribed description and that in any such case a prescribed authority shall assign one or more legal representatives in accordance with regulations under section 2(7) to the person entitled to receive such representation.

(9) None of the following persons may be selected or assigned under this section—

    (a) a solicitor who is for the time being excluded from legal aid work under section 47(2) of the Solicitors Act 1974 (powers of Solicitors Disciplinary Tribunal);

    (b) a barrister excluded from such work under section 42 of the Administration of Justice Act 1985 (exclusion of barristers from legal aid work);

    (c) any other legal representative excluded from such work for disciplinary reasons by an authorised body.

(10) Notwithstanding subsection (1) above, a legal representative who has been selected to act for a person under that subsection may himself select to act for that person, as the legal representative's agent, any other legal representative who is not for the time being excluded from selection.

Legal aid complaints against barristers and their exclusion from legal aid work

33.—(1) The following sections shall be substituted for sections 41 and 42 of the Administration of Justice Act 1985—

    "**Application to legal aid complaints against barristers of disciplinary provisions** 41.—(1) The disciplinary provisions applicable to barristers shall apply to legal aid complaints relating to the conduct of barristers as they apply to other complaints about their conduct.

    (2) Subject to any exclusion or restriction made by those provisions, any disciplinary tribunal which hears a legal aid complaint relating to the conduct of a barrister may, if it thinks fit and whether or not it makes any other order, order that any fees—

        (a) otherwise payable in connection with his services under or in accordance with the Legal Aid Act 1988, or

        (b) otherwise chargeable in connection with his services in respect of advice or assistance made available under Part III of that Act, shall be reduced or cancelled.

(3) Accordingly, in so far as any of sections 9, 11, 15(6) and (7) and 25(2) of the Legal Aid Act 1988 (which relate to remuneration for legal aid work) has effect in relation to any fees reduced or cancelled by an order under subsection (2) above, it shall so have effect subject to the provisions of that order.

(4) An appeal shall lie in the case of an order under subsection (2) above in the same manner as an appeal would lie in the case of any other order of such a tribunal.

(5) The reference in subsection (2) above to a disciplinary tribunal is a reference to a tribunal acting under the disciplinary provisions applicable to barristers and it includes a reference to a member exercising any functions of the tribunal delegated to him.

Exclusion of barristers from legal aid work 42.—(1) Subject to any exclusion or restriction made by the disciplinary provisions applicable to barristers, where a disciplinary tribunal hears a charge of professional misconduct or breach of professional standards against a barrister, it may order that he shall be excluded from legal aid work, either temporarily or for a specified period, if it determines that there is good reason for the exclusion arising out of—

(a) his conduct in connection with any such services as are mentioned in section 40(1); or

(b) his professional conduct generally.

(2) Subsection (4) of section 41 shall apply to an order under subsection (1) as it applies to an order under subsection (2) of that section.

(3) The disciplinary provisions applicable to barristers shall include provision enabling a barrister who has been excluded from legal aid work under this section to apply for an order terminating his exclusion from such work.

(4) In this section—

(a) the reference to a disciplinary tribunal shall be construed in accordance with section 41(5); and

(b) references to a person being excluded from legal aid work are references to his being excluded from those who may be selected or assigned under section 32 of the Legal Aid Act 1988."

Regulations

34.—(1) The Lord Chancellor may make such regulations as appear to him necessary or desirable for giving effect to this Act or for preventing abuses of it.

(2) Without prejudice to the generality of subsection (1) above, any such regulations may—

(a) make provision as to the matters which are or are not to be treated as distinct matters for the purposes of advice or assistance under Part III, as to the proceedings which are or are not to be treated as distinct proceedings for the purposes of representation under Part IV, and as to the apportionment of sums recoverable or recovered by virtue of any order for costs made generally with respect to matters or proceedings treated as distinct;

(b) regulate the procedure of any court or tribunal in relation to advice, assistance or representation under this Act or orders for costs made thereunder and authorise the delegation (subject to appeal) or the exercise of their functions by members, officers or other courts or the judges or members of other courts;

(c) regulate the availability of advice, assistance, mediation or representation (other than for the purposes of proceedings for contempt) and the making of contributions towards its provision by reference to the financial resources or, in prescribed cases, the aggregate financial resources, of persons and provide for the courts, persons or bodies who are to determine the financial resources of persons and the persons who are to be required or permitted to furnish information for those purposes;

(d) provide for the cases in which a person may be refused advice, assistance, mediation or representation or have the grant of it withdrawn or revoked by reason of his conduct when seeking or receiving advice, assistance or representation (whether in the same or a different matter);

(e) make provision for the remuneration and payment of the expenses of legal representatives and for the courts, persons or bodies by whom, and the manner in which, any determinations which may be required for those purposes are to be made, reviewed or appealed;

(f) make provision for the recovery of sums due to the Board and for making effective the charge created by this Act on property recovered or preserved for a legally assisted person and regulating the release or postponement of the enforcement of any charge (however created) in favour of the Board.

(3) Regulations may also modify this Act for the purposes of its application to prescribed description of persons or in prescribed circumstances.

(4) Without prejudice to subsection (3) above, regulations may also modify this Act for the purposes of its application—

(a) in cases where its modification appears to the Lord Chancellor necessary for the purpose of fulfilling any obligation imposed on the United Kingdom or Her Majesty's Government in the United Kingdom by any international agreement; or

(b) in relation to proceedings for securing the recognition or enforcement in England and Wales of judgments given outside the United Kingdom for whose recognition or enforcement in the United Kingdom provision is made by any international agreement.

(5) Regulations made for the purposes mentioned in subsection (2)(b) above may include provisions—

(a) as to the determination of costs incurred in connection with proceedings not actually begun; and

(b) as to the cases in which and extent to which a person receiving advice, assistance or representation may be required to give security for costs, and the manner in which it may be so given.

(6) Regulations made for the purposes mentioned in subsection (2)(c) above

309

may provide that the income or capital of a person in receipt of prescribed social security benefits is to be taken as not exceeding a prescribed amount.

(7) Regulations made for the purposes mentioned in subsection (2)(e) above may include provisions—

(a) imposing conditions for the allowance of remuneration and expenses;

(b) attaching financial penalties in the event of appeals or reviews of determinations being unsuccessful;

(c) authorising the making of interim payments of remuneration or in respect of expenses.

(8) Regulations made for the purposes mentioned in subsection (2)(f) above may include provisions—

(a) for the enforcement for the benefit of the Board of an order or agreement for costs made in favour of a legally assisted person;

(b) for making a legal representative's right to payment by the Board wholly or partly dependent on his performance of the duties imposed on him by regulations made for the purposes of that paragraph; and

(c) requiring interest to be charged at a prescribed rate in circumstances where enforcement of a charge in favour of the Board is postponed.

(9) The Lord Chancellor, in making regulations for the purposes mentioned in subsection (2)(e) above as respects any description of legal aid work, shall have regard, among the matters which are relevant, to—

(a) the time and skill which it requires;

(b) the general level of fee income arising from it;

(c) the general level of expenses of legal representatives which is attributable to it;

(d) the number and general level of competence of legal representatives undertaking it;

(e) the effect of the regulations on the handling of the work; and

(f) the cost to public funds of any provision made by the regulations.

(10) Before making regulations for the purposes mentioned in subsection (2)(e) above, the Lord Chancellor shall consult the General Council of the Bar and the Law Society.

(11) Regulations under this Act may make different provision for different description of advice, assistance, mediation or representation, for different cases or classes of case, for different areas or for other different circumstances and for different descriptions of persons.

(12) Before making regulations as to the procedure of any court or tribunal, the Lord Chancellor shall so far as practicable consult any rule committee or similar body by whom or on whose advice rules of procedure for the court or tribunal may be made apart from this provision or whose consent or concurrence is required to any such rules so made.

(13) No regulations shall be made under this section which include provision for the purposes mentioned in subsection (2)(c) or (e) above except with the consent of the Treasury.

(14) *[Repealed by the Social Security (Consequential Provisions) Act 1992.]*

Amended by Schedule 8 to the Family Law Act 1996.

Advisory Committee*

35.—(1) The existing advisory committee shall continue in being to advise the Lord Chancellor on such questions relating to the provision of advice, assistance or representation under this Act as he may from time to time refer to them and to make recommendations or furnish comments to him on such matters as they consider appropriate.

(2) Appointments to the committee by the Lord Chancellor, whether by way of replacing existing members or making additional appointments, shall be made so as to secure that the committee is constituted of persons having knowledge of the work of the courts and social conditions.

(3) The Lord Chancellor may pay to the members of the advisory committee such travelling and other allowances as he may, with the consent of the Treasury, determine; and any expenses of the Lord Chancellor under this subsection shall be defrayed out of money provided by Parliament.

(4) It shall be the duty of the advisory committee to provide to the Lord Chancellor, as soon as possible after 31st March in each year, a report containing any advice, recommendations or comments of theirs on questions or matters arising during the preceding twelve months.

(5) The Lord Chancellor shall lay before each House of Parliament a copy of the annual report of the committee made to him under subsection (4) above.

(6) The Lord Chancellor may, by order dissolve the advisory committee on such day as is specified in the order and on that day this section shall cease to have effect except as regards the defrayal out of money provided by Parliament of the allowances falling to be paid thereafter under subsection (3) above.

(7) In this section "the existing advisory committee" means the advisory committee in existence under section 21 of the Legal Aid Act 1974 at the passing of this Act.

*The advisory committee was dissolved by the Legal Aid Advisory Committee (Dissolution) Order 1995 (S.I. 1995 No. 162) with effect from January 26, 1995.

Orders and regulations: general

36.—(1) Any power under this Act to make an order or regulations shall be exercisable by statutory instrument.

(2) As respects orders under this Act other than orders under section 47—

    (a) except in the case of an order under section 3(4) and 35(6), any instrument containing the order shall be subject to annulment in pursuance of a resolution of either House of Parliament;

    (b) in the case of an order under section 3(4) or 35(6), no such order shall be made unless a draft of it has been laid before and approved by resolution of each House of Parliament.

(3) As respects regulations under this Act—

    (a) except in the case of regulations under section 8, 14(2) and 32(7), any instrument containing the regulations shall be subject to annulment in pursuance of a resolution of either House of Parliament;

    (b) in the case of regulations under section 8, 14(2) or 32(7), no such regulations shall be made unless a draft of them has been laid before and approved by resolution of each House of Parliament.

Laying of Board's annual reports before Parliament

37. The Lord Chancellor shall lay before each House of Parliament a copy of the annual report of the Board made to him under section 5(3).

Restriction of disclosure of information

38.—(1) Subject to the following provisions of this section, no information furnished for the purposes of this Act to the Board or any court or other person or body of persons upon whom functions are imposed or conferred by regulations and so furnished in connection with the case of a person seeking or receiving advice, assistance, mediation or representation shall be disclosed otherwise than—

(a) for the purpose of enabling or assisting the Lord Chancellor to perform his functions under or in relation to this Act;

(b) for the purpose of enabling the Board to discharge its functions under this Act;

(c) for the purpose of facilitating the proper performance by any court, tribunal or other person or body of persons of functions under this Act;

(d) with a view to the institution of, or otherwise for the purpose of, any criminal proceedings for an offence under this Act;

(e) in connection with any other proceedings under this Act; or

(f) for the purpose of facilitating the proper performance by any tribunal of disciplinary functions as regards legal representatives or mediators.

(2) This section does not apply to information in the form of a summary or collection of information so framed as not to enable information relating to any particular person to be ascertained from it.

(3) Subsection (1) above shall not prevent the disclosure of information for any purpose with the consent of the person in connection with whose case it was furnished and, where he did not furnish it himself, with that of the person or body of persons who did.

(4) A person who, in contravention of this section, discloses any information furnished to the Board or any court or other person or body of persons for the purposes of this Act shall be liable on summary conviction to a fine not exceeding level 4 on the standard scale.

(5) Proceedings for an offence under this section shall not be brought without the written consent of the Attorney General.

(6) For the avoidance of doubt it is hereby declared that information furnished to a legal representative or mediator as such by or on behalf of a person seeking or receiving advice, assistance, mediation or representation under this Act is not information furnished to the Board or a person upon whom functions are imposed or conferred as mentioned in subsection (1) above.

Amended by Schedule 8 to the Family Law Act 1996.

Proceedings for misrepresentation, etc.

39.—(1) If any person seeking or receiving advice, assistance, mediation or representation under this Act—

(a) intentionally fails to comply with regulations as to the information to be furnished by him; or

(b) in furnishing any information required by regulations knowingly makes any false statement or false representation,

he shall be liable on summary conviction to a fine not exceeding level 4 on the standard scale or to imprisonment for a term not exceeding three months or to both.

(2) Notwithstanding anything in the Magistrates' Courts Act 1980, proceedings in respect of an offence under subsection (1) above may be brought at any time within the period of six months beginning with the date on which evidence sufficient in the opinion of the prosecutor to justify a prosecution comes to his knowledge.

(3) Nothing in subsection (2) above shall authorise the commencement of proceedings for an offence at a time more than two years after the date on which the offence was committed.

(4) A county court shall have jurisdiction to hear and determine any action brought by the Board to recover the loss sustained by it on account of its legal aid fund by reason of—

(a) the failure of a person seeking or receiving advice, assistance, mediation or representation to comply with regulations as to the information to be furnished by him; or

(b) a false statement or false representation made by such a person in furnishing information for the purposes of this Act.

Amended by S.I. 1997 No. 724 and Schedule 8 to the Family Law Act 1996.

Adaptation of rights of indemnity in cases of advice, assistance or representation in civil proceedings

40.—(1) This section shall have effect for the purpose of adapting in relation to Parts III and IV any right (however and whenever created or arising) which a person may have to be indemnified against expenses incurred by him.

(2) In determining for the purposes of any such right the reasonableness of any expenses, the possibility of avoiding them or part of them by taking advantage of Part III or Part IV shall be disregarded.

(3) Where a person having any such right to be indemnified against expenses incurred in connection with any proceedings receives in connection with those proceedings advice, assistance or representation then (without prejudice to the effect of the indemnity in relation to his contribution, if any, under section 9 or 16) the right shall endure also for the benefit of the Board as if any expenses incurred by the Board on his account in connection with the advice, assistance or representation had been incurred by him.

(4) Where a person's right to be indemnified enures for the benefit of the Board under subsection (3) above in a case where he has been represented in pursuance of a contract made with the Board on terms which do not differentiate between the remuneration for his and other cases, the reference in that subsection to any expenses incurred by the Board on his account shall be construed as a reference to such part of the remuneration payable under the contract as may be specified in writing by the Board.

(5) Where—

(a) a person's right to be indemnified against expenses incurred in connection with any proceedings arises by virtue of an agreement and is subject to any express condition conferring on those liable under it any right with respect to the bringing or conduct of the proceedings; and

(b) those liable have been given a reasonable opportunity of exercising the right so conferred and have not availed themselves of the opportunity,

the right to be indemnified shall be treated for the purpose of subsection (3) above as not being subject to that condition.

(6) Nothing in subsections (3) and (5) above shall be taken as depriving any person or body of persons of the protection of any enactment or, except as provided in subsection (5), as conferring any larger right to recover money in respect of any expenses than the person receiving advice, assistance or representation would have had if the expenses had been incurred by him.

Application to Crown
41. This Act binds the Crown.

Finance
42.—(1) The Lord Chancellor shall pay to the Board out of money provided by Parliament—

(a) such sums as are required (after allowing for payments by the Board into its legal aid fund under paragraphs (a), (b), (c), (d) and (f) of section 6(3)) to meet the payments which, under subsection (2) of that section, are to be paid by the Board out of that fund; and

(b) such sums as he may, with the approval of the Treasury, determine are required for the other expenditure of the Board.

(2) The Lord Chancellor may, with the approval of the Treasury—

(a) determine the manner in which and times at which the sums referred to in subsection (1)(a) above shall be paid to the Board; and

(b) impose conditions on the payment of the sums referred to in subsection (1)(b) above.

Definitions
43. In this Act—

"advice," "assistance", "mediation" and "representation" have the meanings assigned to them by section 2(2), (3), (3A) and (4) respectively subject, however, to the other provisions of that section;

"authorised body" has the meaning assigned by section 119(1) of the Courts and Legal Services Act 1990;

"the Board" has the meaning assigned to it by section 3(1);

"determination," in relation to the costs of advice or assistance or representation for the purposes of proceedings, includes taxation and assessment;

"family matters," has the meaning assigned by section 13A(2);

"financial resources," in relation to any person, includes any valuable facility which is available to him;

"legal representative" means an authorised advocate or authorised litigator, as defined by section 119(1) of the Courts and Legal Services Act 1990;

"mediator" means a person with whom the Board contracts for the provision of mediation by any person;

"order for costs" includes any judgment, order, decree, award or direction for the payment of the costs of one party to any proceedings by another party, whether given or made in those proceedings or not;

"prescribed" means prescribed by regulations made by the Lord Chancellor under this Act;

"proceedings for contempt" has the meaning assigned to it by section 29(1);

"regulations" means regulations made by the Lord Chancellor under this Act;

"sentence," in relation to a person, includes any order made on his conviction of an offence;

"solicitor" means solicitor of the Supreme Court;

"statutory inquiry" has the meaning assigned to it by section 16(1) of the Tribunals and Inquiries Act 1992; and

"tribunal" includes an arbitrator or umpire, however appointed, and whether the arbitration takes place under a reference by consent or otherwise.

Amended by Schedule 8 to the Family Law Act 1996.

PART VIII

MISCELLANEOUS

Scottish provisions

Scottish provisions

44. The Legal Aid (Scotland) Act 1986 shall have effect subject to the amendments specified in Schedule 4 to this Act.

Supplementary

Amendments, repeals and transitional provisions

45.—(1) The enactments specified in Schedule 5 to this Act shall have effect subject to the amendments there specified.

(2) Subject to subsection (4) below, the enactments specified in Schedule 6 to this Act are repealed to the extent specified in the third column of that Schedule.

(3) Where any enactment amended or repealed by subsection (1) or (2) above extends to the United Kingdom or any part of it, the amendment or repeal has a corresponding extent.

(4) Schedule 7 to this Act shall have effect for the purpose of making the transitional and saving provisions set out there.

Amendments of Legal Aid Act 1974 pending repeal

46. The Legal Aid Act 1974 shall have effect subject to the amendments specified in Schedule 8 to this Act.

Short title, commencement and extent

47.—(1) This Act may be cited as the Legal Aid Act 1988.

(2) Subject to subsections (3) and (4) below, this Act shall come into force on such day as the Lord Chancellor appoints by order and different days may be appointed for different provisions.

(3) Section 44 and Schedule 4 shall come into force on such day as the Secretary of State appoints by order and different days may be appointed for different provisions.

(4) Sections 35 (together with the repeal of section 21 of the Legal Aid Act 1974) and 465 shall come into force on the date on which this Act is passed.

(5) An order under subsection (2) or (3) above may contain such transitional and saving provisions as appear to the Lord Chancellor or, as the case may be, the Secretary of State necessary or expedient.

(6) This Act, with the exception of sections 12(3) and 17(3), section 44 and Schedule 4 and the amendments or repeals of the enactments referred to in section 45(3), extends to England and Wales only and section 44 and Schedule 4 extend to Scotland only.

SCHEDULES

SCHEDULE 1

THE LEGAL AID BOARD

Incorporation and Status

1. The Board shall be a body corporate.

2. The Board shall not be regarded as the servant or agent of the Crown or as enjoying any status, immunity or privilege of the Crown; and the Board's property shall not be regarded as property of, or held on behalf of, the Crown.

Tenure of Members

3. Subject to paragraphs 4 and 5 any member of the Board shall hold and vacate office in accordance with the terms of his appointment, but a person shall not be appointed a member of the Board for a period of more than five years.

4.—(1) The chairman or a member may resign office by giving notice in writing to the Lord Chancellor, and if the chairman ceases to be a member he shall cease to be the chairman.

(2) A person who ceases to be the chairman or a member shall be eligible for reappointment.

5. The Lord Chancellor may terminate the appointment of a member of the Board if satisfied that—

(a) he has become bankrupt or made an arrangement with his creditors;

(b) he is unable to carry out his duties as a Board member by reason of physical or mental illness;

(c) he has been absent from meetings of the Board for a period longer than six consecutive months without the permission of the Board; or

(d) he is otherwise unable or unfit to discharge the functions of a member of the Board.

Members' interests

6.—(1) Before appointing a person to be a member of the Board, the Lord Chancellor shall satisfy himself that that person will have no such financial or other interest as is likely to affect prejudicially the exercise or performance by him of his functions as a member of the Board.

(2) The Lord Chancellor shall from time to time satisfy himself with respect to every member of the Board that he has no such interest as is referred to in sub-paragraph (1) above.

(3) Any person whom the Lord Chancellor proposes to appoint as, and who has consented to be, a member of the Board, and any member of the Board, shall, whenever requested by the Lord Chancellor to do so, supply him with such information as the Lord Chancellor considers necessary for the performance by the Lord Chancellor of his duties under this paragraph.

7.—(1) A member of the Board who is in any way directly or indirectly interested in a contract made or proposed to be made by the Board shall disclose the nature of his interest at a meeting of the Board; and the disclosure shall be recorded in the minutes of the Board, and the member shall not take any part in any deliberation or decision of the Board with respect to that contract.

(2) For the purposes of sub-paragraph (1) above, a general notice given at a meeting of the Board by a member of the Board to the effect that he is a member of a specified company or firm and is to be regarded as interested in any contract which may, after the date of the notice, be made with the company or firm shall be regarded as a sufficient disclosure of his interest in relation to any contract so made.

(3) A member of the Board need not attend in person at a meeting of the Board in order to make any disclosure which he is required to make under this paragraph if he takes reasonable steps to secure that the disclosure is made by a notice which is brought up and read out at the meeting.

Remuneration of members

8.—(1) The Board may—

    (a) pay to its members such remuneration; and

    (b) make provision for the payment of such pensions, allowances or gratuities to or in respect of its members,

as the Lord Chancellor may, with the approval of the Treasury, determine.

(2) Where a person ceases to be a member of the Board otherwise than on the expiry of his term of office, and it appears to the Lord Chancellor that there are special circumstances which make it right for that person to receive compensation, the Lord Chancellor may, with the consent of the Treasury, direct the Board to make that person a payment of such amount as the Lord Chancellor may, with the consent of the Treasury, determine.

Staff

9.—(1) The Board shall appoint a person to be the chief executive of the Board who shall be responsible to the Board for the exercise of its functions.

(2) The Board may appoint such other employees as it thinks fit.

(3) The Board may only appoint a person to be its chief executive or the holder of any other employment of a specified description after consultation with, and subject to the approval of, the Lord Chancellor.

(4) The reference in sub-paragraph (3) above to employment of a specified description is a reference to any employment for the time being specified by the Lord Chancellor in a direction given for the purposes of that sub-paragraph.

(5) An appointment under this paragraph may be made on such terms and conditions as the Board, with the approval of the Lord Chancellor and consent of the Treasury, may determine.

10.—(1) The Board shall make, in respect of such of its employees as, with the approval of the Lord Chancellor and the consent of the Treasury, it may determine such arrangements for providing pensions, allowances or gratuities, including pensions, allowances or gratuities by way of compensation for loss of employment, as it may determine.

(2) Arrangements under sub-paragraph (1) above may include the establishment and administration, by the Board or otherwise, of one or more pension schemes.

317

(3) If an employee of the Board—

    (a) becomes a member of the Board; and

    (b) was by reference to his employment by the Board a participant in a pension scheme established and administered by it for the benefit of its employees,

the Board may determine that his service as a member shall be treated for the purposes of the scheme as service as an employee of the Board whether or not any benefits are to be payable to or in respect of him by virtue of paragraph 8.

(4) Where the Board exercises the power conferred by sub-paragraph (3) above, any discretion as to the benefits payable to or in respect of the member concerned which the scheme confers on the Board shall be exercised only with the approval of the Lord Chancellor and consent of the Treasury.

Proceedings

11.—(1) Subject to anything in regulations, the Board may regulate its own proceedings.

(2) The Board may make such arrangements as it considers appropriate for the discharge of its functions, including the delegation of specified functions and shall make such arrangements for the delegation of functions to committees and persons as may be prescribed.

(3) Subject to anything in regulations, committees may be appointed and may be dissolved by the Board, and may include, or consist entirely of, persons who are not members of the Board.

(4) A committee shall act in accordance with such directions as the Board may from time to time give, and the Board may provide for anything done by a committee to have effect as if it had been done by the Board.

(5) The validity of any proceedings of the Board or of any committee appointed by the Board shall not be affected by any vacancy among its members or by any defect in the appointment of any member.

Instruments

12.—(1) The fixing of the seal of the Board shall be authenticated by the chairman or another member of the Board and by some other person authorised either generally or specially by the Board to act for that purpose.

(2) A document purporting to be duly executed under the seal of the Board, or to be signed on the Board's behalf, shall be received in evidence and, unless the contrary is proved, be deemed to be so executed or signed.

Allowances

13. The Board may pay to the members of any committee such fees and allowances as the Lord Chancellor may, with the consent of the Treasury, determine.

SCHEDULE 2

Civil Proceedings: Scope of Part IV Representation

Part I

Description of Proceedings

1. Proceedings in, or before any person to whom a case is referred in whole or in part by, any of the following courts, namely:

    (a) the House of Lords in the exercise of its jurisdiction in relation to appeals from courts in England and Wales;

    (b) the Court of Appeal;

(c) the High Court;

(d) any county court.

2. The following proceedings in a magistrates' court, namely—

(a) *[Repealed by the Children Act 1989.]*

(b) proceedings under section 43 of the National Assistance Act 1948, section 22 of the Maintenance Orders Act 1950, section 4 of the Maintenance Orders Act 1958, or section 18 of the Supplementary Benefits Act 1976;

(c) proceedings in relation to an application for leave of the court to remove a child from a person's custody under section 27 or 28 of the Adoption Act 1976 or proceedings in which the making of an order under Part II or section 29 or 55 of the Adoption Act 1976 is opposed by any party to the proceedings;

(d) proceedings under Part I of the Maintenance Orders (Reciprocal Enforcement) Act 1972 relating to a maintenance order made by a court of a country outside the United Kingdom;

(e) *[Repealed by the Children Act 1989.]*

(f) proceedings for or in relation to an order under Part I of the Domestic Proceedings and Magistrates' Courts Act 1978;

(g) proceedings under the Children Act 1989;

(h) appeals under section 20, where they are to be made to a magistrates' court, and proceedings under section 27 of the Child Support Act 1991;

(i) proceedings under section 30 of the Human Fertilisation and Embryology Act 1990.

3. Proceedings in the Employment Appeal Tribunal.

4. Proceedings in the Lands Tribunal.

5. Proceedings before a Commons Commissioner appointed under section 17(1) of the Commons Registration Act 1965.

6. Proceedings in the Restrictive Practices Court under Part III of the Fair Trading Act 1973, and any proceedings in that court in consequence of an order made, or undertaking given to the court, under that Part of that Act.

PART II

EXCEPTED PROCEEDINGS

1. Proceedings wholly or partly in respect of defamation, but so that the making of a counterclaim for defamation in proceedings for which representation may be granted shall not of itself affect any right of the defendant to the counterclaim to representation for the purposes of the proceedings and so that representation may be granted to enable him to defend the counterclaim.

2. Relator actions.

3. Proceedings for the recovery of a penalty where the proceedings may be taken by any person and the whole or part of the penalty is payable to the person taking the proceedings.

4. Election petitions under the Representation of the People Act 1983.

5. In a county court, proceedings for or consequent on the issue of a judgment summons and, in the case of a defendant, proceedings where the only question to be brought before the court is as to the time and mode of payment by him of a debt (including liquidated damages) and costs.

5A. Proceedings for a decree of divorce or judicial separation unless the cause is defended, or the petition is directed to be heard in open court, or it is not practicable by reason of physical or mental incapacity for the applicant to proceed without representation; except that representation shall be available for the purpose of making or opposing an application—

(a) for an injunction;

(b) for ancillary relief, excluding representation for the purpose only of inserting a prayer for ancillary relief in the petition;

(c) for an order relating to the custody of (or access to) a child, or the education or care or supervision of a child, excluding representation for the purpose only of making such an application where there is no reason to believe that the application will be opposed;

(d) for an order declaring that the court is satisfied as to arrangements for the welfare of the children of the family, excluding representation for the purpose only of making such an application where there is no reason to believe that the application will be opposed; or

(e) for the purpose of making or opposing any other application, or satisfying the court on any other matter which raises a substantial question for determination by the court.

5B. Proceedings to the extent that they consist in, or arise out of, an application to the court under section 235A of the Trade Union and Labour Relations (Consolidation) Act 1992.

6. Proceedings incidental to any proceedings excepted by this Part of this Schedule.

SCHEDULE 3

CRIMINAL PROCEEDINGS: ENFORCEMENT OF CONTRIBUTION ORDERS

PART I

ORDERS MADE BY A COURT

Collecting court

1. In this Part "collecting court," in relation to a contribution order, means a magistrates' court specified in the order; and the court so specified shall be:

(a) in a case where the court making the order is itself a magistrates' court, that court;

(b) in a case where the order is made on an appeal from a magistrates' court, or in respect of a person who was committed (whether for trial or otherwise by a magistrates' court) to the Crown Court, the court from which the appeal is brought or, as the case may be, which committed him; and

(c) in any other case, a magistrates' court nominated by the court making the order.

Enforcement proceedings

2.—(1) Any sum required to be paid by a contribution order shall be recoverable as if it had been adjudged to be paid by an order of the collecting court, subject to and in accordance with the provisions of this paragraph.

(2) Sections 17 (not more than one committal for same arrears) and 18 (power to review committal) of the Maintenance Orders Act 1958 shall apply as if a contribution order were a maintenance order.

(3) The collecting court may exercise, in relation to a contribution order, the power conferred by section 75 of the Magistrates' Courts Act 1980 (power to dispense with immediate payment); and for the purposes of that section any provisions made by the

authority which made the order as to time for payment, or payment by instalments, shall be treated as made by the collecting court.

(4) The following provisions of the Magistrates' Courts Act 1980 shall apply as if a contribution order were enforceable as an affiliation order:

> section 80 (application of money found on defaulter to satisfy sum adjudged);
>
> section 93 (complaint for arrears);
>
> section 94 (effect of committal on arrears); and
>
> section 95 (power to remit arrears).

(5) Any costs awarded under section 64 of the Magistrates' Courts Act 1980 on the hearing of a complaint for the enforcement of a contribution order shall be enforceable as a sum required to be paid by that order.

3.—(1) Without prejudice to paragraph 2, any sum required to be paid by a contribution order shall be enforceable by the High Court or a county court as if the sum were due to the clerk of the collecting court in pursuance of a judgment or order of the High Court or county court, as the case may be.

(2) The clerk of the collecting court shall not take proceedings by virtue of this paragraph unless authorised to do so by the court.

(3) This paragraph shall not authorise—

(a) the enforcement of a sum required to be paid by a contribution order by issue of a writ of fieri facias or other process against goods or by imprisonment or attachment of earnings;

(b) *[Repealed by S.I. 1991 No. 724.]*

4.—(1) Any expenses incurred by the clerk of a magistrates' court in recovering any sum required to be paid by a contribution order shall be treated for the purposes of Part VI of the Justices of the Peace Act 1979 as expenses of the magistrates' courts committee.

(2) Any sum paid to a clerk of a magistrates' court in or towards satisfaction of a liability imposed by a contribution order shall be paid by him to the Lord Chancellor and section 61(4) of the Justices of the Peace Act 1979 (regulations as to accounts of justices' clerks) shall apply in relation to sums payable to the Lord Chancellor under this sub-paragraph as it applies in relation to sums payable to the Secretary of State under that section.

Transfer of enforcement proceedings to different court

5.—(1) Where in relation to any contribution order it appears to the collecting court that the person subject to it is residing in a petty sessions area other than that for which the court acts, the court may make an order under this paragraph ("a transfer order") with respect to the contribution order specifying the other petty sessions area.

(2) Where a court makes a transfer order in relation to any contribution order—

(a) payment under the contribution order shall be enforceable in the petty sessions area specified in the transfer order; and

(b) as from the date of the transfer order, a magistrates' court for that petty sessions area shall be substituted for the court which made the transfer order as the collecting court in relation to the contribution order.

Limitations on enforcement by proceedings

6. Any sum due under a contribution order shall not be recoverable, and payment of any such sum shall not be enforced, under paragraph 2 or 3 until—

(a) the conclusion of the proceedings for the purposes of which the relevant grant of representation was made; or

(b) if earlier, the revocation or withdrawal of the relevant grant of representation.

7. Where a contribution order has been made in respect of a member of Her Majesty's armed forces and the Secretary of State notifies the collecting court that any sum payable under the order will be recovered by deductions from the person's pay, the collecting court shall not enforce payment of any sum unless and until the Secretary of State subsequently notifies it that the person is no longer a member of those forces and that sum has not been fully recovered.

Power to defer enforcement proceedings

8. The collecting court may defer recovering any sum due under a contribution order if—

(a) an appeal is pending in respect of the proceedings for the purposes of which the relevant grant of representation was made; or

(b) the person granted representation has been ordered to be retried.

Interpretation

9. In this Part:

(a) "relevant grant of representation," in relation to a contribution order, means the grant of representation in connection with which the order was made; and

(b) references to the proceedings for the purposes of which a grant of representation has been made include, where the proceedings are proceedings before a magistrates' court which result:

(i) in the legally assisted person being committed to the Crown Court for trial or sentence, or

(ii) in his case being remitted to a youth court in pursuance of section 56(1) of the Children and Young Persons Act 1933,

the proceedings before the Crown Court or that youth court.

PART II

ORDERS MADE BY THE BOARD

Limitations on enforcement by proceedings

10.—(1) Any sum due under a contribution order shall not be recoverable, and payment of any such sum shall not be enforced until:

(a) the conclusion of the proceedings for the purposes of which the relevant grant of representation was made; or

(b) if earlier, the revocation or withdrawal of the relevant grant of representation.

(2) In this paragraph—

(a) "relevant grant of representation," in relation to a contribution order, means the grant of representation in connection with which the order was made; and

(b) the reference to the proceedings for the purposes of which the relevant grant of representation was made includes, where the proceedings are proceedings before a magistrates' court which result:

(i) in the legally assisted person being committed to the Crown Court for trial or sentence, or

(ii) in his case being remitted to a youth court in pursuance of section 56(1) of the Children and Young Persons Act 1933,

the proceedings before the Crown Court or that youth court.

11. Where a contribution order has been made in respect of a member of Her Majesty's armed forces and the Secretary of State notifies the Board that any sum payable under the order will be recovered by deductions from the person's pay, the Board shall not enforce payment of any sum unless and until the Secretary of State subsequently notifies it that the person is no longer a member of those forces and that sum has not been fully recovered.

SCHEDULE 4

AMENDMENTS OF LEGAL AID (SCOTLAND) ACT 1986 (C. 47)

PART I

Direct payment of fees and outlays by legally assisted person

1. In section 4(2) (payments out of the Scottish Legal Aid Fund):

  (a) in paragraph (a), after the word "due" there shall be inserted the words "out of the Fund;"

  (b) in paragraph (c), the words "for the purposes of this Act" are repealed.

2. In section 16—

  (a) subsection (1) is repealed;

  (b) in subsection (2), the words "In this section and" are repealed.

3. In section 17 (contributions, etc.)—

  (a) in subsection (1), for the words from "by the Board" to "the Fund" there shall be substituted the word "to contribute to the fees and outlays incurred by them (or on their behalf)";

  (b) subsections (3) to (8) are repealed;

  (c) at the end there shall be added the following subsections—

  "(9) Except insofar as regulations made under this section otherwise provide—

  (a) any award of expenses to a legally assisted person; and
  (b) any property (wherever situated) recovered or preserved for him in the proceedings for which he is legally assisted,

  shall be paid initially to the Fund, to be applied towards:

  (i) the fees and outlays incurred by or on behalf of the legally assisted person in those proceedings;
  (ii) recouping any sums paid out of the fund on his behalf in respect of advice and assistance in relation to those proceedings or to any matter to which those proceedings relate.

  (10) Where the solicitor acting for a legally assisted person is employed by the Board for the purposes of Part V of this Act, references in subsection (1) above and in section 33 of this Act to "fees and outlays" include references to sums which would have been payable to that solicitor had he not been so employed.

  (11) Nothing in subsection (9) above shall prejudice the power of the court to allow any damages or expenses to be set off.

  (12) An account of expenses which:

  (a) has been agreed between the board and the solicitor acting for the legally assisted person; or
  (b) has been taxed,

  shall not be liable to taxation by an auditor of court in any proceedings."

4. In section 32(a) (restriction on payment etc.), the words, "out of the Fund" are repealed.

5. In section 33 (fees and outlays of solicitors and counsel) in subsection (1), for the words from "out" to the end there shall be substituted the words—

"in respect of any fees or outlays properly incurred by him in so acting—

   (a) by the person concerned, to the extent to which a contribution has been determined for him under section 17 of this Act;

   (b) to the extent that such fees and outlays exceed any such contribution out of the Fund in accordance with section 4(2)(a) of this Act."

6. In section 36(2) (regulations), in paragraph (b) at end add—

"and the power to substitute different amounts for the amount specified in section 10(2) of this Act includes power to substitute different amounts in relation to different cases or classes of case."

Part II

Liability of legally assisted person for expenses to be assessed in all cases
7. In section 18 (expenses)—

   (a) subsection (1) is repealed;

   (b) in subsection (2), for the words "in proceedings to which this section applies," there shall be substituted the words "in any proceedings."

8. In section 19(1) (expenses out of the Fund), for the words "to which this section applies" there shall be substituted the words "to which a legally assisted person is party and which are finally decided in favour of an unassisted party."

9. In section 20(1) (supplementary), for the words "sections 18 and" there shall be substituted the word "section."

Part III

Board's property to be rateable
10. In Schedule 1, paragraph 2(4) is repealed.

SCHEDULE 5

Minor and Consequential Amendments

Public Records Act 1958 (c. 51)
1. In Schedule 1 to the Public Records Act 1958 (definition of public records), there shall be inserted at the end of Part I of the Table at the end of paragraph 3 the following entry—

"Lord Chancellor's Department.	Legal Aid Board."

Parliamentary Commissioner Act 1967 (c. 13)
2. In Schedule 2 to the Parliamentary Commissioner Act 1967 (which lists the bodies subject to the jurisdiction of the Parliamentary Commissioner), there shall be inserted (at the appropriate place in alphabetical order) the following entry—

"Legal Aid Board."

Attachment of Earnings Act 1971 (c. 32)
3. In section 25(1) of the Attachment of Earnings Act 1971, for the words "section 7 or

8(2) of the Legal Aid Act 1982" there shall be substituted the words "section 23 of the Legal Aid Act 1988."

House of Commons Disqualification Act 1975 (c. 24)

4. In Part III of Schedule 1 to the House of Commons Disqualification Act 1975 (other disqualifying offices), there shall be inserted (at the appropriate places in alphabetical order) the following entries—

"Chairman of the Legal Aid Board."

"Member of the Legal Aid Board."

Northern Ireland Assembly Disqualification Act 1975 (c. 25)

5. In Part III of Schedule 1 to the Northern Ireland Assembly Disqualification Act 1975 (other disqualifying offices), there shall be inserted (at the appropriate places in alphabetical order) the following entries—

"Chairman of the Legal Aid Board."

"Member of the Legal Aid Board."

Sex Discrimination Act 1975 (c. 65)

6. In section 75(4) of the Sex Discrimination Act 1975—

(a) for the words "Legal Aid Act 1974" there shall be substituted the words "Legal Aid Act 1988"; and

(b) for the words "any of those Acts for payment of any sum into the legal aid fund" there shall be substituted the words "either of those Acts for payment of any sum to the Legal Aid Board or into the Scottish Legal Aid Fund."

Race Relations Act 1976 (c. 74)

7. In section 66(6) of the Race Relations Act 1976—

(a) for the words "Legal Aid Act 1974" there shall be substituted the words "Legal Aid Act 1988"; and

(b) for the words "any of those Acts for payment of any sum into the legal aid fund" there shall be substituted the words "either of those Acts for payment of any sum to the Legal Aid Board or into the Scottish Legal Aid Fund."

Child Care Act 1980 (c. 5)

8. In section 21A of the Child Care Act 1980, after subsection (8), there shall be inserted the following subsection—

"(9) In this section "legal aid" means representation for the purposes of care proceedings under Part VI of the Legal Aid Act 1988."

Magistrates' Courts Act 1980 (c. 43)

9. In section 92(1)(b) of the Magistrates' Courts Act 1980, for the words "section 7 or 8(2) of the Legal Aid Act 1982" there shall be substituted the words "section 23 of the Legal Aid Act 1988."

Supreme Court Act 1981 (c. 54)

10. In section 47(7) of the Supreme Court Act 1981, for the words "legal aid contribution order made under section 7 or 8(2) of the Legal Aid Act 1982" there shall be substituted the words "contribution order made under section 23 of the Legal Aid Act 1988."

Telecommunications Act 1984 (c. 12)

11. In section 52 of the Telecommunications Act 1984, the following subsection shall be substituted for subsection (5)—

"(5) A charge conferred by subsection (4) above is subject to:

(a) any charge under the Legal Aid Act 1988 and any provision of that Act for payment of any sum to the Legal Aid Board;

(b) any charge or obligation for payment in priority to other debts under the Legal Aid (Scotland) Act 1986 and any provision of that Act for payment of any sum into the Scottish Legal Aid Fund; or

(c) any charge under the Legal Aid, Advice and Assistance (Northern Ireland) Order 1981 and any provision of that Order for payment of any sum into the legal aid fund."

Prosecution of Offences Act 1985 (c. 23)

12. In section 19(2)(b) of the Prosecution of Offences Act 1985, the words "(including any legal aid order)" shall be omitted and at the end of that paragraph there shall be inserted the words "or any grant of representation for the purposes of the proceedings which has been made under the Legal Aid Act 1988."

13. In section 20(2) of that Act, for the words "out of the legal aid fund or" there shall be substituted the words "by the Legal Aid Board or out of."

14. In section 21(1) of that Act, for the definition of "legally assisted person" there shall be substituted the following—

" 'legally assisted person,' in relation to any proceedings, means a person to whom representation under the Legal Aid Act 1988 has been granted for the purposes of the proceedings."

15. In section 21 of that Act, after subsection (4), there shall be inserted the following subsection—

"(4A) Where one party to any proceedings is a legally assisted person then:

(a) for the purposes of sections 16 and 17 of this Act, his costs shall be taken not to include either the expenses incurred on his behalf by the Legal Aid Board or the Lord Chancellor or, if he is liable to make a contribution under section 23 of the Legal Aid Act 1988, any sum paid or payable by way of contribution; and

(b) for the purposes of sections 18 and 19 of this Act, his costs shall be taken to include the expenses incurred on his behalf by the Legal Aid Board or the Lord Chancellor (without any deduction on account of any contribution paid or payable under section 23 of the Legal Aid Act 1988), but, if he is liable to make such a contribution his costs shall be taken not to include any sum paid or payable by way of contribution."

Child Abduction and Custody Act 1985 (c. 60)

16. In section 11 of the Child Abduction and Custody Act 1985, for the words "Part I of the Legal Aid Act 1974" there shall be substituted the words "Part III or IV of the Legal Aid Act 1988."

Administration of Justice Act 1985 (c. 61)

17. In section 40 of the Administration of Justice Act 1985 (preliminary provisions concerning legal aid complaints), for the words from the beginning of paragraph (a) to the end there shall be substituted the words "the provision for any person of services under the Legal Aid Act 1988 including, in the case of a solicitor, provision for any person of such services in the capacity of agent for that person's solicitor."

18. In section 43 of that Act (jurisdiction and powers of Solicitors Disciplinary Tribunal in relation to complaints against solicitors)—

(a) in subsection (3), for paragraphs (a), (b) and (c) there shall be substituted the following—

"(a) otherwise payable under or in accordance with the Legal Aid Act 1988, or

(b) otherwise chargeable in respect of advice or assistance made available under Part III of that Act"; and

(b) in subsection (4), for paragraphs (a) and (b) there shall be substituted the words "any of sections 9, 11, 15(6) and (7) and 25(2) of, or any provision made under, the Legal Aid Act 1988."

19. In section 44 of that Act—

(a) in subsection (3), in the inserted subsection (2A), for the words from the beginning of paragraph (a) to the end there shall be substituted the words:

"(a) his conduct, including conduct in the capacity of agent for another solicitor, in connection with the provision for any person of services under the Legal Aid Act 1988; or

(b) his professional conduct generally;" and

(b) in subsection (4), in the inserted subsection (6), for the words from "each" to the end there shall be substituted the words "those who may be selected or assigned for the purpose of providing for any person services under the Legal Aid Act 1988."

Housing Act 1985 (c. 68)

20. In section 170(5) of the Housing Act 1985:

(a) for the words "Legal Aid Act 1974" there shall be substituted the words "Legal Aid Act 1988;" and

(b) for the words "into the legal aid fund" there shall be substituted the words "to the Legal Aid Board."

Family Law Act 1986 (c. 55)

21. Section 64 of the Family Law Act 1986 (family proceedings rules) shall cease to have effect.

Criminal Justice Act 1987 (c. 38)

22. In section 4(1) of the Criminal Justice Act 1987, for the words "section 28(7A) of the Legal Aid Act 1974" there shall be substituted the words "section 20(4) of the Legal Aid Act 1988."

SCHEDULE 6

Repeals

Chapter	Short title	Extent of repeal
1967 c. 80.	The Criminal Justice Act 1967.	Section 90.
1974 c. 4.	The Legal Aid Act 1974.	The whole Act.
1974 c. 47.	The Solicitors Act 1974.	Section 75(d). In Schedule 3, paragraph 10.
1975 c. 72.	The Children Act 1975.	Section 65. In Schedule 3, paragraph 82.
1976 c. 36.	The Adoption Act 1976.	In Schedule 3, paragraph 18.
1976 c. 63.	The Bail Act 1976.	Section 11.
1976 c. 71.	The Supplementary Benefits Act 1976.	In Schedule 7, paragraphs 33 and 35.
1977 c. 38.	The Administration of Justice Act 1977.	In Schedule 1, Part I.

Chapter	Short title	Extent of repeal
1977 c. 45.	The Criminal Law Act 1977.	In Schedule 12, the entry relating to the Legal Aid Act 1974.
1978 c. 22.	The Domestic Proceedings and Magistrates' Courts Act 1978.	In Schedule 2, paragraphs 45 and 52.
1979 c. 26.	The Legal Aid Act 1979.	The whole Act.
1979 c. 55	The Justices of the Peace Act 1979.	In Schedule 2, paragraph 27.
1980 c. 5.	The Child Care Act 1980.	In Schedule 5, paragraph 36.
1980 c. 30.	The Social Security Act 1980.	In Schedule 4, paragraph 9.
1980 c. 43.	The Magistrates' Courts Act 1980.	In Schedule 7, paragraphs 126 to 129.
1981 c. 49.	The Contempt of Court Act 1981.	Section 13. In Schedule 2, Part 1.
1982 c. 27.	The Civil Jurisdiction and Judgments Act 1982.	Section 40(1).
1982 c. 44.	The Legal Aid Act 1982.	The whole Act.
1982 c. 48.	The Criminal Justice Act 1982.	Section 25(2). Section 29(3). Section 60(4).
1983 c. 41.	The Health and Social Services and Social Security Adjudications Act 1983.	In Schedule 1, paragraph 3.
1984 c. 42.	The Matrimonial and Family Proceedings Act 1984.	In Schedule 1, paragraph 18.
1984 c. 60.	The Police and Criminal Evidence Act 1984.	Section 59.
1985 c. 23.	Prosecution of Offences Act 1985.	Section 16(8). In section 19(2)(b), the words "(including any legal aid order)". In section 21(1), the definition of "legal aid order".
1985 c. 61.	The Administration of Justice Act 1985.	Sections 45 and 46. In Schedule 7, paragraphs 1 to 3.
1986 c. 28.	The Children and Young Persons (Amendment) Act 1986.	Section 3(3).
1986 c. 47.	The Legal Aid (Scotland) Act 1986.	In section 4(2)(c), the words "for the purposes of this Act". In section 16, subsection (1) and, in subsection (2), the words "in this section and". In section 17, subsections (3) to (8).

Chapter	Short title	Extent of repeal
		Section 18(1). In section 32(1), the words ", out of the Fund". In Schedule 1, paragraph 2(4).
1986 c. 50.	The Social Security Act 1986.	In Schedule 10, paragraphs 46, 47 and 56.
1986 c. 55.	The Family Law Act 1986.	Section 64.
1987 c. 38.	The Criminal Justice Act 1987.	In Schedule 2, paragraphs 7 and 8.

SCHEDULE 7

TRANSITION

Preliminary

1. In this Schedule—

"the 1974 Act" means the Legal Aid Act 1974; and

"the appointed day" means the day appointed by the Lord Chancellor under section 47(2) of this Act for the coming into force of section 3(2) thereof.

The Legal Aid Fund

2.—(1) On the appointed day the legal aid fund ("the Old Fund") maintained by the Law Society under section 17 of the 1974 Act shall be wound up.

(2) If, as at the appointed day, after taking account of all receipts and expenses of the Law Society attributable to their functions under the 1974 Act and the Legal Aid Act 1982 ("the 1982 Act"), there is in relation to the Old Fund any surplus or deficit—

 (a) such surplus shall be paid by the Law Society to the Lord Chancellor; and

 (b) such deficit shall be made up by payment to the Law Society by the Lord Chancellor of the amount of the deficit.

(3) Notwithstanding their repeal by this Act—

 (a) sections 15(9) and 18 of the 1974 Act shall continue to have effect for the purposes of requiring the Law Society to account for the Old Fund and to report on the discharge of its functions under that Act up to the appointed day; and

 (b) section 17(5) of that Act shall continue to have effect for the purposes of any determination as to the expenses of receipts of the Law Society;

and, if the appointed day falls on a day which is not the last day of the financial year (for the purposes of the said section 18), references in those sections to the financial year shall be construed as references to the period commencing on the day immediately following the end of the last complete financial year and ending with the appointed day.

(4) The Lord Chancellor shall pay to the Law Society such expenses incurred after the appointed day in connection with their functions under sections 15(9) and 18 of the 1974 Act as appear to him to be reasonable.

(5) Any payments received by the Lord Chancellor under sub-paragraph (2)(a) above shall be paid by him into the legal aid fund established by the Board under section 6.

(6) Any amount required to be paid by the Lord Chancellor under sub-paragraph (2)(b) or (4) above shall be defrayed out of money provided by Parliament.

Rights, obligations and property

3.—(1) Subject to paragraph 2, on the appointed day all rights, obligations and property of the Law Society which are referable to its functions under the 1974 Act and the 1982 Act shall become rights, obligations and property of the Board.

(2) Any payments which are required to be made into or out of the Old Fund in connection with legal aid or advice or assistance under the 1974 Act shall, on and after the appointed day, be paid to or by the Board.

Transfer of functions

4.—(1) Any grant of legal aid under Part I of the 1974 Act which is in force immediately before the appointed day shall, on and after the appointed day, have effect as a grant by the Board of representation under Part IV of this Act.

(2) Any approval given in connection with the grant of legal aid or advice or assistance under Part I of the 1974 Act which is in force immediately before the appointed day shall, on and after the appointed day, have effect as an approval by the Board in connection with the corresponding advice, assistance or representation under Part III or IV of this Act.

(3) Anything which, immediately before the appointed day, is in the process of being done by or in relation to the Law Society in connection with any function which it has relating to legal aid or advice or assistance under Part I of the 1974 Act, may be continued, on and after the appointed day, by or in relation to the Board.

Legal aid contribution orders

5. Notwithstanding their repeal by this Act, the provisions of the 1974 Act and the 1982 Act with respect to legal aid contribution orders shall continue to have effect in relation to any such order made in connection with a legal aid order made by virtue of section 28(11A) of the 1974 Act (legal aid for proceedings for contempt).

The Board: transfers of employment

6.—(1) The Board shall make, not later than such date as the Lord Chancellor may determine, an offer of employment by the Board to such of the persons employed immediately before that date by the Law Society for the purpose of their functions under the 1974 Act as fall within such descriptions as the Lord Chancellor designates for the purposes of this paragraph or are persons whom the Board wishes to employ.

(2) The terms of the offer shall be such that they are, taken as a whole, not less favourable to the person to whom the offer is made than the terms on which he is employed on the date on which the offer is made.

(3) An offer made in pursuance of this paragraph shall not be revocable during the period of three months commencing with the date on which it is made.

7.—(1) Where a person becomes an employee of the Board on acceptance of an offer made under paragraph 6, then, for the purposes of the Employment Protection (Consolidation) Act 1978, his period of employment with the Law Society shall count as a period of employment by the Board, and the change of employment shall not break the continuity of the period of employment.

(2) Where an offer is made under paragraph 6 to any person, none of the agreed redundancy procedures applicable to employees of the Law Society shall apply to him.

(3) Where a person employed by the Law Society ceases to be so employed—

    (a) on becoming a member of the staff of the Board on accepting an offer under paragraph 6; or

    (b) having unreasonably refused such an offer;

Part VI of the Employment Protection (Consolidation) Act 1978 shall not apply to him and he shall not be treated for the purposes of any scheme in force under section 19 of the 1974 Act as having been retired on redundancy.

(4) Where a person to whom an offer under paragraph 6 has been made continues in employment in the law Society after having not unreasonably refused that offer he shall be treated for all purposes as if no offer under paragraph 6 had been made to him.

8.—(1) Any dispute as to whether an offer purporting to be made under paragraph 6 complies with that paragraph shall be referred to and be determined by an industrial tribunal.

(2) An industrial tribunal shall not consider a complaint referred to it under sub-paragraph (1) above unless the complaint is presented to the tribunal before the end of the period of three months beginning with the date of the offer of employment or within such further period as the tribunal considers reasonable in a case where it is satisfied that it was not reasonably practicable for the complaint to be presented before the end of the period of three months.

(3) An appeal shall lie to the Employment Appeal Tribunal on a question of law arising from the decision of, or in proceedings before, an industrial tribunal under this paragraph.

(4) Except as mentioned in sub-paragraph (3) above, no appeal shall lie from the decision of an industrial tribunal under this paragraph.

9.—(1) In the event of the Board assuming under section 3(4) any of the functions specified in that subsection the Lord Chancellor shall by regulations make such provision corresponding to paragraphs 6, 7 and 8 in respect of employees to whom this paragraph applies as appears to him to be appropriate.

(2) This paragraph applies to persons employed—

    (a) in civil service of the State; or

    (b) by a magistrates' courts committee,

and so employed wholly or mainly in connection with the functions referred to in sub-paragraph (1) above.

Pensions

10. Any arrangements made by the Law Society under section 19 of the 1974 Act in respect of any pension shall be treated on and after the appointed day (so far as may be necessary to preserve their effect) as having been made under paragraph 10(2) of Schedule 1 to this Act, and any pension scheme administered by the Law Society immediately before the appointed day shall be deemed to be a pension scheme established and administered by the Board under that paragraph and shall continue to be administered accordingly.

Representation in affiliation proceedings: transitory provision

11. Until the repeal of the Affiliation Proceedings Act 1957 by the Family Law Reform Act 1987 takes effect, Schedule 2 to this Act shall be taken to include proceedings in the Crown Court or a magistrates' court for or in relation to an affiliation order within the meaning of the Affiliation Proceedings Act 1957.

SCHEDULE 8

Transitory Amendments of Legal Aid Act 1974

Preliminary

1. In this Schedule "the 1974 Act" means the Legal Aid Act 1974.

Regulation of charges on property

2. In section 20(2)(e) of the 1974 Act (regulation of charge on property):

    (a) after the words "receiving advice or assistance or legal aid" there shall be inserted the words "and regulating the release or postponement of the enforcement of any charge (however created) for the benefit of the legal aid fund"; and

    (b) at the end there shall be inserted the words; "and

        (iii) requiring interest to be charged at a prescribed rate in circumstances where enforcement of a charge for the benefit of the legal aid fund is postponed."

Remuneration

3. In section 39 of the 1974 Act, for subsection (3) (fair remuneration in criminal and certain other legal aid cases) there shall be substituted the following:

"(3) The Lord Chancellor, in making regulations under this section as to the amounts payable to council, or solicitors undertaking any description of legal aid work under this Part of this Act, shall have regard, among the matters which are relevant, to:

(a) the time and skill which it requires;

(b) the general level of fee income arising from it;

(c) the general level of expenses of barristers and solicitors which is attributable to it;

(d) the number and general level of competence of barristers and solicitors undertaking it;

(e) the effect of the regulations on the handling of the work; and

(f) the cost to public funds of any provision made by the regulations.".

4.—(1) In Schedule 2 to the 1974 Act (remuneration in civil legal aid cases):

(a) in paragraph 1(1), for the words "95 per cent. of the" there shall be substituted the words "the full"; and

(b) in paragraph 2(1), for the words "95 per cent. of the" there shall be substituted the words "the full."

(2) The amendments made by this paragraph have effect in relation to any case in which the order or direction for taxation is made on or after the date on which this Act is passed.

Legal Advice and Assistance (Scope) Regulations 1989*

Came into force April 1, 1989

ARRANGEMENT OF REGULATIONS

PART I

GENERAL

Citation and Commencement

1. These Regulations may be cited as the Legal Advice and Assistance (Scope) Regulations 1989 and shall come into force on April 1, 1989.

Interpretation

2. In these Regulations, unless the context otherwise requires—

"ABWOR" means assistance by way of representation;

"the Act" means the Legal Aid Act 1988;

"client" means a person seeking or receiving advice or assistance or on whose behalf advice or assistance is sought;

---

* S.I. 1989 No. 550 as amended by the Legal Advice and Assistance (Scope) (Amendment) Regulations 1990 (S.I. 1990 No. 1477) with effect from August 1, 1990, the Legal Advice and Assistance (Scope) (Amendment) Regulations 1992 (S.I. 1992 No. 2874) with effect from November 23, 1992, and the Legal Aid (Scope) Regulations 1994 (S.I. 1994 No. 2768), the Legal Advice and Assistance (Scope) (Amendment) Regulations 1997 (S.I. 1997 No. 997) and the Legal Advice and Assistance (Scope) (Amendment) (No. 2) Regulations 1997 (S.I.1997 No. 1731).

"conditional sale agreement" has the meaning assigned to it in section 189 of the Consumer Credit Act 1974;

"Controller" means a person appointed by the Secretary of State pursuant to section 85(1)(b) of the Criminal Justice Act 1991;

"conveyancing services" has the meaning assigned to it in section 11 of the Administration of Justice Act 1985;

"discretionary life prisoner" has the meaning assigned by section 34(1) of the Criminal Justice Act 1991;

"governor" has the meaning assigned by rule 99 of the Prison Rules 1964;

"mental disorder" has the meaning assigned to it in section 1 of the Mental Health Act 1983;

"the Parole Board" has the meaning assigned by section 32 of the Criminal Justice Act 1991;

"rental purchase agreement" has the meaning assigned to it in section 88 of the Housing Act 1980;

"will" has the meaning assigned to it in section 1 of the Wills Act 1837;

Amended by the Legal Aid (Scope) Regulations 1994 (S.I. 1994 No. 2768).

PART II

EXCLUSIONS FROM PART III OF THE ACT

Conveyancing Services

3.—(1) Subject to paragraphs (2) and (3), advice and assistance consisting of conveyancing services are excluded from Part III of the Act.

(2) Paragraph (1) does not exclude from Part III of the Act advice or assistance relating to a rental purchase agreement or a conditional sale agreement for the sale of land.

(3) Paragraph (1) does not exclude from Part III of the Act advice or assistance consisting of such conveyancing services as are necessary in order to give effect to an order of the court or, in proceedings under the Matrimonial Causes Act 1973 or the Matrimonial and Family Proceedings Act 1984, the terms of an agreement.

Wills

4.—(1) Except as provided by paragraph (2), advice and assistance in the making of wills are excluded from Part III of the Act.

(2) Advice and assistance in the making of a will are not excluded by paragraph (1) from Part III of the Act where they are given to a client who is:

(a) aged 70 or over; or

(b) blind (or partially sighted), deaf (or hard of hearing), or dumb, or who suffers from mental disorder of any description, or who is substantially and permanently handicapped by illness, injury or congenital deformity; or

(c) a parent or guardian within the meaning of section 87 of the Child Care Act 1980 of a person to whom any description in (b) applies, where the client wishes to provide in the will for that person; or

(d) the mother or father of a minor who is living with the client, where the client is not living with the minor's other parent, and the client wishes to appoint a guardian for that minor under section 4 of the Guardianship of Minors Act 1971.

Services under contracts and grants

4A.—(1) Advice and assistance provided under a contract or grant to which this regulation applies are excluded from Part III of the Act.

(2) This regulation applies to any contract or grant under Part II of the Act which—

(a) secures the provision of advice and assistance under Part II of the Act, and

(b) does not relate to the provision of advice, assistance or representation under any other Part of the Act.

Inserted by the Legal Advice and Assistance (Scope) (Amendment) (No. 2) Regulations 1997 (S.I. No. 1731).

Transition

5. Where advice or assistance has been given before these Regulations come into force, nothing in this Part shall affect further advice or assistance given in relation to the same matter.

PART III

ABWOR

Application of Part III of the Act to ABWOR

6. Part III of the Act does not apply to ABWOR except as provided in this Part.

Proceedings in magistrates' courts

7.—(1) Part III of the Act applies to ABWOR given—

(a) to a client for the purposes of the proceedings in magistrates' courts specified in the Schedule;

(b) at a hearing in any proceedings in a magistrates' court to a party who is not receiving and has not been refused representation in connection with those proceedings, where the court—
   (i) is satisfied that the hearing should proceed on the same day;
   (ii) is satisfied that that party would not otherwise be represented; and
   (iii) requests a solicitor who is within the precincts of the court for purposes other than the provision of ABWOR in accordance with this sub-paragraph, or approves a proposal from such a solicitor, that he provide that party with ABWOR; or

(c) to a person in connection with an application for a warrant of further detention, or for an extension of such a warrant, made in respect of that person to a magistrates' court under section 43 or 44 of the Police and Criminal Evidence Act 1984.

(2) Subject to paragraph (3), Part III of the Act also applies, in criminal proceedings in magistrates' courts where the client has not previously received and is not otherwise receiving representation or ABWOR in connection with the same proceedings, to ABWOR given to a client—

(a) in making an application for bail;

(b) at an appearance in court where the client is in custody and wishes the case to be concluded at that appearance, unless the solicitor who is advising him considers that the case should be adjourned in the interests of justice or of the client;

(c) who is before the court as a result of a failure to obey an order of the court, where such failure may lead to his being at risk of imprisonment;

(d) who is not in custody and who in the opinion of the solicitor requires ABWOR.

(3) Paragraph (2) does not apply to committal proceedings, to proceedings in which the client pleads not guilty, nor, unless the solicitor considers the circumstances to be exceptional, to proceedings in connection with a nonimprisonable offence.

(4) Part III also applies to ABWOR given to a party in proceedings in a magistrates' court where he is before the court as a result of a failure to—

(a) pay a fine or other sum which he was ordered to pay; or

(b) to obey an order of the court,

and such failure is likely to lead to his being at risk of a term of imprisonment being fixed in his case (whether at the hearing for which ABWOR is given or subsequently).

Amended by the Legal Advice and Assistance (Scope) (Amendment) Regulations 1997 (S.I. 1997 No. 997).

Proceedings in county courts

8. Part III of the Act applies to ABWOR given by a solicitor at a hearing in any proceedings in a county court to a party who is not receiving and has not been refused representation in connection with those proceedings, where the court—

(a) is satisfied that the hearing should proceed on the same day;

(b) is satisfied that that party would not otherwise be represented; and

(c) requests a solicitor who is within the precincts of the court for purposes other than the provision of ABWOR in accordance with this regulation, or approves a proposal from such a solicitor, that he provide that party with ABWOR.

Other proceedings

9. Part III of the Act applies to ABWOR given—

(a) to a person in proceedings before a Mental Health Review Tribunal under the Mental Health Act 1983 whose case or whose application to the Tribunal is or is to be the subject of the proceedings;

(b) to a prisoner who has been permitted by the governor or Controller to be legally represented in proceedings before him;

(c) to a discretionary life prisoner whose case is referred to the Parole Board under sections 34(4) or (5) or 39(4) of the Criminal Justice Act 1991.

(d) to a person serving a sentence of detention during Her Majesty's

Pleasure whose case is referred to the Parole Board under section 32(2) or 39(4) of the Criminal Justice Act 1991.

Amended by the Legal Aid (Scope) Regulations 1994 (S.I. 1994 No. 2768) and the Legal Advice and Assistance (Scope) (Amendment) Regulations 1997 (S.I. 1997 No. 997).

SCHEDULE

PROCEEDINGS IN MAGISTRATES' COURTS IN WHICH ABWOR IS AVAILABLE

1. In this Schedule "proceedings in a magistrates' court" includes giving notice of appeal or applying for a case to be stated within the ordinary time for so doing, and matters preliminary thereto.

2. The proceedings in which Part III of the Act applies to ABWOR under regulation 7(1)(a) are proceedings—

(a) for or in relation to an affiliation order within the meaning of the Affiliation Proceedings Act 1957;

(b) for or in relation to an order under the Matrimonial Proceedings (Magistrates' Courts) Act 1960 or Part I of the Domestic Proceedings and Magistrates' Courts Act 1978;

(c) under the Guardianship of Minors Act 1971 and 1973;

(d) under sections 43 or 47 of the National Assistance Act 1948, section 22 of the Maintenance Orders Act 1950, section 4 of the Maintenance Orders Act 1958, section 18 of the Supplementary Benefits Act 1976, or section 24 of the Social Security Act 1986;

(e) in relation to an application for leave of the court to remove a child from a person's custody under section 27 or 28 of the Adoption Act 1976 or proceedings in which the making of an order under Part II or section 29 or 55 of the Adoption Act 1976 is opposed by any party to the proceedings;

(f) under Part I of the Maintenance Orders (Reciprocal Enforcement) Act 1972 relating to a maintenance order made by a court of a country outside the United Kingdom;

(g) under Part II of the Children Act 1975;

(h) under section 10A of the Fire Precautions Act 1971.

Amended by the Legal Advice and Assistance (Scope) (Amendment) Regulations 1997 (S.I. 1997 No. 997).

EXPLANATORY NOTE

(This note is not part of the Regulations)

These Regulations replace, with amendments, the provisions in the Legal Advice and Assistance Regulations (No. 2) 1980 (S.I. 1980 No. 1898) which prescribe the scope of advice and assistance (including assistance by way of representation). The other provisions of those Regulations are replaced, with amendments, by the Legal Advice and Assistance Regulations 1989 (S.I. 1989 No. 340).

The main changes are to disapply (with certain exceptions) the provisions of Part III of the Act from advice and assistance consisting of conveyancing services (regulation 3) or in the making of wills (regulation 4).

In accordance with section 8(2) of the Legal Aid Act 1988, the Regulations apply Part III of the Act to assistance by way of representation (as to proceedings in magistrates' courts, regulation 7; as to proceedings in county courts, regulation 8; as to proceedings before Mental Health Review Tribunals and proceedings before boards of prison visitors, regulation 9).

[These Regulations have since been amended.]

Legal Advice and Assistance Regulations 1989*

Came into force April 1, 1989

ARRANGEMENTS OF REGULATIONS

---

* S.I. 1989 No. 340 as amended by the Legal Advice and Assistance (Amendment) Regulations 1989 (S.I. 1989 No. 560), the Legal Advice and Assistance (Amendment) Regulations 1990 (S.I. 1990 No. 486), the Legal Advice and Assistance (Amendment) Regulations 1991 (S.I. 1991 No. 636), the Legal Advice and Assistance (Amendment) (No. 2) Regulations 1991 (S.I. 1991 No. 2305), the Legal Advice and Assistance (Amendment) Regulations 1992 (S.I. 1992 No. 591), the Legal Advice and Assistance (Amendment) (No. 2) Regulations 1992 (S.I. 1992 No. 719), the Legal Advice and Assistance (Amendment) (No. 3) Regulations 1992 (S.I. 1992 No. 2654), the Legal Advice and Assistance (Amendment) Regulations 1993 (S.I. 1993 No. 790), the Legal Advice and Assistance (Amendment) Regulations 1994 (S.I. 1994 No. 805), the Legal Advice and Assistance (Amendment) (No. 2) Regulations 1994 (S.I. 1994 No. 1823), the Legal Advice and Assistance (Amendment) Regulations 1995 (S.I. 1995 No. 795), the Legal Advice and Assistance (Amendment) (No. 2) Regulations 1995 (S.I. 1995 No. 949), the Legal Advice and Assistance (Amendment) Regulations 1996 (S.I. 1996 No. 435), the Legal Advice and Assistance (Amendment) (No. 2) Regulations 1996 (S.I. 1996 No. 641), the Legal Advice and Assistance (Amendment (No. 3) Regulations 1996 (S.I. 1996 No. 2308), the Legal Advice and Assistance (Amendment) Regulations 1997 (S.I. 1997 No. 751) and the Legal Advice and Assistance (Amendment) Regulations 1998 (S.I. 1998 No. 663).

Citation, commencement, and transitional provisions

1.—(1) These Regulations may be cited as the Legal Advice and Assistance Regulations 1989 and shall come into force on April 1, 1989.

(2) Where a review under paragraph (7) of regulation 29 relates to a claim made before June 1, 1989, paragraphs (8) and (9) of that regulation shall not apply and the solicitor may appeal in writing within 21 days of receipt of notification of the decision on the review to a committee appointed by the Board.

Revocations

2. The Regulations specified in Schedule 1 are hereby revoked.

Interpretation

3.—(1) In these Regulations, unless the context otherwise requires—

"ABWOR" means assistance by way of representation;

"the Act" means the Legal Aid Act 1988;

"appropriate area committee" means the area committee in whose area an application for advice and assistance, or a claim for costs has been dealt with by an Area Director;

"area committee" has the meaning assigned to it in the Civil Legal Aid (General) Regulations 1989;

"Area Director" has the meaning assigned to it in the Civil Legal Aid (General) Regulations 1989;

"assessed deficiency" means the amount by which the sum allowed to the solicitor by the Area Director in assessing his claim under regulation 29 exceeds any contribution payable by the client to the solicitor under section 9 of the Act together with the value of any charge arising under section 11 of the Act;

"board of visitors" means a board of visitors appointed by the Secretary of State under section 6(2) of the Prison Act 1952;

"child" means a person under the age that is for the time being the upper limit of compulsory school age by virtue of section 35 of the Education Act 1944 together with any Order in Council made under that section;

"client" means a person seeking or receiving advice and assistance or on whose behalf advice and assistance is sought;

"contract" means a contract entered into by the Board with other persons or bodies pursuant to its powers under section 4 of the Act;

"costs" means the cost of giving advice or assistance, including disbursements, charges and fees;

"Costs Regulations" means the Legal Aid in Criminal and Care Proceedings (Costs) Regulations 1989;

"disability working allowance" means a disability working allowance under the Social Security Contributions and Benefits Act 1992;

"extension" means the grant of prior authority to exceed the limit prescribed under section 10(1) of the Act and, where appropriate, the grant of prior authority to exceed any further limit imposed under regulation 21(3) or 22(8);

"family credit" means family credit under the Social Security Contributions and Benefits Act 1992;

"franchisee" means a person or body (other than the Board) acting under the terms of a franchising contract;

"fund" means the legal aid fund;

"income-based jobseeker's allowance" has the meaning given by section 1(4) of the Jobseekers Act 1995, but excludes any sum treated as payable by way of a jobseeker's allowance by virtue of section 26 of that Act;

"income support" means income support under the Social Security Contributions and Benefits Act 1992;

"patient" means a person who by reason of mental disorder within the meaning of the Mental Health Act 1983 is incapable of managing and administering his property and affairs;

"Scope Regulations" means the Legal Advice and Assistance (Scope) Regulations 1989;

"serious service offence" means an offence under any of the Army Act 1955, the Air Force Act 1955, or the Naval Discipline Act 1957 which cannot be dealt with summarily or which appears to an interviewing service policeman to be serious;

"volunteer" means a person who, for the purpose of assisting with an investigation, attends voluntarily at a police station or at any other place where a constable is present or accompanies a constable to a police station or any such other place without having been arrested.

(2) Any reference in these Regulations to a regulation or Schedule by number means the regulation or Schedule so numbered in these Regulations.

Amended by the Legal Advice and Assistance (Amendment) (No. 2) Regulations 1994 and the Legal Advice and Assistance (Amendment) (No. 3) Regulations 1996 (S.I. 1996 No. 2308).

Exercise of Area Director's functions by franchisee

3A. Where and to the extent that a franchising contract so provides, any functions of an Area Director are conferred on a franchisee, the functions may be exercised by the franchisee on the Area Director's behalf.

Inserted by the Legal Advice and Assistance (Amendment) (No. 2) Regulations 1994.

Limit on cost of advice and assistance

4.—(1) Subject to paragraph (2), the limit applicable under section 10(1) of the Act is—

(a) in respect of advice and assistance given in accordance with regulation 6(1), £90;

(b) in respect of advice and assistance provided to a petitioner for divorce or judicial separation which includes advice or assistance in the preparation of the petition, three times the relevant sum specified for preparation in the table in paragraph 1 (or paragraph 2 in the case of a franchisee) of Schedule 6;

(c) in respect of all other advice and assistance, twice the relevant sum referred to in sub-paragraph (b);

(2) Section 10(1) of the Act shall not apply to—

(a) advice or assistance specified in regulation 5(1)(b) of the Legal Advice and Assistance at Police Stations (Remuneration) Regulations 1989 where the interests of justice require such advice or assistance to be given as a matter of urgency; or

(b) ABWOR provided under arrangements made by the Board under regulation 7; or

(c) advice or assistance given under arrangements made by the Board under regulation 8.

Amended by the Legal Advice and Assistance (Amendment) (No. 2) Regulations 1995 (S.I. 1995 No. 949).

ABWOR relating to applications for further detention

5.—ABWOR to which Part III of the Act applies by virtue of regulation 7(1)(c) of the Scope Regulations (application for warrant of further detention) shall be available without reference to the client's financial resources.

ABWOR in proceedings before a Mental Health Review Tribunal

5A.—ABWOR to which Part III of the Act applies by virtue of regulation 9(a) of the Scope Regulations shall be available without reference to the client's financial resources.

Inserted by the Legal Advice and Assistance (Amendment) Regulations 1994 (S.I. 1994 No. 805).

Provision of advice and assistance at police stations, etc.

6.—(1) A solicitor may give advice and assistance to any person who—

   (a) is arrested and held in custody at a police station or other premises; or

   (b) is being interviewed in connection with a serious service offence; or

   (c) is a volunteer.

(2) Subject to any arrangements made by the Board under paragraph (3), an application for advice and assistance in the circumstances specified in paragraph (1) may be made by telephone to the solicitor from whom the advice and assistance is sought.

(3) The Board may make arrangements for solicitors designated by the Board to attend at police stations or other premises in order to provide advice and assistance under paragraph (1).

(4) Advice and assistance given under this regulation shall be available without reference to the client's financial resources.

ABWOR in proceedings in magistrates' courts

7.—(1) The Board may make arrangements for the provision of ABWOR to which Part III of the Act applies by virtue of regulation 7(2) and (4) of the Scope Regulations.

(2) Arrangements under paragraph (1) may provide for solicitors designated by the Board to attend at magistrates' courts.

(3) ABWOR under this regulation shall be available without reference to the client's financial resources.

Amended by the Legal Advice and Assistance (Amendment) Regulations 1997 (S.I. 1997 No. 751).

Advice and assistance in criminal proceedings in magistrates' courts

8.—(1) Arrangements under regulation 7 may provide for a solicitor who gives ABWOR in accordance with them also to give—

   (a) advice to a defendant who is in custody;

   (b) advice to a defendant who is before the court as a result of a failure to pay a fine or other sum which he was ordered on conviction to pay, or to obey an order of the court, where such failure may lead to his being at risk of imprisonment;

   (c) advice, where in the opinion of the solicitor the defendant requires it, to a defendant who is not in custody;

   (d) assistance to a defendant to make an application for representation under the Act in respect of any subsequent appearance of the defendant before the court.

(2) Advice and assistance given under this regulation shall be available without reference to the client's financial resources.

Applications for advice and assistance

9.—(1) An application for advice and assistance to which this regulation applies shall be made in accordance with its provisions to the solicitor from whom the advice and assistance is sought.

(2) This regulation applies to all advice and assistance except—

(a) advice or assistance given under regulation 6 or 8; and

(b) ABWOR given under regulation 7, or to which Part III of the Act applies by virtue of regulation 7(1)(c) of the Scope Regulations (warrants of further detention).

(3) Subject to paragraph 3A and regulations 10 and 15, the application under paragraph (1) shall be made by the client in person.

(3A) Where a franchising contract so provides and subject to compliance with any provisions specified in the contract, an application for advice and assistance may be made by telephone or by post.

(4) Where a client makes an application under paragraph (1) he shall provide the solicitor with the information necessary to enable the solicitor to determine—

(a) his disposable capital;

(b) where appropriate, whether he is in receipt of income support, income-based jobseeker's allowance, family credit or disability working allowance, and

(c) where he is not in receipt of income support, income-based jobseeker's allowance, family credit or disability working allowance, his disposable income.

(5) Where an application under paragraph (1) is for advice or assistance relating to the making of a will, the client shall provide the solicitor with the information necessary to enable the solicitor to determine whether the advice or assistance would fall within regulation 4(2) of the Scope Regulations.

(6) The information required by this regulation shall be furnished on a form approved by the Board.

Amended by the Legal Advice and Assistance (Amendment) (No. 2) Regulations 1994 and the Legal Advice and Assistance (Amendment) (No. 3) Regulations 1996 (S.I. 1996 No. 2308).

Attendance on behalf of a client

10.—(1) Where a client cannot for good reason attend on the solicitor in order to apply for advice and assistance in accordance with paragraph (3) of regulation 9, he may authorise another person to attend on his behalf.

(2) Where a person authorised in accordance with paragraph (1) attends on a solicitor, he shall furnish the solicitor with the information necessary to enable the solicitor to determine—

(a) the client's disposable capital;

(b) where appropriate, whether the client is in receipt of income support, income-based jobseeker's allowance, family credit or disability working allowance; and

(c) where the client is not in receipt of income support, income-based jobseeker's allowance, family credit or disability working allowance, the client's disposable income.

(3) Where the application is for advice or assistance relating to the making

of a will, the person authorised in accordance with paragraph (1) shall provide the solicitor with the information necessary to enable the solicitor to determine whether the advice or assistance would fall within regulation 4(2) of the Scope Regulations.

(4) The information required by this regulation shall be furnished on a form approved by the Board.

Amended by the Legal Advice and Assistance (Amendment) (No. 2) Regulations 1996 (S.I. 1996 No. 2308).

Eligibility for advice and assistance to which regulation 9 applies

11.—(1) A client is eligible for advice and assistance (excluding ABWOR) to which regulation 9 applies if his weekly disposable income does not exceed £80, and his disposable capital does not exceed £1,000.

(2) A client is eligible for ABWOR to which regulation 9 applies if his weekly disposable income does not exceed £172, and his disposable capital does not exceed £3,000.

Amended by the Legal Advice and Assistance (Amendment) (No. 2) Regulations 1992 (S.I. 1992 No. 719), the Legal Advice and Assistance (Amendment) Regulations 1993 (S.I. 1993 No. 790), the Legal Advice and Assistance (Amendment) Regulations 1994 (S.I. 1994 No. 805), the Legal Advice and Assistance (Amendment) Regulations 1995 (S.I. 1995 No. 795) and the Legal Advice and Assistance (Amendment) (No. 2) Regulations 1996 (S.I. 1996 No. 641), the Legal Advice and Assistance (Amendment) Regulations 1997 (S.I. 1997 No. 751) and the Legal Advice and Assistance (Amendment) Regulations 1998 (S.I. 1998 No. 663).

Contributions

12.—(1) A client shall be liable to pay weekly contributions towards the cost of ABWOR if his weekly disposable income exceeds £72 but does not exceed £172.

(2) The amount of any contribution under paragraph (1) shall be one third of the amount by which his weekly disposable income exceeds £72.

(3) The period during which contributions shall be payable shall start on the date of approval of ABWOR and shall continue until the conclusion of the proceedings to which ABWOR related or until ABWOR is withdrawn.

(4) For ABWOR to which Part III of the Act applies by virtue of regulation 7(1)(b) or 8 of the Scope Regulations, a client shall be liable (subject to paragraphs (1), (2) and (5) of this regulation) to pay one week's contribution towards the cost of ABWOR.

(5) A client whose weekly disposable income does not exceed £72 is not liable to pay any contribution under section 9(6) of the Act towards the cost of ABWOR.

(6) A client shall in no case be liable to pay any contribution towards the cost of advice and assistance other than ABWOR.

Amended by the Legal Advice and Assistance (Amendment) Regulations 1993 (S.I. 1993 No. 790), the Legal Advice and Assistance (Amendment) Regulations 1994 (S.I. 1994 No. 805), the Legal Advice and Assistance (Amendment) Regulations 1995 (S.I. 1995 No. 795), the Legal Advice and Assistance (Amendment) (No. 2) Regulations 1996 (S.I. 1996 No. 641), the Legal Advice and Assistance (Amendment) Regulations 1997 (S.I. 1997 No. 751) and the Legal Advice and Assistance (Amendment) Regulations 1998 (S.I. 1998 No. 663).

Assessment of disposable income, disposable capital and contribution

13.—(1) Subject to paragraphs (2) and (3), a solicitor to whom an application under regulation 9 is made shall assess the disposable income and disposable capital of the client and, where appropriate, of any person whose financial resources may be treated as those of the client in accordance with Schedule 2.

(2) Where the solicitor is satisfied that any of the persons whose disposable incomes are to be assessed under paragraph (1) is directly or indirectly in receipt of income support, income-based jobseeker's allowance, family credit or disability working allowance, he shall take that person's disposable income as not exceeding the sum for the time being specified in regulation 11(1).

(3) Where, in the case of an application for ABWOR to which regulation 9 applies, the solicitor is satisfied that any of the persons whose disposable capital is to be assessed under paragraph (1) is directly or indirectly in receipt of income support or income-based jobseeker's allowance, he shall take that person's disposable capital as not exceeding the capital sum specified in regulation 11(2).

(4) The solicitor shall also determine in accordance with the provisions of regulation 12 the weekly contribution, if any, payable to him by the client under section 9(6) of the Act.

(5) The solicitor shall not provide advice and assistance to any person until either the form referred to in regulation 9(6) has been signed by the client or, where appropriate, the form referred to in regulation 10(4) has been signed on behalf of the client, and in any case, until the solicitor has assessed disposable income and disposable capital in accordance with paragraph (1).

Amended by the Legal Advice and Assistance (Amendment) Regulations 1993 (S.I. 1993 No. 790) and the Legal Advice and Assistance (Amendment) (No. 3) Regulations 1996 (S.I. 1996 No. 2308).

Children and patients

14.—(1) A solicitor shall not, except where paragraph (2) or (2A) applies, accept an application for advice and assistance from a child unless he has been authorised to do so by the Area Director and the Area Director shall withhold such authority unless he is satisfied that it is reasonable in the circumstances that the child should receive advice and assistance.

(2) A solicitor may accept an application for advice and assistance from a child who—

(a) is arrested and held in custody at a police station or other premises;

(b) is being interviewed in connection with a serious service offence; or

(c) is a volunteer;

where the solicitor is satisfied that the application cannot reasonably be made by any of the persons specified in paragraph (3)(a), (c) or (d).

(2A) A solicitor may accept an application for advice and assistance from a child in relation to proceedings in which that child is entitled to begin, prosecute or defend without a next friend or guardian *ad litem*.

(3) A solicitor may accept an application for advice and assistance on behalf of a child or patient from—

(a) in the case of a child, his parent or guardian or other person in whose care he is; or

(b) in the case of a patient, a receiver appointed under Part VII of the Mental Health Act 1983 or the patient's nearest relative or guardian within the meaning of Part II of the Mental Health Act 1983; or

(c) in the case of a child or patient, a person acting for the purposes of any proceedings as his next friend or guardian *ad litem*; or

(d) in the case of a child or a patient, any other person where the Area Director is satisfied that it is reasonable in the circumstances and has given prior authority for the advice and assistance to be given to such other person on behalf of the child or patient.

Amended by the Legal Advice and Assistance (Amendment) Regulations 1992 (S.I. 1992 No. 591).

Clients resident outside England and Wales

15.—Where the client resides outside England and Wales, the Area Director may give the solicitor prior authority to accept a postal application for advice and assistance if the Area Director is satisfied that it is reasonable in the circumstances to do so.

Advice and assistance from more than one solicitor

16.—(1) A person shall not, except where regulation 6, 7 or 8 applies, be given advice and assistance for the same matter by more than one solicitor without the prior authority of the Area Director, and such authority may be given on such terms and conditions as the Area Director may in his discretion see fit to impose.

(2) Where regulation 6 applies, a person may be given advice and assistance for the same matter by more than one solicitor without the prior authority of the Area Director, provided that the cost of that advice and assistance shall not exceed the cost that would have been incurred had it been given by one solicitor.

Separate matters

17. Where two or more separate matters are involved, each matter shall be the subject of a separate application for advice and assistance provided that matters connected with or arising from proceedings for divorce or judicial separation, whether actual or prospective between the client and his spouse, shall not be treated as separate matters for the purpose of advice and assistance.

Refusal of advice and assistance

18. A solicitor may for good cause either refuse to accept an application for advice and assistance or (having accepted an application) decline to give, or to continue to give advice and assistance and may, if he thinks fit, refuse to disclose his reasons for doing so to the client or person seeking advice and assistance on his behalf; but he shall give the Area Director such information about such a refusal as the Area Director may require.

Power to require information

19. The Area Director may require a solicitor who has given advice and assistance to furnish such information as he may from time to time require for the purposes of his functions under these Regulations; and the solicitor shall not be precluded, by reason of any privilege arising out of the relationship between solicitor and client, from disclosing such information to him.

Entrusting functions to others

20. Subject to any arrangements made by the Board under regulations 6, 7 or

8, nothing in these Regulations shall prevent a solicitor from entrusting any function under these Regulations to a partner of his or to a competent and responsible representative of his who is employed in his office or is otherwise under his immediate supervision.

Extensions

21.—(1) Subject to regulation 22(8), and except where regulation 6, 7 or 8 applies, where it appears to the solicitor that the cost of giving advice or assistance is likely to exceed the limit applicable under section 10(1) of the Act, he shall apply to the Area Director for an extension and shall furnish such information as may enable him to consider and determine that application.

(2) Where an Area Director receives an application in accordance with paragraph (1) he shall consider—

    (a) whether it is reasonable for the advice and assistance to be given; and

    (b) whether the estimate of the costs to be incurred in giving advice and assistance is reasonable.

(3) If the Area Director is satisfied that it is reasonable for the advice or assistance to be given and that the estimate of the costs to be incurred in giving it is reasonable, he shall grant an extension and shall prescribe such higher limit as he thinks fit and may limit the advice and assistance to such subject matter as he thinks fit.

Applications for approval of ABWOR

22.—(1) The approval of the Board shall not be required for ABWOR to be given in accordance with arrangements made by the Board under regulation 7.

(2) The approval of the Board shall not be required for ABWOR to which Part III of the Act applies by virtue of regulation 7(1)(b), 7(1)(c), or 8 of the Scope Regulations.

(3) Subject to paragraph (1), where it appears to the solicitor that the client needs ABWOR to which Part III of the Act applies by virtue of regulation 7(1)(a), 7(2), 7(4) or 9 of the Scope Regulations, he shall apply to the Area Director for approval.

(4) The application for approval shall be on a form approved by the Board and the solicitor shall supply such information as may enable the Area Director to consider and determine it.

(5) An application for approval, except in respect of ABWOR to which Part III of the Act applies by virtue of regulation 7(4) or 9 of the Scope Regulations, shall be refused unless it is shown that the client has reasonable grounds for taking, defending or being a party to the proceedings to which it relates.

(6) Subject to paragraph (6A) below, an application for approval may be refused if it appears unreasonable that approval should be granted in the particular circumstances of the case.

(6A) In respect of ABWOR to which Part III of the Act applies by virtue of regulation 7(4) of the Scope Regulations, an application for approval may be refused if—

    (a) it appears unreasonable that approval should be granted in the particular circumstances of the case (because, for example, ABWOR is available in accordance with arrangements made by the Board under regulation 7(1)), or

    (b) it is not in the interests of justice that approval should be granted (because, for example, the applicable law is not unduly complex or there is no real risk of imprisonment).

(7) The Area Director may grant an application for approval in whole or in part and may impose such conditions as to the conduct of the proceedings to which his approval relates as he thinks fit, and in particular it shall be a condition of every approval that the prior permission of the Area Director shall be required—

(a) to obtain a report or opinion of an expert; or

(b) to tender expert evidence; or

(c) to perform an act which is either unusual in its nature or involves unusually large expenditure;

unless such permission has been included in the grant of approval.

(8) An approval of ABWOR shall include an extension in respect of the matter to which it relates and, without prejudice to paragraph (7), the Area Director may prescribe such higher limit as he thinks fit.

Amended by the Legal Advice and Assistance (Amendment) Regulations 1990 (S.I. 1990 No. 486) and the Legal Advice and Assistance (Amendment) Regulations 1997 (S.I. 1997 No. 751).

Counsel

23. Where it appears to the solicitor that the proper conduct of proceedings in respect of which ABWOR has been granted under regulation 22 requires the instruction of counsel, he may apply to the Area Director for approval and the Area Director shall grant approval if he considers that the proper conduct of the proceedings requires counsel.

Notification of approval of assistance by way of representation

24. Where ABWOR has been approved in respect of proceedings specified in regulation 7(1)(a) of the Scope Regulations and the client becomes a party to proceedings or is already a party to proceedings the solicitor shall as soon as practicable give notice of the approval to any other party to the proceedings and the court in which the proceedings are pending.

Withdrawal of approval of assistance by way of representation

25.—(1) The Area Director shall withdraw approval of ABWOR granted under regulation 22 from such date as he considers appropriate where, as a result of information which has come to his knowledge, he considers that:

(a) in respect of proceedings specified in regulation 7(1)(a) of the Scope Regulations, the client no longer has reasonable grounds for taking, defending or being a party to the proceedings, or for continuing to do so; or

(b) the client has required the proceedings to be conducted unreasonably so as to incur an unjustifiable expense to the fund; or

(c) it is unreasonable in the particular circumstances that the client should continue to receive ABWOR.

(2) When approval of ABWOR is withdrawn, the Area Director shall notify the solicitor who shall forthwith—

(a) inform his client; and

(b) in respect of proceedings specified in regulation 7(1)(a) of the Scope Regulations, if proceedings have been commenced, send a copy of the notice to the court and to any other party to the proceedings to which the approval related.

(3) Withdrawal of approval shall not affect or prejudice any subsequent application for representation or for approval of ABWOR in respect of the same proceedings.

Appeals against refusal of ABWOR, etc.

26.—(1) Where the Area Director—

(a) refuses an application under regulation 22 for the approval of ABWOR; or

(b) refuses authority in respect of any of the matters set out in paragraph (7)(a) to (c) of regulation 22; or

(c) withdraws approval of ABWOR under regulation 25;

the client may appeal to the appropriate area committee.

(2) An appeal shall be made by giving notice on a form approved by the Board within 14 days of the Area Director's decision to refuse the application or authority or withdraw approval.

Determination of appeals

27.—(1) The area committee shall, on an appeal under regulation 26, reconsider the application for approval or authority or the circumstances set out in paragraph (1)(a) to (c) of regulation 25 and shall—

(a) dismiss the appeal; or

(b) in the case of an application for approval or authority, grant the application subject to such terms and conditions as the committee thinks fit; or

(c) in the case of a decision to withdraw approval, quash that decision.

(2) The decision of the area committee on an appeal shall be final and it shall give notice in writing of its decision, and the reasons for it, to the client and to any solicitor acting for him.

(3) Where the Area Director's decision to withdraw approval is quashed on appeal by the area committee, the solicitor shall, in respect of proceedings specified in regulation 7(1)(a) of the Scope Regulations, notify any other party to the proceedings and the court, if any, in which the proceedings are pending.

Collection and refund of contributions

28.—(1) Where a client is required to pay contributions, the solicitor may collect them in weekly instalments or by such other periodic instalments as may be agreed between him and the client.

(1A) Where the total contribution is likely to exceed the cost of giving ABWOR, the solicitor shall not require the client to pay a sum higher than would be expected to defray his reasonable costs.

(2) Where the reasonable costs of the ABWOR are less than any contribution made by the client, the solicitor shall refund the balance.

Amended by the Legal Advice and Assistance (Amendment) Regulations 1993 (S.I. 1993 No. 790).

Costs payable out of the fund

29.—(1) Where the reasonable costs of the advice or assistance, including charges for disbursements, exceed any contribution payable by the client to the solicitor under section 9 of the Act together with the value of any charge arising under section 11 of the Act, the solicitor shall, except where paragraph (2) applies, submit a claim to the Area Director requesting payment of the deficiency.

(2) A claim for charges or fees properly chargeable for advice and assistance given in the circumstances specified in regulation 6 shall be made in accordance with the Legal Advice and Assistance at Police Stations (Remuneration) Regulations 1989.

(3) A claim for the costs of advice and assistance given in accordance with arrangements made by the Board under regulation 7 or 8 shall be made in accordance with the Legal Advice and Assistance (Duty Solicitor) (Remuneration) Regulations 1989.

(4) Where the claim does not relate to ABWOR in respect of which counsel has been instructed, the Area Director shall assess it and pay the assessed deficiency, if any, to the solicitor.

(5) Where the claim relates to ABWOR in respect of which counsel has been instructed and the Area Director considers that the proper conduct of the proceedings required counsel, or the instruction of counsel has been approved under regulation 23, the Area Director shall—

(a) assess the solicitor's claim excluding counsel's fee, and pay the assessed deficiency, if any, to the solicitor; and

(b) assess counsel's fee and pay him the amount so allowed less the amount, if any, by which the value of any charge arising under section 11 of the Act together with the amount of any contribution payable by the client under section 9(6) of the Act exceeds the amount allowed to the solicitor on the assessment of his claim.

(6) Where the claim relates to ABWOR in respect of which counsel has been instructed without obtaining prior approval under regulation 23, and the Area Director considers that the proper conduct of the proceedings did not require counsel, the Area Director shall—

(a) determine the assessed deficiency on the basis that counsel had not been instructed and the solicitor had conducted the case on his own;

(b) allow the amount which it would have allowed counsel under paragraph (5) above and pay counsel what it would have paid him under that paragraph to the extent of the assessed deficiency; and

(c) pay the balance of the net assessed deficiency if any to the solicitor.

(7) If any solicitor or counsel is dissatisfied with any decision of the Area Director as to the payment of an assessed deficiency in the costs of advice and assistance, he may within 21 days of receipt of notification of that decision make written representations to the appropriate area committee; and that committee shall review the assessment of the Area Director whether by confirming, increasing or decreasing the amount assessed by the Area Director.

(8) A solicitor or counsel who is dissatisfied with the decision of an area committee on a review under paragraph (7) may within 21 days of receipt of notification of the decision apply to that committee to certify a point of principle of general importance.

(9) Where an area committee certifies a point of principle of general importance the solicitor or counsel may, within 21 days of receipt of notification of that certification, appeal in writing to a committee appointed by the Board against the decision of the area committee under paragraph (7).

(10) On an appeal under this regulation the committee appointed by the Board may reverse, affirm or amend the decision of the area committee under paragraph (7).

Basis of assessments

30.—(1) Subject to paragraphs (2), (3) and (4), in any assessment or review of a claim for costs made under these Regulations the amount to be allowed shall be assessed under the Costs Regulations as if the work done was work done by a solicitor in criminal proceedings in a magistrates' court, save that:

(a) any reference in regulation 7 to regulation 54 of the General Regulations shall be construed as a reference to regulation 22(7) of these Regulations;

(b) the words from "in taking" to "given or" in regulation 7(6) shall not apply;

(c) Schedule 6 to these Regulations shall apply instead of Part I to Schedule 1 to the Costs Regulations.

(2) Where the claim is in respect of ABWOR to which regulation 5 applies and which is given in unsocial hours (as defined in regulation 2 of the Legal Advice and Assistance at Police Stations (Remuneration) Regulations 1989), by a solicitor designated in accordance with arrangements made by the Board under regulation 6(3), the amount to be allowed under paragraph (1) shall be increased by one third.

(3) Omitted.

(4) Where advice and assistance is provided under a franchising contract, regulations 29 and 30 shall apply except to the extent that the contract makes different express provision.

Amended by the Legal Aid Advice and Assistance (Amendment) Regulations 1989 (S.I. 1989 No. 560), the Legal Advice and Assistance (Amendment) (No. 2) Regulations 1991 (S.I. 1991 No. 2305), the Legal Advice and Assistance (Amendment) Regulations 1992 (S.I. 1992 No. 591), the Legal Advice and Assistance (Amendment) (No. 3) Regulations 1992 (S.I. 1992 No. 2654), the Legal Advice and Assistance (Amendment) (No. 2) Regulations 1994 and the Legal Advice and Assistance (Amendment) (No. 2) Regulations 1995 (S.I. 1995 No. 949).

Payment on account

30A.—(1) A solicitor acting for a client who is in receipt of ABWOR may apply to the Area Director for the payment of a sum on account of disbursements incurred or about to be incurred in connection with the proceedings to which the approval of ABWOR relates.

(1A) Where ABWOR is provided under a franchising contract, the franchisee may apply to the Area Director for the payment of a sum on account of his charges and fees.

(1B) Where advice and assistance (other than ABWOR) is provided under a franchising contract, the franchisee may apply to the Area Director for the payment of a sum on account of his costs.

(2) Where a payment is made under this regulation, then notwithstanding

that there is no deficiency, the solicitor shall, at the conclusion of the case, submit to the Area Director a statement of his costs, the amount of any contribution payable and the value of any charge arising under section 11 of the Act.

(3) In the event of any payment under this regulation proving to be greater than the assessed deficiency (if any) found to be due, the solicitor shall, on demand, repay the excess to the fund and, where the assessed deficiency exceeds any payment made under this regulation, the balance shall be paid from the fund.

(4) In this regulation "deficiency" and "assessed deficiency" shall have the meanings assigned by regulation 29.

Inserted by the Legal Advice and Assistance (Amendment) Regulations 1992 (S.I. 1992 No. 591) and amended by the Legal Advice and Assistance (Amendment) (No. 2) Regulations 1994.

Recovery of costs

31.—(1) Where any sum is payable to the client by virtue of an order for costs made in connection with proceedings for which ABWOR has been approved under regulation 22, the sum shall be paid to the clerk to the justices, who shall pay it to the Board; and only the clerk to the justices shall be able to give a good discharge for it.

(2) The Board shall, except where a payment has been made under paragraph (3), pay to the solicitor such portion of the sum paid to the Board under paragraph (1) as corresponds to the charge created in his favour on that sum by section 11(2)(a) of the Act, and pay any balance to the client.

(3) The Board may in addition to any payment under regulation 29, pay the solicitor a sum not greater than the sum payable to the Board under paragraph (1) and where such a payment is made, the Board shall require the solicitor to assign his charge under section 11(2)(a) of the Act to the Board.

Exceptions to charge on property recovered or preserved

32. The provisions of section 11(2)(b) of the Act shall not apply to the matters specified in Schedule 4.

Authority not to enforce the charge

33.—Where in the opinion of the solicitor—

(a) it would cause grave hardship or distress to the client to enforce the charge on any money or property recovered or preserved for him; or

(b) the charge on any property recovered or preserved could be enforced only with unreasonable difficulty because of the nature of the property,

the solicitor may apply to the appropriate area committee for authority not to enforce, either wholly or in part, the charge and, if the committee gives authority, any deficiency in the solicitor's costs shall be computed as if section 11(2)(b) of the Act did not apply to that money or property or to such part of it as the committee may have authorised.

Costs awarded against a client

34.—Where proceedings have been concluded in which a client is or was in receipt of ABWOR and an order for costs has been made against him in those proceedings, the amount of his liability for costs (if any) shall be determined in accordance with Schedule 5.

Costs of successful unassisted parties out of the fund

35.—Before making any order under section 13 of the Act, the Court shall afford the Area director who dealt with the application under regulation 22 an opportunity to make representations.

False statements, etc.

36.—Where a client has wilfully failed to comply with the provisions of these Regulations as to the information to be furnished by him or, in furnishing such information, has knowingly made a false statement or false representation, and after the failure occurred or the false statement or false representation was made the client received advice or assistance, the appropriate area committee may declare that the advice or assistance so given was not given under the Act and these Regulations and, if it does, shall so inform the client and the solicitor; and thereafter the Board shall be entitled to recover from the client any sums paid out of the fund in respect of the advice and assistance so given.

Computation of time

37.—(1) Where, under these Regulations, an act is required to be done within a specified period after or from a specified date, the period of time so fixed starts immediately after that date.

(2) The period within which an act is required or authorised to be done under these Regulations may, if the Area Director thinks fit, be extended and any such period may be extended although the application for extension is not made until after the expiration of the period.

Inserted by the Legal Advice and Assistance (Amendment) Regulations 1992 (S.I. 1992 No. 591).

SCHEDULES

SCHEDULE 1

Regulations revoked	*References*
The Legal Advice and Assistance Regulations (No. 2) 1980.	S.I. 1980/1898.
The Legal Advice and Assistance (Amendment) Regulations 1982.	S.I. 1982/1592.
The Legal Advice and Assistance (Amendment) (No. 2) Regulations 1983.	S.I. 1983/470.
The Legal Advice and Assistance (Financial Conditions) Regulations 1983.	S.I. 1983/618.
The Legal Advice and Assistance (Amendment) (No. 3) Regulations 1983.	S.I. 1983/1142.
The Legal Advice and Assistance (Financial Conditions) (No. 2) Regulations 1983.	S.I. 1983/1784.

Regulations revoked	References
The Legal Advice and Assistance (Prospective Cost) (No. 2) Regulations 1983.	S.I. 1983/1785.
The Legal Advice and Assistance (Amendment) (No. 5) Regulations 1983.	S.I. 1983/1935.
The Legal Advice and Assistance (Amendment) (No. 6) Regulations 1983.	S.I. 1983/1963.
The Legal Advice and Assistance (Amendment) Regulations 1984.	S.I. 1984/241.
The Legal Advice and Assistance (Amendment) (No. 2) Regulations 1984.	S.I. 1984/637.
The Legal Advice and Assistance (Amendment) Regulations 1985.	S.I. 1985/1491.
The Legal Advice and Assistance (Prospective Cost) Regulations 1985.	S.I. 1985/1840.
The Legal Advice and Assistance (Amendment) (No. 2) Regulations 1985.	S.I. 1985/1879.
The Legal Advice and Assistance (Amendment) Regulations 1986.	S.I. 1986/275.
The Legal Advice and Assistance (Financial Conditions) (No. 2) Regulations 1987.	S.I. 1987/396.
The Legal Advice and Assistance (Financial Conditions) Regulations 1988.	S.I. 1988/666.
The Legal Advice and Assistance (Financial Conditions) (No. 2) Regulations 1988.	S.I. 1988/459.
The Legal Advice and Assistance (Amendment) Regulations 1988.	S.I. 1988/461.

SCHEDULE 2

Assessment of Resources

1. In this Schedule, unless the context otherwise requires—

"capital" means the amount or value of every resource of a capital nature;

"income" means the total income from all sources which the person concerned has received or may reasonably expect to receive in respect of the seven days up to and including the date of his application;

"the person concerned" means the person whose disposable capital and disposable income are to be assessed.

2. The provisions of this Schedule apply to a man and a woman who are living with each other in the same household as husband and wife as they apply to the parties to a marriage.

3. Any question arising under this Schedule shall be decided by the solicitor to whom the client has applied and that solicitor, in deciding any such question, shall have regard to any guidance which may from time to time be given by the Board as to the application of this Schedule.

4. The disposable capital and disposable income of the person concerned shall be the capital and income as assessed by the solicitor after deducting any sums which are to be left out of account or for which allowance is to be made under the provisions of this Schedule.

5. The resources of any person who, under section 26(3) and (4) of the Social Security

Act 1986 is liable to maintain a child or who usually contributes substantially to a child's maintenance, or who has care and control of the child, not being a person who has such care and control by reason of any contract or for some temporary purpose, may be treated as the resources of the child, if, having regard to all the circumstances, including the age and resources of the child and to any conflict of interest it appears just and equitable to do so.

6. If it appears to the solicitor that the person concerned has, with intent to reduce the amount of his disposable capital or disposable income, whether for the purpose of making himself eligible for advice and assistance, reducing his liability to pay a contribution in respect of the costs of advice and assistance or otherwise—

(a) directly or indirectly deprived himself of any resources; or

(b) converted any part of his resources into resources which are to be left out of account wholly or partly;

the resources of which he has so deprived himself or which he has so converted shall be treated as part of his resources or as not so converted as the case may be.

Amended by the Legal Advice and Assistance (Amendment) Regulations 1990 (S.I. 1990 No. 486).

7.—(1) In computing the capital and income of the person concerned, there shall be left out of account the value of the subject matter of any claim in respect of which he is seeking advice or assistance.

(2) In computing the capital and income of the person concerned, the resources of any spouse of his shall be treated as his resources unless—

(i) the spouse has a contrary interest in the matter in respect of which he is seeking advice and assistance, or

(ii) the person concerned and his spouse are living separate and apart, or

(iii) in all the circumstances of the case it would be inequitable or impractical to do so.

(3) In computing the capital and income of the person concerned, there shall be left out of account so much of any back to work bonus received under section 26 of the Jobseekers Act 1995 as is by virtue of that section to be treated as payable by way of a jobseeker's allowance.

Inserted by the Legal Advice and Assistance (Amendment) (No. 3) Regulations 1996 (S.I. 1996 No. 2308).

8. In computing the capital of the person concerned—

(a) there shall be left out of account the value of his household furniture and effects, of his clothes and of tools and implements of his trade;

(aa) the value of the main or only dwelling in which he resides shall be taken to be the amount for which that interest could be sold in the open market, subject to the following rules:—

(i) the amount to be allowed in respect of any mortgage debt or heritable security shall not exceed £100,000;

(ii) the first £100,000 of the value of that interest, after the application of the rule in paragraph (i), shall be disregarded;

(b) where the person concerned resides in more than one dwelling in which he has an interest there shall be taken into account the amount for which any interest in a dwelling which is not the main dwelling could be sold in the open market; provided that the total amount to be allowed in respect of any mortgage debts or heritable securities over all such dwellings, together with any amount allowed under paragraph (aa)(i) in respect of the main dwelling, shall not exceed £100,000;

(c) where the person concerned has living with him one or more of the following persons, namely, a spouse whose resources are required to be aggregated with his, a dependent child or a dependent relative wholly or substantially maintained by him, a deduction shall be made of £335 in respect of the first person, £200 in respect of the second and £100 in respect of each further person.

Paragraph (aa) was inserted by and paragraph (b) amended the Legal Advice and Assistance (Amendment) Regulations 1996 (S.I. 1996 No. 435) in respect of applications made on or after June 1, 1996.

9. In computing the income of the person concerned—

    (a) there shall be left out of account—

        (i) any income tax paid or payable on income treated under the provisions of this Schedule as his income;

        (ii) contributions estimated to have been paid under the Social Security Acts 1975–1988 or any scheme made under those Acts during or in respect of the seven days up to and including the date of the application for advice and assistance;

    (b) there shall be a deduction in respect of the spouse of the person concerned, if the spouses are living together, in respect of the maintenance of any dependent child and in respect of the maintenance of any dependent relative of the person concerned, being (in either of such cases) a member of his or her household, at the following rates—

        (i) in the case of a spouse at a rate equivalent to the difference between the income support allowance for a couple where both members are aged not less than 18 (which is specified in column 2 of paragraph 1(3)(c) of Schedule 2 Part I of the Income Support (General) Regulations 1987), and the allowance for a single person aged not less than 25, (which is specified in column 2 of paragraph 1(1)(e) of Schedule 2 Part I of those Regulations);

        (ii) in the case of a dependent child or a dependent relative aged 18 or under, at a rate equivalent to the amount specified for the time being in paragraph 2 of Part I of Schedule 2 to the Income Support (General) Regulations 1987 appropriate to the age of the child or relative.

        (iii) in the case of a dependent child or a dependent relative aged 19 or over, at a rate equivalent to the amount which would have been specified for the time being in accordance with paragraph 9(b)(ii) immediately before he attained the age of 19.

Amended by the Legal Advice and Assistance (Amendment) Regulations 1993 (S.I. 1993 No. 790) and the Legal Advice and Assistance (Amendment) Regulations 1998 (S.I. 1998 No. 663).

9A.—(1) In computing disposable income the following payments made under the Social Security Contributions and Benefits Act 1992 shall be disregarded:

    (a) disability living allowance;

    (b) attendance allowance paid under section 64 or Schedule 8 paragraphs 4 or 7(2);

    (c) constant attendance allowance paid under section 104 as an increase to a disablement pension; or

    (d) any payment made out of the social fund.

Inserted by the Legal Advice and Assistance (Amendment) Regulations 1993 (S.I. 1993 No. 790).

(2) In computing disposable income, a payment made under the Community Care (Direct Payments) Act 1996 shall be disregarded.

Inserted by the Legal Advice and Assistance (Amendment) Regulations 1997 (S.I. 1997 No. 751).

9B. In computing the disposable income of any person there shall be disregarded any payment made by the Secretary of State under the Earnings Top-up Scheme 1996.

Inserted by the Legal Advice and Assistance (Amendment) (No. 3) Regulations 1996 (S.I. 1996 No. 2308).

10. If the person concerned is making bona fide payments for the maintenance of a spouse who is living apart, of a former spouse, of a child or relative who is not (in any such case) a member of the household of the person concerned, there shall be a deduction of such payment as was or will be made in respect of the seven days up to and including the date of the application for advice and assistance.

11. Where it appears to the solicitor that there has been some error or mistake in the assessment of the disposable income, disposable capital or contribution of the person concerned, he may reassess the disposable income or disposable capital or contribution or, as the case may be, amend the assessment and in the latter case the amended assessment shall for all purposes be substituted for the original assessment.

Amended by the Legal Advice and Assistance (Amendment) Regulations 1993 (S.I. 1993 No. 790).

SCHEDULE 3

Omitted by the Legal Advice and Assistance (Amendment) Regulations 1993 (S.I. 1993 No. 790).

SCHEDULE 4

EXCEPTIONS TO CHARGE ON PROPERTY RECOVERED OR PRESERVED

The provisions of section 11(2)(b) of the Act shall not apply to—

(a) any periodical payment of maintenance, which for this purpose means money or money's worth paid towards the support of a spouse, former spouse, child or any other person for whose support the payer has previously been responsible or has made payments;

(b) any property recovered or preserved for the client as a result of advice and assistance given to him by the solicitor which comprises the client's main or only dwelling, or any household furniture or tools of trade;

(c) (without prejudice to (b) above) the first £2,500 of any money or of the value of any property recovered or preserved by virtue of—

(i) an order made or deemed to be made, under the provisions of section 23(1)(c) or (f), 23(2), 24, 27(6)(c) or (f), or 35 of the Matrimonial Causes Act 1973;

(ii) an order made, or deemed to be made, under the provisions of section 2 or 6 of the Inheritance (Provision for Family and Dependants) Act 1975;

(iii) an order made, or deemed to be made, under section 17 of the Married Women's Property Act 1882; or

(iv) an order made, or deemed to be made, under the provisions of section 4(2)(b) of the Affiliation Proceedings Act 1957; or

(v) an order for the payment of a lump sum made, or deemed to be made, under the provisions of section 60 of the Magistrates' Courts Act 1980; or

(vi) an order made, or deemed to be made, under the provisions of section 2(1)(b) or (d), 6(1) or (5), 11(2)(b) or (3)(b) or 20(2) of the Domestic Proceedings and Magistrates' Courts Act 1978; or

(vii) an order made, or deemed to be made, under section 9(2)(b), 10(1)(b)(ii), 11(b)(ii) of the Guardianship of Minors Act 1971 or under section 11B, 11C or 11D of that Act; or

(viii) an order made, or deemed to be made, under section 34(1)(c) or 35 of the Children Act 1975; or

(ix) an agreement which has the same effect as an order made, or deemed to be made, under any of the provisions specified in this sub-paragraph;

(d) one-half of any redundancy payment within the meaning of Part VI of the Employment Protection (Consolidation) Act 1978 recovered or preserved for the client;

(e) any payment of money in accordance with an order made under section 136 of the Employment Protection (Consolidation) Act 1978 by the Employment Appeal Tribunal;

(f) any sum, payment or benefit which, by virtue of any provision of or made under an Act of Parliament, cannot be assigned or charged.

SCHEDULE 5

COSTS AWARDED AGAINST A CLIENT

1. No costs attributable to the period during which a client was in receipt of ABWOR shall be recoverable from him until the court has determined the amount of his liability in accordance with section 12 of the Act:

Provided that where the ABWOR does not relate to or has been withdrawn so that it no longer relates to the whole of the proceedings the court shall nevertheless make a determination in respect of that part of the proceedings to which the approval of ABWOR relates.

2. The court may, if it thinks fit, refer to the clerk to the justices for investigation any question of fact relevant to the determination, requiring him to report his findings on that question to the court.

3. In determining the amount of the client's liability his dwelling-house, clothes, household furniture and the tools and implements of his trade shall be left out of account to the like extent as they are left out of account by the solicitor in determining the client's disposable capital.

4. Any person, not being himself a client, who is a party to proceedings to which the client is a party may, at any time before the judgment, lodge with the clerk to the justices an affidavit exhibiting thereto a statement setting out the rate of his own income and amount of his own capital and any other facts relevant to the determination of his means in accordance with section 12 of the Act and shall serve a copy thereof together with the exhibit upon the client's solicitor and such affidavit and exhibit shall be evidence of the facts stated therein.

5. The court may, if it thinks fit, order the client and any party who has filed an affidavit in accordance with paragraph (4) of this Schedule to attend for oral examination as to his means and as to any other facts relevant to the determination of the amount of the client's liability and may permit any party to give evidence and call witnesses thereon.

6. The court may direct—

(a) that payment under the order for costs shall be limited to such amount payable in instalments or otherwise as the court thinks reasonable having regard to all the circumstances; or

(b) where the court thinks it reasonable for payment under sub-paragraph (a) not to be made immediately, that payment under the order for costs be suspended either until such date as the court may determine or sine die.

7. The party in whose favour an order is made may within six years from the date thereof apply to the court for the order to be varied on the grounds that—

(a) material additional information as to the client's means, being information which could not have been obtained by that party with reasonable diligence at the time the order was made, is available; or

(b) there has been a change in the client's circumstances since the date of the order, and on any such application the order may be varied as the court thinks fit but save as aforesaid the determination of the court shall be final.

8. Where an order for costs is made against a client who is concerned in the proceedings solely in a representative, fiduciary or official capacity, he shall have the benefit of section 12(1) of the Act and his personal resources shall not (unless there is reason to the contrary) be taken into account for that purpose, but regard shall be had to the value of the property or estate, or the amount of the fund out of which he is entitled to be indemnified.

9. Where a client is a child, his means for the purpose of determining his liability for costs under section 12(1) of the Act shall be taken as including the means of any person whose disposable income and disposable capital has, by virtue of Schedule 2 been included in assessing the child's resources.

10. Where an order for costs is made against a next friend or guardian *ad litem* of a client who is a child or patient, he shall have the benefit of section 12(1) of the Act in like manner as it applies to a client, and the means of the next friend or guardian *ad litem* shall be taken as being the means of the child as defined in paragraph 9 or, as the case may be, of the patient.

SCHEDULE 6

1. Subject to paragraphs 2, 3 and 4, the amount to be allowed shall be assessed at the following prescribed rates:

Class of work	Rate	
Preparation	£44.00 per hour—	(£46.50 per hour for a fee-earner whose office is situated within legal aid area 1)
Advocacy	£55.25 per hour	
Attendance at court where counsel assigned	£30.00 per hour	
Travelling and waiting	£24.50 per hour	
Routine letters written and routine telephone calls	£3.40 per item—	(£3.55 per item for a fee-earner whose office is situated within legal aid area 1)

2. Subject to paragraph 4, where advice and assistance is provided by a franchisee, the following rates shall apply instead of those contained in paragraph 1:

Class of work	Rate	
Preparation	£45.50 per hour—	(£48.25 per hour for a fee-earner whose office is situated within legal aid area 1)
Advocacy	£57.25 per hour	
Attendance at court where counsel assigned	£31.00 per hour	
Travelling and waiting	£25.50 per hour	
Routine letters written and routine telephone calls	£3.55 per item—	(£3.70 per item for a fee-earner whose office is situated within legal aid area 1)

3. Subject to paragraph 4, where the claim is in respect of ABWOR to which Part III of the Act applies by virtue of regulation 9(a), (c) or (d) of the Scope Regulations, the following rates shall apply instead of those contained in paragraph 1:

Class of work	Rate	
Preparation	£52.75 per hour—	(£56.25 per hour for a fee-earner whose office is situated within legal aid area 1)
Advocacy	£64.00 per hour	
Attendance at court where counsel assigned	£30.00 per hour	
Travelling and waiting	£24.50 per hour	
Routine letters written and routine telephone calls	£3.75 per item	

4. Where the claim is in respect of ABWOR to which Part III of the Act applies by virtue of regulation 9(a), (c) or (d) of the Scope Regulations and the work is done by a franchisee, the following rates shall apply instead of those contained in paragraphs 1, 2 and 3:

Class of work	Rate	
Preparation	£54.50 per hour—	(£58.25 per hour for a fee-earner whose office is situated within legal aid area 1)
Advocacy	£66.25 per hour	
Attendance at court where counsel assigned	£31.00 per hour	
Travelling and waiting	£25.50 per hour	
Routine letters written and routine telephone calls	£3.90 per item	

5. In paragraphs 1 to 4, "legal aid area" means an area specified by the Board under regulation 4(1) of the Civil Legal Aid (General) Regulations 1989, and legal aid area 1 means the area so numbered by the Board.

Substituted by the Legal Advice and Assistance (Amendment) (No. 2) Regulations 1995 (S.I. 1995 No. 949) and amended by the Legal Advice and Assistance (Amendment) (No. 2) Regulations 1996 (S.I. 1996 No. 641) and the Legal Advice and Assistance (Amendment) Regulations 1997 (S.I. No. 751).

EXPLANATORY NOTE
(This note is not part of the Regulations)
These Regulations replace, with amendments, the Legal Advice and Assistance Regulations (No. 2) 1980 (S.I. 1980 No. 1898) (as amended) (except their provisions as to the scope of advice and assistance), which are replaced, with amendments, by the Legal Advice and Assistance (Scope) Regulations 1989 (S.I. 1989 No. 560).

The main changes reflect the transfer of responsibility for administration of legal aid from the Law Society to the Legal Aid Board established by the Legal Aid Act 1988.

Other important changes are—

(a) to enable the Board to make duty solicitor arrangements replacing those made by the Law Society under the Legal Aid (Duty Solicitor) Scheme 1988 (regulations 6(3) and 7);

(b) to require the provision of information to enable the solicitor to determine whether advice or assistance relating to the making of a will would fall within the scope of Part III of the Act (regulations 9(5), 10(3));

(c) to require the Board to be given an opportunity to make representations before any order for costs against the Board is made under section 13 of the Act (regulation 35);

(d) to set out in the Regulations the financial limits on advice and assistance which can be given without the approval of the Board (regulation 4);

(e) to set out in the Regulations all the provisions for eligibility for advice and assistance and contributions (regulations 11 to 13 and Schedules 2 and 3);

(f) to provide for the purposes of eligibility and contributions that the resources of a man and a woman living together as husband and wife are to be treated as if they were married (paragraph 2 of Schedule 2); and

(g) to provide (subject to the transitional provision in regulation 1(2)) for the assessment of costs by Area Directors, for reviews of such assessments by area committees, and for appeals from such reviews to a committee appointed by the Board (regulation 29).

Legal Aid (Mediation in Family Matters) Regulations 1997*

Came into force May 1, 1997

Citation, commencement and interpretation

1.—(1) These Regulations may be cited as the Legal Aid (Mediation in Family Matters) Regulations 1997 and shall come into force on May 1, 1997.

(2) In these Regulations, unless the context otherwise requires—

"Area Director" has the meaning assigned to it in the Civil Legal Aid (General) Regulations 1989;

"client" means a person seeking or receiving mediation;

"disability working allowance" means a disability working allowance under the Social Security Contributions and Benefits Act 1992;

"family credit" means family credit under the Social Security Contributions and Benefits Act 1992;

"income-based jobseeker's allowance" has the meaning given by section 1(4) of the Jobseekers Act 1995, but excludes any sum treated as payable by way of a jobseeker's allowance by virtue of section 26 of that Act;

"income support" means income support under the Social Security Contributions and Benefits Act 1992.

Applications

2.—(1) An application for mediation under Part IIIA of the Legal Aid Act 1988 shall be made in accordance with the provisions of these Regulations to the mediator from whom mediation is sought.

(2) The application under paragraph (1) shall be made by the client in person.

(3) Where a client makes an application under paragraph (1), he shall provide the mediator with the information necessary to enable the mediator to determine:

(a) his disposable capital;

(b) where appropriate, whether he is in receipt of income support, income-based jobseeker's allowance, family credit or disability working allowance, and

(c) where he is not in receipt of income support, income-based jobseeker's allowance, family credit or disability working allowance, his disposable income.

(4) The information required by this regulation shall be furnished on a form approved by the Board.

* S.I. 1997 No. 1078 as amended by the Legal Aid (Mediation in Family Matters) (Amendment) Regulations 1998 (S.I. 1998 No. 900).

Eligibility for mediation to which regulation 2 applies

3. A client is eligible for mediation under regulation 2 if his weekly disposable income does not exceed £172, and his disposable capital does not exceed £3,000.

Amended by the Legal Aid (Mediation in Family Matters) (Amendment) Regulations 1998 (S.I. 1998 No. 900).

Assessment of disposable income and disposal capital

4.—(1) Subject to paragraphs (4) and (5), a mediator to whom an application under regulation 2 is made shall assess the disposable income and disposable capital of the client and, where appropriate, of any person whose financial resources may be treated as those of the client.

(2) The assessment under paragraph (1) shall be made in accordance with Schedule 2 to the Legal Advice and Assistance Regulations 1989 with the modifications set out in paragraph (3).

(3) For the purposes of these Regulations, Schedule 2 to the Legal Advice and Assistance Regulations 1989 shall be modified as follows:

(a) any references to a solicitor shall be references to a mediator;

(b) "client" shall have the meaning assigned to it by regulation 1(2) of these Regulations;

(c) any references to advice and assistance shall be references to mediation;

(d) any references to a contribution shall be omitted;

(e) in paragraph 11 of Schedule 2 "for all purposes" shall be omitted.

(4) Where the mediator is satisfied that any of the persons whose disposable incomes are to be assessed under paragraph (1) is directly or indirectly in receipt of income support, income-based jobseeker's allowance, family credit or disability working allowance, he shall take that person's disposable income as not exceeding the sum for the time being specified in regulation 3.

(5) Where, in the case of an application to which regulation 2 applies, the mediator is satisfied that any of the persons whose disposable capital is to be assessed under paragraph (1) is directly or indirectly in receipt of income support or income-based jobseeker's allowance, he shall take that person's disposable capital as not exceeding the capital sum specified in regulation 3.

(6) The mediator shall not provide mediation to any person until the form referred to in regulation 2(4) has been signed by the client and until the mediator has assessed disposable income and disposable capital in accordance with paragraphs (1) and (2).

(7) Where the mediator is satisfied that any of the persons whose disposable income or disposable capital is to be assessed under paragraph (1) is an assisted person within the meaning of the Civil Legal Aid (General) Regulations 1989, he shall take that person's disposable income and disposable capital as not exceeding the amounts specified in regulation 3.

Paragraph (7) inserted by the Legal Aid (Mediation in Family Matters) (Amendment) Regulations 1998 (S.I. 1998 No. 900).

Disclosure of information

5. Notwithstanding the relationship between or rights of a mediator and client or any privilege arising out of such relationship, the mediator shall not be precluded from disclosing to any person authorised by the Board to request it, any information which relates to mediation provided to a client or former client of his where that client is or was a legally assisted person which is requested for the purpose of enabling the Board to discharge its functions under the Legal Aid Act 1988.

Civil Legal Aid (General) Regulations 1989*

Came into force April 1, 1989

ARRANGEMENT OF REGULATIONS

PART I

GENERAL

PART II

APPLICATIONS FOR CERTIFICATES

---

* S.I. 1989 No. 339 as amended by the Civil Legal Aid (General) (Amendment) Regulations 1991 (S.I. 1991 No. 524), the Civil Legal Aid (General) (Amendment) (No. 2) Regulations 1991 (S.I. 1991 No. 2036), the Civil Legal Aid (General) (Amendment) (No. 3) Regulations 1991 (S.I. 1991 No. 2784), the Civil Legal Aid (General) (Amendment) Regulations 1992 (S.I. 1992 No. 590), the Civil Legal Aid (General) (Amendment) (No. 2) Regulations 1992 (S.I. 1992 No. 721), the Civil Legal Aid (General) (Amendment) Regulations 1993 (S.I. 1993 No. 565) [for applications where the period of computation begins on or after April 12, 1993 and in respect of applications for payments on account under regulation 100 from April 1, 1993], the Civil Legal Aid (General) (Amendment) (No. 2) Regulations 1993 (S.I. 1993 No. 1756), the Civil Legal Aid (General) (Amendment) Regulations 1994 (S.I. 1994 No. 229) [in respect of certificates granted on or after February 25, 1994 unless the assisted person's solicitor represents any other assisted person in the same proceedings under a legal aid certificate granted before February 25, 1994], the Civil Legal Aid (General) (Amendment) (No. 2) Regulations 1994 (S.I. 1994 No. 1822), the Civil Legal Aid (General) (Amendment) Regulations 1996 (S.I. 1996 No. 649) which apply to proceedings in respect of which a certificate is granted on or after April 1, 1996, the Civil Legal Aid (General) (Amendment) (No. 2) Regulations 1996 (S.I. 1996 No. 1257), the Civil Legal Aid (General) (Amendment) Regulations 1997 (S.I. 1997 No. 416) and the Civil Legal Aid (General) (Amendment) (No. 2) Regulations 1997 (S.I. 1997 No. 1079).

SCHEDULES

1. Regulations revoked.

2. Matters to be included in an affidavit of costs and resources.

PART I

GENERAL

Citation, commencement, revocations and transitional provisions

1.—(1) These Regulations may be cited as the Civil Legal Aid (General) Regulations 1989 and shall come into force on April 1, 1989.

(2) The Regulations specified in Schedule 1 are hereby revoked.

(3) Where a review by an area committee under regulation 104, 105 or 106 relates to an assessment made before June 1, 1989, paragraphs (5) and (6) of regulation 105 shall not apply and the assisted person's solicitor or counsel may, within 21 days of the area committee's decision, appeal in writing to a committee appointed by the Board.

Scope

2.—(1) Subject to section 15(7)(a) of the Act and paragraph (2) below, these Regulations apply for the purposes of the provision of civil legal aid under Part IV of the Act.

(2) Where the Board has entered into a franchising contract, regulations relevant to the remuneration and payment of expenses of legal representatives and the manner in which any determination which may be required for those purposes may be made, reviewed or appealed shall apply except to the extent that the franchising contract makes different express provision.

Substituted by the Civil Legal Aid (General) (Amendment) (No. 2) Regulations 1994.

Interpretation

3.—(1) In these Regulations, unless the context otherwise requires—

"the Act" means the Legal Aid Act 1988;

"affidavit of costs and resources" means an affidavit which includes the matters specified in Schedule 2 and which is sworn by a person in support of his application for an order under section 18 of the Act;

"appropriate area committee" means the area committee in whose area an application for a certificate has been granted or refused and includes an area committee to whose area an application has been transferred under these Regulations;

"area committee" means an area committee appointed by the Board in accordance with regulation 4;

"Area Director" means an Area Director appointed by the Board in accordance with regulation 4 and includes any person duly authorised to act on his behalf;

"assessment officer" means a person authorised by the Secretary of State or the Board to assess the disposable income, disposable capital and contribution of the person concerned;

"assisted person" means a person in respect of whom a certificate issued under these Regulations is in force and, for the purposes of Part XI only, includes a person in respect of whom a certificate has been, but is no longer, in force;

"authorised summary proceedings" means proceedings in a magistrates' court for which legal aid is available by virtue of Part I of Schedule 2 to the Act;

"certificate" means a legal aid certificate issued in accordance with these Regulations (or any regulations revoked by these Regulations) and includes an amendment to a certificate issued under Part VII and, unless the context otherwise requires, an emergency certificate;

"contract" means a contract entered into by the Board with other persons or bodies pursuant to its powers under section 4 of the Act;

"contribution" means the contribution payable under section 16(1) of the Act in respect of the costs of representation;

"court" includes:

(a) in relation to proceedings tried or heard at first instance by a master or taxing master of the Supreme Court, a registrar of the Family Division of the High Court, a district registrar or the registrar of a county court, that master or registrar;

(b) in relation to proceedings on appeal to the Court of Appeal, the registrar of civil appeals;

"disposable capital" and "disposable income" mean the amounts of capital and income available for the making of a contribution after capital and income have been computed in accordance with the Civil Legal Aid (Assessment of Resources) Regulations 1989;

"EEC lawyer" has the same meaning as in the European Communities (Services of Lawyers) Order 1978;

"emergency certificate" means a certificate issued under Part III of these Regulations;

"family proceedings" has the meaning assigned by section 32 of the Matrimonial and Family Proceedings Act 1984;

"franchisee" means a person or body (other than the Board) acting under the terms of a franchising contract;

"fund" means the legal aid fund;

"legal aid" means representation under Part IV of the Act;

"legal aid area" has the meaning assigned by regulation 4(1);

"legal aid only costs" means those costs which would not be allowed as inter partes costs, but which are payable from the fund subject to determination under regulation 107A(2);

"legal executive" means a fellow of the Institute of Legal Executives;

"master" in relation to an application for an order under section 18 of the Act in respect of proceedings in or on appeal from the Chancery or Queen's Bench Division of the High Court, means a taxing master of the Supreme Court or a district registrar of the High Court; and in relation to such an application made in respect of proceedings in or on appeal from the Family Division of the High Court, means a registrar of the said Division or a district registrar of the High Court;

"patient" means a person who, by reason of mental disorder within the meaning of the Mental Health Act 1983, is incapable of managing and administering his property and affairs;

"recognised mediator" means a mediator who is recognised by the Board for the purposes of conducting a meeting described in section 15(3F) of the Act;

"relevant authority" means the Area Director in the case of an assessment and the taxing officer in the case of a taxation;

"special Children Act proceedings" means proceedings under the Children Act 1989 for which representation must be granted to the applicant regardless of sections 15(1) to (3) of the Act;

"standard basis" and "indemnity basis," in relation to the taxation of costs, have the meanings assigned by Order 62, rule 12 of the Rules of the Supreme Court 1965;

"substantive certificate" means a certificate issued to replace an emergency certificate which is still in force.

"taxing officer" has the same meanings in relation to proceedings governed by Order 38 of the County Court Rules 1981, Order 62 of the Rules of the Supreme Court 1965 and the Matrimonial Causes (Costs) Rules 1988 respectively, as it has in those Rules.

(2) Any reference in these Regulations to a regulation or Schedule by number means the regulation or Schedule so numbered in these Regulations.

(3) References in these Regulations to costs shall, unless the context otherwise requires, be construed as including references to fees, charges, disbursements, expenses and remuneration.

Amended by the Civil Legal Aid (General) (Amendment) Regulations 1993 (S.I. 1993 No. 565) in relation to applications where the period of computation begins on or after April 12, 1993, the Civil Legal Aid (General) (Amendment) Regulations 1994 (S.I. 1994 No. 229), the Civil Legal Aid (General) (Amendment) (No. 2) Regulations 1994 and the Civil Legal Aid (General) (Amendment) (No. 2) Regulations 1997 (S.I. 1997 No. 1079).

Exclusion from civil legal aid of prescribed bodies

3A. Representation under Part IV of the Act shall not be available to any body acting in a representative, fiduciary or official capacity for the purposes of proceedings under the Children Act 1989.

Area committees, Area Directors and legal aid areas

4.—(1) The Board shall, for the purposes of administering the Act, appoint—

(a) area committees; and

(b) Area Directors,

in respect of areas (in these Regulations referred to as "legal aid areas") to be specified by the Board.

(2) Area committees and Area Directors so appointed shall exercise func-

tions respectively delegated to them by the Board or conferred on them by these Regulations.

(3) Where and to the extent that a franchising contract permits the franchisee to exercise any of the functions of an Area Director, the functions may be exercised by the franchisee on the Area Director's behalf.

Amended by the Civil Legal Aid (General) (Amendment) (No. 2) Regulations 1994.

Powers exercisable by courts

5. Where the power to do any act or exercise any jurisdiction or discretion is conferred by any provision of these Regulations on a court, it may, unless it is exercisable only during the trial or hearing of the action, cause or matter, be exercised—

(a) in respect of proceedings in a county court or the Family Division of the High Court, by the registrar;

(b) in respect of proceedings in the Chancery or Queen's Bench Division of the High Court, by a judge, master or district registrar;

(c) in respect of proceedings in the Court of Appeal, by a single judge of that Court or by the registrar of civil appeals;

(d) in respect of proceedings in the House of Lords, by the Clerk of the Parliaments;

(e) by any person who, under any enactment or rules of court, is capable of exercising the jurisdiction of the court in relation to the proceedings in question.

Powers exercisable by Area Directors

6.—(1) Where an area committee is required or entitled to perform any function under these Regulations, that function may, subject to paragraph (2), be performed on behalf of that committee by the Area Director.

(2) Paragraph (1) shall not empower an Area Director to determine an appeal under regulation 39.

Computation of time

7.—(1) Where, under these Regulations, an act is required to be done within a specified period after or from a specified date, the period of time so fixed starts immediately after that date.

(2) The period within which an act is required or authorised to be done under these Regulations may, if the Area Director thinks fit, be extended and any such period may be extended although the application for extension is not made until after the expiration of the period.

Service of notices

8.—(1) Where by virtue of these Regulations any document is required to be served (whether the expression "serve" or the expression "send" or "send by post" or any other expression is used) the document may be served—

(a) if the person to be served is acting in person, by delivering it to him personally or by delivering it at, or sending it by post to, his address for service or, if he has no address for service:

(i) by delivering the document at his residence or by sending it by post to his last known residence, or

(ii) in the case of a proprietor of a business, by delivering the document at his place of business or by sending it by post to his last known place of business;

(b) if the person to be served is acting by a solicitor:

(i) by delivering the document at, or by sending it by post to, the solicitor's address for service, or

(ii) where the solicitor's address for service includes a numbered box at a document exchange, by leaving the document at that document exchange or at a document exchange which transmits documents daily to that document exchange.

(2) Any document which is left at a document exchange in accordance with paragraph (1)(b)(ii), shall, unless the contrary is proved, be deemed to have been served on the second day after the day on which it is left.

Availability of documents to the court

9. Any document sent to a court office or registry or filed or exhibited under the provisions of these Regulations may, on request, be made available for the use of the court at any stage of the proceedings.

PART II

APPLICATIONS FOR CERTIFICATES

Applications to be made to Area Directors

10. Any person who wishes to be granted legal aid for the purposes of proceedings may apply for a certificate—

(a) if resident in the United Kingdom, to any Area Director; or

(b) if resident elsewhere, to the Area Director of one of the legal aid areas nominated by the Board for this purpose.

Form and lodgment of application

11. Every application—

(a) shall be made in writing on a form approved by the Board or in such other written form as the Area Director may accept; and

(b) shall be lodged with the Area Director.

Contents of application

12.—(1) Subject to regulation 12A, every application shall—

(a) state the name of the solicitor selected by the applicant to act for him;

(b) contain such information and be accompanied by such supporting documents (including any welfare report) as may be necessary to enable:

(i) the Area Director to determine the nature of the proceedings in respect of which legal aid is sought and whether it is reasonable that representation should be granted; and

(ii) the assessment officer to assess the disposable income, disposable capital and contribution of the applicant.

(2) *[Omitted by the Civil Legal Aid (General) (Amendment) (No. 2) Regulations 1991.]*

(3) An applicant shall, if required to do so for the purpose of providing additional material, supply such further information or documents as may be required or attend for an interview.

Amended by the Civil Legal Aid (General) (Amendment) Regulations 1993 (S.I. 1993 No. 565).

Certificates relating to special Children Act proceedings

12A.—(1) Where a person is entitled to legal aid for special Children Act proceedings, his solicitor shall lodge with the Area Director an application on a form approved by the Board at the first available opportunity and in any event within three working days of receiving instructions to act for that person in such proceedings.

(2) The application shall—

> (a) state the name of the solicitor selected by the applicant to act for him; and

> (b) contain a statement signed by the solicitor to the effect that legal aid is sought in respect of proceedings to which section 15(1) to (3) of the Act do not apply.

(3) Work done by a solicitor in relation to special Children Act proceedings prior to the issue of a certificate shall be deemed to be work done while such a certificate is in force provided that the application was lodged at the first available opportunity and in any event within the time specified in paragraph (1).

Applications by persons resident outside United Kingdom

13.—(1) Subject to paragraph (2), where the applicant resides outside the United Kingdom and cannot be present in England or Wales while his application is considered, his application shall be—

> (a) written in English or in French; and

> (b) except where the applicant is a member of Her Majesty's armed forces, sworn—

>> (i) if the applicant resides within the Commonwealth or the Republic of Ireland, before any justice of the peace or magistrate or any person for the time being authorised by law in the place where he resides to administer an oath for any judicial or other legal purpose, or

>> (ii) if the applicant resides elsewhere, before a British consular officer or any other person for the time being authorised to exercise the functions of such an officer or having authority to administer an oath in that place; and

> (c) accompanied by a statement in writing, signed by some responsible person who has knowledge of the facts, certifying that part of the application which relates to the applicant's disposable income and disposable capital.

(2) The requirements of paragraph (1) may be waived by the Area Director where compliance with them would cause serious difficulty, inconvenience

or delay and the application otherwise satisfies the requirements of regulations 11 and 12.

Child Abduction and Custody Act 1985

14.—(1) A person whose application under the Hague Convention or the European Convention has been submitted to the Central Authority in England and Wales pursuant to section 3(2) or section 14(2) of the Child Abduction and Custody Act 1985 and on whose behalf a solicitor in England and Wales has been instructed in connection with the application—

(a) shall be eligible to receive legal aid whether or not his financial resources are such as to make him eligible to receive it under regulations made under the Legal Aid Act 1988;

(b) shall not be refused legal aid by virtue of subsections (2) and (3) of section 15 of the said Act of 1988; and

(c) shall not be required to pay a contribution to the legal aid fund;

and these Regulations (with the exception of those provisions relating to assessment of disposable income and capital, eligibility on their merits and payment of contribution) shall apply accordingly.

(2) In this regulation the "Hague Convention" means the convention defined in section 1(1) of the Child Abduction and Custody Act 1985 and the "European Convention" means the convention defined in section 12(1) of that Act.

Registration of certain foreign orders and judgments

15.—(1) This regulation applies to any person who—

(a) appeals to a magistrates' court against the registration of or the refusal to register a maintenance order made in a Hague Convention country pursuant to the Maintenance Orders (Reciprocal Enforcement) Act 1972; or

(b) applies for the registration of a judgment under section 4 of the Civil Jurisdiction and Judgments Act 1982.

(2) Subject to paragraph (3), a person to whom this regulation applies—

(a) shall be eligible to receive legal aid whether or not his financial resources are such as to make him eligible to receive it under regulations made under the Legal Aid Act 1988;

(b) shall not be refused legal aid by virtue of subsections (2) and (3) of section 15 of the said Act of 1988;

(c) shall not be required to pay a contribution to the legal aid fund,

and these Regulations (with the exception of those provisions relating to assessment of disposable income and capital, eligibility on the merits and payment of contribution) shall apply accordingly.

(3) A person shall not be given legal aid under this regulation in respect of any appeal or application as is mentioned in paragraph (1) unless he benefited from complete or partial legal aid or exemption from costs or expenses in the country in which the maintenance order was made or the judgment was given.

(4) In this regulation, "Hague Convention country" has the same meaning

as in the Reciprocal Enforcement of Maintenance Orders (Hague Convention Countries) Order 1979 and "the Maintenance Orders (Reciprocal Enforcement) Act 1972" means that Act as applied with such exceptions, adaptations and modifications as are specified in the said 1979 Order.

Application on behalf of minors and patients

16.—(1) Subject to paragraph (5), an application for legal aid for a minor or patient shall be made on his behalf by a person of full age and capacity and:

   (a) where the application relates to proceedings which are required by rules of court to be brought or defended by a next friend or guardian *ad litem*, the person making the application shall be the next friend or guardian *ad litem*; or,

   (b) where the application relates to proceedings which have not actually begun, the person who, subject to any order of the court, intends to act in either of those capacities when the proceedings begin, shall make the application; or,

   (c) where the application is made by a minor who is entitled to begin, prosecute or defend any proceedings without a next friend or guardian *ad litem*, the person making the application shall be that minor's solicitor.

(2) *[Deleted by the Civil Legal Aid (General) (Amendment) Regulations 1992 (S.I. 1992 No. 590).]*

(3) Any certificate issued to a minor or patient shall be in his name, stating the name of the person who has applied for it on his behalf.

(4) In any matter relating to the issue, amendment, revocation or discharge of a certificate issued to a minor or patient, and in any other matter which may arise between an assisted person who is a minor or patient and the Area Director, the person who is named in the certificate as the next friend or guardian *ad litem* or (where there is no next friend or guardian *ad litem*) solicitor of the minor or patient shall be treated for all purposes (including the receipt of notices) as the agent of the minor or patient.

(5) An Area Director may, where the circumstances appear to make it desirable, waive all or any of the requirements of the preceding paragraphs of this regulation.

Power to transfer application to another area office

17. If it appears to an Area Director that an application could, without prejudice to the applicant, be more conveniently or appropriately dealt with in another area office, the papers relating to the application shall be transferred to that other office.

Reference to the assessment officer for assessment of resources

18.—(1) Subject to section 15(3B) to (3D) of the Act and except where he has previously refused the application, the Area Director shall refer to the assessment officer so much of it as is relevant to the assessment of the applicant's disposable income and disposable capital; and (subject to paragraph (2) and regulation 21) no application shall be approved until the assessment officer has assessed the applicant's disposable income, disposable capital and contribution in accordance with the Civil Legal Aid (Assessment of Resources) Regulations 1989.

(2) Where an Area Director approves an application relating to proceedings:

(a) in the House of Lords or on appeal from a magistrates' court in any action, cause or matter in which the applicant was an assisted person in the court below; or

(b) by way of a new trial ordered by a court in any action, cause or matter in which the applicant was an assisted person;

he shall not require the assessment officer to re-assess the assisted person's disposable income and disposable capital.

Amended by the Civil Legal Aid (General) (Amendment) Regulations 1993 (S.I. 1993 No. 565).

PART III

EMERGENCY CERTIFICATES

Application for emergency certificate

19.—(1) Any person who desires legal aid as a matter of urgency may apply to any Area Director for an emergency certificate on a form approved by the Board or in such other manner as the Area Director may accept as sufficient in the circumstances of the case.

(2) Subject to paragraph (3), an application for an emergency certificate shall contain such information and be accompanied by such documents as may be necessary to enable the Area Director to determine the nature of the proceedings for which legal aid is sought and the circumstances in which it is required and whether—

(a) the applicant is likely to fulfil the conditions under which legal aid may be granted under the Act and these Regulations; and

(b) it is in the interests of justice that the applicant should, as a matter of urgency, be granted legal aid;

and the applicant shall furnish such additional information and documents (if any) as may be sufficient to constitute an application for a certificate under Part II of these Regulations.

(3) If it appears to the Area Director that the applicant cannot at the time of making the application reasonably furnish the information required under paragraph (2), or any part of it, that Area Director shall nevertheless have the power to issue an emergency certificate subject to such conditions as to the furnishing of additional information as he thinks fit.

Refusal of emergency certificate

20. An application for an emergency certificate may be refused—

(a) on one of the grounds on which a substantive certificate may be refused under regulation 34; or

(b) on the ground that the applicant is unlikely to fulfil the conditions under which legal aid may be granted; or

(c) on the ground that it is not in the interests of justice that legal aid be granted as a matter of urgency.

Issue and effect of emergency certificate

21.—(1) An Area Director shall have power to approve an application made under regulation 19 and to issue an emergency certificate without reference to the assessment officer.

(2) [*Omitted.*]

(3) Where an Area Director issues an emergency certificate, he shall send the emergency certificate (together with a copy) to the solicitor selected by the applicant, and a copy of the certificate to the applicant.

(4) An emergency certificate shall have the same effect in all respects as a substantive certificate and any person holding an emergency certificate shall, while it is in force, be deemed for the purposes of the proceedings to which the emergency certificate relates to be an assisted person.

Duration of emergency certificate

22. An emergency certificate shall remain in force until—

(a) it is discharged or revoked in accordance with Part X of these Regulations; or

(b) it is merged in a substantive certificate under regulation 23; or

(c) the expiry of any period (including any extension of that period granted under regulation 24(1)) allowed for the duration of the emergency certificate.

Merger in substantive certificate

23.—(1) Where a substantive certificate is issued, the emergency certificate shall merge in the substantive certificate and the substantive certificate shall take effect from the date upon which the emergency certificate was issued in respect of the proceedings specified in the emergency certificate.

(2) Where an emergency certificate is merged in a substantive certificate, the substantive certificate shall state—

(a) the date of issue of the emergency certificate; and

(b) that the emergency certificate has been continuously in force from that date until the date of the substantive certificate.

Extension and expiry of emergency certificate

24.—(1) The Area Director (whose decision shall be final) may extend the period allowed for the duration of an emergency certificate where—

(a) the applicant is offered a substantive certificate in respect of the proceedings to which the emergency certificate relates and either fails to signify his acceptance or appeals against the terms of the offer; or

(b) the application for a substantive certificate in respect of the proceedings to which the emergency certificate relates has been refused and either notice of appeal has been given to the appropriate area committee within the time limits laid down by regulation 36 or the time limit for doing so has not expired; or

(c) there are exceptional circumstances.

(2) Where an emergency certificate is extended under paragraph (1)(a) or (b), no further work may be done or steps taken under the certificate.

Notification of extension of emergency certificate

25.—(1) Where an emergency certificate is extended, the Area Director shall:

(a) forthwith issue a notice to that effect;

(b) send the notice (together with a copy) to the solicitor acting for the person to whom the emergency certificate was issued; and

(c) send a copy of the notice to the person to whom the emergency certificate was issued.

(2) It shall be the duty of the solicitor to notify forthwith any counsel whom he may have instructed that the certificate has been extended.

(3) A solicitor who receives notice that an emergency certificate has been extended under regulation 24 shall, if proceedings have begun or otherwise upon their commencement—

(a) send a copy of the notice by post to the appropriate court office or registry; and

(b) serve notice of the fact upon any other persons who are parties to the proceedings;

and, if any other person becomes a party to the proceedings, serve a similar notice upon that person.

PART IV

DETERMINATION OF APPLICATIONS

Power to notify other parties of application

26.—(1) On receiving an application for a certificate, the Area Director may, if he thinks fit—

(a) notify any party to the proceedings in respect of which the application is made; and

(b) ask that party whether he is willing to delay taking any further step in, or in relation to, the proceedings until the application has been determined.

(2) When the Area Director has determined the application, he shall so inform any party notified under this regulation.

Meeting with a mediator in family matters

26A. Subsection (3F) of section 15 of the Act shall not apply—

(a) where there is no recognised mediator available to the applicant or any other party to the proceedings to hold a meeting under that subsection; or

(b) where—

(i) the applicant is likely to fulfil the conditions under which legal aid may be granted under the Act and these Regulations;

(ii) it is in the interests of justice that the applicant should, as a matter of urgency, be granted legal aid; and

(iii) an application for an emergency certificate under regulation 19 has been made.

Regulation 26A inserted by the Civil Legal Aid (General) (Amendment) (No. 2) Regulations 1997 (S.I. 1997 No. 1079).

Financial eligibility

27.—(1) Where the assessment officer assesses that an applicant has disposable income of an amount which makes him ineligible for legal aid, the Area Director shall refuse the application.

(2) Where the assessment officer assesses that an applicant, having disposable income of an amount which makes him eligible for legal aid, has disposable capital of an amount which renders him liable to be refused legal aid, the Area Director shall refuse the application if it appears to him that the probable costs of the applicant in the proceedings in respect of which the application was made would not exceed the contribution payable by the applicant.

Eligibility on the merits

28.—(1) Without prejudice to the generality of sections 15(2) to (3C) and (3E) of the Act and subject to paragraph (2), an application for a certificate shall only be approved after the Area Director has considered all the questions of fact or law arising in the action, cause or matter to which the application relates and the circumstances in which the application was made.

(2) Where the application relates to proceedings to which section 15(3B), (3C) or (3E) of the Act apply, provided that the Area Director is satisfied that it does so relate and subject to regulation 27 (where applicable) he shall grant the application and Parts IV and V of these Regulations shall apply with any necessary modifications.

Refusal where advantage trivial or on account of nature of proceedings

29. Without prejudice to regulations 28 and 32, an application may be refused where it appears to the Area Director that—

(a) only a trivial advantage would be gained by the applicant from the proceedings to which the application relates; or

(b) on account of the nature of the proceedings a solicitor would not ordinarily be employed.

Refusal where other rights or facilities available

30.—(1) Without prejudice to regulation 28, an application may be refused where it appears to the Area Director that—

(a) the applicant has available to him rights or facilities which make it unnecessary for him to obtain legal aid; or

(b) the applicant has a reasonable expectation of obtaining financial or other help from a body of which he is a member,

and that he has failed to take all reasonable steps to enforce or obtain such rights, facilities or help (including permitting the Area Director to take those steps on his behalf).

(2) Where it appears that the applicant has a right to be indemnified against expenses incurred in connection with any proceedings, it shall not, for the purposes of paragraph (1), be deemed to be a failure to take reasonable steps if he has not taken proceedings to enforce that right, whether for a declaration as to that right or otherwise.

Determination of contribution

31.—(1) The Area Director shall, when determining an application, also determine the sums for the time being payable on account of the applicant's contribution.

Amended by the Civil Legal Aid (General) (Amendment) Regulations 1993 (S.I. 1993 No. 565).

Proceedings in which others have an interest

32.—(1) When determining an application, the Area Director shall consider whether it is reasonable and proper for persons concerned jointly with or having the same interest as the applicant to defray so much of the costs as would be payable from the fund in respect of the proceedings if a certificate were issued.

(2) In determining an application made by, or on behalf of, a person in connection with an action, cause or matter in which—

(a) numerous persons have the same interest; and

(b) in accordance with rules of court, one or more persons may sue or be sued, or may be authorised by a court to defend any such action, cause or matter on behalf of or for the benefit of all persons so interested,

the Area Director shall consider whether the rights of the applicant would be substantially prejudiced by the refusal of his application.

(3) Where an application has been approved and the Area Director considers that it is reasonable that persons concerned jointly with or having the same interest as the applicant should contribute to the cost of the proceedings, he shall add the amount which would be payable by such persons to the sums (if any) payable by the applicant under regulation 31 and shall so notify him under regulation 43(2).

(4) The Area Director may subsequently redetermine the amount of any additional sums payable under paragraph (3) where he is satisfied that the applicant has, without success, taken all reasonable steps (including permitting the Area Director to take those steps on his behalf) to obtain such payment.

Application in representative, fiduciary or official capacity

33. Where an application is made in a representative, fiduciary or official capacity, the Area Director—

(a) shall take into account the value of any property or estate or the amount of any fund out of which the applicant is entitled to be indemnified and the financial resources of any persons (including the applicant if appropriate) who might benefit from the proceedings; and

(b) may (without prejudice to regulation 28) either—

(i) approve the application, subject to the payment from the property or resources specified in sub-paragraph (a) of any sums which he may in his discretion determine, or

(ii) refuse the application, if he concludes that to do so would not cause hardship.

Refusal where assignment made to obtain legal aid

33A. Without prejudice to regulation 28, an application may be refused where it appears to the Area Director that

(a) any cause of action in respect of which the application was made has been transferred to the applicant by assignment or otherwise from a body of persons corporate, or unincorporate, or by another person who would not be entitled to receive legal aid; and

(b) the assignment or transfer was entered into with a view to allowing the action to be commenced or continued with the benefit of a legal aid certificate.

Inserted by the Civil Legal Aid (General) (Amendment) (No. 2) Regulations 1996 (S.I. 1996 No. 1257).

PART V

REFUSAL OF APPLICATIONS

Notification of refusal

34.—(1) Where an application for a certificate is refused on one or more of the following grounds, namely, that—

(a) the assessment officer has assessed that the applicant has disposable income which makes him ineligible for legal aid; or

(b) the assessment officer has assessed that the applicant, having disposable income of an amount which makes him eligible for legal aid, has disposable capital of an amount which renders him liable to be refused legal aid and it appears to the Area Director that, without legal aid, the probable costs to the applicant of the proceedings in respect of which the application was made would not exceed the sums payable by the applicant on account of his contribution; or

(c) the proceedings to which the application relates are not proceedings for which legal aid may be given; or

(d) the applicant has not shown that he has reasonable grounds for taking, defending or being a party to the proceedings; or

(e) it appears unreasonable that the applicant should receive legal aid in the particular circumstances of the case,

the Area Director shall notify the applicant of the grounds on which the application has been refused and inform him of the circumstances in which he may appeal to the appropriate area committee for the decision to be reviewed.

(2) Where an application is refused on either of the grounds specified in sub-paragraphs (d) and (e) of paragraph (1), the notification given under that paragraph shall include a brief statement of the reasons why that ground applies to the applicant's case.

Right of appeal against refusal

35.—(1) Where an Area Director refuses an application for a certificate or an applicant is dissatisfied with the terms upon which the Area Director would be prepared to issue it, the applicant may, subject to paragraph (2), appeal to the appropriate area committee.

(2) No appeal shall lie to an area committee from—

(a) an assessment of the assessment officer, or

(b) any decision by an Area Director as to the sums payable on account of the applicant's contribution or the method by which they shall be paid except a decision as to sums payable under regulation 32(3) or 33, or

(c) the refusal of an application for an emergency certificate.

Amended by the Civil Legal Aid (General) (Amendment) (No. 2) Regulations 1994.

Time and form of appeal
36. Every appeal shall be brought by giving to the appropriate Area Committee, within 14 days of the date of notice of refusal of a certificate or of the terms upon which a certificate would be issued (or such longer period as the appropriate area committee may allow), notice of appeal in writing either on a form approved by the Board or in such other written form as the Area Director may accept as sufficient in the circumstances of the case.

Nature of appeal
37. Every appeal shall be by way of reconsideration of the application.

Representation at appeal or other final application
38.—(1) Upon an appeal the appellant may—

(a) furnish further statements, whether oral or in writing, in support of his application; and

(b) conduct the appeal himself, with or without the assistance of any person whom he may appoint for the purpose, or be represented by counsel or a solicitor or legal executive.

(2) With any necessary modifications, paragraph (1)(a) shall apply to any appeal to an area committee and, subject to regulation 58(3), paragraph (1)(b) shall apply to any appeal to an area committee on which the committee finally determines the applicant's right to receive legal aid.

Determination of appeal
39.—(1) The area committee shall determine the appeal in such manner as seems to it to be just and, without prejudice to the generality of the foregoing, may—

(a) dismiss the appeal; or

(b) direct the Area Director to offer a certificate subject to such terms and conditions as the area committee thinks fit;

(c) direct the Area Director to settle terms and conditions on which a certificate may be offered; or

(d) refer the matter, or any part of it, back to the Area Director for his determination or report.

(2) Any decision of an area committee with regard to an appeal shall be final, and it shall give notice of its decision, and the reasons for it, to the appellant and to any solicitor acting for him on a form approved by the Board.

Repeated refusal of certificates
40.—(1) Where a person has applied for and been refused a certificate on three separate occasions and it appears to the Area Director to whom such person applies that his conduct may amount to an abuse of the facilities pro-

vided by the Act, then the Area Director may report the matter to the appropriate area committee.

(2) If a report under paragraph (1) has been made, the area committee may:

(a) enquire whether any other area office has received an application from the person named in the report;

(b) call for a report as to the circumstances of any other such application; and

(c) if it considers that the person named in the report has abused the facilities provided by the Act, report thereon to the Board, making such recommendations as seem to the area committee to be just.

Power to make prohibitory directions

41.—(1) The Board, on receipt of a report made under regulation 40(2)(c), shall give the person named in it an opportunity of making (either by himself or by some other person acting on his behalf) representations in writing on the matter, and shall make such other enquiries as seem to be necessary; and, if they are satisfied that his conduct has amounted to an abuse of the facilities provided by the Act, may make a direction (in this regulation referred to as a "prohibitory direction") that no consideration shall, for a period not exceeding five years, be given by any Area Director or area committee either—

(a) to any future or pending application by that person for a certificate with regard to any particular matter; or

(b) in exceptional circumstances, to any future or pending application by him whatsoever.

(2) The Board may in its discretion—

(a) include within the terms of any prohibitory direction any receiver, next friend or guardian *ad litem* who applies for a certificate on behalf of the person referred to in the prohibitory direction; and

(b) at any time vary or revoke any prohibitory direction in whole or in part.

(3) Where the Board makes a prohibitory direction, it shall inform the Lord Chancellor and shall, if so requested, give him its reasons for making it.

Amended by the Civil Legal Aid (General) (Amendment) (No. 2) Regulations 1994.

PART VI

ISSUE AND EFFECT OF CERTIFICATES

Issue of certificate where no contribution may be payable

42. Where an application is approved relating to special Children Act proceedings or proceedings where no contribution is (for the time being) payable, the Area Director shall—

(a) issue a certificate;

(b) send the certificate (together with a copy) to the solicitor selected by the applicant; and

(c) send a copy of the certificate to the applicant together with a notice drawing the applicant's attention to the provisions of sections 16(6) and 17(1) of the Act.

Offer of certificate where contribution payable

43.—(1) Where an application is approved for any proceedings where a contribution will be payable, the Area Director shall require—

(a) any sums payable out of capital to be paid forthwith if the sum is readily available or, if it is not, by such time as seems to him reasonable in all the circumstances; and

(b) the first contribution payable out of income to be paid forthwith, with further contributions payable at monthly intervals thereafter.

(2) The Area Director shall notify the applicant—

(a) of the sums payable under regulation 31; and

(b) of the terms upon which a certificate will be issued to him;

and draw to his attention the provisions of sections 16(1) and (6) and 17(1) of the Act.

Amended by the Civil Legal Aid (General) (Amendment) Regulations 1993 (S.I. 1993 No. 565).

Undertaking to account for sums received from third parties

44. Where the applicant—

(a) appears to be a member of an organisation or body which might reasonably be expected to give him financial assistance in meeting the cost of the proceedings for which the applicant has applied for legal aid; and

(b) does not appear to have any right to be indemnified by that organisation or body against expenses incurred in connection with those proceedings,

the Area Director shall require the applicant, as a term upon which the certificate will be issued, to sign an undertaking to pay to the Board (in addition to any sums payable under regulations 31 and 32) any sum which he receives from that organisation or body on account of the cost of those proceedings.

Acceptance and issue of certificate where contribution payable

45.—(1) An applicant who desires that a certificate should be issued to him on the terms notified to him by an Area Director shall, within 28 days of being so notified—

(a) signify his acceptance of those terms on a form approved by the Board and lodge it with the Area Director; and

(b) if those terms require the payment of any sums of money, give an undertaking, on a form approved by the Board, to pay those sums by the method stated in the terms and, if any sum is required to be paid before the certificate is issued, make that payment accordingly.

(2) When an applicant has complied with so many of the requirements of paragraph (1) as are relevant to his case, the Area Director shall issue a certificate and send it to the solicitor selected by the applicant.

(3) *[Omitted by the Civil Legal Aid (General) (Amendment) (No. 2) Regulations 1991.]*

Scope of certificates

46.—(1) A certificate may be issued in respect of the whole or part of proceedings and may be extended to cover appellate proceedings other than those mentioned in paragraph (2).

(2) Except in the case of special Children Act proceedings a certificate shall not be extended to cover proceedings in the House of Lords or on appeal from a magistrates' court.

(3) A certificate shall not relate to more than one action, cause or matter except in the case of—

   (a) family proceedings; or

  (b)–(c) *[Omitted by the Civil Legal Aid (General) (Amendment) (No. 2) Regulations 1991]*;

   (d) an application for a grant of representation which is necessary to enable the action, which is the subject matter of the certificate, to be brought;

   (e) an application under section 33 of the Supreme Court Act 1981 or section 52 of the County Courts Act 1984 and subsequent court proceedings; or

   (f) proceedings which, under the Act, may be taken to enforce or give effect to any order or agreement made in the proceedings to which the certificate relates; and, for the purposes of this sub-paragraph, proceedings to enforce or give effect to an agreement or order shall include proceedings in bankruptcy or to wind-up a company.

Certificates to specify parties to proceedings

47. A certificate other than one relating to family proceedings shall specify the parties to the proceedings in respect of which it is issued.

Power to restrict costs allowable to distant solicitor

48.—(1) Where the solicitor selected by the applicant to whom a certificate is issued carries on his practice at a place which is so far away from where his services will be required in acting under the certificate that his selection will result in significantly greater expense to the fund than would have been incurred if the applicant had selected another solicitor, the certificate may provide that the solicitor shall not be entitled to payment in respect of any additional costs or disbursements incurred by reason of the fact that he does not carry on his practice at or near the place where his services are required in acting under the certificate.

(2) Where a certificate includes a provision under paragraph (1), payment of such additional costs or disbursements shall not be allowed on determination of the costs.

Effect of certificates

49. Any document purporting to be a certificate issued in accordance with these Regulations shall, until the contrary is proved, be deemed to be a valid certificate issued to the person named in it and for the purposes there set out and shall be received in evidence without further proof.

Notification of issue of certificates

50.—(1) Whenever an assisted person becomes a party to proceedings, or a party to proceedings becomes an assisted person, his solicitor shall forthwith—

(a) serve all other parties to the proceedings with notice of the issue of a certificate in a form approved by the Board; and

(b) if at any time thereafter any other person becomes a party to the proceedings, forthwith serve a similar notice on that party.

(2) Copies of the notices referred to in paragraph (1) shall form part of the papers for the use of the court in the proceedings.

(3) Where an assisted person's solicitor—

(a) commences any proceedings for the assisted person in a county court; or

(b) commences proceedings in accordance with Order 112, rule 3 or 4 of the Rules of the Supreme Court 1965 or rule 101 or 103 of the Matrimonial Causes Rules 1977;

and at the same time files a copy of the notice to be served in accordance with paragraph (1), a copy of that notice shall be annexed to the originating process for service.

(4) A solicitor who receives a certificate from an Area Director shall, if proceedings have begun, or otherwise upon their commencement, send a copy of it by post to the appropriate court office or registry.

(5) *[Omitted by the Civil Legal Aid (General) (Amendment) (No. 2) Regulations 1991.]*

Amended by the Civil Legal Aid (General) (Amendment) (No. 2) Regulations 1994.

Part VII

Amendment of Certificate and Adjustment of Contribution

Power to amend certificates

51. The Area Director may amend a certificate where in his opinion—

(a) there is some mistake in the certificate; or

(b) it has become desirable for the certificate to extend to

(i) proceedings; or

(ii) other steps; or

(iii) subject to regulation 46(3), other proceedings; or

(iv) proceedings which under the Act may be taken to enforce or give effect to any order or agreement made in the proceedings in respect of which the certificate was issued; or

(v) the bringing of an interlocutory appeal; or

(vi) proceedings in the Court of Justice of the European Communities on a reference to that Court for a preliminary ruling; or

(vii) representation by an EEC lawyer; or

(c) it has become desirable to add or substitute parties to the proceedings in respect of which the certificate was issued; or

(d) it has become desirable for the certificate to extend to any steps having the same effect as a cross-action or as a reply thereto, or a cross-appeal; or

(e) it has become desirable for the certificate not to extend to certain of the proceedings in respect of which it was issued; or

(f) a change of solicitor should be authorised.

Power to alter contribution and amend certificate

52.—(1) Without prejudice to the provisions of the Civil Legal Aid (Assessment of Resources) Regulations 1989, where the assisted person's disposable income and disposable capital have been assessed, the Area Director may, if he considers it to be desirable, request the assessment officer to re-assess the assisted person's financial resources and contribution.

(2) Where at any time during which a certificate is in force the Area Director is of opinion that the costs incurred or likely to be incurred under the certificate will not be more than the contribution which the assisted person has already paid he may waive (and, where necessary, subsequently revive) the requirement for further payments on account of the assisted person's contribution.

(3) Without prejudice to regulation 51, the Area Director shall amend the certificate from such date as he considers appropriate—

(a) where he re-determines the amount payable on account of the assisted person's contribution whether as a result of a re-assessment pursuant to paragraph (1) or otherwise; or

(b) where he waives or revives (following a period of waiver) the requirement for further payments on account of the assisted person's contribution under paragraph (2).

Amended by the Civil Legal Aid (General) (Amendment) Regulations 1993 (S.I. 1993 No. 565).

Making and determination of applications for amendment

53. Parts II and V of these Regulations shall apply, with any necessary modifications, to applications for the amendment of certificates as they apply to applications for certificates.

Procedure on issue of amendment

54.—(1) Where an Area Director amends a certificate, he shall send two copies of the amendment to the assisted person's solicitor and one copy to the assisted person.

(2) A solicitor who receives an amendment sent to him under paragraph (1) shall forthwith—

(a) if proceedings have begun or otherwise upon their commencement, send a copy of the amendment by post to the appropriate court office or registry; and

(b) except in the case of an amendment made under regulation 52, serve notice of the fact of the amendment in a form approved by the Board upon all other parties to the proceedings, and, if any other person becomes a party to the proceedings, serve similar notice upon that person.

(3) The copy of the amendment sent to the appropriate court office or registry shall form part of the papers for the court in the proceedings.

(4) Paragraphs (2) and (3) shall not apply to authorised summary proceedings, and, where an assisted person is a party to such proceedings, his solicitor

shall, before or at the first hearing that takes place after the amendment has been issued, file the amendment with the clerk to the justices.

Amended by the Civil Legal Aid (General) (Amendment) (No. 2) Regulations 1994.

Right to show cause on application to remove limitation

55. An Area Director shall not refuse an application to amend a certificate (other than an emergency certificate) by removing a limitation imposed upon it until—

(a) notice has been served on the assisted person that the application may be refused and his certificate discharged and that he may show cause why the application should be granted; and

(b) the assisted person has been given an opportunity to show cause why his application should be granted.

Procedure on refusal of amendment

56. Where an Area Director refuses an application for the amendment of a certificate, he shall notify the assisted person's solicitor in writing, stating his reasons for so doing.

Right of appeal against refusal of amendment

57.—(1) Where an Area Director refuses an application for the amendment of a certificate, the assisted person may appeal to the appropriate area committee.

(2) An appeal shall be brought by giving notice on a form approved by the Board within 14 days of the Area Director's decision to refuse the application.

Determination of appeal against refusal of amendment

58.—(1) Subject to paragraph (3), the area committee shall, on an appeal under regulation 57, reconsider the application and determine the appeal in such manner as seems to it to be just and, without prejudice to the generality of the foregoing, may—

(a) dismiss the appeal; or

(b) direct the Area Director to amend the certificate in such manner as the area committee thinks fit.

(2) Any decision of an area committee with regard to an appeal shall be final, and it shall give notice of its decision, and the reasons for it, to the assisted person and to his solicitor in a form approved by the Board.

(3) Nothing in this regulation or regulation 53 shall require the area committee to allow the assisted person to conduct an appeal under this regulation himself or to be represented on any such appeal if the area committee considers that such steps are unnecessary.

PART VIII

AUTHORITY TO INCUR COSTS

Instructing counsel

59.—(1) Where it appears to an assisted person's solicitor that the proper conduct of the proceedings so requires, he may instruct counsel; but, unless authority has been given in the certificate or by the Area Director—

(a) counsel shall not be instructed in authorised summary proceedings; and

   (b) a Queen's Counsel or more than one counsel shall not be instructed.

(2) Any instructions delivered to counsel under paragraph (1) shall:

   (a) include a copy of the certificate (and any amendments to it) and any authority to incur costs under this Part of these Regulations;

   (b) be endorsed with the legal aid reference number; and

   (c) in the case of authorised summary proceedings, show the authority for counsel to be instructed;

but no fees shall be marked on any set of papers so delivered.

Power of Board to give general authority

60. The Board may give general authority to solicitors acting for assisted persons in any particular class of case to incur costs by—

   (a) obtaining a report or opinion from one or more experts or tendering expert evidence;

   (b) employing a person to provide a report or opinion (other than as an expert); or

   (c) requesting transcripts of shorthand notes or tape recordings of any proceedings;

and, if such authority is given, the Board shall specify the maximum fee payable for any such report, opinion, expert evidence or transcript.

Other cases where authority may be sought

61.—(1) Where it appears to an assisted person's solicitor to be necessary for the proper conduct of the proceedings to incur costs by taking any of the steps specified in paragraph (2), he may, unless authority has been given in the certificate, apply to the Area Director for prior authority.

(2) The steps referred to in paragraph (1) are—

   (a) obtaining a report or opinion of an expert or tendering expert evidence in a case of a class not included in any general authority given under regulation 60; or

   (b) paying a person, not being an expert witness, a fee to prepare a report and, if required, to give evidence in a case of a class not included in any general authority given under regulation 60; or

   (c) in a case of a class included in a general authority given under regulation 60, paying a higher fee than that specified by the Board or obtaining more reports or opinions or tendering more evidence (expert or otherwise) than has been specified; or

   (d) performing an act which is either unusual in its nature or involves unusually large expenditure; or

   (e) bespeaking any transcripts of shorthand notes or tape recordings of any proceedings not included in any general authority given under regulation 60.

(3) Where the Area Director gives prior authority for the taking of any step referred to in paragraph (2)(a), (b), (c) or (e), he shall specify

   (a) the number of reports or opinions that may be obtained or the number of persons who may be authorised to give expert evidence, and

(b) the maximum fee to be paid for each report, opinion, transcript or to each person for tendering evidence, as the case may be.

Amended by the Civil Legal Aid (General) (Amendment) (No. 2) Regulations 1994.

Reasons to be given for refusing authority

62. If an Area Director refuses an application for authority made under regulation 59 or 61, he shall give written reasons for his decision.

Effect of obtaining and failing to obtain authority

63.—(1) Subject to paragraph (2), no question as to the propriety of any step or act in relation to which prior authority has been obtained under regulation 59, 60 or 61 shall be raised on any taxation of costs.

(2) Where costs are incurred in accordance with and subject to the limit imposed by a prior authority given under regulation 59, 60 or 61, no question shall be raised on any taxation as to the amount of the payment to be allowed for the step or act in relation to which the authority was given unless the solicitor or the assisted person knew or ought reasonably to have known that the purpose for which the authority was given had failed or become irrelevant or unnecessary before the costs were incurred.

(3) Without prejudice to regulation 59, where costs are incurred in instructing a Queen's Counsel or more than one counsel, without authority to do so having been given in the certificate or under regulation 59(1), no payment in respect of those costs shall be allowed on any taxation unless it is also allowed on an inter partes taxation.

(4) Where costs are incurred in instructing counsel or in taking any step or doing any act for which authority may be given under regulation 60 or 61, without authority to do so having been given in the certificate or under regulation 59, 60 or 61, payment in respect of those costs may still be allowed on taxation.

Restriction on payment otherwise than from the fund

64. Where a certificate has been issued in connection with any proceedings, the assisted person's solicitor or counsel shall not receive or be party to the making of any payment for work done in those proceedings during the currency of that certificate (whether within the scope of the certificate or otherwise) except such payments as may be made out of the fund.

PART IX

CONDUCT OF PROCEEDINGS

Restrictions on entrusting case to others

65.—(1) No solicitor or counsel acting for an assisted person shall entrust the conduct of any part of the case to any other person except another solicitor or counsel selected under section 32(1) of the Act.

(2) Nothing in paragraph (1) shall prevent a solicitor from entrusting the conduct of any part of the case to a partner of his or to a competent and responsible representative of his employed in his office or otherwise under his immediate supervision.

Duty to report changes of circumstances

66. The assisted person shall forthwith inform his solicitor of any change in his circumstances or in the circumstances of his case, which he has reason to believe might affect the terms or the continuation of his certificate.

Provision of information

66A. The Area Director or the assessment officer may at any time after the grant of a certificate require the assisted person to

(a) provide further evidence of any information given in relation to his application for a certificate;

(b) attend for an interview for the purpose of providing such information;

(c) provide such additional information as the Area Director or the assessment officer may require.

Inserted by the Civil Legal Aid (General) (Amendment) (No. 2) Regulations 1996 (S.I. 1996 No. 1257).

Duty to report abuse of legal aid

67.—(1) Where an assisted person's solicitor or counsel has reason to believe that the assisted person has—

(a) required his case to be conducted unreasonably so as to incur an unjustifiable expense to the fund or has required unreasonably that the case be continued; or

(b) intentionally failed to comply with any provision of regulations made under the Act concerning the information to be furnished by him or in furnishing such information has knowingly made a false statement or false representation,

the solicitor or counsel shall forthwith report the fact to the Area Director.

(2) Where the solicitor or counsel is uncertain whether it would be reasonable for him to continue acting for the assisted person, he shall report the circumstances to the Area Director.

Power of court to refer abuse to Area Director

68.—(1) Subject to paragraph (2), at any time during the hearing of any proceedings to which an assisted person is a party, the court may, on the application of the Board or of its own motion, make an order referring to the Area Director the question whether the assisted person's certificate should continue where the court considers that the assisted person has—

(a) in relation to any application for a certificate, made an untrue statement as to his financial resources or had failed to disclose any material fact concerning them, whether the statement was made or the failure occurred before or after the issue of the certificate and notwithstanding that it was made or occurred in relation to an application to another area office in connection with the same proceedings; or

(b) intentionally failed to comply with these Regulations by not furnishing to his solicitor or the Area Director any material information concerning anything other than his financial resources; or

(c) knowingly made an untrue statement in furnishing such information;

and the court shall notify the Area Director of the terms of any order so made.

(2) No order shall be made under paragraph (1) by reason of any such mis-statement or failure as is referred to in paragraph (1)(a) if the assisted person satisfies the court that he used due care or diligence to avoid such mis-statement or failure but the assisted person's solicitor shall nevertheless report the circumstances to the Area Director.

Duty to report on refusing or giving up case

69.—(1) A solicitor shall inform the Area Director of his reasons for refusing to act or for giving up a case after being selected.

(2) Counsel, where he has been selected to act or is acting for an assisted person, shall inform the Area Director of his reasons for refusing to accept instructions or for giving up the case or shall, if required so to do, inform that Area Director of his reasons for entrusting it to another.

(3) Without prejudice to any other right of a solicitor or counsel to give up a case, any solicitor or counsel may give up an assisted person's case in the circumstances specified in regulation 67.

(4) Where any solicitor or counsel exercises his right to give up an assisted person's case in the circumstances specified in regulation 67, the solicitor shall make a report to the Area Director of the circumstances in which that right was exercised.

(5) Where the Area Director to whom a report is made under paragraph (4) does not discharge or revoke the assisted person's certificate, he shall require the assisted person to select another solicitor to act for him.

Duty to report progress of proceedings

70.—(1) An assisted person's solicitor and his counsel (if any) shall give the Area Director such information regarding the progress and disposal of the proceedings to which the certificate relates as the Area Director may from time to time require for the purpose of performing his functions under these Regulations and, without being required so to do, the assisted person's solicitor shall—

(a) make a report where the assisted person declines to accept a reasonable offer of settlement or a sum which is paid into court;

(b) notify the Area Director where a legal aid certificate is issued to another party to the proceedings.

(2) Without prejudice to the generality of paragraph (1), an assisted person's solicitor shall, when required so to do by the Board, make a report to the Area Director, on a form approved by the Board, specifying the grounds on which he certifies that it is reasonable for the assisted person to continue to receive legal aid in respect of the proceedings to which the certificate relates.

(3) Where an assisted person's solicitor fails to make a report under paragraph (2) within 21 days of the Board's request, the Area Director shall—

(a) give notice to him and to the assisted person that the legal aid certificate may be discharged; and

(b) invite the assisted person to show cause why the certificate should not be discharged,

and the provisions of Part X of these Regulations shall apply, with any necessary modifications, where notice is given under sub-paragraph (a) above.

Duty to report death, etc., of assisted person

71. A solicitor who has acted or is acting for an assisted person shall, on becoming aware that the assisted person—

(a) has died; or

(b) has had a bankruptcy order made against him, report that fact to the Area Director.

Duty to report completion of case

72. A solicitor shall report forthwith to the Area Director either—

(a) upon the completion of the case if he has completed the work authorised by the certificate; or

(b) if, for any reason, he is unable to complete the work.

Privilege, etc., not to prevent disclosure

73.—(1) No solicitor or counsel shall be precluded, by reason of any privilege arising out of the relationship between counsel, solicitor and client, from disclosing to an Area Director or an area committee any information, or from giving any opinion, which he is required to disclose or give to the Area Director or that committee under the Act or these Regulations, or which may enable them to perform their functions under the Act or these Regulations.

(2) For the purpose of providing information under the Act or these Regulations or to enable an Area Director or an area committee to perform its functions under the Act or these Regulations, any party may disclose to an Area Director or an area committee communications in relation to the proceedings concerned sent to or by the assisted person's solicitor, whether or not they are expressed to be "without prejudice."

PART X

REVOCATION AND DISCHARGE OF CERTIFICATES

Effect of revocation or discharge

74.—(1) An Area Director may terminate a certificate by revoking or discharging it under this Part of these Regulations.

(2) Subject to this Part of these Regulations, a person whose certificate is revoked shall be deemed never to have been an assisted person in relation to those proceedings except for the purposes of section 18 of the Act; and a person whose certificate is discharged shall, from the date of the discharge, cease to be an assisted person in the proceedings to which the certificate related.

Revocation or discharge of emergency certificate

75.—(1) The Area Director shall revoke an emergency certificate where the assessment officer assesses that the person to whom it was issued has disposable income of an amount which makes him ineligible for legal aid.

(2) The Area Director shall revoke an emergency certificate where the assessment officer assesses that the person to whom it was issued, having disposable income of an amount which makes him eligible for legal aid, has disposable capital of an amount which renders him liable to be refused legal aid, and it appears to the Area Director that, without legal aid, the probable cost to him of the proceedings in respect of which the emergency certificate was issued would not exceed the contribution which would be payable by him.

(3) The Area Director may revoke or discharge an emergency certificate if

he is satisfied that the assisted person has failed to attend for an interview or to provide information or documents when required to do so under these Regulations, or has failed to accept an offer of a substantive certificate.

(4) The Area Director may revoke or discharge an emergency certificate upon the expiry of such period (including any extension of that period granted under regulation 24(1)) as he may have allowed for the duration of the certificate.

(5) No emergency certificate shall be revoked under paragraph (3) until—

(a) notice has been served on the assisted person and his solicitor that the Area Director may do so and that the assisted person may show cause why the certificate should not be revoked; and

(b) the assisted person has been given an opportunity to show cause why his certificate should not be revoked.

(6) Where notice is served under paragraph (5), no further work may be done or steps taken under the certificate unless authorised by the Area Director.

Discharge of certificate on financial grounds

76.—(1) The Area Director shall discharge a certificate (other than an emergency certificate) from such date as he considers appropriate where the assessment officer assesses that the person to whom it was issued has disposable income of an amount which makes him ineligible for legal aid.

(2) The Area Director shall discharge a certificate (other than an emergency certificate) from such date as he considers appropriate where the assessment officer assesses that the person to whom it was issued, having disposable income of an amount which makes him eligible for legal aid, has disposable capital of an amount which renders him liable to be refused legal aid, and it appears to the Area Director that, without legal aid, the probable cost to him of continuing the proceedings in respect of which the certificate was issued would not exceed the contribution which would be payable.

(3) Subject to section 15(3B) to (3D) of the Act, where the Area Director considers that the current financial circumstances of the assisted person are such that he could afford to proceed without legal aid, he may, with a view to discharging the certificate, require the assessment officer to assess the assisted person's current financial resources in accordance with the Civil Legal Aid (Assessment of Resources) Regulations 1989 and may discharge the certificate from such date as he considers appropriate.

Discharge on the merits

77.—(1) The Area Director shall discharge a certificate from such date as he considers appropriate where, as a result of information which has come to his knowledge, he considers that—

(a) the assisted person no longer has reasonable grounds for taking, defending or being a party to the proceedings, or for continuing to do so; or

(b) the assisted person has required the proceedings to be conducted unreasonably so as to incur an unjustifiable expense to the fund; or

(c) it is unreasonable in the particular circumstances that the assisted person should continue to receive legal aid.

Power to revoke or discharge for abuse of legal aid

78.—(1) Subject to paragraph (2), the Area Director may revoke or discharge a certificate where, as a result of information which has come to his knowledge, whether by a reference from the court under regulation 68 or otherwise, it appears to the Area Director that the assisted person has—

(a) in relation to any application for a certificate (whether for the same or different proceedings), made an untrue statement as to his financial resources or has failed to disclose any material fact concerning them, whether the statement was made or the failure occurred before or after the issue of the certificate and notwithstanding that it was made or occurred in relation to an application to another area office; or

(b) intentionally failed to comply with these Regulations by not furnishing to the Area Director or the solicitor any material information concerning any matter other than his financial resources; or

(c) knowingly made an untrue statement in furnishing such information.

(2) No certificate shall be revoked or discharged under paragraph (1) by reason of any such mis-statement or failure as is referred to in paragraph (1)(a) if the assisted person satisfies the Area Director that he used due care or diligence to avoid such mis-statement or failure.

Paragraph (1)(a) amended by the Civil Legal Aid (General) (Amendment) Regulations 1997 (S.I. 1997 No. 416).

Power to revoke or discharge for failure to provide information, etc.

79. The Area Director may revoke or discharge a certificate if he is satisfied that the assisted person has failed to attend for an interview or to provide information or documents when required to do so under these Regulations, whether in respect of the same or different proceedings.

Amended by the Civil Legal Aid (General) (Amendment) Regulations 1997 (S.I. 1997 No. 416).

Further power to discharge

80. The Area Director may discharge a certificate from such date as he considers appropriate—

(a) with the consent of the assisted person; or

(b) where the assisted person has been required to make a contribution and any payment in respect of it is more than 21 days in arrears; or

(c) on being satisfied, by the report of the assisted person's solicitor or otherwise, that—

(i) the assisted person has died; or

(ii) the assisted person has had a bankruptcy order made against him; or

(iii) the proceedings to which the certificate relates have been disposed of; or

(iv) the work authorised by the certificate has been completed.

Opportunity to show cause against revocation or discharge

81.—(1) Except where a certificate is discharged or revoked under regulation 75 or discharged under regulation 76 or 80(a), (b), (c)(i), (iii) or (iv), no certificate shall be revoked or discharged until—

(a) notice has been served on the assisted person that the Area Director may revoke or discharge his certificate (as the case may be) and that he may show cause why it should not be revoked or discharged; and

(b) the assisted person has been given an opportunity to show cause why his certificate should not be revoked or discharged.

(2) Where an Area Director revokes or discharges a certificate after notice has been given under paragraph (1), the assisted person may appeal to the appropriate area committee against such revocation or discharge and the provisions of regulations 36 to 39 shall, with the necessary modifications, apply to the conduct of such appeals.

(3) Any decision with regard to an appeal under paragraph (2) shall be final, and the area committee shall give notice of its decision and the reasons for it to the appellant and to any solicitor acting for him on a form approved by the Board.

Notification of revocation or discharge

82.—(1) Where an Area Director revokes or discharges an assisted person's certificate, he shall, unless the costs have already been determined, forthwith issue a notice of revocation or a notice of discharge (as the case may be), and shall send the notice (together with a copy) to his solicitor, and shall (except where the certificate has been discharged because the assisted person has died) send a further copy of the notice to the assisted person.

(2) A solicitor who receives a notice of revocation or a notice of discharge sent to him under paragraph (1) shall either forthwith, or if an appeal has been brought under regulation 81(2) which has been dismissed, forthwith upon receipt by him of a notice of dismissal—

(a) service notice of such revocation or discharge in a form approved by the Board upon any other persons who are parties to the proceedings; and

(b) inform any counsel, and if proceedings have been commenced, send a copy of the notice by post to the appropriate court office or registry.

(3) The copy of the notice sent to the appropriate court office or registry shall form part of the papers for the use of the court in the proceedings.

(4) *[Omitted by the Civil Legal Aid (General) (Amendment) (No. 2) Regulations 1991.]*

(5) Where the Area Director has considered revoking or discharging a certificate in consequence of information brought to his knowledge by any person, he may, if he thinks fit, inform that person whether or not the certificate has been revoked or discharged.

Amended by the Civil Legal Aid (General) (Amendment) (No. 2) Regulations 1994.

Effect of revocation or discharge on retainer

83.—(1) Upon receipt by him of a notice of revocation or discharge of a certificate, the retainer of any solicitor and counsel selected by or acting on behalf of the assisted person shall, subject to paragraph (2), either forthwith determine or, if an appeal had been brought under regulation 81(2) which had been dismissed, forthwith determine after receipt by him of a notice of such dismissal.

(2) If an Area Director revokes or discharges a certificate and proceedings

have commenced, the retainer of the solicitor shall not determine until he has sent to the appropriate court office or registry, and has served, any notice required by regulation 82.

Costs to be taxed or assessed on revocation or discharge

84. Upon the determination of a retainer under regulation 83—

(a) the costs of the proceedings to which the certificate related, incurred by or on behalf of the person to whom it was issued, shall, as soon as is practicable after the determination of the retainer, be submitted for taxation or assessment; and

(b) the fund shall remain liable for the payment of any costs so taxed or assessed.

Operation of statutory charge

85.—(1) Where a certificate has been revoked or discharged, section 16(6) of the Act (which provides for a charge upon property recovered or preserved for an assisted person) shall apply to any property recovered or preserved as a result of the person whose certificate has been revoked or discharged continuing to take, defend or be a party to the proceedings to which the certificate related.

(2) For the purpose of paragraph (1), the reference to a person whose certificate has been discharged shall, where the certificate has been discharged under regulation 80(c)(i) or (ii), include his personal representatives, his trustee in bankruptcy or the Official Receiver, as the case may be.

Right to recover costs and contribution

86.—(1) Where a certificate has been revoked—

(a) the Board shall have the right to recover from the person to whom the certificate was issued the costs paid or payable under regulation 84(b) less any amount received from him by way of contribution; and

(b) the solicitor who has acted under the certificate shall have the right to recover from that person the difference between the amount paid or payable out of the fund and the full amount of his solicitor and own client costs.

(2) Where a certificate has been discharged, the person to whom the certificate was issued shall remain liable for the payment of his contribution (if any) as determined or redetermined, up to the amount paid or payable by the Board under regulation 84(b) and, where he continues to take, defend or be a party to the proceedings to which the certificate related, section 17(1) of the Act shall apply in so far as the costs were incurred while he was an assisted person.

PART XI

PROPERTY AND COSTS RECOVERED FOR ASSISTED PERSONS

Money recovered to be paid to solicitor or the Board

87.—(1) Subject to regulations 89 and 94, all moneys payable to an assisted person—

(a) by virtue of any agreement or order made in connection with the action, cause or matter to which his certificate relates, whether such agreement was made before or after the proceedings were taken; or

(b) being moneys payable in respect of the action, cause or matter to which his certificate relates upon the distribution of property of a person who had been adjudicated bankrupt or has entered into a deed of arrangement, or of a company in liquidation; or

(c) being moneys which were paid into court by him or on his behalf in any proceedings to which his certificate relates and which have been ordered to be repaid to him; or

(d) being moneys standing in court to the credit of any proceedings to which his certificate relates,

shall be paid or repaid, as the case may be, to the solicitor of the assisted person or, if he is no longer represented by a solicitor, to the Board, and only the solicitor, or, as the case may be, the Board, shall be capable of giving a good discharge for moneys so payable.

(2) Where the assisted person's solicitor has reason to believe that an attempt may be made to circumvent the provisions of paragraph (1), he shall inform the Board.

Notice to trustee in bankruptcy, etc.

88.—(1) Where moneys become payable under regulation 87(b), the solicitor or the Board, as the case may be, shall send to the trustee in bankruptcy, the trustee or assignee of the deed of arrangement or the liquidator of the company in liquidation, as the case may be; notice that a certificate has been issued to the assisted person.

(2) A notice sent under paragraph (1) shall operate as a request by the assisted person for payment of the moneys payable under regulation 87(b) to the assisted person's solicitor or the Board, as the case may be, and shall be a sufficient authority for that purpose.

Exceptions to regulation 87

89. Notwithstanding the requirements of regulation 87—

(a) payment of any sum under an order for costs in favour of an assisted person in authorised summary proceedings shall be made to the clerk to the justices, who shall pay it to the Board or as the Board shall direct, and only the clerk to the justices shall be able to give a good discharge therefor; and

(b) where any moneys recovered or preserved for an assisted person in any proceedings have been paid into or remain in court and invested for the benefit of the assisted person, such part of those moneys as is not subject to the charge created by section 16(6) of the Act in accordance with regulation 93 may be paid to the assisted person.

Solicitor to pay moneys recovered to the Board

90.—(1) An assisted person's solicitor shall forthwith—

(a) inform the Area Director of any property recovered or preserved for the assisted person and send to him a copy of the order or agreement by virtue of which the property was recovered or preserved; and

(b) subject to paragraphs (2) and (4), pay all moneys received by him under the terms of the order or agreement made in the assisted person's favour to the Board.

(2) Where the Area Director considers that the rights of the fund will thereby be safeguarded, he may direct the assisted person's solicitor to—

(a) pay to the Board under paragraph (1)(b) only such sums as, in the opinion of the Area Director, should be retained by the Board in order to safeguard the rights of the fund under any provisions of the Act and these Regulations; and

(b) pay any other moneys to the assisted person.

(3) Where:

(a) in proceedings under any of the enactments referred to in regulation 96(1) the property recovered or preserved for the assisted person includes money which by order of the court or under the terms of any agreement reached is to be used for the purpose of purchasing a home for himself or his dependants; or

(b) in any proceedings the property recovered or preserved for the assisted person includes property which, by order of the court or under the terms of any agreement reached, is to be used as a home for the assisted person or his dependants,

the assisted person's solicitor shall forthwith so inform the Area Director.

(3) *Where in proceedings under any of the enactments referred to in regulation 96(1) the property recovered or preserved for the assisted person includes—*

(a) *property which by order of the court or under the terms of any agreement reached is to be used as a home for the assisted person or his dependants; or*

(b) *money which by order of the court or under the terms of any agreement reached is to be used to purchase a home for the assisted person or his dependants,*

the assisted person's solicitor shall forthwith so inform the Area Director.

The words in bold were inserted and the words in italic omitted by regulation 14 of the Civil Legal Aid (General) (Amendment) (No. 2) Regulations 1994—see p. 437 for transitionals.

(4) If the Area Director considers and directs that the provisions of regulation 96 apply to any sum of money, paragraph (1)(b) above shall not apply to it and the assisted person's solicitor shall release the money only in accordance with the provisions of regulation 96.

(5) Where the assisted person's solicitor pays moneys to the Board in accordance with this Regulation, he shall identify what sums relate to costs and what to damages.

Amended by the Civil Legal Aid (General) (Amendment) Regulations 1994 (S.I. 1994 No. 229).

Enforcement of orders, etc., in favour of assisted person

91.—(1) Where in any proceedings to which an assisted person is a party—

(a) an order or agreement is made providing for the recovery or preservation of property for the benefit of the assisted person and, by virtue of the Act, there is a first charge on the property for the benefit of the Board; or

(b) an order or agreement is made for the payment of costs to the assisted person,

the Board may take such proceedings in its own name as may be necessary to enforce or give effect to such an order or agreement.

(2) An assisted person may, with the consent of the appropriate Area Director, take proceedings (being proceedings for which representation may be granted under the Act) to give effect to an order or agreement referred to in regulation **87(1)(a)** *87(a)*.

The words in bold were inserted and the words in italic omitted by the Civil Legal Aid (General) (Amendment) (No. 2) Regulations 1994—see p. 437 for transitionals.

(2A) The assisted person's solicitor may take proceedings for the recovery of costs in the circumstances to which regulation 107B applies.

(2B) Where the Board has paid costs to which regulation 92(1)(b) refers, but those costs have not been reimbursed by payment from any other party in favour of the assisted person, the solicitor shall require the consent of the Area Director before taking proceedings to which paragraph (2A) refers.

(3) Where the Board takes proceedings, it may authorise any person to swear an affidavit, file a proof, receive a dividend or take any other step in the proceedings in its name and the costs incurred by the Board in any such proceedings shall be a first charge on any property or sum so recovered.

Amended by the Civil Legal Aid (General) (Amendment) Regulations 1994 (S.I. 1994 No. 229).

Retention and payment out of moneys by the Board

92.—(1) The costs payable by the Board in respect of any work done under a certificate, after deduction of any sums paid under regulations 100 or 101 (payments on account), shall be—

(a) the legal aid only costs;
(b) any other costs determined under regulation 107A(2);
(c) where inter partes costs paid in favour of the assisted person are received by the Board, a sum equal to the amount by which the costs received exceed the costs referred to in sub-paragraph (b) above;
(d) where all the inter partes costs as agreed or determined in accordance with any direction or order given or made in the proceedings in favour of the assisted person are received by the Board together with interest, a sum equal to the balance of interest after deduction of interest on the costs to which sub-paragraph (b) refers.

(2) Upon receipt of moneys paid to it under this Part of the Regulations the Board shall retain—

(a) subject to regulation 103 and to paragraph (1)(c) and (d) above, any sum paid under an order or agreement for costs made in favour of the assisted person in respect of the period covered by his certificate;
(b) a sum equal to the amount (if any) by which any property recovered or preserved is charged for the benefit of the Board by virtue of section 16(6) of the Act;
(c) any costs of proceedings taken by the Board under regulation 91(1),

and shall pay the balance to the assisted person.

Substituted by the Civil Legal Aid (General) (Amendment) Regulations 1994 (S.I. 1994 No. 229) which apply to proceedings in respect of which a civil legal aid certificate is issued on or after February 25, 1994.

In circumstances where a legal aid certificate has been issued before February 25, 1994, the italicised provisions below will apply.

Retention and payment out of moneys by the Board

92. Upon receipt of moneys paid to it under this Part of these Regulations, the Board shall retain—

> *(a) subject to regulation 103, any sum paid under an order or agreement for costs made in the assisted person's favour in respect of the period covered by his certificate;*

> *(b) a sum equal to the amount (if any) by which any property recovered or preserved is charged for the benefit of the Board by virtue of section 16(6) of the Act; and*

> *(c) any costs of proceedings taken by the Board under regulation 91(1);*

and shall pay the balance to the assisted person.

Omitted by the Civil Legal Aid (General) (Amendment) Regulations 1994 (S.I. 1994 No. 229).

Interest on damages

92A.—(1) Where the Board receives damages paid in favour of an assisted person it shall, subject to the provisions of this regulation, pay to the assisted person a sum representing gross interest earned while the damages are being held by the Board.

(2) Without prejudice to its other powers to invest money, the Board shall maintain and may deposit in one general account at a bank or building society damages to which this regulation refers.

(3) The rate of interest payable to the assisted person by virtue of this regulation shall be ½ per cent. per annum less than the rate payable on damages deposited in the general account.

(4) The Board shall not be required to pay interest where the damages received do not exceed £500 or where the period during which they are held by the Board is less than 28 days.

(5) Interest shall be payable for the period beginning on the third business day after the date on which the damages are received by the Board down to (and including) the date on which the Board determines the amount to be retained under regulation 92(2).

(6) In this regulation—

> "bank" means the Bank of England, or the branch, situated in England or Wales, of any institution authorised under the Banking Act 1987;
> "building society" means the branch, situated in England or Wales, of a building society within the meaning of the Building Societies Act 1986;
> "business day" means a day other than a Saturday, a Sunday, Christmas day, Good Friday or a bank holiday under the Banking and Financial Dealings Act 1971;
> "general account" means an interest bearing account opened in the name of the Board, the title of which account does not identify any assisted person.

Inserted by regulation 16 of the Civil Legal Aid (General) (Amendment) (No. 2) Regulations 1994.

Operation of statutory charge on moneys in court

93. Where any moneys recovered or preserved for an assisted person in any proceedings are ordered to be paid into or remain in court and invested for the benefit of the assisted person, the charge created by section 16(6) of the Act shall attach only to such parts of those moneys as, in the opinion of the Area Director, will be sufficient to safeguard the rights of the Board under any provisions of the Act or these Regulations and the Area Director shall notify the court in writing of the amount so attached.

Exemptions from the statutory charge

94. The charge created by section 16(6) of the Act shall not apply to—

   (a) any interim payment made in accordance with an order made under Order 29, rule 11 or 12 of the Rules of the Supreme Court 1965, or Order 13, rule 12 of the County Court Rules 1981, or in accordance with an agreement having the same effect as such an order;

   (b) any sum or sums ordered to be paid under section 5 of the Inheritance (Provision for Family and Dependants) Act 1975;

   (c) any periodical payment of maintenance which, for this purpose, means money or money's worth paid towards the support of a spouse, former spouse, child or any other person for whose support the payer has previously been responsible or has made payments;

   (d) the first £2,500 of any money, or of the value of any property, recovered or preserved by virtue of—

   (i) an order made, or deemed to be made, under the provisions of section 23(1)(c) or (f), 23(2), 24, 27(6)(c) or (f), or 35 of the Matrimonial Causes Act 1973; or

   (ii) an order made, or deemed to be made, under the provisions of section 2 or 6 of the Inheritance (Provision for Family and Dependants) Act 1975 or any provision repealed by that Act; or

   (iii) an order made, or deemed to be made, after September 30, 1977, under section 17 of the Married Women's Property Act 1882; or

   (iv) *[Omitted by the Civil Legal Aid (General) (Amendment) (No. 2) Regulations 1991]*;

   (v) an order for the payment of a lump sum made, or deemed to be made, under the provisions of section 60 of the Magistrates' Courts Act 1980; or

   (vi) an order made, or deemed to be made, under the provisions of section 2(1)(b) or (d), 6(1) or (5) or 20(2) of the Domestic Proceedings and Magistrates' Courts Act 1978; or

   (vii) *[Omitted by the Civil Legal Aid (General) (Amendment) (No. 2) Regulations 1991]*;

   (viii) an order made, or deemed to be made, under the provisions of Schedule 1 to the Children Act 1989; or

   (ix) an agreement made after March 1, 1981 which has the same effect as an order made, or deemed to be made under any of the provisions specified in sub-paragraph (d)(i) to (viii);

   (dd) any tools of the assisted person's trade;

   (e) where the certificate was issued before May 3, 1976, any money or property, of whatever amount or value, recovered or preserved by the virtue of an order made, or deemed to be made, under any of the provisions specified in sub-paragraph (d)(i) or (ii) before August 1, 1976 or which, if made on or after that date, gives effect to a settlement entered into before that date;

(f) any payment made in accordance with an order made by the Employment Appeal Tribunal, or in accordance with a settlement entered into after November 1, 1983 which has the same effect as such an order;

(ff) any payment made by the Secretary of State under the Earnings Top-up Scheme 1996; or

(g) any sum, payment or benefit which, by virtue of any provision of, or made under, an Act of Parliament, cannot be assigned or charged.

Amended by the Civil Legal Aid (General) (Amendment) Regulations 1997 (S.I. 1997 No. 416).

Vesting and enforcement of charges

95.—(1) Any charge on property recovered or preserved for an assisted person arising under section 16(6) of the Act or created by virtue of regulation 96, 97 or 98 shall vest in the Board.

(2) The Board may enforce any such charge in any manner which would be available to a chargee in respect of a charge given inter partes, but the Board shall not agree to the release or postponement of the enforcement of any such charge except where regulation 96, 97 or 98 applies and then only in accordance with the provisions of those regulations.

(3) Any such charge shall according to its nature—

(a) in the case of unregistered land, be a Class B land charge within the meaning of section 2 of the Land Charges Act 1972;

(b) in the case of registered land, be a registrable substantive charge; or

(c) in a case in which the conditions specified in **section 53(1) or 54(1)** *section 54(1)* of the Land Registration Act 1925 are met, be protected by lodging a caution in accordance with the provisions of **the relevant section** *that section,*

and references to registration in regulations 96 to 98 shall be construed as references to registration or protection in accordance with paragraph (a), (b) or (c) of this regulation.

(3A) Where, in any of the circumstances described in regulation 96, 97 or 98, the property charged or to be charged is land to which the Conveyancing and Feudal Reform (Scotland) Act 1970 applies—

(a) **references in those regulations to a charge executed in favour of the Board shall be construed as references to a standard security in favour of the Board within the meaning of Part II of that Act; and**

(b) **references in those regulations to registration shall be construed as references to the recording of a standard security in the Register of Sasines.**

The words in bold were inserted and the words in italic omitted by regulation 17 of the Civil Legal Aid (General) (Amendment) (No. 2) Regulations 1994—see p. 437 for transitionals.

(4) Without prejudice to the provisions of the Land Registration Act 1925 and the Land Charges Act 1972, all conveyances and acts done to defeat, or

operating to defeat, any such charge shall, except in the case of a bona fide purchaser for value without notice, be void as against the Board.

Postponement of enforcement of charges over money

96.—(1) This regulation applies where in proceedings under—

(a) the Married Women's Property Act 1882;

(b) the Matrimonial Causes Act 1973;

(c) the Inheritance (Provision for Family and Dependants) Act 1975; *or*

(d) Schedule 1 to the Children Act 1989;

(e) **Part III of the Matrimonial and Family Proceedings Act 1984; or**

(f) **section 30 of the Law of Property Act 1925,**

there is recovered or preserved for the assisted person a sum of money which by order of the court or under the terms of any agreement reached is to be used for the purpose of purchasing a home for himself or his dependants.

(2) Where the assisted person—

(a) wishes to purchase a home in accordance with the order or agreement; and

(b) agrees in writing on a form approved by the Board to comply with the conditions set out in paragraph (3),

the Board may, if the Area Director is satisfied that the property to be purchased will provide adequate security for **the amount of the charge created by section 16(6) of the Act** *the sum referred to in paragraph (3)(b)*, agree to defer enforcing any charge over that sum.

(3) The conditions referred to in paragraph (2) are that—

(a) the property to be purchased shall be subject to a charge executed in favour of the Board and registered in accordance with regulation **95** 95*(3)*; and

(b) **interest shall accrue for the benefit of the Board in accordance with regulation 99(4).**

(b) *from the date on which the charge is first registered, simple interest shall accrue for the benefit of the Board at the rate of 8 per cent. per annum (or such other rate as may from time to time be prescribed) on such sum as, but for the provisions of this regulation, the Board would have retained under regulation 92(b) in respect of its charge over the property to which this regulation applies.*

(4) Where the Board has agreed to defer enforcement under paragraph (2), the assisted person's solicitor may release any money received by him under regulation 87 and which is the subject of the order or agreement, to the vendor or the vendor's representative on completion of the purchase of the property purchased in accordance with the order or agreement.

(5) Where—

(a) the Area Director has directed (under regulation 90(4)) that this regulation applies; and

(b) **an agreement** *no agreement* to defer enforcement under paragraph (2) above has been made, the assisted person's solicitor may release any money received by him under regulation 87 and which is the subject of the order or agreement to another solicitor or to a person providing conveyancing services to whom section 22(1) of the Solicitors Act 1974 does not apply, who has given an undertaking to, and on a form approved by, the Board that he will fulfil the obligations imposed by this regulation on the assisted person's solicitor.

(6) Where the assisted person's solicitor releases any money under paragraph (4) or (5), he shall so inform the Area Director as soon as practicable and either—

(a) provide the Area Director with sufficient information to enable him to register a charge on the property purchased in accordance with the order or agreement; or

(b) send to the Area Director a copy of any undertaking given under paragraph (5).

(7) Where any sum of money retained by the assisted person's solicitor by virtue of this regulation has not been used for the purchase of a home after a period of one year from the date of the order or agreement under which it was recovered or preserved for the assisted person, the assisted person's solicitor shall pay that sum to the Board.

Amended by the Civil Legal Aid (General) (Amendment) Regulations 1994 (S.I. 1994 No. 229).

The words in bold were inserted and the words in italic omitted by regulation 18 of the Civil Legal Aid (General) (Amendment) (No. 2) Regulations 1994—see p. 437 for transitionals.

Postponement of enforcement of charges over land

97.—(1) This regulation applies where, **in any proceedings** *in proceedings under any of the enactments referred to in regulation 96(1)*, there is recovered or preserved for the assisted person property which, by order of the court or under the terms of any agreement reached, is to be used as a home for the assisted person or his dependants.

(2) Where the Area Director considers that the provisions of this regulation apply to any property, he shall so direct.

(3) Where the Area Director has directed that this regulation applies to property and the assisted person—

(a) wishes to use the property as a home for himself or his dependants; and

(b) agrees in writing on a form approved by the Board to comply with the condition set out in paragraph (4),

the Board may, if the Area Director is satisfied that the property will provide adequate security for the sum referred to in paragraph (4), agree to defer enforcing *of* any charge over that property.

(4) The condition referred to in paragraph (3) is that interest shall accrue for the benefit of the Board in accordance with regulation 99(4).

(4) The condition referred to in paragraph (3) is that from the date on which the charge is first registered where that date is after December 1, 1988, simple interest shall accrue for the benefit of the Board at the rate of 8 per cent per annum (or such other rate as may from time to time be prescribed) on such sum as, but for the provisions of this regulation, the Board would

have retained under regulation 92(b) in respect of the property to which this regulation applies.

(5) Where, in a case to which this regulation applies, the charge in favour of the Board has not yet been registered in accordance with regulation 95(3) and the assisted person—

    (a) wishes to purchase a different property in substitution for the property which is the subject of the order or agreement referred to in paragraph (1); and

    (b) agrees in writing on a form approved by the Board to comply with the conditions set out in paragraph (6),

the Board may, if the Area Director is satisfied that the property to be purchased will provide adequate security for **the amount of the charge created by section 16(6) of the Act** *the sum referred to in paragraph (4)*, agree to defer enforcing any charge over that property.

(6) The conditions referred to in paragraph (5) are that—

    (a) the property to be purchased shall be subject to a charge executed in favour of the Board and registered in accordance with regulation 95 *95(3)*; and

    (b) interest shall accrue for the benefit of the Board in accordance with regulation 99(4).

    (b) from the date on which the charge is first registered where that date is after December 1, 1988, simple interest shall accrue for the benefit of the Board at the rate referred to in paragraph (4) on the sum referred to in that paragraph.

Amended by the Civil Legal Aid (General) (Amendment) Regulations 1994 (S.I. 1994 No. 229).

The words in bold were inserted and the words in italic omitted by regulation 19 of the Civil Legal Aid (General) (Amendment) (No. 2) Regulations 1994—see p. 437 for transitionals.

Substitution of charged property

98.—(1) This regulation applies where the Board has agreed under regulation 96 or 97 to defer enforcing a charge created by section 16(6) of the Act and a charge over any property (whether created by the said section 16(6) or in pursuance of regulation 96 or 97 or this regulation) has been registered in favour of the Board in accordance with regulation 95(3).

(1) This regulation applies where a charge has been registered in favour of the Board in pursuance of an agreement made under regulation 96 or 97.

(2) Where, in a case to which this regulation applies—

    (a) the assisted person wishes to purchase a different property in substitution for that over which a charge already exists;

    (b) the assisted person agrees in writing on a form approved by the Board to comply with the conditions set out in paragraph (3); and

    (c) the Area Director is satisfied that the property to be purchased will provide adequate security for **the amount of the charge created by section 16(6) of the Act** *the sum referred to in regulation 96(3)(b) or regulation 97(4)*, as the case may be, the Board may agree to release that charge.

(3) The conditions referred to in **paragraph 2** *paragraphs (2) and (4)* are that—

(a) the property to be purchased shall be subject to a charge executed in favour of the Board and registered in accordance with regulation **95** *95(3);* and

(b) simple interest shall accrue or continue to accrue for the benefit of the Board from the same date, on the same amounts and at the same rate as would apply if the assisted person were to retain the property over which the charge exists and the charge were not to be released.

(b) *where simple interest has accrued, it shall continue to accrue for the benefit of the Board at the rate prescribed for the time being for the purposes of regulation 96(3)(b) on the sum referred to in that regulation or in regulation 97(4), as the case may be.*

(4) Where, after a charge has been registered in favour of the Board in pursuance of an agreement made under this regulation—

(a) the assisted person wishes to purchase a different property in substitution for the property over which that charge exists;

(b) the assisted person agrees in writing on a form approved by the Board to comply with the conditions set out in paragraph (3) above; and

(c) the Area Director is satisfied that the property to be purchased will provide adequate security for the sum referred to in regulation 96(3)(b) or regulation 97(4), as the case may be,

the Board may agree to release that charge.

The words in bold were inserted and the words in italic omitted by regulation 20 of the Civil Legal Aid (General) (Amendment) (No. 2) Regulations 1994—see p. 437 for transitionals.

Payment and recovery of interest

99.—(1) Where interest is payable by the assisted person pursuant to the provisions of regulations 96, 97 or 98, such interest shall continue to accrue until **the amount of the charge created by section 16(6) of the Act** *the sum referred to in regulation 96(3)(b) or regulation 97(4), as the case may be,* is paid and the Board shall not seek to recover interest until such payment is made.

(2) The Board may take such steps as may be necessary to enforce, give effect to or terminate any agreement made under regulation 96, 97 or 98.

(3) Nothing in regulations 96 to 99 shall prevent the assisted person from making interim payments of interest or capital in respect of **the amount outstanding on the charge** *any sum referred to in regulation 96(3)(b) or 97(4),* whether such payments are made at regular intervals or not, and any such payment of capital shall reduce **that amount** *those sums* accordingly except that no interim payment shall be used to reduce any such sum while interest on that sum remains outstanding.

(4) Where interest is payable by the assisted person pursuant to the provisions of regulation 96 or 97—

(a) it shall run from the date on which the charge is first registered;

(b) it shall accrue at the rate of 8 per cent. per annum (or such other rate as may from time to time be prescribed), and

(c) the capital on which it is calculated shall be the amount outstanding on the charge from time to time.

(5) In paragraphs (3) and (4), the amount outstanding on the charge at any given time means the amount of the charge created by section 16(6) of the Act, calculated so as to take into account only those sums which up to that time have been either—

(a) paid by the Board in accordance with an assessment or taxation of costs, or

(b) recouped by the Board in the circumstances described in section 16(9) of the Act or in accordance with paragraph (3) of this regulation.

(6) In regulations 96 to 99 references to the amount of any charge created by section 16(6) of the Act shall be construed as references to the amount determined in accordance with sections 16(6) and (9) of the Act or to the value of the property to which it applies at the time when it was recovered or preserved whichever is the less.

The words in bold were inserted and the words in italic omitted by regulation 21 of the Civil Legal Aid (General) (Amendment) (No. 2) Regulations 1994—see p. 437 for transitionals.

PART XII

COSTS OF ASSISTED PERSONS

Payment on account

100.—(1) A solicitor acting for an assisted person under a certificate to which this regulation applies may submit a claim to the Board on a form approved by the Board for the payment of sums on account of profit costs incurred in connection with the proceedings to which the certificate relates.

(2) Counsel instructed on behalf of an assisted person under a certificate to which this regulation applies may submit a claim to the Board on a form approved by the Board for the payment of sums on account of his fees for work done in connection with the proceedings to which the certificate relates.

(3) A payment may only be made under paragraph (1) or (2) when—

(a) a period of 12 months has elapsed since the date on which the certificate was issued; or

(b) further periods of 12 months and 24 months have elapsed since that date.

(4) A claim may only be made under paragraph (1) or (2) within the period of 2 months before to 4 months after any period specified in paragraph (3).

(5) The maximum payment to be made for each claim under paragraph (1) or (2) in any one financial year shall be:

for the financial year 1993/94	62%
for the financial year 1994/95	70%
for the financial year 1995/96 and thereafter.	75%

(6) Where a solicitor's retainer has been determined and another solicitor (who is not a member of the same firm) is acting on behalf of the assisted

person, the appropriate area committee may authorise payment of a sum on account of the original solicitor's costs where it appears unlikely that the costs will be taxed within six months of the date on which the retainer was determined.

(7) The making of a payment under this regulation shall not release a solicitor from any obligation under these Regulations to submit his costs and counsel's fees for taxation or assessment on conclusion of the case.

(8) Where, after taxation or assessment, payments made under this regulation are found to exceed the final costs of the case, the solicitor or counsel (if any) shall, on demand, repay the balance due to the fund and, where the total costs exceed any payment made under this regulation, the balance shall be paid from the fund.

(9) Claims for payments on account made under regulation 100(1), (2) or (6) or regulation 101(1)(b) shall be made at prescribed rates where such rates are prescribed for solicitors or counsel, as the case may be, in

  (a) the Legal Aid in Civil Proceedings (Remuneration) Regulations 1994; or

  (b) the Legal Aid in Family Proceedings (Remuneration) Regulations 1991.

Amended by the Civil Legal Aid (General) (Amendment) Regulations 1992 (S.I. 1992 No. 590), the Civil Legal Aid (General) (Amendment) Regulations 1993 (S.I. 1993 No. 565), for proceedings in respect of which a legal aid certificate is granted on or after February 25, 1994, the Civil Legal Aid (General) (Amendment) Regulations 1994 (S.I. 1994 No. 229) and the Civil Legal Aid (General) (Amendment) (No. 2) Regulations 1994.

Payment on account of disbursements, in cases of hardship, etc.

101.—(1) Without prejudice to regulation 100, a solicitor acting for an assisted person may apply to the appropriate area committee for the payment of a sum on account of

  (a) disbursements incurred or about to be incurred in connection with the proceedings to which the certificate relates;

  (b) profit costs or counsel's fees where the proceedings to which the certificate relates have continued for more than 12 months and it appears unlikely that an order for taxation will be made within the next 12 months and delay in the taxation of those costs or fees will cause hardship to the solicitor or counsel.

(1A) A solicitor who has acted for an assisted person may make an application under paragraph 1(a) notwithstanding that the proceedings to which the certificate related have concluded and that the certificate has been revoked or discharged.

(2) Without prejudice to regulation 100, where—

  (a) the proceedings to which the certificate related have concluded or the solicitor is otherwise entitled to have his costs taxed; and

  (b) counsel acting for the assisted person has not received payment in respect of his fees for at least six months since the event which gave rise to the right to taxation,

counsel may apply to the appropriate area committee for payment of 75 per cent. of the amount claimed on account of his fees for work done in connection with the proceedings to which the certificate related.

(3) Without prejudice to regulation 100, where—

(a) the proceedings to which the certificate related have concluded or the solicitor acting for the assisted person is otherwise entitled to have his bill of costs taxed;

(b) the solicitor commenced proceedings for taxation in accordance with the time limits laid down by rules of court; and

(c) the solicitor has not received payment in respect of his costs for at least six months since he submitted his bill for taxation,

he may apply to the appropriate area committee for payment of 75 per cent of the amount claimed account of his profit costs for work done in connection with the proceedings to which the certificate related.

Paragraph (1A) inserted by the Civil Legal Aid (General) (Amendment) Regulations 1997 (S.I. 1997 No. 416). Paragraph (3) inserted by the Civil Legal Aid (General) (Amendment) Regulations 1996 (S.I. 1996 No. 649) and applicable to certificates granted on or after April 1, 1996.

Deferment of solicitor's profit costs

102. Where an assisted person's solicitor has failed to comply with any provision of these Regulations and, as a result of his default or omission, the fund incurs loss—

(a) the appropriate area committee may defer payment of all or part of the solicitor's profit costs in connection with the proceedings to which the certificate relates until he has complied with such provisions; and

(b) if the Board refers the conduct of the solicitor to the Solicitors' Disciplinary Tribunal and the solicitor is disciplined, the Board may retain any sum, payment of which has been deferred under sub-paragraph (a), in accordance with the finding of the Tribunal.

Legal aid granted after costs incurred

103.—(1) Where, after proceedings have been instituted in any court, a party becomes an assisted person in relation to those proceedings, the provisions of section 17(1) of the Act shall apply only to so much of the costs of the proceedings as are incurred while a certificate is in force.

(2) Any solicitor who has acted on behalf of the assisted person in the proceedings to which a certificate relates before the date of the certificate, and any solicitor who has a lien on any documents necessary for the proceedings and who has delivered them up subject to his lien, may give notice of that fact to the appropriate area committee.

(3) Subject to paragraph (4), if moneys are recovered for the assisted person, the Board shall pay to any solicitor who has given notice under paragraph (2) out of the sum so recovered the costs to which he would have been entitled following a solicitor and own client taxation.

(4) In any case where the sums so recovered are insufficient to pay the solicitor's costs in full in accordance with paragraph (3) and also to meet the sums paid out or payable out of the fund on the assisted person's account, the sums recovered in the proceedings shall be divided between the fund and the solicitor in the same proportions as the solicitor's costs and the cost to the fund bear to the aggregate of the two, and the first charge for the benefit of the Board

imposed by virtue of section 16(6) of the Act on property recovered or preserved in the proceedings shall take effect accordingly.

(5) In any case in which the amount of—

(a) the costs payable to a solicitor under this regulation; or

(b) the inter partes costs incurred during the period in which the certificate was in force,

have not been ascertained on taxation, they shall, for the purpose of this regulation, be assessed by the appropriate area committee and, where the committee makes an assessment under this regulation, it shall do so with a view
to allowing, for the costs referred to in sub-paragraph (a) above, such costs as
the solicitor would have been entitled to on a solicitor and own client taxation and, for the costs referred to in sub-paragraph (b) above, such costs as
would have been allowed on a taxation **under regulation 107A(2)** *on the standard basis.*

The words in bold were inserted and the words in italic omitted by the Civil Legal Aid
(General) (Amendment) Regulations 1994 (S.I. 1994 No. 229) which apply to proceedings in respect of which a civil legal aid certificate is granted on or after February 25,
1994.

(6) For the purposes of this regulation, work done by a solicitor—

(a) immediately prior to the issue of an emergency certificate; and

(b) at a time when no application for an emergency certificate could be
made because the appropriate area office was closed,

shall be deemed to be work done while such a certificate is in force if the
solicitor applies for an emergency certificate at the first available opportunity
and the application is granted.

Remuneration of legal representatives in magistrates' courts *and family proceedings*

104.—(1) The sums to be allowed to legal representatives in connection
with authorised summary proceedings shall be assessed by the Area Director.

*(2) In the case of any family proceedings any assessment, review or tax-
ation shall be made in accordance with the Legal Aid in Family Proceedings
(Remuneration) Regulations 1991 and Part XII of these Regulations shall
apply subject to the provisions of those Regulations.*

The heading to regulation 104 was amended and Regulation 104(2) was omitted by
the Civil Legal Aid (General) (Amendment) Regulations 1994 (S.I. 1994 No. 229) for
proceedings in respect of which a legal aid certificate is granted on or after February 25,
1994.

(3) In the case of authorised summary proceedings which are not family
proceedings any assessment, review or appeal under this regulation shall be
made in accordance with the provisions of regulation 6 of and Schedule 1 Part
I paragraph 1(1)(a) to the Legal Aid in Criminal and Care Proceedings (Costs)
Regulations 1989 as if the work done was work to which these provisions
apply, save that paragraphs 2 and 3 of Schedule 1, Part I shall not apply.

(4) Paragraphs (4) to (8) of regulation 105 and regulation 105A shall apply
where costs are assessed by an Area Director under paragraph (1) as they apply

to an assessment under that regulation.

(5) Subject to paragraph (4), regulations 105 to 110 shall not apply to costs in respect of authorised summary proceedings.

Assessment of costs*

105.—(1) In this regulation and in regulation 106A, "assessment" means an assessment of costs with a view to ensuring that the amounts of costs to be allowed are those which would be allowed on a taxation under regulation 107A(2).

(2) Subject to regulation 106A where the retainer of an assisted person's solicitor or counsel is determined before proceedings are actually begun and there has been no subsequent change of solicitor or counsel under the certificate, the amount of the solicitor's costs and counsel's fees (if any) shall be assessed by the Area Director.

(2A) Where proceedings have begun and the solicitor is of the opinion that the total amount which he and counsel (if any) would receive after taxation under regulation 107A(2) would not be more than £500 he must apply to the Area Director for an assessment of the amount of his costs and counsel's fees (if any) in respect of the work done.

(3) Subject to paragraph (2A) and regulation 106A where proceedings have begun and—

(a) the solicitor is of the opinion that the total amount which he and counsel (if any) would receive after taxation under regulation 107A(2) would not be more than £1,000; or

(b) *[Omitted]*

(c) there are special circumstances where a taxation would be against the interest of the assisted person or would increase the amount payable from the fund; or

(d) after a direction or order that the assisted person's costs shall be taxed under regulation 107A(2), the solicitor incurs costs for the purpose of recovering moneys payable to the fund,

the solicitor may apply to the Area Director for an assessment of the amount of his costs and counsel's fees (if any) in respect of the work done.

(4) If any solicitor or counsel is dissatisfied with any decision on an assessment in accordance with paragraph (2) or (3), he may, within 21 days of that decision, make written representations to the appropriate area committee; and that committee shall review the assessment of the Area Director whether by confirming, increasing or decreasing the amount assessed by the Area Director.

(5) A solicitor or counsel who is dissatisfied with the decision of an area committee on a review under paragraph (4) may, within 21 days of the decision, apply to that committee to certify a point of principle of general importance.

(6) Where an area committee certifies a point of principle of general importance, the solicitor or counsel may, within 21 days of the certification, appeal in writing to a committee appointed by the Board against the decision of the area committee under paragraph (4).

(7) On an appeal under pargraph (6) the committee appointed by the Board

---

* The Civil Legal Aid (General) (Amendment) Regulations 1994 (S.I. 1994 No. 229) which apply to proceedings in respect of which a civil legal aid certificate is granted on or after February 25, 1994.

may reverse, affirm or amend the decision of the area committee under paragraph (4).

(8) The assisted person's solicitor shall within seven days after an assessment or review under this regulation notify counsel in writing where the fees claimed on his behalf have been reduced or disallowed on assessment or review.

Assessment of costs

105.—*(1) In this regulation and in regulation 106, "assessment" means an assessment of costs with a view to ensuring that the amounts of costs to be allowed are those which would be allowed on a taxation on the standard basis under rules of court.*

(2) Where the retainer of an assisted person's solicitor or counsel is determined before proceedings are actually begun and there has been no subsequent change of solicitor or counsel under the certificate, the amount of the solicitor's costs and counsel's fees (if any) shall be assessed by the Area Director.

(2A) Where proceedings have begun and the solicitor is of the opinion that the total amount which he and counsel (if any) would receive after taxation on the standard basis would not be more than £500 he must apply to the Area Director for an assessment of the amount of his costs and counsel's fees (if any) in respect of the work done.

(3) Subject to paragraph (2A) where proceedings have begun and—

 (a) the solicitor is of the opinion that the total amount which he and counsel (if any) would receive after taxation on the standard basis would not be more than £1,000; or

 (b) the case of an assisted person (who is not such a person as is referred to in Order 62, rule 16, of the Rules of the Supreme Court 1965) has been settled after the commencement of proceedings without any direction of the court as to costs on terms that include provision for an agreed sum in respect of costs to be paid to the assisted person which the solicitor and counsel (if any) is willing to accept in full satisfaction of the work done; or

 (c) there are special circumstances where a taxation would be against the interest of the assisted person or would increase the amount payable from the fund; or

 (d) after a direction or order that the assisted person's costs shall be taxed on the standard basis, the solicitor incurs costs for the purpose of recovering moneys payable to the fund,

the solicitor may apply to the Area Director for an assessment of the amount of his costs and counsel's fees (if any) in respect of the work done.

(4) If any solicitor or counsel is dissatisfied with any decision on an assessment in accordance with paragraph (2) or (3), he may, within 21 days of that decision, make written representations to the appropriate area committee; and that committee shall review the assessment of the Area Director whether by confirming, increasing or decreasing the amount assessed by the Area Director.

(5) A solicitor or counsel who is dissatisfied with the decision of an area committee on a review under paragraph (4) may, within 21 days of the decision, apply to that committee to certify a point of principle of general importance.

418

(6) Where an area committee certifies a point of principle of general importance, the solicitor or counsel may, within 21 days of the certification, appeal in writing to a committee appointed by the Board against the decision of the area committee under paragraph (4).

(7) On an appeal under paragraph (6) the committee appointed by the Board may reverse, affirm or amend the decision of the area committee under paragraph (4).

(8) The assisted person's solicitor shall within seven days after an assessment or review under this regulation notify counsel in writing where the fees claimed on his behalf have been reduced or disallowed on assessment or review.

Assisted person having financial interest in assessment

105A.—(1) Where an assisted person has a financial interest in any assessment, review or appeal under regulation 105 he shall have a right to make written representations to the Area Director, appropriate area committee or committee appointed by the Board as the case may be within 21 days of being notified of the right to make such representations.

(2) On an assessment to which paragraph (1) applies it shall be the duty of an assisted person's solicitor:

(a) to supply him with a copy of his bill;

(b) to inform him of the extent of his financial interest and his right to make written representations; and

(c) to endorse on the bill that the assisted person has a financial interest in the assessment and that he has complied with sub-paragraphs (a) and (b) above.

(3) Where a legal representative wishes to apply for a review of the assessment of the Area Director or appeal against a decision of the area committee under regulation 105 and the assisted person has exercised his right to make representations prior to the assessment, the legal representative shall notify the assisted person of the decision to be reviewed or appealed, the grounds of appeal and his right to make further representations.

Amended by the Civil Legal Aid (General) (Amendment) (No. 3) Regulations 1991 (S.I. 1991 No. 2784).

Agreement in respect of costs*

106.—*(1) Where, in proceedings to which an assisted person (or a former assisted person) has been a party and which have been brought to an end by a judgment, decree or final order, there has been an agreement as to the costs to be paid by any other party to the assisted person (or former assisted person) which that person's solicitor and counsel (if any) is willing to accept in full satisfaction of the costs of the work done, the amount of those costs shall be assessed by the Area Director.*

(2) Where costs are to be assessed in the circumstances specified in paragraph (1), the Area Director may, if he thinks fit, request the taxing officer of the court in which the proceedings were conducted to assess the costs on the standard basis without a taxation.

* Regulation 106 is omitted by the Civil Legal Aid (General) (Amendment) Regulations 1994 (S.I. 1994 No. 229) which apply to proceedings in respect of which a civil legal aid certificate is granted on or after February 25, 1994.

(3) Paragraphs (4) to (8) of regulation 105 shall apply where costs are assessed by an Area Director under paragraph (1) as they apply to an assessment under that regulation.

Assessment and taxation where agreed costs have been paid

106A.—(1) In the circumstances described in paragraph (2) below, there shall be no taxation or assessment except in accordance with this regulation.

(2) The circumstances are—

   (a) where proceedings to which an assisted person has been a party are, as regards an assisted person (other than a person referred to in Order 62, rule 16 of the Rules of the Supreme Court 1965), settled without any direction of the court as to costs on terms including a provision for the payment of agreed costs in favour of the assisted person;

   (b) where proceedings to which an assisted person has been a party are brought to an end by a judgment, decree or final order and there has been agreement as to the costs to be paid in favour of the assisted person; or

   (c) where the retainer of an assisted person's solicitor or counsel is determined in circumstances to which regulation 105(2) refers and there is an agreement for the payment of agreed costs in favour of the assisted person,

and the agreed costs have been paid.

(3) The assisted person's solicitor may apply to the Area Director for an assessment limited to legal aid only costs if the solicitor is of the opinion that the amount of those costs, when determined, including counsel's fees (if any) would not be more than £1,000.

(4) The assisted person's solicitor may apply for a taxation under regulation 107A(2) limited to legal aid only costs if the solicitor is of the opinion that the amount of those costs, when determined, including counsel's fees (if any) would be more than £500.

(5) Before any assessment of taxation under paragraphs (3) or (4), the assisted person's solicitor shall confirm in writing to the relevant authority that the agreed costs have been paid.

(6) The relevant authority may require the production of any information which it considers relevant for the purposes of discharging its functions with respect to a determination under this regulation.

(7) Paragraphs (4) to (8) of regulation 105 shall apply where costs are assessed by an Area Director under paragraph (3) above as they apply under that regulation.

Inserted by the Civil Legal Aid (General) (Amendment) Regulations 1994 (S.I. 1994 No. 229) which apply to proceedings in respect of which a civil legal aid certificate is granted on or after February 25, 1994.

Taxation of costs*

107.—(1) The costs of proceedings to which an assisted person is a party

* The words in bold replaced the words in italic in accordance with the Civil Legal Aid (General) (Amendment) Regulations 1994 (S.I. 1994 No. 229) which apply to proceedings in respect of which a civil legal aid certificate is granted on or after February 25, 1994.

shall be taxed in accordance with any direction or order given or made in the proceedings irrespective of the interest (if any) of the assisted person in the taxation; and, for the purpose of these Regulations, an order for the taxation of the costs of a review of taxation or of the costs of an appeal from a decision of a judge on such a review shall be deemed to be a final order.

(2) Any certificate or notice of revocation or discharge, or a copy of any such certificate or notice, shall be made available on the taxation.

(3) Where in any proceedings to which an assisted person is a party—

(a) judgment is signed in default, the judgment shall include a direction that the costs of any assisted person shall be taxed *on the standard basis*;

(b) the court gives judgment or makes a final decree or order in the proceedings, the judgment, decree or order shall include a direction (in addition to any other direction as to taxation) that the costs of any assisted person shall be taxed **under regulation 107A(2)** *on the standard basis*;

(c) the plaintiff accepts money paid into court, the costs of any assisted person shall be taxed **under regulation 107A(2)** *on the standard basis.*

(4) Where in any proceedings to which an assisted person or a former assisted person is a party and—

(a) the proceedings are, or have been, brought to an end without a direction having been given, whether under paragraph (3) or otherwise, as to the assisted person's costs being taxed **under regulation 107A(2)** *on the standard basis*; or

(b) a judgment or order in favour of an opposing party, which includes a direction that the assisted person's costs be so taxed, has not been drawn up or, as the case may be, entered by him; or

(c) a retainer is determined under regulation 83 in such circumstances as to require a taxation in accordance with the provisions of these Regulations;

the costs of that person shall be taxed **under regulation 107A(2)** *on the standard basis* on production of a copy of the notice of discharge or revocation of the certificate at the appropriate taxing office.

Basis of Taxation

107A.—(1) This regulation applies on any assessment, review or taxation of the costs of an assisted person in proceedings where the costs are, or may be, paid out of the fund.

(2) Costs to which this regulation applies shall be determined on the standard basis subject to—

(a) the Legal Aid in Civil Proceedings (Remuneration) Regulations 1994 in proceedings to which those Regulations apply;

(b) the Legal Aid in Family Proceedings (Remuneration) Regulations 1991 in proceedings to which those Regulations apply.

(3) Any assessment, review or taxation under this Regulation shall—

(a) subject to the provisions of sub-paragraphs (a) and (b) of paragraph (2), be in accordance with Part XII of these Regulations;

421

(b) be conducted together with any determination of the costs of the proceedings required in accordance with any direction or order given or
made in the proceedings.

Inserted by the Civil Legal Aid (General) (Amendment) Regulations 1994 (S.I. 1994
No. 229) which apply to proceedings in respect of which a civil legal aid certificate is
granted on or after February 25, 1994.

Recovery of costs

107B.—(1) Where an agreement or order provides for costs to be paid by any
other party (in this regulation referred to as "the paying party") in favour of
the assisted person, the assisted person's solicitor may recover a sum in
respect of costs from the paying party subject to the provisions of this regulation and regulation 91(2B).

(2) The costs which the assisted person's solicitor may recover by virtue of
this regulation shall not exceed the total of the sums referred to in sub-paragraphs (c) and (d) of regulation 92(1).

(3) The assisted person's legal representatives shall not be prevented from
recovering from the paying party the sums in respect of costs to which this
regulation refers by

(a) any rule of law which limits the costs recoverable by a party to proceedings to the amount which he is liable to pay his legal representatives; or

(b) regulation 64 (restriction on payment otherwise than from the fund).

(4) Subject to reimbursement of the Board in respect of costs to which regulation 92(1)(b) refers and any interest thereon, any costs recovered from the
paying party by virtue of this Regulation shall belong to the solicitor.

Inserted by the Civil Legal Aid (General) (Amendment) Regulations 1994 (S.I. 1994
No. 229) which apply to proceedings in respect of which a civil legal aid certificate is
granted on or after February 25, 1994.

Failure to apply for taxation

108. Where, in any proceedings to which a former assisted person was a
party, an order or agreement was made for the payment to him of costs and he
has failed to ask for the costs to be taxed or his certificate is discharged before
taxation, the Board may authorise the making of the application for taxation
on his behalf and the costs of the application and of taxation shall be deemed
to be costs in the proceedings to which the certificate related.

Disallowance or reduction of costs

109.—(1) Without prejudice to section 51(6) of the Supreme Court Act 1981,
Order 62, rules 10 and 11 of the Rules of the Supreme Court 1965 or to Order
38, rule 1(3) of the County Court Rules, on any taxation of an assisted person's
costs in connection with proceedings (which are not authorised summary
proceedings) any wasted costs shall be disallowed or reduced, and where the
solicitor has without good reason delayed putting in his bill for taxation the
whole of the costs may be disallowed or reduced.

(2) No costs shall be disallowed or reduced under paragraph (1) until notice
has been served by the taxing officer on the solicitor whose name appears on
the assisted person's certificate and, in a case where those costs relate to
counsel's fees, on the assisted person's counsel, requiring the solicitor or, as
the case may be, counsel to show cause orally or in writing why those costs
should not be disallowed or reduced.

(3) In this regulation "wasted costs" has the same meaning as in section 51(7) of the Supreme Court Act 1981.

Solicitor's duty to safeguard the interests of the fund

110. It shall be the duty of an assisted person's solicitor to safeguard the interests of the fund on any inter partes taxation pursuant to an order for costs made in favour of the assisted person where that person may himself have no interest in the result of the taxation, and for this purpose to take such steps as may appear to the solicitor to be necessary to obtain a review of taxation under regulation 113 or 114.

Costs of applications, reports, etc., under these Regulations

111. Costs incurred by reason of any application made under Part VIII, and of any report made by an assisted person's solicitor under Part IX, of these Regulations shall be taxed **under regulation 107A(2)** *on the standard basis* and costs incurred by reason of regulation 25, 50, 54, 82 or 124 shall be costs in the cause.

The words in bold replaced the words in italic in accordance with the Civil Legal Aid (General) (Amendment) Regulations 1994 (S.I. 1994 No. 229) which apply to proceedings in respect of which a civil legal aid certificate is granted on or after February 25, 1994.

Duty to inform counsel

112.—(1) The assisted person's solicitor shall within seven days after the taxation (or provisional taxation) notify counsel in writing where the fees claimed on his behalf have been reduced or disallowed on taxation, and shall endorse the bill of costs with the date on which such notice was given or that no such notice is necessary.

(2) Where the bill of costs is endorsed that no notice under paragraph (1) is necessary, the taxing officer may issue the certificate or allocatur but, where such a notice has been given, the taxing officer shall not issue the certificate or allocatur until 14 days have elapsed from the date so endorsed.

Application to carry in objections to the taxation

113.—(1) In this regulation, in regulation 114 and in regulation 116, "legal aid taxation" means the taxation **under regulation 107A(2)** of a solicitor's bill to his own client where that bill is to be paid out of the fund.

(2) Where—

   (a) an assisted person is dissatisfied with any decision of a taxing officer *(except a decision under regulation 106)* as to the amount which he is entitled to recover by virtue of an order or agreement for costs made in his favour or for which he is liable by virtue of an order for costs made against him; or

   (b) the assisted person's solicitor is dissatisfied with any decision of the taxing officer:

   (i) on an inter partes taxation pursuant to an order for costs made in favour of the assisted person, or
   (ii) on a legal aid taxation,

the solicitor shall apply to the appropriate area committee for authority to carry in objections to the taxation; and if the area committee gives authority (but not otherwise) the solicitor may carry in objections in accordance with rules of court.

The words in bold in regulation 113(1) and in italic in regulation 113(2)(a) were respectively inserted and omitted by the Civil Legal Aid (General) (Amendment) Regulations 1994 (S.I. 1994 No. 229) which apply to proceedings in respect of which a civil legal aid certificate is issued on or after February 25, 1994.

Application to judge to review taxation

114. Where the assisted person or his solicitor, as the case may be, is dissatisfied with the decision of the taxing officer on any matter to which objection has been taken under regulation 113, the solicitor shall apply to the Board for authority to have the taxation reviewed; and, if the Board gives authority (but not otherwise), the solicitor may apply (or instruct counsel to apply) to a judge to review the taxation in accordance with rules of court.

Appeal from review of taxation

115.—(1) Subject to paragraph (2) and notwithstanding that the assisted person may have no interest in the appeal or would, but for regulation 118, have an interest adverse to that of his solicitor, an assisted person's solicitor:

    (a) may, with the authority of the Board, appeal from the decision of the judge on a review of taxation under regulation 114; or

    (b) shall be entitled to be heard on an appeal brought by any other party,

and, on any such appeal, the solicitor may appear by counsel.

(2) Nothing in this regulation shall be deemed to confer a right of appeal in proceedings to which an assisted person is not a party where no such right exists.

(3) Where an assisted person's solicitor applies for authority under paragraph (1), he shall do so before the expiration of the time allowed by rules of court for an appeal from the decision of a judge and, for this purpose, the time so allowed shall be extended by two months.

Amended by the Civil Legal Aid (General) (Amendment) (No. 2) Regulations 1994.

Counsel dissatisfied with taxation

116.—(1) Where counsel acting for an assisted person is dissatisfied with any decision on a legal aid taxation, it shall be the duty of the assisted person's solicitor to report the matter to the appropriate area committee or to the Board, as the case may be, and, if the committee or the Board give authority to do so—

    (a) to carry in objections to the taxation;

    (b) to apply to a judge to review the taxation; or

    (c) to appeal from the decision of the judge,

as the case may be, and regulations 113 to 115 and 120 shall apply as if the solicitor were the person dissatisfied.

(2) Paragraph (1) shall apply to a provisional taxation with the necessary modifications and in particular with the insertion of the words "to inform the taxing officer that he wishes to be heard on the taxation and to attend on the taxation," after the words "the assisted person's solicitor."

Objection by other party

117. If, in proceedings to which an assisted person is a party, any other party carries in objections to the inter partes taxation or applies to a judge to review that taxation, the assisted person's solicitor may be heard on the objections or review notwithstanding that the assisted person himself may have no interest in the taxation.

Assisted person having no interest or adverse interest in taxation

118. Where the assisted person has no interest in the taxation or would, but for the provisions of this regulation, have an interest adverse to that of his solicitor—

(a) it shall be the duty of the solicitor carrying in objections under regulation 113 or applying for a review under regulation 114 to ensure that all matters which are proper to be taken into account in consideration of the objections or on the review are placed before the taxing officer or the judge, as the case may be;

(b) the assisted person shall not be required to make any contribution to the fund on account of the costs of any proceedings arising under regulations 113 to 117 or in consequence of any order made in such proceedings; and

(c) the charge created by section 16(6) of the Act shall not apply in relation to any resulting increase in the net liability of the fund arising out of the costs of any proceedings under regulations 113 to 117 or in consequence of any order made in such proceedings.

Assisted person having financial interest in taxation

119.—(1) Where the assisted person has a financial interest in the taxation it shall be the duty of his solicitor:

(a) to supply him with a copy of his bill;

(b) to inform him of the extent of his financial interest and the steps which can be taken to safeguard that interest and, if the assisted person so requests, to give notice in accordance with rules of court to the taxing officer that the assisted person has such an interest; and

(c) to endorse on the bill that the assisted person has a financial interest in the taxation and that he has complied with sub-paragraphs (a) and (b) above.

(2) Where the assisted person has a financial interest in the taxation he shall not be required to make any contribution to the fund on account of the costs of the taxation proceedings and the charge created by section 16(6) of the Act shall not apply in relation to any resulting increase in the net liability of the fund arising out of the costs of the taxation proceedings.

Amended by the Civil Legal Aid (General) (Amendment) (No. 3) Regulations 1991 (S.I. 1991 No. 2784).

Costs to be paid out of the fund

120. Any proceedings under regulations 113 to 119 shall be deemed to be proceedings to which the assisted person's certificate relates, whether or not it has been discharged or revoked, and the costs of such proceedings shall be paid out of the fund.

Time limits, etc.

121.—(1) Subject to regulation 112 where any party to a taxation is an assisted person, the certificate or allocatur shall not, unless the parties agree, be signed until 21 days after the taxing officer's decision; and where an assisted person's solicitor applies under regulation 113, 114 or 115 (or under regulation 116) for authority to carry in objections or to have a taxation reviewed, he shall do so before the expiration of the time allowed under rules of court for applying to the taxing officer for review of the taxation and the time so allowed shall, for this purpose, be extended by two months, or such longer period as the taxing officer may allow.

(2) Notice of any application made under regulation 113, 114, 115 or 116 shall be given to the taxing officer and to any opposing party.

Amended by the Civil Legal Aid (General) (Amendment) (No. 2) Regulations 1994.

Appointment of solicitor to intervene

122.—(1) The Lord Chancellor may appoint a solicitor to intervene in any review by a judge of a taxation of the costs of proceedings to which an assisted person is a party, and any such appointment may be made in respect of a particular review or may extend to any review of taxation during the period for which the solicitor is appointed.

(2) Whenever the Board gives authority to an assisted person's solicitor to apply to a judge to review a taxation, it shall notify the Lord Chancellor and inform him of the name and address of the assisted person's solicitor.

(3) If, in proceedings to which an assisted person is a party, any other party applies to a judge to review the inter partes taxation or the assisted person's solicitor applies to a judge to review any such taxation as is referred to in regulation 113, the assisted person's solicitor shall so inform the Board and the Board shall notify the Lord Chancellor and inform him of the name and address of the assisted person's solicitor and, where the subject of the review is an inter partes taxation, the name and address of the solicitor acting for the other party.

(4) The solicitor appointed by the Lord Chancellor to intervene in a review of taxation shall be entitled to production of all documents relevant to the matters in issue before the judge and to delivery of copies thereof and to appear by counsel and be heard on the review, with a view to ensuring that all considerations which are proper to be taken into account are placed before the court, whether they relate to the interests of the fund or of the assisted person or to the remuneration of solicitors and counsel acting for assisted persons.

(5) On any review in which a solicitor appointed by the Lord Chancellor has intervened, the judge may make such order as may be just for the payment to or by that solicitor of the costs incurred by him or any other party, and any sum due to the solicitor by virtue of any such order shall be paid by him to the Board and any sum so payable by the solicitor shall be paid out of the fund, and the solicitor shall be entitled to receive from the fund the costs he has incurred on the intervention.

(6) A solicitor appointed by the Lord Chancellor under paragraph (1) may appeal from the decision of the judge on a review of taxation under regulation 115 and paragraphs (2) to (5) above shall apply to such an appeal as it applies to a review.

PART XIII

COSTS AWARDED AGAINST AN ASSISTED PERSON

Security for costs given by assisted person

123. Where in any proceedings an assisted person is required to give security for costs, the amount of such security shall not exceed the amount which could be ordered under section 17(1) of the Act.

Assisted person's liability for costs

124.—(1) Where proceedings have been concluded in which an assisted person (including, for the purpose of this regulation, a person who was an assisted person in respect of those proceedings) is liable or would have been liable for costs if he had not been an assisted person, no costs attributable to the period during which his certificate was in force shall be recoverable from him until the court has determined the amount of his liability in accordance with section 17(1) of the Act.

(2) Where the assisted person's certificate does not relate to, or has been amended so that it no longer relates to the whole of the proceedings, the court shall nevertheless make a determination under section 17(1) of the Act in respect of that part of the proceedings to which the certificate relates.

(3) The amount of an assisted person's liability for costs shall be determined by the court which tried or heard the proceedings.

Affidavit of means by unassisted party

125.—(1) Any person, not being himself an assisted person, who is a party to proceedings (other than authorised summary proceedings) to which an assisted person is a party, may file in the appropriate court office or registry an affidavit exhibiting a statement setting out the rate of his own income and amount of his own capital and any other facts relevant to the determination of his means in accordance with section 17(1) of the Act.

(2) Any person filing an affidavit under paragraph (1) shall serve a copy of it, together with the exhibit, upon the assisted person's solicitor, who shall forthwith serve him with a copy of the certificate and shall send a copy of the affidavit to the Area Director.

Determination of liability for costs

126. In determining the amount of the assisted person's liability for costs—

(a) his dwelling-house, clothes, household furniture and the tools and implements of his trade shall be left out of account to the like extent as they are left out of account by the assessment officer in determining his disposable income and disposable capital; and

(b) any document which may have been sent to the court office or registry or filed or exhibited under these Regulations shall, subject to regulation 128, be evidence of the fact stated therein.

Postponement, adjournment or referral of determination

127. The court may, if it thinks fit—

(a) postpone or adjourn the determination for such time and to such place (including chambers) as the court thinks fit; or

(b) refer to a master, registrar or the Clerk of the Parliaments or (in the case of an appeal from a decision of the Crown Court or a court of summary jurisdiction) to the chief clerk or clerk to the justices of the court from which the appeal is brought, for investigation (in chambers or elsewhere) any question of fact relevant to the determination, and require him to report his findings on that question to the court.

Oral examination of parties

128.—(1) The court may, if it thinks fit, order the assisted person and any party who has filed an affidavit pursuant to regulation 125 to attend for oral examination as to his means and as to any other facts (whether stated in any document before the court or otherwise) which may be relevant to the determination of the amount of the assisted person's liability for costs and may permit any party to give evidence and call witnesses.

(2) Where the court has made an order under regulation 127(b), the person to whom the matter has been referred for investigation may exercise the power conferred on the court by this regulation.

Order for costs

129. The court may direct—

    (a) that payment under the order for costs shall be limited to such amount, payable in instalments or otherwise (including an amount to be determined on taxation), as the court thinks reasonable having regard to all the circumstances; or

    (b) where the court thinks it reasonable that no payment should be made immediately or that the assisted person should have no liability for payment, that payment under the order for costs be suspended either until such date as the court may determine or indefinitely.

Variation of order for costs

130. The party in whose favour an order for costs is made may, within six years from the date on which it was made, apply to the court for the order to be varied on the ground that—

    (a) material additional information as to the assisted person's means, being information which could not have been obtained by that party with reasonable diligence at the time the order was made, is available; or

    (b) there has been a change in the assisted person's circumstances since the date of the order;

and on any such application the order may be varied as the court thinks fit; but save as aforesaid the determination of the court shall be final.

Assisted person acting in representative, fiduciary or official capacity

131. Where an order for costs is made against an assisted person who is concerned in the proceedings in a representative, fiduciary or official capacity, he shall have the benefit of section 17(1) of the Act and his personal resources shall not (unless there is reason to the contrary) be taken into account for that purpose, but regard shall be had to the value of the property or estate, or the amount of the fund out of which he is entitled to be indemnified.

Assisted person a minor

132. Where a minor is an assisted person, his means for the purpose of determining his liability for costs under section 17(1) of the Act shall be taken as including the means of any person whose resources have been taken into account under the Civil Legal Aid (Assessment of Resources) Regulations 1989 by the assessment officer in assessing the disposable income and disposable capital of the minor.

Order against next friend or guardian ad litem

133. Where an order for costs is made against a next friend or guardian *ad* *litem* of an assisted person who is a minor or patient, he shall have the benefit of section 17(1) of the Act as it applies to an assisted person and the means of the next friend or guardian *ad litem* shall, for the purposes of regulation 132, be taken as being the means of the minor or, as the case may be, of the patient.

PART XIV

COSTS OF UNASSISTED PARTIES OUT OF THE FUND

Time and form of application

134.—(1) An application for an order under section 18 of the Act may be made at any time and in any manner in which an application for an order for costs might be made in respect of the same proceedings if none of the parties were receiving legal aid.

(2) Any proceedings in respect of which a separate certificate could properly be issued shall be treated as separate proceedings for the purposes of section 18 of the Act.

Unassisted party acting in representative, fiduciary or official capacity

135. Where an unassisted party is concerned in proceedings only in a representative, fiduciary or official capacity, then for the purposes of section 18(4)(b) of the Act the court shall not take into account his personal resources, but shall have regard to the value of the property, estate or fund out of which the unassisted party is entitled to be indemnified and may in its discretion also have regard to the resources of the persons, if any, including the unassisted party where appropriate, who are beneficially interested in that property, estate or fund.

Appearance by unassisted party and Area Director

136.—(1) The unassisted party and the Area Director may appear at any hearing or inquiry under Parts XIII and XIV of these Regulations.

(2) The Area Director may, instead of appearing, submit written representations concerning the application and such representations shall be:

(a) supported by an affidavit sworn by the Area Director; and

(b) sent to the proper officer of the court, with a copy to the unassisted party, not less than seven days before the hearing or inquiry to which they relate.

Applications in respect of magistrates' court proceedings

137.—(1) Where an application for an order under section 18 of the Act is made in respect of authorised summary proceedings, the court, instead of making an order forthwith, may in its discretion either—

(a) adjourn the hearing of the application; or

(b) dismiss the application.

(2) If the court adjourns the hearing of the application, the unassisted party shall swear an affidavit of costs and resources containing the matters specified in Schedule 2, which he shall produce at the adjourned hearing and, not less than 21 days before the adjourned hearing, the unassisted party shall serve notice of the date and time of the hearing on the Area Director, with a copy of his affidavit of costs and resources together with any exhibits and supporting documents.

Applications in respect of county court proceedings

138. On application for an order under section 18 of the Act made in respect of proceedings in or on appeal from a county court, the court shall not make an order under that section forthwith, but may in its discretion—

(a) refer the application to the registrar for hearing and determination; or

(b) adjourn the application; or

(c) dismiss the application,

and, in this regulation and regulations 139 to 142, "registrar" means the registrar of the county court in which the proceedings were tried or determined or from which the appeal was brought.

Procedure where application referred to registrar for determination

139. Where a court in accordance with regulation 138(a) refers an application to the registrar for hearing and determination—

(a) the provisions of regulation 142 shall apply as if the registrar were the court and the court had adjourned the hearing of the application to a date to be fixed; and

(b) the unassisted party or the Area Director may appeal to the judge on a point of law from the registrar's determination within 14 days of the date on which it was given.

Reference to registrar for inquiry and report

140. The court may, if it adjourns the hearing of an application in accordance with regulation 138(b), make an order referring it to the registrar for inquiry and report; and, if such an order is made—

(a) the court shall serve a copy of its order on the unassisted party;

(b) within 21 days of the court making its order (or such longer time as the court may allow), the unassisted party shall file an affidavit of costs and resources (with any exhibits and supporting documents) together with a copy; and

(c) the court shall serve a copy of its order and of the unassisted party's affidavit of costs and resources filed under sub-paragraph (b) on the Area Director.

Procedure on inquiry and report

141.—(1) As soon as a copy of the order of the court and the affidavit of costs and resources have been served on the Area Director in accordance with regulation 140(1)(c), the registrar shall give the unassisted party and the Area Director not less than 21 days' notice of the date and time when he proposes to conduct his inquiry.

(2) In exercising his functions under this regulation, the registrar shall have the same powers as a taxing officer has in the exercise of his functions under the County Court Rules 1981.

(3) On completing his inquiry, the registrar shall report to the court in writing, and shall at the same time send a copy of his report to the unassisted party and the Area Director.

(4) When the court has received the registrar's report, it shall give the unassisted party and the Area Director 21 days' notice of the day appointed for the hearing and determination of the application in chambers.

Procedure where application adjourned

142. If the court adjourns the hearing of an application in accordance with regulation 138(b) but does not refer it to the registrar for inquiry and report:

(a) within 21 days of the adjournment, the unassisted party shall file an affidavit of costs and resources (with any exhibits and supporting documents) together with a copy; and

(b) not less than 21 days before the adjourned hearing, the court shall serve on the Area Director notice of the date fixed together with a copy of the affidavit of costs and resources filed under sub-paragraph (a).

Applications in respect of proceedings in the Supreme Court and House of Lords

143.—(1) On an application for an order under section 18 of the Act made in respect of proceedings in the Supreme Court (except proceedings on appeal from a county court) or in the House of Lords, the court shall not make an order forthwith, but may in its discretion—

(a) refer the application to a master or registrar for hearing and determination; or

(b) adjourn the hearing of the application; or

(c) dismiss the application,

and, in relation to proceedings in the Court of Appeal, "registrar" means the registrar of civil appeals, or, in respect of appeals from the Employment Appeal Tribunal or from the Restrictive Practices Court, the registrar of that Tribunal or Court, as the case may be.

(2) Where the application is referred to a registrar under paragraph (1)(a), the provisions of regulations 139 and 142 shall apply with any necessary modifications.

Procedure where application referred to master for determination

144. Where the court in accordance with regulation 143(1)(a) refers the application to a master for hearing and determination—

(a) the provisions of regulation 147 shall apply as if the master were the court and the court had adjourned the hearing of the application to a date to be fixed; and

(b) the master shall have the same powers as a taxing officer has in the exercise of his functions under Order 62 of the Rules of the Supreme Court 1965; and

(c) the unassisted party or the Area Director may appeal to a judge in chambers on a point of law within 14 days from the determination of the master.

Reference to master for inquiry and report

145. The court may, if it adjourns the hearing of an application in accordance with regulation 143(1)(b), make an order referring it to the master for inquiry and report; and if, such an order is made, then within 21 days of the court making the order (or such longer time as the master may allow) the unassisted party shall:

(a) file an affidavit of costs and resources;

(b) lodge a copy of the order of the court and of his affidavit of costs and resources, together with original exhibits and any other documents necessary to support the affidavit, with the master; and at the same time

(c) serve a copy of the order of the court and of his affidavit of costs and resources (and of any exhibits and supporting documents) on the Area Director.

Procedure on inquiry and report

146.—(1) Where the unassisted party has complied with the requirements of regulation 145, the master shall give the unassisted party and the Area Director not less than 21 days' notice of the date and time when he proposes to conduct his inquiry.

(2) In exercising his functions under this regulation, the master shall have the same powers as a taxing officer has in the exercise of his functions under Order 62 of the Rules of the Supreme Court 1965.

(3) On completing his inquiry, the master shall report to the court in writing, and shall at the same time send a copy of his report to the unassisted party and to the Area Director.

(4) When the court has received the report of the master, the unassisted party shall seek an appointment for the hearing and determination of the application in chambers, and shall give the Area Director not less than 21 days' notice of the date and time so fixed.

Procedure where application adjourned

147. If the court adjourns the hearing of an application in accordance with regulation 143 but does not refer it for inquiry and report, then—

(a) within 21 days of the adjournment, the unassisted party shall file an affidavit of costs and resources together with original exhibits and any other documents necessary to support the affidavit; and

(b) not less than 21 days before the adjourned hearing, the unassisted party shall serve notice on the Area Director of the date and time of the adjourned hearing together with a copy of his affidavit of costs and resources (and of any exhibits and supporting documents).

PART XV

PARTICULAR COURTS AND TRIBUNALS

The Lands Tribunal

148.—(1) In this regulation—

"the tribunal" means the Lands Tribunal established by section 1(1)(b) of the Lands Tribunal Act 1949 and

"the registrar" means the registrar of the tribunal.

(2) Except in so far as otherwise provided by this regulation, these Regulations shall apply to applications for legal aid for proceedings in the tribunal

and in the conduct of all proceedings in it for which a certificate is granted in like manner as they apply to applications for legal aid for, and the conduct of, proceedings in any court.

(3) Where any power to do any act or exercise any jurisdiction or discretion is conferred by these Regulations on a court it shall be exercised by the tribunal and may, unless it is exercisable only during the hearing of the proceedings, be exercised by the registrar.

(4) Notwithstanding anything in regulation 105 or 107, the following provisions shall have effect in relation to proceedings in the tribunal to which an assisted person is a party:

(a) where a final decision is given in writing by the tribunal, it shall, in addition to any direction as to costs, contain a direction that the costs of any assisted person shall be taxed on the standard basis and the costs shall be so taxed by the registrar;

(b) where the proceedings are brought to an end without a direction having been given under sub-paragraph (a), the costs of any assisted person shall be taxed by the registrar on the standard basis; and

(c) in taxing the costs of any assisted person the registrar shall have power to determine as the appropriate scale for the taxation, one of the scales of costs for the time being prescribed by the County Court Rules 1981.

The Employment Appeal Tribunal

149.—(1) In this regulation—

"the Appeal Tribunal" means the Employment Appeal Tribunal established under section 135(1) of the Employment Protection (Consolidation) Act 1988; and

"the registrar" means the registrar of the Appeal Tribunal and includes any officer of the Appeal Tribunal authorised to act on behalf of the registrar.

(2) Except in so far as otherwise provided by this regulation, these Regulations shall apply to applications for legal aid for proceedings in the Appeal Tribunal and to the conduct of all proceedings in it for which a certificate is granted, in the same way as they apply to applications for legal aid for, and the conduct of, proceedings in any court.

(3) Where any power to do any act or exercise any jurisdiction or discretion is conferred by these Regulations on a court, it shall in relation to proceedings in the Appeal Tribunal, be exercised by the Tribunal and may, unless it is exercisable only during the hearing of the proceedings by a judge or member of the Appeal Tribunal or by the Appeal Tribunal as required to be constituted by paragraph 16 of Schedule 11 to the Employment Protection (Consolidation) Act 1978, be exercised by the registrar.

(4) Where it appears to the Area Director that an application for a certificate relates to proceedings in the Appeal Tribunal which are likely to be conducted in Scotland, he shall transmit the application forthwith to the Chief Executive of the Legal Aid Board in Scotland and shall notify the applicant and his solicitor accordingly.

(5) Where it appears to the Area Director doubtful whether the proceedings to which an application for a certificate relates will be conducted in the Appeal Tribunal in England and Wales or in Scotland, he shall request the

registrar to determine that question and that determination shall be binding upon the Area Director.

(6) Where a certificate has been issued and there is a change of circumstances regarding the conduct of the proceedings in that, by direction of the Appeal Tribunal, they will be wholly or partly conducted in Scotland—

(a) the certificate shall remain in force;

(b) the assisted person shall continue to be represented in the proceedings in Scotland by the solicitor who represented him in England and that solicitor may instruct either a member of the English or the Scottish Bar; and

(c) no question as to the propriety of appearing in Scotland shall be raised on a taxation or on an assessment in accordance with regulation 105.

(7) The costs of an assisted person in respect of proceedings in the Appeal Tribunal shall be assessed in accordance with regulation 105 or taxed on the standard basis by a taxing master of the Supreme Court and the provisions of Order 62 of the Rules of the Supreme Court 1965 shall apply, with the necessary modifications, to the taxation of those costs as if the proceedings in the Appeal Tribunal were a cause or matter in the Supreme Court.

The Commons Commissioners

150.—(1) In this regulation, "a commissioner" means a Commons Commissioner appointed under section 17(1) of the Commons Registration Act 1965.

(2) Except in so far as otherwise provided by this regulation, these Regulations shall apply to applications for legal aid for proceedings before a commissioner and to the conduct of all proceedings before him for which a certificate is granted, in the same way as they apply to applications for legal aid for, and the conduct of, proceedings in any court.

(3) Where any power to do any act or exercise any jurisdiction or discretion is conferred on a court by these Regulations, it shall, in relation to proceedings before a commissioner, be exercised by him.

(4) The costs of an assisted person in respect of proceedings before a commissioner shall be taxed (or assessed) as if they were costs of proceedings in a county court.

The Restrictive Practices Court

151.—(1) In this regulation—

"the Court" means the Court established by section 1 of the Restrictive Practices Court Act 1976, and

"the proper officer of the Court" shall have the same meaning as in the Restrictive Practices Court Rules 1976.

(2) Except in so far as otherwise provided by this regulation, these Regulations shall apply to applications for legal aid for proceedings in the Court under Part III of the Fair Trading Act 1973 and to any proceedings in the Court in consequence of an order made, or undertaking given to the Court, under that Part of the Act, and to the Conduct of all such proceedings for which a certificate is granted, in the same way as they apply to applications for legal aid for, and the conduct of, proceedings in any court.

(3) Where any power to do any act or exercise any jurisdiction or discretion

is conferred by these Regulations on a court it shall in relation to proceedings in the Court be exercised by that Court and may, unless it is exercisable only during the hearing of any proceedings by a judge or by the Court, be exercisable by the proper officer of the Court.

(4) Where it appears to the Area Director that an application for a certificate relates to proceedings in the Court which are likely to be conducted in Scotland or Northern Ireland, he shall transmit the application forthwith to the Chief Executive of the Legal Aid Board in Scotland or the Secretary of the Legal Aid Department of the Incorporated Law Society of Northern Ireland, as the case may be, and shall notify the applicant and his solicitor accordingly.

(5) Where it appears to the Area Director doubtful whether the proceedings to which an application for a certificate relates will be conducted in the Court in England and Wales or in Scotland or Northern Ireland, he shall request the proper officer of the Court to determine that question and that determination shall be binding upon the Area Director.

(6) Where a certificate has been issued and there is a change of circumstances regarding the conduct of the proceedings in that, by order of the Court, they will be wholly or partly conducted in Scotland or Northern Ireland—

(a) the certificate shall remain in force; and

(b) for any proceedings in Scotland—

    (i) the assisted person shall continue to be represented in the proceedings by the solicitor who represented him in England and Wales and that solicitor may instruct a member of the English or the Scottish Bar; and

    (ii) as to the propriety of appearing in Scotland shall be raised on a taxation or on an assessment in accordance with regulation 105; and

(c) for any proceedings in Northern Ireland, the assisted person shall continue to be represented in the proceedings by the solicitor who represented him in England and Wales and that solicitor shall instruct as his agent a solicitor on the panel maintained by the Incorporated Law Society of Northern Ireland of solicitors willing to act for assisted persons before the Court.

(7) The costs of an assisted person in respect of proceedings in the Court shall be assessed in accordance with regulation 105 or taxed on the standard basis by a taxing master of the Supreme Court, and the provisions of Order 62 of the Rules of the Supreme Court 1965 shall apply, with the necessary modifications, to the taxation of those costs as if the proceedings in the Court were a cause or matter in the Supreme Court.

PART XVI

REPRESENTATION BY MEANS OF CONTRACTS

Extent of power to contract

152.—(1) The classes of case in respect of which the Board may enter contracts for the provision of representation under Part IV of the Act shall be any proceedings for the time being specified in Part I of Schedule 2 to the Act except—

(a) proceedings listed at 5. or 6. of Part I of that Schedule;

(b) proceedings for the time being specified in Part II of that Schedule.

Substituted by the Civil Legal Aid (General) (Amendment) (No. 2) Regulations 1994.

SCHEDULES

SCHEDULE 1

REGULATIONS REVOKED

Title	Reference
The Legal Aid (General) Regulations 1980	S.I. 1980/1894
The Legal Aid (General) (Amendment) Regulations 1981	S.I. 1981/173
The Legal Aid (General) (Amendment) Regulations 1982	S.I. 1982/1892
The Legal Aid (General) (Amendment) Regulations 1983	S.I. 1983/424
The Legal Aid (General) (Amendment) (No. 2) Regulations 1983	S.I. 1983/1483
The Legal Aid (General) (Amendment) Regulations 1986	S.I. 1986/272
The Legal Aid (General) (Amendment) (No. 2) Regulations 1986	S.I. 1986/1186
The Legal Aid (General) (Amendment) (No. 3) Regulations 1986	S.I. 1986/2135
The Legal Aid (General) (Amendment) Regulations 1988	S.I. 1988/460
The Legal Aid (General) (Amendment) (No. 2) Regulations 1988	S.I. 1988/1938

SCHEDULE 2

MATTERS TO BE INCLUDED IN AN AFFIDAVIT OF COSTS AND RESOURCES

1. An estimate of the unassisted party's inter partes costs of the proceedings in respect of which his application is made, supported by—

(a) particulars of the estimated costs in the form of a summary bill of costs; and

(b) all necessary documentary evidence to substantiate each item in the bill.

2. A statement, supported by evidence, of the unassisted party's financial resources of every kind during the period beginning three years before his application is made, and of his estimated future financial resources and expectations.

3. A declaration that to the best of his knowledge and belief the unassisted party has not, and at any relevant time has not had and will not have any financial resources or expectations not specified in the statement described in paragraph 2 above.

4. A declaration that the unassisted party has not at any time deliberately forgone or deprived himself of any financial resources or expectations with a view to furthering his application.

5. A statement supported by evidence of the unassisted party's reasonable financial commitments during the period covered by his statement described in paragraph 2 above, including, if desired, his estimated solicitor and own client costs of the proceedings in respect of which his application is made.

6.—(1) If the unassisted party has, or at any relevant time has had, a spouse, his statements and declarations described in paragraphs 2 to 5 above shall also take account of and (to the best of this knowledge and belief) specify that spouse's financial resources, expectations and commitments, unless he or she had a contrary interest to the unassisted party in the proceedings in respect of which his application is made, or the unassisted party and his spouse are or at the relevant time were living separate and apart, or for some other reason it would be either inequitable or impracticable for the unassisted party to comply with the requirements of this paragraph.

(2) Paragraph (1) shall apply to a man and woman who are living with each other in the same household as husband and wife as it applies to the parties to a marriage.

7. Full particulars of any application for legal aid made by the unassisted party in connection with the proceedings in respect of which his application is made, including the date and reference number of any such application and the Area Director to whom it was made.

EXPLANATORY NOTE

(This note is not part of the Regulations)

These Regulations replace, with amendments, the Legal Aid (General) Regulations 1980 (as subsequently amended). The main changes made reflect the transfer of responsibility for administration of the legal aid scheme from the Law Society to the Legal Aid Board established by the Legal Aid Act 1988.

Other important changes are—

(a) to require an assisted person's solicitor, where the Board makes such a request, to certify that it is reasonable for the assisted person to continue to receive legal aid (regulation 70(2), (3));

(b) to make provision for payments on account of costs and fees incurred by solicitors and counsel and of disbursements (regulations 100, 101);

(c) to make fresh provision for the deferment of solicitors' profit costs (regulation 102));

(d) to provide for work done immediately prior to the issue of an emergency certificate to be deemed in certain circumstances to be work done under the certificate (regulation 103(6));

(e) to provide (subject to the transitional provision in regulation 1(3)) for the assessment of costs by Area Directors, for reviews of such assessments by area committees, and for appeals from such reviews to a committee appointed by the Board (regulations 104, 105 and 106);

(f) to require solicitors to inform counsel where counsel's fees are reduced or disallowed on assessment or taxation (regulations 105(8), 106(3) and 112); and

(g) to enable assisted persons who have a financial interest in the taxation of costs to take steps to safeguard their interest (regulation 119).

Transitional provisions—Civil Legal Aid (General) (Amendment) (No. 2) Regulations 1994:

(1) Regulations 14, 17, 18, 19 and 21 of these Regulations shall apply to all charges arising under section 16(6) of the Act, whether before or after 1st August 1994, unless—

(a) the amount charged has been paid in full to the Board before 1st August 1994; or

(b) the Board has by an agreement entered into before that date agreed to defer enforcing the charge.*

(2) Regulation 20 of these Regulations shall apply to charges registered in favour of the Board in accordance with regulation 95(3), whether before or after 1st August 1994, unless—

(a) the amount charged has been paid in full to the Board before 1st August 1994; or

(b) the Board has by an agreement entered into before that date agreed to release the charge.*

(3) The principal Regulations shall apply in the circumstances referred to in sub-paragraphs (a) and (b) of paragraphs (1) and (2) as if regulations 14 and 17 to 21 of these Regulations had not been made.

(4) Interest shall not be payable by reason only of regulations 14 and 17 to 21 of these Regulations in respect of any period before 1st August 1994.

(5) Where—

    (a) in any proceedings under Part III of the Matrimonial and Family Proceedings Act 1984 or section 30 of the Law of Property Act 1925 a sum of money is recovered or preserved for an assisted person; and

    (b) the order of the court or agreement under which the sum of money is recovered or preserved was made before 1st August 1994,

the Board shall have power to agree under regulation 96 to defer enforcement of its charge notwithstanding that the order of the court or agreement does not contain any term to the effect that the sum of money is to be used for the purpose of purchasing a home for the assisted person or his dependants.

(6) Where—

    (a) in any proceedings (other than proceedings under any of the enactments mentioned in sub-paragraphs (a) to (d) of regulation 96(1)) property is recovered or preserved for an assisted person; and

    (b) the order of the court or agreement under which the property is recovered or preserved was made before 1st August 1994,

the Board shall have power to agree under regulation 97 to defer enforcement of its charge notwithstanding that the order of the court or agreement does not contain any term to the effect that the property is to be used as a home for the assisted person or his dependants.

---

* Regulation 14 substitutes regulation 90(3) in the principal regulations.
Regulation 17 amends regulation 95(3) and inserts regulation 95(3A) in the principal regulations.
Regulations 18, 19, 20 and 21 amend regulations 96, 97, 98 and 99 respectively in the principal regulations.

Civil Legal Aid (Assessment of Resources) Regulations 1989*

Came into force April 1, 1989

ARRANGEMENT OF REGULATIONS

1. Citation and commencement.

2. Revocations.

3. Interpretation.

4. Computation of disposable income, disposable capital and contribution.

5. Subject matter of dispute.

6. Application in representative, fiduciary or official capacity.

7. Resources of spouses, etc.

8. *[Omitted]*.

9. Deprivation or conversion or resources.

10. Notification of the assessment officer's decision.

11. Duty of the person concerned to report change in financial circumstances.

---

* S.I. 1989 No. 338 as amended by the Civil Legal Aid (Assessment of Resources) (Amendment) Regulations 1990 (S.I. 1990 No. 484), the Civil Legal Aid (Assessment of Resources) (Amendment) Regulations 1991 (S.I. 1991 No. 635), the Civil Legal Aid (Assessment of Resources) (Amendment) Regulations 1992 (S.I. 1992 No. 718) and the Civil Legal Aid (Assessment of Resources) (Amendment) Regulations 1993 (S.I. 1993 No. 788), the Civil Legal Aid (Assessment of Resources) (Amendment) Regulations 1994 (S.I. 1994 No. 806), the Civil Legal Aid (Assessment of Resources) (Amendment) Regulations 1995 (S.I. No. 797), the Civil Legal Aid (Assessment of Resources) (Amendment) Regulations 1996 (S.I. 1996 No. 434), the Civil Legal Aid (Assessment of Resources) (Amendment) (No. 2) Regulations 1996 (S.I. 1996 No. 642), the Civil Legal Aid (Assessment of Resources) (Amendment) (No. 3) Regulations 1996 (S.I. 1996 No. 2309), the Civil Legal Aid (Assessment of Resources) (Amendment) Regulations 1997 (S.I. 1997 No.753) and the Civil Legal Aid (Assessment of Resources) (Amendment) Regulations 1998 (S.I. 1998 No. 664). The 1993 Amendment Regulations apply to applications for legal aid where the period of computation begins on or after 12th April 1993 but not to:
  (a) assessments, re-assessments under regulations 12 and amended assessments under regulation 14 in respect of applications where the period of computation began before 12th April 1993; and
  (b) further assessments under regulation 13 in respect of a certificate granted before 12th April 1993.
The complete paragraphs of the Regulations which are omitted by the 1993 Amendment Regulations but still apply to some cases are shown in italics.

12. Further assessments.

13. *[Omitted]*.

14. Amendment of assessment due to error or receipt of new information.

15. Power of assessment officer to estimate the resources of the person concerned.

SCHEDULES:
1. Regulations revoked.

2. Computation of income.

3. Computation of capital.

Citation and commencement

1. These Regulations may be cited as the Civil Legal Aid (Assessment of Resources) Regulations 1989 and shall come into force on April 1, 1989.

Revocations

2. The Regulations specified in Schedule 1 are hereby revoked.

Interpretation

3.—(1) In these Regulations, unless the context otherwise requires—

"the Act" means the Legal Aid Act 1988;
"area committee," "Area Director" and "assessment officer" have the meanings assigned to them by the Civil Legal Aid (General) Regulations 1989;
"certificate" means a legal aid certificate issued in accordance with the Civil Legal Aid (General) Regulations 1989;
"child" means a person—

(a) under the age that is for the time being the upper limit of compulsory school age within the meaning of the Education Act 1944; or

(b) over the limit of compulsory school age and either receiving full-time instruction at an educational establishment or undergoing training for a trade, profession; or vocation;

"contribution" has the meaning assigned to it by the Civil Legal Aid (General) Regulations 1989;
"disposable capital" and "disposable income" have the meanings assigned to them by regulation 4;
"income" includes:

(a) benefits,

(b) privileges, and

(c) any sum payable (whether voluntarily or under a court order, the terms of any instrument or otherwise) for the purpose of the maintenance of a child;

"income-based jobseeker's allowance" has the meaning given by section 1(4) of the Jobseekers Act 1995, but excludes any sum treated as payable by way of a jobseeker's allowance by virtue of section 26 of that Act *[Inserted by the Civil Legal Aid (Assessment of Resources) (Amendment) (No. 3) Regulations 1996 (S.I. 1996 No. 2309).]*;

"legal aid" means representation under Part IV of the Act;

"make an assessment," in relation to the assessment officer, means to assess the disposable income, disposable capital and contribution of the person concerned;

"period of computation" means the period of 12 months next ensuing from the date of the application for a certificate, or such other period of 12 months as in the particular circumstances of any case the assessment officer may consider to be appropriate;

"person concerned" means the person—

(a) whose disposable income and disposable capital are to be assessed or reassessed; or

(b) whose resources are to be treated as the resources of any other person under these Regulations.

(2) Any reference in these Regulations to a regulation or Schedule by number means the regulation or Schedule so numbered in these Regulations.

Amended by the Civil Legal Aid (Assessment of Resources) (Amendment) Regulations 1993 (S.I. 1993 No. 788).

Computation of disposable income, disposable capital and contribution

4.—(1) Subject to the provisions of these Regulations, the assessment officer shall—

(a) take into account the financial resources of the person concerned; and

(b) compute his income and capital in accordance with Schedules 2 and 3;

and, in these Regulations, "disposable income" and "disposable capital" mean the amounts of income and capital available for the making of a contribution after the person concerned's income and capital have been computed in accordance with those Schedules.

(2) Subject to paragraph (3) below, legal aid shall be available to a person whose disposable income does not exceed £7,777 a year but a person may be refused legal aid where—

(a) his disposable capital exceeds £6,750; and

(b) it appears to the Area Director that he could afford to proceed without legal aid.

(3) Where the subject matter of the dispute in respect of which the legal aid application has been made includes a claim in respect of personal injuries, legal aid shall be available to a person whose disposable income does not exceed £8,571 a year but a person may be refused legal aid where—

(a) his disposable capital exceeds £8,560; and

(b) it appears to the Area Director that he could afford to proceed without legal aid.

(4) A person who desires to receive legal aid shall be liable to make the following contributions—

(a) where his disposable income in the period of computation exceeds £2,625, a monthly contribution in respect of disposable income payable throughout the period while the certificate is in force of one thirty-sixth of the excess;

(b) where his disposable capital exceeds £3,000, a contribution in respect of disposable capital not greater than the excess.

(5) In this regulation "personal injuries" includes any death and any disease or other impairment of a person's physical or mental condition.

Amended by the Civil Legal Aid (Assessment of Resources) (Amendment) Regulations 1992 (S.I. 1992 No. 718), the Civil Legal Aid (Assessment of Resources) (Amendment) Regulations 1993 (S.I. 1993 No. 788), the Civil Legal Aid (Assessment of Resources) (Amendment) Regulations 1994 (S.I. 1994 No. 806), the Civil Legal Aid (Assessment of Resources) (Amendment) Regulations 1995 (S.I. 1995 No. 797) and the Civil Legal Aid (Assessment of Resources) (Amendment) (No. 2) Regulations 1996 (S.I. 1996 No. 642), the Civil Legal Aid (Assessment of Resources) (Amendment) Regulations 1997 (S.I. 1997 No. 753) and the Civil Legal Aid (Assessment of Resources) (Amendment) Regulations 1998 (S.I. 1998 No. 664).

Subject matter of dispute

5.—(1) In computing the income or capital of the person concerned, there shall be excluded the value of the subject matter of the dispute in respect of which the legal aid application has been made.

(2) Periodical payments of maintenance (whether made voluntarily or otherwise) shall not be treated as the subject matter of the dispute for the purposes of paragraph (1).

Application in representative, fiduciary or official capacity

6. Where an application for legal aid is made by a person who is concerned in the proceedings only in a representative, fiduciary or official capacity, the assessment officer shall, in computing the income and capital of that person and the amount of any contribution to be made—

(a) where so requested by the Area Director, assess the value of any property or estate or the amount of any fund out of which that person is entitled to be indemnified and the disposable income, disposable capital and contribution of any persons (including that person if appropriate), who might benefit from the outcome of the proceedings; and

(b) except in so far as they are assessed under paragraph (a), disregard the personal resources of that person.

Amended by the Civil Legal Aid (Assessment of Resources) (Amendment) Regulations 1993 (S.I. 1993 No. 788).

Resources of spouses, etc.

7.—(1) Subject to paragraph (2), in computing the income and capital of the person concerned the resources of his or her spouse shall be treated as his or her resources.

(2) The resources of the spouse of the person concerned shall not be treated as his or her resources if—

(a) the spouse has a contrary interest in the dispute in respect of which the legal aid application is made; or

(b) the person concerned and the spouse are living separate and apart.

(3) Paragraphs (1) and (2) above and Schedules 2 and 3 shall apply to a man and a woman who are living with each other in the same household as husband and wife as it applies to the parties to a marriage.

7A.—(1) Where it appears to the assessment officer that:

(a) the person concerned has transferred any resources to another person;

(b) another person is or has been maintaining the person concerned in the proceedings to which the application relates or any other proceedings, or

(c) any of the resources of another person are or have been made available to the person concerned,

the assessment officer shall have power to treat all or any part of the resources of that other person as the resources of the person concerned.

(2) Where paragraph (1) applies:

(a) the question of what is or is not a resource of that other person shall be determined, as nearly as the circumstances permit, in accordance with the provisions of these Regulations excluding this regulation, and

(b) the assessment officer shall assess or estimate the value of those resources to the best of his judgment.

(3) In this regulation "person" (except in the phrase "person concerned") includes a company, partnership, body of trustees and any body of persons whether corporate or not corporate.

Paragraph 7A was added by the Civil Legal Aid (Assessment of Resources) (Amendment) Regulations 1996 (S.I. 1996 No. 434) which apply to applications made on or after June 1, 1996.

Resources of an applicant who is a child

8.—*[Omitted by the Civil Legal Aid (Assessment of Resources) (Amendment) Regulations 1990 (S.I. 1990 No. 484).]*

Deprivation or conversion of resources

9. Where it appears to the assessment officer that the person concerned has with intent to reduce the amount of his disposable income or disposable capital, whether for the purpose of making himself eligible for legal aid, reducing his liability to pay a contribution towards legal aid or otherwise—

(a) directly or indirectly deprived himself of any resources; or

(b) converted any part of his resources into resources which under these Regulations are to be wholly or partly disregarded, or in respect of which nothing is to be included in determining the resources of that person;

the resources of which he has so deprived himself or which he has so converted shall be treated as part of his resources or as not so converted as the case may be and, for this purpose, resources which are to be wholly or partly disregarded shall include the repayment of money borrowed on the security of a dwelling.

Amended by the Civil Legal Aid (Assessment of Resources) (Amendment) Regulations 1990 (S.I. 1990 No. 484).

Notification of the assessment officer's decision

10.—(1) The assessment officer shall make an assessment of the disposable capital, disposable income and contribution of the person concerned.

(2) The assessment made under paragraph (1) shall be communicated in writing to the Area Director and the assessment officer may draw attention to any special circumstances affecting the manner in which any contribution is to be made.

Amended by the Civil Legal Aid (Assessment of Resources) (Amendment) Regulations 1993 (S.I. 1993 No. 788).

Duty of the person concerned to report change in financial circumstances

11. The person concerned shall forthwith inform the Area Director of any change in his financial circumstances which has occurred since the original assessment was made and which he has reason to believe might affect the terms on which the certificate was granted or its continuation.

Amended by the Civil Legal Aid (Assessment of Resources) (Amendment) Regulation 1998 (S.I 1998 No. 664).

Further assessments

12.—(1) Where—

(a) it appears that the circumstances upon which the assessment officer has assessed the disposable income or disposable capital of the person concerned have altered so that:

   (i) his disposable income may have increased by an amount greater than £750 or decreased by an amount greater than £300; or
   (ii) his disposable capital may have increased by an amount greater than £750;

or

(b) the Area Director considers that the current financial circumstances of the person concerned are such that he could afford to proceed without legal aid,

the assessment officer shall make a further assessment of the person's disposable income or disposable capital or contribution as the case may be in accordance with the provisions of Schedules 2 and 3, unless (in relation to sub-paragraph (a)) it appears to him unlikely that any significant change in that person's liability to make a contribution will result from any such further assessment.

(2) For the purposes of the further assessment, the period of computation shall be the period of 12 months following from the date of the request for a reassessment or such other period of twelve months as in the particular circumstances of the case the assessment officer may consider to be appropriate.

(3) Where a further assessment is made the amount and value of every resource of a capital nature acquired since the date of the legal aid application shall be ascertained as at the date of receipt of that resource.

Substituted by the Civil Legal Aid (Assessment of Resources) (Amendment) Regulations 1993 (S.I. 1993 No. 788).

Re-assessment on change of circumstances

12.—(1) Where:

   (a) it appears that the circumstances upon which the assessment officer

has assessed the disposable income or disposable capital of the person concerned have altered so that:

    (i) his disposable income may have increased by an amount greater than £750 or decreased by an amount greater than £300; or

    (ii) his disposable capital may have increased by an amount greater than £750;

or

    (b) new information which is relevant to the assessment has come to light;

the assessment officer shall re-assess that person's disposable income or disposable capital and maximum contribution, as the case may be, unless it appears to him to be unlikely that any significant change in that person's liability to make a contribution will result from such a re-assessment.

(2) For the purpose of making a re-assessment under paragraph (1), the amount and value of every resource of a capital nature acquired since the date of the legal aid application shall be ascertained as at the date of receipt of that resource.

[Applicable to re-assessments under regulation 12 where the period of computation began before April 12, 1993.]

Further assessment of resources outside the original period of computation

13.—(1) Where a certificate is still in force after the expiration of the period of computation and the Area Director considers that the current financial circumstances of the person concerned are such that he could afford to proceed without legal aid, he may request the assessment officer to make a further assessment of the current disposable income and current disposable capital of the person concerned with a view to discharging the certificate.

(2) Where a request under paragraph (1) is made, the assessment officer shall make a further assessment in accordance with the provisions of Schedules 2 and 3 and, for this purpose—

    (a) the period of computation shall be the period of twelve months following the date of the Area Director's request; and

    (b) the amount and value of every resource of a capital nature acquired since the date of the legal aid application shall be ascertained as at the date of receipt of that resource.

Omitted by the Civil Legal Aid (Assessment of Resources) (Amendment) Regulations 1993 (S.I. 1993 No. 788) but applicable to further assessments under regulation 13 in respect of a certificate granted before April 12, 1993.

Amendment of assessment due to error or receipt of new information

14. Where—

    (a) it appears to the assessment officer that there has been some error or mistake in the assessment of a person's disposable income, disposable capital or contribution or in any computation or estimate upon which such assessment was based, and that it would be just and equitable to correct the error or mistake; or

(b) new information which is relevant to the assessment has come to light,

the assessment officer shall make an amended assessment and give written notice to the Area Director of the amended assessment and of any of the circumstances giving rise to it which he considers to merit special attention.

Amended by the Civil Legal Aid (Assessment of Resources) (Amendment) (No. 3) Regulations 1996 (S.I. 1996 No. 2309).

Amendment of assessment due to error or mistake

14. Where it appears to the assessment officer that—

(a) there has been some error or mistake in the assessment of a person's disposable income, disposable capital or maximum contribution or in any computation or estimate upon which such assessment was based; and

(b) it would be just and equitable to correct the error or mistake,

the officer may make an amended assessment which shall, for all purposes, be substituted for the original assessment and have effect in all respects as if it were the original assessment.

[Applicable to amended assessments under regulation 14 in respect of applications where the period of computation began before April 12, 1993.]

Power of assessment officer to estimate the resources of the person concerned

15.—(1) Where the Area Director informs the assessment officer that the person concerned requires a certificate as a matter of urgency and the officer is not satisfied that he can make an assessment and communicate it to the Area Director by the time that he is requested so to do, the officer may, on the basis of the information then available to him, make an estimate of the disposable income and disposable capital of the person concerned and of his contribution.

(2) The assessment officer shall communicate any estimate made under paragraph (1) to the Area Director in writing and, until the making of a full assessment, the estimate shall be treated as if it were an assessment and section 17(1) of the Act and regulation 4(2) to (4) above shall have effect as if the disposable income, disposable capital and contribution of the person concerned were of the amounts specified in the estimate.

(3) In any case in which the assessment officer makes an estimate under paragraph (1) he shall, upon receiving such additional information as he may require, make an assessment and shall communicate it to the Area Director in writing and the assessment shall for all purposes take the place of the estimate.

Amended by the Civil Legal Aid (Assessment of Resources) (Amendment) Regulations 1990 (S.I. 1990 No. 484) and the Civil Legal Aid (Assessment of Resources) (Amendment) Regulations 1993 (S.I. 1993 No. 788).

SCHEDULES

SCHEDULE 1

REGULATIONS REVOKED

Title	Reference
The Legal Aid (Assessment of Resources) Regulations 1980	S.I. 1980/1630
The Legal Aid (Assessment of Resources) (Amendment) Regulations 1983	S.I. 1983/423
The Legal Aid (Assessment of Resources) (Amendment) Regulations 1986	S.I. 1986/276
The Legal Aid (Assessment of Resources) (Amendment) Regulations 1988	S.I. 1988/467
The Legal Aid (Financial Conditions) Regulations 1988	S.I. 1988/667

SCHEDULE 2

COMPUTATION OF INCOME

1. The income of the person concerned from any source shall be taken to be the income which that person may reasonably expect to receive (in cash or in kind) during the period of computation and, in the absence of other means of ascertaining it, shall be taken to be the income received during the preceding year.

2. The income in respect of any emolument, benefit or privilege which is received otherwise than in cash shall be estimated at such sum as in all the circumstances is just and equitable.

3.—(1) The income from a trade, business or gainful occupation other than an employment at a wage or salary shall be deemed to be the profits there from which have accrued or will accrue to the person concerned in respect of the period of computation, and, in computing such profits, the assessment officer may have regard to the profits of the last accounting period of such trade, business or gainful occupation for which accounts have been prepared.

(2) In ascertaining the profits under paragraph (1), there shall be deducted all sums necessarily expended to earn those profits, but no deduction shall be made in respect of the living expenses of that person or of any member of his family or household, except in so far as such member of his family or household is wholly or mainly employed in such trade or business and such living expenses form part of his remuneration.

4.—(1) In computing the income of the person concerned, there shall be deducted the total amount of tax which it is estimated would be payable by the person concerned if his income (as computed in accordance with paragraphs 1 to 3 above but not taking into account the provisions of regulation 5) were his income for a fiscal year and his liability for tax in that year were to be ascertained by reference to that income and not by reference to his income in any other year or period.

(2) For the purposes of this paragraph, tax shall be estimated at the rate provided by and after making all appropriate allowances, deductions or reliefs in accordance with the statutory provisions relating to income tax in force for the fiscal year in which the legal aid application is made.

4A. In computing the income of the person concerned, there shall be deducted any sums payable (net of council tax benefit) by the person concerned in respect of the council tax to which he is liable by virtue of section 6 of the Local Government Finance Act 1992.

Amended by the Civil Legal Aid (Assessment of Resources) (Amendment) Regulations 1990 (S.I.

1990 No. 484) and the Civil Legal Aid (Assessment of Resources) (Amendment) Regulations 1993 (S.I. 1993 No. 788).

5. Where the person concerned or his spouse is in receipt of income-based job-seeker's allowance or income support paid under the Social Security Contributions and Benefits Act 1992, the person concerned shall, for the period during which income-based job-seeker's allowance or income support is received, be deemed to have a disposable income which does not exceed the figure for the time being specified in regulation 4(4)(a).

Amended by the Civil Legal Aid (Assessment of Resources) (Amendment) Regulations 1990 (S.I. 1990 No. 484), the Civil Legal Aid (Assessment of Resources) (Amendment) Regulations 1993 (S.I. 1993 No. 788) and the Civil Legal Aid (Assessment of Resources) (Amendment) (No. 3) Regulations 1996 (S.I. 1996 No. 2309).

6.—(1) In computing disposable income the following payments made under the Social Security Contributions and Benefits Act 1992 shall be disregarded—

(a) disability living allowance;

(b) attendance allowance paid under section 64 or Schedule 8 paragraphs 4 or 7(2);

(c) constant attendance allowance paid under section 104 as an increase to a disablement pension;

(d) any payment made out of the social fund.

(2) In computing disposable income, a payment under the Community Care (Direct Payments) Act 1996 shall be disregarded.

Amended by the Civil Legal Aid (Assessment of Resources) (Amendment) Regulations 1993 (S.I. 1993 No. 788) and the Civil Legal Aid (Assessment of Resources) (Amendment) Regulations 1997 (S.I 1997 No. 753).

6A. In computing disposable income there shall be disregarded—

(a) so much of any back to work bonus received under section 26 of the Jobseekers Act 1995 as is by virtue of that section to be treated as payable by way of a jobseeker's allowance;

(b) any payment made by the Secretary of State under the Earnings Top-up Scheme 1996.

Paragraph 6A inserted by the Civil Legal Aid (Assessment of Resources) (Amendment) (No. 3) Regulations 1996 (S.I. 1996 No. 2309).

7. Where the income of the person concerned consists, wholly or in part, of a wage or salary from employment, there shall be deducted—

(a) the reasonable expenses of travelling to and from his place of employment;

(b) the amount of any payments reasonably made for membership of a trade union or professional organisation; and

(c) where it would be reasonable so to do, an amount to provide for the care of any dependant child living with the person concerned during the time that person is absent from home by reason of his employment; and

(d) the amount of any contribution paid, whether under a legal obligation or not, to an occupational pension scheme within the meaning of the Social Security Pensions Act 1975 or to a personal pension scheme within the meaning of the Social Security Act 1986.

8. There shall be a deduction in respect of contributions payable by the person concerned (whether by deduction or otherwise) under the Social Security Acts 1975 to 1988, of the amount estimated to be so payable in the 12 months following the application for a certificate.

9.—(1) In the case of a householder, there shall be a deduction in respect of rent of the main or only dwelling of the amount of the net rent payable, or such part thereof as is reasonable in the circumstances, and the assessment officer shall decide which is the main dwelling where the person concerned resides in more than one dwelling in which he has an interest.

(2) For the purposes of this paragraph, "rent" includes—

(a) the annual rent payable; and

(b) a sum in respect of yearly outgoings borne by the householder including, in particular, any water and sewerage charges, a reasonable allowance towards any necessary expenditure on repairs and insurance and any annual instalment (whether of interest or of capital) payable in respect of a mortgage debt or heritable security charged on the house in which the householder resides or has an interest;

and, in calculating the amount of rent payable, any housing benefit paid under the Social Security Contributions and Benefits Act 1992 shall be deducted from the amount of rent payable.

(3) In this paragraph, the expression "net rent" means the rent less any proceeds of sub-letting any part of the premises in respect of which the said rent is paid or the outgoings are incurred except that, where any person or persons other than the person concerned, his or her spouse or any dependant of his or hers is accommodated, otherwise than as a sub-tenant, in the premises for which the rent is paid, the rent may be deemed to be reduced by an amount reasonably attributable to such other person or persons.

(4) In sub-paragraph (2)(b) above, the amount to be included as "rent" in respect of any annual instalment payable in respect of a mortgage debt or heritable security shall not exceed an amount bearing the same proportion to the amount of the annual instalment as £100,000 bears to the debt secured.

Amended by the Civil Legal Aid (Assessment of Resources) (Amendment) Regulations 1990 (S.I. 1990 No. 484) and the Civil Legal Aid (Assessment of Resources) (Amendment) Regulations 1993 (S.I. 1993 No. 788). Paragraph 9(4) was added by the Civil Legal Aid (Assessment of Resources) (Amendment) Regulations 1996 (S.I. 1996 No. 434) which apply to applications made on or after June 1, 1996.

10. If the person concerned is not a householder, there shall be a deduction in respect of the cost of his living accommodation of such amount as is reasonable in the circumstances.

Amended by the Civil Legal Aid (Assessment of Resources) (Amendment) Regulations 1990 (S.I. 1990 No. 484) and the Civil Legal Aid (Assessment of Resources) (Amendment) Regulations 1993 (S.I. 1993 No. 788).

11.—(1) Subject to paragraph (2), in computing the income of the person concerned there shall be a deduction—

(a) in respect of the maintenance of the spouse of the person concerned, where the spouses are living together;

(b) in respect of the maintenance of any dependent child and of any dependent relative aged 18 or under of the person concerned, where such persons are members of his household;

at the following rates—

(i) in the case of a spouse at a rate equivalent to the difference between the income support allowance for a couple where both members are aged not less than 18 (which is specified in column 2 of paragraph 1(3)(c) of Schedule 2 Part I of the Income Support (General) Regulations 1987), and the allowance for a single person aged not less than 25, (which is specified in column 2 of paragraph 1(1)(e) of Schedule 2 Part I of those Regulations) which applied at the beginning of the computation period;

(ii) in the case of a dependent child or a dependent relative aged 18 or under, at a rate equivalent to the amount specified in paragraph 2 of Part I of Schedule 2 to the Income Support (General) Regulations 1987 which applied at the beginning of the computation period appropriate to the age of the child or relative.

(iii) in the case of a dependent child or a dependent relative aged 19 or over, at a rate equivalent to the amount which would have been specified in accordance with paragraph 11(1)(b)(ii) immediately before he attained the age of 19.

Amended by the Civil Legal Aid (Assessment of Resources) (Amendment) Regulations 1990 (S.I 1990 No. 484), the Civil Legal Aid (Assessment of Resources) (Amendment) Regulations 1993 (S.I. 1993 No. 788) and the Civil Legal Aid (Assessment of Resources) (Amendment) Regulations 1998 (S.I. 1998 No. 664).

(2) The assessment officer may reduce any rate provided by virtue of sub-paragraph (1) by taking into account the income and other resources of the dependent child or other dependant to such extent as appears to the officer to be just and equitable.

(3) In ascertaining whether a child is a dependent child or whether a person is a dependent relative for the purposes of this paragraph, regard shall be had to their income and other resources.

12. Where the person concerned is making and, throughout such period as the assessment officer may consider to be adequate, has regularly made *bona fide* payments for the maintenance of—

(a) a spouse who is living apart;

(b) a former spouse;

(c) a child; or

(d) a relative;

who is not a member of the household of the person concerned, there shall be a deduction at the rate of such payments or at such rate (not exceeding the rate of such payments) as in all the circumstances is reasonable.

13. Where the person concerned is required to, or may reasonably provide for any other matter, the assessment officer may make an allowance of such amount as he considers to be reasonable in the circumstances of the case.

14. In computing the income from any source, there shall be disregarded such amount, if any, as the assessment officer considers to be reasonable having regard to the nature of the income or to any other circumstances of the case.

SCHEDULE 3

Computation of Capital

1.—(1) Subject to paragraph (2) and to the provisions of these Regulations, in computing the capital of the person concerned, there shall be included the amount or value of every resource of a capital nature belonging to him on the date the legal aid application is made.

(2) Where it comes to the attention of the assessment officer that, between the date the legal aid application is made and the assessment, there has been a substantial fluctuation in the value of a resource or there has been a substantial variation in the nature of a resource affecting the basis of computation of its value, or any resource has ceased to exist or a new resource has come into the possession of the person concerned, the officer shall compute the capital resources of that person in the light of such facts and the resources as so computed shall be taken into account in the assessment.

2. In so far as any resource of a capital nature does not consist of money, its amount or value shall be taken to be—

(a) the amount which that resource would realise if sold in the open market or, if there is only a restricted market for that resource, the amount which it would realise in that market, or

(b) the amount or value assessed in such manner as appears to the assessment officer to be just and equitable.

3. Where money is due to the person concerned, whether it is payable immediately or otherwise and whether payment is secured or not, its value shall be taken to be its present value.

4. Where the person concerned stands in relation to a company in a position analogous to that of a sole owner or partner in the business of that company, the assessment officer may, in lieu of ascertaining the value of his stocks, shares, bonds or debentures in that company, treat that person as if he were a sole owner or partner and compute the amount of his capital in respect of that resource in accordance with paragraph 5 below.

5. Where the person concerned is or is to be treated as sole owner of, or a partner in, any business, the value of such business to him or his share shall be taken to be either—

(a) such sum, or his share of such sum, as the case may be, as could be withdrawn from the assets of such business without substantially impairing the profits of such business or its normal development; or

(b) such sum as that person could borrow on the security of his interest in such business without substantially injuring the commercial credit of that business;

whichever is the greater.

6. The value of any interest in reversion or remainder on the termination of a prior estate, whether legal or equitable, in any real or personal property or in a trust or other fund, whether the person concerned has the sole interest or an interest jointly or in common with other persons or whether his interest is vested or contingent, shall be computed in such manner as is both equitable and practicable.

7. Where the person concerned or his spouse is in receipt of income-based jobseeker's allowance or income support paid under the Social Security Contributions and Benefits Act 1992, the person concerned shall, for the period during which income-based jobseeker's allowance or income support is received, be deemed to have disposable capital not exceeding the figure for the time being specified in regulation 4(4)(b).

Amended by the Civil Legal Aid (Assessment of Resources) (Amendment) 1990 (S.I. 1990 No. 484), the Civil Legal Aid (Assessment of Resources) (Amendment) Regulations 1993 (S.I. 1993 No. 788), the Civil Legal Aid (Assessment of Resources) (Amendment) (No. 3) Regulations 1996 (S.I. 1996 No. 2309) and the Civil Legal Aid (Assessment of Resources) (Amendment) Regulations 1998 (S.I. 1998 No. 664).

8. In computing the amount of capital of the person concerned, there shall be disregarded—

(a) so much of any back to work bonus received under section 26 of the Jobseekers Act 1995 as is by virtue of that section to be treated as payable by way of a jobseeker's allowance; and

(b) the whole of any payment made out of the socal fund under the Social Security Contributions and Benefits Act 1992 or any arrears of payments made under the Community Care (Direct Payments) Act 1996.

Substituted by the Civil Legal Aid (Assessment of Resources) (Amendment) (No. 3) Regulations 1996 (S.I. 1996 No. 2309) and amended by the Civil Legal Aid (Assessment of Resources) (Amendment) Regulations 1997 (S.I. 1997 No. 753).

9. Save in exceptional circumstances, no sum shall be included in the amount of the capital of the person concerned in respect of—

(a) the household furniture and effects of the dwelling house occupied by him;

(b) articles of personal clothing; and

(c) the tools and equipment of his trade, unless they form part of the plant or equipment of a business to which the provisions of paragraph 5 of this Schedule apply.

10.—(1) In computing the amount of capital of the person concerned, the value of any interest in the main or only dwelling in which he resides shall be **taken to be the amount for which that interest could be sold in the open market, subject to the following rules—**

(a) **the amount to be allowed in respect of any mortgage debt or heritable security shall not exceed £100,000;**

(b) **the first £100,000 of the value of that interest, after the application of the rule in paragraph (a), shall be** *wholly disregarded.*

(2) Where the person concerned resides in more than one dwelling in which he has an interest, the assessment officer shall decide which is the main dwelling and shall take into account **the amount for which any interest in a dwelling which is not the main dwelling could be sold in the open market; provided that the total amount to be allowed in respect of any mortgage debts or heritable securities over all such dwellings, together with any amount allowed under sub-paragraph (1)(a) in respect of the main dwelling, shall not exceed £100,000** *in respect of the value to him of any interest in a dwelling which is not the main dwelling any sum which might be obtained by borrowing money on the security thereof.*

The words in italic were deleted and those in bold substituted by the Civil Legal Aid (Assessment of Resources) (Amendment) Regulations 1996 (S.I. 1996 No. 434) which apply to applications made on or after June 1, 1996.

11. Where the person concerned has received or is entitled to receive from a body of which he is a member a sum of money by way of financial assistance towards the cost of the proceedings in respect of which the legal aid application is made, such sum shall be disregarded.

12. The value to the person concerned of any life assurance or endowment policy shall be taken to be the amount which the person concerned could readily borrow on the security thereof.

13. Where under any statute, bond, covenant, guarantee or other instrument, the person concerned is under a contingent liability to pay any sum or is liable to pay a sum not yet ascertained, an allowance shall be made of such an amount as is reasonably likely to become payable within the 12 months immediately following the date of the application for a certificate.

14. Where the person concerned produces evidence which satisfies the assessment officer that the debt or part of the debt will be discharged within the twelve months immediately following the date of the legal aid application, an allowance may be made in respect of any debt owing by the person concerned (other than a debt secured on the dwelling or dwellings in which he resides) to the extent to which the assessment officer considers reasonable.

14A.—(1) Where the person concerned is of pensionable age and his annual disposable income (excluding any net income derived from capital) is less than the figure for the time being prescribed in regulation 4(4)(a) there shall be disregarded the amount of capital as specified in the following table:—

annual disposable income (excluding net income derived from capital)	amount of capital disregard
up to £370	£35,000
£371–670	£30,000
£671–970	£25,000
£971–1,270	£20,000
£1,271–1,570	£15,000
£1,571–£1,870	£10,000
£1,871 and above	£ 5,000

Amended by the Civil Legal Aid (Assessment of Resources) (Amendment) Regulations 1992 (S.I. 1992 No. 718) and the Civil Legal Aid (Assessment of Resources) (Amendment) Regulations 1993 (S.I. 1993 No. 788).

(2) in this Schedule "pensionable age" means—

   (a) in the case of a man, the age of 60; and

   (b) in the case of a woman, the age of 60.

Amended by the Civil Legal Aid (Assessment of Resources) (Amendment) Regulations 1998 (S.I 1998 No. 664).

14B. *[Omitted by the Civil Legal Aid (Assessment of Resources) (Amendment) (No. 3) Regulations 1996 (S.I. 1996 No. 2309).]*

15. In computing the capital of the person concerned, there may also be disregarded such an amount of capital (if any) as the assessment officer may, in his discretion, decide having regard to all the circumstances of the case.

EXPLANATORY NOTE
(This note is not part of the Regulations)

These Regulations replace, with amendments, the Legal Aid (Assessment of Resources) Regulations 1980 (as subsequently amended). These Regulations, together with the Civil Legal Aid (General) Regulations 1989, govern the provision of representation under Part IV of the Legal Aid Act 1988 (legal aid in civil proceedings).

These Regulations make provision for the assessment of the financial resources of the person concerned in order to determine eligibility to receive legal aid and to assess the maximum contribution payable towards the cost of providing representation in the proceedings in respect of which the legal aid application is made.

The main changes made are as follows:

   (a) the income and capital eligibility limits (which determine whether a person is eligible to receive legal aid and provide the financial limits above which a contribution is to be payable) are set out in the Regulations and not in the Act *(regulation 4)*;

   (b) the resources of persons living together as husband and wife are to be treated as if those persons were married *(regulation 7(3))*.

Legal Aid (Disclosure of Information) Regulations 1991*

Came into force August 19, 1991

1. These Regulations may be cited as the Legal Aid (Disclosure of Information) Regulations 1991 and shall come into force on August 19, 1991.

2. Notwithstanding the relationship between or rights of a legal representative and client or any privilege arising out of such relationship, the legal representative shall not be precluded from disclosing to any person authorised by the Board to request it, any information which relates to advice, assistance and representation provided to a client or former client of his where that client is or was a legally assisted person which is requested for the purpose of enabling the Board to discharge its functions under the Legal Aid Act 1988.

EXPLANATORY NOTE

(*This note is not part of the Regulations*)

These Regulations waive the rules of privilege and confidentiality thereby to permit legal representatives to disclose to Legal Aid Board representatives information relating to the cases of clients or former clients who were legally aided.

---

* S.I. 1991 No. 1753.

Legal Aid in Contempt Proceedings (Remuneration) Regulations 1995*

Came into force April 24, 1995

Citation, commencement and revocations

1.—(1) These Regulations may be cited as the Legal Aid in Contempt Proceedings (Remuneration) Regulations 1995 and shall come into force on April 24, 1995.

(2) The Legal Aid in Contempt Proceedings (Remuneration) Regulations 1991 and the Legal Aid in Contempt Proceedings (Remuneration) (Amendment) Regulations 1992 are hereby revoked.

Scope and transitional provisions

2. These Regulations shall apply to the determination of remuneration for any work done by a legal representative pursuant to an order for representation under section 29 of the Act made on or after 24th April 1995, and where an order under that section was made before that date the remuneration payable shall be determined as if these Regulations had not come into force.

Interpretation

3. In these Regulations—

"the Act" means the Legal Aid Act 1988;

"area committee" has the meaning assigned to it by regulation 4 of the Civil Legal Aid (General) Regulations 1989;

"the Costs Regulations" means the Legal Aid in Criminal and Care Proceedings (Costs) Regulations 1989 as in force on any day of appearance in respect of which a legal representative claims remuneration under these Regulations;

"day of appearance", in relation to a legal representative, means a day or any part of a day on which he represents any person pursuant to an order for representation made under section 29 of the Act;

"fee-earner" means an authorised litigator within the meaning of section 119(1) of the Courts and Legal Services Act 1990 or any person who regularly does work in respect of which it is appropriate for an authorised litigator to make a direct charge to a client, and any reference to grades of fee-earner shall be construed in accordance with regulation 6(4) of the Costs Regulations as nearly as the circumstances permit;

* S.I. 1995 No. 948. These Regulations revoke and replace The Legal Aid in Contempt Proceedings (Remuneration) Regulations 1991 (S.I. 1991 No. 837) and the Legal Aid in Contempt Proceedings (Remuneration) (Amendment) Regulations 1992 (S.I. 1992 No. 595) and have been amended by the Legal Aid in Contempt Proceedings (Remuneration) (Amendment) Regulations 1996 (S.I. 1996 No. 643).

"franchisee" means a person or body (other than the Board) acting under the terms of a franchising contract.

The appropriate authority

4.—(1) Subject to paragraph (2), the appropriate authority for the purposes of these Regulations shall be—

   (a) in the case of proceedings in the Court of Appeal, Criminal Division, the registrar of criminal appeals;

   (b) in the case of proceedings in the Crown Court, an officer appointed by the Lord Chancellor for the purposes of regulation 3(1)(b) of the Costs Regulations;

   (c) in any other case, the Board.

(2) The appropriate authority shall appoint or authorise the appointment of determining officers to act on its behalf under these Regulations in accordance with directions given by it or on its behalf.

Claims for remuneration

5.—(1) Any claim for remuneration shall be submitted to the appropriate authority in such form and manner as it may direct and shall be submitted within 3 months of the completion of the work in respect of which the claim is made.

(2) The legal representative shall supply such further information and documents as the appropriate authority may require.

(3) The time limit within which the claim for remuneration must be submitted may, for good reason, be extended by the appropriate authority.

Standard fee

6.—(1) Subject to regulation 7, the total remuneration payable under these Regulations shall be a standard fee of £72.75 for each day of appearance.

(2) Where the assisted person is represented by two legal representatives, that standard fee shall be divided into £46.50 for each day of appearance for the legal representative appearing as an advocate and £26.25 for each day of appearance for the other legal representative.

Amended by the Legal Aid in Contempt Proceedings (Remuneration) (Amendment) Regulations 1996 (S.I. 1996 No. 643).

Exceptional remuneration

7.—(1) A legal representative may, when he claims remuneration for work done pursuant to an order under section 29 of the Act, claim that there are exceptional circumstances which justify remuneration greater than the standard fee specified in regulation 6.

(2) The appropriate authority shall consider the claim, any further particulars, information or documents submitted by the legal representative under regulation 5(2) and any other relevant information and shall decide whether there are such exceptional circumstances.

(3) If the appropriate authority decides that there are such exceptional circumstances, it may allow any legal representative such fee as appears to it to be reasonable (having regard to the amount of the standard fee specified in regulation 6) for such work as appears to it to have been reasonably done. If it decides that there are not such exceptional circumstances, no fee shall be

payable under this regulation and the standard fee specified in regulation 6 shall apply.

(4) The fee allowed to a legal representative (other than counsel) under this regulation for any work shall not exceed the rates set out in paragraphs 1(1)(a) and (b) and 1A of Part I of Schedule 1 to the Costs Regulations as appropriate to the type of work, the court in which the proceedings took place, the grade and the situation of the office of the fee-earner who did the work and whether the work was done by a franchisee.

(5) In the application of paragraph (4) the rates appropriate to the Crown Court shall apply to proceedings in all courts other than magistrates' courts.

(6) Where the fee-earner who did the work was not assigned by the court under section 32(5) of the Act, the fee allowed for his work shall not exceed the rate set out in paragraphs 1(1)(a) and (b) and 1A of Part I of Schedule 1 to the Costs Regulations as appropriate to the lowest grade of fee-earner which the appropriate authority considers would have been competent to do the work.

(7) The total of the fees allowed to counsel under this regulation in respect of proceedings covered by any one order for representation under section 29 of the Act shall not exceed the amounts set out in the Table in Part II of Schedule 2 to the Costs Regulations as appropriate to a single junior counsel instructed in an appeal to the Crown Court against conviction.

Review and appeal

8. A legal representative who is dissatisfied with a decision made under regulation 5(3) or regulation 7(2) or with the remuneration allowed under regulation 7(3) may proceed—

(a) where the Board is the appropriate authority, in accordance with regulations 12, 13 and 17 of the Costs Regulations, except that any application for review shall be made to, and any review shall be carried out by, an area committee nominated by the Board;

(b) in any other case, in accordance with regulations 14 to 17 of the Costs Regulations;

as if those regulations referred to remuneration allowed under these Regulations.

Payment of costs and recovery of overpayments

9. Regulations 10 and 10A of the Costs Regulations shall apply with the necessary modifications to the remuneration payable to any legal representative under these Regulations.

EXPLANATORY NOTE

(This note is not part of the Regulations)

These Regulations provide for payment of a standard fee in contempt proceedings where representation is granted under section 29 of the Legal Aid Act 1988. They supersede and revoke earlier Regulations, and come into force on 24th June 1995. The principal changes are—

(a) the regulations introduce a fixed division of the standard fee between the advocate and any other legal representative instructed;

(b) they create rights of review and appeal where a legal representative is dissatisfied with the remuneration allowed under these Regulations;

(c) they provide increased rates for remuneration payable under these Regulations.

457

Legal Aid in Civil Proceedings (Remuneration) Regulations 1994[*]

Came into force February 25, 1994

Citation, commencement and transitional provisions

1. These Regulations may be cited as the Legal Aid in Civil Proceedings (Remuneration) Regulations 1994 and shall come into force on 25th February, 1994.

(2) Subject to paragraph (3) below, these Regulations apply to proceedings in respect of which a certificate is granted on or after 25th February, 1994.

(3) Where a certificate was granted before 25th February, 1994 to an assisted person whose solicitor represents any other assisted person in the same proceedings under a certificate granted on or after 25th February, 1994, the provisions of these Regulations shall not apply as regards the costs payable under the later certificate.

(4) Proceedings in respect of which a certificate was granted before 25th February, 1994 shall be treated as if these Regulations had not been made notwithstanding any amendment issued under Part VII of the General Regulations on or after that date.

Interpretation

2.—(1) In these Regulations—

> "CCR Order 38" means Order 38 of the County Court Rules 1981;
> "General Regulations" means the Civil Legal Aid (General) Regulations 1989;
> legal aid area" means an area specified by the Board under regulation 4(1) of the General Regulations and "legal aid area 1" means the area so numbered by the Board;
> "prescribed rate" means the fee or hourly rate specified in the Schedules to these Regulations corresponding to the relevant item or class of work, the level of court and the location of the solicitor's office;
> "relevant authority" means the Area Director in the case of an assessment and the taxing officer in the case of a taxation;
> "RSC Order 62" means Order 62 of the Rules of the Supreme Court 1965.

(2) Unless the context otherwise requires, expressions used in RSC Order 62, CCR Order 38 or in the General Regulations shall have the same meanings as in those Rules or Regulations.

Amended by the Legal Aid in Civil Proceedings (Remuneration) (Amendment) Regulations 1996 (S.I. 1996 No. 645).

---

[*] S.I. 1994 No. 228, amended by the Legal Aid in Civil Proceedings (Remuneration) (Amendment) Regulations 1996 (S.I. 1996 No. 645).

Scope

3. These regulations apply to proceedings to which Part IV of the Legal Aid Act 1988 applies except—

(a) proceedings in the House of Lords;

(b) proceedings in the Court of Appeal;

(c) proceedings in magistrates' courts;

(d) proceedings to which regulation 3(2)(a) or 3(2)(b) of the Legal Aid in Family Proceedings (Remuneration) Regulations 1991 applies;

(e) proceedings to which section 29 of the Legal Aid Act 1988 applies;

(f) proceedings to which Part XV of the General Regulations (Particular Courts and Tribunals) applies.

Remuneration

4.—(1) The amounts to be allowed to solicitors on a determination of the costs of an assisted person under regulation 107A of the General Regulations shall be—

(a) in accordance with the Schedule 1 to these Regulations or, where the work done was done by a person or body (other than the Board) acting under the terms of a franchising contract which was entered into by the Board pursuant to its powers under section 4 of the Legal Aid Act 1988, in accordance with Schedule 2;

(b) in accordance with paragraph (2) of RSC Order 62, rule 17 where the costs incurred relate to the kind of work to which that paragraph applies;

(c) in accordance with paragraph 1(1) of Appendix 2, Part I to RSC Order 62, or CCR Order 38 rule 3(3A) or (3B), whichever is applicable, where no provision is made in the Schedules to these Regulations for the kind of work to which the costs relate.

(2) The relevant authority, in determining costs referred to at 3. in the Schedules to these Regulations, shall allow costs at the higher rate specified where the office of the solicitor for the assisted person where the work was done is situated within legal aid area 1.

(3) The relevant authority shall determine disbursements (including counsel's fees) in accordance with RSC Order 62 or CCR Order 38, whichever is applicable.

(4) Subject to these regulations, the sums to be allowed to legal representatives in connection with the representation of an assisted person in proceedings to which these Regulations apply, shall be determined in accordance with Part XII of the General Regulations, RSC Order 62 and CCR Order 38.

Amended by the Legal Aid in Civil Proceedings (Remuneration) (Amendment) Regulations 1996 (S.I. 1996 No. 645).

Enhancement

5.—(1) Upon a determination the relevant authority may allow fees at more than the prescribed rate subject to the provisions of this regulation where it appears to the relevant authority, taking into account all the relevant circumstances, that

(a) the work was done with exceptional competence, skill or expertise;

(b) the work was done with exceptional dispatch; or

(c) the case involved exceptional circumstances or complexity.

(2) Where the relevant authority considers that any item or class of work should be allowed at more than the prescribed rate, it shall apply to that item or class of work a percentage enhancement in accordance with the following provisions of this regulation.

(3) In determining the percentage by which fees should be enhanced above the prescribed rate the relevant authority shall have regard to—

(a) the degree of responsibility accepted by the solicitor;

(b) the care, speed and economy with which the case was prepared;

(c) the novelty, weight and complexity of the case.

(4) Except in proceedings to which paragraph (5) applies, the percentage above the prescribed rate by which fees for work may be enhanced shall not exceed 100%.

(5) In proceedings in the High Court, the relevant authority may allow an enhancement exceeding 100% where it considers that, in comparision with work in other High Court proceedings which would merit 100% enhancement, the item or class of work relates to exceptionally complex matters which have been handled with exceptional competence or dispatch.

(6) In proceedings to which paragraph (5) applies, the percentage above the prescribed rate by which fees for work may be enhanced may exceed 100% but shall not exceed 200%.

(7) The relevant authority may have regard to the generality of proceedings to which these Regulations apply in determining what is exceptional within the meaning of this regulation.

Reduction of costs

6.—(1) Upon a determination the relevant authority may allow costs in respect of any item or class of work at less than the prescribed rate where it appears reasonable to do so having regard to the competence or dispatch with which the item or class of work was done.

(2) Paragraph (1) is without prejudice to regulation 109 of the General Regulations.

SCHEDULE 1

Column 1	Column 2 High Court	Column 3 County Court or Magistrates' Court
WORK		
1. Routine letters out	£7.40 per item	£6.50 per item
2. Routine telephone calls	£4.10 per item	£3.60 per item

Column 1	Column 2 High Court	Column 3 County Court or Magistrates' Court
3. All other preparation work including any work which was reasonably done arising out of or incidental to the proceedings, interviews with client, witnesses, and other parties; obtaining evidence; preparation and consideration of, and dealing with, documents, negotiations and notices; dealing with letters written and received and telephone calls which are not routine	£74.00 per hour (£78.50 per hour where solicitor's office situated within legal aid area 1)	£65.00 per hour £69.00 per hour
4. Attending counsel in conference or at the trial or hearing of any summons or application at court, or other appointment.	£36.40 per hour	£32.00 per hour
5. Attending without counsel at the trial or hearing of any cause or the hearing of any summons or other application at court, or other appointment.	£74.00 per hour	£65.00 per hour
6. Travelling and waiting in connection with the above matters.	£32.70 per hour	£28.75 per hour

SCHEDULE 2

Column 1	Column 2 High Court	Column 3 County Court or Magistrates' Court
WORK		
1. Routine letters out	£7.50 per item	£6.60 per item
2. Routine telephone calls	£4.15 per item	£3.65 per item
3. All other preparation work including any work which was reasonably done arising out of or incidental to the proceedings, interviews with client, witnesses, and other parties; obtaining evidence; preparation and consideration of, and dealing with, documents, negotiations and notices; dealing with letters written and received and telephone calls which are not routine	£75.00 per hour (£79.50 per hour where solicitor's office situated within legal aid area 1)	£66.00 per hour £70.00 per hour

Column 1	Column 2 High Court	Column 3 County Court or Magistrates' Court
4. Attending counsel in conference or at the trial or hearing of any summons or application at court, or other appointment	£37.00 per hour	£32.50 per hour
5. Attending without counsel at the trial or hearing of any cause or the hearing of any summons or other application at court, or other appointment	£75.00 per hour	£66.00 per hour
6. Travelling and waiting in connection with the above matters	£33.25 per hour	£29.20 per hour

Inserted by The Legal Aid in Civil Proceedings (Remuneration) (Amendment) Regulations 1996 (S.I. 1996 No. 645).

EXPLANATORY NOTE
(*This note is not part of the Regulations*)

These Regulations provide that on a legal aid determination under regulation 107A of the Civil Legal Aid (General) Regulations 1989, solicitors will be paid fixed fees for certain items of work and prescribed hourly rates for preparation, advocacy, travelling and waiting and attending on counsel.

The prescribed fees and hourly rates which are specified in the Schedule to the Regulations apply to High Court and county court proceedings. There is a separate London rate for preparation work. Costs may be enhanced or reduced in specified circumstances.

Legal Aid in Family Proceedings (Remuneration) Regulations 1991*

Came into force October 14, 1991 (Rates shown in italics apply to work done on or after July 8, 1996 and rates shown in bold apply to certificates issued on or after November 1, 1997 (solicitor attending a county court appointment without counsel)).

Citation, commencement and transitional provisions

1.—(1) These Regulations may be cited as the Legal Aid in Family Proceedings (Remuneration) Regulations 1991 and shall come into force on October 14, 1991.

(2) Subject to paragraph (3), these Regulations shall apply to remuneration payable in respect of work done on or after October 14, 1991 and remuneration payable in respect of work done in proceedings commenced before that date shall be determined as if these Regulations and the Legal Aid in Criminal and Care Proceedings (Costs) (Amendment) (No. 3) Regulations 1991 had not been made.

Provided that regulation 3 of, and Schedule 1 to, these Regulations shall apply to remuneration payable in respect of work done on or after October 14, 1991 in relation to care proceedings (within the meaning of section 27 of the Legal Aid Act 1988) as if those proceedings were care proceedings within the meaning of these Regulations.

(3) For the purposes of determining remuneration payable in respect of work done before October 14, 1991 in relation to proceedings of a kind described in paragraph (a) of the definition of "prescribed family proceedings", Schedule 2 to the Rules shall have effect as if that Schedule were substituted for Schedule 2(a) to these Regulations and Schedule 2 (as so substituted) shall have effect as it had effect during the year in which the work in question was done.

Interpretation

2.—(1) In these Regulations, unless the context otherwise requires—

"the relevant authority" means the Area Director in the case of an assessment and the taxing officer in the case of a taxation, and "determination" shall mean an assessment or taxation as the case may be;

* S.I. 1991 No. 2038 as amended by the Legal Aid in Family Proceedings (Remuneration) (Amendment) Regulations 1991 (S.I. 1991 No. 2112), the Legal Aid in Family Proceedings (Remuneration) (Amendment) Regulations 1992 (S.I. 1992 No. 596), the Legal Aid in Family Proceedings (Remuneration) (Amendment) Regulations 1993 (S.I. 1993 No. 1117), the Legal Aid in Family Proceedings (Remuneration) (Amendment) Regulations 1994 (S.I. 1994 No. 230) (in respect of certificates granted on or after February 25, 1994 unless the assisted person's solicitor represents any other assisted person in the same proceedings under a legal aid certificate granted before February 25, 1994), the Legal Aid in Family Proceedings (Remuneration) (Amendment) Regulations 1996 (S.I. 1996 No. 650), the Legal Aid in Family Proceedings (Remuneration) (Amendment) (No. 2) Regulations 1996 (S.I. 1996 No. 1555) and the Legal Aid in Family Proceedings (Remuneration) (Amendment) Regulations 1997 (S.I. 1997 No. 2394) (applicable to certificates issued on or after November 1, 1997 only).

"care proceedings" means proceedings for an order under Parts IV or V of the Children Act 1989 and includes proceedings under section 25 of that Act (secure accommodation orders);

"fee-earner" means a solicitor, a legal executive or any clerk who regularly does work for which it is appropriate to make a direct charge to a client;

"the General Regulations" means the Civil Legal Aid (General) Regulations 1989;

"prescribed family proceedings" means—

    (a) proceedings commenced before October 14, 1991 with respect to which rules made under section 50 of the Matrimonial Causes Act 1973 applied immediately before the date of the coming into force of these Regulations;

    (b) proceedings commenced on or after October 14, 1991 to which those rules would have applied if they had continued in force on and after that date, other than proceedings under Part IV of the Family Law Act 1996;

    (c) proceedings under the Children Act 1989, excluding care proceedings;

    (d) proceedings under sections 20 or 27 of the Child Support Act 1991 in the High Court, a county court or a magistrates' court.

    (e) proceedings under section 30 of the Human Fertilisation and Embryology Act 1990 in the High Court, a county court or a magistrates' court.

"the Rules" means the Matrimonial Causes (Costs) Rules 1988.

(2) Unless the context otherwise requires—

    (a) expressions used in the Rules, the Family Proceedings Rules 1991 and in the General Regulations shall have the same meanings as in those Rules or Regulations; and

    (b) any reference in these Regulations to a regulation, Part or Schedule by number means the regulation, Part or Schedule so numbered in these Regulations.

Amended by the Legal Aid in Family Proceedings (Remuneration) (Amendment) Regulations 1993 (S.I. 1993 No. 1117), the Legal Aid in Family Proceedings (Remuneration) (Amendment) Regulations 1994 (S.I. 1994 No. 230), the Legal Aid in Family Proceedings (Remuneration) (Amendment) Regulations 1996 (S.I. 1996 No. 650) and the Legal Aid in Family Proceedings (Remuneration) (Amendment) Regulations 1997 (S.I. 1997 No. 2394).

Remuneration*

3.—(1) The sums to be allowed to legal representatives in connection with family proceedings shall be determined in accordance with these Regulations, Part XII of the General Regulations, the Family Proceedings (Costs)

---

* Paragraph (1A) was inserted and the words in italic in paragraph 2(c) removed by the Legal Aid in Family Proceedings (Remuneration) (Amendment) Regulations 1994 (S.I. 1994 No. 230) which apply to certificates granted on or after February 25, 1994 unless the assisted person's solicitor represents any other assisted person in the same proceedings under a legal aid certificate granted before February 25, 1994.

Rules 1991 and paragraphs 1(3), (4)(a) and (5) and paragraph 2(2)(a) of Part I of Schedule 1 to the Rules.

(1A) The following paragraphs of this regulation shall apply solely on a determination under regulation 107A of the General Regulations.

(2) Subject to the following paragraphs, the amounts to be allowed on determination under this regulation shall be—

    (a) in accordance with Schedule 1 where the certificate was issued in relation to care proceedings;

    (b) in accordance with Schedule 2 where the certificate was issued in relation to prescribed family proceedings, or, in relation to proceedings in a magistrates' court, any family proceedings other than care proceedings or proceedings under Part IV of the Family Law Act 1996;

    (bb) in accordance with the county court rate in column 3 of Schedule 2(a) where the certificate was issued in relation to proceedings in the High Court, a county court or a magistrates' court under Part IV of the Family Law Act 1996;

    (c) in accordance with *R.S.C., Order 62 or C.C.R., Order 38* the Legal Aid in Civil Proceedings (Remuneration) Regulations 1994 where the certificate was issued in relation to family proceedings not falling within sub-paragraph (a), (b) or (bb);

    (d) in accordance with paragraph (2) of rule 8 of the Rules where the costs incurred relate to the kind of work to which that paragraph applies;

    (e) in accordance with paragraph 1(1) of Part I of Schedule 1 to the Rules where no provision is made in the Schedules to these Regulations for the kind of work to which the costs relate.

(3) Where a certificate relating to proceedings under paragraph (2)(c) is extended to cover proceedings falling within sub-paragraphs (a) or (b), the amounts to be allowed on determination shall be in accordance with Schedule 1 or 2 as the case may be, or, if it is extended to cover proceedings falling within both sub-paragraphs, in accordance with Schedule 2.

(3A) Where a certificate relating to proceedings under paragraph (2)(c) is extended to cover proceedings falling within sub-paragraph (bb), the amounts to be allowed on determination shall be in accordance with that sub-paragraph.

(4) On determination the relevant authority—

    (a) in allowing costs under item 4 of Part I of Schedule 1, shall allow costs at the higher rate where the work was done by a fee-earner whose office is situated within legal aid area 1;

    (b) in allowing costs under item 4 of Part I of Schedule 2(a), shall allow costs at the higher rate where at the time when the relevant work was done the proceedings were conducted in the principal registry or in another court on the South-Eastern Circuit;

    (bb) in allowing costs under Parts I to III and V of Schedule 1 and Parts I to III and V of Schedule 2, shall allow the rates specified for franchisees in Schedules 1A and 2A where the work done was done by a person or body (other than the Board) acting under the terms of a franchising contract which was entered into by the Board pursuant to its powers under section 4 of the Legal Aid Act 1988 and references in these Regulations to Schedule 1 or 2 shall, in relation to work done by franchisees, be construed as references to Schedule 1A or, as the case may be, 2A;

Inserted by the Legal Aid in Family Proceedings (Remuneration) (Amendment) Regulations 1996 (S.I. 1996 No. 650).

(c) may allow a larger amount than that specified in column 2 or column 3, as the case may be, of Parts I, II, III and V of Schedules 1 and 2(a) where it appears to him reasonable to do so having regard to—

(i) the exceptional competence with which the work was done, or

(ii) the exceptional expedition with which the work was done, or

(iii) any other exceptional circumstances of the case including, in the case of care proceedings, the fact that the solicitor was a member of the Law Society's Children Act panel.

but, without prejudice to regulation 109 of the General Regulations or rules 15 or 16 or the Rules, the relevant authority may in respect of any item in Part I, II, III or V of Schedule 1 or 2(a) allow a lower amount than that specified in column 2 or column 3 of that Part, as the case may be, where it appears to him reasonable to do so having regard to any failure on the part of the solicitor to provide timely preparation or advice, or for any similar reason.

(5) Without prejudice to regulation 109 of the Legal Aid General Regulations or rules 15 or 16 of the Rules, where a standard fee is specified in Part IV of Schedules 1 or 2(a) for work done by junior counsel that fee shall be allowed unless the relevant authority considers that it would be unreasonable to do so, in which case he shall allow such lesser or greater fee as may be reasonable—

Provided that the fee allowed shall not exceed any maximum fee which is specified unless the relevant authority considers that, owing to the time and labour expended by counsel or to any other special circumstance of the case, the maximum fee specified would not provide reasonable remuneration for some or all of the work done, in which case the fee to be allowed shall be in the discretion of the relevant authority.

(6) For the purpose of determining which of the brief fees provided by item 13 of Schedules 1 and 2(a) should be allowed—

(a) a one hour fee shall be allowed where the hearing lasts for one hour or less than one hour;

(b) a half day fee shall be allowed where the hearing lasts for more than one hour and

(i) begins and ends before the luncheon adjournment, or

(ii) begins after the luncheon adjournment and ends before 5.30 p.m.;

(c) a full day fee shall be allowed where the hearing lasts for more than one hour and

(i) begins before and ends after the luncheon adjournment but before 5.30 p.m., or

(ii) begins after the luncheon adjournment and ends after 5.30 p.m.; and

(d) a more than a full day fee shall be allowed where the hearing

    (i) begins before the luncheon adjournment and ends after 5.30 p.m. on the same day, or

    (ii) begins on one day and continues into a subsequent day.

(7) In exercising his discretion under this regulation or in relation to any provision of the Schedules where the amount of costs to be allowed is in his discretion, the relevant authority shall exercise his discretion in accordance with paragraph 1(2) of Part I of Schedule 1 to the Rules.

(8) Disbursements (other than counsel's fees) for which no allowance is made in Schedules 1 or 2(a) shall be determined and allowed, or disallowed, according to the general principles applicable to the taxation of costs in R.S.C., Order 62.

Amended by the Legal Aid in Family Proceedings (Remuneration) (Amendment) Regulations 1997 (S.I. 1997 No. 2394) which applies only to certificates issued on or after November 1, 1997.

SCHEDULE 1

CARE PROCEEDINGS

PART I

PREPARATION

Column 1	Column 2 High Court	Column 3 County Court or Magistrates' Court
ITEM		
1. Writing routine letters.	£4.25 per item	£3.65 per item
2. Receiving routine letters.	*£2.10 per item*	*£1.85 per item*
3. Routine telephone calls.	£4.25 per item	£3.65 per item
4. All other preparation work including any work which was reasonably done arising out of or incidental to the proceedings, interviews with client, witnesses, and other parties; obtaining evidence; preparation and consideration of, and dealing with, documents, negotiations and notices; dealing with letters written and received and telephone calls which are not routine.	£65.50 per hour (£69.75 per hour for a fee-earner whose office is situated within legal aid area 1)	£58.00 per hour £61.25 per hour
5. Travelling and waiting time in connection with the above matters.	£32.00 per hour	£29.25 per hour

PART II

CONFERENCES WITH COUNSEL

6. Attending counsel in conference.	£37.00 per hour	£32.50 per hour
7. Travelling and waiting.	£32.00 per hour	£29.25 per hour

PART III
ATTENDANCES

Column 1	Column 2 High Court	Column 3 County Court or Magistrates' Court
8. Attending with counsel at the trial or hearing of any cause or the hearing of any summons or other application at court, or other appointment.	£37.00 per hour	£32.50 per hour
9. Attending without counsel at the trial or hearing of any cause or the hearing of any summons or other application at court, or other appointment.	£64.00 per hour	£64.00 per hour
10. Travelling and waiting.	£32.00 per hour	£29.25 per hour

PART IV
FEES FOR JUNIOR COUNSEL

11. With a brief on an unopposed application for an injunction, or procedural issue.	Standard Maximum	£88.25 £146.25	£76.25 £127.00
12. With a brief on the trial of a cause or matter or on the hearing of an application where the hearing lasts for			
(a) one hour	Standard Maximum	£133.50 £268.00	£114.25 £228.50
(b) a half day	Standard Maximum	£184.75 £304.50	£159.25 £268.00
(c) a full day	Standard Maximum	£368.50 £584.75	£317.75 £508.50
(d) more than a full day.	Discretionary		Discretionary
13. For each day or part of a day on which the trial of a cause or matter, or the hearing of an ancillary application, or a children appointment, is continued after the first day.	Discretionary		Discretionary
14. Conference (including time reasonably spent in preparation and conference, but not otherwise remunerated).	Standard £20.25 per ½ hour		Standard £17.75 per ½ hour
15. (a) Complex items of written work (such as advices on evidence, opinions and affidavits of a substantial nature, requests for particulars or answers).	Standard £96.25 per item		Standard £82.75 per item
(b) All other written work.	Standard £57.00 per item		Standard £50.25 per item

Column 1	Column 2 High Court	Column 3 County Court or Magistrates' Court
16. Except where the court is within 40 kilometres of Charing Cross or where there is no local Bar in the court town, or within 40 kilometres thereof, for travelling time.	Standard £18.50 per hour + expenses	Standard £15.85 per hour + expenses

PART V
TAXATION AND REVIEW OF TAXATION
(HIGH COURT AND COUNTY COURT ONLY)

17. Preparing the bill (where allowable) and completing the taxation (excluding preparing for and attending the taxation).	£32.00–£89.25	£32.00–£51.00
18. Preparing for and attending the taxation (including travelling and waiting).	Discretionary	Discretionary
19. Review by district judge or judge (including preparation).	Discretionary	Discretionary

SCHEDULE 1A
CARE PROCEEDINGS

PART I
PREPARATION

Column 1	Column 2 High Court	Column 3 County Court or Magistrates' Court

ITEM

1. Writing routine letters.	£4.25 per item	£3.70 per item
2. Receiving routine letters.	£2.10 per item	£1.85 per item
3. Routine telephone calls.	*£4.25 per item*	£3.70 per item
4. All other preparation work including any work which was reasonably done arising out of or incidental to the proceedings, interviews with client, witnesses, and other parties; obtaining evidence; preparation and consideration of, and dealing with, documents, negotiations and notices; dealing with letters written and received and telephone calls which are not routine.	£66.50 per hour (£70.75 per hour for a fee-earner whose office is situated within legal aid area 1)	£59.00 per hour £62.00 per hour
5. Travelling and waiting time in connection with the above matters.	£32.50 per hour	£29.50 per hour

Column 1	Column 2 *High Court*	Column 3 *County Court or* *Magistrates' Court*

PART II
CONFERENCES WITH COUNSEL

6. Attending counsel in conference.	£37.50 per hour	£33.00 per hour
7. Travelling and waiting.	£32.50 per hour	£29.50 per hour

PART III
ATTENDANCES

8. Attending with counsel at the trial or hearing of any cause or the hearing of any summons or other application at court, or other appointment.	£37.50 per hour	£33.00 per hour
9. Attending without counsel at the trial or hearing of any cause or the hearing of any summons or other application at court, or other appointment.	£65.00 per hour	£65.00 per hour
10. Travelling and waiting.	£32.50 per hour	£29.50 per hour

PART V
TAXATION AND REVIEW OF TAXATION
(HIGH COURT AND COUNTY COURT ONLY)

17. Preparing the bill (where allowable) and completing the taxation (excluding preparing for and attending the taxation).	£32.50–£90.75	£32.50–£51.75
18. Preparing for and attending the taxation (including travelling and waiting).	Discretionary	Discretionary
19. Review by district judge or judge (including preparation).	Discretionary	Discretionary

470

SCHEDULE 2

PRESCRIBED FAMILY PROCEEDINGS

(a) High Court and county court proceedings

PART I
PREPARATION

Column 1	Column 2 High Court	Column 3 County Court
ITEM		
1. Writing routine letters.	£4.25 per item	£3.65 per item
2. Receiving routine letters.	*£2.10 per item*	*£1.85 per item*
3. Routine telephone calls.	£4.25 per item	£3.65 per item
4. All other preparation work including any work which was reasonably done arising out of or incidental to the proceedings, interviews with client, witnesses, and other parties; obtaining evidence; preparation and consideration of, and dealing with, documents, negotiations and notices; dealing with letters written and received and telephone calls which are not routine.	Where the proceedings were conducted in the divorce registry or in another court on the South-Eastern Circuit at the time when the relevant work was done: £46.75 per hour All other circuits: £43.75 per hour	£41.00 per hour £38.75 per hour
5. In addition to items 1–4 above, to cover the general care and conduct of the proceedings.	+50%	+50%
6. Travelling and waiting time in connection with the above matters.	£32.00 per hour	£29.25 per hour

PART II
CONFERENCES WITH COUNSEL

7. Attending counsel in conference.	£37.00 per hour	£32.50 per hour
8. Travelling and waiting.	£32.00 per hour	£29.25 per hour

PART III
ATTENDANCES

9. Attending with counsel at the trial or hearing of any cause or the hearing of any summons or other application at court, or other appointment.	£37.00 per hour	£32.50 per hour
10. Attending without counsel at the trial or hearing of any cause or the hearing of any summons or other application at court, or other appointment.	£55.75 per hour	**£55.25 per hour**
11. Travelling and waiting.	£32.00 per hour	£29.25 per hour

471

Column 1	*Column 2* *High Court*		*Column 3* *County Court*

PART IV
FEES FOR JUNIOR COUNSEL

12. With a brief on an unopposed application for an injunction, or procedural issue.	Standard Maximum	£88.25 £146.25		£76.25 £127.00
13. With a brief on the trial of a cause or matter or on the hearing of an application or on a children appointment where the hearing lasts for				
(a) one hour	Standard Maximum	£133.50 £268.00		£114.25 £228.50
(b) a half day	Standard Maximum	£184.75 £304.50		£159.25 £268.00
(c) a full day	Standard Maximum	£368.50 £584.75		£317.75 £508.50
(d) more than a full day.	Discretionary			Discretionary
14. For each day or part of a day on which the trial of a cause or matter, or the hearing of an ancillary application, or a children appointment, is continued after the first day.	Discretionary			Discretionary
15. Conference (including time reasonably spent in preparation and conference, but not otherwise remunerated).	Standard £20.25 per ½ hour			Standard £17.75 per ½ hour
16. (a) Complex items of written work (such as advices on evidence, opinions and affidavits of a substantial nature, requests for particulars or answers).	Standard £96.25 per item			Standard £82.75 per item
(b) All other written work.	Standard £57.00 per item			Standard £50.25 per item
17. Except where the court is within 40 kilometres of Charing Cross or where there is no local Bar in the court town, or within 40 kilometres thereof, for travelling time.	Standard £18.50 per hour + expenses			Standard £15.85 per hour + expenses

PART V
TAXATION AND REVIEW OF TAXATION

18. Preparing the bill (where allowable) and completing the taxation (excluding preparing for and attending the taxation).	£32.00–£89.25		£32.00–£51.00
19. Preparing for and attending the taxation (including travelling and waiting).	Discretionary		Discretionary

Column 1	Column 2 High Court	Column 3 County Court
20. Review by district judge or judge (including preparation).	Discretionary	Discretionary

(b) Magistrates' court proceedings

Class of work	Rate
Preparation	£44.00 per hour—(£46.75 per hour for a fee-earner whose office is situated within legal aid area 1)
Advocacy	£55.25 per hour
Attendance at court where counsel assigned	£30.00 per hour
Travelling and waiting	£24.60 per hour
Routine letters written and routine telephone	£3.40 per item—(£3.55 per item for a fee-earner whose office is situated within legal aid area 1)

SCHEDULE 2A

PRESCRIBED FAMILY PROCEEDINGS

(a) High Court and county court proceedings

PART I
PREPARATION

Column 1	Column 2 High Court	Column 3 County Court
ITEM		
1. Writing routine letters.	£4.25 per item	£3.70 per item
2. Receiving routine letters.	£2.10 per item	£1.85 per item
3. Routine telephone calls.	*£4.25 per item*	£3.70 per item
4. All other preparation work including any work which was reasonably done arising out of or incidental to the proceedings, interviews with client, witnesses, and other parties; obtaining evidence; preparation and consideration of, and dealing with, documents, negotiations and notices; dealing with letters written and received and telephone calls which are not routine.	Where the proceedings were conducted in the divorce registry or in another court on the South Eastern Circuit at the time when the relevant work was done: £47.50 per hour All other circuits: £44.25 per hour	£41.50 per hour £39.25 per hour
5. In addition to items 1–4 above, to cover the general care and conduct of the proceedings.	+50%	+50%
6. Travelling and waiting time in connection with the above matters.	£32.50 per hour	£29.50 per hour

Column 1	Column 2 High Court	Column 3 County Court

PART II
CONFERENCES WITH COUNSEL

7. Attending counsel in conference.	£37.50 per hour	£33.00 per hour
8. Travelling and waiting.	£32.50 per hour	£29.50 per hour

PART III
ATTENDANCES

9. Attending with counsel at the trial or hearing of any cause or the hearing of any summons or other application at court, or other appointment.	£37.50 per hour	£33.00 per hour
10. Attending without counsel at the trial or hearing of any cause or the hearing of any summons or other application at court, or other appointment.	£56.75 per hour	**£56.25 per hour**
11. Travelling and waiting.	£32.50 per hour	£29.50 per hour

PART V
TAXATION AND REVIEW OF TAXATION

18. Preparing the bill (where allowable) and completing the taxation (excluding preparing for and attending the taxation).	£32.50–£90.75	£32.50–£51.75
19. Preparing for and attending the taxation (including travelling and waiting).	Discretionary	Discretionary
20. Review by district judge or judge (including preparation).	Discretionary	Discretionary

(b) Magistrates' court proceedings

Class of work	Rate
Preparation	£44.50 per hour—(£47.50 per hour for a fee-earner whose office is situated within legal aid area 1)
Advocacy	£56.25 per hour
Attendance at court where counsel assigned	£30.25 per hour
Travelling and waiting	£25.00 per hour
Routine letters written and routine telephone	£3.45 per item—(£3.60 per item for a fee-earner whose office is situated within legal aid area 1)

Schedules substituted by the Legal Aid in Family Proceedings (Remuneration) (Amendment) Regulations 1996 (S.I. 1996 No. 650) and amended by the Legal Aid in Family Proceedings (Remuneration) (Amendment) (No. 2) Regulations 1996 (S.I. 1996 No. 1555) and the Legal Aid in Family Proceedings (Remunderation) (Amendment) Regulations 1997 (S.I. 1997 No. 2394).

EXPLANATORY NOTE
(This note is not part of the Regulations)

These Regulations make provision for the remuneration of legal representatives of persons granted legal aid in family proceedings.

The rates applicable in care proceedings are in Schedule 1 (regulation 3(2)(a)).

The rates applicable in matrimonial proceedings and non-care proceedings under the Children Act 1989 are in Schedule 2. These consist of the same rates previously applicable in matrimonial proceedings in the High Court and county courts. All magistrates' court family proceedings (other than care proceedings) are paid at the same rates as in criminal proceedings, as previously authorised by regulation 104 of the Civil Legal Aid (General) Regulations 1989 which applied the rates from the Legal Aid in Criminal and Care (Costs) Regulations 1989 (regulation 3(2)(b).

Family proceedings not falling within the above categories (such as domestic violence injunctions) continue to be taxed in accordance with rules of court (regulation 3(1)(c)).

The appropriate rate is that applicable to the proceedings for which the certificate was originally issued save that where a legal aid certificate in family proceedings which do not attract either of the prescribed rates is extended to cover proceedings that attract one or other of those rates, then that rate is applicable for the whole of the proceedings covered by that certificate. Where the certificate is extended to cover proceedings covered by the Schedule 2 rate as well as care proceedings, the Schedule 2 rate prevails (regulation 3(3)).

The appropriate rate can be summarised as follows:

Proceedings (for which the certificate was issued)	Rate
Care (proceedings under Parts IV and V of the Children Act)	Schedule 1
Matrimonial and non-care Children Act (High Court and county courts)	Schedule 2
Family proceedings other than care (magistrates' courts)	Schedule 2
Other family proceedings (High Court and county courts) where no proceedings attracting a rate are added	Rules of Court
Other family proceedings (High Court and county courts) where care proceedings are added	Schedule 1
Other family proceedings (High Court and county courts) where matrimonial and non-care proceedings are added (whether or not care proceedings are added)	Schedule 2

The mechanism for assessment or taxation of the fees continues to be in accordance with the relevant parts of the rules of court, the Civil Legal Aid (General) Regulations 1989 and the Matrimonial Causes Costs Rules 1988, as they take effect through the Family Proceedings (Costs) Rules 1991 (regulation 3(1)). The parts of the 1988 Rules relating purely to legal aid are replaced by provisions in these Regulations (regulations 3(2)(d) and (e) and (4) to (8)).

NOTE: The contents of this Note are no longer correct in that prescribed hourly rates apply to family proceedings within regulation 3(2)(c)—see page 465.

Legal Aid in Criminal and Care Proceedings (General) Regulations 1989*

Came into force April 1, 1989

ARRANGEMENT OF REGULATIONS

PART I

GENERAL

* S.I. 1989 No. 344 as amended by the Legal Aid in Criminal and Care Proceedings (General) (Amendment) Regulations 1991 (S.I. 1991 No. 637), the Legal Aid in Criminal and Care Proceedings (General) (Amendment) (No. 2) Regulations 1991 (S.I. 1991 No. 1925), the Legal Aid in Criminal and Care Proceedings (General) (Amendment) Regulations 1992 (S.I. 1992 No. 720), the Legal Aid in Criminal and Care Proceedings (General) (Amendment) Regulations 1993 (S.I. 1993 No. 789), the Legal Aid in Criminal and Care Proceedings (General) (Amendment) (No. 2) Regulations 1993 (S.I. 1993 No. 1895), the Legal Aid in Criminal and Care Proceedings (General) (Amendment) Regulations 1994 (S.I. 1994 No. 807), the Legal Aid in Criminal and Care Proceedings (General) (Amendment) (No. 2) Regulations 1994 (S.I. 1994 No. 3136), the Legal Aid in Criminal and Care Proceedings (General) (Amendment) Regulations 1995 (S.I. 1995 No. 542), the Legal Aid in Criminal Aid Care Proceedings (General) (Amendment) (No. 2) Regulations 1995 (S.I. 1995 No. 796), the Legal Aid in Criminal and Care Proceedings (General) (Amendment) Regulations 1996 (S.I. 1996 No. 436), the Legal Aid in Criminal and Care Proceedings (General) (Amendment) (No. 2) Regulations 1996 (S.I. 1996 No. 646), the Legal Aid in Criminal and Care Proceedings (General) (Amendment) (No. 3) Regulations 1996 (S.I. 1996 No. 1258), the Legal Aid in Criminal and Care Proceedings (General) (Amendment) Regulations 1996 (No. 4) (S.I. 1996 No. 2307) and the Legal Aid in Criminal and Care Proceedings (General) (Amendment) (No. 5) Regulations 1996 (S.I. 1996 No. 2656), the Legal Aid in Criminal and Care Proceedings (General) (Amendment) Regulations 1997 (S.I. 1997 No. 752) and the Legal Aid in Criminal and Care Proceedings (General) (Amendment)(No. 2) Regulations 1997 (S.I. 1997 No. 1485), the Legal Aid in Criminal and Care Proceedings (General) (Amendment) (No. 3) Regulations 1997 (S.I. 1997 No. 1985), the Legal Aid in Criminal and Care Proceedings (General) (Amendment) (No. 4) Regulations 1997 (S.I. 1997 No. 2647) and the Legal Aid in Criminal and Care Proceedings (General) (Amendment) Regulations 1998 (S.I. 1998 No. 662).

PART I

GENERAL

Citation, commencement and application

1.—(1) These Regulations may be cited as the Legal Aid in Criminal and Care Proceedings (General) Regulations 1989 and shall come into force on April 1, 1989.

(2) *[Omitted by the Legal Aid in Criminal and Care Proceedings (General) (Amendment) (No. 2) Regulations 1991.]*

Revocations

2. The Regulations specified in Schedule 1 are hereby revoked.

Interpretation

3.—(1) In these Regulations, unless the context otherwise requires—

"the Act" means the Legal Act 1988;

"applicant" means, in relation to an application for legal aid made on behalf of a person who has not attained the age of 17 by his parent or guardian, that person and, in the case of any other application for legal aid, the person making the application;

"appropriate authority" means an officer or body authorised to determine costs under the Legal Aid in Criminal and Care Proceedings (Costs) Regulations 1989;

"appropriate contributor," in relation to a person who has not attained the age of 16, means—

(a) his father (or any person who has been adjudged to be his father) or his mother; or

(b) his guardian;

"appropriate officer" means, in the case of the Crown Court, the Court Manager or an officer designated by him to act on his behalf;

"appropriate area committee" means the area committee in whose area is situated the court to which an application for or concerning a legal aid order has been made;

"area committee" and "Area Director" have the meanings assigned to them by regulation 4 of the Civil Legal Aid (General) Regulations 1989;

"Area Director" includes any person duly authorised to act on his behalf;

"attendance allowance" means an allowance paid under section 64 or Schedule 8 paragraphs 4 or 7(2) of the Social Security Contributions and Benefits Act 1992;

"contribution" means the contribution payable under section 23(1) of the Act in respect of the costs of representation;

"Court of Appeal" means the criminal division of the Court of Appeal or the Courts-Martial Appeal Court as the case may be;

"disability living allowance" means a disability living allowance under the Social Security Contributions and Benefits Act 1992;

"disability working allowance" means a disability working allowance under the Social Security Contributions and Benefits Act 1992;

"disposable capital" and "disposable income" mean the amounts of capital and income which are available for the making of a contribution after capital and income have been computed in accordance with Schedule 3;

"family credit" means family credit under the Social Security Contributions and Benefits Act 1992;

"guardian" has the meaning assigned by section 87 of the Child Care Act 1980;

"income-based jobseeker's allowance" has the meaning given by section 1(4) of the Jobseekers Act 1995, but excludes any sum treated as payable by way of a jobseeker's allowance by virtue of section 26 of that Act;

"income support" means income support under the Social Security Contributions and Benefits Act 1992;

"interests of justice criteria" means factors which the competent authority is required to take into account by section 22(2) of the Act;

"judge of the court" means—

(a) in the case of the Court of Appeal, a single judge of that Court or a judge of the High Court;

(b) in the case of the Crown Court, a judge of the High Court, a Circuit judge, a recorder, or an assistant recorder.

"justices' clerk" includes a person duly authorised by the justices' clerk of a magistrates' court to act on his behalf to the extent that he is so authorised;

"legal aid" means representation under Part V of the Act or representation in care proceedings, as the case may be, and

"legal aid order" means an order granting such representation;

"period of computation" means the period of 3 months next ensuing from the date of the application for a legal aid order;

"person concerned" means the person whose disposable income and disposable capital are to be determined or the person whose resources are to be treated as the resources of any other person under these Regulations;

"proper officer" means—

(a) in respect of proceedings in the House of Lords, the Clerk of the Parliaments;

(b) in respect of proceedings in the Court of Appeal, the registrar;

(c) in respect of proceedings in the Crown Court, the appropriate officer;

(d) in respect of proceedings in a magistrates' court, the justices' clerk.

"registrar" means the registrar of criminal appeals or the registrar of the Courts-Martial Appeal Court, as the case may be, and includes any person duly authorised to act on his behalf to the extent that he is so authorised;

"statement of means" means a statement of means submitted in accordance with regulation 23;

(2) Unless the context otherwise requires, any reference in these Regulations to a regulation, Part or Schedule by number means the regulation, Part or Schedule so numbered in these Regulations and a form referred to by number means the form so numbered in Schedule 2.

(3) In these Regulations (including the forms contained in Schedule 2) unless the context otherwise requires—

(a) references to a solicitor shall be construed as extending to any authorised litigator as defined by section 119(1) of the Courts and Legal Services Act 1990;

(b) references to counsel shall be construed as extending to any authorised advocate as defined by section 119(1) of the Courts and Legal Services Act 1990.

(4) Paragraph (3) shall not apply in the interpretation of regulations 44(4) to (6) and 47.

Amended by the Legal Aid in Criminal and Care Proceedings (General) (Amendment) Regulations 1993 (S.I. 1993 No. 789), the Legal Aid in Criminal and Care Proceedings (General) (Amendment) Regulations 1995 (S.I. 1995 No. 542), the Legal Aid in Criminal and Care Proceedings (General) (Amendment) (No. 3) Regulations 1996 (S.I. 1996 No. 1258), the Legal Aid in Criminal and Care Proceedings (General) (Amendment) (No. 4) Regulations 1996 (S.I. 1996 No. 2307), the Legal Aid in Criminal and Care Proceedings (General) (Amendment) (No. 5) Regulations 1996 (S.I. 1996 No. 2656) and the Legal Aid in Criminal and Care Proceedings (General) (Amendment) Regulations 1998 (S.I. 1998 No. 662).

Forms
4.—(1) Forms 1, 1A and 5 in Schedule 2 shall be used where applicable and the remaining forms in Schedule 2, or forms to the like effect, may be used with such variations as the circumstances may require.

Amended by the Legal Aid in Criminal and Care Proceedings (General) (Amendment) Regulations 1992 (S.I. 1992 No. 720) and the Legal Aid in Criminal and Care Proceedings (General) (Amendment) Regulations 1998 (S.I. 1998 No. 662).

(2) Each magistrates' court shall make copies of Forms 1 and 5 available free of charge to persons (whether solicitors, prospective applicants or appropriate contributors) intending to use them for the purpose of making legal aid applications to that court or of notifying the court or the proper officer of a change in financial circumstances.

Amended by the Legal Aid in Criminal and Care Proceedings (General) (Amendment) Regulations 1995 (S.I. 1995 No. 542).

Applicants reaching the age of 16
5. An applicant who attains the age of 16 after the date on which an application for legal aid is made but before the making of a legal aid order shall be treated for the purposes of these Regulations as not having attained that age.

Exclusion of solicitors and counsel
6.—(1) The proper officer of each court shall keep a list of solicitors and counsel, notified to him by the Lord Chancellor, who are for the time being excluded from legal aid work under section 47(2) of the Solicitors Act 1974 or section 42 of the Administration of Justice Act 1985.

(2) Any reference in these Regulations to solicitors or counsel shall be construed as not including any solicitor or counsel who is so excluded.

Determination in private and in absence of legally assisted person, etc.
7. Where it is provided by these Regulations that any matter may be determined otherwise than by a court, it may be determined in private and in the absence of the applicant, the appropriate contributor, the person concerned or the legally assisted person as the case may be.

Legal aid records
8.—(1) The proper officer of each court shall keep a record of every application to that court for a legal aid order.

(2) That record shall state whether the application

(a) was granted;

(b) was refused on the ground that it did not appear that it was desirable to make an order in the interests of justice, or

(c) was refused on the ground that it did not appear that the applicant's disposable income and disposable capital were such that, in accordance with regulation 26(1), he was eligible for legal aid,

and, in the circumstances referred to in sub-paragraphs (a) and (b), shall state the factors relied upon by the applicant and the reasons for the decision.

(3) Where a legal aid order was granted or refused by an area committee following an application for review under regulation 15, the proper officer shall keep a record of the decision and reasons of the area committee as notified pursuant to regulation 17(4)(b).

(4) In the case of proceedings to which section 22 of the Act applies, the statement of reasons required by paragraph (2) shall include specific reference to such of the interests of justice criteria as appear to be relevant to the decision.

(5) The proper officer shall send to the Lord Chancellor such information from the records required to be kept by this regulation as the Lord Chancellor shall request.

Substituted by the Legal Aid in Criminal and Care Proceedings (General) (Amendment) Regulations 1995 (S.I. 1995 No. 542) in respect of all legal aid applications made on or after May 1, 1995.

Area committees and powers of Area Directors

9.—(1) Area Committees and Area Directors appointed by the Board pursuant to regulation 4 of the Civil Legal Aid (General) Regulations 1989 shall exercise functions respectively delegated to them by the Board or conferred on them by these Regulations and, where an area committee is required or entitled to perform any function under these Regulations, that function may, subject to paragraph (3), be performed on behalf of the committee by the Area Director.

(2) An Area Director so appointed shall act as the secretary to the area committee for his area.

(3) Paragraph (1) shall not empower an Area Director to refuse—

(a) an application for review under regulation 17(1);

(b) an application under regulation 52; or

(c) an application referred to the committee under regulation 54.

General power to grant legal aid

10. Subject to the provisions of section 21(2), (3) and (5) of the Act and to regulation 23, nothing in Part II or in regulation 36 shall affect the power of a court, a judge of the court or of the registrar to make a legal aid order, whether an application has been made for legal aid or not, or the right of an applicant whose application has been refused or whose legal aid order has been revoked under section 24(2) to apply to the court at the trial or in other proceedings.

PART II

APPLICATIONS FOR LEGAL AID

Proceedings in magistrates' courts

11.—(1) An application for a legal aid order in respect of proceedings in a magistrates' court shall be made:

(a) to the justices' clerk in Form 1, or

(b) orally to the court,

and the justices' clerk or the court may grant or refuse the application.

(2) Where an application for a legal aid order is made under paragraph (1)(b), the court may refer it to the justices' clerk for determination.

(3) Except where the applicant is not required to furnish a statement of means under regulation 23(4), a legal aid order shall not be made on an application under paragraph (1) until the court or the justices' clerk has considered the applicant's statement of means.

Notification of refusal of legal aid by a magistrates' court

12.—(1) Where an application for a legal aid order is refused by a magistrates' court or a justices' clerk, the court or the justices' clerk shall notify the applicant on Form 2 that the application has been refused on one or both of the following grounds, namely that it does not appear to the court or the justices' clerk—

(a) desirable to make an order in the interests of justice; or

(b) that the applicant's disposable income and disposable capital are such that, in accordance with regulation 26(1), he is eligible for legal aid,

and shall inform him of the circumstances in which he may renew his application or apply to an area committee for the decision to be reviewed.

(2) Copies of the following documents shall be sent to the applicant and to his solicitor, if any:—

(a) Form 2;

(b) if the application was refused on the ground specified in paragraph (1)(a), the record required to be kept by regulation 8(1);

(c) where an application for review under regulation 15 may be made, the completed Form 1.

Amended by the Legal Aid in Criminal and Care Proceedings (General) (Amendment) (No. 2) Regulations 1993 (S.I. 1993 No.1895).

Regulation 12(2) was substituted by the Legal Aid in Criminal and Care Proceedings (General) (Amendment) Regulations 1995 (S.I. 1995 No. 542) in respect of all legal aid applications made on or after May 1, 1995.

Determination of contribution where legal aid is refused by a magistrates' court

13. Where a magistrates' court or a justices' clerk has refused to make a legal aid order, the court or the justices' clerk shall determine—

(a) the applicant's disposable income and disposable capital, and

(b) the amount of any contribution which would have been payable and the manner in which it would be payable by the applicant or an appropriate contributor had a legal aid order been made,

and shall notify the applicant of the amounts so determined.

Renewal of application

14.—(1) Without prejudice to the provisions of regulation 15, an applicant whose application under regulation 11 has been refused may renew his application either orally to the court or to the justices' clerk.

(2) Where an application is renewed under paragraph (1), the applicant shall return the notice of refusal which he received under regulation 12 or any such notice received under regulation 17(4).

(3) Where an application is renewed to the justices' clerk, he may either grant the application or refer it to the court or to a justice of the peace.

(4) Where an application is renewed to the court, the court may grant or refuse the application or refer it to the justices' clerk.

(5) The court or a justice of the peace to whom an application is referred under paragraph (3) or (6), may grant or refuse the application.

(6) A justices' clerk to whom an application is referred under paragraph (4), may grant the application or refer it either back to the court or to a justice of the peace.

(7) Except where the applicant is not required to furnish a statement of means under regulation 23(4), a legal aid order shall not be made where an application is renewed under paragraph (1) until the court, a justice of the peace or the justices' clerk has considered the applicant's statement of means.

(8) Regulation 12 shall apply where an application is refused under this regulation with the modification that references to a magistrates' court shall be construed as including references to a justice of the peace.

(9) In this regulation, "a justice of the peace" means a justice of the peace who is entitled to sit as a member of the magistrates' court.

Application for review

15.—(1) Where an application for a legal aid order has been refused after having been considered for the first time by a magistrates' court or a justices' clerk, the applicant may, subject to paragraphs (2) and (3), apply for review to the appropriate area committee.

(2) An application for review shall only lie to an area committee where—

(a) the applicant is charged with an indictable offence or an offence which is triable either way or appears or is brought before a magistrates' court to be dealt with in respect of a sentence imposed or an order made in connection with such an offence; and

(b) the application for a legal aid order has been refused on the ground specified in regulation 12(1)(a); and

(c) the application for a legal aid order was made no later than 21 days before the date fixed for the trial of an information or the inquiry into an offence as examining justices, where such a date had been fixed at the time that the application was made.

(3) An application for review shall not lie to an area committee where the offence is one of those mentioned in Schedule 2 to the Magistrates' Courts Act 1980 and by virtue of section 22 of that Act, the offence is triable only summarily.

(Amended by the Legal Aid in Criminal and Care Proceedings (General) (Amendment) Regulations 1998 (S.I. 1998 No. 662).

Procedure on application for review

16.—(1) An application for review shall be made by giving notice in Form 3 to the appropriate area committee within 14 days of the date of notification of the refusal to make a legal aid order and the applicant shall send a copy of Form 3 to the justices' clerk of the magistrates' court to which the first application for legal aid was made.

(2) An application under paragraph (1) shall be accompanied by the following documents—

(a) a copy of the completed Form 1 returned by the court under regulation 12(2); and

(b) a copy of the notice of refusal received under regulation 12.

(3) The time limit within which the application for review is to be made may, for good reason, be waived or extended by the area committee.

(4) The justices' clerk and the applicant shall supply such further particulars, information and documents as the area committee may require in relation to an application under paragraph (1).

Determination of review

17.—(1) On a review, the area committee shall consider the application for legal aid and either—

(a) refuse the application; or

(b) make a legal aid order.

(2) Where the area committee makes a legal aid order, it shall make a contribution order in accordance with any determination made under regulation 13.

(3) Where a magistrates' court or a justices' clerk has determined under regulation 13 that any legal aid order which is made shall not take effect until a contribution from disposable capital is paid, the area committee shall send the legal aid order to the appropriate justices' clerk.

(4) The area committee shall give notice of its decision and the reasons for it in Form 4 to—

(a) the applicant and his solicitor, if any, and

(b) the justices' clerk of the magistrates' court to which the application for legal aid was made.

(5) In the case of proceedings to which section 22 of the Act applies, the statement of reasons required by paragraph (4) shall comply with regulation 8(4).

Amended by the Legal Aid in Criminal and Care Proceedings (General) (Amendment) Regulations 1995 (S.I. 1995 No. 542).

Proceedings in the Crown Court

18.—(1) An application for a legal aid order in respect of proceeding in the Crown Court shall be made either to the appropriate officer of the Crown Court in Form 1 or

(a) orally to the Crown Court or to a magistrates' court at the conclusion of any proceedings in that magistrates' court; or

(b) where a magistrates' court has been given a notice of transfer under section 4 of the Criminal Justice Act 1987 (serious fraud cases), to the justices' clerk of that magistrates' court in form 1; or

(c) in the case of an appeal to the Crown Court from a magistrates' court, to the justices' clerk of that magistrates' court in Form 1; or

(d) where the applicant was granted legal aid for proceedings in the magistrates' court and was committed for trial in the Crown Court under section 6(2) of the Magistrates' Courts Act 1980, to the justices' clerk of the magistrates' court ordering the committal in such form as may be required; or

(e) in the case of a retrial ordered under section 7 of the Criminal Appeal Act 1968, orally to the court ordering the retrial,

and the appropriate officer, the court or the justices' clerk may grant or refuse the application.

(2) Where an application for a legal aid order is made orally to the court, the court may refer it to the proper officer of the court for determination.

(3) Except where the applicant is not required to furnish a statement of means under regulation 23(4), a legal aid order shall not be made on an application under paragraph (1) until the appropriate officer, the court or the justices' clerk has considered the applicant's statement of means.

Notification of refusal of legal aid

19.—(1) Where an application for a legal aid order is refused by the appropriate officer of the Crown Court, the court or a justices' clerk, the appropriate officer, the court or the justices' clerk shall notify the applicant on Form 2 that the application has been refused on one or both of the following grounds, namely that it does not appear to the officer, the court or the justices' clerk—

(a) desirable to make an order in the interests of justice; or

(b) that the applicant's disposable income and disposable capital are such that, in accordance with regulation 26(1), he is eligible for legal aid,

and shall inform him of the circumstances in which he may renew his application.

(2) Copies of the following documents shall be sent to the applicant and to his solicitor, if any:—

(a) Form 2;

(b) if the application was refused on the ground specified in paragraph (1)(a), the record required to be kept by regulation 8(1).

Amended by the Legal Aid in Criminal and Care Proceedings (General) (Amendment) (No. 2) Regulations 1993 (S.I. 1993 No. 1895) and the Legal Aid in Criminal and Care Proceedings (General) (Amendment) Regulations 1995 (S.I. 1995 No. 542).

Determination of contribution where legal aid is refused

20. Where the appropriate officer of the Crown Court, the court or a justices' clerk has refused to make a legal aid order, the officer, the court or the justices' clerk shall determine—

(a) the applicant's disposable income and disposable capital, and

(b) the amount of any contribution which would have been payable and the manner in which it would be payable by the applicant or an appropriate contributor had a legal aid order been made,

and shall notify the applicant of the amounts so determined.

Renewal of application

21.—(1) An applicant whose application under regulation 18 has been refused may renew his application either orally to the court or to the appropriate officer of the Crown Court.

(2) Where an application is renewed under paragraph (1), the applicant shall return the notice of refusal which he received under regulation 19.

(3) Where an application is renewed to the appropriate officer, he may either grant the application or refer it to a judge of the court.

(4) Where an application is renewed to the court, the court may grant or refuse the application or refer it to the appropriate officer.

(5) A judge of the court to whom an application is referred under paragraph (3) or (6), may grant or refuse the application.

(6) An appropriate officer to whom an application is referred under paragraph (4), may grant the application or refer it to a judge of the court.

(7) Except where the applicant is not required to furnish a statement of means under regulation 23(4), a legal aid order shall not be made where an application is renewed under paragraph (1) until the court or the appropriate officer has considered the applicant's statement of means.

(8) Regulation 19 shall apply where an application is refused under this regulation as if references to a justice's clerk were omitted.

Proceedings in the Court of Appeal or the House of Lords

22.—(1) An application for a legal aid order in respect of proceedings in the Court of Appeal or the House of Lords may be made—

(a) orally to the Court of Appeal, to a judge of the court or the registrar, or

(b) by giving written notice of the application to the registrar in such form as he may direct.

(1A) Where section 44A of the Criminal Appeal Act 1968 (death of convicted person) applies and the applicant is the personal representative of the dead person, the application for legal aid shall be made to the registrar in Form 1A.

(2) Where an application for a legal aid order is made orally to the Court of Appeal, the court may refer it to a judge of the court or the registrar for determination; and, where such an application is made orally to a judge of the court, he may refer it to the registrar for determination.

(3) Where a judge of the court refuses to make a legal aid order, the applicant may renew his application to the Court of Appeal.

(4) The registrar considering an application for a legal aid order shall—

(a) make an order; or

(b) refer the application to the Court of Appeal or to a judge of the court.

(5) A legal aid order shall not be made until—

(a) a notice of appeal or application for leave to appeal to the Court of Appeal or the House of Lords, as the case may be, has been given, and

(b) except where the applicant is not required under regulation 23(4) to furnish a statement of means, the Court of Appeal, a judge of the court or the registrar has considered the applicant's statement of means.

(6) In making a legal aid order in respect of proceedings in the Court of Appeal, the court, a judge of the court or the registrar may specify the stage of the proceedings at which legal aid shall commence.

(7) Subject to the provisions of this regulation, the powers of the Court of Appeal to determine an application for a legal aid order may be exercised by a judge of the court or the registrar.

(8) The powers of the Court of Appeal to revoke a legal aid order may be exercised by a judge of the court or, where the legally assisted person applies for the order to be revoked, by the registrar.

(Amended by the Legal Aid in Criminal and Care Proceedings (General) (Amendment) Regulations 1998 (S.I. 1998 No. 662).

Reports by the Board

22A.—(1) Where the court or the proper officer is considering an application for a legal aid order or at any time after making a legal aid order, the court or the proper officer may refer an applicant, a legally assisted person or an appropriate contributor to the Board for a report on his financial resources.

(2) Where an application is referred under paragraph (1), the Board may make a report to the court or to the proper officer on the financial resources of the person referred to it.

(3) In compiling a report under this regulation, the Board may investigate the financial resources of the person referred to it and may require him to provide further evidence of any information given in a statement of means or of any change in his financial circumstances together with such additional information as the Board may require.

Inserted by the Legal Aid in Criminal and Care Proceedings (General) (Amendment) Regulations 1998 (S.I. 1998 No. 662).

PART III

STATEMENT OF MEANS AND PAYMENT OF CONTRIBUTIONS

Statement of means

23.—(1) A statement of means submitted by an applicant or an appropriate contributor shall be in Form 5 and shall be accompanied by supporting documentary evidence in respect of such matters as may be specified in that Form.

(1A) Where section 44A of the Criminal Appeal Act 1968 (death of convicted person) applies and the applicant is the personal representative of the dead person, the statement of means shall be in Form 1A and not in Form 5.

(2) Subject to paragraphs (3) and (4), where an applicant does not submit a statement of means when he applies for legal aid, the proper officer or the court to which the application is being made shall require him to do so.

(2A) Subject to paragraphs (3) and (4), where an applicant submits a statement of means but neither provides supporting documentary evidence nor supplies an explanation in writing of why it was not reasonably practicable to do so, the proper officer or the court to which the application is being made shall require him to provide such evidence or else supply such written explanation.

(3) Where an applicant is under 16, the proper officer may require either the applicant or an appropriate contributor, or both, to submit a statement of means in accordance with this regulation.

(4) A statement of means and supporting documentary evidence shall be required unless—

    (a) it appears to the court or the proper officer that, by reason of his physical or mental condition, the applicant is for the time being incapable of furnishing such a statement;

    (b) the applicant has already submitted such a statement in connection with a previous application in respect of the same case and his financial circumstances have not changed; or

(c) it appears to the court or the proper officer that the circumstance specified in regulation 26(3) obtains.

(5) Nothing in paragraph (4)(a) shall prevent the court or the proper officer from requiring an applicant to furnish a statement of means after a legal aid order has been made where it appears that he is no longer incapable of furnishing such a statement.

Amended by the Legal Aid in Criminal and Care Proceedings (General) (Amendment) (No. 2) Regulations 1993 (S.I. 1993 No. 1895), the Legal Aid in Criminal and Care Proceedings (General) (Amendment) Regulations 1994 (S.I. 1994 No. 807), the Legal Aid in Criminal and Care Proceedings (General) (Amendment) Regulations 1995 (S.I. 1995 No. 542) and the Legal Aid in Criminal and Care Proceedings (General) (Amendment) Regulations 1998 (S.I. 1998 No. 662).

Provision of information

24.—(1) The court or the proper officer may at any time the court or the proper officer may require the applicant, the legally assisted person or the appropriate contributor to provide further evidence of any information given in a statement of means or of any change in his financial circumstances together with such additional information as the court or the proper officer may require.

(2) Where representation is granted to an applicant who provided a reasonable explanation of why, at the time of submission of the statement of means, it was not reasonably practicable to provide supporting documentary evidence, the court or proper officer may subsequently require the assisted person to provide documentary evidence where it appears that it has become reasonably practicable to do so.

(3) Where, pursuant to paragraph (2), documentary evidence is provided, the determination or redetermination of any contribution payable or the amount of any contribution order, shall be in accordance with regulations 32 and 33.

Amended by the Legal Aid in Criminal and Care Proceedings (General) (Amendment) (No. 2) Regulations 1993 (S.I. 1993 No. 1895), the Legal Aid in Criminal and Care Proceedings (General) (Amendment) Regulations 1994 (S.I. 1994 No. 807) and the Legal Aid in Criminal and Care Proceedings (General) (Amendment) (No. 3) Regulations 1996 (S.I. 1996 No. 1258).

Determination of contributions

25.—(1) The court or the proper officer shall, when making a legal aid order, determine the amount of any contribution payable by the applicant, the legally assisted person or the appropriate contributor in accordance with regulation 26.

(2) Where the applicant or the legally assisted person has paid or is liable to pay a contribution under section 9(6) of the Act in respect of advice and assistance given in relation to the same proceedings, any contribution which he or an appropriate contributor is liable to make under section 23(1) of the Act in respect of the costs of representation shall be reduced by the total amount of any contribution paid or liable to be paid under section 9(6).

Assessment of resources and method of determining contributions

26.—(1) Representation shall not be granted to a person for any purpose unless it appears that his financial resources are such that he requires assistance in meeting the costs which he may incur for that purpose.

(2) The court or the proper officer shall—

(a) consider the statement of means and supporting documentary evidence submitted by the applicant or the appropriate contributor and any other relevant information; and

(b) subject to paragraphs (2A) and (3), determine his disposable income and disposable capital in accordance with Schedule 3.

(2A) Where the documentary evidence or information which an applicant or legally assisted person or appropriate contributor is required to produce under regulations 23, 24(1) or 22A(3) is deficient and no reasonable explanation is given for the deficiency, the court or proper officer may—

(a) refuse representation if the court or proper officer considers, on the basis of the information available, that the applicant's financial-resources are not such that he requires assistance; or

(b) deem his disposable income and disposable capital as exceeding the limits below which no contribution is payable by virtue of Schedule 4, and fix the contribution payable by him at such an amount as the court or the proper officer may determine or (in the case of a legally assisted person) redetermine.

(3) The court or the proper officer shall not make a determination under paragraph (2)(b) where—

(a) the applicant,

(b) the appropriate contributor, or

(c) the spouse of the applicant or appropriate contributor, is in receipt of income-based jobseeker's allowance, income support, family credit or disability working allowance and this paragraph shall apply to a man and a woman who are living with each other in the same household as husband and wife as it applies to the parties to a marriage.

(4) Subject to paragraph (3), the applicant or the appropriate contributor shall pay a contribution in accordance with the provisions of Schedule 4.

Amended by the Legal Aid in Criminal and Care Proceedings (General) (Amendment) (No. 2) Regulations 1993 (S.I. 1993 No. 1895), the Legal Aid in Criminal and Care Proceedings (General) (Amendment) (No. 3) Regulations 1996 (S.I. 1996 No. 1258) and the Legal Aid in Criminal and Care Proceedings (General) (Amendment) Regulations 1998 (S.I. 1998 No. 662).

Contribution orders

27.—(1) The court or the proper officer of the court shall make a contribution order, in Form 6, in respect of any contribution determined under regulation 26 above and shall endorse the legal aid order accordingly.

(2) A copy of the contribution order shall be sent to the person ordered to make the contribution, to the legally assisted person's solicitor or counsel (where counsel only is assigned) and to the collecting court.

Earlier contribution orders

28. *[Omitted by the Legal Aid in Criminal and Care Proceedings (General) (Amendment) Regulations 1993 (S.I. 1993 No. 789).]*

Payment of contributions

29.—(1) Any contribution which is to be paid out of disposable income shall be payable by weekly (or, at the discretion of the court or the proper officer of the court, by fortnightly or monthly instalments) for the period during which a legal aid order is in force, and the first such instalment shall fall due 7 days from the making of the legal aid order or of the contribution order, whichever is the later.

(2) Any contribution which is to be paid out of disposable capital shall be paid immediately if the sum is readily available or, if it is not, at such time as the court or the proper officer of the court considers to be reasonable in all the circumstances.

(3) Where a contribution out of disposable capital is to be paid immediately, the legal aid order shall not take effect until such payment is made and the court or the proper officer of the court shall give notice of this fact in Form 7 to—

(a) the applicant and the appropriate contributor, and

(b) the solicitor assigned or, where counsel only is assigned, counsel.

(4) The period referred to in paragraph (1) above means the period from the grant of a legal aid order to—

(a) the final conclusion of the proceedings whether in the court in which the legal aid order was made or in another court following a committal for trial or sentence or remittal; or,

(b) where the legal aid order is withdrawn or revoked, the date of such withdrawal or revocation.

Amended by the Legal Aid in Criminal and Care Proceedings (General) (Amendment) Regulations 1993 (S.I. 1993 No. 789).

Method of payment of contributions

30.—(1) Subject to paragraph (2), payment of contributions shall be made to the proper officer of the collecting court.

(2) Where a legal aid order is not to take effect until a contribution out of disposable capital is paid, such payment shall be made to the proper officer of the court making the legal aid order unless that court otherwise directs.

Change in financial circumstances

31. The legally assisted person or the appropriate contributor shall forthwith inform the court or the proper officer of the court of any change in his financial circumstances which has occurred since he applied for a legal aid order and which he has reason to believe—

(a) might make him liable to pay a contribution where such a contribution is not already payable; or

(b) might affect the terms of any contribution order made in connection with a legal aid order.

Amended by the Legal Aid in Criminal and Care Proceedings (General) (Amendment) (No. 3) Regulations 1996 (S.I. 1996 No. 1258) and the Legal Aid in Criminal and Care Proceedings (General) (Amendment) Regulations 1998 (S.I. 1998 No. 662).

Determination where no contribution previously payable

32.—(1) The court or the proper officer of the court shall determine the amount of any contribution payable by a legally assisted person or an appropriate contributor who is not already liable to make such a contribution where—

(a) further information or a report from the Board under regulation 22A(2) has become available as to the amount of disposable income and disposable capital available at the time when the legal aid order was made; or

(b) the circumstances upon which the disposable income or disposable capital were determined at the time the legal aid order was made have altered during the period in which the legal aid order was in force;

and it appears likely that, were such a determination to be made, the legally assisted person or the appropriate contributor would be liable to make a contribution.

(2) Regulation 26 shall apply where a contribution is determined under paragraph (1) as it applies where a contribution is determined on the making of a legal aid order.

Amended by the Legal Aid in Criminal and Care Proceedings (General) (Amendment) Regulations 1993 (S.I. 1993 No. 789) and the Legal Aid in Criminal and Care Proceedings (General) (Amendment) Regulations 1998 (S.I. 1998 No. 662).

Redetermination of contribution

33. Except where it appears unlikely that any significant change in liability to make a contribution would result, the court or the proper officer of the court shall redetermine the amount of any contribution payable by a legally assisted person or an appropriate contributor under a legal aid order where—

(a) further information or a report from the Board under regulation 22A(2) has become available as to the amounts of disposable income and disposable capital available at the time when the contribution order was made; or

(b) the circumstances upon which the disposable income or disposable capital were determined at the time when the contribution order was made have altered so that—

 (i) his disposable income may have increased by an amount greater than £750 a year or decreased by an amount greater than £300 a year; or

 (ii) his disposable capital may have increased by an amount greater than £750;

and shall vary or revoke the contribution order accordingly.

Amended by the Legal Aid in Criminal and Care Proceedings (General) (Amendment) Regulations 1993 (S.I. 1993 No. 789) and the Legal Aid in Criminal and Care Proceedings (General) (Amendment) Regulations 1998 (S.I. 1998 No. 662).

Effect of error or mistake

34. Where it appears to the court or the proper officer that there has been some error or mistake in the determination of the legally assisted person's or the appropriate contributor's disposable income, disposable capital or contribution and that it would be just and equitable to correct the error or mistake, the court or the proper officer may vary the contribution order accordingly, may revoke it or may make a contribution order.

Variation and revocation of contribution orders

35.—(1) At the conclusion of the proceedings the court in which those proceedings are concluded may, if it thinks fit—

(a) remit any sum due under a contribution order which falls to be paid after the conclusion of the proceedings; or

(b) remit or order the repayment of any sum due or paid under a contribution order where the legally assisted person has been acquitted or where the proceedings were discontinued or withdrawn.

(2) Where the legal aid order in connection with which a contribution order was made is revoked, paragraph (1) shall apply as if the proceedings had been concluded.

(3) Where a legally assisted person—

(a) successfully appeals against his conviction; or

(b) is respondent to an appeal which is unsuccessful,

the court hearing the appeal may remit or order the repayment of any sum due or paid under a contribution order.

(4) Where a contribution order has been varied and the sum of the total contributions paid up to the conclusion of the proceedings exceeds the amount which was due taking into account the variation, the court or the proper officer shall order repayment of an amount equal to the difference between the sums paid and the amount due.

(5) Where—

(a) a contribution order is varied to an amount greater than that which was previously payable; or

(b) a contribution order is made after a determination under regulation 32,

the payment of any contributions shall be made in accordance with the provisions of regulation 29, save that in respect of payments to be made out of disposable income, the court or the proper officer may extend the period within which such payment is to be made beyond the conclusion of the proceedings.

Amended by the Legal Aid in Criminal and Care Proceedings (General) (Amendment) Regulations 1993 (S.I. 1993 No. 789) and the Legal Aid in Criminal and Care Proceedings (General) (Amendment) (No. 4) Regulations 1997 (S.I. 1997 No. 2647).

Refusal to pay contribution

36.—(1) Where any sums which are due under a contribution order before the conclusion of the proceedings have not been paid by the legally assisted person, the court or the proper officer of that court may—

(a) serve notice on the legally assisted person requiring him to comply with the contribution order and pay any sums due under it within 7 days of receiving such notice; and

(b) if he does not do so, serve notice on him inviting him to make representations as to why he cannot comply with the contribution order.

(2) A notice given under paragraph (1)(a) shall be in Form 9 and a notice given under paragraph (1)(b) in Form 10 and copies of any notices so given shall be sent to the legally assisted person and to his solicitor or, where counsel only is assigned, to counsel.

(3) The court shall consider any representations made under paragraph (1)(b) and, if satisfied that the legally assisted person—

(a) was able to pay the relevant contribution when it was due; and

(b) is able to pay the whole or part of it but has failed or refused to do so,

may revoke the grant of representation.

(4) The revocation of the grant of representation under paragraph (3) shall not affect the right of any legal representative previously assigned to the legally assisted person to remuneration for work done before the date of the revocation.

Termination of contribution period

37.—(1) Where a legal aid order is still in force and—

(a) the legally assisted person, the appropriate contributor or the spouse of the legally assisted person or appropriate contributor begins to receive **income-based jobseeker's allowance**, income support, family credit or disability working allowance (in this regulation referred to as "income-related benefits"); or

(b) the court remits any sum due under a contribution order which falls to be paid after the conclusion of the relevant proceedings; or

(c) the legally assisted person is sentenced in the proceedings to which the legal aid order relates to an immediate term of imprisonment or a sentence of detention in a young offender institution,

the liability to pay any further contributions shall end on the date receipt of income-related benefits commenced or on the date of that remission or sentence, as the case may be.

(2) The court making any such remission or passing any such sentence shall inform the collecting court that the liability to pay further contributions ended on the date of the remission or sentence.

(3) Without prejudice to regulation 31, the legally assisted person or the appropriate contributor shall inform the collecting court of the date on which receipt of income-related benefits commenced.

(4) Paragraph (1)(a) shall apply to a man and a woman who are living with each other in the same household as husband and wife as it applies to the parties to a marriage.

Amended by the Legal Aid in Criminal and Care Proceedings (General) (Amendment) Regulations 1993 (S.I. 1993 No. 789) and, from October 7, 1996 as to the words in bold by the Legal Aid in Criminal and Care Proceedings (General) (Amendment) (No. 3) Regulations 1996 (S.I. 1996 No. 1258).

Disposal of sums received from legally assisted persons after conviction

38.—(1) Where a legally assisted person or an appropriate contributor to whom this regulation applies has been ordered to make a contribution, any amounts falling due under the contribution order after the conclusion of the relevant proceedings and any extension of the period for the purposes of regulation 35(5) shall, unless remitted or specifically appropriated by the person paying the money to payment of the contribution, be applied (when paid) first, in accordance with the provisions of section 139 of the Magistrates' Court Act 1980 and any sum paid in addition to the sums referred to in paragraph (2) below shall be paid to the Lord Chancellor in accordance with paragraph 4(2) of Schedule 3 to the Act.

(2) This regulation applies to a legally assisted person who is ordered to pay any sum adjudged to be paid on conviction and to an appropriate contributor who is ordered to pay a fine, compensation or costs under the provisions of section 55 of the Children and Young Persons Act 1933 or section 3 of the Children and Young Person Act 1969.

Amended by the Legal Aid in Criminal and Care Proceedings (General) (Amendment) Regulations 1993 (S.I. 1993 No. 789).

Repayment of contributions

39. On receiving notification of the amount of the costs of representation determined by the appropriate authority under the Legal Aid in Criminal and Care Proceedings (Costs) Regulations 1989, the collecting court or the proper officer of that court shall, in accordance with section 23(7) of the Act, repay to the legally assisted person or the appropriate contributor, as the case may be, the amount, if any, by which any contribution paid exceeds those costs.

PART IV

LEGAL AID ORDERS

Legal aid orders

40.—(1) A magistrates' court inquiring into an offence as examining justices may make a legal aid order which applies, or amend an order so that it applies, both to proceedings before the court and, in the event of the defendant being committed for trial, to his trial before the Crown Court and, where such an order is made,—

    (a) Form 11 shall be used; and

    (b) copies of the order shall be sent in accordance with paragraph (2) below or with regulation 50(3), as the case may be.

(2) A legal aid order for the purposes of proceedings in a magistrates' court, the Crown Court or the Court of Appeal shall be in Form 11, 11A, 12 or 13 as the case may be and, subject to regulations 17(3) and 29(3), the court or the proper officer shall send—

    (a) one copy to the legally assisted person; and

    (b) one copy to the solicitor assigned or to counsel (where counsel only is assigned); and

where the legal aid order is made for the purposes of proceeding before a magistrates' court, a further copy (endorsed "Board copy") shall be sent under sub-paragraph (b) above.

(3) Where a legal aid order is made by an area committee for the purposes of proceedings in a magistrates' court, one copy shall be sent to the proper officer of the court to which the application for legal aid was made.

(4) Where a legal aid order is amended under regulation 50, copies of the amended order shall be sent in accordance with paragraph (3) of that regulation.

(5) Where the solicitor assigned instructs counsel, the instructions which are delivered to counsel shall include a copy of the legal aid order and the solicitor shall inform counsel of any amendments made to the legal aid order.

Withdrawal and revocations legal aid orders

41.—(1) A legal aid order may be withdrawn—

(a) where the legally assisted person declines to accept the terms on which a grant of representation may be made;

(b) at the request of the legally assisted person;

(c) in accordance with the provisions of regulation 50.

(d) where, as a result of information which has been provided under these Regulations or otherwise, it appears to the court or proper officer that the legally assisted person's resources are not such that he requires assistance.

Amended by the Legal Aid in Criminal and Care Proceedings (General) (Amendment) (No. 3) Regulations 1996 (S.I. 1996 No. 1258).

(2) Where two legal aid orders are made in respect of the same proceedings, the second order so made shall be deemed to be of no effect and shall be withdrawn as if the legally assisted person had made a request under paragraph (1)(b) above.

(3) An order withdrawing a legal aid order shall be in Form 14 and a copy of it shall be sent to—

(a) the legally assisted person, or

(b) the solicitor assigned or to counsel (where counsel only is assigned); and

(c) where the legal aid order is withdrawn by the area committee, to the proper officer of the court to which the application for withdrawal was made.

(4) Where a legal aid order is withdrawn—

(a) the counsel assigned shall send all papers and other items in his possession relating to the proceedings to the solicitor assigned or (where no solicitor was assigned) to the legally assisted person; and

(b) the solicitor assigned shall send all papers and other items in his possession relating to the proceedings to the legally assisted person.

(5) Where a legal aid order is revoked under regulation 36(3), the foregoing paragraphs of this regulation shall apply, with any necessary modifications, as if the order had been withdrawn.

Amended by the Legal Aid in Criminal and Care Proceedings (General) (Amendment) (No. 2) Regulations 1993 (S.I. 1993 No. 1895).

Withdrawal for abuse of legal aid or for failure to provide information

41A.—(1) Without prejudice to regulation 41, a legal aid order may be withdrawn where, as a result of information which has been provided under these Regulations or otherwise, it appears that the legally assisted person has—

(a) in relation to any application for a legal aid order, made an untrue statement as to his financial resources or has failed to disclose any material fact concerning them; or

(b) intentionally failed to comply with any provision of regulations made under the Act by not furnishing any material information concerning any matter other than his financial resources or in furnishing such information has knowingly made a false statement or false representation, and, in this regulation, "legally assisted person" includes an appropriate contributor.

(2) A legal aid order shall not be withdrawn under paragraph (1)(a) where the legally assisted person satisfies the court that he used due care or diligence to avoid such mis-statement or failure.

(3) A legal aid order may be withdrawn where the court is satisfied that the legally assisted person has failed to attend for an interview or to provide information or documents when required to do so under these Regulations.

(4) Regulation 41(3) and (4) shall apply where a legal aid order is withdrawn under this regulation as it applies where an order is withdrawn under that regulation.

Inserted by the Legal Aid in Criminal and Care Proceedings (General) (Amendment) (No. 3) Regulations 1996 (S.I. 1996 No. 1258). Paragraph (2) amended by the Legal Aid in Criminal and Care Proceedings (General) (Amendment) (No. 4) Regulations 1996 (S.I. 1996 No. 2307).

Notes of evidence and depositions

42. Where a legal aid order is made in respect of an appeal to the Crown Court, the justices clerk shall supply, on the application of the solicitor assigned to the appellant or respondent on whose application such an order was made, copies of any notes of evidence or depositions taken in the proceedings in the magistrates' court.

Transfer of documents

43. Where a person is committed by a lower court to a higher court or appeals or applies for leave to appeal from a lower court to a higher court, the proper officer of the lower court shall send to the proper officer of the higher court the following documents—

(a) a copy of any legal aid order previously made in respect of the same proceeding;

(b) a copy of any contribution order made;

(c) a copy of any legal aid application which has been refused;

(d) any statement of means already submitted.

PART V

LEGAL REPRESENTATION

Nature of representation

44.—(1) Subject to the following paragraphs of this regulation, a grant of representation shall provide for the services of two legal representatives, whether expressed as such or in equivalent terms, namely solicitor and counsel or authorised litigator and authorised advocate.

(2) A legal aid order granting representation for the purpose of such part of any proceedings before a magistrates' court as relates to the giving of bail shall not include representation by counsel.

(3) A legal aid order granting representation for the purposes of proceedings before a magistrates' court shall not include representation by counsel except—

(a) in the case of any indictable offence, where the court is of the opinion that, because of circumstances which make the case unusually grave or difficult, representation by both solicitor and counsel would be desirable or,

(b) in the case of proceedings under section 9 of the Extradition Act 1989 or paragraph 6 of Schedule 1 to that Act, where the court is of the opinion that, because of circumstances which make the proceedings unusually grave or difficult, representation by both solicitor and counsel would be desirable.

Paragraph (1) amended by the Legal Aid in Criminal and Care Proceedings (General) (Amendment) (No. 5) Regulations 1996 (S.I. 1996 No. 2656).

Paragraph (b) removed by the Legal Aid in Criminal and Care Proceedings (General) (Amendment) (No. 2) Regulations 1991 and reinserted by the Legal Aid in Criminal and Care Proceedings (General) (Amendment) (No. 3) Regulations 1997 (S.I. 1997 No. 1985.)

(4) Where a court grants representation for purposes of appeal to the Court of Appeal, the court may order that representation shall be by counsel only.

(5) Where the Crown Court grants representation for the purposes of—

(a) an appeal to that court;

(b) proceedings in which a person is committed to or appears before that court for trial or sentence or appears or is brought before the Crown Court to be dealt with;

the court may, in cases of urgency where it appears to the court that there is no time to instruct a solicitor, order that representation shall be by counsel only.

(6) Where the Crown Court or a magistrates' court grants representation for the purposes specified in paragraph (5), the court may, if the proceedings are proceedings in which solicitors have a right of audience, order that representation shall be by a solicitor only.

(7) Where in proceedings in a magistrates' court representation or advice is given before a legal aid order is made, that representation or advice shall be deemed to be representation or advice given under the order if—

(a) the interests of justice required that the representation or advice be provided as a matter of urgency;

(b) there was no undue delay in making an application for legal aid; and

(c) the representation or advice was given by the solicitor who was subsequently assigned under the legal aid order.

Assignment of solicitor and selection of counsel

45.—(1) Subject to regulations 46 and 49, any person who is granted representation entitling him to the services of a solicitor, may select any solicitor who is willing to act and such solicitor shall be assigned to him.

(2) Subject to regulations 46 and 49, where a legal aid order is made providing for the services of solicitor and counsel, the solicitor may instruct any counsel who is willing to act.

Assignment of solicitor or counsel for the Court of Appeal or the House of Lords

46.—(1) In the case of proceedings in the Court of Appeal or the House of Lords, counsel may be assigned by the court, a judge of the court or the proper officer making or amending the legal aid order.

(2) In assigning Counsel or a solicitor to a legally assisted person in respect of an appeal to the Court of Appeal or the House of Lords, the court, a judge of the court or the proper officer shall have regard, as far as is reasonably practicable, to the wishes of the legally assisted person, the identity of the solicitor or counsel, if any, who represented him in any earlier proceedings and the nature of the appeal.

Assignment of counsel only

47.—(1) Where a legal aid order granting representation for the purposes of proceedings in the Crown Court is made or amended so as to provide for representation by counsel only, counsel shall be assigned by the court or proper officer making or amending the legal aid order.

(2) Where a legal aid order granting representation for the purposes of proceedings in the Court of Appeal or the Courts-Martial Appeal Court is made or amended so as to provide for representation by counsel only, counsel shall be assigned by the court, a judge of the court or the proper officer.

Assignment of Queen's Counsel or more than one counsel

48.—(1) A legal aid order may provide for the services of a Queen's Counsel or of more than one counsel in respect of the whole or any specified part of any proceedings only in the cases specified and in the manner provided for by the following paragraphs of this regulation.

(2) The cases specified for the purposes of this regulation are trials in the Crown Court or proceedings in the Court of Appeal or the House of Lords—

- (a) on a charge of murder;
- (b) where it appears to the court making the order that the case is one of exceptional difficulty, gravity or complexity and that a legal aid order for the provision of services in the terms provided for by paragraph (3)(a) or (b) of this regulation is required in the interests of justice; or
- (c) where the prosecution is being brought by the Serious Fraud Office.

(3) Subject to paragraphs (4) to (9), a legal aid order may provide for the services of a Queen's Counsel or of more than one counsel in any of the following terms—

- (a) a Queen's Counsel alone;
- (b) where two counsel are required—
  - (i) a Queen's Counsel with a junior counsel, or
  - (ii) a Queen's Counsel with a noting junior counsel, or
  - (iii) two junior counsel, or
  - (iv) a junior counsel with a noting junior counsel.

(4) In proceedings to which paragraph (2)(c) applies, a court making a legal order may, if it considers that three counsel are required, provide for the services of three counsel in any of the terms provided for in paragraph (3)(b) plus an extra junior counsel or noting junior counsel.

(5) The fact that a Queen's Counsel has been or is proposed to be assigned under this regulation shall not by itself be a reason for making an order in any of the terms provided for by paragraph (3)(b) or (4).

(6) Where a Queen's Counsel has been or is proposed to be assigned under this regulation, no order in any of the terms provided for by paragraph (3)(b) or (4) shall be made where it appears to the court at the time of making the order that—

(a) there is reasonable certainty that the indictment will be disposed of by a guilty plea and there are no special circumstances requiring the provision of the services of more than one counsel, or

(b) the case relates to an appeal to the Court of Appeal or to the House of Lords and representation can properly be undertaken by a Queen's Counsel alone.

(7) Unless the court to which the application is made otherwise directs, every application for a legal aid order in any of the terms provided for by paragraph (3) or (4) or for an amendment under paragraph (10) or (11) shall be in writing specifying—

(a) the terms of the order sought and the grounds of the application; and

(b) if the order sought is for the provision of services in any terms provided for by paragraph (3)(b) or (4), the reasons why two counsel are required or an extra junior counsel or noting junior counsel is required as the case may be.

(8) A court may, before making a legal aid order in the terms provided for by paragraph (3) or (4) or amending the order under paragraph (10) or (11), require written advice from any counsel already assigned to the applicant on the question of what representation is needed in the proceedings.

(9) A magistrates' court which is competent as respects any proceedings by virtue of section 20(4) or (5) of the Act may make a legal aid order providing for the services of a Queen's Counsel with one junior counsel where:—

(a) the proceedings are a trial for murder and the order is made upon committal or transfer for trial, or

(b) the prosecution is brought by the Serious Fraud Office and the order is made upon receiving a notice of transfer under section 4 of the Criminal Justice Act 1987

but shall have no other power to make an order under this regulation.

(10) In proceedings to which paragraph (2)(a) or (b) applies, a legal aid order which provides—

(a) for one counsel only may be amended to provide for the services of a Queen's Counsel or of more than one counsel in any terms provided for by paragraph (3),

(b) for two counsel in any terms provided for by paragraph (3)(b) may be amended to provide for the services of the same number of counsel but in other terms provided for by that paragraph, or for a Queen's Counsel alone, or for one counsel only in accordance with regulation 47.

(11) In proceedings to which paragraph (2)(c) applies, a legal aid order which provides—

(a) for one counsel only may be amended to provide for the services of a Queen's Counsel or of more than one counsel in any terms provided for by paragraph (3) or (4);

(b) for two counsel in any terms provided for by paragraph (3)(b) may be amended to provide for the services of three counsel in any terms provided for by paragraph (4), for two counsel but in other terms provided for by paragraph (3)(b), or for a Queen's Counsel alone, or for one counsel only in accordance with regulation 47;

(c) for three counsel in any terms provided for by paragraph (4) may be amended to provide for the same number of counsel but in other terms provided for by paragraph (4), or for two counsel in any terms provided for by paragraph (3)(b), or for a Queen's Counsel alone, or for one counsel only in accordance with regulation 47.

(12) In every case in which a legal aid order is made under this regulation for the provision of services in terms provided for by paragraph (3) or (4), it shall be the duty of—

(a) each legal representative—

    (i) to keep under review the need for more than one counsel to be present in court or otherwise providing services, and

    (ii) to consider whether the legal aid order should be amended as provided for in paragraph (10) or (11);

(b) Queen's Counsel, where the services of a Queen's Counsel are provided, to keep under review whether he could act alone.

(13) It shall be the duty of each legal representative, if of the opinion that the legal aid order should be amended as provided for in paragraphs (10) and (11), to notify that opinion in writing

(a) to the other legal representatives for the assisted person, and

(b) to the court;

and the court shall, after considering the opinion and any representations made by any other legal representatives for the assisted person determine whether and in what manner the legal aid order should be amended.

(14) A decision to make or amend a legal aid order so as to provide for the services of a Queen's Counsel or of more than one counsel may only be made:

(a) in the cases specified in paragraph (2)(a) or (b), by a circuit judge or a High Court judge where the proceedings are in the Crown Court, or by a judge of the Court of Appeal or the Registrar where the proceedings are in the Court of Appeal;

(b) in the case specified in paragraph (2)(c), by the judge expected to try the case or a High Court judge where the proceedings are in the Crown Court, or by a High Court judge or a judge of the Court of Appeal where the proceedings are in the Court of Appeal.

Substituted by the Legal Aid in Criminal and Care Proceedings (General) (Amendment) (No. 2) Regulations 1994 (S.I. 1994 No. 3136).

Assignment of one solicitor or counsel to more than one legally assisted person

49. A solicitor or counsel may be assigned to two or more legally assisted persons whose cases are to be heard together, unless the interests of justice require that such persons be separately represented.

Amendment of legal aid orders

50.—(1) A court having power to make a legal aid order may, on application, amend any such order by substituting for any legal representative or representatives previously assigned under the order any legal representative or representatives whom the court could have assigned if it had then been making the legal aid order.

(2) A court having power to make a legal aid order may withdraw any such order if the only legal representative or all the legal representatives for the time being assigned under the order withdraws or withdraw from the case and it appears to the court that, because of the legally assisted person's conduct, it is not desirable to amend the order under paragraph (1) above.

(3) An order amending a legal aid order shall be in Form 15 and a copy of it shall be sent to—

(a) the legally assisted person;

(b) the solicitor assigned by the legal aid order or to counsel (where counsel only is assigned) and to any solicitor and counsel assigned by the amended legal aid order; and

(c) where the legal aid order is amended by an area committee, to the proper officer of the court to which the application for amendment was made.

(4) Where a new solicitor or counsel (where counsel only was assigned) is assigned by an order amending a legal aid order, the solicitor or counsel originally assigned shall send all papers and other items in his possession relating to the proceedings to the new solicitor or counsel.

Applications for amendment of legal aid orders, etc.

51.—(1) An application for—

(a) representation by counsel in any proceedings of a kind specified in regulation 44(3); or

(b) the amendment or withdrawal of a legal aid order under regulation 50(1) or (2),

shall be made to the proper officer stating the grounds on which the application is made and the proper officer may grant or refuse the application.

(2) Where an application under paragraph (1) is refused, the applicant may renew his application both to the court and (except where paragraph (6) applies) to an area committee, and the proper officer shall notify the applicant of the circumstances in which an application may be renewed.

(3) Where an application is renewed to the court, the court may grant or refuse the application or refer it to the proper officer.

(4) The proper officer to whom an application is referred under paragraph (3), may—

(a) grant the application; or

(b) where the proper officer is a justices' clerk, refer it either back to the court or to a justice of the peace; or

(c) where the proper officer is not a justices' clerk, refer it to a judge of the court.

(5) The court, a judge of the court or a justice of the peace to whom an application is referred under paragraph (4) may grant or refuse the application.

(6) An application may be renewed under paragraph (2) to an area committee except where—

(a) an application under the same sub-paragraph of paragraph (1) in the same proceedings has previously been refused by an area committee or by the court; or

(b) the application was made—

  (i) in the case of proceedings in the Crown Court, more than 14 days after the committal for trial or sentence or the date of giving of notice of appeal; or

  (ii) in the case of proceedings in a magistrates' court, less than 14 days before the date fixed for the trial of an information or the inquiry into an offence as examining justices, where such a date had been fixed at the time the application was made; or

(c) the application is an application in respect of proceedings in the Court of Appeal, the Courts-Martial Appeal Court or the House of Lords.

Renewal to area committee of application for amendment of legal aid order, etc.

52.—(1) Where an application under regulation 51 is renewed to an area committee, the legally assisted person shall send to the Area Director the following documents—

(a) a copy of the legal aid order and of the notice of refusal;

(b) any papers presented to the proper officer by the legally assisted person or his solicitor in support of the application; and

(c) any other relevant documents or information.

(2) The proper officer and the legally assisted person or his solicitor shall supply such further particulars, information and documents as the area committee may require.

Consideration by area committee

53.—(1) The area committee shall consider the application and any further particulars, information or documents submitted to it under regulation 52 and any other relevant information and shall grant or refuse the application and, where necessary, amend or revoke the legal aid order accordingly.

(2) The area committee shall notify the proper officer of the court and the legally assisted person and his solicitor of its decision.

PART VI

AUTHORITY TO INCUR COSTS AND RESTRICTIONS ON PAYMENT OF LEGAL REPRESENTATIVES

Powers of area committee to authorise expenditure

54.—(1) Where it appears to a legally assisted person's solicitor necessary for the proper conduct of proceedings in a magistrates' court or in the Crown Court for costs to be incurred under the legal aid order by taking any of the following steps—

(a) obtaining a written report or opinion of one or more experts;

(b) employing a person to provide a written report or opinion (otherwise than as an expert);

(c) bespeaking transcripts of shorthand notes or of tape recordings of any proceedings, including police questioning of suspects;

(d) where a legal aid order provides for the services of solicitor and counsel, instructing a Queen's Counsel alone without junior counsel; or

(e) performing an act which is either unusual in its nature or involves unusually large expenditure;

he may apply to the appropriate area committee for prior authority so to do.

(2) Where an area committee authorises the taking of any step specified in paragraph (1)(a), (b), (c) or (e), it shall also authorise the maximum fee to be paid for any such report, opinion, transcript or act.

Prior approval for travelling and accommodation expenses

54A. A legal representative assigned to a legally assisted person in any proceedings in the Crown Court may apply to the appropriate authority for prior approval for the incurring of travelling and accommodation expenses in order to attend at the trial or other main hearing in those proceedings.

Inserted by the Legal Aid in Criminal and Care Proceedings (General) (Amendment) (No. 2) Regulations 1997 (S.I. 1997 No. 1485).

Restriction on payment

55. Where a legal aid order has been made, the legally assisted person's solicitor or counsel shall not receive or be a party to the making of any payment for work done in connection with the proceedings in respect of which the legal aid order was made except such payments as may be made—

(a) out of the legal aid fund or by the Lord Chancellor, or

(b) in respect of any expenses or fees incurred in—

(i) preparing, obtaining or considering any report, opinion or further evidence, whether provided by an expert witness or otherwise; or

(ii) bespeaking transcripts of shorthand notes or tape recordings of any proceedings, including police questioning of suspects;

where an application under regulation 54 for authority to incur such expenses or fees has been refused by the area committee.

Duty to report abuse of legal aid

56. Notwithstanding the relationship between or rights of a legal representative and client or any privilege arising out of such relationship, where the legal representative for an applicant or legally assisted person knows or suspects that that person has intentionally failed to comply with any provision of regulations made under the Act concerning the information to be furnished by him or in furnishing such information has knowingly made a false statement or false representation, the legal representative shall forthwith report the circumstances to the proper officer.

Inserted by the Legal Aid in Criminal and Care Proceedings (General) (Amendment) (No. 2) Regulations 1993 (S.I. 1993 No. 1895) and amended by the Legal Aid in Criminal and Care Proceedings (General) (Amendment) (No. 3) Regulations 1996 (S.I. 1996 No. 1258).

SCHEDULES

SCHEDULE 1

REGULATIONS REVOKED

Title	Reference
The Legal Aid in Criminal Proceedings (General) Regulations 1968	S.I. 1968/1231

The Courts-Martial Appeal Legal Aid (General) Regulations 1969	S.I. 1969/177
The Legal Aid in Criminal Proceedings (General) (Amendment) Regulations 1970	S.I. 1970/1980
The Legal Aid in Criminal Proceedings (General) (Amendment) Regulations 1976	S.I. 1976/790
The Legal Aid in Criminal Proceedings (General) (Amendment) Regulations 1980	S.I. 1980/661
The Legal Aid in Criminal Proceedings (General) (Amendment No. 2) Regulations 1980	S.I. 1980/1651
The Legal Aid in Criminal Proceedings (General) (Amendment) Regulations 1983	S.I. 1983/1863
The Legal Aid in Criminal Proceedings (General) (Amendment) Regulations 1984	S.I. 1984/1716
The Legal Aid in Criminal Proceedings (General) (Amendment) Regulations 1985	S.I. 1985/1632
The Legal Aid in Criminal Proceedings (General) (Amendment) Regulations 1986	S.I. 1986/274
The Legal Aid in Criminal Proceedings (General) (Amendment) Regulations 1987	S.I. 1987/422
The Legal Aid in Criminal Proceedings (General) (Amendment) Regulations 1988	S.I. 1988/468
The Legal Aid in Criminal Proceedings (General) (Amendment) (No. 2) Regulations 1988	S.I. 1988/2303

SCHEDULE 2

FORMS

Application for Legal Aid in Criminal Proceedings Magistrates' or Crown Court

Form 1
Regs 11 & 18
(also known as
Crown Court Form 5131)

I apply for Legal Aid—

For the purposes of proceedings before the | Crown/Magistrates'/Youth Court*

1. Personal Details: *(Please use BLOCK letters and BLACK ink)*

a) Surname

e) Date of birth

b) Forenames

c) Permanent address

d) Present address
   (if different from above)

2. Case Details:

a) Describe briefly what it is
   you are accused of doing, e.g.
   "stealing £50 from my
   employer", "kicking a door
   causing £50 damage".

b) The following other person(s)
   is/are charged in this case

c) Give reasons why you and
   the other persons charged in
   this case, if any, should not
   be represented by the same
   solicitor.

3. Court Proceedings: *(Complete section a or b whichever applies)*

a) I am due to appear before

the		Magistrates/Youth Court*
on	19	at	am/pm

or

b) I appeared before

the		Magistrates/Youth Court*
on	19	at	am/pm

and
*(tick
whichever
applies)*

☐ my case has been transferred to the Crown Court for trial

☐ I was convicted and committed for sentence to the Crown Court

☐ I was convicted and/or sentenced and I wish to appeal | conviction and/or sentence* |
   against the

*Cross out whichever does not apply

4. Outstanding Matters:

a) If there are any other
   outstanding criminal
   charges or cases against
   you, give details including
   the court where you are
   due to appear (only those
   cases that are not yet
   concluded)

5. Your Financial Position *(Tick the box which applies)*

a) ☐ I receive INCOME-BASED JOBSEEKER'S ALLOWANCE, Income Support, Family Credit or Disability
   Working Allowance, and I attach documentary evidence that I am receiving such a benefit *(e.g. order
   book)*.
   *(You may also tick this box if your spouse or partner receives any of these benefits and you are living
   together)*

   Give:
   i) the address of the Social Security office OR JOBCENTRE dealing with the
      benefit

   ii) National Insurance number
       of person receiving benefit

iii)   Type of benefit

If you do not produce documentary evidence that you are receiving benefit, the court will assume that you are not receiving benefit and you will also have to complete a Form 5 (statement of means). If you cannot produce evidence you should give your reasons below

b) [ ]   I have already given a statement of my means to the   Court

in a previous application for legal aid in this case and there has been no change in my financial position. *(A new statement is required if there has been any change)*

c) [ ]   I attach a statement of my means in these proceedings *(details of your income and expenditure)*

d) [ ]   I am under 16 and I attach a statement of my parents' means. If you are unable to provide a statement of their means give their name and address

6. Legal Representation:

------- **Note:** -------

a) **If you do not give the name of a solicitor the court will select a solicitor for you.**
b) **You must tell the solicitor that you have named him, unless he has helped you complete this form.**
c) **If you have been charged together with another person or persons, the court may assign a solicitor other than the solicitor of your choice.**

a)   The solicitor I wish to act for me is

b)   Give the firm's name and address (if known)

7. Reasons for wanting Legal Aid

- To avoid the possibility of your application being delayed or legal aid being refused because the court does not have enough information about the case, you must complete the rest of this form.
- When deciding whether to grant you legal aid, the court will need to know the reasons why it is in the interests of justice for you to be represented.
- If you need help completing this form, and especially if you have previous convictions, you should see a solicitor. He may be able to advise you free of charge or at a reduced fee.

Note: If you plead **NOT GUILTY** neither the information in this form nor that in your statement of means will be made available to the members of the court trying your case unless you are convicted or you consent. If you are acquitted, only the financial information you have given in your statement of means will be given to the court.

Tick any boxes which apply and give brief details or reasons in the space provided

	Details	Reasons for grant or refusal *(for court use only)*
a) It is likely that I will lose my liberty *(You should consider seeing a solicitor before answering this question)* [ ]		

		Details	Reasons for grant or refusal *(for court use only)*
b)	I am subject to a: suspended or partly suspended prison sentence ☐ conditional discharge ☐ probation order ☐ supervision order ☐ deferment of sentence ☐ community service order ☐ care order ☐ combination order ☐ *Give details as far as you are able, including the nature of offence and when the order was made*		
c)	It is likely that I will lose my livelihood ☐		
d)	It is likely that I will suffer serious damage to my reputation ☐		
e)	A substantial question of law is involved ☐ *(You will need the help of a solicitor to answer this question)*	*(Please give authorities to be quoted with law reports references)*	
f)	I shall be unable to understand the court proceedings or state my own case because: i) My understanding of English is inadequate ☐ ii) I suffer from a disability ☐ *(Give full details)*		
g)	Witnesses have to be traced and/or interviewed on my behalf *(State circumstances)* ☐		
h)	The case involves expert cross examination of a prosecution witness *(Give brief details)* ☐		

i) It is in
   someone else's
   interests that
   I am represented

j) Any other
   reasons:
   (give full particulars)

8. Declaration:

If you knowingly make a statement which is false, or knowingly withhold information, you may be prosecuted.
If convicted, you may be sent to prison for up to three months or be fined or both *(section 39(1) Legal Aid Act 1988)*. After your application has been considered by the court, you may be asked to give further information or to clarify information or to provide further proof of the information you have given.
If you stop receiving INCOME-BASED JOBSEEKER'S ALLOWANCE, Income Support, Family Credit, Disability Working Allowance or if your financial position changes in any way after you have submitted this form, you must tell the court. This is a requirement of the Legal Aid regulations. I understand that, if I do not produce all the information which the court needs, it may make such enquiries of the Benefits Agency as it considers necessary and I authorise it so to do. I consent to the disclosure of information to confirm that I am in receipt of benefit.

I understand that the court may order me to make a contribution to the costs of Legal Aid, or to pay the whole costs if it considers that I can afford to do so and, if I am under 16, may make a similar order with respect to my parents.

Signed | **Dated:**

For Court use only

Any additional factors considered when determining the application, including any information given orally.

Decision on the interests of justice test

I have considered all available details of all the charges and it is / is not* in the interests of justice that representation be granted because:

Signed | Proper Officer

Date

*Cross out whichever does not apply

Substituted by the Legal Aid in Criminal and Care Proceedings (General) (Amendment) Regulations 1995 (S.I. 1995 No. 542) in respect of all legal aid applications made on or after May 1, 1995 and amended by the Legal Aid in Criminal and Care Proceedings (General) (Amendment) (No. 3) Regulations 1996 (S.I. 1996 No. 1258) and the Legal Aid in Criminal and Care Proceedings (General) (Amendment) Regulations 1998 (S.I. 1998 No. 662).

Application for legal aid in criminal proceedings after the death of a defendant or appellant

Form 1A
(also known as Form 5131A)
Regulations 22 and 23

Use this form

if you are the personal representative of a deceased defendant and you wish to apply for legal aid in order to make, or continue, an appeal on behalf of the estate of the deceased. The court may order the estate to contribute to the costs of legal aid, or to pay the whole costs.

Before you fill in the form

read through it carefully because you may need the help of a solicitor. If you think you need help to fill in the form you may be able to obtain a solicitor's services free of charge or at a reduced fee.

When you fill in the form

Please use black ink because the form will be copied. Answer each part and give as much information as you can. If you do not give all the information which the court needs, it may make enquiries. After the application has been considered by the court, you may be asked to give proof of the information you have given, or asked for further information.

Warning: If you knowingly make a statement which is false, or knowingly withhold information, you may be prosecuted. If you are convicted you may be sent to prison for up to three months or fined, or both (section 39(1)

1 Details of the deceased

a Surname or family name
b Other names
c Title
d Date of death

in BLOCK LETTERS
in BLOCK LETTERS
Mr ☐ Mrs ☐ Miss ☐ Ms ☐

2 About you (the personal representative)

a Surname or family name
b Other names
c Title

d Permanent Address

e Present Address

f Telephone number (daytime)
g You are the personal representative by

in BLOCK LETTERS
in BLOCK LETTERS
Mr ☐ Mrs ☐ Miss ☐ Ms ☐

Letters of Administration granted on
Probate granted on

3 You solicitors

If you do not choose a solicitor the court will select one for you.
You must tell the solicitors that you have named them in this form (unless they have helped you to complete it)

a Name and reference
b Address

c Telephone number
d Fax number

Ref.

Form 5131A

510

4 Details of your appeal

a You intend to

☐ **make an appeal** to the Court of Appeal (Criminal Division)

☐ **continue an appeal** before the Court of Appeal (Criminal Division)

☐ **take over the conduct of an appeal** begun by reference to the Criminal Cases Review Commission

b The deceased was

convicted ☐   sentenced ☐   convicted and sentenced ☐

by the crown court at _____

on _____

c The appeal is against the

conviction ☐   sentence ☐   conviction and sentence ☐

d Are there any co-defendants who have appealed?

No ☐   Yes ☐

If **Yes,** the name(s):

_____

e Did the deceased receive legal aid in these proceedings at any time before death?

No ☐   Yes ☐

5 Reason for wanting legal aid:

	Details of your reason(s)	*For court use only*
a To restore the good name and reputation of the deceased		
b A substantial question of law is involved *You will need the held of a solicitor to give the details. Please give authorities and law report references*		
c I shall be unable to understand the court proceedings or state my own case because: (i) my understanding of English is inadequate (ii) I suffer from a disability *Please say which and give details*		
d Witnesses had to be traced and/or interviewed on my behalf, or on behalf of the deceased		
e The case involves expert cross examination of a prosecution witness *Please give brief details*		
f Any other reason(s): *Please give full particulars*		

Form 5131A

511

6 The estate of the deceased

a You must give full details of the estate of the deceased

You may provide this information by enclosing copies of the Inland Revenue forms which you submitted with either a personal application, or an application through a solicitor, for a Grant of Probate or Letters of Administration.

Please enclose copies of other documents that may be of assistance in assessing the present value of the estate.

I enclose copies of the following Inland Revenue forms:

b If the present value of the estate is different from that shown on the above forms then please state what the present value is and why it has changed.

c If you do not have all the information at present, say why and give details of the information for which you are waiting.

If the value of the estate changes in any way after you have submitted this form then you must tell the court. *This is a requirement of the Legal Aid Regulations.*

7 Other documents

I enclose a

☐ a sealed copy of the Letters of Administration or

☐ the Grant of Probate with the will attached

☐ the indictment and court record (if available)

8 Declaration

I declare to the best of my knowledge and belief that I have given a complete and correct statement of the estates of the deceased. I apply for legal aid as the personal representative of the estate of

insert the name of the deceased

deceased

I authorise the court to make any enquiries it considers necessary.

Signed——————————— Date ———————

(The Personal Representative of the estate of

Insert the name of the deceased

deceased)

Form 5131A

512

For Court use only

Any additional factors considered when determining the application, including any information given orally:

Decision on the interests of justice test

* *cross out whichever does not apply*

I have considered all available details of the application and it is* / is not* in the interests of justice that representation be granted because.

Signed ————————————(Proper Officer)

Date ————————

Form 5131A

Form 1A inserted by regulation 13 of the Legal Aid in Criminal and Care Proceedings (General) (Amendment) Regulations 1998 (S.I. 1998 No. 662).   513

Notification of Refusal to grant Legal Aid and determination of Contribution

Form 2

Regs. 12, 13, 19 and 20

To

Your application for legal aid has been refused by the court/a judge of the court/a justice of the peace/a proper officer of the court on the following grounds:

* (a) it does not appear desirable to make an order in the interests of justice. A statement of reasons for this decision is enclosed; and/or

* (b) it does not appear that your means are such that you require assistance in meeting the costs you may incur.

If legal aid had been granted you would have been orderd to pay a contribution of £   per week from income and £   from capital [payable on   ] towards the costs of your case/legal aid would have been conditional on immediate payment of £

You are entitled:
* (i) to apply for legal aid to an area committee (in some cases where your application has been refused under paragraph (a) above). If you wish to do this you should complete Form 3 overleaf. You must apply within 14 days of the date of this notification.
  (ii) to renew your application to the court [to the Crown Court] at any time. If you wish to do so you should complete the bottom section of this form and return the whole form to the Court at the address stated.
  (iii) in any event to apply for legal aid to the court of trial on the day of the trial.

* Delete as necessary

Signed:
Justices' Clerk/An officer of the Crown Court

Date:

I wish to renew my application for legal aid to the court.

I have/have not* made an application to an area committee.

Signed:

Date:

NOTE: (i) You should enclose any additional or new information you think is relevant to your application.
  (ii) If there has been any change in your financial circumstances you must complete and enclose a new statement of means form.
  (iii) If you have made an application to an area committee you should enclose a copy of the notification decision.

*Delete as appropriate

Substituted by the Legal Aid in Criminal and Care Proceedings (General) (Amendment) Regulations 1995 (S.I. 1995 No. 542) in respect of all legal aid applications made on or after May 1, 1995.

Form 3

Court Code

Offence Code

Solicitor's acc. no.

Application for Review of Refusal to grant Legal Aid

Reg. 16

To the Area Director, Area Committee for Area No. ....

(Address)

I wish to

apply for a review by the area committee of the refusal by the court on the .... 19... to grant

me legal aid in connection with a charge of

My case is due to be heard on*

*(Delete if date has yet to be fixed)

I have/have not* renewed my application for legal aid to the court.

Signed:

Dated:

NOTE: (i)   This application must be made within 14 days of the date of the notice of the refusal to make a legal aid order.

(ii) You should send the enclosed copy of your original application, and any additional or new information you think is relevant to your application.

(iii) A copy of this completed form and any other information you supply must be forwarded to the Clerk to the Justices of the court which refused legal aid.

Substituted by the Legal Aid in Criminal and Care Proceedings (General) (Amendment) Regulations 1995 (S.I. 1995 No. 542) in respect of all legal applications made on or after May 1, 1995.

Notification for decision of the Area Committee on Review of Refusal to grant Legal Aid

Form 4.
Reg. 17

To:

Your application for legal aid has been granted/refused because it appears/does not appear desirable to make an Order in the interests of justice on any of the following grounds:-

(1) You are likely to lose your liberty.

(2) You are likely to lose your livelihood.

(3) You are likely to suffer serious damage to your reputation.

(4) A substantial question of law is involved.

(5) You are unable to understand the proceedings or state your own case because:-

(a) Your knowledge of English is inadequate

(b) You suffer from a disability

(6) Your case involves tracing and/or interviewing witnesses or expert cross-examination of a prosecution witness.

(7) It is in someone else's interests that you are represented.

(8) Any other reasons.

*Delete as appropriate.

The Committee reached this decision because:-

Date: Secretary to the Area Committee

Substituted by the Legal Aid in Criminal and Care Proceedings (General) (Amendment) Regulations 1995 (S.I. 1995 No. 542) in respect of all legal aid applications made on or after May 1, 1995.

Statement of Means
by Applicant or Appropriate Contributor
for Legal Aid purposes

Form 5
Regulation 23
(also known as
Crown Court Form 5132)

To apply for criminal legal aid you must complete this form *unless* you can prove that you are in receipt of Income-based Jobseeker's Allowance, Income Support, Family Credit or Disability Working Allowance and have provided documentary evidence that you receive one of those benefits when you completed Form 1. *(See Section 5 of Form 1 headed* **Your Financial Position.***)* If you are not yet sixteen, then your mother or father may also be asked to complete one. If you have applied for legal aid for a child of yours who is aged sixteen or over **you** do not need to fill in this form. **Your child** should complete it, giving details of his or her **own income**.

To avoid delay in your application being considered please complete the form as fully and carefully as possible and provide the information and documentary evidence the form requires. If you cannot provide the documentary evidence you must explain why at Section 5.

1 Personal details (please use BLOCK letters)

1. Surname   Mr ☐ Mrs ☐ Miss ☐ Ms ☐

2. Forenames

3. Date of birth

4. Home address

5. Marital status
   (please tick one box)   Single ☐   Single and living together ☐   Widow(er) ☐

   Married ☐   Married but separated ☐   Divorced ☐

6. Are you claiming legal aid for a dependant child who is not yet sixteen?   YES ☐

   If YES, give the following details about the child   NO ☐ (go to section 2)

   Surname

   Forenames

   Date of birth

   Home address
   (if different
   from yours)

   Your relationship to the child (e.g. father)

1

2 Financial details—Part A: Income

In this section you are asked to give details of the money you receive. If you are living with your spouse or partner then you must provide details of the income of your spouse or partner as well. The details will be used to work out whether you have to pay a contribution towards legal aid and if so how much. The assessment is based on weekly income so your answers must show the amount you get *each week*. If any of the sections do not apply, write NONE in the space.

Amount received

Work	Employer's name and address	Your income	Income of Spouse or Partner	Official use
Enter gross earnings *per week* (before tax and insurance), including overtime, commission or bonuses. You must attach documentary evidence of the pay you have received over the past 13 weeks. Three monthly or 13 weekly wage slips would be the best evidence.		£	£	
If you are self employed write SELF EMPLOYED. Show your gross earnings and attach the most recent accounts, showing gross income.		£	£	
Part time work Enter gross earnings *per week* (before tax and insurance) from any part time job not included above and attach documentary evidence.		£	£	
State Benefits Enter *weekly amounts*, e.g. from unemployment benefit, child benefit etc. Say which benefit(s) you get in the space provided. You should produce evidence of the benefit payment (e.g. order book).	Types of benefit	£	£	
		£	£	
		£	£	
Money from property Enter *weekly amounts* (before any deductions) of money from sub-letting a house or rooms and attach documentary evidence.		£	£	
Any other income Please give details and *weekly amounts* and attach documentary evidence.		£	£	

Important: If the information you have given above is going to change soon, please give details of the changes in Section 4 of this form.

2

2 Financial details—Part B: Capital and Savings

Please give details of all your capital and savings.
If you are also living with your spouse or partner you must also give details of their capital and savings.

Amount | Official use

Property

**Note* In the questions which follow the value of the equity means the sum which you would receive from the sale of the property after paying the mortgage or other loan on it.

1. Main dwelling

Do you or your spouse/partner own the house or property which you treat as your main dwelling? *(tick appropriate box)*

You YES ☐ NO ☐ **Spouse/Partner** YES ☐ NO ☐

If so, please provide the following information.

i) What is the value of the equity* in your main dwelling? ☐

ii) What is your main dwelling worth now, that is, what is its market value? ☐

iii) What is the mortgage on your main dwelling? ☐

2. Other houses or property

Do you or your spouse/partner own a house or property other than the house or property which you treat as your main dwelling? *(tick appropriate box)*

You YES ☐ NO ☐ **Spouse/Partner** YES ☐ NO ☐

If so, please provide the following information.

i) What is the value of the equity* in the house(s)/other property? ☐

ii) What are the house(s)/other property worth now, that is, what are their market values? ☐

iii) What are the mortgages on the house(s)/other property? ☐

Savings Give details of where your savings are, and the amounts. Include money in any bank, building society, National Savings Certificates, cash, stocks and shares or any other investments. You should produce pass books etc.		£	£
Articles of value Give details of any articles of value that you own (e.g. jewellery, furs, paintings) with their approximate value. You may be asked to produce valuation certificates.		£	£

3 Allowances and Deductions

1. Enter Tax and National Insurance Contributions deducted from your earnings ***per week***.

You		**Spouse or Partner**	
Tax	☐	Tax	☐
N.I.	☐	N.I.	☐

2. Enter the NUMBER of dependants **who are living with you**. If you are claiming legal aid for a child, please include that child. ***N.B. Dependants are the people you and your spouse or partner look after financially***.

Spouse or Partner ☐ Children under 19 ☐ Date of birth for each child ☐ Children and other Relatives 19 and over ☐

Other relatives under 19 ☐ Date of birth for each relative ☐

Others (please say who) ☐

3 Allowances and Deductions (continued)

3. **If you pay maintenance to any dependant who does NOT** live with you, please give details of the amounts you, or your spouse or partner, pay.

| Age(s) of dependant(s) | .... | Your relationship to the dependant | .... | Amount per week | £ .... |

You should supply copies of agreements or court orders.

4. Give the amounts of Council Tax which you and your spouse or partner pay.

(a) The amount of Council Tax paid. You must provide evidence of this (e.g. the demand from the local authority).

£ ___

☐ a week
☐ a month
☐ a year

(b) Is Council Tax benefit received?

☐ YES   ☐ NO

(please say how much)

£ ___

☐ a week
☐ a month
☐ a year

5. Give the following details of housing expenses of you and your spouse/partner. If you own more than one house only give details for the house in which you live. If you are paying the expenses of a dependant who is not living with you, enter the details in the spaces on the right. You should produce rent books, evidence of mortgage instalments, and evidence of water and sewerage charges. It is in your interests to provide evidence of any other expenses claimed and you may be required to provide this.

Rent	£	/week	Amount for dependant(s)	£	/week
Mortgage payment	£	/week		£	/week
Ground rent	£	/week		£	/week
Service charge	£	/week		£	/week
Water and sewerage charges	£	/week		£	/week
Board and lodging	£	/week		£	/week
Bed and Breakfast	£	/week		£	/week

	You	Your spouse or partner
6. How much does it cost you and your spouse or partner **each week** to travel to and from work?	£	£

7. Give details of any other expenses which you think the court should know about. You may include any payments on court orders, and contributions to approved pension schemes, **but not**: money for food, clothing or heating. You should produce documentary evidence of the payments.

£ ___   £ ___

4

4 Further information

1. Have you directly or indirectly transferred any resources (such as sums of money, stocks or shares, the equity value in your home or any other valuable items) to another person since you became aware that these proceedings would be brought? If so, please give details.

2. Has another person been paying your legal fees and expenses in respect of these or other proceedings before you applied for legal aid? If so, please give details.

3. Are the resources of another person available to you e.g. is another person providing you with free accommodation or paying your bills? If so, please give details.

4. Please give any other financial information that you think that the court should have when deciding upon your application for legal aid. You should also include any future changes in circumstances that might alter your position.

5 If you have not produced documentary evidence of all income/benefits that you receive and each allowance you have claimed, you must explain why you cannot do so.

6 Declaration

If you knowingly make a statement which is false, or knowingly withhold information, you may be prosecuted. If convicted, you may be sent to prison for up to three months, or be fined, or both (*section 39(1) Legal Aid Act 1988*). After your application has been considered by the court, you may be asked to give further information or to clarify information or to provide further proof of the information that you have given.
If your financial position changes in any way after you have submitted this form, you must tell the court. This is a requirement of the Legal Aid Regulations.

I declare that to the best of my knowledge and belief, I have given a complete and correct statement of my income, savings and capital (and that of my spouse or partner)* (and that of my child).**
I authorise the court to make such enquiries of the Benefits Agency as it considers necessary and I consent to the disclosure of information to confirm that I am in receipt of benefit.

Signed   Date

* Delete if you are single or if you are not living with your spouse or partner
** Delete if legal aid is not sought for your child

Substituted by the Legal Aid in Criminal and Care Proceedings (General) (Amendment) Regulations 1995 (S.I. 1995 No. 542) in respect of all legal aid applications made on or after May 1, 1995 and amended by the Legal Aid in Criminal and Care Proceedings (General) (Amendment) (No. 3) Regulations 1996 (S.I. 1996 No. 1258) and the Legal Aid in Criminal and Care Proceedings (General) (Amendment) Regulations 1998 (S.I. 1998 No. 662).

5

Legal Aid Contribution Order

Form 6.
Reg. 27

To

In accordance with the provisions of section 23(1) of the Legal Aid Act 1988 the Court/area committee (a) orders you to contribute towards the costs of representation to be provided for you under a legal aid order:-

The contribution required is:-

* a contribution from disposable capital payable is one lump sum of £...... This must be paid on or before
* contributions from disposable income payable at the rate of £...... per week/per month (a) for so long as the legal aid order is in force. The first instalment must be paid on or before
* Delete as necessary.

This money should be paid to the Clerk to the Justices .... Magistrates' Court.

Signed

(Secretary to the area committee)(a)

Date

(a) Delete as necessary.

NOTES
The figures overleaf show how the contribution was calculated. If you are not satisfied with the calculations used, you may apply to this court for your means to be redetermined. If your means change, you must inform the court which is hearing your case IMMEDIATELY so that you contribution can be reassessed and changed if necessary. If you do not want legal aid on these terms, you MUST inform the court IMMEDIATELY by tearing off and returning the slip overleaf. If your legal aid order is revoked, you may still have to pay some money towards any costs already incurred.

If you should prefer to pay monthly, you should inform the Clerk to the Justices who will decide whether you should pay weekly or monthly.

Legal Aid Contribution Order—calculations used

Part One— (1)	Figures used Average weekly net INCOME			£	(A)
(2)	Allowances against income	—dependants —housing —travel —others Total allowances	£ £ £ £ £	£	(B)
				£	
(3)	Total CAPITAL				
Part Two— (1)	Calculation of contribution from INCOME Disposable income is (A) - (B) = Contribution is Disposable Income - £50, divided by 3 =			£ £	

Note: A contribution of £1 is payable for each £3 (or part of £3) by which average disposable income exceeds the weekly limit but no contribution is payable where average disposable income does not exceed £51.

Part Three—   Summary

Your contribution from INCOME is £   per week/month

Your contribution from CAPITAL is £

Please turn to the front sheet for details of how and when to pay.

Tear off along here ....

I   of (address)

have been granted legal aid by the   Court at

I hereby apply for my legal aid order to be withdrawn. I understand that I may be required to pay towards any costs already incurred.

Return this form IMMEDIATELY to:

Signed

Date

Amended by the Legal Aid in Criminal and Care Proceedings (General) (Amendment) Regulations 1992 (S.I. 1992 No. 720), the Legal Aid in Criminal and Care Proceedings (General) (Amendment) Regulations 1993 (S.I. 1993 No. 789), the Legal Aid in Criminal and Care Proceedings (General) (Amendment) (No. 2) Regulations 1996 (S.I. 1996 No. 646), the Legal Aid in Criminal and Care Proceedings (General) (Amendment) Regulations 1997 (S.I. 1997 No. 752) and the Legal Aid in Criminal and Care Proceedings (General) (Amendment) Regulations 1998 (S.I. 1998 No. 662).

Notice of Withholding of Legal Aid Order

Form 7.
Reg. 29

To

The   Court has made an order granting you legal aid in respect of the proceedings before it/ the   Court. It has also made an order, a copy of which is attached, requiring you to make a contribution out of capital towards the cost of your case.

In accordance with regulation 29(3) of the Legal Aid in Criminal and Care Proceedings (General) Regulations 1989 the court requires you to make immediate payment of that capital contribution to the Clerk to the Justices.

Note: *You will NOT receive the legal aid order until you have made this payment and your solicitor and counsel will not be covered by the order until it has been received.*

A copy of this notice has been sent to your solicitor/counsel.

Signed

Date

Variation or Revocation of Contribution Order

Form 8.
Reg. 12

To

In accordance with the provisions of regulation 33 or 34 of the Legal Aid in Criminal and Care Proceedings (General) Regulations 1989, your means have been reassessed.

*   Your contribution order has been varied. The revised amount you must pay is:
* £   on or before   (contribution from disposable capital)
* £   at the rate of £   per week/month (contribution from disposable income) for as long as the legal aid order is in force. The first instalment at the revised rate must be paid to the Clerk to the Justices at   on or before

     NOTE: If your instalments have now increased, and you do not want legal aid on these terms, you must inform the Court IMMEDIATELY.

*   The court hereby revokes the contribution order made on

*   Should your means change again, you MUST inform this court, which will then determine whether you should start to pay instalments again.

*   If at the conclusion of the proceedings the total contributions paid exceed your liability for contributions, taking into account this variation, the excess will be returned to you by the Clerk to the Justices at

*   Delete as appropriate

Signed

Date

Substituted by the Legal Aid in Criminal and Care Proceedings (General) (Amendment) Regulations 1993 (S.I. 1993 No. 789).

Notification of Arrears of Payment of Contribution Order

Form 9.
Reg. 36(1)(a)

To

You have fallen into arrears in the payment of instalments in respect of your legal aid contribution order. You have missed   instalments of £   and are now £   in arrears.

You must pay this sum to the Clerk to the Justices at   WITHIN SEVEN DAYS OF RECEIPT OF THIS NOTICE. If you fail to do so, this court will consider revoking legal aid.

A copy of this form has been sent to your solicitor(s)/counsel.

Signed

Date

Warning of Revocation of Legal Aid Order for Non-payment of Contribution

Form 10.
Reg. 36(1)(b)

To

You were recently sent a warning of arrears in respect of your legal aid contribution order. The arrears now stand at £   . The court is now considering revoking your legal aid. You are entitled to explain to the court why you have fallen into arrears, and to invite the court not to revoke your legal aid.

If you with to do this, YOU MUST RETURN THIS FORM TO THIS COURT WITHIN SEVEN DAYS OF RECEIPT otherwise your legal aid might be revoked.

A copy of this form has been sent to your solicitors.

Signed

Date

I have fallen into arrears because:

Signed

Date

Legal Aid Order (Magistrates' Court)

Form 11.
Reg. 40

In accordance with the Legal Aid Act 1988 the Court now grants legal aid, to   for the following purpose.

Delete (1) to (4) as necessary.

(1) Proceedings before a magistrates' court in connection with

(2) Appealing to the Crown Court against a decision of the
    Magistrates' Court on

(3) Resisting an appeal to the Crown Court against a decision of the
    Magistrates' Court.

(4) Proceedings for (both a magistrates' court and*) the Crown Court in connection with

including in the event of his being convicted or sentenced in those proceedings, advice and assistance in regard to the making of an appeal to the criminal division of the Court of Appeal.

* Delete as necessary

The legal aid granted shall consist of the following representation:-

Magistrates' court proceedings—   Solicitor/solicitor and counsel

Crown Court Proceedings—   Solicitor/solicitor and counsel/solicitor, junior counsel and Queen's Counsel/counsel only

including advice on the preparation of the case for the proceedings.

The solicitor/Counsel assigned is

of

The legally assisted person has been committed to   prison/released on bail and may be communicated with at

Dated this   day of   19

(Signed)

A contribution order was made in respect of this order as follows.

Amended by the Legal Aid in Criminal and Care Proceedings (General) (Amendment) Regulations 1993 (S.I. 1993 No. 789).

Legal Aid Order (Crown Court)

Form 11A.
Reg. 40

In accordance with the Legal Aid Act 1988 the Court now grants legal aid to   for the following purpose.

Delete (1) to (4) as necessary.

(1) Appealing to the Crown Court against a decision of the Magistrates' Court on

(2) Resisting an appeal to the Crown Court against a decision of the Magistrates' Court.

(3) Proceedings before the Crown Court in connection with

including, in the event of his being convicted or sentenced in those proceedings, advice and assistance in regard to the making of an appeal to the criminal division of the Court of Appeal.

(4) A retrial by the Crown Court ordered by the Court of Appeal or the House of Lords.

The legal aid granted shall consist of the following representation:-

Solicitor/solicitor and counsel/solicitor and Queen's Counsel/solicitor, junior counsel and Queen's Counsel/solicitor and two junior counsel/counsel only/solicitor and three counsel (state permutation of counsel within regulation 48(4))*

including advice on the preparation of the case for the proceedings.* Only available where prosecution brought by Serious Fraud Office.

The solicitor/Counsel assigned is

of

The legally assisted person has been committed to   prison/released on bail and may be communicated with at

Dated this   day of   19

(Signed)

A contribution order was made in respect of this order as follows.

Amended by the Legal Aid in Criminal and Care Proceedings (General) (Amendment) Regulations 1993 (S.I. 1993 No. 789) and the Legal Aid in Criminal and Care Proceedings (General) (Amendment) (No. 2) Regulations 1994 (S.I. 1994 No. 3136).

Legal Aid Order (Area Committee)

Form 12.
Reg. 40

The area committee now grants legal aid to

for proceedings before a magistrates' court in connection with

The legal aid granted shall consist of representation by a solicitor [and Counsel].

The solicitor assigned is

of

A contribution order was made in respect of this order as follows.

Signed

Secretary to the area committee

Date

Amended by the Legal Aid in Criminal and Care Proceedings (General) (Amendment) Regulations 1993 (S.I. 1993 No. 789).

Legal Aid Order (Court of Appeal/Courts—Martial Appeal Court)

Form 13.
Reg. 38

| APPELLANT Forenames | Surname (block letters) | |

| WHERE DETAINED | Number | Address if not detained |

CROWN COURT/   before whom tried
Date(s)
COURT MARTIAL   or sentenced

The   , in accordance with part V of the Legal Aid Act 1988 now grants legal aid to the appellant for the following purposes:-

The legal aid granted consists of representation by

Solicitors   Counsel
Two Counsel

Who are assigned as follows:-

      Name   Address

Solicitor

Counsel

Counsel

A contribution order of £   was made in respect of this order.

Date:

Signed: Registrar of Criminal Appeals/Courts-Martial Appeal Court of Royal Courts of Justice, London, WC2.

Order Withdrawing Legal Aid

Form 14.
Reg. 41

The   Court/area committee now withdraws, from this date, the order granting
legal aid to

of

For the purpose of

because:

     (i) he/she has applied for legal aid to be withdrawn.
     (ii) his/her legal representative(s) has/have withdrawn and it is not in the interests of justice to assign new representatives.
     (iii) he/she has failed to pay sums due under legal aid contribution order.
     (iv) the provisions of regulation 41A apply (withdrawal for abuse of legal aid etc.).

     (Delete as necessary)
          Signed

          Date

NOTE TO LEGALLY ASSISTED PERSON

You are no longer entitled to legal aid. You may be required to pay towards any costs already incurred. Your solicitor and Counsel (if any) will cease to act further for you unless you yourself re-employ them, and if you do so, you will be responsible for their costs from the above date.

Amended by the Legal Aid in Criminal and Care Proceedings (General) (Amendment) (No. 3) Regulations 1996 (S.I. 1996 No. 1258).

Order Amending Legal Aid Order

Form 15.
Reg. 50

To

The order granting legal aid to

of
is hereby amended, by substituting for the solicitor named in the order another solicitor, namely
of

and by authorising the instruction of counsel (in place of counsel already instructed)*

Signed

(Secretary to the area committee)*

Date

* Delete as necessary.

Application for Legal Aid in care proceedings in the Juvenile Court or Crown Court

Form 16.

Deleted by the Legal Aid in Criminal and Care Proceedings (General) (Amendment) Regulations 1992 (S.I. 1992 No. 720).

SCHEDULE 3

DETERMINATION OF DISPOSABLE INCOME AND DISPOSABLE CAPITAL

General

1.—(1) In computing the disposable income and disposable capital of the person concerned, the financial resources of any spouse of his shall be treated as his resources except where—

(a) the person concerned and his spouse are living separate and apart; or

(b) the spouse has a contrary interest in the proceedings in respect of which an application for legal aid has been made; or

(c) in all the circumstances of the case, it would be inequitable so to do.

(2) Where a spouse fails to provide information as to his financial resources in response to the request of the proper officer, the proper officer may make an estimate of the likely resources of the spouse on the basis of any information which is available.

2. Paragraph 1(1) and (2) above and the provisions of this Schedule shall apply to a man and a woman who are living with each other in the same household a husband and wife as they apply to the parties to a marriage.

2A.—(1) Where it appears to the proper officer that:

(a) the person concerned has directly or indirectly transferred any resources to another person;

(b) another person is or has been maintaining the person concerned in the proceedings to which the application relates or any other proceedings, or

(c) any of the resources of another person are or have been made available to the person concerned,

the proper officer shall have power to treat all or any part of the resources of that other person as the resources of the person concerned.

(2) Where sub-paragraph (1) applies:

(a) the question of what is or is not a resource of that other person shall be determined, as nearly as the circumstances permit, in accordance with the provisions of this Schedule excluding this paragraph, and

(b) the proper officer shall assess or estimate the value of those resources to the best of his judgment.

(3) In this paragraph, "person" (except in the phrase "person concerned") includes a company, partnership, body of trustees and any body of persons whether corporate or not corporate.

Paragraph 2A was inserted by the Legal Aid in Criminal and Care Proceedings (General) (Amendment) Regulations 1996 (S.I. 1996 No. 436).

2B. Where section 44A of the Criminal Appeal Act 1968 (death of convicted person) applies—

(a) if the applicant is the personal representative of the dead person, the financial resources to be taken into account shall be those forming part of the estate of the dead person, and not the resources belonging to the applicant in another capacity or to any other person;

(b) otherwise, the financial resources to be taken into account shall be those belonging to the applicant or treated as belonging to him in accordance with the other provisions of this Schedule.

Paragraph 2B was inserted by the Legal Aid in Criminal and Care Proceedings (General) (Amendment) Regulations 1998 (S.I. 1998 No. 662).

3. Where it appears to the proper officer that the person concerned has with intent to reduce the amount of his disposable income or disposable capital, whether for the purpose of reducing his liability to pay a contribution towards legal aid or otherwise—

(a) directly or indirectly deprived himself of any resources; or

(b) converted any part of his resources into resources which under these Regulations are to be wholly or partly disregarded, or in respect of which nothing is to be included in determining the resources of that person;

the resources of which he has so deprived himself or which he has so converted shall be treated as part of his resources or as not so converted as the case may be.

Amended by the Legal Aid in Criminal and Care Proceedings (General) (Amendment) Regulations 1990 (S.I. 1990 No. 489).

Disposable income

4.—(1) The income which the person concerned receives during the period of computation shall be taken to his income for the purposes of this Schedule.

(2) The income received during the contribution period may be estimated on the basis of the income received by the person concerned during the three months prior to the commencement of the contribution period.

Amended by the Legal Aid in Criminal and Care Proceedings (General) (Amendment) Regulations 1993 (S.I. 1993 No. 789).

5.—(1) Where the person concerned receives the profits from any trade, business or gainful occupation other than employment at a wage or salary, the profit which accrues during the period of computation shall be taken to be his income for the purposes of this Schedule.

Amended by the Legal Aid in Criminal and Care Proceedings (General) (Amendment) Regulations 1993 (S.I. 1993 No. 789).

(2) The income received during the contribution period may be estimated on the basis of the profits made during the last accounting period for which accounts have been prepared.

6.—(1) In computing disposable income the following payments made under the Social Security Contributions and Benefits Act 1992 shall be disregarded—

(a) disability living allowance;

(b) attendance allowance;

(c) constant attendance allowance paid under section 104 as an increase to a disablement pension;

(d) housing benefit;

(e) any payment made out of the social fund.

(2) In computing disposable income, a payment made under the Community Care (Direct Payments) Act 1996 shall be disregarded.

Amended by the Legal Aid in Criminal and Care Proceedings (General) (Amendment) Regulations 1993 (S.I. 1993 No. 789). Paragraph 6(2) inserted by the Legal Aid in Criminal and Care Proceedings (General) (Amendment) Regulations 1997 (S.I. 1997 No. 752).

6A. In computing disposable income there shall be disregarded—

    (a) so much of any back to work bonus received under section 26 of the Jobseekers Act 1995 as is by virtue of that section to be treated as payable by way of a jobseeker's allowance;

    (b) any payment made by the Secretary of State under the Earnings Top-up Scheme 1996.

Paragraph 6A inserted by the Legal Aid in Criminal and Aid Care Proceedings (General) (Amendment) (No. 4) Regulations 1996 (S.I. 1996 No. 2307).

7. In computing disposable income there shall be deducted—

    (a) the total amount of any tax payable on that income;

    (b) the total amount of any contributions payable under the Social Security Contributions and Benefits Act 1992;

    (c) reasonable expenses of travelling to and from the place of employment;

    (d) the amount of any contribution paid, whether under a legal obligation or not, to an occupational pension scheme within the meaning of the Social Security Pensions Act 1975 or to a personal pension scheme within the meaning of the Social Security Act 1986; and

    (e) reasonable expenses in respect of the making of reasonable provision for the care of any dependent child living with the person concerned because of that person's absence from home by reason of employment.

Amended by the Legal Aid in Criminal and Care Proceedings (General) (Amendment) Regulations 1993 (S.I. 1993 No. 789).

7A. In computing the income of the person concerned, there shall be deducted any sums payable (net of council tax benefit) by the person concerned in respect of the council tax to which he is subject by virtue of section 6 of the Local Government Finance Act 1992.

Substituted by the Legal Aid in Criminal and Care Proceedings (General) (Amendment) Regulations 1993 (S.I. 1993 No. 789).

8.—(1) In computing disposable income there shall be a deduction in respect of the main or only dwelling in the case of a household of the amount of the net rent payable, or such part thereof as is reasonable in the circumstances.

(2) For the purposes of this paragraph, "rent" includes—

    (a) the annual rent payable; and

    (b) a sum in respect of yearly outgoings borne by the householder including, in particular, any domestic rates and water and sewerage charges, a reasonable allowance towards any necessary expenditure on repairs and insurance and any annual instalment (whether of interest or of capital) payable in respect of a mortgage debt or heritable security charged on the house in which the householder resides or has an interest and,

in calculating the amount of rent payable, any housing benefit paid under the Social Security Contributions and Benefits Act 1992 shall be deducted from amount of rent payable.

(3) In this paragraph, the expression "net rent" means the rent less any proceeds of sub-letting any part of the premises in respect of which the said rent is paid or the out-

goings are incurred except that, where any person or persons other than the person concerned, his or her spouse or any dependant of his or hers is accommodated, otherwise than as a sub-tenant, in the premises for which the rent is paid, the rent may be deemed to be reduced by an amount reasonably attributable to such other person or persons.

(4) In sub-paragraph (2)(b) above, the amount to be included as "rent" in respect of any annual instalment payable in respect of a mortgage debt or heritable security shall not exceed an amount bearing the same proportion to the amount of the annual instalment as £100,000 bears to the debt secured.

Amended by the Legal Aid in Criminal and Care Proceedings (General) (Amendment) Regulations 1990 (S.I. 1990 No. 489) and the Legal Aid in Criminal and Care Proceedings (General) (Amendment) Regulations 1993 (S.I. 1993 No. 789). Paragraph 8(4) was inserted by the Legal Aid in Criminal and Care Proceedings (General) (Amendment) Regulations 1996 (S.I. 1996 No. 436) which apply to applications for legal aid made on or after June 1, 1996.

9. Where the person concerned is not a householder, there shall be a deduction in respect of the costs of his living accommodation of such an amount as is reasonable in the circumstances.

Amended by the Legal Aid in Criminal and Care Proceedings (General) (Amendment) Regulations 1990 (S.I. 1990 No. 489) and the Legal Aid in Criminal and Care Proceedings (General) (Amendment) Regulations 1993 (S.I. 1993 No. 789).

10.—(1) Subject to sub-paragraph (2) below, in computing disposable income, there shall be a deduction—

(a) in respect of the maintenance of the spouse of the person concerned, where the spouses are living together;

(b) in respect of the maintenance of any dependent child and of any dependent relative of the person concerned where such persons are members of his household;

at the following rates—

(i) in the case of a spouse at the rate equivalent to the difference between the income support allowance for a couple where both members are aged not less than 18 (which is specified in column 2 of paragraph 1(3)(c) of Schedule 2 Part I of the Income Support (General) Regulations 1987), and the allowance for a single person aged not less than 25, (which is specified in column 2 of paragraph 1(1)(e) of Schedule 2 Part I of those Regulations);

(ii) in the case of a dependent child or a dependent relative aged 18 or under, at the rate equivalent to the amount specified for the time being in paragraph 2 of Part I of Schedule 2 to the Income Support (General) Regulations 1987 appropriate to the age of the child or relative.

(iii) in the case of a dependent child or a dependant relative aged 19 or over, at the rate equivalent to the amount which would have been specified in accordance with paragraph 10(1)(b)(ii) immediately before he attained the age of 19.

(2) The proper officer may reduce any rate provided by virtue of sub-paragraph (1) by taking into account the income and other resources of the dependent child or other dependant to such extent as appears to the officer to be just and equitable.

(3) In ascertaining whether a child is a dependent child or whether a person is a dependent relative for the purposes of this paragraph, regard shall be had to their income and other resources.

Amended by the Legal Aid in Criminal and Care Proceedings (General) (Amendment) Regulations 1993 (S.I. 1993 No. 789) and the Legal Aid in Criminal and Care Proceedings (General) (Amendment) Regulations 1998 (S.I. 1998 No. 662).

11. Where the person concerned is making and, throughout such period as the proper officer may consider to be adequate, has regularly made bona fide payments for the maintenance of

(a) a spouse who is living apart;

(b) a former spouse;

(c) a child; or

(d) a relative;

who is not a member of the household of the person concerned, there shall be a deduction at the rate of such payments or at such rate (not exceeding the rate of such payments) as in all the circumstances is reasonable.

12. In computing disposable income, there shall be a deduction in respect of any sum or sums payable by the person concerned under an order made by, or arising from any conviction before, the High Court, the Crown Court, a county court, or a magistrates' court in any proceedings other than those in respect of which the legal aid order was made.

13. Where the person concerned is required to, or may reasonably, provide for any other matter, the proper officer may make an allowance of such amount as he considers to be reasonable in the circumstances of the case.

14. In computing the income from any source, there shall be disregarded such amount, if any, as the proper officer considers to be reasonable having regard to the nature of the income or to any other circumstances of the case.

Disposable capital

15.—(1) In computing the capital of the person concerned, there shall be included the amount or value of every resource of a capital nature belonging to him on the date of the assessment.

(2) In so far as any resource of a capital nature does not consist of money, its amount or value shall be taken to be—

(a) the amount which that resource would realise if sold in the open market, or if there is only a restricted market for the resource, the amount which it would realise in that market, after deduction of any expenses incurred in the sale, or

(b) if such an amount cannot be ascertained, an amount which appears to the property officer to be reasonable.

15A. A resource of a capital nature shall not be treated as not belonging to the person concerned by reason only that that person is restrained from using or disposing of it by the order of any court, unless—

(a) that person has requested the court which made the order to release assets forming all or part of that resource for use in connection with the proceedings to which the legal aid application relates; and

(b) that request has been refused.

Paragraph 15A inserted by the Legal Aid in Criminal and Care Proceedings (General) (Amendment) Regulations 1998 (S.I. 1998 No. 662).

16. In computing the capital of the person concerned, there shall be disregarded—

(a) any savings of mobility allowance paid under the Social Security Act 1975 or disability living allowance which the person concerned intends to use in connection with mobility or his disability;

(b) for a period not exceeding 12 months from the date of receipt, any arrears of—

(i) attendance or mobility allowance paid under the Social Security Act 1975–1988 or disability living allowance;

(ii) income-based jobseeker's allowance, income support, family credit or disability working allowance;

(iii)   payments under the Community Care (Direct Payments) Act 1996 and;

(c)   any payments made out of the social fund under section 32 of the Social Security Contributions and Benefits Act 1992; and

(d)   so much of any back to work bonus received under section 26 of the Jobseekers Act 1995 as is by virtue of that section to be treated as payable by way of a jobseeker's allowance.

Amended by the Legal Aid in Criminal and Care Proceedings (General) (Amendment) Regulations 1993 (S.I. 1993 No. 789), and from October 7, 1996 as to words in italics by the Legal Aid in Criminal and Care Proceedings (General) (Amendment) (No. 3) Regulations 1996 (S.I. 1996 No. 1258). Also amended by the Legal Aid in Criminal and Care Proceedings (General) (Amendment) (No. 5) Regulations 1996 (S.I. 1996 No. 2307) and the Legal Aid in Criminal and Care Proceedings (General) (Amendment) Regulations 1997 (S.I. 1997 No. 752).
Paragraph 16(d) inserted by the Legal Aid in Criminal and Care Proceedings (General) (Amendment) (No. 4) Regulations 1996 (S.I. 1996 No. 2307).

17. Except where it is reasonable in the circumstances so to do, no sum shall be included in the amount of the capital of the person concerned in respect of the value of the assets of any business owned in whole or in part by him.
18. Save in exceptional circumstances, no sum shall be included in the amount of the capital of the person concerned in respect of—

(a)   household furniture and effects of the main or only residence occupied by him;

(b)   articles of personal clothing; and

(c)   tools and equipment of his trade.

19. In computing the amount of the capital of the person concerned, the value of any interest in the main or only residence in which he resides shall be **taken to be the amount for which that interest could be sold in the open market, subject to the following rules—**

(a)   **the amount to be allowed in respect of any mortgage debt or heritable security shall not exceed £100,000;**

(b)   **the first £100,000 of the value of that interest, after the application of the rule in paragraph (a), shall be** *wholly disregarded.*

19A. **Where the person concerned resides in more than one dwelling in which he has an interest, the proper officer shall decide which is the main dwelling and shall take into account the amount for which any interest in a dwelling which is not the main dwelling could be sold in the open market; provided that the total amount to be allowed in respect of any mortgage debts or heritable securities over all such dwellings, together with any amount allowed under paragraph 19(a) in respect of the main dwelling, shall not exceed £100,000.**

The words in italic were deleted and the words in bold substituted/inserted by the Legal Aid in Criminal and Care Proceedings (General) (Amendment) Regulations 1996 (S.I. 1996 No. 436) which apply to applications for legal aid made on or after June 1, 1996.

20. In computing the capital of the person concerned, there may also be disregarded such an amount of capital (if any) as the proper officer decides to disregard taking into account the nature of the capital or any other circumstances of the case.

SCHEDULE 4

Contributions

Contributions from disposable income
The weekly instalment of contribution payable by the applicant or the appropriate

contributor shall be £1 for each £3 or part of £3 by which his average weekly disposable income exceeds £50; but any applicant or appropriate contributor whose weekly disposable income does not exceed £51 shall not be liable to pay a contribution.

Amended by the Legal Aid in Criminal and Care Proceedings (General) (Amendment) Regulations 1992 (S.I 1992 No. 720), the Legal Aid in Criminal and Care Proceedings (General) (Amendment) Regulations 1993 (S.I. 1993 No. 789), the Legal Aid in Criminal and Care Proceedings (General) (Amendment) Regulations 1994 (S.I. 1994 No. 807), the Legal Aid in Criminal and Care Proceedings (General) (Amendment) (No. 2) Regulations 1995 (S.I. 1995 No. 796) and the Legal Aid in Criminal and Care Proceedings (General) (Amendment) (No. 2) Regulations 1996 (S.I. 1996 No. 646), the Legal Aid in Criminal and Care Proceedings (General) (Amendment) Regulations 1997 (S.I. 1997 No. 752) and the Legal Aid in Criminal and Care Proceedings (General) (Amendment) Regulations 1998 (S.I. 1998 No. 662).

Contributions from disposable capital
The contribution from capital payable by the applicant or the appropriate contributor shall be such an amount as is equal to the amount by which his disposable capital exceeds £3,000.

EXPLANATORY NOTE
(This note is not part of the Regulations)
These Regulations replace, with amendments, the Legal Aid in Criminal Proceedings (General) Regulations 1968 (as subsequently amended). These Regulations govern the provision of representation under Part V and Sections 27 and 28 of the Legal Aid Act 1988 (legal aid in criminal and care proceedings).

These Regulations make provision for the assessment of the financial resources of the applicant or the appropriate contributor in order to determine eligibility to receive legal aid and to determine the contribution payable towards the cost of providing representation in the proceedings in respect of which the application for a legal aid order is made.

The main changes made are as follows:

(a) a single form of application for a legal aid order is prescribed, the use of which is mandatory (regulation 4 and Schedule 2 Part I);

(b) court clerks are given power to refuse an application for a legal aid order subject to a right to renew the application (regulations 11, 14, 18, and 21);

(c) the resources of persons living together as husband and wife are to be treated as if those persons were married (regulations 26, 37 and Schedule 3, paragraph 2);

(d) a solicitor assigned under a legal aid order who instructs counsel is to provide counsel with a copy of the legal aid order (regulation 40);

(e) Parts I to VI of the Regulations are applied, subject to a number of modifications, to the grant of representation in care proceedings and, in the exercise of the power conferred by section 27(2), section 27(1)(f) of the Act is varied to exclude from the categories of care proceedings for the purposes of which representation is available under sections 27 and 28 of the Act appeals from decisions of juvenile courts to the High Court (regulations 56 and 57).

Legal Aid in Criminal and Care Proceedings (Costs) Regulations 1989*

Came into force April 1, 1989

ARRANGEMENT OF REGULATIONS

---

* S.I. 1989 No. 343 as amended by the Legal Aid in Criminal and Care Proceedings (Costs) (Amendment) Regulations 1990 (S.I. 1990 No. 488), the Legal Aid in Criminal and Care Proceedings (Costs) (Amendment) Regulations 1991 (S.I. 1991 No. 529), the Legal Aid in Criminal and Care Proceedings (Costs) (Amendment) (No. 2) Regulations 1991 (S.I. 1991 No. 838), the Legal Aid in Criminal and Care Proceedings (Costs) (Amendment) (No. 3) Regulations 1991 (S.I. 1991 No. 2037), the Legal Aid in Criminal and Care Proceedings (Costs) (Amendment) Regulations 1992 (S.I. 1992 No. 592), the Legal Aid in Criminal and Care Proceedings (Costs) (Amendment) Regulations 1993 (S.I. 1993 No. 934), the Legal Aid in Criminal and Care Proceedings (Costs) (Amendment) Regulations 1994 (S.I. 1994 No. 1477), the Legal Aid in Criminal and Care Proceedings (Costs) (Amendment) (No. 2) Regulations 1994 (S.I. 1994 No. 1825), the Legal Aid in Criminal and Care Proceedings (Costs) (Amendment) (No. 3) Regulations 1994 (S.I. 1994 No. 2218), the Legal Aid in Criminal and Care Proceedings (Costs) (Amendment) Regulations 1995 (S.I. 1995 No. 952), the Legal Aid in Criminal and Care Proceedings (Costs) (Amendment) Regulations 1996 (S.I. 1996 No. 644), the Legal Aid in Criminal and Care Proceedings (Costs) (Amendment) (No. 2) Regulations 1996 (S.I. 1996 No. 2655), the Legal Aid in Criminal and Care Proceedings (Costs) (Amendment) Regulations 1997 (S.I. 1997 No. 754) and the Legal Aid in Criminal and Care Proceedings (Costs) (Amendment) (No. 2) Regulations 1997 (S.I. 1997 No. 1010), the Legal Aid in Criminal and Care Proceedings (Costs) (Amendment) (No. 3) Regulations 1997 (S.I. 1997 No. 1484) and the Legal Aid in Criminal and Care Proceedings (Costs) (Amendment) Regulations 1998 (S.I. 1998 No. 1191).

Items 4F–4J inserted by the Legal Aid in Criminal and Care Proceedings (Costs) (Amendment) (No. 2) Regulations 1996 (S.I. 1996 No. 2655).

SCHEDULES

Item 3 inserted by the Legal Aid in Criminal and Care Proceedings (Costs) (Amendment) (No. 2) Regulations 1996 (S.I. 1996 No. 2655).

Citation, commencement, revocations and transitional provisions

1.—(1) These Regulations may be cited as the Legal Aid in Criminal and Care Proceedings (Costs) Regulations 1989 and shall come into force on 1st April 1989.

(2) Subject to paragraph (3), the Legal Aid in Criminal Proceedings (Costs) Regulations 1988 and the Legal Aid in Criminal Proceedings (Costs) (Amendment) Regulations 1988 shall be revoked.

(3) These Regulations shall apply for the determination of costs which are payable in respect of work done on or after 1st April 1989 and costs payable in respect of work done before that date shall be determined as if these Regulations had not been made.

(4) Where a review under regulation 12 relates to a claim made before 1st June 1989, regulation 13(1) and (2) shall not apply and the solicitor may appeal in writing within 21 days of receipt of notification of the decision on the review to a committee appointed by the Board.

Interpretation

2.—(1) In these Regulations, unless the context otherwise requires—

"the Act" means the Legal Aid Act 1988;

"appropriate authority" has the meaning assigned by regulation 3;

"area committee" has the meaning assigned to it by regulation 4 of the Civil Legal Aid (General) Regulations 1989;

"appropriate area committee" means the area committee in whose area is situated the magistrates' court at which a legal aid order was made;

"contract" means a contract entered into by the Board with other persons or bodies pursuant to its powers under section 4 of the Act;

"costs" means, in the case of a solicitor, the fees and disbursements payable under section 25 of the Act and, in the case of counsel, the fees payable under that section;

"counsel" means counsel assigned under the legal aid order;

"Court of Appeal" means the criminal division of the Court of Appeal or the Courts-Martial Appeal Court as the case may be;

"determining officer" means an officer appointed under regulation 3(2);

"disbursements" means travelling and witness expenses and other out of pocket expenses incurred by a fee-earner in giving legal aid;

"fee-earner" means a solicitor, a legal executive or any clerk who regularly does work for which it is appropriate to make a direct charge to a client;

"franchisee" means a person or body (other than the Board) acting under the terms of a franchising contract;

"legal aid" and "legal aid order" have the meanings respectively assigned by the General Regulations;

"legal aid area" has the meaning assigned by paragraph 1(2) of Schedule 1 Part I;

"legal executive" means a fellow of the Institute of Legal Executives;

"pleas and directions hearing" means any hearing which is fixed for the purpose of arraigning any person, unless it has been arranged that if that person pleads not guilty to one or more counts his trial shall follow immediately. *[Inserted by the Legal Aid in Criminal and Care Proceedings (Costs) (Amendment) (No. 2) Regulations 1996 (S.I. 1996 No. 2655)]*;

"registrar" means the registrar of criminal appeals or the registrar of the Courts-Martial Appeal Court, as the case may be;

"the General Regulations" means the Legal Aid in Criminal and Care Proceedings (General) Regulations 1989;

"solicitor" means a solicitor assigned under the legal aid order;

"trial judge" means the judge who presided at the hearing at which the defendant was substantively dealt with and in respect of which the costs are payable;

"taxing master" means a taxing master of the Supreme Court;

"wasted costs order" has the meaning assigned to it by regulation 3A of the Costs in Criminal Cases (General) Regulations 1986.

(2) Unless the context otherwise requires, any reference in these Regulations to a Regulation or Schedule by number means the Regulation or Schedule so numbered to these Regulations and any reference to a Part of a Schedule by number means the Part so numbered in that Schedule.

Amended by the Legal Aid in Criminal and Care Proceedings (Costs) (Amendment) (No. 2) Regulations 1994 (S.I. 1994 No. 1825).

The appropriate authority

3.—(1) Subject to paragraphs (2), (3) and (4) the appropriate authority shall be—

(a) the registrar in the case of proceedings in the Court of Appeal;

(b) an officer appointed by the Lord Chancellor in the case of criminal proceedings in the Crown Court;

(c) the Board in the case of criminal proceedings in a magistrates' court.

(2) The appropriate authority may appoint or authorise the appointment of determining officers to act on its behalf under these Regulations in accordance with directions given by it or on its behalf.

(3) For costs claimed in respect of advice or assistance as to an appeal from the Crown Court to the Court of Appeal, the appropriate authority shall be:—

(a) (except in the case of an appeal under section 9(11) of the Criminal Justice Act 1987) the registrar where, on the advice of any legal representative assigned, notice of appeal is given, or application for leave to appeal is made, whether or not such appeal is later abandoned;

(b) an officer appointed by the Lord Chancellor under paragraph (1)(b) in all other cases.

(4) For costs claimed in respect of advice or assistance as to an appeal from a magistrates' court to the Crown Court, the appropriate authority shall be the Board.

Paragraph (3)(a) amended by the Legal Aid in Criminal and Care Proceedings (Costs) (Amendment) (No. 2) Regulations 1996 (S.I. 1996 No. 2655).

General

4.—(1) Costs in respect of work done under a legal aid order shall be determined by the appropriate authority in accordance with these Regulations.

(2) In determining costs, the appropriate authority shall, subject to and in accordance with these Regulations—

(a) take into account all the relevant circumstances of the case including the nature, importance, complexity or difficulty of the work and the time involved, and

(b) allow a reasonable amount in respect of all work actually and reasonably done.

Interim payment of disbursements

4A.—(1) A solicitor may submit a claim to the appropriate authority for payment of a disbursement for which he has incurred liability in criminal proceedings in the Crown Court in accordance with the provisions of this regulation.

(2) A claim for payment may be made where—

(a) a solicitor has obtained prior authority to incur expenditure of £100 or more under regulation 54(1)(a), (b), (c) or (e) of the General Regulations; and

(b) he has incurred liability for a disbursement under that authority of £100 or more.

(3) Without prejudice to regulation 7(6), a claim under paragraph (1) above shall not exceed the maximum fee authorised under the prior authority.

(4) A claim for payment under paragraph (1) may be made at any time before the solicitor submits a claim for costs under regulation 5(2).

(5) A claim under paragraph (1) shall be submitted to the appropriate authority in such form and manner as it may direct and shall be accompanied by the authority to incur expenditure and any invoices or other documents in support of the claim.

(6) The appropriate authority shall allow the disbursement subject to the limit in paragraph (3) above if it appears to have been reasonably incurred in accordance with the prior authority.

(7) Where the appropriate authority allows the disbursement, it shall notify the solicitor and, where the disbursement includes the fees or charges of any person, that person, of the amount payable and shall authorise payment to the solicitor accordingly.

(8) Regulations 14 to 16 (redetermination etc.) shall not apply to a claim for payment under this regulation.

Interim disbursements and final determination of costs

4B.—(1) On a final determination of costs, paragraphs (2) and (3)(e) of regulation 5 and regulation 7 shall apply notwithstanding that a payment has been made under regulation 4A.

(2) Where the amount found to be due under regulation 7 in respect of a disbursement is less than the amount paid under regulation 4A ("the interim disbursement"), the appropriate authority shall deduct the difference from the sum otherwise payable to the solicitor on the determination of costs, and where the amount due under regulation 7 exceeds the interim disbursement, the appropriate authority shall add the difference to the amount otherwise payable to the solicitor.

Interim payments in cases awaiting determination

4C.—(1) The appropriate authority shall make an interim payment in respect of a claim for costs in criminal proceedings in the Crown Court in accordance with the following provisions of this regulation.

(2) Entitlement to a payment arises in respect of a claim for costs—

(a) in the case of a solicitor, where the total claim for costs is £4,000 or more (exclusive of Value Added Tax);

(b) in the case of a barrister, where the basic fee claimed is £4,000 or more (exclusive of Value Added Tax);

(c) where the claim for costs is for less than the amounts mentioned in (a) or (b) but is related to any claim falling under (a) or (b).

(3) Entitlement to a payment under paragraph (1) of this regulation shall not arise until three months have elapsed from—

(a) the date on which the bill is ready to tax or, if earlier,

(b) the date three months after the conclusion of the last of any related proceedings.

(4) A bill shall be regarded as being ready to tax on the date on which it is received by the appropriate authority for determination except that where there are related claims for costs all the bills relating thereto shall be regarded as ready to tax on the date the last bill is received.

(5) A solicitor or barrister may submit a claim for an interim payment under this regulation if no payment has been made under paragraph (1) and six months have elapsed from the conclusion of the proceedings against the defendant whom he represented under the legal aid order.

(6) For the purposes of this regulation, proceedings are related to each other in the circumstances set out in paragraph (7) and claims for costs are related to each other in the circumstances set out in paragraph (8).

(7) Proceedings are related to each other:—

(a) where different proceedings involving the same defendant are prepared or heard or dealt with together;

(b) where proceedings involving more than one defendant arose out of the same incident, so that the defendants are charged or tried or disposed of together.

(8) The following claims for costs are related to each other:—

(a) the claims of a solicitor and counsel acting in the same proceedings for a defendant;

(b) the claims of any solicitor or counsel acting in any proceedings mentioned in paragraph (7)(a);

(c) the claims of all the solicitors or counsel acting for the defendants in the circumstances mentioned in paragraph (7)(b).

(9) No payment shall be made under this regulation unless (subject to regulation 17) the solicitor or barrister has submitted his claim in accordance with the provision of regulations 5(1) and 8(1).

Amount of interim payment in cases awaiting determination

4D.—(1) Where entitlement to a payment arises under regulation 4C, the amount payable shall be—

(a) 40 per cent of the total claim for costs

less

(b) any sum already paid.

(2) Regulations 14 to 16 (redetermination etc.) shall not apply to a payment under this regulation.

Inserted by the Legal Aid in Criminal and Care Proceedings (Costs) (Amendment) Regulations 1993 (S.I. 1993 No. 934).

Interim payments under franchising contracts

4E.—(1) Where representation under Part V of the Act is provided under a franchising contract for criminal proceedings in a magistrates' court, the franchisee may apply to the Board when the legal aid order is granted for an interim payment in respect of a claim for costs in accordance with the contract.

Inserted by the Legal Aid in Criminal and Care Proceedings (Costs) (Amendment) (No. 2) Regulations 1994 (S.I. 1994 No. 1825).

Staged payments in long Crown Court cases

4F.—(1) A legal representative may submit a claim to the appropriate authority for a staged payment of his fees in relation to criminal proceedings in the Crown Court.

(2) Where a claim is submitted in accordance with the provisions of this regulation, a staged payment shall be allowed where the appropriate authority is satisfied—

  (a) that the claim relates to fees for a period of preparation of 100 hours or more, for which the legal representative will, subject to final determination of the costs payable, be entitled to be paid in accordance with these Regulations, and

  (b) that the period from committal or transfer for trial (or from the date of the legal aid order, if this is later) to the conclusion of the Crown Court proceedings will be likely to exceed 12 months, having regard amongst other matters to the number of defendants, the anticipated pleas and the weight and complexity of the case.

(3) In this regulation "preparation" means—

  (a) all work falling within the definition of "preparation" in paragraph 1(1) of Schedule 3;

  (b) attendance at pre-trial reviews and other hearings (other than a pleas and directions hearing) prior to the main hearing;

  (c) preparation of applications, statements or notices for the purposes of section 6 or 9(5) of the Criminal Justice Act 1987, and

  (d) all preparation within the meaning of regulation 6(1)(a) not falling within the preceding sub-paragraphs,

and is limited to preparation done before the commencement of the trial, except in proceedings in which a preparatory hearing has been ordered under section 8 of the Criminal Justice Act 1987 in which case it is limited to preparation done before the date on which the jury is sworn (or on which it became certain, by reason of pleas of guilty or otherwise, that the matter would not proceed to trial).

(4) The amount to be allowed for preparation falling within paragraph (3)(a), (b) or (c) shall be computed by reference to the number of hours of preparation which it appears to the appropriate authority, without prejudice to final determination of the costs payable, has been reasonably done multiplied by the relevant hourly rate namely—

  (a) in the case of an authorised advocate who is a Queen's Counsel, the hourly rate for subsidiary fees for Queen's Counsel in the Crown Court prescribed in Table 2 in Schedule 2 Part II;

  (b) in the case of an authorised advocate instructed as leading junior counsel pursuant to an order made under regulation 48 of the General Regulations, 75 per cent of the hourly rate for subsidiary fees for

Queen's Counsel in the Crown Court prescribed in Table 2 in Schedule 2 Part II;

(c) in the case of any other authorised advocate, the hourly rate for subsidiary fees for junior counsel in the Crown Court prescribed in Table 1 in Schedule 2 Part II.

(5) The amount to be allowed for preparation falling within paragraph (3)(d) shall be computed by reference to the number of hours of preparation which it appears to the appropriate authority, without prejudice to the final determination of the costs payable, has been reasonably done multiplied by the relevant hourly rate prescribed in Schedule 1 Part I, paragraph 1(1)(b) applicable to the class of work and the grade and office location of the fee-earner.

(6) A claim shall be submitted in such form and manner as the appropriate authority may direct, including such case plan as the appropriate authority may require for the purposes of paragraph (2)(a).

(7) A legal representative may claim further staged payments in accordance with this regulation in respect of further periods of preparation exceeding 100 hours which were not included in an earlier claim.

(8) Regulations 14 to 16 (redetermination etc.) shall not apply to a payment under this regulation.

Inserted by the Legal Aid in Criminal and Care Proceedings (Costs) (Amendments) (No. 2) Regulations 1996 (S.I. 1996 No. 2655).

Interim payment for attendance at trial and refreshers

4G.—(1) A legal representative may submit a claim to the appropriate authority for an interim payment in respect of attendance at court or refreshers where a Crown Court trial lasts for a qualifying period.

(2) Where a claim is submitted in accordance with the provisions of this regulation, an interim payment shall, without prejudice to the final determination of the costs payable, be allowed—

(a) to an authorised litigator, where he or a fee-earner representing him has attended at court on each day of the qualifying period;

(b) to an authorised advocate, where he has done work falling within paragraph 6(2)(b) or (c) of Schedule 3 on each day of the qualifying period.

(3) The qualifying period for the purposes of this regulation shall be 20 days (which need not be continuous), and a day will qualify as part of that period if the hearing begins at any time on that day.

(4) The amount payable in respect of each day which qualifies as part of the qualifying period shall be

(a) in the case of an authorised litigator—

(i) where the hearing begins before and ends after the luncheon adjournment, five times the hourly rate for an articled clerk or fee-earner of equivalent experience attending court where more than one legal representative is assigned as prescribed in Schedule 1 Part I, paragraph 1(1)(b);

(ii) where the hearing begins and ends before the luncheon adjournment, or begins after the luncheon adjournment, two and a half times the hourly rate referred to in (i) above;

(b) in the case of an authorised advocate who is a Queen's Counsel, the maximum amount of the full day refresher fee for Queen's Counsel in the Crown Court prescribed in Table 2 in Schedule 2 Part II;

(c) in the case of an authorised advocate instructed as leading junior counsel pursuant to an order made under regulation 48 of the General Regulations, 75 per cent of the maximum amount of the full day refresher fee for Queen's Counsel in the Crown Court prescribed in Table 2 in Schedule 2 Part II;

(d) in the case of an authorised advocate retained solely for the purpose of making a note of any hearing, one-half of the maximum amount of the full day refresher fee for junior counsel in the Crown Court prescribed in Table 1 in Schedule 2 Part II;

(e) in the case of any other authorised advocate, the maximum amount of the full day refresher fee for junior counsel in the Crown Court prescribed in Table 1 in Schedule 2 Part II.

(5) A claim for an interim payment may be made in respect of a qualifying period and shall be submitted in such form and manner as the appropriate authority may direct.

(6) Further interim payments under this regulation may be claimed if the trial lasts for further qualifying periods.

(6A) A legal representative who has obtained prior approval under regulation 54A of the General Regulations for the incurring of travelling or accommodation expenses may, at the same time as he submits a claim for an interim payment under this regulation, submit a claim for interim payment of all such expenses incurred to date (less any expenses previously recovered by him by way of interim payment under this paragraph).

(6B) A claim under paragraph (6A) shall be submitted in such form and manner as the appropriate authority may direct, and shall be supported by such evidence of the expenses claimed as the appropriate authority may require.

(7) Regulations 14 to 16 (redetermination etc.) shall not apply to a payment under this regulation.

Inserted by the Legal Aid in Criminal and Care Proceedings (Costs) (Amendments) (No. 2) Regulations 1996 (S.I. 1996 No. 2655) and amended by the Legal Aid in Criminal and Care Proceedings (Costs) (Amendment) (No. 3) Regulations 1997 (S.I. 1997 No. 1484).

Advance payments for early preparation in Crown Court cases

4H.—(1) An advance payment under this regulation shall be payable in respect of every case in the Crown Court in which—

(a) a pleas and directions hearing is held;

(b) on or before the date of the pleas and directions hearing, a legal aid order has been made providing for an authorised advocate to represent the legally assisted person at the trial and a person (referred to in this regulation as "the advocate") has been instructed for that purpose, and

(c) the advocate satisfies the appropriate authority that he has, in his capacity as an advocate, and at least 5 days before the date of the pleas and directions hearing, done work of all the types listed in paragraphs (a) to (d) of the definition of "preparation" in paragraph 1(1) of Schedule 3 (whether or not he also does work of those types afterwards), unless at the pleas and directions hearing the legally assisted person pleads guilty to all counts or the prosecution declares an intention not to proceed to trial.

(2) Subject to paragraph (3), the amount of the advance payment under this regulation in respect of any such case shall be

    (a) £250 where the advocate is a Queen's Counsel;

    (b) £170 where the advocate is not a Queen's Counsel, but appears as leader to another advocate;

    (c) £100 for any other advocate.

(3) Where the same advocate is instructed in two or more cases which are to be heard concurrently the advance payment shall be the amount specified in paragraph (2) in respect of the first case and one-fifth of that amount in respect of each of the other cases.

(4) In this regulation, a "case" means proceedings against any one legally assisted person on one or more counts of a single indictment.

Inserted by the Legal Aid in Criminal and Care Proceedings (Costs) (Amendments) (No. 2) Regulations 1996 (S.I. 1996 No. 2655).

Hardship payments

4I.—(1) The appropriate authority may allow a hardship payment to a legal representative in the circumstances set out in paragraph (2), subject to the other provisions of this regulation.

(2) Those circumstances are—

    (a) the legal representative represents the legally assisted person in pro- ceedings in the Crown Court;

    (b) the legal representative applies for such a payment, in such form and manner as the appropriate authority may direct, not less than six months after he was first instructed in those proceedings (or in any related proceedings, if he was instructed in those proceedings earlier than in the proceedings to which the application relates);

    (c) the legal representative is not, at the date of the application, entitled to any payment under regulation 4C (interim payments in cases awaiting determination), 4F (staged payments) or 4G (interim payments);

    (d) the legal representative is unlikely to receive final payment in respect of the proceedings, as determined under regulation 6 or regulation 9, within the three months following the application for the hardship payment, and

    (e) the legal representative satisfies the appropriate authority that, by reason of the circumstance in paragraph (d), he is likely to suffer finan- cial hardship.

(3) Every application for a hardship payment shall be accompanied by such information and documents as the appropriate authority may require as evi- dence of

    (a) the work done by the legal representative in relation to the proceed- ings up to the date of the application, and

    (b) the likelihood of financial hardship.

(4) The amount of any hardship payment shall be in the discretion of the appropriate authority, but shall not exceed such sum as would be reasonable remuneration for the work done by the legal representative in relation to the proceedings up to the date of the application.

(5) No hardship payment shall be made if it appears to the appropriate authority that the sum which would be reasonable remuneration for the legal representative, or the sum required to relieve his financial hardship, is less than £5,000 (excluding any value added tax).

(6) Any hardship payment shall be set off against the remuneration finally payable to the legal representative under regulation 6 or regulation 9.

(7) The question of whether proceedings are related to each other for the purposes of this regulation shall be determined in accordance with regulation 4C(7).

Inserted by the Legal Aid in Criminal and Care Proceedings (Costs) (Amendments) (No. 2) Regulations 1996 (S.I. 1996 No. 2655).

Computation of final claim

4J.—(1) At the conclusion of a case in which one or more payments have been made to a legal representative under regulation 4F, 4G, 4H or 4I, he shall submit a claim under regulation 5 or regulation 8 for the determination of his overall remuneration, whether or not such a claim will result in any payment additional to those already made.

(2) In the determination of the amount payable to a legal representative under regulation 6 or regulation 9, the appropriate authority shall deduct the amount of any advance payment made under regulation 4F, 4G, 4H or 4I in respect of the same case from the amount that would otherwise be payable; and if the amount of the advance payment is greater than the amount that would otherwise be payable, the appropriate authority shall be entitled to recover the amount of the difference, either by way of repayment by the advocate or by way of deduction from any other amount that may be due to him.

Inserted by the Legal Aid in Criminal and Care Proceedings (Costs) (Amendments) (No. 2) Regulations 1996 (S.I. 1996 No. 2655).

Claims for costs by solicitors

5.—(1) Subject to regulation 17 and paragraph (1A), no claim by a solicitor for costs in respect of work done under a legal aid order shall be entertained unless the solicitor submits it within three months of the conclusion of the proceedings to which the legal aid order relates.

(1A) Where proceedings in a magistrates' court have not been concluded but a warrant of arrest has been issued, a claim by a solicitor for costs in respect of work done under a legal aid order shall be made not earlier than 6 weeks and not later than 19 weeks from the date of issue of the warrant and the provisions of Schedule 1 Part III shall apply.

(2) Subject to paragraph (3), a claim for costs shall be submitted to the appropriate authority in such form and manner as it may direct and shall be accompanied by the legal aid order and any receipts or other documents in support of any disbursements claimed.

(3) A claim shall—

(a) summarise the items of work done by a fee-earner in respect of which fees are claimed according to the classes specified in regulation 6(1), paragraph 4(2) of Schedule 1, Part III;

   (b) state, where appropriate, the dates on which the items of work were done, the time taken, the sums claimed and whether the work was done for more than one assisted person;

   (c) in the case of proceedings in the Crown Court or Court of Appeal, specify, where appropriate, the fee-earner who undertook each of the items of work claimed;

   (d) give particulars of any work done in relation to more than one indictment or a retrial;

   (e) specify any disbursements claimed, the circumstances in which they were incurred and the amounts claimed in respect of them.

   (f) where counsel has been instructed by the solicitor although not assigned under the legal aid order, state

      (i) the amount agreed in respect of counsel's fee;

     (ii) the time spent by counsel in preparation, advocacy, travelling and waiting;

    (iii) the amounts agreed for counsel's travelling and waiting time and travelling costs in proceedings specified in paragraph 2(2) of Schedule 1 Part III.

   (f) state the amount agreed in respect of counsel's fee (including the time spent in preparation, advocacy and waiting) in proceedings where counsel has been instructed by the solicitor although not assigned under the legal aid order.

  (4) Where the solicitor claims that—

   (a) regulation 44(7) of the General Regulations, or

   (b) paragraph 3 of Schedule 1 Part I, should be applied in relation to an item of work, he shall give full particulars in support of his claim.

  (5) Where there are any special circumstances which should be drawn to the attention of the appropriate authority, the solicitor shall specify them.

  (6) The solicitor shall supply such further particulars, information and documents as the appropriate authority may require.

Amended by the Legal Aid in Criminal and Care Proceedings (Costs) (Amendment) Regulations 1993 (S.I. 1993 No. 934) and the Legal Aid in Criminal and Care Proceedings (Costs) (Amendment) (No. 3) Regulations 1994 (S.I. 1994 No. 2218). Sub-paragraph (f) in italics was replaced by the substitute paragraph applicable to orders made on or after October 1, 1994.

Determination of solicitors' fees

  6.—(1) The appropriate authority may allow work done by fee-earners in the following classes—

   (a) preparation, including taking instructions, interviewing witnesses, ascertaining the prosecution case, advising on plea and mode of trial, preparing and perusing documents, dealing with letters and telephone calls which are not routine, preparing for advocacy, instructing counsel and expert witnesses, conferences, consultations, views and work done in connection with advice on appeal or case stated;

   (b) advocacy, including applications for bail and other applications to the court;

  (c) attendance at court where counsel is assigned, including conferences with counsel at court;

  (d) travelling and waiting;

  (e) dealing with routine letters written and routine telephone calls.

(2) The appropriate authority shall consider the claim, any further particulars, information or documents submitted by the solicitor under regulation 5 and any other relevant information and shall allow—

  (a) such work as appears to it to have been reasonably done under the legal aid order (including any representation or advice which is deemed to be work done under that order) by a fee-earner, classifying such work according to the classes specified in paragraph (1) as it considers appropriate; and

  (b) such time in respect of each class of work allowed by it (other than dealing with routine letters written and routine telephone calls) as it considers reasonable.

(2A) Subject to paragraph (2C), in any proceedings which are specified in paragraph 1(2) of Schedule 1 Part II, the appropriate authority shall proceed in accordance with the provisions of paragraph 3 of that Part of that Schedule.

(2B) In any proceedings in a magistrates' court which are specified in the Table in paragraph 2(2) of Schedule 1 Part III, the provisions of that Part of that Schedule shall apply.

(2C) In any proceedings in the Crown Court—

  (a) in respect of the classes of work specified in paragraph 6(2) of Schedule 3 (whether or not the proceedings are ones to which that Schedule applies), the appropriate authority shall proceed in accordance with the provisions of regulation 9 as if the fee-earner who did the work had been a barrister;

  (b) in respect of all other classes of work, the provisions of this regulation (excluding paragraph (2C)(a)) shall apply.

(3) Subject to paragraphs (2), (2A), (2B), (2C) and (4), the appropriate authority shall allow fees for work allowed by it under this regulation in accordance with Schedule 1 Part I; provided that, where any work allowed was done after 30th June 1999, it may allow such fees as appear to it to be reasonable for such work having regard to the rates specified in that Part of Schedule 1.

(4) In the case of criminal proceedings in the Crown Court and the Court of Appeal, the fees allowed in accordance with Part I of Schedule 1 shall be those appropriate to such of the following grades of fee-earner as the appropriate authority considers reasonable—

  (a) senior solicitor,

  (b) solicitor, legal executive or fee-earner of equivalent experience,

  (c) articled clerk or fee-earner of equivalent experience.

(5) *[Omitted by the Legal Aid in Criminal and Care Proceedings (Costs) (Amendment) (No. 3) Regulations 1991.]*

(6) This regulation applies to work in respect of which standard fees are payable under Part II or Part III of Schedule 1 or a graduated or fixed fee is payable under Schedule 3 only to the extent that those Parts or that Schedule specifically so provide.

Amended by the Legal Aid in Criminal and Care Proceedings (Costs) (Amendment) Regulations 1993 (S.I. 1993 No. 934), the Legal Aid in Criminal and Care Proceedings (Costs) (Amendment) Regulations 1994 (S.I. 1994 No. 1477), the Legal Aid in Criminal and Care Proceedings (Costs) (Amendment) Regulations 1995 (S.I. 1995 No. 952), the Legal Aid in Criminal and Care Proceedings (Costs) (Amendment) Regulations 1996 (S.I. 1996 No. 644), the Legal Aid in Criminal and Care Proceedings (Costs) (Amendment) (No. 2) Regulations 1996 (S.I. 1996 No. 2655), the Legal Aid in Criminal and Care Proceedings (Costs) (Amendment) (No. 2) Regulation 1997 (S.I. 1997 No. 1010) and the Legal Aid in Criminal and Care Proceedings (Costs) (Amendment) Regulations 1998 (S.I. 1998 No. 1191).

Paragraph (2C) inserted by the Legal Aid in Criminal and Care Proceedings (Costs) (Amendment) (No. 2) Regulations 1996 (S.I. 1996 No. 2655).

Determination of solicitors' disbursements

7.—(1) Subject to the provisions of this regulation, the appropriate authority shall allow such disbursements claimed under regulation 5 as appear to it to have been reasonably incurred; provided that:

(a) if they are abnormally large by reason of the distance of the court or the assisted person's residence or both from the solicitor's place of business, reimbursement of the expenses may be limited to what would otherwise, having regard to all the circumstances, be a reasonable amount; and

(b) in the case of an appeal to the Court of Appeal, the cost of a transcript, or any part thereof, of the proceedings in the court from which the appeal lies obtained otherwise than through the registrar shall not be allowed except where the appropriate authority considers that it is reasonable in all the circumstances for such disbursement to be allowed.

(2) *[Omitted by the Legal Aid in Criminal and Care Proceedings (Costs) (Amendment) Regulations 1993 (S.I. 1993 No. 934)].*

(3) *[Omitted by the Legal Aid in Criminal and Care Proceedings (Costs) (Amendment) Regulations 1993 (S.I. 1993 No. 934)].*

(4) No question as to the propriety of any step or act in relation to which prior authority has been obtained under regulation 54 of the General Regulations shall be raised on any determination of costs, unless the solicitor knew or ought reasonably to have known that the purpose for which the authority was given had failed or become irrelevant or unnecessary before the costs were incurred.

(5) Where costs are reasonably incurred in accordance with and subject to the limit imposed by a prior authority given under regulation 54 of the General Regulations, no question shall be raised on any determination of costs as to the amount of the payment to be allowed for the step or act in relation to which the authority was given.

(6) Where costs are incurred in taking any steps or doing any act for which authority may be given under regulation 54 of the General Regulations, without authority to do so having been given or in excess of any fee authorised under regulation 54 of the General Regulations, payment in respect of those costs may nevertheless be allowed on a determination of costs.

Costs in proceedings involving counsel not assigned under the legal aid order

7A.—(1) Where counsel has not been assigned under the legal aid order but has been instructed by the solicitor in proceedings in a magistrates' court, the appropriate authority shall, subject to paragraph (4), pay counsel the fees agreed between him and the solicitor.

(1A) In proceedings specified in paragraph 2(2) of Schedule 1 Part III, counsel's agreed fees shall also include any fees agreed in respect of counsel's travelling and waiting time and travelling costs.

(2) The solicitor shall claim his costs (including the time spent by counsel in *preparation, advocacy and waiting* preparation and advocacy) at the rates applicable to solicitors' fees in magistrates' courts proceedings in accordance with the provisions of Schedule 1 Part I.

(3) Where costs are determined in circumstances to which this regulation applies, the appropriate authority shall determine the costs which would have been payable to the solicitor had he undertaken the case without counsel, *but as regards the costs payable in respect of travelling shall allow only such costs as have actually been incurred by the solicitor.*

(4) The costs payable in respect of counsel's agreed fee shall be reduced only where, and to the extent that, they would exceed—

    (a) the costs determined in accordance with paragraph (3);

or

    (b) where a standard fee is payable, the total of the relevant standard fee plus the other costs referred to in paragraph 6(a) of Schedule 1 Part III and the travelling costs allowed in respect of counsel.

(5) The costs payable by the appropriate authority shall be applied as follows:

    (a) payment in respect of counsel shall be paid to counsel direct;

    (b) the balance of the costs payable shall be paid to the solicitor.

(6) In this regulation, except in the phrase "solicitor's fees":—

    (a) references to a solicitor shall be construed as extending to any authorised litigator as defined by section 119(1) of the Courts and Legal Services Act 1990;

    (b) references to counsel shall be construed as extending to any authorised advocate as defined by section 119(1) of the Courts and Legal Services Act 1990.

Amended by the Legal Aid in Criminal and Care Proceedings (Costs) (Amendment) Regulations 1993 (S.I. 1993 No. 934) and by the Legal Aid in Criminal and Care Proceedings (Costs) (Amendment) (No. 3) Regulations 1994 (S.I. 1994 No. 2218); in the latter case to add paragraph 1A and the words "and the travelling costs allowed in respect of counsel" in paragraph (4)(b) and to omit the words in italics in respect of orders made on or after October 1, 1994.

Paragraph (6) inserted by the Legal Aid in Criminal and Care Proceedings (Costs) (Amendment) (No. 2) Regulations 1996 (S.I. 1996 No. 2655).

Claims for fees by counsel

8.—(1) Subject to regulation 17, no claim by counsel for fees for work done under a legal aid order shall be entertained unless counsel submits it within three months of the conclusion of the proceedings to which the legal aid order relates.

(2) Subject to paragraph (3), a claim for fees shall be submitted to the appropriate authority in such form and manner as it may direct.

A claim shall—

(a) summarise the items of work in respect of which fees are claimed according to the classes specified in regulation 9(4);

(b) state the dates on which the items of work were done, the time taken where appropriate, the sums claimed and whether the work was done for more than one assisted person;

(c) give particulars of any work done in relation to more than one indictment or a retrial.

(4) Where counsel claims that—

(a) it would be inappropriate to allow a standard fee under regulation 9(2); or

(b) regulation 9(5)(b) should be applied in relation to an item of work, he shall give full particulars in support of his claim.

(5) Where there are any special circumstances which should be drawn to the attention of the appropriate authority, counsel shall specify them.

(6) Counsel shall supply such further particulars, information and documents as the appropriate authority may require.

Determination of counsel's fees

9.—(1) The appropriate authority shall consider the claim, any further particulars, information or documents submitted by counsel under regulation 8 and any other relevant information and shall allow such work as appears to it to have been reasonably done.

(2) In any proceedings specified in paragraph 2 or 3 of Schedule 3, the appropriate authority shall allow a graduated or fixed fee calculated in accordance with that Schedule in respect of all such work allowed by it as falls into the classes specified in paragraph 6(2) of that Schedule.

(2A) Where in any proceedings specified in paragraph 2 of Schedule 3, the trial judge makes adverse observations concerning the advocate's conduct of the case, the appropriate authority may reduce any fee which would otherwise be payable in accordance with that Schedule by such proportion as it shall see fit, having first given the advocate the opportunity to make representations about the extent to which the fee should be reduced.

(3) Where it appears to the appropriate authority that the fixed fee allowed by Schedule 3 in respect of any proceedings specified in paragraph 3 of that Schedule would be inappropriate taking into account all the relevant circumstances of the case, it may instead allow fees in accordance with paragraphs (4) and (5) of this regulation.

(4) The appropriate authority may, except in relation to work for which a graduated or fixed fee is allowed under paragraph (2), allow any of the following classes of fee to counsel in respect of work allowed by it under this regulation—

(a) a basic fee for preparation including preparation for a pre-trial review and, where appropriate, the first day's hearing including, where they took place on that day, short conferences, consultations, applications and appearances (including bail applications), views and any other preparation;

(b) a refresher fee for any day or part of a day during which a hearing continued, including, where they took place on that day, short conferences, consultations, applications and appearances (including bail applications), views and any other preparation;

(c) subsidiary fees for—

    (i) attendance at conferences, consultations and views not covered by sub-paragraph (a) or (b);

    (ii) written advice on evidence, plea, appeal, case stated or other written work;

    (iii) attendance at pre-trial reviews, applications and appearances (including bail applications and adjournments for sentence) not covered by sub-paragraph (a) or (b).

(5) In the case of proceedings in the Crown Court or a magistrates' court, the appropriate authority shall, except in relation to work for which a graduated or fixed fee is allowed under paragraph (2), allow such fees in respect of such work as it considers reasonable in such amounts as it may determine in accordance with Part II of Schedule 2; provided that:

(a) where any work allowed was done after 30th June 1999, the appropriate authority may allow such fees in such amounts as appear to it to be reasonable remuneration for such work having regard to the amounts specified in Part II of Schedule 2; or

(b) where it appears to the appropriate authority, taking into account all the relevant circumstances of the case, that owing to the exceptional circumstances of the case the amount payable by way of fees in accordance with Part II of Schedule 2 would not provide reasonable remuneration for some or all of the work it has allowed, it may allow such amounts as appears to it to be reasonable remuneration for the relevant work.

(6) In the case of proceedings in the Court of Appeal, the appropriate authority shall allow such fees in respect of such work as it considers reasonable in such amount as appear to it to be reasonable remuneration for such work.

(7) Where prior authority has been obtained to instruct a Queens Counsel alone under regulation 54 of the General Regulations, no question as to the propriety of that act shall be raised on any determination of counsel's fees, unless the solicitor knew or ought reasonably to have known that the purpose for which the authority was given had failed or become irrelevant or unnecessary before the fees were incurred.

Paragraphs (2), (2A) and (3) substituted by the Legal Aid in Criminal and Care Proceedings (Costs) (Amendment) (No. 2) Regulations 1996 (S.I. 1996 No. 2655). Paragraphs (4) and (5) amended by the Legal Aid in Criminal and Care Proceedings (Costs) (Amendment) (No. 2) Regulations 1996 (S.I. 1996 No. 2655), the Legal Aid in Criminal and Care Proceedings (Costs) (Amendment) (No. 2) Regulations 1997 (S.I. 1997 No. 1010) and the Legal Aid in Criminal and Care Proceedings (Costs) (Amendment) Regulations 1998 (S.I. 1998 No. 1191).

9A.—(1) Subject to paragraph (2), where the court has disallowed the whole or any part of any wasted costs under section 19A of the Prosecution of Offences Act 1985 the appropriate authority, in determining costs in respect of work done by the legal representative against whom the wasted costs order was made, shall deduct the amount of the order from the amount otherwise payable in accordance with these Regulations.

(2) Where the appropriate authority, in accordance with these Regulations, is minded to disallow any amount of a claim for work done to which the wasted costs order relates it shall disallow that amount or the amount of the wasted costs order, whichever is the greater.

Amended by the Legal Aid in Criminal and Care Proceedings (Costs) (Amendment) Regulations 1990 (S.I. 1990 No. 488), the Legal Aid in Criminal and Care Proceedings (Costs) (Amendment) Regulations 1993 (S.I. 1993 No. 934), the Legal Aid in Criminal and Care Proceedings (Costs) (Amendment) Regulations 1994 (S.I. 1994 No. 1477), the Legal Aid in Criminal and Care Proceedings (Costs) (Amendment) Regulations 1995 (S.I. 1995 No. 952) and the Legal Aid in Criminal and Care Proceedings (Costs) (Amendment) Regulations 1996 (S.I. 1996 No. 644).

Payment of costs

10.—(1) Having determined the costs payable to a solicitor or counsel in accordance with these Regulations, the appropriate authority shall notify the solicitor or counsel of the costs payable and authorise payment accordingly.

(2) Where the costs payable under paragraph (1) are varied as a result of any review, redetermination or appeal made or brought pursuant to these Regulations, then—

(a) where the costs are increased, the appropriate authority shall authorise payment of the increase;

(b) where the costs are decreased, the solicitor or counsel shall repay the amount of such decrease; and

(c) where the payment of any costs of the solicitor or counsel is ordered under regulation 15(14) or 16(8) or under paragraph 8(4) of Schedule 1 Part II, the appropriate authority shall authorise such payment.

Amended by the Legal Aid in Criminal and Care Proceedings (Costs) (Amendment) Regulations 1993 (S.I. 1993 No. 934).

Recovery of overpayments

10A.—(1) This regulation applies where a solicitor or barrister is entitled to be paid a certain sum ("the amount due") by virtue of these Regulations and, for whatever reason, he is paid an amount greater than that sum.

(2) Where the circumstances in paragraph (1) arise, the appropriate authority may—

(a) require immediate repayment of the amount in excess of the amount due ("the excess amount") and a solicitor or barrister shall on demand repay the excess amount to the appropriate authority, or

(b) deduct the excess amount from any other sum which is or becomes payable to the solicitor or barrister by virtue of these Regulations.

(3) The appropriate authority may proceed under paragraph (2)(b) without first proceeding under paragraph 2(a).

(4) Paragraph (2) shall apply notwithstanding that the solicitor or barrister to whom the excess amount was paid is exercising, or may exercise, a right under regulations 12 to 16 (redetermination etc.).

Inserted by the Legal Aid in Criminal and Care Proceedings (Costs) (Amendment) Regulations 1993 (S.I. 1993 No. 934).

Notification of collecting court

11.—Having determined the costs payable to a solicitor or counsel in accordance with these Regulations, the appropriate authority shall notify the collecting court of the amount determined in each case in which a contribution order under section 23(1) of the Act has been made.

Review of determinations by the Board

12.—(1) If, in a case in which the Board is the appropriate authority, a solicitor or counsel is dissatisfied with a determination (including a decision concerning the application of the provisions for standard fees under Schedule 1 Part III) made under these Regulations, the solicitor or counsel may within 21 days of receipt of notification of the costs payable under regulation 10(1) apply to the appropriate area committee to review that determination.

(2) On an application under paragraph (1), the appropriate area committee shall review the determination whether by confirming, increasing or decreasing the amount of it or in the case of a decision of the type referred to in paragraph (1), by confirming or amending the decision.

Amended by the Legal Aid in Criminal and Care Proceedings (Costs) (Amendment) Regulations 1993 (S.I. 1993 No. 934).

Appeals to committee appointed by the Board

13.—(1) A solicitor or counsel who is dissatisfied with the decision of an area committee on a review under regulation 12 may within 21 days of receipt of notification of the decision apply to that committee to certify a point of principle of general importance.

(2) Where an area committee certifies a point of principle of general importance, the solicitor or counsel may within 21 days of receipt of notification of that certification appeal in writing to a committee of the Board against the decision of the area committee under regulation 12.

(3) On an appeal under this regulation the committee appointed by the Board may reverse, affirm or amend the decision of the area committee under regulation 12.

Redetermination of costs by appropriate authority other than the Board

14.—(1) Where—

(a) a solicitor or counsel is dissatisfied with the costs (other than standard fees allowed under Schedule 1 Part II or graduated or fixed fees allowed under Schedule 3) determined under these Regulations by an appropriate authority for proceedings other than criminal proceedings before a magistrates' court;

(b) an authorised advocate in proceedings in the Crown Court is dissatisfied with the decision that Schedule 3 does or does not apply to those proceedings or with the calculation of the remuneration payable under that Schedule; or

(c) an authorised advocate in proceedings in the Crown Court is dissatisfied with the decision not to allow one of the following fees, or with the number of hours allowed in the calculation of such a fee, namely—
   (i) a special preparation fee under paragraph 17 of Schedule 3;
   (ii) a wasted preparation fee under paragraph 18 of Schedule 3; or
   (iii) an hourly fee under either paragraph of paragraph 19(1) of Schedule 3.

he may apply to the appropriate authority to redetermine those costs or to review that decision as the case may be.

(2) Subject to regulation 17, the application shall be made, within 21 days of the receipt of notification of the costs payable under regulation 10(1), by giving notice in writing to the appropriate authority specifying the matters in respect of which the application is made and the grounds of objection and shall be made in such form and manner as the appropriate authority may direct.

(3) The notice of application shall be accompanied by—

(a) in the case of a solicitor, the particulars, information and documents supplied under regulation 5; and

(b) in the case of counsel, the particulars, information and documents supplied under regulation 8.

(4) The notice of application shall state whether the applicant wishes to appear or to be represented and, if the applicant so wishes, the appropriate authority shall notify the applicant of the time at which it is prepared to hear him or his representative.

(5) The solicitor or counsel shall supply such further particulars, information and documents as the appropriate authority may require.

(6) The appropriate authority shall—

(a) redetermine the costs, whether by way of increase, decrease or in the amounts previously determined; or

(b) review the decision to allow standard fees under regulation 9(2) and confirm it or allow fees in accordance with regulation 9(4) and (5),

in the light of the objections made by the applicant or on his behalf and shall notify the applicant of its decision.

(7) The applicant may request the appropriate authority to give reasons in writing for its decision and, if so requested, the appropriate authority shall comply with the request.

(8) Subject to regulation 17, any request under paragraph (7) shall be made within 21 days of receiving notification of the decision.

Amended by the Legal Aid in Criminal and Care Proceedings (Costs) (Amendment) Regulations 1993 (S.I. 1993 No. 934), the Legal Aid in Criminal and Care Proceedings (Costs) (Amendment) (No. 2) Regulations 1996 (S.I. 1996 No. 2655) and the Legal Aid in Criminal and Care Proceedings (Costs) (Amendment) (No. 3) Regulations 1997 (S.I. 1997 No. 1484).

Paragraph (1)(c) substituted by the Legal Aid in Criminal and Care Proceedings (Costs) (Amendment) (No. 3) Regulations 1997 (S.I. 1997 No. 1484).

Appeals to a taxing master

15.—(1) Where the appropriate authority has given its reasons for its decisions under regulation 14, a solicitor or counsel who is dissatisfied with that decision may appeal to a taxing master.

(2) Subject to regulation 17, an appeal shall be instituted, within 21 days of the receipt of the appropriate authority's reasons, by giving notice in writing to the Chief Taxing Master.

(3) The appellant shall send a copy of any notice given under paragraph (2) to the appropriate authority.

(4) The notice of appeal shall be accompanied by—

(a) a copy of the written representations given under regulation 14(2),

(b) the appropriate authority's reasons for its decision given under regulation 14(7); and

(c) the particulars, information and documents supplied to the appropriate authority under regulation 14.

(5) The notice of appeal shall—

(a) be in such form as the Chief Taxing Master may direct,

(b) specify separately each item appealed against, showing (where appropriate) the amount claimed for the item, the amount determined and the grounds of objection to the determination, and

(c) state whether the appellant wishes to appear or to be represented or whether he will accept a decision given in his absence.

(6) The Chief Taxing Master may, and if so directed by the Lord Chancellor either generally or in a particular case shall, send to the Lord Chancellor a copy of the notice of appeal together with copies of such other documents as the Lord Chancellor may require.

(7) With a view to ensuring that the public interest is taken into account, the Lord Chancellor may arrange for written or oral representations to be made on his behalf and, if he intends to do so, he shall inform the Chief Taxing Master and the appellant.

(8) Any written representations made on behalf of the Lord Chancellor under paragraph (7) shall be sent to the Chief Taxing Master and the appellant and, in the case of oral representations, the Chief Taxing Master and the appellant shall be informed of the grounds on which such representations will be made.

(9) The appellant shall be permitted a reasonable opportunity to make representations in reply.

(10) The taxing master shall inform the appellant (or his representative) and the Lord Chancellor, where representations have been or are to be made on his behalf, of the date of any hearing and, subject to the provisions of this regulation, may give directions as to the conduct of the appeal.

(11) The taxing master may consult the trial judge, the appropriate authority or the determining officer and may require the appellant to provide any further information which he requires for the purpose of the appeal and, unless the taxing master otherwise directs, no further evidence shall be received on the hearing of the appeal and no ground of objection shall be valid which was not raised under regulation 14.

(12) The taxing master shall have the same powers as the appropriate authority under these Regulations and, in the exercise of such powers, may—

(a) alter the redetermination of the appropriate authority in respect of any sum allowed, whether by increase or decrease as he thinks fit;

(b) confirm the decision to allow standard fees under regulation 9(2) or allow fees in accordance with regulation 9(4) and (5).

(13) The taxing master shall communicate his decision and the reasons for it in writing to the appellant, the Lord Chancellor and the appropriate authority.

(14) Except where he confirms or decreases the sums redetermined under regulation 14 or confirms a decision to allow standard fees, the taxing master

may allow the appellant a sum in respect of part or all of any reasonable costs (including any fee payable in respect of an appeal) incurred by him in connection with the appeal.

Appeals to the High Court

16.—(1) A solicitor or counsel who is dissatisfied with the decision of a taxing master on an appeal under regulation 15 may apply to a taxing master to certify a point of principle of general importance.

(2) Subject to regulation 17, an application under paragraph (1) shall be made within 21 days of notification of a taxing master's decision under regulation 15(13).

(3) Where a taxing master certifies a point of principle of general importance, the solicitor or counsel may appeal to the High Court against the decision of a taxing master on an appeal under regulation 15, and the Lord Chancellor shall be a respondent to such an appeal.

(4) Subject to regulation 17, an appeal under paragraph (3) shall be instituted within 21 days of receiving a taxing master's certificate under paragraph (1).

(5) Where the Lord Chancellor is dissatisfied with the decision of a taxing master on an appeal under regulation 15, he may, if no appeal has been made by the solicitor or counsel under paragraph (3), appeal to the High Court against that decision, and the solicitor or counsel shall be a respondent to the appeal.

(6) Subject to regulation 17, an appeal under paragraph (5) shall be instituted within 21 days of receiving notification of the taxing master's decision under regulation 15(13).

(7) An appeal under paragraph (3) and (5) shall be instituted by originating summons in the Queen's Bench Division and shall be heard and determined by a single judge whose decision shall be final.

(8) The judge shall have the same powers as the appropriate authority and a taxing master under these Regulations and may reverse, affirm or amend the decision appealed against or make such other order as he thinks fit.

Time limits

17.—(1) Subject to paragraph (2), the time limit within which any act is required or authorised to be done may, for good reason, be extended:—

   (a) in the case of acts required or authorised to be done under regulation 15 or 16 by a taxing master or the High Court as the case may be;

   (b) in the case of acts required or authorised to be done by a solicitor or counsel under any other regulation, the appropriate authority.

(2) Where a solicitor or counsel without good reason has failed (or, if an extension were not granted, would fail) to comply with a time limit, the appropriate authority, a taxing master or the High Court, as the case may be, may, in exceptional circumstances, extend the time limit and shall consider whether it is reasonable in the circumstances to reduce the costs; provided that costs shall not be reduced unless the solicitor or counsel has been allowed a reasonable opportunity to show cause orally or in writing why the costs should not be reduced.

(3) A solicitor or counsel may appeal to a taxing master against a decision made under this regulation by an appropriate authority in respect of proceedings other than proceedings before a magistrates' court and such an appeal shall be instituted within 21 days of the decision being given by giving notice in writing to the Chief Taxing Master specifying the grounds of appeal.

House of Lords

18.—(1) In the case of proceedings in the House of Lords, the costs payable to a solicitor or counsel under section 25 of the Act shall be determined by such officer as may be prescribed by order of the House of Lords.

(2) Subject to paragraph (1), these Regulations shall not apply to proceedings in the House of Lords.

SCHEDULES

SCHEDULE 1

Solicitors' Fees

Part I

FEES DETERMINED UNDER REGULATION 6

1.—(1) Subject to paragraphs 1A, 2 and 3, the appropriate authority shall allow fees for work allowed by it under regulation 6 at the following prescribed rates:

(a) Magistrates' court proceedings

Class of work	Rate
Preparation	£44.75 per hour—(£47.25 per hour for a fee-earner whose office is situated within legal aid area 1)
Advocacy	£56.50 per hour
Attendance at court where more than one legal representative assigned	£30.50 per hour
Travelling and waiting	£24.75 per hour
Routine letters written and routine telephone calls	£3.45 per item—(£3.60 per item for a fee-earner whose office is situated within legal aid area 1)

(b) Crown Court and Court of Appeal proceedings

Class of work	Grade of fee-earner	Rate
Preparation	Senior solicitor	£53.00 per hour—(£55.75 per hour for a fee-earner whose office is situated within legal aid area 1)
	Solicitor, legal executive or fee-earner of equivalent experience	£45.00 per hour—(£47.25 per hour for a fee-earner whose office is situated within legal aid area 1)

Class of work	Grade of fee-earner	Rate
	Articled clerk or fee-earner of equivalent experience	£29.75 per hour—(£34.00 per hour for a fee-earner whose office is situated within legal aid area 1)
Advocacy (other than in the Crown Court) Attendance at court where more than one legal representative assigned	Senior solicitor	£64.00 per hour
	Solicitor	£56.00 per hour
	Senior solicitor	£42.25 per hour
	Solicitor, legal executive or fee-earner of equivalent experience	£34.00 per hour
	Articled clerk or fee-earner of equivalent experience	£20.50 per hour
Travelling and waiting	Senior solicitor	£24.75 per hour
	Solicitor, legal executive or fee-earner of equivalent experience	£24.75 per hour
	Articled clerk or fee-earner of equivalent experience	£12.50 per hour
Routine letters written and routine telephone calls		£3.45 per item—(£3.60 per item for a fee-earner whose office is situated within legal aid area 1)

(2) In paragraphs 1(1) and 1A, "legal aid area" means an area specified by the Board under regulation 4(1) of the Civil Legal Aid (General) Regulations 1989 and legal aid area 1, means the area so numbered by the Board.

1A. Subject to paragraphs 2 and 3, the following prescribed rates shall apply to work done by a franchisee instead of the corresponding rates in paragraph 1(1)(a):

Class of work	Rate
Preparation	£46.00 per hour—(£48.50 per hour for a fee-earner whose office is situated within legal aid area 1)
Advocacy	£57.75 per hour
Attendance at court where more than one legal representative assigned	£31.50 per hour
Travelling and waiting	£25.50 per hour
Routine letters written and routine telephone calls	£3.55 per item—(£3.70 per item for a fee-earner whose office is situated within legal aid area 1)

Amended by the Legal Aid in Criminal and Care Proceedings (Costs) (Amendment) Regulations 1992 (S.I. 1992 No. 592), the Legal Aid in Criminal and Care Proceedings (Costs) (Amendment) Regulations 1995 (S.I. 1995 No. 952), the Legal Aid in Criminal and Care Proceedings (Costs) (Amendment) Regulations 1996 (S.I. 1996 No. 644) and the Legal Aid in Criminal and Care Proceedings (Costs) (Amendment) (No. 2) Regulations 1996 (S.I. 1996 No. 2655).

2. In respect of any item of work, the appropriate authority may allow fees at less than the relevant *basic* prescribed rates specified in paragraph 1 or 1A where it appears to the appropriate authority reasonable to do so having regard to the competence and dispatch with which the work was done.

3.—(1) Upon a determination the appropriate authority may allow fees at more than the relevant prescribed rate specified in paragraph 1 or 1A subject to the provisions of this regulation where it appears to the appropriate authority, taking into account all the relevant circumstances of the case, that

   (a) the work was done with exceptional competence, skill or expertise;

   (b) the work was done with exceptional dispatch; or

   (c) the case involved exceptional circumstances or complexity.

(2) Where the appropriate authority considers that any item or class of work should be allowed at more than the prescribed rate, it shall apply to that item or class of work a percentage enhancement in accordance with the following provisions of this regulation.

(3) In determining the percentage by which fees should be enhanced above the prescribed rate the appropriate authority shall have regard to:—

   (a) the degree of responsibility accepted by the solicitor and his staff;

   (b) the care, speed and economy with which the case was prepared;

   (c) the novelty, weight and complexity of the case.

(4) Except in proceedings to which paragraph (5) applies, the percentage above the relevant prescribed rate by which fees for work may be enhanced shall not exceed 100 per cent.

(5) Where the proceedings relate to serious or complex fraud, the percentage above the relevant prescribed rate by which fees for work may be enhanced shall not exceed 200 per cent.

(6) The appropriate authority may have regard to the generality of proceedings to which these Regulations apply in determining what is exceptional within the meaning of this regulation.

3. *In respect of any item of work, the appropriate authority may allow fees at more than the relevant basic rate specified in paragraph 1 where it appears to the appropriate authority that, taking into account all the relevant circumstances of the case, the amount of fees payable at such specified rate would not reasonably reflect—*

   (a) the exceptional competence and dispatch with which the work was done, or

   (b) the exceptional circumstances of the case.

Amended by the Legal Aid in Criminal and Care Proceedings (Costs) (Amendment) (No. 3) Regulations 1994 (S.I. 1994 No. 2218) by deleting the words in italics and substituting the words/paragraph in respect of orders made on or after October 1, 1994, and by the Legal Aid in Criminal and Care Proceedings (Costs) (Amendment) Regulations 1995 (S.I. 1995 No. 952).

PART II

STANDARD FEES IN THE CROWN COURT

Application

   1.—(1) Subject to sub-paragraphs (3) and (4), this Part of this Schedule applies to the fees for work done by a fee-earner regardless of his grade in relation to the proceedings in the Crown Court specified in sub-paragraph (2).

(2) The following proceedings are specified for the purposes of sub-paragraph (1)—

    (a) committals for trial in which the indictment consisted of counts in respect of an offence which is classified as a class 3 or 4 offence in accordance with directions given by the Lord Chief Justice under section 75 of the Supreme Court Act 1981 and

        (i) where the trial (including any case prepared for trial in which no jury was sworn) lasted two days or less and at the time of listing was reasonably expected to last two days or less; or

        (ii) where the case was listed and disposed of as a plea of guilty;

    (b) appeals against conviction;

    (c) appeals against sentence, and

    (d) committals for sentence (including proceedings which arose out of a breach of an order of the Crown Court, proceedings in which sentence was deferred and other similar matters).

(3) Where in any proceedings specified in sub-paragraph (2), the trial judge—

    (a) is dissatisfied with the solicitor's conduct of the case; or

    (b) considers that, for exceptional reasons, the fees should be determined under regulation 6,

he may direct that the fees should be determined under regulation 6 and in that event this Part of this Schedule shall not apply.

(4) If a solicitor so elects, he may claim standard fees under this Part of this Schedule in respect of work done by him notwithstanding that the proceedings in relation to which the work was done are not specified in sub-paragraph (2), and the provisions of this Part of this Schedule shall apply to such a claim with the necessary modifications, save that, where a solicitor elects to claim the principal standard fee for preparation in respect of a trial which lasted more than two days, he shall be paid that fee (together with the appropriate standard fee for the other classes of work specified in paragraph 4(2)) and paragraph 2 shall not apply.

(5) For the purposes of this Part of this Schedule, the standard fees which are payable and the classes of work for which such fees may be paid are specified in paragraph 4 and the "lower fee limit" and the "upper fee limit" have the meanings given by paragraph 4(3).

Allowance of standard fees

    2.—(1) The appropriate authority shall allow the standard fees for preparation which has been claimed by a solicitor (together with the appropriate standard fees for the other classes of work specified in paragraph 4(2)) unless, where the principal standard fee for preparation has been claimed, such a fee is considered to be excessive in which case the lower standard fee shall be allowed.

(2) A solicitor who has been allowed the lower standard fee instead of the principal fee claimed may—

    (a) accept that lower fee;

    (b) request the appropriate authority in writing to review its decision; or

    (c) provide the appropriate authority with a detailed claim in the form directed by the appropriate authority requesting in writing that the fees for preparation be determined under regulation 6.

(3) Where the appropriate authority is requested to review its decision under subparagraph (2)(b), the authority shall either—

    (a) allow the principal fee; or

    (b) request the solicitor to provide a detailed claim in the form directed by the appropriate authority.

(4) Where a solicitor fails to make a request under sub-paragraph (2)(b) or to supply a detailed claim for the purposes of sub-paragraph (2)(c) or (3)(b) within six weeks of the decision to allow the lower fee or the request to supply a detailed claim, whichever is the later, the decision to allow the lower standard fee shall be deemed to be confirmed.

3.—(1) Where a solicitor—

(a) submits a claim for determination under regulation 6 in a case to which paragraph 1(2) applies; or

(b) disputes the allowance of the lower standard fee and provides a detailed claim under paragraph 2(2)(c) or (3)(b),

the appropriate authority shall first determine the fees for preparation work within the meaning of paragraph 4(2)(a) of this Part of this Schedule.

(2) If the fees so determined are—

(a) less than the lower fee limit, the appropriate authority shall allow and pay the lower standard fee together with the standard fees for all other classes of work specified in paragraph 4(2);

(b) not less than the lower fee limit and not more than the upper fee limit, the appropriate authority shall allow and pay the principal standard fee together with the standard fees for all other classes of work specified in paragraph 4(2);

(c) more than the upper fee limit, no standard fees shall be payable and all fees shall be determined in accordance with regulation 6.

Standard fees

4.—(1) The classes of work for which standard fees shall be payable are those specified in sub-paragraph (2) and the fees for classes of work which are not so specified shall be determined in accordance with regulation 6.

(2) The classes of work specified for the purposes of sub-paragraph (1) are—

(a) preparation within the meaning of regulation 6(1)(a) but including routine letters written and routine telephone calls, within the meaning of regulation 6(1)(e);

(b) *[Omitted by the Legal Aid in Criminal and Care Proceedings (Costs) (Amendment) (No. 2) Regulations 1996 (S.I. 1996 No. 2655)]*;

(c) attendance at court (including waiting) where more than one legal representative is assigned;

(d) travelling except—
   (i) to undertake work for which standard fees are not payable; or
   (ii) where sub-paragraph (2)(b) applies,
   and, for the purpose of this paragraph, "travelling" shall be deemed to include waiting in connection with preparation work, within the meaning of sub-paragraph (2)(a) above.

(3) The standard fees payable under this Part of this Schedule are the fees specified in the Table below and in this Part of this Schedule the "lower fee limit" and the "upper fee limit" mean the lower and upper fee limits specified in the Table.

TABLE

PREPARATION

Type of proceedings		Lower standard fee	Lower fee limit	Principal standard fee	Upper fee limit
Jury trials (including any case prepared for trial in which no jury was sworn)		£129.50	£179	£249.50	£312
	London rate	£139.00	£186	£261.50	£326
Guilty pleas		£81.50	£110	£175.00	£226
	London rate	£87.50	£114	£185.50	£235
Appeals against conviction		£51.00	£68	£153.00	£233
	London rate	£54.50	£70	£159.00	£244
Appeals against sentence		£36.25	£52	£93.00	£131
	London rate	£39.25	£54	£98.00	£135
Committals for sentence		£42.50	£51	£97.75	£141
	London rate	£45.00	£53	£103.00	£145
ATTENDANCE AT COURT (INCLUDING WAITING) WHERE MORE THAN ONE LEGAL REPRESENTATIVE ASSIGNED		£21.40	per hour		
TRAVELLING		£18.50	per hour		

Amended by the Legal Aid in Criminal and Care Proceedings (Costs) (Amendment) Regulations 1995 (S.I. 1995 No. 952), the Legal Aid in Criminal and Care Proceedings (Costs) (Amendment) Regulations 1996 (S.I. 1996 No. 644) and the Legal Aid in Criminal and Care Proceedings (Costs) (Amendment) (No. 2) Regulations 1996 (S.I. 1996 No. 2655).

(4) A solicitor shall be entitled to the "London rate" of the standard fees specified in the Table where his office is situated within legal aid area 1, within the meaning of paragraph 1(2) of Schedule 1, Part I.

(5) The hourly rate specified in the Table for attendance at court shall, subject to sub-paragraph (6), be paid in respect of the period of time beginning 30 minutes before the case was listed and ending

(a) where the client was present at court, 15 minutes after the hearing ended on that day, or

(b) where the client was not present at court, when the hearing ended on that day,

and, save in exceptional circumstances, shall not be payable during the luncheon adjournment.

(6) Where a fee-earner attends a court centre for the purposes of more than one case, the solicitor may claim the attendance fee in respect of the second or subsequent case only for the time actually spent in attendance in addition to the time for which payment is made under sub-paragraph (5).

(7) The hourly rate specified in the Table shall be paid for time spent travelling (within the meaning of sub-paragraph (2)(d)).

(8) Where a solicitor acts for more than one defendant, the appropriate authority shall—

(a) allow whichever of the appropriate standard preparation fees is the greater and increase that fee by 20 per cent. for each additional defendant;

(b) [Omitted by the Legal Aid in Criminal and Care Proceedings (Costs) (Amendment) (No. 2) Regulations 1996 (S.I. 1996 No. 2655).]

but no percentage increase shall be made to the standard fees for attendance at court or for travelling.

(9) Where a solicitor acts for a defendant in respect of more than one—

(a) indictment,

(b) appeal against conviction,

(c) appeal against sentence, or

(d) committal for sentence

or in respect of any combination of (a) to (d) above, the appropriate authority shall allow whichever of the appropriate standard preparation fees is the greater and increase that fee by 20 per cent for each additional indictment, appeal or committal for sentence as the case may be.

(10) Where a solicitor prepares a case with a view to counsel appearing at the substantive hearing without the solicitor or his representative attending court, the standard preparation fee payable after application of any increase required by paragraphs (8)(a) or (9) shall be further increased by £30.00 (or by £32.00 for a solicitor whose office is situated within legal aid area 1).

(11) Where a fee-earner listens to a tape recording of an interview conducted under a code issued by the Secretary of State under section 60 of the Police and Criminal Evidence Act 1984, the standard preparation fee payable after application of any increase required by paragraph 8(a) or 9 shall be further increased by £10.90 for every 10 minutes of the total running time of all tapes or parts of tapes listened to and by the same amount for any remaining period.

Amended by the Legal Aid in Criminal and Care Proceedings (Costs) (Amendment) Regulations 1992 (S.I. 1992 No. 592), the Legal Aid in Criminal and Care Proceedings (Costs) (Amendment) Regulations 1995 (S.I. 1995 No. 952) and the Legal Aid in Criminal and Care Proceedings (Costs) (Amendment) Regulations 1996 (S.I. 1996 No. 644).

(12) Where the standard fee payable is increased by virtue of sub-paragraph (8)(a), (9), (10) or (11), then for the purposes of paragraphs 3, 6 and 8—

(a) the upper fee limit shall be increased by the same amount by which the principal standard fee has been increased, and

(b) the lower fee limit shall be increased by the same amount by which the lower standard fee has been increased.

Amended by the Legal Aid in Criminal and Care Proceedings (Costs) (Amendment) Regulations 1990 (S.I. 1990 No. 488).

Disbursements

5. Nothing in this Part of this Schedule applies to disbursements which shall be determined in accordance with regulation 7.

Re-determinations and appeals

6.—(1) A solicitor who is dissatisfied with a decision on a determination under paragraph 3 may apply for the costs to be re-determined and, subject to sub-paragraph (2), the provisions of regulation 14(2) to (8) shall apply with the necessary modifications to an application under this paragraph as they apply to an application under regulation 14.

(2) On a re-determination under this paragraph, the appropriate authority shall determine the fees for preparation work within the meaning of paragraph 4(2)(a) and if the fees so determined are—

(a) less than the lower fee limit, the lower standard fee shall be allowed together with the standard fees for all other classes of work specified in paragraph 4(2),

(b) not less than the lower fee limit and not more than the upper fee limit, the principal standard fee shall be allowed together with the standard fees for all other classes of work specified in paragraph 4(2);

(c) more than the upper fee limit, the fees for all classes of work shall be determined in accordance with regulation 6.

7. Irrespective of any dispute under paragraph 2 as to whether the principal standard fee should have been allowed instead of the lower standard fee, where a solicitor is satisfied with a decision to allow a standard fee but contends that—

(a) a standard fee which is not apt for the type of work done has been allowed, or

(b) the provisions of paragraph 4(4) to (12) have been incorrectly applied,

he may, within six weeks of receipt of notification of the decision, make a written request setting out his reasons why the decision should be reviewed and, if the appropriate authority confirms its decision, written reasons shall be given.

8.—(1) A solicitor may appeal to a taxing master where he is dissatisfied with—

(a) a decision on a re-determination under paragraph 6, or

(b) a decision on a review under paragraph 7.

(2) Where a solicitor appeals to a taxing master in respect of a decision under paragraph 6, the taxing master shall determine the fees for preparation within the meaning of paragraph 4(2)(a) and if the fees so determined are—

(a) less than the lower fee limit, the lower standard fee shall be allowed by the taxing master together with the standard fees for all other classes of work specified in paragraph 4(2);

(b) not less than the lower fee limit and not more than the upper fee limit, the principal standard fee shall be allowed by the taxing master together with the standard fees for all other classes of work specified in paragraph 4(2);

(c) more than the upper fee limit, the fees for all classes of work shall be determined by the taxing master in accordance with regulation 6.

(3) Where a solicitor appeals to a taxing master in respect of a decision made on a review under paragraph 7, the taxing master shall allow whichever standard fee he considers to be apt for the type of work done or, as the case may be, re-apply the provisions of paragraph 4(4) to (12).

(4) Where a taxing master allows an appeal in whole or in part, he may allow the solicitor a sum in respect of part or all of any reasonable costs (including any fee payable in respect of the appeal) incurred by him in connection with the appeal.

(5) This paragraph only applies to appeals in proceedings for which standard fees are payable and the provisions of regulation 15 shall apply to appeals in proceedings for which standard fees are not payable.

(6) Subject to the foregoing provisions of this paragraph, the provisions of regulations 15 to 17 relating to appeals by solicitors shall apply with the necessary modifications to appeals in proceedings for which standard fees are payable under this Part of this Schedule as they apply to appeals in proceedings for which standard fees are not payable.

PART III

STANDARD FEES IN MAGISTRATES' COURTS

Interpretation

1. In this Part of this Schedule—

a "case" (except where the context otherwise requires) comprises proceedings relating to one or more charges or informations which are preferred or laid at the same time or which are founded on the same facts or which form or are part of a series of offences;

"Category 1 proceedings" means proceedings of the types referred to in column 1 of the Table in paragraph 2(2), and in paragraph 2(6) and (7);

"Category 2 proceedings" means proceedings of the type referred to in column 2 of the Table in paragraph 2(2);

"Category 3 proceedings" means proceedings of the type referred to in column 3 of the Table in paragraph 2(2),

and references to a category or to a category by number shall be construed accordingly;

"core costs" mean the costs relating to the classes of work specified in paragraph 4(2);

"lower limit" and "higher limit" mean the lower and higher limits specified in the Table in paragraph 8(1) (or paragraph 8(1A) in the case of a franchisee);

"relevant standard fee" means the fee shown in the Table in paragraph 8(1) (or paragraph 8(1A) in the case of a franchisee) which corresponds to the type of proceedings, the location and the limit within which the core costs have been allowed under this Part;

"unassigned counsel" means counsel who is not assigned under the legal aid order but who is instructed by the solicitor.

Amended by the Legal Aid in Criminal and Care Proceedings (Costs) (Amendment) Regulations 1995 (S.I. 1995 No. 952).

Proceedings to which standard fees apply

2.—(1) Subject to paragraph 3, standard fees under this Part of this Schedule shall apply to work done in proceedings in a magistrates' court as specified in sub-paragraph (2).

(2) The proceedings (which include any proceedings preliminary or incidental thereto whether before that or another court including bail applications made either in a magistrates' court or the Crown Court) are the proceedings specified in the following Table:

TABLE: CATEGORIES AND TYPES OF PROCEEDINGS

Column 1	Column 2	Column 2
Category 1	**Category 2**	**Category 3**
1.1 guilty pleas	2.1 contested trials	3.1 committal proceedings including those which are discontinued or withdrawn
1.2 uncontested proceedings arising out of a breach of an order of a magistrates' court (including proceedings in a magistrates' court relating to a breach of a Crown Court probation order, community service order or suspended sentence)	2.2 proceedings which were listed and fully prepared for trial in a magistrates' court but disposed of by a guilty plea on the day of trial before the opening of the prosecution case	3.2 *[Omitted by the Legal Aid in Criminal and Care Proceedings (Costs) (Amendment) Regulations 1997 (S.I. 1997 No. 754).]*
1.3 proceedings (other than committal proceedings) which are discontinued or withdrawn	2.3 proceedings which were listed and fully prepared for trial in a magistrates' court but are discontinued or withdrawn or where the prosecution offers no evidence or which result in a bind over on the day of trial before the opening of the prosecution case	3.3 proceedings transferred under section 4 of the Criminal Justice Act 1987 or section 53 of the Criminal Justice Act 1991
1.4 proceedings (other than committal proceedings) relating to summary or either way offences which result in a bind over		
1.5 proceedings arising out of a deferment of sentence (including any subsequent sentencing hearing) under section 1 of the Powers of Criminal Courts Act 1973	2.4 contested proceedings relating to a breach of an order of a magistrates' court (including proceedings relating to a breach of a Crown Court probation order, community service order or suspended sentence)	
	2.5 proceedings where mixed pleas are entered	

(3) Proceedings shall be treated for the purposes of this Part of this Schedule as forming part of one case where they relate to one or more charges or informations which are preferred or laid at the same time or which are founded on the same facts or which form or are part of a series of offences.

(4) Subject to sub-paragraph (5), where proceedings forming one case fall within more than one category, the proceedings shall be treated as forming part of the higher or highest in value of the categories concerned.

(5) Where a case includes proceedings referred to in the Table in sub-paragraph (2) above at items 3.1 and 3.2, the case shall be treated as if all the proceedings were Category 3 proceedings.

(6) Subject to sub-paragraph (5), where there is a change of solicitor assigned under a legal aid order in proceedings to which sub-paragraph (2) applies, the proceedings shall be treated as Category 1 proceedings for the purposes of a claim for costs in respect of work done under the legal aid order by the solicitor formerly assigned.

(7) Subject to sub-paragraph (5), where proceedings have not been concluded but a warrant of arrest has been issued, the proceedings shall be treated as Category 1 proceedings.

Proceedings to which standard fees do not apply

3. Standard fees shall not apply to proceedings—

(a) in which counsel has been assigned under a legal aid order; or

(b) in which costs are allowed at an enhanced rate in accordance with paragraph 3 of Schedule 1 Part I.

Classes of work covered by the standard fee

4.—(1) The classes of work covered by the standard fee are specified in sub-paragraph (2).

(2) The classes of work are:—

(a) any preparation within the meaning of regulation 6(1)(a), including listening to, or viewing, any tape or video recording of interviews or evidence;

(b) routine letters written and routine telephone calls within the meaning of regulation 6(1)(e);

(c) advocacy, including bail and other application made in either a magistrates' court or the Crown Court;

(d) work done by a fee-earner acting as agent for the solicitor assigned under the legal aid order;

(e) unassigned counsel's *preparation, advocacy and waiting time*/preparation and advocacy.

Amended by the Legal Aid in Criminal and Care Proceedings (Costs) (Amendment) (No. 3) Regulations 1994 (S.I. 1994 No. 2218) by deleting the words in italics in respect of orders made on or after October 1, 1994.

Standard fees: further provisions

5.—(1) Where the solicitor acts for more than one defendant in the proceedings, the claim for payment of a standard fee shall cover all the legally aided defendants whom he represents.

(2) Where a legal aid order is granted to a defendant in respect of more than one charge or information, the claim for payment of a standard fee shall cover all the charges or informations which form part of one case.

Costs additional to the standard fee

6. The following costs shall be payable in addition to the standard fee, and shall be determined in accordance with regulations 6, 7 and 7A:—

(a) travelling and waiting time of fee-earners and unassigned counsel, which shall be payable at the rate provided in paragraph 1(1)(a) (or paragraph 1A in the case of a franchisee) of Schedule 1 Part I; and

(b) disbursements.

Amended by the Legal Aid in Criminal and Care Proceedings (Costs) (Amendment) (No. 3) Regulations 1994 (S.I. 1994 No. 2218) by inserting the words "and unassigned counsel" and substituting the words "6, 7 and 7A" for "6 and 7" in respect of orders made on or after October 1, 1994. Also amended by the Legal Aid in Criminal and Care Proceedings (Costs) (Amendment) Regulations 1995 (S.I. 1995 No. 952).

Allowance of standard fees

7.—(1) The appropriate authority shall allow a lower standard fee where the core costs would not, if they had been determined, have exceeded the lower limit.

(2) Where the core costs claimed by the solicitor exceed the lower limit, the appropriate authority shall determine the core costs in accordance with regulation 6(2) and, if the core costs so determined—

(a) do not exceed the lower limit, allow the lower standard fee;

(b) exceed the lower limit but do not exceed the higher limit, allow the higher standard fee;

(c) exceed the higher limit, allow the core costs as determined.

(3) The rates specified in paragraph 1(1)(a) (or paragraph 1A in the case of a franchisee) of Schedule 1 Part I shall apply to the costs claimed, subject to the provisions of paragraph 2 of that Part of that Schedule.

Amended by the Legal Aid in Criminal and Care Proceedings (Costs) (Amendment) Regulations 1995 (S.I. 1995 No. 952).

Fees payable

8.—(1) Subject to sub-paragraph (1A), standard fees are payable in accordance with the Table below:—

TABLE

Type of proceedings	Lower standard fee	Lower limit	Higher standard fee	Higher limit
Category 1	£144.25	£268	£346.00	£463.75
London rate	£185.50	£344	£440.00	£581.50
Category 2	£254.50	£460	£583.00	£767.25
London rate	£326.50	£584	£732.50	£934.75
Category 3	£229.75	£406	£520.25	£709.50
London rate	£290.50	£493	£611.00	£755.25

(1A) Where the work was done by a franchisee, standard fees are payable in accordance with the Table below:—

TABLE

Type of proceedings	Lower standard fee	Lower limit	Higher standard fee	Higher limit
Category 1	£148.25	£276	£357.00	£478
London rate	£191.00	£354	£453.00	£598
Category 2	£262.25	£474	£601.00	£790
London rate	£336.25	£602	£755.00	£963

Type of proceedings	Lower standard fee	Lower limit	Higher standard fee	Higher limit
Category 3	£236.50	£418	£536.00	£730
London rate	£299.25	£507	£629.00	£778

(2) A solicitor shall be entitled to the relevant standard fee at the "London rate" specified in the appropriate Table where his office is situated within legal aid area 1, within the meaning of paragraph 1(2) of Schedule 1 Part I.

(3) The costs payable in proceedings to which this Part applies shall (subject to any deductions or reductions made pursuant to regulations 9A or 17(2)) be:—

  (a) the relevant standard fee together with the costs determined in accordance with the provisions of paragraph 6; or

  (b) where the core costs allowed exceed the higher limit of the relevant standard fee, the costs as determined in accordance with regulations 6 and 7.

(4) Where, in circumstances to which regulation 5(1A) or paragraph 2(7) of this Part applies, a solicitor has been paid prior to the final disposal of the proceedings, any costs which would have been payable to that solicitor upon the final disposal of the proceedings shall be reduced to the extent that they formed part of the costs previously claimed.

Inserted by the Legal Aid in Criminal and Care Proceedings (Costs) (Amendment) Regulations 1993 (S.I. 1993 No. 934) and amended by the Legal Aid in Criminal and Care Proceedings (Costs) (Amendment) Regulations 1995 (S.I. 1995 No. 952) and the Legal Aid in Criminal and Care Proceedings (Costs) (Amendment) Regulations 1996 (S.I. 1996 No. 644).

SCHEDULE 2

COUNSEL'S FEES

PART I

[Omitted by the Legal Aid in Criminal and Care Proceedings (Costs) (Amendment) (No. 2) Regulations 1996 (S.I. 1996 No. 2655).]

PART II

DETERMINATION OF OTHER FEES

1. The appropriate authority shall allow such fee in respect of an item of work allowed under regulation 9(5), not exceeding the maximum amount specified in respect of that item of work, as appears to it to provide reasonable remuneration.

2. Where an hourly rate is specified in a Table in this Part of this Schedule in respect of an item of work allowed under regulation 9(5), the appropriate authority shall determine any fee for such work in accordance with that hourly rate; provided that the fee determined shall not be less than the minimum amount specified.

3. Where a refresher fee is claimed in respect of less than a full day, the appropriate authority shall allow such fee as appears to it reasonable having regard to the fee which would be allowable for a full day.

4. The fees allowed to junior counsel for proceedings in the Crown Court arising out of a breach of an order of the Crown Court or other similar matters shall not exceed the maximum amounts specified for "committals for sentence."

5. Paragraph 24 of Schedule 3 shall apply where counsel's fees are determined in accordance with this Part of the Schedule as it applies where a graduated or fixed fee is allowed in accordance with Schedule 3.

The following table 1 was amended by the Legal Aid in Criminal and Care Proceedings (Costs) (Amendment) Regulations 1996 (S.I. 1996 No. 644), the Legal Aid in Criminal and Care Proceedings (Costs) (Amendment) (No. 2) Regulations 1996 (S.I. 1996 No. 2655) and the Legal Aid in Criminal and Care Proceedings (Costs) (Amendment) (No. 3) Regulations 1997 (S.I. 1997 No. 1484).

Paragraph 5 was substituted by the 1996 (No. 2) (Amendment) Regulations.

TABLE 1: JUNIOR COUNSEL

Court	Type of proceedings	Basic fee	Full day refresher fee	Subsidiary fees		
				Attendance at consultations, conferences & views	Written work	Attendance at pre-trial reviews, applications and other appearances
Magistrates' Court	All cases	Maximum amount: £468	Maximum amount: £162	£29.25 per hour Minimum amount: £14.50	Maximum amount: £51.25	Maximum amount: £94.00
Crown Court	Jury trials	Maximum amount: £545.50				
	Cases prepared for trial in which no jury is sworn	Maximum amount: £317.75				
	Guilty pleas	Maximum amount: £192.25		£33.50 per hour Minimum amount: £16.75	Maximum amount: £58.25	Maximum amount: £110.00
	Appeals against conviction	Maximum amount: £210	Maximum amount: £178.75			
	Appeals against sentence	Maximum amount: £107.50				
	Committals for sentence	Maximum amount: £107.50				

TABLE 2: QUEEN'S COUNSEL

Court	Type of proceedings	Basic fee	Full day refresher fee	Subsidiary fees		
				Attendance at consultations, conferences & views	Written work	Attendance at pre-trial reviews, applications and other appearances
Magistrates' Court	All cases	Maximum amount: £4,446	Maximum amount: £297	£54.50 per hour Minimum amount £28	Maximum amount: £105	Maximum amount: £205
Crown Court	All cases	Maximum amount: £5,400	Maximum amount: £330.50	£62.50 per hour Minimum amount: £32	Maximum amount: £119.50	Maximum amount: £257.50

SCHEDULE 3

FEES FOR ADVOCACY IN THE CROWN COURT

PART I

DEFINITIONS AND SCOPE

1.—(1) In this Schedule:

"advocate" means a person instructed in accordance with a legal aid order to represent the legally assisted person at the main hearing in any case;

"case" means proceedings in the Crown Court against any one legally assisted person:

(a) on one or more counts of a single indictment;

(b) arising out of a single notice of appeal against conviction or sentence, or a single committal for sentence, whether on one or more charges, or

(c) arising out of a single alleged breach of an order of the Crown Court

and a case falling within paragraph (c) shall be treated as a separate case from the proceedings in which the order was made;

"cracked trial" and "guilty plea" have the meanings given in paragraph 9(3), (4) and (5) of this Schedule;

"main hearing" means:

(a) in relation to a case which goes to trial, the trial;

(b) in relation to a guilty plea or cracked trial, the hearing at which pleas are taken or, where there is more than one such hearing, the last such hearing;

(c) in relation to an appeal against conviction or sentence, the hearing of the appeal;

(d) in relation to proceedings arising out a committal for sentence, the sentencing hearing;

(e) in relation to proceedings arising out of an alleged breach of an order of the Crown Court, the final hearing;

"Newton hearing" means a hearing at which evidence is heard for the purpose of determining the sentence of a convicted person in accordance with the principles of *R. v. Newton* (1982) 77 Cr.App.R. 13);

"preparation" means work of any of the following types when done by an advocate;

(a) reading the papers in the case;

(b) the first conference with the legally assisted person;

(c) contact with prosecution representatives;

(d) written or oral advice on plea;

(e) researching the law, preparation for examination of witnesses and preparation of oral submissions for the main hearing;

(f) viewing exhibits or undisclosed material at police stations;

(g) conferences with the legally assisted person, after the first such conference;

(h) written advice on evidence;

(i) written and oral advice on appeal (where covered under the same legal aid order as the main hearing);

(j) preparation of written submissions, notices or other documents for use at the main hearing;

(k) views.

(2) For the purposes of this Schedule, the number of pages of prosecution evidence shall include all witness statements, documentary and pictorial exhibits and records of interview with the legally assisted person and with other defendants forming part of the committal documents or included in any notice of additional evidence.

(3) In the case of proceedings on indictment in the Crown Court initiated otherwise than by committal for trial, the appropriate authority shall determine the number of pages of prosecution evidence as nearly in accordance with the preceding sub-paragraph as the nature of the case permits.

2.—(1) Subject to the following sub-paragraphs of this paragraph and to paragraph 4, this Schedule applies to every case on indictment in which:

(a) every count (apart from any count which is withdrawn before the pleas and directions hearing) is for an offence referred to in paragraph 5 below, or

(b) one or more counts is for an offence referred to in paragraph 5 below, and the advocate elects that the remaining counts should be disregarded for the purposes of calculating his remuneration.

(2) This Schedule does not apply to a case which goes to trial where—

(a) the prosecution evidence exceeds 1,000 pages;

(b) the number of prosecution witnesses exceeds 80, or

(c) it was accepted at the pleas and directions hearing that the trial would exceed 10 days (or 5 days where one of the counts is for an offence falling within Class I), and the trial did not exceed that length by reason only that it came to an end without the jury being required to consider their verdict.

(3) This Schedule does not apply to a guilty plea where:

(a) the prosecution evidence exceeds 400 pages, or

(b) the number of prosecution witnesses exceeds 80.

(4) This Schedule does not apply to a cracked trial where:

(a) at the pleas and directions hearing, it was accepted by the court that the trial would exceed 10 days in length (or 5 days where one of the counts is for an offence falling within Class I);

(b) the prosecution evidence exceeds 250 pages, or

(c) the number of prosecution witnesses exceeds 80.

(5) Where following a trial an order was made for a new trial, and the same advocate appeared for a legally assisted person at both trials, this Schedule shall not apply in relation to the remuneration of that advocate for—

(a) the original trial, unless remuneration for that trial has been paid in full prior to the making of the order for a new trial, or

(b) the new trial, in any event.

(6) Where following a case on indictment a Newton hearing takes place—

(a) the case shall for all the purposes of this Schedule be treated as having gone to trial;

(b) the length of the trial shall be taken to be the combined length of the main hearing and of the Newton hearing;

(c) the provisions of this Schedule relating to cracked trials and guilty pleas shall not apply, and

(d) no fee shall be payable under paragraph 15 in respect of that hearing.

(7) A case on indictment which is discontinued at the pleas and directions hearing other than by reason of pleas of guilty being entered shall for all the purposes of this Schedule be treated as a guilty plea.

3. This Schedule also applies to the following proceedings in the Crown Court, subject to paragraph 4:

(a) an appeal against conviction or sentence;

(b) a sentencing hearing following a committal to the Crown Court for sentence;

(c) proceedings arising out of an alleged breach of an order of the Crown Court (whether or not this Schedule applies to the proceedings in which the order was made).

4. This Schedule does not apply to any case where:

(a) the legal aid order provides for the services of more than two advocates;

(b) (without prejudice to regulation 55 of the General Regulations) any of the advocate's work in connection with the case is done or remunerated otherwise than under a legal aid order;

(c) a hearing is held to determine the question of whether the legally assisted person is unfit to plead or unfit to be tried;

(d) one or more registered medical practitioners has given oral evidence for the purposes of section 37(2)(a) of the Mental Health Act 1983; or

(e) the length of the main hearing, or the combined length of the main hearing and of any hearing to which paragraph 2(6), 13 or 14 applies, exceeds 10 days (or 5 days where one of the counts is for an offence falling within Class I),

Paragraph 4(d) amended by the Legal Aid in Criminal and Care Proceedings (Costs) (Amendment) Regulations 1998 (S.I. 1998 No. 1191).

5.—(1) The offences to which this paragraph refers are:

(a) those listed in the Table of Offences following paragraph 24 of this Schedule;

(b) conspiracy to commit any of the offences in the Table of Offences, contrary to section 1 of the Criminal Law Act 1977;

(c) incitement to commit any of the offences in the Table of Offences;

(d) attempt to commit any of the offences in the Table of Offences, contrary to section 1 of the Criminal Attempts Act 1981.

(2) For the purposes of this Schedule:

(a) every offence within sub-paragraph (1)(a) falls within the Class under which it is listed in the Table of Offences;

(b) every offence within sub-paragraph (1)(b), (c) or (d) falls within the same Class as the substantive offence to which it relates;

(c) where the Table specifies that the Class within which an offence falls depends on whether that value involved exceeds a stated limit, the value shall be presumed not to exceed that limit unless the person claiming remuneration proves otherwise to the satisfaction of the appropriate authority;

(d) where more than one count of an indictment is for an offence in relation to which the Class depends on the value involved, that value shall be taken to be the total value involved in all those offences, so however that where two or more counts relate to the same property the value of that property shall be taken into account once only;

(e) where an entry in the Table of Offences specifies an offence as being contrary to a statutory provision, then subject to any express limitation in the entry that entry shall include every offence contrary to that statutory provision whether or not the words of description in the entry are apt to cover all such offences.

6.—(1) The classes of work for which a graduated or fixed fee calculated in accordance with the following paragraphs of this Schedule shall be allowed in accordance with regulation 9(2) are those specified in sub-paragraph (2), and the fees for classes of work which are not so specified shall be determined in accordance with regulation 6.

(2) The classes of work specified for the purposes of sub-paragraph (1) are:

(a) all preparation not falling within paragraph (c) below;

(b) advocacy on the first day of the main hearing;

(c) preparation and advocacy on the second and subsequent days of the main hearing;

(d) appearing at the pleas and direction hearing if any;

(e) appearing at other hearings and applications;

(f) listening to or viewing evidence recorded on tape or video cassette;

(g) attending conferences with expert witnesses.

PART II

GRADUATED FEES FOR TRIALS

7.—(1) The amount of the graduated fee for a single advocate representing one legally assisted person being tried on one indictment in the Crown Court shall be calculated according to the following formula:

$$G = B + (d \times D) + (e \times E) + (w \times W) + (d \times R).$$

(2) In the formula in sub-paragraph (1):

G is the amount of the graduated fee;

B is the basic fee specified in paragraph 8 as appropriate to the offence for which the legally assisted person is tried and the category of advocate instructed;

d is the number of days or parts of a day by which the trial exceeds one day;

e is the number of pages of prosecution evidence excluding the first 50;

w is the number of prosecution witnesses excluding the first 10;

D is the length of trial uplift specified in paragraph 8 as appropriate to the offence for which the legally assisted person is tried and the category of advocate instructed;

E is the evidence uplift specified in paragraph 8 as appropriate to the offence for which the legally assisted person is tried and the category of advocate instructed;

W is the witnesses uplift specified in paragraph 8 as appropriate to the offence for which the legally assisted person is tried and the category of advocate instructed;

R is the refresher specified in paragraph 8 as appropriate to the offence for which the legally assisted person is tried and the category of advocate instructed;

8. For the purposes of paragraph 7 the basic fee, refresher, length of trial uplift, evidence uplift and witnesses uplift appropriate to any offence shall be those specified in the Table below as appropriate to the Class within which that offence falls according to paragraph 5 and the category of advocate instructed.

TABLE OF FEES AND UPLIFTS

(a) Trials—Queen's Counsel

Offence falling within	Basic fee	Refresher	Length of trial uplift: per day	Evidence uplift: per page	Witnesses uplift: per witness
Class A	£1,616.50	£413.50	£835.50	£1.44	£6.12
Class B	£1,091.00	£510.00	£636.50	£4.93	£46.47
Class C	£839.50	£431.50	£581.00	£8.47	£55.12
Class D	£1,550.50	£413.50	£574.50	£2.75	£18.13
Class E	£875.00	£431.50	£345.50	£3.55	£23.45
Class F	£847.50	£431.50	£467.00	£5.00	£17.12
Class G	£1,561.50	£510.00	£929.00	£7.71	£63.30
Class H	£1,000.50	£431.50	£637.00	£6.91	£60.18
Class I	£1,032.00	£510.00	£462.00	£10.83	£71.45

(b) Trials—other advocate

Offence falling within	Basic fee	Refresher	Length of trial uplift:	Evidence uplift:	Witnesses uplift
Class A	£808.50	£207.00	£418.00	£0.72	£3.06
Class B	£311.50	£145.50	£182.00	£1.41	£13.28
Class C	£240.00	£123.50	£166.00	£2.42	£15.75
Class D	£446.00	£145.50	£282.00	£1.08	£7.14
Class E	£250.00	£123.50	£98.50	£1.02	£6.70
Class F	£242.00	£123.50	£133.50	£1.43	£4.89
Class G	£446.00	£145.50	£265.50	£2.20	£18.09
Class H	£286.00	£123.50	£182.00	£1.97	£17.19
Class I	£295.00	£145.50	£132.00	£3.09	£20.41

PART III

GRADUATED FEES FOR GUILTY PLEAS AND CRACKED TRIALS

9.—(1) The amount of the graduated fee for a single advocate representing one legally assisted person in a guilty plea or cracked trial shall be the basic fee specified in paragraph 10 as appropriate to the offence with which the legally assisted person is charged, the category of advocate instructed and whether the case is a guilty plea or a cracked trial, increased by the evidence uplift.

(2) The evidence uplift shall be calculated as follows:

(a) there shall be no uplift in respect of the first 10 pages;

(b) the uplift set out in the third column of the applicable Table in paragraph 10 shall be payable in respect of each page from the 11th to the 50th;

(c) the uplift set out in the fourth column of the applicable Table in paragraph 10 shall be payable in respect of each page from the 51st to the 100th;

(d) the uplift set out in the fifth column of the applicable Table in paragraph 10 shall be payable in respect of each page from and after the 101st.

(3) A case on indictment in which a pleas and directions hearing takes place is a cracked trial if it fulfils the following conditions:

(a) the matter did not proceed to trial (whether by reason of pleas of guilty or for other reasons) or the prosecution offered no evidence, and

(b) (i) in respect of one or more counts to which the legally assisted person pleaded guilty, he did not so plead at the pleas and directions hearing, or

(ii) in respect of one or more counts which were not proceeded with, the prosecution did not, before or at the pleas and directions hearing, declare an intention of not proceeding with them.

(4) A case on indictment in which no pleas and directions hearing takes place is a cracked trial if it was listed for trial but the case was disposed of without a trial (whether by reason of pleas of guilty or for other reasons) or the prosecution offered no evidence.

(5) A case on indictment is a guilty plea if it was disposed of without a trial because the legally assisted person pleaded guilty to one or more counts and is not a cracked trial.

10. For the purposes of paragraph 9 the basic fee and evidence uplifts appropriate to any offfence shall be those specified in the Table below as appropriate to the Class within which that offence falls according to paragraph 5 and the category of advocate instructed.

TABLE OF FEES AND UPLIFTS

(a) Guilty plea—Queen's Counsel

Offence falling within	Basic fee	Evidence uplift per page (pages 11 to 50)	Evidence uplift per page (pages 51 to 100)	Evidence uplift per page (pages 101 to 400)
Class A	£1,619.50	£6.14	£3.06	£2.04
Class B	£715.50	£6.03	£4.02	£2.68
Class C	£595.00	£6.03	£4.02	£2.68
Class D	£998.00	£6.03	£4.02	£2.68
Class E	£446.00	£4.02	£2.68	£1.79
Class F	£438.50	£3.22	£2.14	£1.43
Class G	£1,242.00	£8.04	£5.36	£3.57
Class H	£504.00	£8.04	£5.36	£3.57
Class I	£403.50	£8.04	£5.36	£3.57

(b) Guilty plea—other advocate

Offence falling within	Basic fee	Evidence uplift per page (pages 11 to 50)	Evidence uplift per page (pages 51 to 100)	Evidence uplift per page (pages 101 to 400)
Class A	£810.00	£3.07	£1.53	£1.02
Class B	£204.50	£1.72	£1.15	£0.77
Class C	£170.00	£1.72	£1.15	£0.77
Class D	£285.00	£1.72	£1.15	£0.77
Class E	£127.50	£1.15	£0.77	£0.51
Class F	£125.50	£0.92	£0.61	£0.41
Class G	£355.00	£2.30	£1.53	£1.02
Class H	£144.00	£2.30	£1.53	£1.02
Class I	£115.00	£2.30	£1.53	£1.02

(c) Cracked trial—Queen's Counsel

Offence falling within	Basic fee	Evidence uplift per page (pages 11 to 50)	Evidence uplift per page (pages 51 to 100)	Evidence uplift per page (pages 101 to 250)
Class A	£1,694.50	£50.72	£17.04	£4.26
Class B	£1,143.50	£22.29	£8.39	£5.59
Class C	£880.00	£21.96	£8.39	£5.59
Class D	£1,625.00	£34.62	£12.78	£3.19
Class E	£917.00	£10.38	£8.39	£5.59
Class F	£888.50	£12.66	£8.39	£5.59
Class G	£1,637.00	£68.65	£16.77	£11.18
Class H	£1,048.50	£24.78	£8.39	£5.59
Class I	£1,081.50	£17.84	£8.39	£5.59

(d) Cracked trial—other advocate

Offence falling within	Basic fee	Evidence uplift per page (pages 11 to 50)	Evidence uplift per page (pages 51 to 100)	Evidence uplift per page (pages 101 to 250)
Class A	£847.00	£25.36	£8.52	£2.13
Class B	£326.50	£6.37	£2.40	£1.60
Class C	£251.50	£6.27	£2.40	£1.60
Class D	£467.50	£10.51	£2.40	£1.60
Class E	£262.00	£2.97	£2.40	£1.60
Class F	£254.00	£3.62	£2.40	£1.60
Class G	£467.50	£19.61	£4.79	£3.19
Class H	£299.50	£7.08	£2.40	£1.60
Class I	£309.00	£5.10	£2.40	£1.60

PART IV

FIXED AND HOURLY FEES

11.—(1) The basic fee payable to any person for appearing at a pleas and directions hearing or a pre-trial review shall be that set out in the Table following paragraph 21 as appropriate to the category of advocate.

(2) *Omitted.*

(3) *Omitted.*

(4) This paragraph does not apply to a pleas and directions hearing which is or forms part of the main hearing in a case.

Paragraph (1) amended and paragraphs (2) and (3) omitted by the Legal Aid in Criminal and Care Proceedings (Costs) (Amendment) Regulations 1998 (S.I. 1998 No. 1191).

12.—(1) The fixed fee set out in the Table following paragraph 21 as appropriate to the category of advocate shall be payable where:

(a) the legally assisted person fails to attend any hearing at which the advocate appears;

(b) at that hearing a bench warrant is issued for the arrest of the legally assisted person, and

(c) that warrant is not executed within the three months beginning on the date on which it was issued.

(2) The fixed fee set out in the Table following paragraph 21 as appropriate to the category of advocate shall be payable in respect of each occasion on which the case was

listed for trial but did not proceed on the day for which it was listed (other than by reason of an application for postponement by the prosecution or the defence).

13.—(1) This paragraph applies to:

(a) the hearing of an application to stay the indictment or any count on the ground that the proceedings constitute an abuse of the process of the court;

(b) any hearing relating to the question of whether any material should be disclosed by the prosecution to the defence, or by the defence to the prosecution (whether or not any claim to public interest immunity is made);

(c) the hearing of an application under section 2(1) of the Criminal Procedure (Attendance of Witnesses) Act 1965 for disclosure of material held by third parties.

(2) Where a hearing to which this paragraph applies is held on any day of the main hearing of a case on indictment, no separate fee shall be payable in respect of attendance at that hearing, but the hearing shall be included in the length of the main hearing for the purpose of calculating remuneration.

(3) Where a hearing to which this paragraph applies is held prior to the first or only day of the main hearing, it shall not be included in the length of the main hearing for the purpose of calculating remuneration, and the advocate shall be remunerated for attendance at such a hearing

(a) in respect of any day where the hearing begins before and ends after the luncheon adjournment, at the daily rate set out in the Table following paragraph 21 as appropriate to the category of advocate;

(b) in respect of any day where the hearing begins and ends before the luncheon adjournment, or begins after the luncheon adjournment, at the half-daily rate set out in the Table following paragraph 21 as appropriate to the category of advocate.

14.—(1) This paragraph applies to:

(a) a hearing to which the court proceeds under section 2 of the Drug Trafficking Act 1994;

(b) a hearing to which the court proceeds under section 71 of the Criminal Justice Act 1988.

(2) A hearing to which this paragraph applies shall not be included in the length of the main hearing or of any sentencing hearing for the purpose of calculating remuneration, and the advocate shall be remunerated for attendance at such a hearing.

(a) in respect of any day where the hearing begins before and ends after the luncheon adjournment, at the daily rate set out in the Table following paragraph 21 as appropriate to the category of advocate;

(b) in respect of any day where the hearing begins and ends before the luncheon adjournment, or begins after the luncheon adjournment, at the half-daily rate set out in the Table following paragraph 21 as appropriate to the category of advocate.

15.—(1) The fee payable to any person for appearing at a hearing to which this paragraph applies shall be that set out in the Table following paragraph 21 as appropriate to the category of person appearing and the circumstances of the hearing.

(2) This paragraph applies to the following hearings—

(a) a sentencing hearing following a case on indictment to which this Schedule applies, where sentence has been deferred under section 1 of the Powers of Criminal Courts Act 1973;

(b) a sentencing hearing following a case on indictment to which this Schedule applies, other than a hearing within paragraph (a) or a sentencing hearing forming part of the main hearing.

16. A fee under this paragraph, of the amount set out in the Table following paragraph 21 as appropriate to the category of person appearing, shall be payable to any person (whether the advocate or not) for appearing in the following hearings in a case on

indictment, when not forming part of the main hearing or a hearing for which a fee is provided elsewhere in this Schedule:

(a) the hearing of a case listed for plea which is adjourned for trial;

(b) any hearing (other than a trial) which is listed but cannot proceed because of the failure of the legally assisted person or a witness to attend, the unavailability of a pre-sentence report or other good reason;

(c) bail and other applications;

(d) the hearing of a case listed for mention only.

17.—(1) Where this paragraph applies, a special preparation fee may be claimed in addition to the graduated fee payable under this Schedule.

(2) This paragraph applies where, in any case on indictment in the Crown Court in respect of which a graduated fee is payable under this Schedule, it has been necessary for the advocate to do work by way of preparation substantially in excess of the amount normally done for cases of the same type because the case involves a very unusual or novel point of law or factual issue.

(3) The amount of the special preparation fee shall be calculated from the number of hours of preparation in excess of the amount normally done for cases of the same type, using the rates of hourly fees set out in the Table following paragraph 21 as appropriate to the category of advocate.

(4) An advocate claiming a special preparation fee shall supply such information and documents as may be required by the appropriate authority as proof of the unusual nature or novelty of the point of law or factual issue and of the number of hours of preparation.

18.—(1) A wasted preparation fee may be claimed where an advocate instructed in any case to which this paragraph applies is prevented from representing the legally assisted person in the main hearing by any of the following circumstances:

(a) the advocate is instructed to appear in other proceedings at the same time as the main hearing in the case and has been unable to secure a change of date for either the main hearing or the other proceedings;

(b) the date fixed for the main hearing is changed by the court despite the advocate's objection;

(c) the advocate has withdrawn from the case with the leave of the court because of his professional code of conduct or to avoid embarrassment in the exercise of his profession;

(d) the advocate has been dismissed by his client;

(e) the advocate is obliged to attend at any place by reason of a judicial office held by him or other public duty.

(2) This paragraph applies to every case on indictment to which this Schedule applies provided that—

(a) the case goes to trial, and the trial lasts for five days or more, or

(b) the case is a cracked trial, and the number of pages of prosecution evidence exceeds 150.

(3) The amount of the wasted preparation fee shall be calculated from the number of hours of preparation reasonably carried out by the advocate, using the rates for hourly fees set out in the Table following paragraph 21; but no such fee shall be payable unless the number of hours of preparation is eight or more.

(4) An advocate claiming a wasted preparation fee shall supply such information and documents as may be required by the determining officer as proof of the circumstances in which he was prevented from representing the legally assisted person and of the number of hours of preparation.

19.—(1) The hourly fee set out in the Table following paragraph 21 as appropriate to the category of advocate shall be payable in respect of work of the following types, provided that the advocate satisfies the appropriate authority that the work was reasonably necessary, namely;

(a) attendance by the advocate at conferences with prospective or actual expert witnesses; or

(b) travel for the purpose of attending a conference with the legally assisted person, where the appropriate authority is satisfied that the legally assisted person was unable or could not reasonably have been expected to attend a conference at the advocate's office or chambers;

and where that fee is allowed the advocate shall also be paid the reasonable expenses of travelling to and from the conference.

(2) In any case on indictment, an advocate shall be entitled to a fee in accordance with the Table following paragraph 21 for the number of periods or parts of a period of 10 minutes of running time of any tape or video cassette or part thereof which he listens to or views as part of the evidence in the case.

Paragraph (1) amended by the Legal Aid in Criminal and Care Proceedings (Costs) (Amendment) Regulations 1998 (S.I. 1998 No. 1191).

20.—(1) Subject to regulation 9(3) and to paragraph 22(2), the remuneration payable to an advocate instructed in any case mentioned in paragraph 3 shall be the fixed fee set out in the Table following paragraph 21.

(2) Where the advocate appears in any case mentioned in paragraph 3 unattended by an authorised litigator or representative, he shall be entitled to the additional fee set out in that Table.

21. The remuneration payable to an authorised advocate retained solely for the purpose of making a note of any hearing shall be the daily fee set out in the Table following this paragraph.

TABLE

Type of work	Paragraph providing for fee	Fee for Queen's Counsel £	Fee for leading advocate (other than Queen's Counsel) £	Fee for junior or sole advocate (other than Queen's Counsel) £
Pleas and directions hearing or pre-trial review—basic fee	11(1)	188.00	127.00	75.00
Attendance where bench warrant issued	12(1)	250.00	170.00	100.00
Appearing at listed trial which did not proceed—basic fee	12(2)	275.00	187.00	110.00
Work for which daily or half-daily fee is payable	13, 14	330.00 per day 185.00 per half day	250.00 per day 140.00 per half day	178.25 per day 99.50 per half day
Appearing at deferred sentencing hearing	15(2)(a)	300.00	204.00	120.00
Appearing at other sentencing hearing	15(2)(b)	150.00	102.00	60.00
Other appearances	16	116.00	79.00	46.50
Work for which hourly fee is payable	17, 18, 19(1)	62.50 per hour	47.00 per hour	33.50 per hour
Listening to or viewing tapes etc.	19(2)	27.15 per 10 minutes	18.50 per 10 minutes	10.90 per 10 minutes
Appearing in appeal against conviction	20(1)	292.25	199.00	117.00
Appearing in other case within paragraph 3	20(1)	184.50	125.00	73.50
Additional fee for unattended advocate	20(2)	19.25	19.25	19.25
Noting brief	21	—	—	100.00 per day

Table amended by the Legal Aid in Criminal and Care Proceedings (Costs) (Amendment) Regulations 1998 (S.I. 1998 No. 1191).

PART V

MISCELLANEOUS

22.—(1) Where a legally assisted person is charged with more than one offence on one indictment, the graduated fee payable to the advocate shall be based on whichever of those offences he shall select for the purpose.

(2) Where two or more cases to which this Schedule applies involving the same advocate are heard concurrently (whether involving the same or different legally assisted persons):

(a) the advocate shall select one case ("the principal case"), which shall be treated for the purposes of remuneration in accordance with the previous paragraphs of this Schedule;

(b) in respect of the main hearing in each of the other cases the advocate shall be paid a fixed fee of one-fifth of:

(i) the basic fee for the principal case, where that is a case falling within paragraph 2, or

(ii) the fixed fee for the principal case, where that is a case falling within paragraph 3.

(3) Where a person appears at a hearing specified in paragraph 11, 12(2), 13, 14, 15, or 16(a) or (b), forming part of two or more cases involving different legally assisted persons, he shall be paid:

(a) in respect of the first such case, the fixed fee for that hearing specified in the Table following paragraph 21;

(b) in respect of each of the other cases, one-fifth of that fee.

(4) Subject to sub-paragraphs (1) to (3), where a person appears at a hearing forming part of two or more cases, he hall be paid the fixed fee for that hearing specified in the Table following paragraph 21 in respect of one such case, without any increase in respect of the other cases.

23.—(1) Where in any case on indictment two advocates are instructed to represent the same legally assisted person:

(a) if the leading advocate is a Queen's Counsel, he shall receive the same graduated fee as if he were appearing alone;

(b) if the leading advocate is not a Queen's Counsel, he shall receive three-quarters of the 5 graduated fee payable to Queen's Counsel appearing alone;

(c) in either case, the junior advocate shall receive one-half of the graduated fee payable to a Queen's Counsel appearing alone.

(2) Where the legally assisted person is represented by a single advocate and another person charged on the same indictment with an offence falling within the same Class is represented by two advocates, the single advocate shall receive the same graduated fee as if he were appearing as junior to another advocate.

(3) Sub-paragraph (2) shall not apply where the charge which the single advocate is instructed to defend (or where there is more than one such charge, the charge forming the basis of remuneration in accordance with paragraph 22(1)) is for an offence falling within Class A.

24. Where a person is instructed to appear in a court which is not within 40 kilometres of his office or chambers, the appropriate authority may allow an amount for travelling and other expenses incidental to that appearance; provided that the amount shall not be greater than the amount, if any, which would be payable to an advocate from the nearest local Bar or the nearest authorised advocate's office (whichever is the nearer) unless the person instructed to appear has obtained prior approval under regulation 54A of the General Regulations for the incurring of such expenses or can justify his attendance having regard to all the relevant circumstances of the case.

Amended by the Legal Aid in Criminal and Care Proceedings (Costs) (Amendment) (No. 3) Regulations 1997 (S.I. 1997 No. 1484).

TABLE OF OFFENCES   Paragraph 5

Offence	Contrary to	Year and chapter
Class A: Homicide and related grave offences		
Murder	Common law	
Manslaughter	Common law	
Soliciting to murder	Offences against the Person Act 1861 s.4	1861 c.100
Child destruction	Infant Life (Preservation) Act 1929 s.1(1)	1929 c.34
Infanticide	Infanticide Act 1938 s.1(1)	1938 c.36
Causing explosion likely to endanger life or property	Explosive Substances Act 1883 s.2	1883 c.3
Attempt to cause explosion, making or keeping explosive etc.	Explosive Substances Act 1883 s.3	as above

Class B: Offences involving serious violence or damage, and serious drugs offences

Offence	Contrary to	Year and chapter
Kidnapping	Common law	
False imprisonment	Common law	
Aggravated criminal damage	Criminal Damage Act 1971 s.1(2)	1971 c.48
Aggravated arson	Criminal Damage Act 1971 s.1(2), (3)	as above
Arson (where value exceeds £30,000)	Criminal Damage Act 1971 s.1(3)	as above
Possession of firearm with intent to endanger life	Firearms Act 1968 s.16	1968 c.27
Use of firearm to resist arrest	Firearms Act 1968 s.17	as above
Possession of firearm with criminal intent	Firearms Act 1968 s.18	as above
Possession or acquisition of certain prohibited weapons etc.	Firearms Act 1968 s.5	1968 c.27
Aggravated burglary	Theft Act 1968 s.10	1968 c.60
Armed robbery	Theft Act 1968 s.8(1)	as above
Assault with weapon with intent to rob	Theft Act 1968 s.8(2)	as above
Blackmail	Theft Act 1968 s.21	as above
Riot	Public Order Act 1986 s.1	1986 c.64
Violent disorder	Public Order Act 1986 s.2	1986 c.64
Contamination of goods with intent	Public Order Act 1986 s.38	1986 c.64
Causing death by dangerous driving	Road Traffic Act 1988 s.1	1988 c.52
Causing death by careless driving while under the influence of drink or drugs	Road Traffic Act 1988 s.3A	as above

Offence	Contrary to	Year and chapter
Aggravated vehicle taking resulting in death	Theft Act 1968 s.12A	1968 c.60
Causing danger to road users	Road Traffic Act 1988 s.22A	1988 c.52
Attempting to choke, suffocate, strangle etc.	Offences against the Person Act 1861 s.21	1861 c.100
Causing miscarriage by poison, instrument	Offences against the Person Act 1861 s.58	as above
Making threats to kill	Offences against the Person Act 1861 s.16	as above
Wounding or grievous bodily harm with intent to cause grievous bodily harm etc.	Offences against the Person Act 1861 s.18	as above
Endangering the safety of railway passengers	Offences against the Person Act 1861 ss.32, 33, 34	as above
Impeding persons endeavouring to escape wrecks	Offences against the Person Act 1861 s.17	as above
Administering chloroform, laudanum etc.	Offences against the Person Act 1861 s.22	as above
Administering poison etc. so as to endanger life	Offences against the Person Act 1861 s.23	1861 c.100
Cruelty to persons under 16	Children and Young Persons Act 1933 s.1	1933 c.12
Aiding and abetting suicide	Suicide Act 1961 s.2	1961 c.60
Placing wood etc. on railway	Malicious Damage Act 1861 s.35	1861 c.97
Exhibiting false signals etc.	Malicious Damage Act 1861 s.47	as above
Prison mutiny	Prison Security Act 1992 s.1	1992 c.25
Assaulting prison officer whilst possessing firearm etc.	Criminal Justice Act 1991 s.90	1991 c.53
Acquiring, possessing etc. the proceeds of criminal conduct	Criminal Justice Act 1988 s.93	1988 c.33
Producing or supplying a Class A or B drug	Misuse of Drugs Act 1971 s.4	1971 c.38
Possession of a Class A or B drug with intent to supply	Misuse of Drugs Act 1971 s.5(3)	as above
Manufacture and supply of scheduled substances	Criminal Justice (International Co-operation) Act 1990 s.12	1990 c.5
Fraudulent evasion of controls on Class A and B drugs	Customs and Excise Management Act 1979 s.170 (2)(b), (c)	1979 c.2
Illegal importation of Class A and B drugs	Customs and Excise Management Act 1979 s.50	as above
Offences in relation to proceeds of drug trafficking	Drug Trafficking Act 1994 ss.49, 50 and 51	1994 c.37
Offences in relation to money laundering investigations	Drug Trafficking Act 1994 ss.52 and 53	as above
Practitioner contravening drug supply regulations	Misuse of Drugs Act 1971 ss.12 and 13	1971 c.38
Cultivation of cannabis plant	Misuse of Drugs Act 1971 s.6	as above
Occupier knowingly permitting drugs offences etc.	Misuse of Drugs Act 1971 s.8	as above
Activities relating to opium	Misuse of Drugs Act 1971 s.9	as above
Drug trafficking offences at sea	Criminal Justice (International Co-operation) Act 1990 s.18	1990 c.5

581

Offence	Contrary to	Year and chapter
Firing on Revenue vessel	Customs and Excise Management Act 1979 s.85	as above
Making or possession of explosive in suspicious circumstances	Explosive Substances Act 1883 s.4(1)	1883 c.3
Causing bodily injury by explosives	Offences against the Person Act 1861 s.28	1861 c.100
Using explosive or corrosives with intent to cause grievous bodily harm	Offences against the Person Act 1861 s.29	as above
Hostage taking	Taking of Hostages Act 1982 s.1	1982 c.28
Assisting another to retain proceeds of terrorist activities	Northern Ireland (Emergency Provisions) Act 1991 s.53	1991 c.24
Concealing or transferring proceeds of terrorist activities	Northern Ireland (Emergency Provisions) Act 1991 s.54	as above
Offences against international protection of nuclear material	Nuclear Material (Offences) Act 1983 s.2	1983 c.18
Placing explosives with intent to cause bodily injury	Offences against the Person Act 1861 s.30	1861 c.100
Membership, support or meeting of proscribed organisations	Prevention of Terrorism (Temporary Provisions) Act 1989 s.2	1989 c.4
Offences involving money or property to be used for acts of terrorism	Prevention of Terrorism (Temporary Provisions) Act 1989 s.9	as above
Offences involving contributions to proscribed organisations	Prevention of Terrorism (Temporary Provisions) Act 1989 s.10	as above
Assisting in the retention or control of terrorist funds	Prevention of Terrorism (Temporary Provisions) Act 1989 s.11	as above
Possession of articles for terrorist purposes	Prevention of Terrorism (Temporary Provisions) Act 1989 s.16A	as above
Unlawful collection of information for terrorist purposes	Prevention of Terrorism (Temporary Provisions) Act 1989 s.16B	as above
Frustrating investigation of terrorist activities	Prevention of Terrorism (Temporary Provisions) Act 1989 s.17	as above

Class C: Lesser offences involving violence or damage, and less serious drugs offences

Robbery (other than armed robbery)	Theft Act 1968 s.8(1)	1968 c.60
Unlawful wounding	Offences against the Person Act 1861 s.20	1861 c.100
Assault occasioning actual bodily harm	Offences against the Person Act 1861 s.47	as above
Concealment of birth	Offences against the Person Act 1861 s.60	as above
Abandonment of children under two	Offences against the Person Act 1861 s.27	as above
Arson (other than aggravated arson) where value does not exceed £30,000	Criminal Damage Act 1971 s.1(3)	1971 c.48

Offence	Contrary to	Year and chapter
Criminal damage (other than aggravated criminal damage)	Criminal Damage Act 1971 s.1(1)	as above
Possession of firearm without certificate	Firearms Act 1968 s.1	1968 c.27
Carrying loaded firearm in public place	Firearms Act 1968 s.19	as above
Trespassing with a firearm	Firearms Act 1968 s.20	as above
Shortening of shotgun or possession of shortened shotgun	Firearms Act 1968 s.4	as above
Shortening of smooth bore gun	Firearms Amendment Act 1988 s.6(1)	1988 c.45
Possession or acquisition of shotgun without certificate	Firearms Act 1968 s.2	1968 c.27
Possession of firearms by person convicted of crime	Firearms Act 1968 s.21(4)	as above
Acquisition by or supply of firearms to person denied them	Firearms Act 1968 s.21(5)	as above
Dealing in firearms	Firearms Act 1968 s.3	as above
Failure to comply with certificate when transferring firearm	Firearms Act 1968 s.42	as above
Permitting an escape	Common law	
Rescue	Common law	
Escaping from lawful custody without force	Common law	
Breach of prison	Common law	
Harbouring escaped prisoners	Criminal Justice Act 1961 s.22	1961 c.39
Assisting prisoners to escape	Prison Act 1952 s.39	1952 c.52
Fraudulent evasion of agricultural levy	Customs and Excise Management Act 1979 s.68A (1) and (2)	1979 c.2
Offender armed or disguised	Customs and Excise Management Act 1979 s.86	as above
Making threats to destroy or damage property	Criminal Damage Act 1971 s.2	1971 c.48
Possessing anything with intent to destroy or damage property	Criminal Damage Act 1971 s.3	as above
Child abduction by connected person	Child Abduction Act 1984 s.1	1984 c.37
Child abduction by other person	Child Abduction Act 1984 s.2	as above
Bomb hoax	Criminal Law Act 1977 s.51	1977 c.45
Cutting away buoys etc.	Malicious Damage Act 1861 s.48	1861 c.97
Producing or supplying Class C drug	Misuse of Drugs Act 1971 s.4	1971 c.38
Possession of a Class C drug with intent to supply	Misuse of Drugs Act 1971 s.5(3)	as above
Fraudulent evasion of controls on Class C drugs	Customs and Excise Management Act 1979 s.170 (2)(b), (c)	1979 c.2
Illegal importation of Class C drugs	Customs and Excise Management Act 1979 s.50	as above
Possession of Class A drug	Misuse of Drugs Act 1971 s.5(2)	1971 c.38

Offence	Contrary to	Year and chapter
Failure to disclose knowledge or suspicion of money laundering	Drug Trafficking Offences Act 1986 s.26B	1986 c.32
Tipping-off in relation to money laundering investigations	Drug Trafficking Offences Act 1986 s.26C	as above
Assaults on officers saving wrecks	Offences against the Person Act 1861 s.37	1861 c.100
Attempting to injure or alarm the Sovereign	Treason Act 1842 s.2	1842 c.51
Assisting illegal entry or harbouring persons	Immigration Act 1971 s.25	1971 c.77
Administering poison with intent to injure etc.	Offences against the Person Act 1861 s.24	1861 c.100
Neglecting to provide food for or assaulting servants etc.	Offences against the Person Act 1861 s.26	as above
Setting spring guns with intent to inflict grievous bodily harm	Offences against the Person Act 1861 s.31	as above
Supplying instrument etc. to cause miscarriage	Offences against the Person Act 1861 s.59	as above
Failure to disclose information about terrorism	Prevention of Terrorism (Temporary Provisions) Act 1989 s.18	1989 c.4
Offences in respect of exclusion orders	Prevention of Terrorism (Temporary Provisions) Act 1989 s.8	as above
Circumcision of females	Prohibition of Female Circumcision Act 1985 s.1	1985 c.38
Breaking or injuring submarine telegraph cables	Submarine Telegraph Act 1885 s.3	1885 c.49
Failing to keep dogs under proper control resulting in injury	Dangerous Dogs Act 1991 s.3	1991 c.65
Making gunpowder etc. to commit offences	Offences against the Person Act 1861 s.64	1861 c.100
Stirring up racial hatred	Public Order Act 1986 ss.18–23	1986 c.64

Class D: Serious sexual offences, offences against children

Offence	Contrary to	Year and chapter
Rape	Sexual Offences Act 1956 s.1(1)	1956 c.69
Administering drugs to obtain intercourse	Sexual Offences Act 1956 s.4	as above
Sexual intercourse with girl under 13	Sexual Offences Act 1956 s.5	as above
Sexual intercourse with girl under 16	Sexual Offences Act 1956 s.6	as above
Sexual intercourse with defective	Sexual Offences Act 1956 s.7	as above
Procurement of a defective	Sexual Offences Act 1956 s.9	as above
Incest	Sexual Offences Act 1956 s.10	as above
Buggery of male of 16 or over without consent	Sexual Offences Act 1956 s.2	as above
Buggery of male under 16, woman or animal	Sexual Offences Act 1956 s.12	as above
Buggery by male of 21 or over of consenting male of 16–18	Sexual Offences Act 1956 s.12	as above
Gross indecency between male of 18 or over and male under 18	Sexual Offences Act 1956 s.13	as above

Offence	Contrary to	Year and chapter
Indecent assault on a woman	Sexual Offences Act 1956 s.14	as above
Indecent assault on a man	Sexual Offences Act 1956 s.15	as above
Indecency with children under 14	Indecency with Children Act 1960 s.1(1)	1960 c.33
Taking, having etc. indecent photographs of children	Protection of Children Act 1978 s.1	1978 c.37
Assault with intent to commit buggery	Sexual Offences Act 1956 s.16	1956 c.69
Abduction of woman by force	Sexual Offences Act 1956 s.17	as above
Permitting girl under 13 to use premises for sexual intercourse	Sexual Offences Act 1956 s.25	as above
Man living on earnings of prostitution	Sexual Offences Act 1956 s.30	as above
Woman exercising control over prostitute	Sexual Offences Act 1956 s.31	as above
Living on earnings of male prostitution	Sexual Offences Act 1967 s.5	1967 c.60
Incitement to commit incest	Criminal Law Act 1977 s.54	1977 c.45
Allowing or procuring child under 16 to go abroad to perform	Children and Young Persons Act 1933 ss.25, 26	1933 c.12
Sexual intercourse with patients	Mental Health Act 1959 s.128	1959 c.72
Ill-treatment of persons of unsound mind	Mental Health Act 1983 s.127	1983 c.20
Abduction of unmarried girl under 18 from parent	Sexual Offences Act 1956 s.19	1956 c.69
Abduction of unmarried girl under 16 from parent	Sexual Offences Act 1956 s.20	as above
Abduction of defective from parent	Sexual Offences Act 1956 s.21	as above
Procuration of girl under 21	Sexual Offences Act 1956 s.23	as above
Permitting girl under 16 to use premises for intercourse	Sexual Offences Act 1956 s.26	as above
Permitting defective to use premises for intercourse	Sexual Offences Act 1956 s.27	as above
Causing or encouraging prostitution of girl under 16	Sexual Offences Act 1956 s.28	as above
Causing or encouraging prostitution of defective	Sexual Offences Act 1956 s.29	as above

Class E: Burglary etc.

Burglary (domestic)	Theft Act 1968 s.9(3)(a)	1968 c.60
Going equipped to steal	Theft Act 1968 s.25	as above
Burglary (non-domestic)	Theft Act 1968 s.9(3)(b)	as above

Classes F and G: Other offences of dishonesty
The following offences are always in Class F

Destruction of registers of births etc.	Forgery Act 1861 s.36	1861 c.98
Making false entries in copies of registers sent to register	Forgery Act 1861 s.37	as above

Offence	Contrary to	Year and chapter
The following offences are always in Class G		
Counterfeiting notes and coins	Forgery and Counterfeiting Act 1981 s.14	1981 c.45
Passing counterfeit notes and coins	Forgery and Counterfeiting Act 1981 s.15	as above
Offences involving custody or control of counterfeit notes and coins	Forgery and Counterfeiting Act 1981 s.16	as above
Making, custody or control of counterfeiting materials etc.	Forgery and Counterfeiting Act 1981 s.175	as above
Illegal importation: counterfeit notes or coins	Customs and Excise Management Act 1979 s.50	1979 c.2
Fraudulent evasion: counterfeit notes or coins	Customs and Excise Management Act 1979 s.170 (2)(b), (c)	as above

The following offences are in Class G if the value involved exceeds £30,000, and in Class F otherwise

Offence	Contrary to	Year and chapter
Theft	Theft Act 1968 s.1	1968 c.60
Removal of articles from places open to the public	Theft Act 1968 s.11	as above
Abstraction of electricity	Theft Act 1968 s.13	as above
Obtaining property by deception	Theft Act 1968 s.15	as above
Obtaining pecuniary advantage by deception	Theft Act 1968 s.16	as above
False accounting	Theft Act 1968 s.17	as above
Handling stolen goods	Theft Act 1968 s.22	as above
Obtaining services by deception	Theft Act 1978 s.1	1978 c.31
Evasion of liability by deception	Theft Act 1978 s.2	as above
Illegal importation: not elsewhere specified	Customs and Excise Management Act 1979 s.50	1979 c.2
Counterfeiting Customs documents	Customs and Excise Management Act 1979 s.168	as above
Fraudulent evasion: not elsewhere specified	Customs and Excise Management Act 1979 s.170 (2)(b), (c)	as above
Forgery	Forgery and Counterfeiting Act 1981 s.1	1981 c.45
Copying false instrument with intent	Forgery and Counterfeiting Act 1981 s.2	as above
Using a false instrument	Forgery and Counterfeiting Act 1981 s.3	as above
Using a copy of a false instrument	Forgery and Counterfeiting Act 1981 s.4	as above
Custody or control of false instruments etc.	Forgery and Counterfeiting Act 1981 s.5	as above
Offences in relation to dies or stamps	Stamp Duties Management Act 1891 s.13	1891 c.38
Counterfeiting of dies or marks	Hallmarking Act 1973 s.6	1973 c.43
Fraudulent application of trade mark	Trade Marks Act 1938 s.58A	1938 c.22

Class H: Miscellaneous lesser offences

Offence	Contrary to	Year and chapter
Possession of offensive weapon	Prevention of Crime Act 1953 s.1	1953 c.14
Affray	Public Order Act 1986 s.3	1986 c.64

Offence	Contrary to	Year and chapter
Assault with intent to resist arrest	Offences against the Person Act 1861 s.38	1861 c.100
Unlawful eviction and harassment of occupier	Protection from Eviction Act 1977 s.1	1977 c.43
Obscene articles intended for publication for gain	Obscene Publications Act 1964 s.1	1964 c.74
Gross indecency between males (other than where one is 18 or over and the other is under 18)	Sexual Offences Act 1956 s.13	1956 c.69
Solicitation for immoral purposes	Sexual Offences Act 1956 s.32	as above
Buggery by male under 21 of consenting male 16–18	Sexual Offences Act 1956 s.12	1956 c.69
Buggery of males of 21 or over otherwise than in private	Sexual Offences Act 1956 s.12	as above
Acts outraging public decency	Common law	
Offences of publication of obscene matter	Obscene Publications Act 1959 s.2	1959 c.66
Keeping a disorderly house	Common law; Disorderly Houses Act 1751 s.8	25 Geo. 2 c.36
Indecent display	Indecent Displays (Control) Act 1981 s.1	1981 c.42
Presentation of obscene performance	Theatres Act 1968 s.2	1968 c.54
Procurement of intercourse by threats etc.	Sexual Offences Act 1956 s.2	1956 c.69
Causing prostitution of women	Sexual Offences Act 1956 s.22	as above
Detention of woman in brothel or other premises	Sexual Offences Act 1956 s.24	as above
Procurement of a woman by false pretences	Sexual Offences Act 1956 s.3	as above
Procuring others to commit homosexual acts	Sexual Offences Act 1967 s.4	1967 c.60
Trade description offences (9 offences)	Trade Descriptions Act 1968 ss.1, 8, 9, 12, 13, 14, 18	1968 c.29
Absconding by person released on bail	Bail Act 1976 s.6(1), (2)	1976 c.63
Misconduct endangering ship or persons on board ship	Merchant Shipping Act 1970 s.27	1970 c.36
Obstructing engine or carriage on railway	Malicious Damage Act 1861 s.36	1861 c.97
Offences relating to the safe custody of controlled drugs	Misuse of Drugs Act 1971 s.11	1971 c.38
Possession of Class B or C drug	Misuse of Drugs Act 1971 s.5(2)	1971 c.38
Wanton or furious driving	Offences against the Person Act 1861 s.35	1861 c.100
Dangerous driving	Road Traffic Act 1988 s.2	1988 c.52
Forgery and misuse of driving documents	Public Passenger Vehicles Act 1981 s.65	1981 c.14
Forgery of driving documents	Road Traffic Act 1960 s.233	1960 c.59
Forgery etc. of licences and other documents	Road Traffic Act 1988 s.173	1988 c.52
Mishandling or falsifying parking documents etc.	Road Traffic Regulations Act 1984 s.115	1984 c.27

Offence	Contrary to	Year and chapter
Aggravated vehicle taking	Theft Act 1968 s.12A	1968 c.60
Forgery, alteration, fraud of licences etc.	Vehicle (Excise) Act 1971 s.26	1971 c.10
Making off without payment	Theft Act 1978 s.3	1978 c.31
Agreeing to indemnify sureties	Bail Act 1976 s.9(1)	1976 c.63
Sending prohibited articles by post	Post Office Act 1953 s.11	1953 c.36
Impersonating Customs officer	Customs and Excise Management Act 1979 s.3	1979 c.2
Obstructing Customs officer	Customs and Excise Management Act 1979 s.16	as above

Class I: Offences against public justice and similar offences

Perverting the course of public justice	Common law	
Perjuries (7 offences)	Perjury Act 1911 s.1–7(2)	1911 c.6
Corrupt transactions with agents	Prevention of Corruption Act 1906 s.1	1906 c.34
Corruption in public office	Public Bodies Corrupt Practices Act 1889 s.1	1889 c.69
Embracery	Common law	
Fabrication of evidence with intent to mislead a tribunal	Common law	
Personation of jurors	Common law	
Concealing an arrestable offence	Criminal Law Act 1967 s.5	1967 c.45
Assisting offenders	Criminal Law Act 1967 s.4(1)	as above
False evidence before European Court	European Communities Act 1972 s.11	1972 c.68
Personating for purposes of bail etc.	Forgery Act 1861 s.34	1861 c.60
Intimidating a witness, juror etc.	Criminal Justice and Public Order Act 1994 s.51(1)	1994 c.33
Harming, threatening to harm a witness, juror etc.	Criminal Justice and Public Order Act 1994 s.51(2)	as above
Prejudicing a drug trafficking investigation	Drug Trafficking Act 1994 s.58(1)	1994 c.37
Giving false statements to procure cremation	Cremation Act 1902 s.8(2)	1902 c.8
False statement tendered under section 9 of the Criminal Justice Act 1967	Criminal Justice Act 1967 s.89	1967 c.80
Making a false statement to obtain interim possession order	Criminal Justice and Public Order Act 1994 s.75(1)	1994 c.33
Making false statement to resist making of interim possession order	Criminal Justice and Public Order Act 1994 s.75(2)	as above
False statement tendered under section 102 of the Magistrates' Courts Act 1980	Magistrates' Courts Act 1980 s.106	1980 c.43
Making false statement to authorised officer	Trade Descriptions Act 1968 s.29(2)	1968 c.29

Schedule 3 was inserted by the Legal Aid Criminal and Care Proceedings (Costs) (Amendment) (No. 2) Regulations 1996 (S.I. 1996 No. 2655) and amended by the Legal Aid in Criminal and Care Proceedings (Costs) (Amendment) (No. 3) Regulations 1997 (S.I. 1997 No. 1484).

EXPLANATORY NOTE

(This note is not part of the Regulations)

These Regulations consolidate the Legal Aid in Criminal Proceedings (Costs) Regulations 1988, as amended, (which are revoked subject to the provisions of regulation 1(3)) and provide for the determination of the costs which may be paid to the legal representatives of a person given legal aid under Parts I and VI of the Legal Aid Act 1988 (legal aid in criminal proceedings and care proceedings).

Regulations 5 and 6 provide for the determination of solicitors' fees, and hourly rates (including separate rates for work in care proceedings) are prescribed together with (in Schedule 1 Part II) a system of standard fees. Regulations 8 and 9 provide for the determination of counsel's fees and scales of payment are prescribed together with a system of standard fees for certain items of work done by junior counsel in the Crown Court. Regulations 12 to 16 and paragraphs 6 to 8 of Schedule 1 Part II provide for the redetermination of fees and for appeals.

These Regulations increase the rates of remuneration previously payable under the 1988 Regulations with an overall increase of 6 per cent.

Since these Regulations were made, a new system for the payment of graduated fees has been introduced. The 1996 Amendment (No. 2) Regulations make provision for this by instituting a new system for the payment of graduated fees for advocacy and preparation work on the occasion of a trial or guilty plea in the Crown Court, with fixed fees for appeals to the Crown Court against conviction or sentence and for committals for sentence. The graduated fees vary with the nature of the offence and a number of indicators designed to reflect the complexity of the case, and apply to both barrister and solicitor advocates.

The Legal Aid in Criminal and Care Proceedings (Costs) (Amendment) (No. 2) Regulations 1996 further amend the Legal Aid in Criminal and Care Proceedings (Costs) Regulations 1989 by:

(a) introducing staged payments in long Crown Court cases, consisting of one payment for each block of 100 hours' preparation;

(b) introducing interim payments for attendance at trial by solicitors and for counsel's refreshers, consisting of one payment for each period of 20 days' attendance at the trial;

(c) allowing an advance payment of £100 to the advocate (£250 to a Queen's Counsel, £170 to a leading junior) where substantial preparation for the trial has been done five days before the pleas and directions hearing;

(d) introducing hardship payments for legal representatives engaged in a case for six months or more when final payment is not likely to be received within three months and staged, interim and advance payments are not available.

Legal Advice and Assistance (Duty Solicitor) (Remuneration) Regulations 1989*

Came into force April 1, 1989

Title, commencement, revocations and transitional provisions

1.—(1) These Regulations may be cited as the Legal Advice and Assistance (Duty Solicitor) (Remuneration) Regulations 1989 and shall come into force on April 1, 1989.

(2) The Regulations specified in the schedule are hereby revoked.

(3) Where a review under regulation 8 relates to a claim made before June 1, 1989, regulation 9(1) and (2) shall not apply and the solicitor may appeal in writing within 21 days of receipt of notification of the decision on the review to a committee appointed by the Board.

Interpretation

2. In these Regulations, unless the context otherwise requires:—

"the 1988 Act" means the Legal Aid Act 1988;

"appropriate area committee" means the area committee in whose area is situated the magistrates' court at which a solicitor has given advice or assistance in accordance with arrangements made by the Board under regulation 7 or 8 of the Legal Advice and Assistance Regulations 1989;

"area committee" has the meaning assigned to it by regulation 4 of the Civil Legal Aid (General) Regulations 1989;

"business day" means any day other than a Saturday, a Sunday, Christmas Day, Good Friday or a bank holiday under the Banking and Financial Dealings Act 1971;

"contract" means a contract entered into by the Board with other persons or bodies pursuant to its powers under section 4 of the 1988 Act;

"duty day" means a day during which a duty solicitor is present at a magistrates' court in accordance with a scheme;

"duty solicitor" means a solicitor who is present at a magistrates' court in accordance with a scheme;

"duty solicitor scheme" means any arrangements made by the Board under regulation 31 or 33 of the Legal Advice and Assistance Regulations 1989;

"franchisee" means a person or body (other than the Board) acting under the terms of a franchising contract;

---

* S.I. 1989 No. 341 as amended by the Legal Advice and Assistance (Duty Solicitor) (Remuneration) (Amendment) Regulations 1991 (S.I. 1991 No. 528), the Legal Advice and Assistance (Duty Solicitor) (Remuneration) (Amendment) Regulations 1992 (S.I. 1992 No. 639), the Legal Advice and Assistance (Duty Solicitor) (Remuneration) (Amendment) Regulations 1995 (S.I. 1995 No. 951) and the Legal Advice and Assistance (Duty Solicitor) (Remuneration) (Amendment) Regulations 1996 (S.I. 1996 No. 647).

"the 1989 regulations" means the Legal Aid in Criminal and Care Proceedings (Costs) Regulations 1989.

Amended by the Legal Advice and Assistance (Duty Solicitor) (Remuneration) (Amendment) Regulations 1995 (S.I. 1995 No. 951).

General
3.—(1) Remuneration shall be determined by the Board in accordance with these Regulations.

(2) The Board shall appoint or authorise the appointment of determining officers to act on its behalf under these Regulations in accordance with directions given by it or on its behalf.

Claims for remuneration
4.—(1) A claim for remuneration by a duty solicitor shall be submitted to the determining officer in such form and manner as the Board may direct and any such claim shall be submitted within three months of the duty day in respect of which the claim is made.

(2) The duty solicitor shall supply such further particulars, information and documents as the determining officer may require.

(3) The time limit within which the claim for remuneration must be submitted may, for good reason, be extended by the determining officer.

(4) Where the solicitor without good reason has failed (or, if an extension were not granted, would fail) to comply with the time limit, the determining officer may, in exceptional circumstances, extend the time limit and shall consider whether it is reasonable in the circumstances to reduce the costs; provided that costs shall not be reduced unless the solicitor has been allowed a reasonable opportunity to show cause orally or in writing why the costs should not be reduced.

Determination of remuneration
5.—(1) The determining officer shall consider the claim, any further particulars, information or documents submitted by the duty solicitor and any other relevant information and allow:—

(a) such time as he considers reasonable in respect of work done, including attendance and waiting, at a magistrates' court which he considers has been actually and reasonably done in accordance with a scheme; and

(b) such time as he considers was reasonably taken by a duty solicitor in travelling from his place of work (or, on a day which is not a business day from his place of residence) to a magistrates' court; and in returning therefrom, where that solicitor is called out to (or, on a day not a business day, attends at) the Court to act as a duty solicitor.

(2) Subject to paragraph (3), the determining officer shall allow remuneration:—

(a) in respect of paragraph (1)(a),

    (i) at £50.75 per hour or, in the case of work done by a franchisee, at £52.25 per hour or

      (ii)   where the fee-earner's office is situated within legal aid area 1, at £52.00 per hour or, in the case of work done by a franchisee, at £53.50 per hour;

    (b) in respect of paragraph (1)(b), at £25.00 per hour or, in the case of work done by a franchisee, at £25.50 per hour.

(3) Remuneration allowed in accordance with paragraph (2)(a) shall be increased by 25 per cent in respect of work done on a day which is not a business day.

(4) In this regulation, "legal aid area" means an area specified by the Board under regulation 4(1) of the Civil Legal Aid (General) Regulations 1989(a) and legal aid area 1, means the area so specified by the Board.

Amended by the Legal Advice and Assistance (Duty Solicitor) (Remuneration) (Amendment) Regulations 1995 (S.I. 1995 No. 951) and the Legal Advice and Assistance (Duty Solicitor) (Remuneration) (Amendment) Regulations 1996 (S.I. 1996 No. 647).

Travelling expenses

6. Where the determining officer allows travelling time under Regulation 5(1)(b) above, he may also allow such travelling expenses as he considers have been actually and reasonably incurred.

Payment of remuneration

7.—(1) The determining officer shall authorise payment to the duty solicitor in the amounts determined (whether by him or on review or appeal) in accordance with these Regulations.

(2) Where the costs payable under paragraph (1) are varied as a result of any review or appeal in accordance with these Regulations, then—

    (a) where the costs are increased, the determining officer shall authorise payment of the increase;

    (b) where the costs are decreased the solicitor shall repay the amount of such decrease.

Review of determination

8.—(1) If a solicitor is dissatisfied with the decision of a determining officer under these Regulations, the solicitor may within 21 days of receipt of notification of the costs payable under regulation 7(1) apply to the appropriate area committee to review that decision.

(2) On an application under paragraph (1), the appropriate area committee shall review the determination of the determining officer whether by confirming, increasing or decreasing the amount of the determination.

Appeals to Committee Appointed by the Board

9.—(1) A solicitor who is dissatisfied with the decision of an area committee on a review under regulation 8 may within 21 days of receipt of notification of the decision apply to that committee to certify a point of principle of general importance.

(2) Where an area committee certifies a point of principle of general import-ance, the solicitor may within 21 days of receipt of notification of that certifi-cation appeal in writing against the decision of the area committee to a committee appointed by the Board.

(3) On an appeal under this regulation the committee appointed by the Board may reverse, affirm or amend the decision of the area committee.

SCHEDULE

REVOCATIONS

Regulations revoked	References
The Legal Advice and Representation (Duty Solicitor) (Remuneration) Regulations 1987.	S.I. 1987/443.
The Legal Advice and Representation (Duty Solicitor) (Remuneration) (Amendment) Regulations 1988.	S.I. 1988/447

EXPLANATORY NOTE

(This note is not part of the Regulations)

These Regulations replace with amendments the Legal Advice and Rep-resentation (Duty Solicitor) (Remuneration) Regulations 1987. They provide for determination and review by the Legal Aid Board of the remuneration pay-able to duty solicitors providing advice and assistance by way of represen-tation at magistrates' court under regulations 7 and 8 of the Legal Advice and Assistance Regulations 1989. The main changes are:—

(a) to reflect the taking over of responsibility for the administration of legal aid by the Legal Aid Board; and

(b) to increase by 25 per cent remuneration for work done at a magis-trates' court on a bank holiday, a Saturday or a Sunday (regulation 5).

The rates of remuneration are fixed by reference to the rates provided for advocacy and for travelling and waiting (currently, *in April 1989*, £46 and £20.50 per hour respectively) in paragraph 1(1)(a) of Part I of Schedule 1 to the Legal Aid in Criminal and Care Proceedings (Costs) Regulations 1989.

[The regulations have since been amended so that the remuneration rates are specified.]

Legal Advice and Assistance at Police Stations (Remuneration) Regulations 1989*

Came into force April 1, 1989 (rates shown in italics apply to work done on or after July 8, 1996).

Citation, commencement, revocations and transitional provisions

1.—(1) These Regulations may be cited as the Legal Advice and Assistance at Police Stations (Remuneration) Regulations 1989 and shall come into force on April 1, 1989.

(2) The Legal Advice and Assistance at Police Stations (Remuneration) Regulations 1988 are hereby revoked except in relation to work done before April 1, 1989.

(3) Where a review under regulation 7 relates to a claim made before June 1, 1989, regulation 8(1) and (2) shall not apply and the solicitor may appeal in writing within 21 days of receipt of notification of the decision on the review to a committee appointed by the Board.

Interpretation

2.—(1) In these Regulations, unless the context otherwise requires—

> "the 1988 Act" means the Legal Aid Act 1988;
> "advice" and "assistance" mean respectively advice and assistance under the 1988 Act;
> "appropriate area committee" means the area committee in whose area is situated the police station or other premises at which a solicitor has given advice or assistance in accordance with arrangements made by the Board under regulation 6 of the Legal Advice and Assistance Regulations 1989;
> "area committee" has the meaning assigned to it by regulation 4 of the Civil Legal Aid (General) Regulations 1989;
> "business day" means any day other than a Saturday, a Sunday, Christmas Day, Good Friday or a bank holiday under the Banking and Financial Dealings Act 1971;

* S.I. 1989 No. 342 as amended by the Legal Advice and Assistance at Police Stations (Remuneration) (Amendment) Regulations 1990 (S.I. 1990 No. 487), the Legal Advice and Assistance at Police Stations (Remuneration) (Amendment) Regulations 1991 (S.I. 1991 No. 527), the Legal Advice and Assistance at Police Stations (Remuneration) (Amendment) Regulations 1992 (S.I. 1992 No. 594), the Legal Advice and Assistance at Police Stations (Remuneration) (Amendment) Regulations 1994 (S.I. 1994 No. 1824), the Legal Advice and Assistance at Police Stations (Remuneration) (Amendment) (No. 2) Regulations 1994 (S.I. 1994 No. 3303) [in respect of advice and assistance given on or after 1st February 1995], the Legal Advice and Assistance at Police Stations (Remuneration) (Amendment) Regulations 1995 (S.I. 1995 No. 950) and the Legal Advice and Assistance at Police Stations (Remuneration) (Amendment) Regulations 1996 (1996 S.I. No. 648) and the Legal Advice and Assistance at Police Stations (Remuneration) (Amendment) (No. 2) Regulations 1996 (S.I. 1986 No. 1554).

"contract" means a franchising contract entered into by the Board with other persons or bodies pursuant to its powers under section 4 of the 1988 Act;

"duty period" means any period of 24 hours during which a duty solicitor holds himself available to give advice and assistance in accordance with a duty solicitor scheme;

"duty solicitor" means any solicitor, and any representative of a solicitor, who provides advice and assistance in accordance with a duty solicitor scheme;

"duty solicitor scheme" means any arrangements made by the Board under section 4 of the 1988 Act for the purposes of regulation 6(3) of the Legal Advice and Assistance Regulations 1989;

"franchisee" means a person or body (other than the Board) acting under the terms of a franchising contract;

"own solicitor" means a solicitor and any representative of a solicitor who gives advice and assistance to a person arrested and held in custody or to a volunteer otherwise than as a duty solicitor;

"own solicitor representatives scheme" means any arrangements made by the Board under section 4 of the 1988 Act applicable to representatives of own solicitors;

"serious service offence" means an offence under any of the Army Act 1955, the Air Force Act 1955 or the Naval Discipline Act 1957 which cannot be dealt with summarily or which appears to an interviewing service policeman to be serious;

"unsocial hours" means between the hours of 5.30 pm and 9.30 am on any business day and any time on a day which is not a business day;

"volunteer" means a person who, for the purpose of assisting with an investigation, attends voluntarily at a police station or at any other place where a constable is present or accompanies a constable to a police station or any such other place without having been arrested.

Amended by the Legal Advice and Assistance at Police Stations (Remuneration) (Amendment) Regulations 1994 (S.I. 1994 No. 1824) and the Legal Advice and Assistance at Police Stations (Remuneration) (Amendment) (No. 2) Regulations 1994 (S.I. 1994 No. 3303).

General

3.—(1) Remuneration shall be determined by the Board in accordance with these Regulations.

(2) The Board shall appoint or authorise the appointment of determining officers to act on its behalf under these Regulations in accordance with directions given by it or on its behalf.

Claims for remuneration

4.—(1) A claim for remuneration by a duty solicitor or an own solicitor shall be submitted to the determining officers in such form and manner as the Board may direct and any such claim shall be submitted within three months of the duty period or of the day on which the advice and assistance was given.

(2) The solicitor shall supply such further particulars, information and documents as the determining officer may require.

(3) The time limit within which the claim must be submitted may, for good reason, be extended by the determining officer.

(4) Where the solicitor without good reason has failed (or, if an extension were not granted, would fail) to comply with the time limit, the determining officer may, in exceptional circumstances, extend the time limit and shall consider whether it is reasonable in the circumstances to reduce the costs; provided that costs shall not be reduced unless the solicitor has been allowed a reasonable opportunity to show cause orally or in writing why the costs should not be reduced.

Determination of remuneration

5.—(1) The determining officer may allow work done in the following classes:

> (a) availability during duty period;
>
> (b) advice and assistance given to a person arrested and held in custody or being interviewed in connection with a serious service offence or to a volunteer;
>
> (c) travelling and waiting;
>
> (d) advising and assisting over the telephone;
>
> (e) routine telephone calls.

(2) The determining officer shall consider the claim, any further particulars, information or documents submitted by the solicitor under regulation 4 and any other relevant information, and allow:

> (a) such work as appears to him to have been actually and reasonably done by a duty solicitor or, subject to paragraph (2A), an own solicitor, classifying it according to the classes specified in paragraph (1); and
>
> (b) such time in respect of each class of work allowed by him (other than advising over the telephone and dealing with routine telephone calls) as he considers reasonable.

(2A) The determining officer shall not allow any charges or fees for advice or assistance given by a representative of an own solicitor to whom any own solicitor representatives scheme applies unless he was registered under and met the other requirements of the scheme when the advice or assistance was given.

(3) Subject to paragraph (5), the determining officer shall allow fees for the work allowed by him under this regulation in accordance with the Schedule.

(4) Subject to paragraphs (2A) and (5), the determining officer may allow a reasonable sum in respect of:

> (a) hotel expenses actually and reasonably incurred by a duty solicitor where attendance in accordance with a rota is allowed under paragraph (1)(a);
>
> (b) travelling expenses actually and reasonably incurred by a duty solicitor or an own solicitor where travelling and waiting is allowed under paragraph (1)(c);
>
> (c) any disbursement actually and reasonably incurred by a duty solicitor or an own solicitor.

596

(5) Subject to paragraphs (6) and (7) the fees allowed under the Schedule, except any fee allowed in respect of work done under paragraph (1)(a), together with any expenses allowed under paragraph (4)(b) and (c), shall not exceed the limit prescribed by regulation 4(1)(a) of the Legal Advice and Assistance Regulations 1989.

(6) Paragraph (5) shall not apply to fees for advice or assistance which the determining officer is satisfied was required in the interests of justice be given as a matter of urgency.

(7) Paragraph (5) shall not apply where a franchisee certifies that advice and assistance was required in the interests of justice to be given as a matter of urgency.

Amended by the Legal Advice and Assistance at Police Stations (Remuneration) (Amendment) Regulations 1994 (S.I. 1994 No. 1824) and the Legal Advice and Assistance at Police Stations (Remuneration) (Amendment) (No. 2) Regulations 1994 (S.I. 1994 No. 3303).

Payment of remuneration

6.—(1) The determining officer shall authorise payment to the duty solicitor or an own solicitor in the amounts determined (whether by him or on review or appeal) in accordance with these Regulations.

(2) Where the costs payable under paragraph (1) are varied as a result of any review or appeal in accordance with these Regulations, then—

(a) where the costs are increased, the determining officer shall authorise payment of the increase;

(b) where the costs are decreased the solicitor shall repay the amount of such decrease.

Review of determination

7.—(1) If a solicitor is dissatisfied with the determination of a determining officer under these Regulations, the solicitor may within 21 days of receipt of notification of the costs payable under regulation 6(1) apply to the appropriate area committee to review that determination.

(2) On an application under paragraph (1), the appropriate area committee shall review the determination of the determining officer whether by confirming, increasing or decreasing the amount of his determination.

Appeal to committee appointed by the Board

8.—(1) A solicitor who is dissatisfied with the decision of an area committee on a review under regulation 7 may within 21 days of receipt of notification of the decision apply to that committee to certify a point of principle of general importance.

(2) Where an area committee certifies a point of principle of general importance, the solicitor may within 21 days of receipt of notification of that certification appeal in writing against the decision of the area committee to a committee appointed by the Board.

(3) On an appeal under this regulation the committee appointed by the Board may reverse, affirm or amend the decision of the area committee.

SCHEDULE

Regulation 5

1.—(1) The Board shall, subject to paragraphs 2 and 3 allow fees for work allowed by it under regulation 5 at the following rates:

Class of work	*Rate*	
(a) availability during duty period	£3.65 per hour— served, to a maximum of £87.60	(£3.75 per hour served to a maximum of *£90.00* in respect of a solicitor whose office is situated within legal aid area 1)
(b) advice and assistance to a person arrested and held in custody, or being interviewed in connection with a serious service offence or to a volunteer, given		
(i) by a duty solicitor in unsocial hours	£60.00 per hour	
(ii) by a duty solicitor in all other hours	£45.50 per hour—	(£48.50 per hour in respect of a solicitor whose office is situated within legal aid area 1)
(iii) by an own solicitor	£45.50 per hour—	(£48.50 per hour in respect of a solicitor whose office is situated within legal aid area 1)
(c) travelling and waiting		
(i) by a duty solicitor in unsocial hours	£60.00 per hour	
(ii) by a duty solicitor in all other hours	£45.50 per hour—	(£48.50 per hour in respect of a solicitor whose office is situated within legal aid area 1)
(iii) by an own solicitor	£25.25 per hour	
(d) advising and assisting over the telephone	£20.75 per item—	(£21.50 per item in respect of a solicitor whose office is situated within legal aid area 1)
(e) routine telephone calls	£3.50 per item—	(£3.60 per item in respect of a solicitor whose office is situated within legal aid area 1)

(2) In paragraphs 1(1) and 3, "legal aid area 1" means the area so numbered by the Board under regulation 4(1) of the Civil Legal Aid (General) Regulations 1989.

2. The fee allowed under paragraph 1(1)(a) shall be reduced by the amount of any other fees allowed under that paragraph for work done as a duty solicitor during that duty period to a maximum of one half of the fee allowed under paragraph 1(1)(a).

3. In the case of a franchisee, the Board shall allow fees for work allowed by it under regulation 5 at the following rates:

Class of work	*Rate*
(a) availability during duty period	£3.80 per hour served, to a maximum of £91.20	—(£3.85 per hour served to a maximum of £92.40 in respect of a solicitor whose office is situated within legal aid area 1)
(b) advice and assistance to a person arrested and held in custody, or being interviewed in connection with a serious service offence or to a volunteer, given	
(i) by a duty solicitor in unsocial hours	£61.75 per hour
(ii) by a duty solicitor in all other hours	£46.50 per hour—(£50.25 per hour in respect of a solicitor whose office is situated within legal aid area 1)
(iii) by an own solicitor	£46.50 per hour—(£50.25 per hour in respect of a solicitor whose office is situated within legal aid area 1)
(c) travelling and waiting	
(i) by a duty solicitor in unsocial hours	£61.75 per hour
(ii) by a duty solicitor in all other hours	£46.50 per hour—(£50.25 per hour in respect of a solicitor whose office is situated within legal aid area 1)
(iii) by an own solicitor	£25.75 per hour
(d) advising and assisting over the telephone	£21.25 per item—(£22.00 per item in respect of a solicitor whose office is situated within legal aid area 1)
(e) routine telephone calls	£3.60 per item—(£3.75 per item in respect of a solicitor whose office is situated within legal aid area 1)

Substituted by the Legal Advice and Assistance at Police Stations (Remuneration) (Amendment) Regulations 1996 (S.I. 1996 No. 648) and amended by the Legal Advice and Assistance at Police Stations (Remuneration) (Amendment) (No. 2) Regulations 1996 (S.I. 1986 No. 1554).

EXPLANATORY NOTE

(This note is not part of the Regulations)

These Regulations replace with amendments the Legal Advice and Assistance at Police Stations (Remuneration) Regulations 1988 (which are revoked except in relation to work done before April 1, 1989).

The Regulations provide for determination and review by the Legal Aid Board of the remuneration of solicitors (including duty solicitors acting in accordance with arrangements made under regulation 6 of the Legal Advice and Assistance Regulations 1989) who give advice and assistance to suspects at police stations, and prescribe rates of payment for that remuneration. The main changes are:—

(a) to reflect the taking over of responsibility for administration of legal aid by the Legal Aid Board;

(b) to remove the lower limit on fees hitherto applied to certain work (regulation 5(1));

(c) to increase the rates previously payable under the 1988 Regulations by six per cent. overall (Schedule).

Legal Aid Board Duty Solicitor Arrangements 1997*

* As amended by the Duty Solicitor (Amendment) Arrangements 1998 with effect from May 1, 1998.

The following arrangements have been approved by the Board and came into effect on June 1, 1997.

PART I—GENERAL

Transitional Arrangements

1. A committee member appointed or reappointed under the Duty Solicitor Arrange-

ments 1994 or any previous Arrangements or Scheme shall be deemed to have been appointed or reappointed under these Arrangements for the remainder of the period for which he or she was so appointed or reappointed and any decision validly made under the Duty Solicitor Arrangements 1994 or any previous Arrangements or Scheme shall be deemed to continue to have been validly made.

Interpretation

2. In these Arrangements, unless the context otherwise requires:

"the 1988 Act" means the Legal Aid Act 1988;

"advice" means "advice and assistance" under Part III of the 1988 Act;

"appropriate area committee" means the area committee in the area of which are situated the magistrates' courts at which advice and representation is provided or police stations at which advice is provided;

"appropriate regional committee" means the regional duty solicitor committee in the region of which are situated the magistrates' courts at which advice and representation is provided and police stations at which advice is provided;

"appropriate local committee" means the local duty solicitor committee appointed by the appropriate regional committee for the purpose of making arrangements whereby advice and representation is provided by duty solicitors at one or more specified magistrates' courts and advice is provided by duty solicitors to persons at police stations;

"appropriate local law society" means the society or societies of the district or districts in which are situated the magistrates' courts at which it is proposed to provide advice and representation or police stations at which it is proposed to provide advice;

"area committee" means the area committee appointed by the Board in respect of each legal aid area;

"Board" means the Legal Aid Board appointed under the 1988 Act;

"clerk of the court" means a justices' clerk or a member of the staff of a justices' clerk acting as a clerk in a magistrates' court;

"duty solicitor" means a solicitor who in accordance with arrangements made by the appropriate local committee is in attendance at a magistrates' court for the purpose of providing advice and representation or giving advice at a police station or both and, in each case, has been selected in accordance with these Arrangements;

"Duty Solicitor Committee" means the committee appointed by the Legal Aid Board;

"duty solicitor's representative" means any person selected in accordance with paragraph 45;

"lay member" means a person neither practising as a barrister or solicitor nor coming within any of the categories specified in paragraphs 7(2), (3), (5), (7), (9) and (10) or 18(3), (4), (6) and (7).

"local committee" means the committee appointed by the appropriate regional committee for the purpose of making arrangements whereby advice and representation is provided by duty solicitors at one or more magistrates' courts and advice is provided at police stations;

"local law society" means a society or group of societies which is for the time being recognised as a local law society by the Law Society and, in London, includes the London Criminal Courts Solicitors' Association;

"panel" and "panel cases" means an arrangement whereby the telephone service telephones the duty solicitors in the order in which they appear on the panel until finding one willing to give advice and assistance at a police station. The telephone service will then start with the next duty solicitor on the panel in respect of the next suspect requiring advice and assistance at a police station. The panel arrangement will also apply where the telephone service is unable to refer to a solicitor on a rota;

"police station" means a police station, or any other place where a constable is present or, except where expressly excluded by these Arrangements, any place where Services personnel are assisting with an investigation under paragraph 56;

"region" means one of the regions referred to in paragraph 3;

"regional committee" means the committee appointed by the Duty Solicitor Committee for each region for the purpose of making arrangements whereby duty solicitors shall be in attendance at magistrates' courts and police stations within that region;

"regulations" means the Legal Advice and Assistance Regulations 1989, the Legal Advice and Assistance (Scope) Regulations 1989; the Legal Advice and Assistance (Duty Solicitor) (Remuneration) Regulations 1989 and the Legal Advice and Assistance at Police Stations (Remuneration) Regulations 1989 and all subsequent amendments to such regulations;

"representation" means "assistance by way of representation" under Part III of the 1988 Act;

"rota" means a rota of duty solicitors to give advice and representation at magistrates' courts and advice at police stations;

"Services Discipline Acts" means the Army Act 1955, the Air Force Act 1955 and the Navy Discipline Act 1957;

"Services police" means members of the Royal Naval Special Investigations Branch, members of the Corps of Royal Military Police or Women's Royal Army Corps Provost, Royal Air Force Provost Officers or members of the Royal Air Force Police;

"Services person" means a person assisting with an investigation by the Services police;

"suspect" means a person who for the purposes of assisting with an investigation attends voluntarily at a police station or at any other place where a constable is present or who accompanies a constable to a police station or any such other place without having been arrested or who has been arrested and is being held in custody in a police station or other premises or a Services person assisting with an investigation by Services police under paragraph 56;

"telephone service" means the telephone service established by the Duty Solicitor Committee to receive initial requests for advice from suspects at police stations.

Regions

3. For the purposes of these Arrangements, England and Wales shall be divided into the regions which are set out in Schedule I.

PART II—THE DUTY SOLICITOR COMMITTEE

Appointment of Duty Solicitor Committee

4. The Duty Solicitor Committee is appointed by the Board and shall perform its duties and exercise its powers in accordance with any guidance and directions issued by the Board.

Powers and duties

5. (1) The Duty Solicitor Committee shall:

(a) undertake reviews and appeals from regional committees under paragraph 16 and appeals from a local committee under paragraph 29. The Duty Solicitor Committee shall give the appellant reasons for its decision in connection with a review or an appeal;

(b) give such directions and guidance to regional and local committees as it considers necessary;

(c) maintain records and call for such reports from the regional and local committees as are necessary for the Committee to fulfil its responsibilities properly; and

(d) make reports and recommendations to the Board in respect of the provisions and operations of these Arrangements.

(2) The Duty Solicitor Committee may:

(a) modify any provision in these Arrangements in connection with the provision of advice and representation at particular courts or advice at particular police stations;

(b) remove from office for due cause any member of a regional committee or local committee.

(3) (a) Whether or not arrangements have been approved under paragraph 14(2) or any such arrangements are still operating, the Duty Solicitor Committee may, if it thinks fit, recommend to the Board that it enter into a contract or contracts for the provision of advice under Part II of the 1988 Act at specified police stations, and the procedure for so doing.

(b) If the Board approves such recommendation the Duty Solicitor Committee shall, at the appropriate time,

(i) where arrangements have been approved under paragraph 14(2), give notice to the appropriate regional committee that from a specified date the approval under paragraph 14(2) for arrangements at specified police stations shall be of no effect; and

(ii) in all cases direct the appropriate regional committee not to approve arrangements for specified police stations without the prior approval of the Duty Solicitor Committee.

(4) (a) Whether or not arrangements have been approved under paragraph 13(1) or any such arrangements are still operating, the Duty Solicitor Committee may, if it thinks fit, recommend to the Board that it enter into a contract or contracts for the provision of advice and representation under Part II of the 1988 Act at specified magistrates' courts and the procedure for so doing.

(b) If the Board approves such recommendation, the Duty Solicitor Committee shall, at the appropriate time,

(i) where arrangements have been approved under paragraph 13(1) give notice to the appropriate regional committee that from a specified date the approval under paragraph 13(1) for arrangements at specified magistrates' courts shall be of no effect; and

(ii) in all cases direct the appropriate regional committee not to approve arrangements for specified magistrates' courts without the prior approval of the Duty Solicitor Committee.

PART III—REGIONAL DUTY SOLICITOR COMMITTEES

Appointment of Regional Committee Members and size of membership

6. The members of a regional committee shall be such as the regional committee shall from time to time appoint but shall not be fewer than 10 nor more than 35.

Categories of membership

7. The members of each regional committee shall be the following:—

(1) at least one member of each local committee in the region following the appointment of a committee or committees under paragraphs 13(1)(c) and 14(1), one or more of such member or members to be a duty solicitor with considerable current experience of advocacy in criminal cases in magistrates' courts to be nominated by the appropriate local committee;

(2) one or more Justices of the Peace, nominated by the Magistrates' Association;

(3) one or more Justices' Clerks, nominated by the Justices' Clerks' Society;

(4) two lay members. Members of court staff are ineligible for appointment under this sub-paragraph;

(5) one or more representatives of the police force or forces in the region nominated by the chief officer(s) of police;

and may include:

(6) one member of the appropriate area committee, such member to be a solicitor advocate experienced in criminal law and nominated by the appropriate area committee;

(7) one or more representatives of the probation service or services in the region nominated by that service or those services;

(8) one or more lay members. Members of court staff are eligible for appointment under this sub-paragraph;

(9) one or more representatives of the Crown Prosecution Service nominated by that Service;

(10) a stipendiary magistrate.

Appointment of regional committee lay members

8. Applicants for membership of the regional committee within the categories set out in paragraphs 7(4) and 7(8) shall, prior to appointment, be interviewed by the chairman or vice-chairman and a majority of members of the regional committee appointed under paragraphs 7(4) and 7(8) in order to ascertain the extent of the applicants' understanding of the role of regional committee lay members and the applicants' suitability for membership of the regional committee.

Majority of members

9. The majority of members of a regional committee shall be solicitors appointed under paragraphs 7(1), (6), and (9).

Adjudication on appeals and exclusions

10. (1) A decision by a regional committee upon an appeal under paragraphs 15(7) or 47(1) or a decision to exclude or suspend under paragraphs 15(5) or 15(14) can only be made by the solicitor members appointed under paragraphs 7(1) and 7(6) and the lay members save that the other members of the regional committee may participate in the deliberations of the regional committee prior to the decision being made.

(2) A member of the local committee which has made the decision from which the appeal is being made shall not participate in the hearing and determination of such appeal.

Period of service

11. (1) Every member of a regional committee shall be appointed for a period not exceeding three years and may be reappointed by the regional committee, sub-

ject to such consultation or nomination as is required by paragraph 7, for successive periods not exceeding three years until he or she has attained 70 years of age.

(2) The regional committee may, on an annual basis and in circumstances considered by the regional committee as exceptional, allow a member to continue past the age of 70 subject to a maximum of 75 years of age.

(3) A member shall be re-appointed only if he or she has attended at least half of all the meetings which were held during his or her membership unless the regional committee considers that there are special circumstances to permit re-appointment despite a lower level of attendance.

Vacancies

12. Any vacancy on a regional committee caused by the retirement or otherwise of members shall be filled by the regional committee in accordance with the provisions of this Part of these Arrangements.

Powers and duties—magistrates' courts

13. In accordance with the provisions of regulations 6 and 7 of the Legal Advice and Assistance Regulations 1989 and subject to any directions and guidance given to it by the Duty Solicitor Committee and in consultation with the appropriate local law society every regional committee shall:

(1) in consultation with the appropriate magistrates' courts:

    (a) decide in which magistrates' courts in the region it would be appropriate, in accordance with guidance laid down by the Duty Solicitor Committee, for duty solicitors to be in attendance whether or not any defendant wishes to consult a duty solicitor;

    (b) in relation to those magistrates' courts in the region which do not come within the provisions of paragraph 13(1)(a), make such arrangements as it thinks fit for the provision of advice and representation in accordance with guidance laid down by the Duty Solicitor Committee;

    (c) the regional committee shall establish and appoint the members of a local committee for the magistrates' courts coming within paragraph 13(1)(a) and (b) and shall supervise such committees; and

    (d) consider and, if satisfied, approve arrangements prepared by the appropriate local committee in accordance with guidance laid down by the Duty Solicitor Committee for the provision of advice and representation by duty solicitors at magistrates' courts.

(2) consider and, if satisfied, approve applications under paragraph 25(4).

(3) if it thinks fit, withdraw its approval of existing arrangements for the provision of advice and representation at magistrates' courts and substitute other arrangements where in its view the substituted arrangements will provide an adequate service to the public taking into account the cost of providing such a service.

Powers and duties—police stations

14. In accordance with the provisions of regulations 6 and 7 of the Legal Advice and Assistance Regulations 1989 and subject to any directions and guidance given to it by the Duty Solicitor Committee and in consultation with the appropriate local law society every regional duty solicitor committee:—

(1) shall consider what arrangements are required for the provision of advice by duty solicitors at police stations in the region, establish and appoint the members of local committees for the purpose of making such arrangements and shall supervise such committees. Such local committees may be either the committees appointed under paragraph 13(1)(c), or committees appointed solely for the purposes of this sub-paragraph;

(2) shall consider and, if satisfied, approve arrangements prepared by the appropriate local committees in accordance with guidance laid down by the Duty Solicitor Committee for the provision of advice by duty solicitors at police stations;

(3) may approve the use of duty solicitors' representatives in connection with the provision of advice at police stations covered by a particular local committee and may limit their use to particular periods of time;

(4) may approve:

   (a) a variation in the requirements in paragraph 33(2) that an applicant shall live or work within 45 minutes' travel time of the relevant police station;
   (b) a modification under paragraph 26(6);

(5) shall if it thinks fit, withdraw its approval of existing arrangements for the provision of advice at police stations and substitute other arrangements, where in its view the substituted arrangements will provide an adequate service to the public taking into account the cost of providing such a service.

Powers and duties—general

15. In accordance with the provisions of regulations 6 and 7 of the Legal Advice and Assistance Regulations 1989 and subject to any directions and guidance given it by the Duty Solicitor Committee in consultation, if appropriate, with the appropriate local law society every regional committee shall administer these Arrangements within its region and in particular, and without prejudice to the generality of the foregoing:—

(1) may if it thinks fit, consent to a proposal by a local committee submitted in accordance with paragraph 25(10), or direct a local committee, to require all solicitors at specified courts or police stations to provide advice at police stations as duty solicitors under paragraph 32(1)(g) or advice and representation at magistrates' courts as duty solicitors under paragraph 33(6) or both subject to the right of appeal against any such direction set out in paragraph 29;

(2) shall monitor the arrangements by local committees for advice and representation at magistrates' courts and advice at police stations;

(3) shall:

   (a) require a local committee to take any steps specified by the regional committee;
   (b) amalgamate two or more local committees if in the view of the regional committee an improved service would be provided to the public by so doing;

(4) shall if not satisfied with the arrangements made by the appropriate local committee for the provision of advice and representation at any magistrates' court or advice at any police station, give notice to the appropriate local committee requiring it to provide adequate arrangements within the period specified in the notice which shall not be less than three calendar months. If at the end of that period the appropriate regional committee is still not satisfied with the arrangements it may, with the consent of the Duty Solicitor Committee, disband the appropriate local committee forthwith and appoint a new committee in its place;

(5) (a) may if it thinks fit, suspend for a period of up to 12 months or exclude a duty solicitor from providing either advice and representation at magistrates' courts or advice at police stations or both in the event of failure to satisfy any of the criteria set out in Part V, failure to carry out his or her duties or for some other good cause provided that the solicitor has been notified of any complaint against him or her and that he or she may make written representations or give notice of his or her intention to make oral

representations within 21 days of the committee having notified him or her of the complaint;

(b) failure to accept a reasonable number of calls while on panel duty may be treated as sufficient reason to justify exclusion or suspension;

(c) if the committee decides to exclude or suspend the duty solicitor it shall provide him or her with a written statement of the reasons for its decision;

(d) when a solicitor is under investigation or has been charged with a criminal offence or is the subject of an investigation by the Solicitors Complaints Bureau, the chairman with the concurrence of two other members of the committee may suspend the solicitor for a period of up to six weeks without his or her having been notified of the complaint against him or her or having the opportunity to be heard. The period of suspension may be extended for good reason on one other occasion for a further period of six weeks by the chairman with the concurrence of two members of the committee;

(e) the effect of a decision to suspend or exclude shall be immediate, subject to the regional committee having a discretion to postpone the effect providing that the solicitor affected undertakes to submit a notice of an appeal under paragraph 16(2) within the period stipulated in that paragraph;

(6) may if it thinks fit, recommend to the Duty Solicitor Committee that any provision in these Arrangements be modified in connection with the provision of advice and representation at any specified magistrates' court or advice at specified police stations;

(7) shall determine appeals under paragraphs 28, 37, and 47, and in connection with such appeals:

(a) each appeal shall be by way of a rehearing;

(b) the appellant shall submit written representations when giving notice of appeal and shall send a copy of such representations to the appropriate local committee;

(c) the appropriate local committee may submit written representations about the appeal to the appropriate regional committee and if it does so shall send a copy of such representations to the appellant;

(d) the Board's staff may obtain and provide information relating to the appeal and they shall ensure that both the appellant and the local committee receive copies;

(e) the appellant shall have the right to make oral representations to the appropriate regional committee in support of the appeal and must do so where the appeal is under paragraph 37(3). If the oral representations or any written representations subsequently submitted cover matters not covered in the written representations referred to in paragraph 15(7)(b) the regional committee has a discretion not to consider such additional matters unless the appellant has given 14 days notice to the Board's staff and the local committee;

(f) the appellant shall be given written reasons for the appeal decision;

(g) where the regional committee is of the opinion that the local committee has not complied with the procedure laid down in paragraphs 35, 36, 38, 45(2) and 48 or with any directions and guidance given by the Duty Solicitor Committee under paragraph 5(1)(b) it may refer the matter back to the appropriate local committee for reconsideration;

(h) the regional committee may exclude the appellant from any other scheme or schemes in the relevant region on the basis of the regional committee's appeal findings and may report such exclusion to other regional committees;

609

(8) shall investigate complaints about the provisions of advice and representation at magistrates' courts and advice at police stations by duty solicitors;

(9) may report to the Duty Solicitor Committee any circumstances where duty solicitors have inadequate access to defendants in custody or suspects at police stations or inadequate facilities to enable them to carry out their functions;

(10) may if it thinks fit, approve local instructions to duty solicitors made by a local committee under paragraph 27(7)(a);

(11) shall supply to the Duty Solicitor Committee such reports, statistics, estimates and other information as the Duty Solicitor Committee may from time to time require;

(12) shall keep the police, courts and other relevant organisations in the region informed about the existence and responsibilities of the regional committee;

(13) may revoke any consent, direction or approval it has given under paragraphs 13(1)(d), 14(2), 14(3), 14(4), 14(5), 15(1), 15(10), 25(4), and 25(6);

(14) (a) may if it thinks fit, suspend for a period of up to 12 months or exclude a duty solicitor's representative from providing advice if satisfied that he or she has failed to satisfy any of the criteria set out in paragraph 45(1), or that there is some other good cause provided that the duty solicitor employing the representative has been notified of the complaint against the representative and that the appropriate duty solicitor may make written representations or give notice of his or her intention to make oral representations within 21 days of the committee having notified him or her of the complaint;

(b) if the committee decides to exclude or suspend the representative, it shall provide the appropriate duty solicitor with a written statement of the reasons for its decision;

(c) where a duty solicitor's representative is under investigation or has been charged with a criminal offence, the chairman with the concurrence of two other members of the committee may suspend a duty solicitor's representative for a period of up to six weeks without his or her having been notified of the complaint against him or her having the opportunity to be heard. The period of suspension may be extended for good reason on one occasion for a further period of six weeks by the chairman with the concurrence of two members of the committee;

(d) the effect of a decision to suspend or exclude shall be immediate subject to the committee having discretion to postpone the effect providing that the appropriate duty solicitor undertakes to submit a notice of an appeal under paragraph 16(2) within the period stipulated in that paragraph;

(15) may for good reason remove an administrator appointed by a local committee under paragraph 27(5) and request the local committee to appoint another administrator;

(16) may in exceptional circumstances waive the relevant paragraph where a local committee makes a recommendation under paragraph 32(1)(f)(vi) subject to the applicant appearing before the regional committee.

Applications for review and appeal by the Duty Solicitor Committee

16. (1) Where a solicitor or representative is dissatisfied with the determination of an appeal under paragraph 15(7) he or she may submit a written request for a review to the Duty Solicitor Committee;

(2) Where a duty solicitor or duty solicitor's representative is excluded or suspended under paragraphs 15(5), 15(7)(h) or 15(14) he or she may appeal to the Duty Solicitor Committee;

(3) The request for a review or notice of an appeal must be given within 28 days of having been notified of the decision of the appropriate regional committee subject to the Duty Solicitor Committee having discretion to accept a request outside the period of 28 days for good reason;

(4) A request for a review shall include a statement of reasons for which it is claimed that the regional committee's decision was unreasonable;

(5) The conduct of an appeal to the Duty Solicitor Committee shall be conducted so far as may be appropriate in the same way as an appeal to a regional committee under paragraph 15(7).

PART IV—LOCAL DUTY SOLICITOR COMMITTEES

Size of membership
17. The members of a local committee shall be such as the appropriate regional committee shall from time to time appoint but shall not be fewer than four or more than 15.

Categories of membership
18. The members of each local committee shall be the following:

(1) at least three solicitors with considerable current experience of advocacy in criminal cases in magistrates' courts of whom the majority shall be duty solicitors but excluding solicitors employed on a full-time basis by the Crown Prosecution Service;

(2) one lay member. Members of court staff are ineligible for appointment under this sub-paragraph;

and may also include:

(3) one or more Justices of the Peace or stipendiary magistrate;

(4) one or more Justices' Clerk or a person nominated by the Justices' Clerk for a court covered by the local committee;

(5) a solicitor with considerable current experience of advocacy in criminal cases in magistrates' courts employed on a full-time basis by the Crown Prosecution Service;

(6) one or more representatives of the Probation Service or Services nominated by that Service or those Services;

(7) one or more representatives of the police force or forces nominated by the chief officer(s) of police; and

(8) not more than two additional lay members. Members of court staff are eligible for appointment under this paragraph.

Solicitor and lay members
19. (1) Solicitor members appointed under paragraph 18(1) shall be appointed after consultation with the appropriate local law society.

(2) The appointment of lay members under paragraphs 18(2) and (8) shall, subject to details of the experience of the member being submitted on a form approved by the Duty Solicitor Committee, be made by the members of the regional committee identified in paragraph 8.

Majority of members and conduct of meetings
20. (1) The majority of members of a local committee shall be solicitors appointed under paragraph 18(1).

(2) A member of the relevant regional committee and/or a member of the Board's staff shall be entitled to attend local committee meetings and shall be given adequate notice of a meeting where notice is given of an intention to attend.

Adjudication on selection or exclusion

21. A decision by a local committee upon selection and reselection under paragraphs 35, 38, 45 or 48 or the exclusion or suspension under paragraphs 27(3) or 27(10) can only be made by the solicitor members appointed under paragraphs 18(1) or (5) and the lay members save that the other members of the local committee may participate in the deliberations of the local committee prior to the decision being made.

Period of service

22. (1) Every member of a local committee shall be appointed for a period not exceeding three years and may be reappointed by the appropriate regional committee, subject to such consultation as is required under paragraph 23(2), for successive periods not exceeding three years until he or she has attained 70 years of age.

(2) The regional committee may, in circumstances considered by the regional committee as exceptional, allow a member of a local committee to continue past the age of 70 subject to a maximum of 75 years of age. The decision to allow a member to continue past the age of 70 shall be made by the members of the regional committee identified in paragraph 8.

Vacancies

23. (1) Any vacancy on a local committee caused by retirement or otherwise may be filled by the appropriate regional committee;

(2) in the case of a solicitor appointed under paragraph 18(1) after consultation with the appropriate local law society.

Duties

24. (1) Each local committee shall help the Board to provide a quality service to the public.

(2) The appropriate local committee shall subject to any directions given to it by the appropriate regional committee, make arrangements for advice and representation to be provided by duty solicitors at the court or courts and advice at police stations in connection with which the committee is appointed under paragraphs 13(1)(c) or 14(1) respectively;

(3) Arrangements made under paragraph 24(2) are subject to approval by the appropriate regional committee and shall come into effect only when they have been approved under paragraph 13 or 14 as appropriate;

(4) Each local committee shall meet a minimum of once a year or:

(a) to consider an application from a solicitor who wishes to become a duty solicitor or an application in respect of a duty solicitor's representative or to undertake the reselection of a duty solicitor or duty solicitor's representative, or

(b) at the request of the chairman of the relevant regional committee, or

(c) if a member of the local committee submits a request in writing to the chairman of the local committee, or

(d) to consider an audit report about the performance of duty solicitors under the arrangements provided by the local committee.

Detailed arrangements—magistrates' courts

25. In connection with providing advice and representation under Part VII the appropriate local committee:

(1) shall ensure that arrangements exist to inform all defendants, who are eligible for advice or representation in accordance with the provisions of paragraph 50, of the availability of the duty solicitor;

(2) shall ensure that arrangements exist for a duty solicitor to be present at court, or available to the court, as the regional committee may specify so as to provide advice and representation as specified in paragraph 50 to defendants who are eligible to receive such advice and representation;

(3) shall ensure that arrangements exist for defendants who wish to receive advice and representation by a duty solicitor as specified in paragraph 50 to receive such advice and representation;

(4) shall apply to the appropriate regional committee for approval where it is proposed that more than one duty solicitor is regularly to be on duty at the same court at the same time;

(5) shall ensure where practicable that arrangements are made to provide advice and representation where sittings in addition to ordinary sittings of courts are involved;

(6) may, with the consent of the appropriate regional committee, specify the maximum number of courts before which a solicitor may appear as duty solicitor;

(7) may require all duty solicitors appointed by the local committee whilst acting as duty solicitor, not to undertake any cases in connection with which he or she has previously received instructions;

(8) may make appropriate arrangements for duty solicitors to be assisted by representatives of voluntary organisations to make initial contact with defendants and provide advice to defendants and their families;

(9) shall use its best endeavours to ensure compliance with Part VII;

(10) may, with the consent of the appropriate regional committee, require all solicitors at specified courts or police stations to provide advice at police stations as duty solicitors under paragraph 32(1)(g) or advice and representation at magistrates' courts as duty solicitors under paragraph 33(6) or both.

Detailed arrangements—police stations

26. In connection with the provision of advice at police stations the appropriate local committee either by itself or in conjunction with other local committees:

(1) shall ensure that arrangements exist for suspects to receive advice at police stations in accordance with paragraphs 53–56;

(2) shall, with the approval of the appropriate regional committee under paragraph 14(2), ensure that arrangements exist for duty solicitors to be available at all times of the day and night to give advice at police stations by means of a rota or a panel arrangement or by a combination of both;

(3) may require a duty solicitor to be available to go to a police station with the least possible delay;

(4) may, with the consent of the appropriate regional committee, permit the provision by duty solicitors' representatives of advice at police stations;

(5) may, where the appropriate regional committee consents to the use of duty solicitors' representatives, decide to select only solicitors as duty solicitors' representatives;

(6) may, with the consent of the regional committee, modify the requirement of home or office in paragraph 33(2) to office only.

Detailed arrangements—general

27. In connection with the provision of advice and representation at magistrates' courts and advice at police stations the appropriate local committee:

(1) shall satisfy itself that duty solicitors are not improperly or unnecessarily prevented from providing advice and representation to defendants and advice to suspects and, if the committee is not so satisfied, it shall report the matter to the appropriate regional committee;

(2) shall be responsible for the selection of duty solicitors in accordance with the procedure specified in Part V;

(3) (a) may suspend for a period of up to 12 months or exclude a duty solicitor from providing advice and representation at magistrates' courts or advice at police stations or both if satisfied that he or she has failed to carry out his or her duties or to meet any of the criteria set out in Part V, or is in breach of any local instructions to duty solicitors made under paragraph 27(7)(a), or that there is some other good cause provided that the solicitor has been notified of the complaint against him or her and that he or she may make written representations or give notice of his or her intention to make oral representations within 21 days of the committee having notified him or her of the complaint;

(b) failure to accept a reasonable number of calls while on panel duty may be treated as sufficient reason to justify exclusion or suspension;

(c) if the committee decides to exclude or suspend the duty solicitor it shall provide him or her with a written statement of the reasons for its decision;

(d) when a solicitor is under investigation for or has been charged with a criminal offence or is the subject of an investigation by the Solicitors Complaints Bureau, the chairman with the concurrence of two other members of the local committee may suspend a duty solicitor for a period of up to six weeks without him or her having been notified of the complaint against him or her or having the opportunity to be heard. The period of suspension may be extended for good reason on one occasion for a further period of six weeks by the chairman with the concurrence of two members of the local committee;

(e) the effect of a determination to suspend or exclude shall be immediate, subject to the local committee having discretion to postpone the effect, providing that the duty solicitor affected undertakes to submit notice of an appeal within the period stipulated in paragraph 28. An exclusion should be notified by the local committee to the relevant regional committee;

(4) shall, where a rota is required, by itself or in conjunction with other local committees, arrange rotas for duty solicitors for periods not exceeding six months such rotas save as mentioned in (a) below to be drawn up on the basis of individual duty solicitors and to include all duty solicitors who are members of that scheme.

(a) Where as at June 30, 1996 rotas based on firms were in existence such rotas may continue provided that:
(i) proper arrangements exist for new duty solicitors to be admitted to the scheme;
(ii) there is an adequate number of firms available to undertake criminal legal aid work in connection with the scheme;
(iii) the scheme continues to achieve the relevant performance targets laid down by the Duty Solicitor Committee; and
(iv) the scheme is in the public interest.
(b) Should any such scheme fail to meet any of these conditions the Duty Solicitor Committee or regional committee may direct the local committee to arrange rotas based on individual duty solicitors.

   (c) Where a rota is based on firms and the local committee receives a request supported by at least 10 per cent of the duty solicitors who are members of the scheme to consider a change to a rota based on individuals the local committee shall:

      (i) invite all solicitors who are members of the scheme to a meeting to consider the proposed changes;

      (ii) within 14 days of such meeting conduct a postal ballot of all duty solicitors who are members of the scheme as to whether they wish to change to a rota based on individuals;

      (iii) if 90 per cent or more of votes received are in favour of retaining a rota based on firms continue to prepare rotas based on firms subject to the conditions set out in (a);

      (iv) if less than 90 per cent of the votes received are in favour of retaining a rota based on firms prepare rotas based on individuals to take effect within no more than four months from the conclusion of the ballot.

   (d) if the rota is to continue to be based on firms following a ballot, no further change to a rota based on individuals can be considered for a period of 12 months from the conclusion of the ballot. The regional committee may consent to a shorter period than 12 months.

Copies of the rota must be sent as appropriate to the court, the telephone service, each solicitor on the rota, to the appropriate office of the Board and such other organisations as the local committee may determine no less than four weeks before the expiration of the previous rota.

(5) may appoint one or more administrators to prepare and issue the rota or rotas of duty solicitors, to receive applications from solicitors who wish to become duty solicitors, to convene meetings of the committee and generally to deal with the day to day matters including liaison with the courts and police, where it wishes these functions to be undertaken by an administrator rather than by the relevant legal aid office;

(6) may apply to the appropriate regional committee to exercise its power of recommendation under paragraph 15(6) where the committee considers that modification of these Arrangements is required;

(7) with the approval of the appropriate regional committee:

   (a) shall prepare local instructions to duty solicitors relating to the procedure to be adopted by duty solicitors to comply with Parts VII and VIII; and

   (b) may issue notes for guidance and publicity;

(8) shall, if so required, submit an annual report to the appropriate regional committee about the operation of the arrangements in the courts or police stations for which it is responsible;

(9) shall supply to the appropriate regional committee or the appropriate office of the Board such reports, statistics, estimates, local instructions to duty solicitors and other information as that committee may from time to time require;

(10) (a) may suspend for a period of up to 12 months or exclude a duty solicitor's representative from providing advice if satisfied that he or she has failed to satisfy any of the criteria set out in paragraph 45(1) or that there is some other good cause provided that the appropriate duty solicitor has been notified of the complaint against him or her and that the appropriate duty solicitor may make written representations or give notice of his or her intention to make oral representations within 21 days of the committee having notified him or her of the complaint;

   (b) if the committee decides to exclude or suspend the representative it shall provide the appropriate duty solicitor with a written statement of the reasons for its decision;

(c) where a duty solicitor's representative is under investigation for or has been charged with a criminal offence, the chairman with the concurrence of two other members of the local committee may suspend a duty solicitor's representative for a period of up to six weeks without him or her having been notified of the complaint against him or her or having the opportunity to be heard. The period of suspension may be extended for good reason on one occasion for a further period of six weeks by the chairman with the concurrence of two members of the local committee;

(d) the effect of a determination to suspend or exclude shall be immediate, subject to the local committee having a discretion to postpone the effect providing that the appropriate duty solicitor undertakes to submit notice of an appeal within the period stipulated by paragraph 28;

(11) Where a duty solicitor or a duty solicitor's representative has been excluded an application under paragraphs 31 and 44 may not be made to a local committee to which the exclusion relates for a period of 12 months from the date of the decision to exclude or any appeal or review relating thereto. If after 12 months an application is made to a local committee to which the exclusion relates and that local committee refuses to remove the exclusion the local committee shall not entertain a further application if made within 12 months of the refusal to remove the exclusion;

(12) shall comply with any revocation by the appropriate regional committee under paragraph 15(13) subject to an appeal to the Duty Solicitor Committee under paragraph 29.

Appeals to Regional Committee

28. (1) Where a duty solicitor has been excluded or suspended from providing advice and representation at magistrates' courts or advice at police stations or both under paragraph 27(3) or not reselected under paragraph 38 he or she may appeal to the appropriate regional committee within 28 days of the decision being notified to him or her subject to that committee having discretion to accept an appeal outside the period of 28 days for good reason;

(2) Where a duty solicitor's representative has been excluded or suspended from providing advice under paragraph 27(10) or not reselected under paragraph 48, the appropriate duty solicitor may appeal in writing to the appropriate regional committee within 28 days of the decision being notified to him or her subject to that committee having discretion to accept an appeal outside the period of 28 days for good reason;

(3) Where a local committee refuses to remove an exclusion under paragraph 27(11) the duty solicitor or the appropriate duty solicitor for a duty solicitor's representative may appeal to the regional committee.

Appeals to Duty Solicitor Committee

29. Where a local committee objects to being required by the appropriate regional committee to exclude solicitors from providing advice and representation at magistrates' courts or advice at police stations under paragraph 15(1), or to a revocation by the appropriate regional committee under paragraph 15(13), the local committee may appeal in writing to the Duty Solicitor Committee within 28 days of the decision being notified to it, subject to the Duty Solicitor Committee having the power to accept an appeal outside the period of 28 days for good reason.

Payment of administrators

30. The administrators appointed under paragraph 27(5) above may be paid for any reasonable expenses actually incurred by them.

PART V—SELECTION OF DUTY SOLICITORS

Application

31. Only a current application form in a form approved by the Duty Solicitor Com-

mittee and obtained from the Board and submitted by the prospective duty solicitor to the Board shall be considered by the appropriate local committee.

Selection criteria—magistrates' courts

32. (1) The criteria for the selection of a duty solicitor to provide advice and representation at a magistrates' court shall be as follows:

(a) the applicant's office shall, in connection with a magistrates' court at which a duty solicitor is required to be in attendance under paragraph 13(1)(a), be within the area of that court or, if it is outside the area of the court, be reasonably accessible to the court for the convenience of any defendant who wishes to instruct the duty solicitor to continue to act for him or her;*

(b) the applicant shall, in connection with a magistrates' court at which a duty solicitor is required to be in attendance under paragraph 13(1)(a), normally be in attendance at the office referred to in paragraph 32(1)(a) and that office shall be open during the majority of normal business hours;

(c) the applicant's office shall, in connection with a magistrates' court or courts not falling within paragraph 13(1)(a), be reasonably accessible to the court or courts taking into account relevant local considerations;

(d) the applicant shall hold a current practising certificate which may (in the discretion of the local committee) be conditional;

(e) the applicant shall be willing to act personally as duty solicitor and to undertake the majority of rota duties allocated to him or her;

(f) (i) the applicant, who must not be a special constable, shall regularly practise in criminal defence work;

(ii) the applicant shall have comprehensive experience of criminal defence work including advocacy in Crown or magistrates' courts throughout the previous 12 months, except in the circumstances in sub-paragraph (iii) below;

(iii) if the applicant has been in recent full-time employment as a prosecuting solicitor or in another similar position for a period of 18 months he or she must have had comprehensive experience of criminal defence work throughout the six months immediately prior to the application;

(iv) the experience of criminal defence work referred to in sub-paragraphs (ii) and (iii) above need not have been gained in the magistrates' court or courts in connection with which the local committee is appointed;

(v) any interval of up to 12 months, during or at the end of the periods of experience required by sub-paragraphs (ii) and (iii) above, when the applicant was absent from work because of sickness, injury, pregnancy or confinement or for other good reason may be disregarded;

(vi) if the applicant does not comply with paragraphs 32(1)(f)(i)–(v) but the local committee considers that the applicant would make a competent duty solicitor the local committee may recommend to the regional committee in exceptional circumstances that the latter exercises its power under paragraph 15(16) to waive the relevant paragraph;

(g) subject to the approval or direction of the appropriate regional committee under paragraph 15(1), the applicant shall provide advice at police stations for which the local committee is responsible as a duty solicitor and, where that paragraph is in effect, the local committee shall exclude a solicitor from providing advice and representation at magistrates' courts as

---

* Alternative arrangements apply in London details of which are available from the Legal Aid Board.

duty solicitor if he or she does not provide advice at police stations for which the local committee is responsible as duty solicitor;

(h) the applicant shall be prepared, if selected as a duty solicitor, to carry out his or her duties so as not to discriminate on grounds of race, gender, sexual orientation, religion, age or disability;

(i) any other criteria as approved by the appropriate regional committee and the Duty Solicitor Committee.

(2) In assessing an application the local committee shall be satisfied that the solicitor is competent to provide advice and representation having regard to the nature, frequency and quality of the solicitor's advocacy including:

(a) an ability to provide advice and representation to a number of defendants in a limited time without the opportunity to prepare the cases before arriving at court;

(b) an adequate knowledge of the procedure in magistrates' courts; and

(c) an adequate knowledge of the law relating to the more common offences coming before the court.

(3) The applicant shall have attended an advocacy training course appropriate to advice and representation at magistrates' courts by a duty solicitor, unless he or she has substantial experience of defence advocacy.

(4) Where the applicant:

(a) has been charged with or convicted of a criminal offence since admission, or

(b) has been the subject of any adverse findings by the Adjudication Committee of the Solicitors Complaints Bureau or by the Solicitors Disciplinary Tribunal, or there are any hearings pending in either forum, or

(c) for other good reason

the committee considering the application has a discretion to reject the application, if it considers that to do so would be in the interests of suspects or defendants provided that it provides the applicant with written reasons for its decision;

(5) The applicant shall possess or have ready access to relevant up to date legal reference material.

Selection criteria—police stations

33. The criteria for the selection of a duty solicitor to provide advice at a police station shall be as follows:

(1) the criteria set out in paragraphs 32(1)(d) to (i) and 32(2), (3), (4) and (5);

(2) the applicant's home or office shall be within 45 minutes travel time of the relevant police station,* and the applicant shall be prepared to make arrangements to be reasonably accessible to the relevant police station when on rota duty, except where adherence to these requirements would make it impracticable for a police station to be covered; in which case the relevant regional committee may agree for the requirement of 45 minutes travel time to be varied under paragraph 14(4). The applicant may, in the discretion of the committee, be required to satisfy the committee that he or she will be in a position to accept panel cases referred by the telephone service;

(3) the applicant shall have attended a course on advice at the police station unless he or she has substantial experience of that area of work;

(4) adequate experience of providing advice to persons arrested and held in custody at police stations;

* Alternative arrangements apply in London details of which are available from the Legal Aid Board.

(5) the applicant shall agree not to provide any money or other gifts to a suspect except items of refreshment and smoking materials for immediate consumption by the suspect.

(6) subject to the approval or direction of the appropriate regional committee under paragraph 15(1), the applicant shall provide advice and representation at magistrates' courts for which the local committee is responsible as a duty solicitor and, where that paragraph is in effect, the local committee shall exclude a solicitor from providing advice at police stations as duty solicitor if he or she does not provide advice and representation at magistrates' courts for which the local committee is responsible as a duty solicitor.

Interview

34. (1) The appropriate local committee shall interview all applicants. Interviews may be conducted by a sub-committee of the local committee. Where the applicant has been approved by another local committee the appropriate local committee is under no duty to interview him or her but may in its discretion do so. An applicant cannot be rejected by the appropriate local committee without an interview;

(2) Any local committee, or sub-committee when interviewing must include a lay member appointed under paragraph 18(2) or (8) provided that any member appointed under paragraph 18(8) is, in this case, not a member of court staff. If no such member can attend, one who is entitled to attend must agree to the interview being conducted in his or her absence;

(3) A member of the relevant regional committee from another part of the region may be included on any local committee or sub-committee when interviewing and selecting applicants;

(4) The composition of the local committee or sub-committee when interviewing applicants is otherwise subject to paragraph 21.

Approval of applications

35. If the applicant meets the criteria set out in paragraph 32 or 33 (whichever is appropriate) the appropriate local committee shall, within 60 days of the submission of the application, approve the application and give notice of such approval to the applicant.

Rejection of applications

36. If the committee decides not to allow the application it shall provide the applicant with a statement of the reasons for its decision, showing which of the criteria in paragraph 32 or 33 he or she does not meet and an explanation of why they have not been met.

Appeals to regional committee

37. (1) Where an application has been rejected under paragraph 36 the applicant may appeal to the appropriate regional committee within 28 days of the decision being notified to him or her subject to the appropriate regional committee having discretion to accept an appeal outside the period of 28 days for good reason;

(2) Where an appeal is referred back to the appropriate local committee under paragraph 15(7)(g), the local committee must approve or reject the application within 60 days;

(3) If the appropriate local committee has not approved an application within a period of 60 days from the date of its submission or from when it was referred back to it under paragraph 15(7)(g) the application shall be deemed to have been rejected (unless the applicant agrees otherwise) and the applicant may within 28 days of the expiration of such period appeal to the appropriate

regional committee subject to that committee having discretion to accept an appeal outside the period of 28 days for good reason.

Reselection

38. (1) A duty solicitor shall be subject to reselection by the appropriate local committee at least every five years;

(2) The duty solicitor shall, when subject to reselection, complete a current form approved by the Duty Solicitor Committee and obtained from the Board and shall return it to the Board within the time scale specified thereon failing which the duty solicitor will be deemed not to be seeking reselection,

(3) If the committee is satisfied that the duty solicitor meets the criteria set out in paragraph 39(1) and/or (2) (whichever is appropriate) and paragraph 40, it shall reselect him or her and give him or her notice of such reselection. If it is not satisfied that he or she meets such criteria, the committee shall give him or her a statement of any representations received under paragraph 41 and shall invite him or her to an interview. Acceptance of the invitation to an interview must be submitted within 21 days of the committee having invited the duty solicitor to the interview. If having interviewed the duty solicitor the committee decides not to reselect the duty solicitor it shall provide him or her with a statement of the reasons for its decision;

(4) Reselection shall take place, in respect of all duty solicitors admitted during a particular year, to take effect on December 31 of the fifth following year.

Reselection criteria—magistrates' courts and police stations

39. (1) The criteria for the reselection of duty solicitors providing advice and representation at magistrates' courts shall be:

(a) continued ability to satisfy the criteria in paragraph 32;
(b) regularity of personal attendance at court as duty solicitor; and
(c) compliance with these Arrangements and instructions to duty solicitors made under paragraph 27(7)(a);

(2) The criteria for the reselection of duty solicitors providing advice at police stations shall be:

(a) continued ability to satisfy the criteria in paragraph 33(1), (2), (4) and (5);
(b) the availability of the duty solicitor to receive telephone calls concerning requests for advice from suspects at police stations, and willingness to accept calls when a panel duty solicitor;
(c) the attendance of the duty solicitor at police stations in the circumstances set out in paragraph 54;
(d) the appropriate use of duty solicitors' representatives at police stations.

Reselection criteria—continuing training

40. Any duty solicitor wishing to be reselected whether providing advice and representation at a magistrates' court or advice at a police station or both must have undertaken a minimum of six hours tuition during the previous five years on a course or courses relevant to advice and representation at magistrates' courts or advice at police stations or both.

Representations about performance

41. The appropriate local committee shall, when considering reselection, take into account any representations received as to the performance of the duty solicitor or duty solicitor's representative, provided that where any such representations are received the duty solicitor, or appropriate duty solicitor where a representative is involved, shall be provided with a written statement of them and shall have an opportunity in any representations he or she may make under paragraphs 38 or 48 to respond.

620

Changes in circumstances—duty to report

42. A duty solicitor, or, in the case of a duty solicitor's representative, the appropriate duty solicitor, shall immediately notify the appropriate local committee in any of the following circumstances:

(a) if his or her practising address changes or if his or her home address changes if the home address was relevant for selection under paragraph 33(2);

(b) if he or she or a representative is unable to comply with the criteria set out in paragraphs 32, 33, 39, or 40 where duty solicitors are concerned, or 45 in the case of representatives;

(c) on resignation giving one month's notice;

(d) if he or she or a representative of him or her is incapable of carrying out his or her duties for more than 28 days;

(e) if he or she or a representative of him or her is charged with or convicted of a criminal offence;

(f) if (where appropriate) a hearing by the Adjudication Committee of the Solicitors Complaints Bureau or by the Solicitors Disciplinary Tribunal is pending in respect of him or her; or

(g) where the Adjudication Committee of the Solicitors Complaints Bureau or the Solicitors Disciplinary Tribunal has made an adverse finding in respect of him or her or a representative of him or her.

Changes in rota

43. A duty solicitor may arrange for another duty solicitor to take his or her place on a rota provided that:

(i) the telephone service is notified in connection with the provision of advice at police stations,

(ii) the court is notified in connection with the provision of advice and representation

and, in either case, if the local committee so request, the local administrator is notified of any such rota change.

PART VI—DUTY SOLICITORS' REPRESENTATIVES

Application

44. When the appropriate regional committee gives its consent to the use of duty solicitors' representatives under paragraph 14(3), only a current application form in a form approved by the Duty Solicitor Committee and obtained from the Board and submitted by the prospective duty solicitor representative to the Board shall be considered by the appropriate local committee.

Selection criteria

45. (1) When an application is received in respect of a duty solicitor's representative, the local committee must be satisfied that the person referred to in the application:

(a) is in the full or part-time employment of, or a partner in the same firm as the duty solicitor or duty solicitors who will deploy the applicant under paragraph 57 and does not represent any other solicitor or firm for the purposes of giving any advice at police stations;

(b) has had experience of providing advice at a police station, having gained such experience as the result of having worked in a solicitor's office;

(c) (i) if a solicitor, has had at least four months experience of criminal cases as a solicitor or trainee solicitor; or

(ii) if a solicitor's clerk, has had at least three years experience of criminal defence work; or

(iii) if a trainee solicitor, has had at least six months experience of which four months are of criminal cases;

(d) is competent to act as a duty solicitor's representative;

(e) has received appropriate training;

(f) possesses or has ready access to relevant up to date legal reference material;

(g) if a solicitor, holds a current practising certificate which may (in the discretion of the local committee) be conditional;

(h) where the proposed representative:

(i) has been charged with or convicted of a criminal offence (in the case of a solicitor, since admission), or

(ii) if a solicitor, has been the subject of any adverse findings by the Adjudication Committee of the Solicitors Complaints Bureau or by the Solicitors Disciplinary Tribunal, or there are any hearings pending in either forum; or

(iii) for other good reason

the committee considering the application has a discretion to reject the application if it considers that to do so would be in the interests of suspects provided that it provides the applicant with written reasons for its decision;

(i) is not a special constable;

(j) has agreed not to provide any money or other gifts to a suspect except items of refreshment and smoking materials for immediate consumption by the suspect;

(k) has registered under the Legal Aid Board's Legal Advice and Assistance at Police Stations Register Arrangements 1995 as specified in Schedule 2 subject to:

(i) thereafter to that person remaining on the register, and

(ii) the requirement to register not applying to an applicant who is a solicitor, and

(l) will carry out his or her duties so as not to discriminate on grounds of race, gender, sexual orientation, religion, age or disability.

(2) If the committee decides not to allow the application it shall provide the applicant with a statement of the reasons for its decision showing which of the criteria in paragraph 45(1) he or she does not meet and an explanation of why they have not been met.

(3) A duty solicitor representative may after selection become employed by a different firm of solicitors subject to the same conditions set out in paragraph 45(1)(a) but without having to apply to the local committee for selection and provided that such employment is in connection with the police stations for which the local committee which selected the duty solicitor representative is responsible and that he or she has notified the local committee and the Board of such change of employment.

Interview

46. (1) The appropriate local committee, or a sub-committee of it, shall require the proposed representative to attend an interview; however, where that person has been approved by any other local committee the appropriate local committee is under no duty to interview him or her but may in its discretion do so. An application cannot be rejected by the appropriate local committee without an interview.

(2) Any local committee or sub-committee when interviewing must include a lay

member appointed under paragraph 18(2) or (8) provided that any member appointed under paragraph 18(8) is not a member of court staff. If no such member can attend, one who is entitled to attend must agree to the interview being conducted in his or her absence.

Appeal to regional committee

47. (1) Where an application has been refused under paragraph 45(2), an appeal may be made by the appropriate duty solicitor to the appropriate regional committee within 28 days of the decision being notified to him or her subject to that committee having a discretion to accept an appeal outside the period of 28 days for good reason;

(2) If the appropriate local committee has not approved the application within a period of 60 days from the date of its submission or from when it was referred back to it under paragraph 15(7)(g) the application shall be deemed to have been rejected (unless the applicant agrees otherwise) and the applicant may, within 28 days of the expiration of such period appeal to the appropriate regional committee subject to that committee having a discretion to accept an appeal outside the period of 28 days for good reason;

(3) Where a duty solicitor's representative has not been reselected under paragraph 48 the appropriate duty solicitor may appeal to the appropriate regional committee within 28 days of the decision being notified to the duty solicitor subject to that committee having a discretion to accept an appeal outside the period of 28 days for good reason;

(4) Where an appeal is referred back to the appropriate local committee under paragraph 15(7)(g), the local committee must approve or reject the application within 60 days.

Reselection criteria

48. (1) A duty solicitor's representative shall be subject to reselection by the appropriate local committee at least every five years;

(2) The appropriate duty solicitor shall, where a representative is subject to reselection, complete a current application form approved by the Duty Solicitor Committee and obtained from the Board and shall return it to the Board within the time scale specified thereon failing which it will be deemed that the appropriate duty solicitor is not seeking reselection of the representative;

(3) If the committee is satisfied that the duty solicitor's representative meets the criteria set out in paragraph 45(1) and that the representative has undertaken a minimum of six hours tuition during the previous five years on a course relevant to advice at police stations it shall reselect him or her and give notice of such reselection to the duty solicitor;

(4) If it is not satisfied that he or she meets such criteria, the committee shall give the appropriate duty solicitor a statement of any representations received under paragraph 41 and shall invite the appropriate duty solicitor and the representative to an interview. Acceptance of the invitation to an interview must be submitted within 21 days of the committee having invited the representative to the interview;

(5) If the committee decides not to reselect the representative it shall provide the appropriate duty solicitor with a statement of the reasons for its decision;

(6) Reselection shall take place, in respect of all representatives admitted during a particular year, to take effect on December 31 of the fifth following year.

PART VII—SCOPE OF SERVICE—MAGISTRATES' COURTS

Defendant's right to instruct another solicitor

49. (1) A duty solicitor at a magistrates' court shall inform every defendant to whom

he or she offers advice or representation that the defendant is entitled to instruct any solicitor. The duty solicitor shall then ask the defendant if he or she has a solicitor whom he or she wishes to represent him or her and if the defendant has such a solicitor the duty solicitor shall not act for the defendant save in the circumstances mentioned in sub-paragraph (2) below;

(2) If the defendant wishes to be represented by a named solicitor or firm but that solicitor or a member of the firm is not available, then provided the defendant so wishes, the duty solicitor may give advice and representation to him or her on that occasion but shall not thereafter act for the defendant in that matter unless the defendant specifically asks him or her to do so in writing.

Services to be provided

50. (1) A duty solicitor at a magistrates' court shall provide the following services to any defendant who wishes to receive advice and representation from the duty solicitor:

(a) advice to a defendant who is in custody;

(b) the making of a bail application unless the defendant has received such assistance on a previous occasion.

(2) The duty solicitor shall subject to paragraph 51(1) also provide:

(a) representation of a defendant who is in custody on a plea of guilty where the defendant wishes the case to be concluded at that appearance in court, unless the duty solicitor considers that the case should be adjourned in the interests of justice or of the defendant;

(b) where necessary, advice and representation to a defendant who is before the court as a result of failure to pay a fine or other sum ordered or to obey an order of the court, and such failure may lead to the defendant being at risk of imprisonment;

(c) advice and, where appropriate, representation of any other defendant who is not in custody where, in the opinion of the duty solicitor, such defendant requires advice or representation;

(d) help to a defendant to make an application for a legal aid order in respect of any subsequent appearance of the defendant before the court. Where such an application is made the duty solicitor shall enquire whether the defendant wishes to instruct another solicitor to act for him or her. If the defendant does so wish, the duty solicitor shall insert the name of that solicitor in the application form.

(e) advice and, where appropriate, representation to the parent or guardian in connection with a proposal by the court to bind over the parent or guardian under section 58, Criminal Justice Act 1991 as amended or the breach of such an order.

Prohibition of certain services

51. (1) A duty solicitor shall not under paragraph 50 provide representation in committal proceedings or on a not guilty plea, nor save in circumstances which the duty solicitor considers exceptional, advice or representation to a defendant in connection with a non-imprisonable offence;

(2) On any adjourned hearing, a duty solicitor shall not, as duty solicitor, represent a defendant to whom he or she or any other duty solicitor has provided advice or representation in the same case except in connection with defendants coming within paragraph 50(2)(b);

(3) A duty solicitor shall not advise or represent any defendant at a sitting when that duty solicitor or any member of his or her firm is representing the Crown Prosecution Service in the same courtroom.

Duty to remain at court

52. A duty solicitor shall remain at the court until it has become clear to him or her

after consulting the clerk of the court where practicable that advice and representation is not required by any defendant under paragraph 50.

PART VIII—SCOPE OF SERVICE—POLICE STATIONS

Initial advice

53. (1) A duty solicitor on a rota shall accept a case referred to him or her by the telephone service unless he or she is already engaged in connection with another suspect at a police station or at a hearing of an application for a warrant of further detention or an extension of such a warrant;

(2) The duty solicitor on rota or a duty solicitor on a panel who accepts a case from the telephone service shall provide initial advice by speaking directly to the suspect on the telephone, unless the duty solicitor is at or adjacent to the police station and can immediately advise the suspect in person. If the suspect is incapable by reason of drunkenness or violent behaviour of speaking to the duty solicitor, initial advice may be postponed. The duty solicitor shall make arrangements to provide initial advice as soon as the suspect is capable of speaking to him or her. Where the case is one to which paragraph 54(1) applies, the duty solicitor shall tell the suspect that the duty solicitor will attend the police station to provide advice and to attend the police interview and any identity parade, group or video identification or confrontation unless the duty solicitor is of the opinion that there are exceptional circumstances for not doing so, in which case the duty solicitor shall explain the circumstances to the suspect;

(3) In addition to the requirements set out in paragraph 53(2), the duty solicitor shall, where a suspect is to be charged with an arrestable office, advise on the implications of the caution which will be given when the suspect is charged and must also consider whether or not he or she should attend the police station at that time bearing in mind whether it is possible to give confidential telephone advice and the possible consequences of not making a statement when being charged.

(4) The duty solicitor may only arrange for a duty solicitor's representative to give advice under paragraph 57 after the duty solicitor has provided advice under paragraph 53(2);

(5) Requests by suspects for the duty solicitor must be referred to the duty solicitor by the telephone service except where the duty solicitor is already at the same police station at which the suspect requests the services of the duty solicitor. In the latter event the duty solicitor must notify the telephone service where he or she has accepted the request from the suspect.

Obligation to attend the suspect at the police station

54. (1) After providing initial advice, the duty solicitor shall attend the suspect at the police station in person or by his or her duly authorised representative if paragraph 57 applies, in the following circumstances:

(a) where the suspect has been arrested in connection with an arrestable offence as defined under Section 24 Police and Criminal Evidence Act 1984, and the police intend to interview the suspect; or

(b) where the police intend to resolve an issue of identification by holding an identity parade, group or video identification or confrontation; or

(c) where the suspect complains of serious maltreatment by the police;

(2) If exceptional circumstances exist which justify non-attendance at the police station, the duty solicitor shall explain his or her decision not to attend on the costs claim form;

(3) If a police interview and any identification parade, group identification or con-

frontation is postponed to a time when the duty solicitor is no longer on duty or, if on a panel, where it is no longer convenient to act as duty solicitor, he or she must make arrangements to ensure that the suspect continues to receive advice in connection with paragraph 53(2) either by the rota duty solicitor continuing to act as duty solicitor or by ensuring that the suspect continues to receive advice from another duty solicitor.

Discretion to attend the suspect at the police station

55. In circumstances other than those set out in paragraph 54 the duty solicitor shall exercise his or her discretion whether it is in the interests of the suspect that he or she, or his or her representative, attends the police station. In assessing whether attendance is necessary the duty solicitor shall have regard to:

(1) whether he or she is satisfied that he or she can provide advice and assistance on the telephone with sufficient confidentiality to deal adequately with the matter, and

(2) where the suspect is a juvenile or a person at risk there shall be a presumption that the duty solicitor will exercise his or her discretion in favour of attendance.

Services personnel

56. Where the suspect is a Services person at a Services establishment or elsewhere assisting with an investigation by the Services police and suspected of offences contrary to the Services Discipline Acts where:

(a) the investigation involves any offences which cannot be dealt with summarily, or

(b) the offence appears to the interviewing Services police to be serious,

the duty solicitor shall attend personally upon the suspect where he or she considers that such attendance is necessary for the protection of the suspect's interests.

Advice by duty solicitor's representative

57. The duty solicitor may, where it is appropriate to do so, arrange for a duty solicitor's representative employed by his or her firm to give advice to the suspect at a police station provided that the representative can attend at the police station within 45 minutes. The suspect must be informed before advice is given in such circumstances of the status of the representative giving such advice. A duty solicitor's representative may not give advice to a Services person unless that representative is a solicitor. The duty solicitor who arranges for a duty solicitor representative to give advice will be responsible for that advice.

Continued instructions

58. The duty solicitor may, when he or she has given advice to the suspect at the police station, indicate to the suspect that he or she may be instructed by the suspect to continue to act for him or her, except in cases under paragraph 56 which are dealt with under summary Service procedures, subject to:

(1) advising the suspect that the suspect is entitled to instruct any solicitor; the duty solicitor should then ask the suspect if he or she has a solicitor whom he or she wishes to instruct and if the suspect has such a solicitor the duty solicitor shall not act for the suspect;

(2) if the suspect initially indicated that he or she wished to receive advice from a named solicitor or firm but that solicitor or a member of the firm was not available, the duty solicitor shall not continue to act for the suspect in that matter unless the suspect specifically asks him or her to do so in writing and such written instructions are filed within seven days with the local committee or the administrator of it;

(3) if the duty solicitor does not continue to act for the suspect he or she must make available to any solicitor subsequently instructed by the suspect any relevant information about the suspect's case.

PART IX—REGIONAL AND LOCAL COMMITTEES—GENERAL PROVISIONS

Election of chairman and vice-chairman

59. A committee shall, at the first meeting after its appointment and thereafter annually, elect a chairman and, in the case of a regional committee, a vice-chairman to hold office for such period not exceeding one year as the Committee may determine. A chairman or vice-chairman shall be eligible for re-election at the expiration of such period provided that no chairman or vice-chairman shall hold office for more than three years.

Quorum

60. A quorum shall consist of not less than one-third of the members of the committee or sub-committee or, where a committee is considering a matter where not all members are entitled to make decisions, one-third of such members who are entitled to make decisions in either case with a minimum of two members.

Minutes

61. A committee or a sub-committee shall keep minutes of its proceedings with the names of the members present at each meeting, and such minutes shall be signed by the chairman of the appropriate meeting.

Regional committee sub-committee and procedure

62. (1) Each regional committee may appoint a sub-committee of at least five members, two of whom must be lay persons (provided that there is a majority of solicitor and lay members) to which it may delegate all decisions, providing that the regional committee shall meet at least twice a year;

(2) Each regional committee may also appoint sub-committees of at least three members of whom one must be a lay person (provided that there is a majority of solicitor and lay members) to whom it may delegate the determination of appeals under paragraph 15(7) and suspensions and exclusions under paragraphs 15(5) and 15(14);

(3) The ruling of the chairman of a committee or sub-committee on any matter of procedure arising at that meeting of such committee or sub-committee shall be final and conclusive.

Resignation

63. A member of a committee may resign by giving notice in writing to the appropriate area office whereupon his or her office shall become vacant.

Disqualification and notification

64. (1) The office of a member of a regional or local committee shall be vacated by disqualification if:

(a) receiving order in bankruptcy is made against him or her;

(b) he or she becomes a patient within the meaning of the Mental Health Act 1959;

(c) he or she abstains without leave of the committee from attending meetings for one year,

(d) he or she ceases to be a nominee of the body or organisation he or she was nominated to represent, or

(e) there is good reason to disqualify him or her.

627

(2) A resolution of the appropriate regional committee declaring a member of a regional or local committee disqualified shall be conclusive as to the fact and ground of disqualification stated in the resolution.

Committee members' expenses and fees

65. (1) When attending meetings and conferences convened by the Board, members of the Duty Solicitor Committee and regional committees including sub-committees of regional committees shall be entitled to receive the following:

    (a) travel expenses;

    (b) subsistence allowances on such scale as the Board shall from time to time direct;

    (c) other proper expenses;

    (d) if they suffer loss, such fees as the Lord Chancellor may with the concurrence of the Treasury from time to time direct;

    (e) if they are lay members who attend to hear appeals under paragraph 15(7) or to consider suspensions or exclusions under paragraphs 15(5) and (14), the fee referred to in paragraph (d) but subject to the meeting of the regional committee:

        (i) being specifically convened to hear such appeals, suspensions and exclusions, or

        (ii) a sub-committee being held outside normal office hours;

(2) When making monitoring visits to magistrates' courts and police stations, members of regional and local committees shall be entitled to receive the following:

    (a) travel expenses;

    (b) subsistence allowances on such scale as the Board shall from time to time direct, and

    (c) other proper expenses.

(3) When attending local committee meetings in accordance with paragraph 20(2) of these Arrangements, regional committee members shall be entitled to receive the following:

    (a) travel expenses;

    (b) subsistence allowances on such scale as the Board shall from time to time direct, and

    (c) other proper expenses;

(4) When attending local committee meetings, members appointed under paragraphs 18(2) and (8) shall be entitled to receive child care expenses and, from a date to be decided by the Board, travel expenses;

(5) Regional committee members from other parts of the region attending interviews under paragraphs 34(3) or 46, and interviewees under paragraph 8, shall be entitled to receive travel expenses;

(6) When attending for interview in accordance with paragraph 8 or paragraph 19(2) of these Arrangements, applicants shall be entitled to receive the following:

    (a) travel expenses;

    (b) subsistence allowances on such scale as the Board shall from time to time direct, and

    (c) other proper expenses.

(7) When attending centralised selection meetings in regions 1, 13 and 14, members appointed under paragraphs 18(1) and (5) shall be entitled to receive travel expenses.

Consultation with local Law Societies

66. Where consultation is required with a local law society under paragraphs 13, 14,

15, 19(1) and 23 the appropriate local law society shall have a period of 21 days in which to notify an intention to respond and 42 days in which to respond.

SCHEDULE 1

Region	Legal Aid Area Covered	Area Office
1.	**No. 1 (London)**	London

The London Boroughs of:

Bexley
Bromley
Croydon
Ealing
Greenwich
Hounslow
Kingston
Lambeth
Lewisham
Merton
Richmond
Southwark
Sutton
Wandsworth

2.	**No. 2 (South Eastern)**	Brighton

East Sussex
Brighton and Hove
Kent
Surrey
West Sussex

3A.	**No. 3 (Southern)**	Reading

Berkshire
Buckinghamshire
Milton Keynes
Oxfordshire

3B.	**No. 3 (Southern)**	Reading

Dorset
Bournemouth
Poole
Hampshire
Portsmouth
Southampton
Isle of Wight

Region	Legal Aid Area Covered	Area Office
4A.	**No. 4 (South Western)**	Bristol

Cornwall
Devon

The following districts
of Somerset:

Sedgemoor
Yeovil
Taunton
Deane

4B.	**No. 4 (South Western)**	Bristol

Gloucestershire
Wiltshire
Thamesdown
Bath and North East Somerset
Bristol
South Gloucestershire
North West Somerset

The following districts
of Somerset:

Glastonbury
Shepton Mallet
Wells
Frome

5.	**No. 5 (South Wales)**	Cardiff

Dyfed
South Glamorgan
Mid Glamorgan
West Glamorgan
Gwent

The following districts
of Powys:

Brecknock
Radnor

6A.	**No. 6 (West Midland)**	Birmingham

Hereford & Worcester
Warwickshire

The following West Midlands
Metropolitan Boroughs:

Solihull
Coventry

Region	Legal Aid Area Covered	Area Office
6B.	**No. 6 (West Midland)**	Birmingham

The following districts
of Staffordshire:

Cannock Chase
Lichfield
South Staffordshire
Tamworth

The following West Midlands
Metropolitan Boroughs:

Birmingham
Sandwell
Dudley
Walsall
Wolverhampton

7A.	**No. 7 (North Western)**	Manchester

Greater Manchester

7B.	**No. 7 (North Western)**	Manchester

The following districts of Cumbria:

Barrow-in-Furness
South Lakeland

The following districts
of Lancashire

Blackburn
Burnley
Chorley
Hyndburn
Lancaster
Pendle
Ribble Valley
Rossendale

8A.	**No. 8 (Northern)**	Newcastle-upon-Tyne

The following districts of Cumbria

Northumberland
Tyne and Wear
Allerdale
Carlisle
Copeland
Eden

631

Region	Legal Aid Area Covered	Area Office
8B.	**No. 8 (Northern)**	Newcastle-upon-Tyne
	Hartlepool Redcar and Cleveland Middlesbrough Stockton-on-Tees Durham Darlington	
	The following districts of North Yorkshire:	
	Hambledon Richmondshire Ryedale Scarborough	
9A.	**No. 9 (North Eastern)**	Leeds
	West Yorkshire City of York	
	The following districts of North Yorkshire:	
	Craven Harrogate Selby York	
9B.	**No. 9 (North Eastern)**	Leeds
	East Riding of Yorkshire Hull	
10A.	**No. 10 (East Midland)**	Nottingham
	Derbyshire Derby Lincolnshire Nottinghamshire North Lincolnshire North East Lincolnshire	
10B.	**No. 10 (East Midland)**	Nottingham
	Leicestershire Leicester Rutland Northamptonshire	
11A.	**No. 11 (Eastern)**	Cambridge
	Cambridgeshire Norfolk Suffolk Bedfordshire Luton	

Region	Legal Aid Area Covered	Area Office
11B.	**No. 11 (Eastern)** Hertfordshire Essex	Cambridge
12A.	**No. 12 (Chester and North Wales)** Clwyd Gwynedd The following district of Powys: Montgomery	Chester
12B.	**No. 12 (Chester and North Wales)** Cheshire Shropshire Stoke-on-Trent The following districts of Staffordshire: East Staffordshire Newcastle-under-Lyme Stafford Staffordshire Moors	Chester
13.	**No. 1 (London)** The City of London The London Boroughs of: Camden Hackney Havering Islington Newham Redbridge Tower Hamlets Waltham Forest	London
14.	**No. 1 (London)** The London Boroughs of: Barnet Brent Enfield Hammersmith Haringey Harrow Hillingdon Kensington & Chelsea Westminster	London

Region	Legal Aid Area Covered	Area Office
15.	**No. 15 (Merseyside)**	Liverpool

Merseyside

The following districts
of Lancashire:

Blackpool
Fylde
Preston
South Ribble
Wyre
West Lancashire

Schedule 2

Category of duty solicitor representative	Requirement for Registration
(i) Duty solicitor representative selected before July 1, 1993.	Register as a probationary or accredited representative from February 1, 1997.
(ii) Duty solicitor representative selected between July 1, 1993 and January 31, 1995.	Register as a probationary or accredited representative from February 1, 1996.
(iii) A duty solicitor representative applicant considered for selection between February 1, 1995 and January 31, 1996.	Register as a probationary or accredited representative from February 1, 1995
(iv) A duty solicitor representative applicant considered for selection after February 1, 1996.	Register as an accredited representative from February 1, 1996.
(v) A person who is no longer a duty solicitor representative but who is within a period of five years of selection or reselection.	Register as a probationary or accredited representative from February 1, 1996
(vi) A person who is no longer a duty solicitor representative and who was last selected or reselected more than five years ago.	Register as a probationary or accredited representative from February 1, 1995.

Legal Aid Board Legal Advice and Assistance at Police Stations Register Arrangements 1995 (as amended)

The following Arrangements were approved by the Legal Aid Board and came into effect on November 1, 1995. They establish a scheme for the registration of representatives who give legal advice at police stations on behalf of solicitors. Insofar as the Arrangements apply to own solicitor representatives, the Arrangements establish an own solicitor representatives scheme within the meaning of the Legal Advice and Assistance at Police Stations (Remuneration) Regulations 1989 as amended. These Arrangements and the Duty Solicitor Arrangements 1994 as amended extend the register to duty solicitor representatives. Solicitors with practising certificates are not subject to these Arrangements.

Interpretation

1. In these Arrangements, unless the context otherwise requires:

"Accredited representative" is a representative the name of whom is included on the police station or immigration register who gives legal advice at police stations or immigration advice having passed the relevant tests;

"application form" is the current form for applying for inclusion on the police station or immigration register issued by the Board to be completed by the applicant;

"Board" means the Legal Aid Board at the current address of its Head Office in London;

"certificate of fitness" is a certificate given by the supervising solicitor that the representative is of suitable character to provide legal advice at police stations or immigration advice and that the applicant should be so regarded by the police in accordance with paragraph 6.13 of the Code of Practice for the Detention, Treatment and Questioning of Persons by Police Officers;

"duty solicitor representative" is a representative selected in accordance with the Board's Duty Solicitor Arrangements 1994 as amended of whom the Board has a record;

"immigration advice" means advice and assistance provided under the Legal Advice and Assistance at Police Stations (Remuneration) Regulations 1989 as amended given where a suspect is interviewed by immigration officers;

"immigration register" is a listing of probationary and accredited immigration representatives maintained by the Board;

"immigration representative" is a probationary or accredited representative included on the immigration register who gives immigration advice and who falls within the categories set out in paragraph 2.2;

"legal advice at police stations" means advice and assistance provided under the Legal Advice and Assistance at Police Stations (Remuneration) Regulations 1989 as amended and given where a suspect is being investigated by the police;

"police station register" is a listing of probationary and accredited police station representatives maintained by the Board;

"police station representative" is a probationary or accredited representative included on the police station register who gives legal advice at police stations or immigration advice and who falls within the categories set out in paragraph 2.2. A police station probationary representative cannot give advice in connection with indictable only cases;

"probationary representative" is a representative who has not passed the relevant tests and the name of whom is included on the police station or immigration register;

"relevant tests" are the tests undertaken by a probationary representative who must have satisfied a testing organisation that he/she has submitted a satisfactory portfolio and has passed the written test and (except for an immigration representative) the critical incidents test the details of which have been prescribed by the relevant testing organisation. Probationary police station representatives who have passed the Law Society's final examination or completed the Legal Practice Course, Fellows and members of the Institute of Legal Executives who have passed the Institute's criminal law and litigation papers, solicitors without practising certificates and barristers are exempt from the written test;

"satisfactory portfolio" means a portfolio of cases which is in a prescribed format and which is accepted by a testing organisation as satisfactory;

"supervising solicitor" means the solicitor who is currently supervising the representative;

"testing organisation" is an organisation approved by the Law Society to apply the relevant tests.

Police Station and Immigration Registers

2.1 The Board will maintain police station and immigration registers of probationary and accredited representatives in respect of whom the Board may pay remuneration for giving legal advice at police stations.

2.2 Representatives who fall within the following categories will be included on the police station or immigration register with effect where relevant from the dates specified:

   (i) a barrister;

   (ii) a trainee solicitor from February 1, 1997;

   (iii) a non-solicitor who gives immigration advice only from September 1, 1995;

   (iv) a non-solicitor who is not a trainee solicitor or a duty solicitor representative;

   (v) a duty solicitor representative as specified in the Board's Duty Solicitor Arrangements for the time being;

   (vi) a representative who is no longer a duty solicitor representative but who is within a period of five years of selection or reselection from February 1, 1996;

   (vii) a representative who is no longer a duty solicitor representative and who was last selected or reselected more than five years ago from February 1, 1995.

2.3 The Board will not include an accredited or probationary representative on the police station or immigration register unless an application has been made on a properly completed application form. Such representatives will be registered from the date the Board receives a properly completed application form and the Board will notify the representative of the date of registration.

2.4 The Board will record the representative as an accredited representative when

it has been notified by a testing organisation that the representative has submitted a satisfactory portfolio and passed the relevant tests.

2.5 Representatives are responsible for notifying the Board of any change of
address or other details recorded on the police station or immigration register
and the Board shall not be liable for the consequences of removing a representative from the relevant register where it has not received a certificate of fitness or has not been notified of a change of address.

Certificate of Fitness

3.1 The application form must include a certificate of fitness which must be
signed by the supervising solicitor.

3.2 No person applying to be registered on the police station or immigration register as a probationary or accredited representative can be so registered without
submitting to the Board a properly completed application form incorporating a
certificate of fitness properly completed.

3.3 The Board will request each accredited representative to provide a new certificate of fitness three years after the last certificate of fitness was received. Such
a request will be sent by the Board to the last address notified by the
representative.

Suspension and Removal from the Police Station and Immigration Registers

4.1 The Board will take the following action in connection with the register:

(i) subject to any suspension under sub-paragraph (iii), suspend a probationary representative where it does not receive notification from a testing
organisation that a portfolio certified by the supervising solicitor as complete has been submitted within six months of the date of registration and
will remove the representative if he or she remains suspended at the
expiration of one year from the date of registration;

(ii) subject to any suspension under sub-paragraph (iii), suspend a probationary representative where it does not receive notification from a testing
organisation that the representative has passed the relevant tests within
one year from the date of registration and will remove the representative
where it does not receive notification from a testing organisation that the
representative has passed the relevant tests within two years from the
date of registration;

(iii) suspend a probationary representative at the request of the representative
(subject to the reason for suspension being for illness, pregnancy or loss of
employment) for a minimum period of three months and will remove the
representative if he or she remains suspended for more than three years
from the date of suspension;

(iv) remove a probationary or an accredited representative at the request of
the representative;

(v) suspend an accredited representative if a certificate of fitness required
under paragraph 3.3 is not received within 28 days and will remove the
representative if he or she remains suspended for more than six months
from the date the certificate of fitness was requested;

(vi) suspend a representative if a certificate of fitness required under paragraph 6.1 is not received within 14 days and will remove the representative from the register if he or she remains suspended for more than three
years from the date the certificate of fitness was requested;

(vii) suspend a representative from the date of an order made by the Solicitors
Disciplinary Tribunal under section 43, Solicitors Act 1974 and will
remove the representative from the register if he or she remains suspended for more than three years from the date of the order.

4.2 A representative who has been suspended or removed from the register shall not be treated as being registered and may therefore not be remunerated for legal advice at police stations or immigration advice.

Reinstatement

5.1 The Board will reinstate a probationary or an accredited representative who has been suspended from the police station or immigration register:

   (i) where a portfolio is certified by the supervising solicitor as complete submitted after six months but before one year from the date of registration subject to any period of suspension under paragraph 4 (iii) reinstatement shall take effect from the date the Board is notified by the testing organisation that a portfolio certified by the supervising solicitor as complete has been submitted to the testing organisation but only for the balance of the probationary period of one year,

   (ii) where a satisfactory portfolio has been submitted within one year of the date of registration and the relevant tests have been passed within two years from the date of registration,

   (iii) at the end of a period of suspension referred to in 4 (iii) but only for the balance of the probationary period of one year,

   (iv) where the representative has not submitted a certificate of fitness under paragraphs 3.3 or 6.1 within the relevant period subject to the certificate being received by the Board, or

   (v) where a representative is suspended under paragraph 4 (vii) and permission has been given by the Law Society for the representative to be employed by the employing solicitor.

5.2 The Board will only reinstate a representative to the register following removal from the register where the representative has obtained accreditation since the date of removal.

Complaints

6.1 Where a complaint is received as to the suitability of character of the representative to give legal advice at police stations or immigration advice the Board will request the representative to obtain from the supervising solicitor a certificate of fitness which must be received by the Board within 14 days.

6.2 If the Board is not satisfied that, either before or after a certificate of fitness is received by it, the representative is fit to remain on the police station or immigration register the Board will refer the matter to the Solicitors' Complaints Bureau.

Miscellaneous

7. The Board shall approve forms for use in connection with the police station or immigration registers.

Legal Aid Board Multi-Party Action Arrangements 1992 (as amended)*

PART I—PRELIMINARY

Introduction

1. These arrangements are made by the Legal Aid Board. They set out the procedures which will apply to representation by means of contracts with the Board pursuant to Part XVI of the Civil Legal Aid (General) Regulations 1989.

2. Parts II to IV of the arrangements deal with the procedures leading up to and including signing of the contract. In particular, firms seeking a contract in a multi-party action must have regard to the requirements set out in Part III.

The procedures which will apply once a contract is in force are set out in Part V of the arrangements. Unless the Board otherwise directs, the provisions of Part V will be incorporated into every contract entered into under these arrangements.

Interpretation

3. In these arrangements, unless the context otherwise requires—

"the Act" means the Legal Aid Act 1988;

"Area Director" means the Area Director of the area office nominated for a particular multi-party action under paragraph 7;

"the Board" means the Legal Aid Board established under the Act;

"claimant" means a person making a claim in a multi-party action with the benefit of a certificate issued under regulations;

"the Committee" means the Committee appointed by the Board in accordance with paragraphs 4 and 6;

"contracting firm" means any firm which has entered into a contract with the Board, whether by itself or as one of a group of firms;

"contract" means a contract between one or more firms and the Board entered into under these arrangements for the provision of representation under Part IV of the Act in a multi-party action;

"contract work" means work of the type specified in the contract in accordance with paragraph 19;

"firm" means a firm of solicitors or other legal representatives duly authorised to provide representation under Part IV of the Act;

"generic work" means representation in respect of the issues common to all claimants or to a particular group of claimants and includes:

    (i) the selection, preparation and trial of lead issues and lead cases; and

    (ii) any work determined to be generic work by the Board.

"group of firms" means a group, consortium or steering committee of firms which propose to enter into a contract;

---

* See note at Note for Guidance 17, p. 226.

"local firm" means any firm representing a claimant in respect of work which is not covered by the contract;

"multi-party action" means any action or actions in which ten or more assisted persons have causes of action which involve common issues of fact or law arising out of the same cause or event;

"nominated contracting firm" means the firm specified in the contract as responsible for a particular obligation;

"paragraph" means a numbered paragraph in these arrangements;

"private client" means a person making a claim in a multi-party action without the benefit of a certificate issued under regulations;

"regulations" means the Civil Legal Aid (General) Regulations 1989 and reference to a regulation by number means a regulation so numbered in those regulations;

"representation" has the meaning assigned to it by section 2(4) of the Act and for the avoidance of doubt includes:

(i) the co-ordination of the action on behalf of claimants; and

(ii) any steps which contracting firms are required to take pursuant to the contract.

"termination" means termination of a contract.

Unless otherwise provided, words and phrases which are defined in the Act or regulations shall have those meanings in these arrangements.

PART II—THE MULTI-PARTY ACTIONS COMMITTEE

4. The Board will appoint a Committee to carry out functions under these Arrangements, in accordance with any guidance and directions issued by the Board. The Committee will include a nominee of the Law Society and a nominee of the National Consumer Council. The Committee may co-opt additional members to serve on it for particular functions or for the purposes of a particular action.

5. [Omitted]

6. The functions of the Committee will include:

(i) selecting firms to enter into contracts;

(ii) monitoring complaints generally and reviewing complaints referred to it in accordance with paragraph 45;

(iii) terminating contracts in appropriate circumstances;

(iv) advising and assisting the Board on any matters relating to particular actions or to multi-party actions generally;

(v) considering any application for a grant from the Board in relation to a multi-party action and making recommendations.

The Chairman of the Committee may if he thinks fit refer any matter before the Committee to the Chairman of the Board or to the Board.

PART III—PROCEDURES PRIOR TO CONTRACT

7. As soon as a multi-party action or potential multi-party action has been identified the Board will normally nominate one area office to deal with all applications for legal aid in that action.

8. When the nominated area office has issued at least ten certificates in the action the Area Director of the nominated office will prepare a report to the Board giving a brief description of the action.

9. The Area Director will at the same time appoint a liaison officer to have overall responsibility for the action in that area office.

10. If on consideration of such a report the Board is satisfied that:

(i) the action is a Multi-Party Action and the criteria for contracting set out in Part XVI of the regulations are satisfied; and

(ii) the action involves significant complexity in terms of assembling statements, undertaking research, obtaining expert evidence, examining and processing large volumes of documentation, or otherwise;

the Board may, if it thinks fit, invoke the procedures set out below.

11. If the Board does so decide, any firm which, on or before such date as the committee may specify ("the set closing date"), was acting for a client who had submitted a bona fide written application for legal aid in the action on or before the set closing date, will be entitled to submit reports detailing their proposals for co-ordinating and progressing the action ("tender reports"). The Board will also consider tender reports from any group of firms which includes at least one firm which has submitted such an application by the set closing date. The Board will set a deadline by which tender reports must be submitted.

12. Each firm or group of firms seeking selection must send to the liaison officer a tender report in a form approved by the Board. Each tender report should include:

(i) details of the firms to undertake the work, the respective responsibilities of the firms involved and a justification of the number of firms involved;

(ii) a nominated firm to be responsible for liaising with the Board, and an individual from each firm to have overall responsibility for the action;

(iii) nominated firms to be responsible for the production of six-monthly reports under paragraph 29 and reports to claimants under paragraph 35;

(iv) details of how the litigation is to be co-ordinated;

(v) details of the number and level of personnel from each firm to be deployed in the action, taking into account other work commitments, with details of how staff will be supervised and of suitable replacement personnel if required;

(vi) details of the relevant litigation and other experience and expertise of firms and of relevant personnel including managerial, IT and public relations experience insofar as it relates to the present action or to multi-party actions generally;

(vii) details of the availability of suitable secretarial, administrative and IT facilities in each firm;

(viii) an assessment of the progress of the action and proposals for the future including, so far as it is available, the information required in the six-monthly reports under paragraph 29;

(ix) details of the firm's proposals for consultation and liaison with claimants and local firms;

(x) details of the firms' complaints procedure having regard to paragraph 44;

(xi) details of any outstanding complaints being investigated by the Solicitors Complaints Bureau;

(xii) proposals as to how private clients will contribute to the costs of the proceedings;

(xiii) details of the present number of certificates held by each firm and the date when the firm first submitted an application for legal aid in the action;

(xiv) such further information as the Board may at that stage require.

13. The liaison officer will make such enquiries as he considers appropriate and then forward the tender report to the Committee.

So far as necessary the liaison officer or the Committee may:

    (i) require further information from any firm which has submitted a tender report;

    (ii) visit or request any person to visit firms which have submitted tender reports to verify or clarify the information contained therein;

    (iii) require the attendance of representatives from such firms to attend any meeting to answer questions.

14. The Committee may then either:

    (i) select a firm or group of firms to enter into a contract under these arrangements;

    (ii) invite firms to agree to a smaller, larger or different group of firms from that proposed and, if the chosen firms agree, select them;

    (iii) make no selection and invite other firms to submit proposal reports; or

    (iv) decide not to proceed to selection for the time being;

and where the Committee makes no selection the Committee will give written reasons for that decision to the firms concerned and, if appropriate, to the claimants.

15. Before making a selection the Committee will take into account, *inter alia*:

    (i) the matters set out in paragraph 12;

    (ii) the contents of the tender reports;

    (iii) any representations by the liaison officer;

    (iv) the number of actual or prospective claimants and their geographical spread;

    (v) the wishes of the claimants (if known);

    (vi) the likely effect, direct or indirect, which a particular selection would have on the general availability of experience and expertise in the handling of multi-party litigation.

16. The Committee may waive or dispense with any of the requirements of this Part of the arrangements if it is of the opinion that to do so would be appropriate for a particular action and would not cause any significant prejudice to claimants.

17. Nothing in these arrangements shall oblige the Board to call for tender reports or enter into any contracts and the Board may choose to limit the number of contracts in force at any time or restrict contracts to particular types of action.

PART IV—ENTRY INTO AND EFFECTS OF CONTRACTS

18. Where the Committee has selected a firm or group of firms, the Board may enter into a contract. The contract will be signed by the Chairman of the Committee on behalf of the Board and by each contracting firm.

19. Contracts entered into under these arrangements will specify the work to which the contract relates and may either:

    (i) limit representation under the contract to the generic work only;

    (ii) cover all representation in the action; or

    (iii) cover such representation as may be specified in the contract.

20. When a contract has been entered into, all relevant certificates will be amended as required. Unless the Board otherwise directs, representation in respect of contract work will be limited to representation by contracting firms in pursuance of the contract.

21. A person may be represented outside these arrangements in respect of work which is not covered by the contract, so that if the contract covers only generic work,

the assisted person may choose and be represented by a local firm as regards non-generic work.

22. While a contract is in force, contracting firms may apply to the Committee to add, substitute or remove firms from the group to meet the needs of the action as it progresses. After consulting with the liaison officer, the Committee may effect the proposed change.

23. Without prejudice to any other terms agreed by the Board and save where the contract provides to the contrary, every contract entered into under these arrangements shall contain and be subject to the provisions of Part V of these arrangements.

24. The Board may amend these arrangements from time to time and unless the contrary is stated such amendments shall apply both to existing and new contracts.

PART V—STANDARD CONTRACTING PROVISIONS

General

25. Contracting firms will carry out only such work as is authorised by the Board and will comply with such limitations on contract work as the Board may from time to time impose.

26. Subject to any directions given by the liaison officer:

   (i) contracting firms shall divide the contract work between them and may amend such division from time to time; but contracting firms shall notify the liaison officer of any major change of responsibilities within a group;

   (ii) each contracting firm shall individually record the contract work which it does;

   (iii) contracting firms may instruct counsel in respect of contract work but may not delegate or assign contract work to non-contracting firms.

27. A nominated contracting firm shall be primarily responsible for liaising with the Board.

28. In carrying out contract work, contracting firms will exercise reasonable skill and care.

Monitoring Multi-Party Actions

29. A nominated contracting firm shall submit a report to the liaison officer every six months (or such shorter period as the Board may prescribe). Such reports shall be divided into two sections:

   (i) legal and financial;

   (ii) management and administration.

30. The legal and financial section of the report shall include:

   (i) an up-to-date appraisal of the current position, including:

      (a) an assessment of the present strength and financial viability of the action, setting out the information which is relevant to the assessment and taking into account any developments since the last report;

      (b) an estimate of costs to date;

      (c) anticipated future costs;

      (d) present estimates of quantum;

      (e) a costs benefit assessment;

   (ii) a description of the work carried out since the last report;

   (iii) statistics, including:

      (a) number of claimants;

      (b) number of private clients in the action;

      (c) number of enquiries from prospective clients;

(d) best estimate of likely numbers of claimants or private clients who have yet to join the action;

(iv) copies of all reports and circulars sent to claimants and local firms over the last six months;

(v) details of unresolved complaints;

(vi) details of any relevant time limits or deadlines in the action, the steps taken to comply with them and the extent to which such deadlines are being or will be complied with;

(vii) a plan to progress the action over the next six months.

31. The management and administration section of the report shall include:

(i) details of how the action has been managed and co-ordinated over the last six months, including any changes in administration, personnel or IT since the last report;

(ii) a plan for the management and administration of the action over the next six months.

32. If the nominated contracting firm fails to provide an adequate report the liaison officer may:

(i) withhold any payments on account pending submission of the report;

(ii) limit work to submitting the report only;

(iii) recommend to the Committee termination of the contract.

33. The liaison officer may during any action make enquiries of claimants as to the standard of service they are receiving from contracting firms.

Keeping Claimants and Local Firms Informed

34. Contracting firms will keep claimants fully informed as to the preparation and prosecution of their claims.

35. Without prejudice to the obligation under paragraph 34, a nominated contracting firm shall make reports on at least a three-monthly basis to claimants on the preparation and progress of their claims. Such reports may be sent via local firms to claimants with an instruction that local firms should pass the reports on and deal with any queries from their clients. Reports sent to claimants must be in language readily understandable to the layman.

36. Contracting firms will keep local firms informed of the progress of the action and will give them sufficient guidance and information to enable them:

(i) properly to advise and assist their clients;

(ii) to make representations on behalf of their clients on the conduct of the litigation;

(iii) to assess so far as possible the likely impact of the statutory charge on claims of their clients;

(iv) to progress the individual claims of their clients in accordance with the latest orders or directions from the Court.

37. Nothing in these arrangements shall oblige contracting firms to comply with all requests for information from local firms or claimants or to disseminate information which in the opinion of contracting firms might prejudice the interests of claimants in the action generally.

Remuneration

38. Save where these arrangements expressly provide otherwise, contracting firms will be paid at the same rates and in the same manner as they would be paid under

regulations, and their fees shall be subject to taxation on the standard basis or assessment in accordance with the provisions of the regulations. For the avoidance of doubt contracting firms may obtain authority to incur costs in accordance with the provisions of Part VIII of the regulations.

39. Contracting firms may apply for payments on account only as provided for by these arrangements. Contracting firms may apply to the liaison officer for the payment of a sum on account of:

(i) disbursements incurred or about to be incurred in connection with contract work;

(ii) profit costs or counsel's fees in respect of contract work as soon as such work has been undertaken, including contract work undertaken under a legal aid certificate prior to the date of the contract.

In relation to applications under sub-paragraph (ii) above the Board will pay 75 per cent. of what it considers to be a reasonable amount for work reasonably done. Payments on account will be made as soon as practicable, provided that sufficient details are submitted to enable the Board to consider the reasonableness of the claim.

40. Where contract work is carried out for the benefit of private clients as well as claimants the Board will be responsible only for the legal aid proportion of the costs of the action and at the conclusion of the action the Board will immediately recoup any excess sums paid on account.

Subject to paragraph 41, payments on account will be reduced by a percentage to take into account the current proportion of private clients in the action as a whole. For this purpose only private clients who have commenced proceedings or are otherwise clearly identified to the satisfaction of the liaison officer will be taken into account, but contracting firms shall provide the liaison officer with such information as he requires to enable a fair estimate of numbers to be given.

41. In exceptional circumstances the Board may, if it thinks fit, agree to payments on account being made as if there were fewer private clients or no private clients in the action, but only if it is satisfied that:

(i) reducing payments on account to take account of private clients would cause delay or otherwise prejudice the interests of claimants; and

(ii) contracting firms have taken all reasonable steps to obtain appropriate levels of funding from private clients in the action generally; and

(iii) it would be reasonable to make payments on account at a higher rate having regard to the proportion of private clients in the action.

42. Contracting firms may apply to the liaison officer for payment of the travelling costs of claimants in connection with:

(i) claimants' meetings organised by contracting firms;

(ii) committees organised by contracting firms which include claimant representatives.

The liaison officer may approve such payment if the purpose of the meeting or committee is clear and will progress the conduct of the litigation, and the objectives of the meeting or committee cannot be achieved as effectively through other procedures. If such approval is given the Board will pay claimants' reasonable travelling costs within the United Kingdom (equivalent to Second Class return rail fare) to contracting firms for distribution to claimants, or reimburse contracting firms for any such reasonable sums as they have paid.

Contracting firms will explain to claimants the effect of the statutory charge should such expenses not be allowed on *inter partes* taxation.

43. Where contracting firms have failed to comply with any relevant provision of the regulations, arrangements or contract:

(i) payments on account may be deferred or suspended; and

(ii) where as a result of such default or omission the Board incurs loss, such loss may be deducted from payment of profit costs in respect of contract work until the loss is recovered.

Complaints

44. Contracting firms shall issue details of their complaints procedure to claimants and should ensure that, so far as possible, the following procedure is adopted in respect of obligations and procedures contained in these arrangements:

(i) claimants should in the first instance complain to their own solicitors;

(ii) complaints unresolved by a local firm should be referred to contracting firms;

(iii) complaints unresolved by contracting firms should be referred to the liaison officer.

45. The liaison officer will monitor and keep records of complaints. The liaison officer will refer complaints to the Committee where the complaints relate to the arrangements themselves or where the volume or severity of the complaints might lead the Committee to consider termination.

Publicity

46. The Board may, in consultation with contracting firms, take such steps as it considers appropriate to publicise a multi-party action.

Conflicting Instructions and Compromises

47. Nothing in these arrangements shall affect the normal professional duties of solicitors to their clients. Where as a result of instructions received contracting firms or local firms consider that they cannot reasonably be expected to act for any claimant they shall inform the liaison officer and certificates may be amended or discharged as appropriate.

48. Where a contracting firm receives conflicting instructions (whether in relation to an offer of compromise or otherwise) and cannot resolve such conflict, it shall report the problem to the liaison officer. The normal procedures as to amendment or discharge of certificates shall apply in such circumstances but where it appears to the liaison officer that there may be grounds for terminating the contract or for dividing the claimants into groups and entering into one or more new contracts, he will inform the Committee and make appropriate recommendations.

Termination

49. The Board may terminate any contract, either in respect of a specific firm within a group or all firms, where in the opinion of the Board:

(i) any contracting firm in the group is in breach of its obligations under the contract or under these arrangements or has otherwise acted or is proposing to act in a way likely to cause substantial prejudice to claimants or to the Board;

(ii) information set out in a tender report is inaccurate or misleading; or

(iii) it is no longer appropriate to continue representation by means of a contract in the action.

By way of examples only, potential grounds for termination are set out in the Schedule hereto.

50. The Board may terminate immediately in case of urgency, but otherwise:

(i) the liaison officer will notify the contracting firm of the area of concern and ask for remedial steps to be taken within 21 days, or such other period as he may specify; and

(ii) failure to remedy the problem will result in the liaison officer referring the matter to the Committee to consider termination.

51. Where a termination has occurred the Committee will consider how best to

proceed in the interests of claimants and the Board may enter into a new contract or contracts without applying the procedures set out in Part III of these arrangements.

52. Subject to paragraph 43, after termination a former contracting firm may apply for payment on account under paragraph 39 in respect of work done up to the date of termination. On termination contracting firms will deliver up documents relating to contract work as required by the Board.

Apportionment of Costs

53. In this and the remaining paragraphs of the arrangements, "costs" refers to all costs, counsel's fees and disbursements incurred in respect of contract work on behalf of claimants, and "generic costs" refers to such costs in respect of generic work. Costs will be apportioned between the accounts of claimants by the Board where required pursuant to sections 16(10) and 40(4) of the Act.

54. Contracting firms will keep such records and supply such information as is necessary to enable the Board to carry out apportionment of costs. When lodging for taxation any bill of costs in respect of contract work, contracting firms will serve a copy of the bill on the liaison officer.

55. When apportioning costs the Board will seek to give effect to any costs sharing order made by the Court. Subject to any such order, the following principles will operate as guidelines only in the apportionment of costs:

(i) subject to the following guidelines, generic costs will be divided equally between all claimants and all other costs will be placed on the account of the individual claimant concerned;

(ii) generic costs attributable to a particular group of claimants will be divided equally between the members of that group. This would apply where there are issues in the action which relate only to that group, or where a group of claimants continue with the action after others have discontinued or accepted offers of settlement;

(iii) generic costs will be apportioned between claimants *ab initio*, regardless of when they joined the action;

(iv) claimants who leave an action before it is concluded, whether by discontinuing, death, accepting an offer of settlement or otherwise ("early leavers") will be liable for their share of generic costs only up to the time they left, or up to the end of the next accounting period chosen for this purpose by the Board;

(v) travelling costs to meetings paid under paragraph 42 will be placed on the account of the claimant concerned; travelling costs to committees under that paragraph will be treated as generic costs.

56. At the request of an early leaver the Board may if it thinks fit specify a figure pursuant to section 16(10) of the Act before the conclusion of the action. Any such determination shall then be binding on both the Board and the claimant, leaving the balance of the costs to be apportioned amongst the remaining claimants at the conclusion of the action.

SCHEDULE

EXAMPLES OF POTENTIAL GROUNDS FOR TERMINATION

1. Serious or persistent failure to comply with relevant provisions of regulations, arrangements or contract after appropriate notice of default. Examples include:

(i) unauthorised delegation of generic work;

(ii) failure to co-operate with other contracting or local firms, including failure to provide information needed for monitoring reports;

(iii) failure to comply with monitoring requirements including material non-disclosure which could substantially prejudice claimants or the Board;

(iv) failure to comply with any complaints procedure;

(v) failure to provide proper information to claimants either as specifically required in the arrangements or in response to reasonable requests;

(vi) failure to maintain accurate records of costs incurred as apportioned between claimants.

2. Material alteration to partnership or team membership of any firm affecting ability to fulfil obligations to the Board or to claimants (e.g. in the case of a split or merger in a contracting firm, the Board may wish to terminate and enter new contracts if the team left its old firm and transferred to a new one which met the selection criteria. Alternatively as a result of the move neither firm might meet the criteria and a completely new firm might be required).

3. Failure properly to control the conduct and progress of the action.

4. Failure/inability to maintain adequate support services for the conduct of the action, *i.e.* the breakdown of suitable secretarial, administrative and information technology facilities.

5. Poor quality of work and advice identified by the Board.

6. Continuing substantiated complaints or an adverse adjudication by the SCB whether regarding work in the multi-party action or otherwise, including an adjudication on delay, or persistent discrimination against staff or clients.

7. Continuing excessive claims for payment, including for payments on account.

8. Major loss of confidence by claimants.

9. The contracting firm being unable on ethical grounds to continue representing the claimants.

10. The firm's financial condition being such that to continue might at worst lead to the bankruptcy of its partners, at best lead to diminished quality of work and advice.

11. Dishonesty or criminal conviction of relevant personnel.

12. Bankruptcy of partner members of the team.

13. Termination requested by contracting firms and agreed to by the Board.

Legal Aid Board Area Committee Arrangements 1998

1. Background

1.1 Regulation 4 of the Civil Legal Aid (General) Regulations 1988 requires the Board to appoint area committees and area directors in respect of legal aid areas specified by the Board. Area committees and area directors must exercise the functions:

1.1.1	delegated to them by the Board; or
1.1.2	conferred on them by regulations.

1.2 The functions of area committees may be exercised by sub-committees of their members.

2. Introduction

2.1 These arrangements

2.1.1	specify legal aid areas;
2.1.2	nominate legal aid areas for specified purposes;
2.1.3	define "area directors" and "area committees";
2.1.4	describe the role of and regulate the composition, powers and processes of area committees.

3. Definitions

3.1	"area director" means such member of the Board's staff as the Board has designated as responsible for a legal aid area. Each of the Board's duly appointed area managers is an area director;
3.2	"area committee" means a committee appointed under these arrangements;
3.3	"panel of chairs" is the panel described in paragraph 14;
3.4	"practicable" and "appropriate" mean practicable or appropriate (as the case may be) having regard to any guidance issued by the Board;
3.5	"sub-committee" means a sub-committee of an area committee.

4. Specification of legal aid areas

4.1 The Board has specified the 13 legal aid areas set out in Appendix A.

4.2 For each legal aid area there shall be:

4.2.1	an area committee; and
4.2.2	an area office managed by an area director responsible for the legal aid area.

5. Nomination of legal aid areas

5.1 Regulation 10 of the Civil Legal Aid (General) Regulations 1989 obliges the Board to nominate a legal aid area to receive applications for legal aid certificates from persons resident outside the United Kingdom.

5.2 The Board has nominated legal aid area 1 (London) to receive applications for legal aid certificates from applicants resident outside the United Kingdom and to receive all applications under the Hague Convention or European Convention which have been submitted to the Lord Chancellor's Department as central authority in England and Wales under the Child Abduction and Custody Act 1985. (Applications for legal aid for proceedings under the Child Abduction and Custody Act 1985 which have not been submitted to the central authority are not covered by this nomination.)

6. Duties and discretion of area director

6.1 In performing his or her duties and in exercising any discretion under these arrangements, the area director shall have regard to such guidance as may be issued by the Board.

7. Size and composition of area committees

7.1 Each area committee shall comprise no fewer than 16 nor more than 120 (240 in the case of area 1 (London)) members.

7.2 Area committees shall comprise solicitors and barristers and may include temporary members.

7.3 A person who is not a solicitor or a barrister may be appointed as a temporary member of an area committee in accordance with these arrangements.

7.4 A person who is a member of one area committee may be appointed as a temporary member of another area committee in accordance with these arrangements.

7.5 An area committee shall comprise competent and experienced solicitors and barristers of good standing and such temporary members as may be appointed in accordance with these arrangements from time to time.

8. Applications and appointment of, and notification by, area committee members

8.1 Area directors shall secure applications for membership of area committees in such manner as they consider practicable. When they are seeking applications, they shall notify the General Council of the Bar and the local law societies in the legal aid area for which they are responsible.

8.2 In appointing members of area committees, area directors shall, so far as they consider practicable, have regard to the desirability not only of retaining members with experience of area committee work, but also the desirability of bringing in new members.

8.3 Area committee members may be appointed by the Board or, where any applicant meets the criteria set by the Board, by the appropriate area director in consultation with the chair of the appropriate area committee. The Board's criteria and guidance are set out in Appendix B (*not reproduced in the Legal Aid Handbook*).

8.4 Area committee members must notify the area director if they cease to be in private practice and of any other matter which is material to their membership of the area committee (*e.g.* any disciplinary findings made against them or any bankruptcy proceedings).

9. Temporary appointments to area committees

9.1 An area director may appoint any member of another area committee as a temporary member of the area committee for the legal aid area for which he or she is responsible.

9.2 An area director may, with the authority of the Board, appoint as a temporary member of the area committee for the legal aid area for which he or she is responsible, a person of good standing who is neither a barrister nor a solicitor. The Board's authority will be given only for a specific purpose and only if it considers that appointing such a temporary member will be expedient for the proper administration of legal aid in a particular area.

9.3 Unless, in any case, the Board directs otherwise, a temporary appointment to an area committee lasts for one month from the date of appointment.

10. Chair and vice-chair of area committees

10.1 Each area committee shall, at the first meeting after its appointment and thereafter on the date of each annual general meeting (or on such earlier date as it may determine), elect a chair and one vice-chair or two vice-chairs to hold office until the date of the following annual general meeting (or such earlier date as the committee may determine). Any chair or vice-chair shall be eligible for re-election at the expiration of such period, provided that no chair or vice-chair shall hold office for more than three consecutive periods.

11. Meetings and decisions of area committees

11.1 It is the responsibility of the area director, in consultation with the area chair, to convene meetings, including annual general meetings, of the area committee for the legal aid area for which he or she is responsible and to give written notice to the members of such meetings.

11.2 The decisions of an area committee shall be by the majority of members present and voting and in the case of an equality of votes, the chair of the meeting shall have a second or casting vote.

11.3 In the absence of the area committee chair and vice-chair from any meeting of the area committee, a chair of the day shall be elected by the members present from their number.

11.4 Three members of an area committee shall form a quorum.

12. Annual general meetings

12.1 There shall be no more than eighteen months between the dates of any two annual general meetings.

12.2 The business of each annual general meeting shall normally include:

12.2.1   the election of the area committee chair and vice-chair;

12.2.2   a review of membership (including appointments, re-appointments, resignations, disqualifications and removals) of the area committee and of the panel of chairs;

12.2.3   a report by the area director on the administration of, and developments in, legal aid in the relevant legal aid area, and nationally; and

12.2.4   updating for the panel of chairs and other committee members;

and may include:

12.2.5   a training session, a review of the performance of the sub-committees of the area committee and such other business as the area committee chair in consultation with the area director considers appropriate.

13. Sub-committees—general

13.1 Area committees shall discharge the functions conferred on them by regulations, through sub-committees of their members.

13.2 The area director is responsible for the convening and composition of sub-committees and for issuing sub-committee agendas.

14. Sub-committees—panel of chairs and specialists

14.1 It is the responsibility of the area director, in consultation with the area committee chair to maintain a panel of area committee members who he or she considers are best qualified among the membership to be chairs of sub-committees.

14.2 The size of the panel of chairs shall be such as the area director, in consultation with the area committee chair, considers appropriate.

14.3 It is the responsibility of the area director to maintain a record of area committee members who have specialist experience or knowledge in particular areas of law.

15. Sub-committees—chairs

15.1 So far as the area director considers is practicable in each case, each sub-committee shall include at least one member of the panel of chairs.

15.2 The chair of each sub-committee shall be such member as is nominated by the area director and shall normally be a member of the panel of chairs.

15.3 In the absence of a chair nominated by the area director, a chair of the day shall be elected by the members of the sub-committee present, from their number.

16. Sub-committees—reasons

16.1 It is the responsibility of the chair of a sub-committee to ensure that the sub-committee gives reasons for its decisions.

17. Sub-committees—clerks

17.1 Each sub-committee shall be assisted by a clerk who is a representative of the area director. The role of the clerk is to assist the sub-committee in performing its functions. The clerk must record the minutes of the meeting, the decisions made by the sub-committee and the reasons for them.

18. Sub-committees—quorum

18.1 Subject to paragraph 18.2, three members of a sub-committee shall form a quorum.

18.2 Where only two members of a sub-committee are present, they shall form a quorum and have power to consider and deal with all matters within the scope of the sub-committee's terms of reference on which they are in agreement as to the decision to be made.

18.3 Subject to paragraph 18.2, the decisions of a sub-committee shall be by the majority of members present and voting and in the case of an equality of votes, the chair of the meeting shall have a second or casting vote.

19. Area committees and sub-committees—minutes, dissenting minority and conflicts of interest

19.1 Every committee and sub-committee shall keep minutes of its procedures with the names of members present at each meeting.

19.2 The chair of any meeting is responsible for ensuring that minutes of the meeting are properly recorded and signed by him or her.

19.3 If any member of an area committee or sub-committee dissents from the majority of its members as to any actions, or any report or parts of a report to be laid before some other committee or the Legal Aid Board (as the case may be), the name of such dissentient member shall, if he or she so requires, appear on the minutes as dissenting and the dissentient member may submit to such other committee or to the Legal Aid Board (as the case may be), an independent report or reports.

19.4 It is the responsibility of each member of an area committee to be alert to the possibility, in any matter, of a conflict of interest and, if he or she identifies a conflict or a possible conflict, to declare it forthwith.

19.5 If any member of an area committee has a conflict of interest in any matter he or she shall withdraw entirely from the meeting while the matter is considered and determined and shall not return until the committee or sub-committee permits them to do so.

19.6 The minutes of each meeting shall record the names of any member who has, or has declared, a conflict of interest or a possible conflict of interest, the matter in respect of which the conflict or potential conflict of interest arose and what steps were taken in respect of that conflict or potential conflict of interest.

20. Procedure

20.1 Except so far as the procedure of any area committee or sub-committee is regulated by the Board, it shall have power to regulate its own procedure and the ruling of its chair on any matter or procedure arising at any meeting shall be final and conclusive.

20.2 The validity of any proceedings of an area committee or a sub-committee shall not be affected by any vacancy among its members or by any defect in the appointment or continued membership of any member.

21. Retirement

21.1 On 31 December each year, one fifth (or if the number of members of an area committee is not a multiple of five, then the nearest to one fifth) of the members of each area committee shall retire.

21.2 The members so to retire shall be those who on 31 December have been members for the longest period since they were last appointed, or re-appointed. If two or more such members have been members for an equal time, both or all such members shall retire.

22. Re-appointment

22.1 Every retiring area committee member shall be eligible for re-appointment unless he or she is 65 years old or older. Any retiring member who is 65 years old or older may be re-appointed, provided he or she is not 70 years old or older, if the area director in consultation with the area committee chair considers it is expedient for the proper administration of legal aid in a particular area.

22.2 In considering whether to re-appoint any member, the area director in consultation with the area committee chair shall have regard to the same criteria as on the appointment of new members (see paragraph 8).

23. Resignation

23.1 A member of an area committee may resign by giving two months' notice in writing to the appropriate area director.

24. Disqualification

24.1 The membership of any member of an area committee is terminated by disqualification if he or she makes a composition with his creditors or a receiving order in bankruptcy is made against him or her or he or she becomes of unsound mind.

24.2 A resolution of the appropriate area committee declaring a member of the committee disqualified shall be conclusive as to the facts, ground and date of disqualification stated in the resolution.

25. Removal from office

25.1 The Legal Aid Board may, if it thinks fit, remove from office any member of an area committee. If it does so, it shall give reasons and shall, without delay, inform the former member and the area director.

25.2 With the agreement of the area director, the chair of an area committee may remove from office any member of the area committee who, having been given reasonable notice to attend has, without the consent of the area director, either:

(a) without securing the attendance of a substitute member, failed to attend a meeting of a sub-committee; or

(b) failed twice consecutively to attend meetings of sub-committees.

26. Attendance fees

26.1 There shall be paid out of the legal aid fund to chairs and vice-chairs of area committees attending any meeting convened by the Board in connection with those committees, and to all members attending meetings of the area committee or a sub-committee, such fees as the Lord Chancellor may, with the concurrence of the Treasury from time to time, authorise.

27. Travelling and other expenses

27.1 Travelling and other proper expenses and subsistence allowances on such scale as the Lord Chancellor shall from time to time direct, shall be paid out of the legal aid fund to members attending meetings of committees or sub-committees and to chairs and vice-chairs of area committees attending any meeting convened by the Board.

Legal Aid Board Regional Legal Services Committee Arrangements 1997

Introduction

1.1 These Arrangements are made by the Legal Aid Board. They set out the composition, powers and procedures of Regional Legal Services Committees.

1.2 A Regional Legal Services Committee is an advisory committee of the Legal Aid Board.

1.3 In these Arrangements:

"Board" means the Legal Aid Board.

"Committee" and "sub-committee" mean a Regional Legal Services Committee or sub-committee thereof.

"Designated legal aid areas" mean the legal aid areas designated under paragraph 2 of the Legal Aid Board Area Committee Arrangements (as amended).

"External member" means a member of a Regional Legal Services Committee who is not a member of the Board or an Area Manager.

"Area Manager" means an employee of the Board designated as "Area Director" under paragraph 4 of the Legal Aid Board Area Committee Arrangements (as amended).

Appointment

2.1 The Board shall appoint a Regional Legal Services Committee in respect of each designated legal aid area to carry out functions under these Arrangements.

2.2 The members of a Regional Legal Services Committee shall be the following:

(a) a member of the Board who shall be Chair;

(b) the Area Manager of the designated legal aid area who shall serve *ex officio*;

(c) external members each of whom shall have knowledge and experience of one or more of the following and who between them shall, so far as reasonably practicable, have knowledge and experience of all of the following:

(i) legal aid private practice;

(ii) provision of legal services in the not for profit sector (advice or law centres);

(iii) the role and function of local authorities;

(iv) the consumer perspective.

2.3 External members of a Regional Legal Services Committee shall be appointed by the Chair of the Committee with the prior approval of the Chair of the Board. The Chair of the Committee shall report all appointments to the Board.

2.4 All members of a Regional Legal Services Committee shall follow the Code of Best Practice for Legal Aid Board members and the Rules of Conduct as approved by the Board from time to time.

2.5 External members shall be bound by the Terms and Conditions of External Appointments to the Legal Aid Board's Regional Legal Services Committees as approved by the Board from time to time.

Period of service

3.1 The Chair of a Regional Legal Services Committee shall be appointed by the Chair of the Board for a period which does not exceed four years and which may be renewed for a further successive period or periods provided that if the Chair ceases to be a member of the Board, his or her appointment as a member of a Regional Legal Services Committee shall automatically cease. In the event of such cessation, or in the event of the temporary incapacity (whether through illness or otherwise) of any Chair of an RLSC, the Chair of the Board may appoint a temporary Chair of the RLSC who need not be a Board member and who shall exercise all relevant powers pending the appointment of a new Chair or the return of the current Chair (as the case may be).

3.2 An external member of a Regional Legal Services Committee shall be appointed for a period of two, three or four years to be determined at the discretion of the Chair of the Committee.

3.3 An external appointment to a Regional Legal Services Committee may be renewed by the Chair with the prior approval of the Chair of the Board for a further successive period or periods of two, three or four years at a time provided that the total period of service shall not exceed eight years.

Functions

4.1 Subject to the remainder of this paragraph, a Regional Legal Services Committee shall have the general function of advising the Board on the nature and extent of the need for legal and related services in its designated legal aid area and recommending to the Board a regional strategy to meet those needs in its area. In carrying out its functions, a Regional Legal Services Committee shall act in accordance with any guidance and directions issued by the Board.

4.2 The Board may determine and assign priorities for the work to be undertaken by a Regional Legal Services Committee by reference to geographical area, category of work, type of client, method of service delivery or otherwise, and may identify specific issues to be addressed by a Regional Legal Services Committee in carrying out its functions.

4.3 The Board may set a timetable for a Regional Legal Services Committee to submit its regional strategy or to report on any specific issue, and shall determine the form in which the regional strategy or any reports are prepared and submitted for approval. The Board may prescribe the scope of the regional strategy.

4.4 A Regional Legal Services Committee is an advisory body and its recommendations are not binding on the Board.

4.5 The Board shall publish the regional strategies for each designated legal aid area once they have been approved by the Board.

4.6 The Board may approve a regional strategy notwithstanding any defect or omission in procedure of a Regional Legal Services Committee if in its discretion the Board considers it appropriate to do so.

Powers and duties of the Committee

5.1 In carrying out its functions a Regional Legal Services Committee shall, in relation to its designated legal aid area and subject to any directions from the Board:

(a) assess the need for legal and related services;
(b) gather information on the supply of legal and related services;
(c) identify regional priorities according to geographical area, category of work and client group need for such services;
(d) develop a regional strategy to meet the assessed need for legal and related services and the identified regional priorities;
(e) monitor implementation of the regional strategy approved by the Board.

5.2 A Regional Legal Services Committee may arrange such conferences and other activities as it considers appropriate to facilitate the consultative process.

5.3 A Regional Legal Services Committee shall carry out such consultation exercises as the Board may from time to time require.

5.4 External members shall carry out such duties as the Chair of a Regional Legal Services Committee may specify and in so doing shall act under the overall direction of the Chair.

5.5 In representing a Regional Legal Services Committee all members shall have regard to the aims and objectives of the Board as set out in its corporate plan, management statement and the statutory provisions set out in the Legal Aid Act 1988 and its supporting regulations.

Regional Legal Services Advisers

6.1 A Regional Legal Services Committee shall be supported by a Regional Legal Services Adviser who is a member of staff of the Board.

6.2 A Regional Legal Services Adviser may attend meetings of the Regional Legal Services Committee and any sub-committee but shall not be a member of a committee or sub-committee.

6.3 A Regional Legal Services Adviser shall assist in carrying out the work of the Regional Legal Services Committee under its guidance.

Frequency of meeting

7.1 A Regional Legal Services Committee shall meet at least four times a year and may hold additional meetings at the discretion of the Chair.

7.2 Meetings of a Regional Legal Services Committee shall take place on dates and in places to be determined by the Chair in conjunction with the Area Manager.

Notice of meeting

8.1 A meeting of a Regional Legal Services Committee shall be convened by posting notices to each member setting out the nature of the business to be discussed on a day at least 10 clear days prior to the date of the meeting.

8.2 Additional items of business may be added to the agenda at any time with the agreement of the Chair. Papers may be circulated after despatch of the notice convening the meeting with the agreement of the Chair.

8.3 An urgent meeting of a Regional Legal Services Committee may be convened by the Chair on a period of less than 10 clear days notice provided that all members of the committee agree in writing

Chair

9.1 Each Chair may be appointed as Chair of more than one Regional Legal Services Committee.

9.2 The Chair shall have authority to refer any matter to the Board at his or her discretion.

Sub-committees

10.1 The Chair of a Regional Legal Services Committee shall have power to appoint any number of members to a sub-committee, who need not be members of the committee.

10.2 The Chair of a sub-committee shall be appointed by the Chair of the Regional Legal Services Committee.

10.3 The Chair of a sub-committee may nominate a member to chair a meeting in his or her absence.

10.4 A sub-committee may be appointed to consider any matter within the Regional Legal Services Committee's terms of reference and report or make recommendations to the committee.

Quorum

11.1 Three members of a Regional Legal Services Committee shall form a quorum provided that this number includes the Chair or the Area Manager, unless the Chair nominates a member to chair a meeting in his or her absence in which case that member shall replace the Chair for the purposes of the quorum.

11.2 Two members of a sub-committee shall form a quorum.

Decision-making

12. Where a vote is necessary, the decisions of a Regional Legal Services Committee or sub-committee shall be made by the majority of members present and voting. In the case of equality of votes the Chair, or any member nominated in the Chair's absence, shall have a second or casting vote.

Minutes

13. A Regional Legal Services Committee or sub-committee shall keep minutes of its proceedings including the names of those present at each meeting.

Procedure

14. Save in so far as the procedure of a Regional Legal Services Committee is regulated by the Board, any such committee shall have power to regulate its own procedure in relation to the conduct of meetings. The ruling of the Chair of a committee or sub-committee on any matter of procedure arising at any meeting of such committee or sub-committee shall be final and conclusive.

Attendance fees

15. There shall be paid out to external members attending Regional Legal Services Committee meetings or any such other meeting or undertaking any other activity as required by the Chair or by the Board under these Arrangements, such fees as the Lord Chancellor may with the concurrence of the Treasury from time to time authorise.

Travelling and other expenses

16. Travelling and other proper expenses and subsistence allowances as may be authorised by the Board may be paid on such scale as the Lord Chancellor shall from time to time direct, to external members and members of a sub-committee attending Regional Legal Services Committee meetings or any such other meeting or activity as required by the Chair or by the Board under these Arrangements.

Vacation of office

17. An external member of a Regional Legal Services Committee may resign by giving notice in writing to the Chair and on the acceptance of such resignation by the Chair his or her office shall become vacant.

Vacancies

18. Any vacancy on a Regional Legal Services Committee shall, as soon as practicable, be filled by the Chair in accordance with paragraph 2 above.

Suspension or termination of appointment of external members

19. The Chair of a Regional Legal Services Committee may review, suspend or terminate the membership of an external member. The basis on which the membership of an external member may be reviewed, suspended or terminated is set out in the Terms and Conditions of External Appointments to the Legal Aid Board's Regional Legal Services Committees as approved by the Board from time to time. The Chair shall notify the Chair of the Board of any investigation conducted under this paragraph.

Retirement

20.1 A member of a Regional Legal Services Committee shall retire if he or she reaches sixty-five years of age during the term of appointment.

20.2 The Chair of a Regional Legal Services Committee may waive the requirement in sub-paragraph 20.1 in relation to any other member of the committee unless the member concerned has attained the age of seventy years.

20.3 The Chair of the Board may waive the requirement in sub-paragraph 20.1 in relation to a Chair of a Regional Legal Services Committee unless the Chair concerned has attained the age of seventy years.

20.4 A decision by the Chair of a Regional Legal Services Committee to waive the requirement in sub-paragraph 20.1 is subject to approval by the Chair of the Board.

Legal Aid Board—Regional Legal Services Committees—Directions for the year to March 31, 1999

1. Introduction

1.1 These directions are issued pursuant to paragraph 4 of the Regional Legal Services Committee Arrangements 1997 (henceforth referred to as the "Arrangements"). Terms used in these directions are, where relevant, as defined in paragraph 1.3 of the Arrangements.

1.2 The directions are in two parts. The first part deals with the immediate programme of work (for 1998/99), the second with the ongoing arrangements.

PROGRAMME OF WORK FOR 1998/99

2. Objective

The primary objective for Committees in 1998/99 will be to produce a draft regional strategy by the end of January 1999 for consideration by the Board. This strategy will inform decisions on contracts to be let within an exclusive contracted regime for civil and family advice and assistance by the end of 1999; excluding personal injury, subject to the outcome of the Lord Chancellor's consultations. (Arrangements 5.1(a) and (b)).

3. Outline and contents of the regional strategy for 1999/2000 (Arrangements4.3) :

3.1 Executive summary

Outline of regional strategy and main conclusions, including table showing priorities by geographical area and categories of law.

An example (for illustrative purposes only) of a table of priorities is shown below:

	Fam	Debt	WB	Hou	Emp	Imm	Cons	Mental Health
District 1	High	High	High	High	Med	Low	Low	Low
District 2	High	Med	Med	Med	Low	Low	Low	High
District 3	High	Low	Low	Med	High	Low	Low	Low
District 4	High	High	High	High	Low	High	Med	Low

3.2 Introduction

Purpose of strategy—defines purpose of strategy and sets in context
Status, remit and role of Committee

3.3 Assessment of need for legal services

Outlines categories of law for which need is to be assessed
Describes methods and data used to assess need
Summarises outcome of need assessment

3.4 Measuring supply of legal services

Describes process of identifying and measuring supply of legal services

Identifies current level of supply

Summarises supply information

3.5 Consultation

Outlines purpose of consultation

Describes methods of consultation

Summarises outcomes of consultation (*i.e.* changes from the consultation draft)

3.6 Cross-boundary issues

3.7 Recommendations

Summarises recommendations of Committee to Area Manager in respect of priorities for contracting, identifying any matters of particular note

Outlines, where relevant, recommendations to be implemented by the Adviser, to develop services other than by contracting

3.8 Committee programme for next year

4. Method of Work

4.1 Draft regional strategy *(Arrangements 5.1(d))*

Each Committee will issue the draft regional strategy by October 31, 1998. The strategy will outline priorities for the provision of services, through contracts to be let in the year 1999/2000.

4.1.1 Assessing needs and priorities

The Committee will assess the need for legal services in its area in the following franchise categories of law:

    (a) Matrimonial/family;

    (b) Housing;

    (c) Debt;

    (d) Immigration;

    (e) Welfare benefits;

    (f) Consumer/general contract;

    (g) Mental health;

    (h) Employment.

4.1.2 The Committee should also consider whether there is need for contracts to cover the provision of services in other specialist categories of law not covered by separate franchise categories. For example, in:

    (a) Education;

    (b) Community care;

    (c) Prisoners' rights;

or any other category identified during the assessment of need process.

4.1.3 The strategy should include a section which discusses any specific client group (for example, ethnic minorities, disabled, elderly, carers, remote communities) needs which should be addressed, and advise on methods of delivery which might be employed in contracts to address need in particular geographical areas, categories of work and client groups.

4.1.4 Adviser's reports

To assist, the Adviser will prepare reports for the Committee summarising local and national data on deprivation generally and the need for legal services in particular. The Adviser will have regard to any predictive needs models prepared by the Board and to any relevant nationally and locally produced information. In preparing reports, Advisers must ensure that they cover broadly the same sets of data as each other.

4.1.5 Levels of supply of legal services

The Committee will also gather information on the current level of supply of legal services, utilising the Board's agreed supplier questionnaire where appropriate. Some information can be derived from the Boards' internal data on legal aid work. However, Committees should also be aware of, and gather relevant information about, the supply of non legally aided services as this will be important in determining the priorities for contracting. Information relating to the quality, siting and accessibility of services should also be gathered.

4.1.6 Prioritisation of need (Arrangements 5.1(c))

The Committee will use the relevant information to determine which geographical areas and categories of work should be accorded priority and in which order. Areas and categories with the greatest need will normally be accorded the highest priority, unless there are exceptional circumstances. The Committee will determine whether or not exceptional circumstances apply and a note to that effect will be included in the draft regional strategy.

4.2 Consultation on draft regional strategy *(Arrangements 5.3)*

4.2.1 Purpose of consultation

The purposes of consultation include gathering further information and validating existing information on need and on the existing supply of services which may meet the identified need, obtaining the views of consumers, potential consumers, suppliers and other funders about need and supply and enabling a wide discussion and debate about which areas and categories of work should be accorded the highest priority.

4.2.2 Written consultation

A copy of the draft regional strategy will be sent to Network members, and any additional organisations and individuals with whom or with which the Committee considers it appropriate to consult. The draft regional strategy will be accompanied by notice of a conference at which the strategy will be discussed. In addition, written submissions will be encouraged. Consultees should be allowed eight weeks to make written comments.

4.2.3 Conferences

Consultative conferences will be held throughout the region covered by the Committee. Consultees (see above) will be invited and given the opportunity to discuss, comment upon and challenge the information and conclusions contained in the draft regional strategy.

4.2.4 Summary of comments

A written summary of comments made on the draft regional strategy will be compiled by the Adviser and sent to the Board with the completed regional strategy. Copies of the summary of comments will be available to members of the public on request.

4.2.5 Cross-boundary issues

Each Committee will send a copy of its draft regional strategy to all the other Committees with which it shares a boundary and will provide comment on the draft regional strategies of its neighbouring Committees. Committees will also work together to facilitate information gathering and consultation on issues which affect two or more areas.

4.3 Finalising the regional strategy *(Arrangements 4.2)*

4.3.1 Following the consultation process outlined above, a final version of the regional strategy will be completed and submitted to the Board by 31 January 1999 for approval.

4.3.2 The Board may approve or amend the regional strategy. If in the opinion of the Board further information or analysis is needed before conclusions can be formed, this will be raised with the Committee which may be requested to resubmit the strategy for approval within a specified time limit. The Board will set out in writing any changes it makes to the regional strategy.

4.4 Publication of regional strategies at relevant stages (*Arrangements 4.3)*

The reports will be available publicly at various stages:

4.4.1 The draft regional strategy will be sent out for consultation by the Committee.

4.4.2 The version finally submitted to the Board, together with a summary of the results of the consultation, will be available from each Committee.

4.4.3 The final approved strategies, incorporating any changes agreed by the Board, will be available from Committees and the Board's Head Office.

4.5 Implementing the strategy

4.5.1 Contracting

The Committee will have no role in awarding individual contracts. The Area Manager will enter into contracts, on behalf of the Board, to address needs and priorities identified in the regional strategy and will monitor the performance of the supplier against the terms of the contract. The Committee will have access to relevant information held by the Board to monitor and evaluate the impact of contracts let by the Area Manager in meeting the need set out in the regional strategy.

4.5.2 Quality suppliers

The regional strategy will inform the development of suppliers able to meet the relevant quality requirements for contracts. It will be an aim of each area office to ensure that there are suitably qualified suppliers to meet the needs and priorities identified in the regional strategy.

ADMINISTRATIVE AND OTHER ARRANGEMENTS

5. External membership *(Arrangements 2.2–3.3)*

5.1 Attendance at meetings

External Committee members are asked to commit up to 24 days a year to the work of the committee. As part of this commitment, members will endeavour to attend all meetings to which they are invited by the Chair, including any conference convened by the Board. External members will sign a record of attendance at meetings, such record to be kept by the Adviser.

5.2 Recruitment

5.2.1 Local information about vacancies

Information about vacancies on the Committee will be publicised locally.

5.2.2 Applications

Applications to join the Committee will be made by CV and covering letter, in accordance with the instructions set out in the nationally agreed application pack. Information about shortlisting, interviews and the criteria for selection will be contained in the pack.

5.3 The selection process

Selection will be via a process of shortlisting and interview. The Chair will recommend appropriate candidates to the Chair of the Board for approval. Subject to this approval and the receipt of satisfactory references (including status inquiries in the case of solicitor applicants), the Chair will make the appointments.

5.4 Induction and training

On appointment, members will be given an induction which covers the role and function of the Committee and its relationship to the Legal Aid Board.

Additional training will be provided as appropriate.

5.5 Decision to reappoint

The Chair may recommend to the Chair of the Board that a member of a Committee is reappointed, if the Chair wishes and the member agrees. The member will be informed of any decision taken at least one month before the end of his or her term of appointment.

5.6 Leaving the Committee

Membership of the Committee ceases when the term of appointment has expired and has not been renewed, written notice of resignation is given to the Chair, membership is terminated by the Chair in writing (see Terms and Conditions of Service) or when the member reaches the age of 65, or 70 if the requirement to retire at 65 has been waived by the Chair.

6. The work of the Committee

6.1 Geographical area

Each Committee covers a Legal Aid Board area. The Committee is primarily concerned with the prioritisation of the need for legal services in its own area, although it may also be asked to consider issues which have a wider regional or national relevance. Neighbouring Committees should be aware of each others' regional strategies and the data on which they are based.

6.2 The Network

The purpose of the Network is to enable those with an interest in legal services to be informed about the work of the Committee, consulted on a range of issues and involved in the development of the regional strategy. The Network is an informal body, organised by the Adviser, through which those interested in the provision of legal and advice services can contribute to the work of the Committee. This contribution may be made by providing information on the need for and supply of services and by involvement in consultation and working groups.

6.2.1 Network members and activities

Membership of the Network is open to all. There is no limit to the size of the Network and any interested individual can join at any time. Members will not be required to make any particular commitment in terms of time or participation, but will be invited to attend consultative meetings and may be asked to participate in projects or studies. Network activities will be focused on the consultation necessary to develop and monitor the implementation of the regional strategy.

6.2.2 Consultation with the Network

Consultation and communication will take place with the Network on an ongoing basis, however in addition members of the Network will each receive a copy of the draft regional strategy and be invited to comment in writing and to attend a conference in their area.

7. Administration of the Committee *(Arrangements 7–14)*

7.1 Administrative support

The area office will provide administrative support to the Committee through the Adviser and support staff who are responsible for the day-to-day work of the Committee. The Adviser will be responsible for ensuring that the Committee has all the information it requires to perform its role. The Adviser will also organise consultative meetings, Committee meetings, conferences and other events as necessary.

7.1 Meetings

The agenda for each Committee meeting will be approved by the Chair. Members may raise matters for discussion with the Chair, for inclusion on the agenda. The Chair will decide whether a matter will be included on the agenda.

7.3 Declaration of interest

Members of the Committee will declare any interest which they have in relation to any matter under consideration by the Committee as soon as it arises and follow the procedures set out in the Rules of Conduct for Legal Aid Board members to Report Conflicts of Interest.

7.4 Scope

The Board will determine which categories of work are within the scope of the Committee's remit. The Board may also ask the Committee to consider other matters, from time to time. Subject to such directions from the Board, it is a matter for the Chair to determine whether or not any matter is within the scope of the Committee's remit.

7.5 Matters referred to the Legal Aid Board

Any matter may be referred to the Legal Aid Board by the Chair, at his or her discretion. Matters to be referred may include complex cross-boundary issues and problems which require resolution at a national level.

8. Open Government

The Committee will follow the Code of Practice on Access to Government information and will have regard to the Board's internal guidance on the Code.

9. Finance

The Area Manager will determine the budget for the Committee activities. The Committee will work within that budget.

Part Three

Part Three

Financial Eligibility—April 1998

Financial Eligibility—April 1998

All income and capital figures are "disposable". The financial eligibility limits and dependants' allowances for legal advice and assistance, civil legal aid, criminal legal aid and the family mediation pilot with effect from April 6, 1998 (April 20, 1998 for the family mediation pilot) are shown below.

LEGAL ADVICE AND ASSISTANCE—SEE KEY CARD NUMBER 30

Disposable Capital

Ineligible if disposable capital exceeds limits.

	no dependants £	one dependant £	two dependants £
Capital limits	1,000.00	1,335.00	1,535.00
	Plus £100 for each additional dependant		

Disposable Income

Ineligible if weekly disposable income exceeds £80.00.

Weekly Dependants' Allowances

Partner:		£28.65		
Dependants*:	Up to 11 yrs.	11–16 yrs.	16–18 yrs.	19 and over
	£17.30	£25.35	£30.30	£30.30

Automatically qualify on income if in receipt of income support, income-based Jobseeker's Allowance, family credit or disability working allowance but may still be out of scope on capital.

---

* Dependants aged 11 or 16 may fall into one of two age bands, according to the following rules:
  11 year olds — Use the higher rate of "11–16" if the child became 11 before September 7, 1998 and the lower rate "up to 11" if the child became 11 on or after that date.
  16 year olds — Use the higher rate of "16–18" if the child became 16 before September 7, 1998 and the lower rate "11–16" if they became 16 on or after that date. The "16–18" allowance is to be used from the September following the child's sixteenth birthday until the day before their nineteenth birthday.
  19 and over — Where a dependent child/relative is 19 or over, the rate to apply is the "16–18" rate.

ABWOR

(ABWOR for proceedings before a Mental Health Review Tribunal is available without reference to the client's financial resources.)

Disposable Capital

	no dependants £	one dependant £	two dependants £
Capital limits	3,000.00	3,335.00	3,535.00
	Plus £100 for each additional dependant		

Disposable Income

Ineligible if weekly disposable income exceeds £172.00.

Weekly Dependants' Allowances

(As for legal advice and assistance—see also note on p. 667.)

Partner:		£28.65		
Dependants:	Up to 11 yrs.	11–16 yrs.	16–18 yrs.	19 and over
	£17.30	£25.35	£30.30	£30.30

Automatically qualify on income, free of contribution, if in receipt of income support, income-based Jobseeker's Allowance, family credit or disability working allowance. Automatically qualify on capital if in receipt of income support or income-based Job-seeker's allowance.

Contribution System

No contribution if weekly disposable income up to £72. If between £72 and £172, weekly contribution of 1/3rd of excess income over £72.

CIVIL LEGAL AID (see Guide to Assessing Financial Eligibility—p. 670)

Income and capital limits

	£
	per year
Lower income limit	2,625.00
Upper income limit	7,777.00
	8,571.00 for personal injury
Lower capital limit	3,000.00
Upper capital limit	6,750.00
	8,560.00 for personal injury

All applicants in receipt of income support or income-based Jobseeker's Allowance are eligible for civil legal aid, regardless of capital.

Capital disregards for pensioners (available to men and women over 60 years of age)

Annual disposable income (excluding net income derived from capital)	*amount of capital disregard*
£	£
up to 370	35,000
371–670	30,000
671–970	25,000
971–1270	20,000
1,271–1,570	15,000
1,571–1,870	10,000
1,871–2,625	5,000

Yearly Dependants' Allowances

(See note on p. 667 regarding the appropriate allowance.)

Partner:		£1,494		
Dependants:	Up to 11 yrs.	11–16 yrs.	16–18 yrs.	18 and over
	£902	£1,322	£1,580	£1,580

Contribution System

Ongoing monthly contribution of 1/36th of excess over £2,625 for the lifetime of the certificate. Contribution from capital of excess over £3,000.

CIVIL LEGAL AID: GUIDE TO ASSESSING FINANCIAL ELIGIBILITY

This is a general guide only and does not guarantee the outcome of any application for a full certificate. Note that the assessment officer may take into account the assets of others where they have transferred resources to the client, maintained the client in the proceedings or have made resources available to the client.

Further details of the key guidance provided to Assessment Officers can be purchased from the Board. For more information please contact the Documentation Production Team, Quality Assurance Department, 85 Grays' Inn Road, London WC1X 8AA, DX 328 LON/CH'RY LN WC2, Fax 0171 813 8647.

Step One: Identify clients in receipt of income support, or income-based Jobseeker's Allowance

Applicants properly in receipt of income support, or income-based Jobseeker's Allowance are eligible for free civil legal aid.

There are two ways to check eligibility, which are by:

(1) Sight of notification from the Benefits Agency—this will be in the form of a letter of entitlement (issued either when income support/income-based jobseeker's allowance was awarded or when benefit was uprated in April).

(2) Proof of payment—either from bank statements showing the benefit paid in or by sight of the orderbook.

If the client is not in receipt of income support, or income-based Jobseeker's Allowance (including applications where the client is still awaiting a decision regarding a claim for such a benefit) move on to step two. Other types of benefit, such as family credit, do not give automatic entitlement.

Step Two: Work out capital

Add together all the capital of the client (and partner if appropriate).

Capital includes:

- land and buildings other than the client's home and including interests in timeshares although the market value of the client's home in excess of £100,000 after allowing for any outstanding mortgage or £100,000 (whichever is the lesser) must be included, and a maximum of £100,000 allowed in respect of the total mortgage debt on any property or properties that the client resides in;
- money in the bank, Building Society, Post Office; premium bonds, National Savings certificates, etc;
- investments, stocks and shares;
- money that can be borrowed against the surrender value of insurance policies;
- money value of valuable items; for example, boat, caravan, antiques, jewellery (but not wedding or engagement rings or usually the client's car, unless of exceptional value);
- money owing to the client;
- money due from an estate or Trust Fund;
- money that can be borrowed against business assets.

Do not include any savings, valuable items or property the ownership of which is the specific subject of the court case; for example, a holiday cottage would normally count but not if it was specifically under attack as part of a disputed divorce settlement.

Do not include:

- loans or grants from the Social Fund;
- home contents, for example (unless exceptionally valuable) furniture and household effects;
- personal clothing;
- personal tools and equipment of trade;
- back to work bonus under Jobseekers Act 1995 s.26;
- payments under the Community Care Direct Payment Scheme;
- any capital disregard for pensioners (men and women over 60):

Annual disposable income (excluding net income derived from capital)	amount of capital disregarded
up to £370	£35,000
£371–£670	£30,000
£671–£970	£25,000
£971–£1,270	£20,000
£1,271–£1,570	£15,000
£1,571–£1,870	£10,000
£1,871–£2,625	£5,000

Total Disposable Capital £ ....

Step Three: Does the disposable capital qualify the client for Civil Legal Aid?

If under £3,000 → no contribution from capital.

If between £3,000 and £6,750 (personal injury £8,560) → Civil Legal Aid subject to a capital contribution.

Over these limits the client will not get Civil Legal Aid unless the area office considers the probable costs would exceed the contribution payable.

Step Four: Work out the size of the client's likely capital contribution

Total disposable capital £ .... deduct £3,000 to give
        (step 2)

Capital Contribution £ ....

Step Five: Work out weekly income

Add together the client's weekly gross income (*i.e.* before tax) and that of his/her partner if appropriate.

Income includes:

- weekly earnings or profits from business;
- maintenance payments;
- pensions;
- all welfare benefits except housing benefit, attendance allowance, disability living allowance, constant attendance allowance, back to work bonus under section 26 of the Jobseekers Act 1995, payments made under Earnings Top-up Scheme and payments under the Community Care Direct Payments Scheme;
- income from savings and investments;
- dividends from shares;
- monies received from friends and relatives;
- student grants and loans.

Weekly Income £ ....

Step Six: Work out deductible allowances and expenses

Deduct the following from *weekly* income:

- Income Tax; National Insurance contributions; pension scheme contributions; trade union membership;
- council tax;
- maintenance payments made;
- fares to and from work;
- child care expenses incurred because of work;
- housing costs:
  — rent (less any housing benefit), water rates and mortgage repayments (interest and capital) although the amount allowed if the client's mortgage debt exceeds £100,000 will be reduced in proportion (e.g. if the client's mortgage debt is £200,000 only half the amount actually paid can be deducted);
  — £5.29 weekly for necessary repairs and house insurance (where payable by the client owner-occupier);
  — endowment policy premiums (if paid in connection with a mortgage);
  — actual costs of accommodation if the client is neither a tenant nor owner-occupier;
  — ground rent and any other applicable charges; and service charges which have to be paid as part of a lease or tenancy agreement.
- fixed amounts for each dependant relative (adult and child) living with the client.

The *weekly* amounts of allowances for dependants are:

> £28.65 for a partner
> £17.30 for each child aged up to 11
> £25.35 for each child aged 11–16
> £30.30 for each child aged 16–18
> £30.30 for each child or dependant aged 19 or over

For children and dependants aged 11, 16 or 19 (or over) at the time legal aid is applied for, the following rules apply:

11 year olds — Use the higher rate of "11–16" if the child became 11 before September 7, 1998 and the lower rate "up to 11" if the child became 11 on or after that date.

16 year olds — Use the higher rate of "16–18" if the child became 16 before September 7, 1998 and the lower rate "11–16" if they became 16 on or after that date. The "16–18" allowance is to be used from the September following the child's sixteenth birthday until the day before their nineteenth birthday.

19 and over — Where a dependant child/relative is 19 or over, the rate to apply is the "16–18" rate.

Total of all deductions £...

Note that other deductions may be made by the Legal Aid Assessment Office, e.g. for membership of professional associations connected with employment, fines and judgments and payments of arrears of tax, mortgage, gas or electricity.

Step Seven: Work out yearly disposable income

Weekly income £................................ minus deductions £.............................. to give
(step 5)   (step 6)

Weekly disposable income £.. multiply by 52 to give

Yearly Disposable Income £ ....

Note that if there are known changes of circumstances (e.g. a pay rise, applicant having a baby or returning to work after sickness) which will affect the income of the applicant during the next 52 weeks then these will be taken into account in the assessment by the assessment officer when determining the actual level of annual disposable income.

Step Eight: Does the yearly disposable income qualify the client for Civil Legal Aid?

If under £2,625 → no contribution from income.

If between £2,625 and £7,777 (£8,571 in personal injury claims) → Civil Legal Aid subject to a contribution from income.

Step Nine: Work out amount of contribution from income

Yearly disposable income £ .... deduct £2,625 = £ ....
(step 8)

divide by 36 to give   *Monthly Contribution* £ ....

Step 10: Work out total initial contribution

Add together:

Monthly Contribution £............................ and Capital Contribution £ ....
                               (step 9)   (step 4)

to give   *Total Initial Contribution* £ ....

FAMILY MEDIATION PILOT*

This only concerns those practitioners/organisations who have contracted with the Board to take part in the pilot and deals with the eligibility for mediation of their clients.

Advice and assistance for mediation in family matters itself (as opposed to legal advice and assistance to support mediation) is covered by a pilot scheme. Eligibility is set at the ABWOR limits but is non-contributory. Those who hold a current civil legal aid certificate also qualify automatically.

Income Limit

(from 20 April 1998) £172.00 per week

Weekly Dependants' Allowances

(from 6 April 1998) as for ABWOR (see page 668)

Capital Limits: no change

No dependants	£3,000
One dependant	£3,335
Two dependants	£3,535
Plus £100 for each additional independent	

Contribution System

None, ineligible if weekly disposable income exceeds £172.00.

State Benefits

As ABWOR (see page 668).

CRIMINAL LEGAL AID

Income and capital limits

	£ per week (average)
Free legal aid income limit *No upper income limit*	50.00

	£
Free legal aid capital limit *No upper capital limit*	3,000.00

Weekly Dependants' Allowances

(See note on p. 667 regarding the appropriate allowance.)

Partner:		£28.65		
Dependants:	Up to 11 yrs.	11–16 yrs.	16–18 yrs.	19 and over
	£17.30	£25.35	£30.30	£30.30

Automatically qualify free of contribution if in receipt of income support, income-based Jobseeker's allowance, family credit or disability working allowance.

Contribution System

Ongoing weekly contribution from income of £1 for every £3 or part of £3 by which weekly disposable income exceeds £50, except that no contribution is payable if the disposable income is less than £51 per week. Contribution from capital of excess over £3,000.

675

Remuneration Rates—April 1996 onwards

The rates quoted are applicable for work done from April 1, 1996 onwards (with the exception of the rates shown in italics which apply to work done on or after July 8, 1996 and the rates in bold, which apply to certificates issued on or after November 1, 1997—advocacy in prescribed family proceedings in the County Court as well as the rates for Part IV Family Law Act 1996.)

The figures in brackets are the London rates applicable to a fee-earner whose office is in the London Legal Aid Area.

GREEN FORM AND ABWOR

1. Green Form

	Franchisees		Non-Franchisees	
	£	£	£	£
Preparation	45.50	(48.25)	44.00	(46.50)
Travelling and waiting	25.50	(25.50)	24.50	(24.50)
Routine letters written and telephone calls	3.55	(3.70)	3.40	(3.55)
Cost limit—Petition prepared	136.50	(144.75)	132.00	(139.50)
—Other cases	91.00	(96.50)	88.00	(93.00)

2. ABWOR—*(other than Mental Health Review Tribunals, Discretionary Life Prisoners, Her Majesty's Pleasure Panel and Warrants of Further Detention—see below)*

	Franchisees		Non-Franchisees	
	£	£	£	£
Preparation	45.50	(48.25)	44.00	(46.50)
Advocacy	57.25	(57.25)	55.25	(55.25)
Attendance at Court where counsel assigned	31.00	(31.00)	30.00	(30.00)
Travelling and waiting	25.50	(25.50)	24.50	(24.50)
Routine letters written and telephone calls	3.55	(3.70)	3.40	(3.55)

3. ABWOR—*Mental Health Review Tribunals, Discretionary Life Prisoners and Her Majesty's Pleasure Panel*

	Franchisees		Non-Franchisees	
	£	£	£	£
Preparation	54.50	(58.25)	52.75	(56.25)
Advocacy	66.25	(66.25)	64.00	(64.00)
Attendance at Court where counsel assigned	31.00	(31.00)	30.00	(30.00)

676

	Franchisees		Non-Franchisees	
	£	£	£	£
Travelling and waiting	25.50	(25.50)	24.50	(24.50)
Routine letters written and telephone calls	3.90	(3.90)	3.75	(3.75)

4. ABWOR—*Warrants of Further Detention**

	Franchisees		Non-Franchisees	
	£	£	£	£
Preparation	60.67	(64.33)	58.67	(62.00)
Advocacy	76.33	(76.33)	73.67	(73.67)
Attendance at Court where counsel assigned	41.33	(41.33)	39.99	(39.99)
Travelling and waiting	33.99	(33.99)	32.67	(32.67)
Routine letters written and telephone calls	4.73	(4.93)	4.53	(4.73)

*Note: these rates apply only to Duty Solicitors providing ABWOR in unsocial hours. ABWOR for warrants of further detention at other times or by own solicitors is paid at the normal ABWOR rates in 2. above.

COURT DUTY SOLICITOR AND ADVICE AND ASSISTANCE AT POLICE STATIONS

Court Duty Solicitor

	Franchisees		Non-Franchisees	
	£	£	£	£
Standard Rate	52.25	(53.50)	50.75	(52.00)
Enhanced Rate	65.31	(66.88)	63.44	(65.00)
Travelling	25.50	(25.50)	25.00	(25.00)

Police Station Duty Solicitor

	Franchisees		Non-Franchisees	
	£	£	£	£
Availability during duty period	3.80*	(3.85)*	3.65	(3.75)
to a maximum of	91.20	(92.40)	87.60	(90.00)
Advice and assistance other than by telephone				
—Duty Solicitor Unsocial Hours	61.75	(61.75)	60.00	(60.00)
—Duty Solicitor Other Hours	46.50	(50.25)	45.50	(48.50)
—Own Solicitor	46.50	(50.25)	45.50	(48.50)
Travelling and waiting				
—Duty Solicitor Unsocial Hours	61.75	(61.75)	60.00	(60.00)
—Duty Solicitor Other Hours	46.50	(50.25)	45.50	(48.50)
—Own Solicitor	25.75	(25.75)	25.25	(25.25)
Telephone advice	21.25	(22.00)	20.75	(21.50)
Routine telephone calls	3.60	(3.75)	3.50	(3.60)
Cost limit per case	90.00*	(90.00)*	90.00*	(90.00)*

*Note: Franchisees are not subject to any clawback of standby payments and do not require authority to exceed £90 costs limit.

CRIMINAL LEGAL AID

MAGISTRATES' COURT—FEE EARNER OUTSIDE LONDON AREA

1. Hourly Rates

	Franchisees £	Non-Franchisees £
Preparation	46.00	44.75
Advocacy	57.75	56.50
Attendance at Court where counsel assigned	31.50	30.50
Travelling and waiting	25.50	24.75
Routine letters written and telephone calls	3.55	3.45

2. Standard Fees for Franchisees

	Lower Standard Fee £	Lower Limit £	Higher Standard Fee £	Higher Limit £
Category 1	148.25	276.00	357.00	478.00
Category 2	262.25	474.00	601.00	790.00
Category 3	236.50	418.00	536.00	730.00

3. Standard Fees for Non-Franchisees

	Lower Standard Fee £	Lower Limit £	Higher Standard Fee £	Higher Limit £
Category 1	144.25	268.00	346.00	463.75
Category 2	254.50	460.00	583.00	767.25
Category 3	229.75	406.00	520.25	709.50

MAGISTRATES' COURT—FEE EARNER IN LONDON AREA

1. Hourly Rates

	Franchisees £	Non-Franchisees £
Preparation	48.50	47.25
Advocacy	57.75	56.50
Attendance at Court where counsel assigned	31.50	30.50
Travelling and waiting	25.50	24.75
Routine letters written and telephone calls	3.70	3.60

2. Standard Fees for Franchisees

	Lower Standard Fee £	Lower Limit £	Higher Standard Fee £	Higher Limit £
Category 1	191.00	354.00	453.00	598.00
Category 2	336.25	602.00	755.00	963.00
Category 3	299.25	507.00	629.00	778.00

3. Standard Fees for Non-Franchisees

	Lower Standard Fee £	Lower Limit £	Higher Standard Fee £	Higher Limit £
Category 1	185.50	344.00	440.00	581.50
Category 2	326.50	584.00	732.50	934.75
Category 3	290.50	493.00	611.00	755.25

CROWN COURT AND COURT OF APPEAL

	£	£
Preparation		
Senior Solicitor	53.00	(55.75)
Solicitor, fee earner (or equivalent)	45.00	(47.25)
Articled clerk (or equivalent)	29.75	(34.00)
Advocacy		
Senior solicitor	64.50	(64.50)
Solicitor	56.00	(56.00)
Attendance at court		
Senior solicitor	42.25	(42.25)
Solicitor	34.00	(34.00)
Articled clerk	20.50	(20.50)
Travelling and waiting		
Senior solicitor	24.75	(24.75)
Solicitor	24.75	(24.75)
Articled clerk	12.50	(12.50)
Letters/Telephone Calls	3.45	(3.60)

STANDARD FEES IN THE CROWN COURT

Outside London

	Lower Fee £	Lower Limit £	Principal Fee £	Upper Limit £
Jury Trial	129.50	179.00	249.50	312.00
Guilty Plea	81.50	110.00	175.00	226.00
Appeal against conviction	51.00	68.00	153.00	233.00
Appeal against sentence	36.25	52.00	93.00	131.00
Committal for sentence	42.50	51.00	97.75	141.00
Advocacy	26.25	—	—	—
Attendance at court (including waiting) where more than one legal representative assigned	21.40	—	—	—
Travelling	18.50	—	—	—
Additional amount for preparation of case for counsel to appear alone	£30.00			
Additional amount for listening to tape recordings	£10.90 for every 10 minutes of total running time (or part thereof)			

STANDARD FEES IN THE CROWN COURT cont—

In London	Lower Fee £	Lower Limit £	Principal Fee £	Upper Limit £
Jury Trial	139.00	186.00	261.50	326.00
Guilty Plea	87.50	114.00	185.50	235.00
Appeal against conviction	54.50	70.00	159.00	244.00
Appeal against sentence	39.25	54.00	159.00	244.00
Committal for sentence	45.00	53.00	103.00	145.00
Advocacy	28.75	—	—	—
Attendance at court (including waiting where more than one legal representative assigned	21.40	—	—	—
Travelling	18.50	—	—	—
Additional amount for preparation of case for counsel to appear alone		£32.00		
Additional amount for listening to tape recordings		£10.90 for every 10 minutes of total running time (or part thereof)		

Criminal Higher Courts—Counsel's Fees*

	£
Jury Trials	221.50
Guilty Pleas	117.00
Appeals against convictions	117.00
Appeals against sentence	73.50
Committals for sentence	73.50
Standard appearance fee	46.50
Standard refresher fee	
(1) Half day	81.75
(2) Full day	158.25
(3) More than full day	238.00
Standard written work fee	30.00

Where counsel appears alone the standard basic fee payable is increased by £19.25.

Where counsel listens to a taped interview the standard basic fee payable is increased by £10.90 for every 10 minutes (or part thereof).

* A system of graduated fees has been introduced for counsel's fees in Crown Court cases. The details are contained in the Legal Aid in Criminal Aid Care Proceedings (Costs) (Amendment) (No. 2) Regulations 1996 (S.I. 1996 No. 2655) which apply to work done under legal aid orders made on or after January 1, 1997.

CIVIL LEGAL AID—HIGH COURT AND COUNTY COURT
(except Family Proceedings within regulations 3(2)(a) or (b) Legal Aid in Family Proceedings (Remuneration) Regulations 1991).

FRANCHISEE RATES

	High Court £	County Court £
Routine letters out	7.50 per item	6.60 per item
Routine telephone calls	4.15 per item	3.65 per item
All other preparation work including any work which was reasonably done arising out of or incidental to the proceedings, interviews with client, witnesses, and other parties; obtaining evidence; preparation and consideration of, and dealing with, documents, negotiations and notices; dealing with letters written and received and telephone calls which are not routine	75.00 per hour (79.50 per hour where solicitor's office situated within legal aid area 1)	66.00 per hour 70.00 per hour
Attending counsel in conference or at the trial or hearing of any summons or application at court, or other appointment	37.00 per hour	32.50 per hour
Attending without counsel at the trial or hearing of any cause or the hearing of any summons or application at court, or other appointment	75.00 per hour	66.00 per hour
Travelling and waiting	33.25 per hour	29.20 per hour

NON-FRANCHISEE RATES

	High Court £	County Court £
Routine letters out	7.40 per item	6.50 per item
Routine telephone calls	4.10 per item	3.60 per item
All other preparation work including any work which was reasonably done arising out of or incidental to the proceedings, interviews with client, witnesses, and other parties; obtaining evidence; preparation and consideration of, and dealing with, documents, negotiations and notices; dealing with letters written and received and telephone calls which are not routine	74.00 per hour (78.50 per hour where solicitor's office situated within legal aid area 1)	65.00 per hour 69.00 per hour

	High Court £	County Court £
Attending counsel in conference or at the trial or hearing of any summons or application at court, or other appointment	£36.40 per hour	£32.00 per hour
Attending without counsel at the trial or hearing of any cause or the hearing of any summons or application at court, or other appointment	£74.00 per hour	£65.00 per hour
Travelling and waiting	£32.70 per hour	£28.75 per hour

CIVIL LEGAL AID—IN FAMILY PROCEEDINGS (except proceedings under Part IV Family Law Act 1996 (see p. 689 below))

Rates from April 1, 1996 onwards, with the exception of the rates in italics, which apply to work done on or after July 8, 1996, and the rates in bold, which apply to certificates issued on or after November 1, 1997. The figures in brackets are the London rates applicable to a fee earner whose office is in the London Legal Aid Area.

FRANCHISEE RATES

Care proceedings—*i.e.* proceedings for an order under Parts IV or V of the Children Act 1989—care and supervision/protection of children but including secure accommodation orders.

	High Court £	County Court or Magistrates' Court £
Preparation		
Writing routine letters	£4.25 per item	£3.70 per item
Receiving routine letters	£2.10 per item	£1.85 per item
Routine telephone calls	*£4.25 per item*	£3.70 per item
All other preparation work including dealing with letters written and received and telephone calls which are not routine	£66.50 per hour (£70.75 per hour)	£59.00 per hour (£62.00 per hour)
Travelling and waiting	£32.50 per hour	£29.50 per hour
Conferences with Counsel		
Attending counsel in conference	£37.50 per hour	£33.00 per hour
Travelling and waiting	£32.50 per hour	£29.50 per hour
Attendances		
Attending with counsel at the trial or hearing of any cause or the hearing of any summons or other application at court, or other appointment	£37.50 per hour	£33.00 per hour

	High Court £	County Court £
Attending without counsel at the trial or hearing of any cause or the hearing of any summons or other application at court, or other appointment	£65.00 per hour	£65.00 per hour
Travelling and waiting	£32.50 per hour	£29.50 per hour
Fees for junior counsel	See non-franchisee rates below	
Taxation and review of taxation (High Court and County Court only)		
Preparing the bill (where allowable) and completing the taxation (excluding preparing for and attending the taxation)	£32.50–£90.75	£32.50–£51.75
Preparing for and attending the taxation (including travelling and waiting)	Discretionary	Discretionary
Review by district judge or judge (including preparation)	Discretionary	Discretionary

Prescribed Family Proceedings

(a) High Court and County Court Proceedings

Preparation

	High Court	County Court
Writing routine letters	£4.25 per item	£3.70 per item
Receiving routine letters	£2.10 per item	£1.85 per item
Routine telephone calls	*£4.25 per item*	£3.70 per item
All other preparation work including dealing with letters written and received and telephone calls which are not routine	Where the proceedings were conducted in the divorce registry or the South Eastern Circuit at the time when the relevant work was done. £47.50 per hour £41.50 per hour All other circuits: £44.25 per hour £39.25 per hour	
In addition to the items 1–4 above, to cover the general care and conduct of the proceedings	+50%	+50%
Travelling and waiting	£32.50 per hour	£29.50 per hour

Conferences with Counsel

	High Court	County Court
Attending counsel in conference	£37.50 per hour	£33.00 per hour
Travelling and waiting	£32.50 per hour	£29.50 per hour

	High Court £	County Court £

Attendances

Attending with counsel at the trial or hearing of any cause or the hearing of any summons or other application at court, or other appointment	£37.50 per hour	£33.00 per hour
Attending without counsel at the trial or hearing of any cause or the hearing of any summons or other application at court, or other appointment	£56.75 per hour	**£56.25 per hour**
Travelling and waiting	£32.50 per hour	£29.50 per hour

Fees for junior counsel See non-franchisee rates below

Taxation and review of taxation (High Court and County Court only)

Preparing the bill (where allowable) and completing the taxation (excluding preparing for and attending the taxation)	£32.50–£90.75	£32.50–£51.75
Preparing for and attending the taxation (including travelling and waiting)	Discretionary	Discretionary
Review by district judge or judge (including preparation)	Discretionary	Discretionary

(b) Magistrates' Court Proceedings

Preparation	£44.50 per hour—(£47.50)
Advocacy	£56.25 per hour
Attendance at court where counsel assigned	£30.25 per hour
Travelling and waiting	£25.00 per hour
Routine letters written and routine telephone	£3.45 per item—(£3.60)

684

NON-FRANCHISEE RATES

Care proceedings—*i.e.* proceedings for an order under Parts IV or V of the Children Act 1989—care and supervision/protection of children including secure accommodation orders.

	High Court £	County Court or Magistrates' Court £
Preparation		
Writing routine letters	£4.25 per item	£3.65 per item
Receiving routine letters	*£2.10 per item*	*£1.85 per item*
Routine telephone calls	£4.25 per item	£3.65 per item
All other preparation work including dealing with letters written and received and telephone calls which are not routine	£65.50 per hour (£69.75 per hour for a fee-earner whose office is situated within legal aid area 1).	£58.00 per hour £61.25 per hour
Travelling and waiting	£32.00 per hour	£29.25 per hour
Conferences with Counsel		
Attending counsel in conference	£37.00 per hour	£32.50 per hour
Travelling and waiting	£32.00 per hour	£29.25 per hour
Attendances		
Attending with counsel at the trial or hearing of any cause or the hearing of any summons or other application at court, or other appointment	£37.00 per hour	£32.50 per hour
Attending without counsel at the trial or hearing of any cause or the hearing of any summons or other application at court, or other appointment	£64.00 per hour	£64.00 per hour
Travelling and waiting	£32.00 per hour	£29.25 per hour
Fees for junior counsel		
With a brief on an unopposed application for an injunction, or procedural issue	Standard £88.25 Maximum £146.25	£76.25 £127.00
With a brief on the trial of a cause or matter or on the hearing of an application where the hearing lasts for		

	High Court £	County Court or Magistrates' Court £
(a) one hour	Standard £133.50 Maximum £268.00	£114.25 £228.50
(b) a half day	Standard £184.75 Maximum £304.50	£159.25 £268.00
(c) a full day	Standard £368.50 Maximum £584.75	£317.75 £508.50
(d) more than a full day	Discretionary	Discretionary
For each day or part of a day on which the trial of a cause or matter, or the hearing of an ancillary application, or a children appointment, is continued after the first day	Discretionary	Discretionary
Conference (including time reasonably spent in preparation and conference, but not otherwise remunerated)	Standard £20.25 per ½ hour	Standard £17.75 per ½ hour
(a) Complex items of written work (such as advices on evidence, opinions and affidavits of a substantial nature, requests for particulars or answers)	Standard £96.25 per item	Standard £82.75 per item
(b) All other written work	Standard £57.00 per item	Standard £50.25 per item
Except where the court is within 40 kilometres of Charing Cross or where there is no local Bar in the court town, or within 40 kilometres thereof, for travelling time	Standard £18.50 per hour + expenses	Standard £15.85 per hour + expenses

Taxation and review of taxation (High Court and County Court only)

Preparing the bill (where allowable) and completing the taxation (excluding preparing for and attending the taxation)	£32.00–£89.25	£32.00–£51.00

	High Court £	County Court £
Preparing for and attending the taxation (including travelling and waiting)	Discretionary	Discretionary
Review by district judge or judge (including preparation)	Discretionary	Discretionary

Prescribed Family Proceedings

(a) High Court and County Court Proceedings

Preparation

	High Court	County Court
Writing routine letters	£4.25 per item	£3.65 per item
Receiving routine letters	*£2.10 per item*	*£1.85 per item*
Routine telephone calls	£4.25 per item	£3.65 per item

All other preparation work including dealing with letters written and received and telephone calls which are not routine	Where the proceedings were conducted in the divorce registry or the South Eastern Circuit at the time when the relevant work was done £46.75 per hour £41.00 per hour All other circuits: £43.75 per hour £38.75 per hour

	High Court	County Court
In addition to the items 1–4 above, to cover the general care and conduct of the proceedings	+50%	+50%
Travelling and waiting	£32.00 per hour	£29.25 per hour

Conferences with Counsel

	High Court	County Court
Attending counsel in conference	£37.00 per hour	£32.50 per hour
Travelling and waiting	£32.00 per hour	£29.25 per hour

Attendances

	High Court	County Court
Attending with counsel at the trial or hearing of any cause or the hearing of any summons or other application at court, or other appointment	£37.00 per hour	£32.50 per hour
Attending without counsel at the trial or hearing of any cause or the hearing of any summons or other application at court, or other appointment	£55.75 per hour	**£55.25 per hour**
Travelling and waiting	£32.00 per hour	£29.25 per hour

687

	High Court £	County Court £
Fees for junior counsel		
With a brief on an unopposed application for an injunction, or procedural issue	Standard £88.25 Maximum £146.25	£76.25 £127.00
With a brief on the trial of a cause or matter or on the hearing of an application where the hearing lasts for		
(a) one hour	Standard £133.50 Maximum £268.00	£114.25 £228.50
(b) a half day	Standard £184.75 Maximum £304.50	£159.25 £268.00
(c) a full day	Standard £368.50 Maximum £584.75	£317.75 £508.50
(d) more than a full day	Discretionary	Discretionary
For each day or part of a day on which the trial of a cause ormatter, or the hearing of an ancillary application, or a children appointment, is continued after the first day	Discretionary	Discretionary
Conference (including time reasonably spent in preparation and conference, but not otherwise remunerated)	Standard £20.25 per ½ hour	Standard £17.75 per ½ hour
(a) Complex items of written work (such as advices on evidence, opinions and affidavits of a substantial nature, requests for particulars or answers)	Standard £96.25 per item	Standard £82.75 per item
(b) All other written work	Standard £57.00 per item	Standard £50.25 per item
Except where the court is within 40 kilometres of Charing Cross or where there is no local Bar in the court town, or within 40 kilometres thereof, for travelling time	Standard £18.50 per hour + expenses	Standard £15.85 per hour + expenses
Taxation and review of taxation (High Court and County Court only)		
Preparing the bill (where allowable) and completing the taxation (excluding preparing for and attending the taxation)	£32.00–£89.25	£32.00–£51.00
Preparing for and attending the taxation (including travelling and waiting)	Discretionary	Discretionary
Review by district judge or judge (including preparation)	Discretionary	Discretionary

(b) Magistrates' Court Proceedings

Preparation	£44.00 per hour—(£46.75 per hour for a fee-earner whose office is situated within legal aid area 1)
Advocacy	£55.25 per hour
Attendance at court where counsel assigned	£30.00 per hour
Travelling and waiting	£24.60 per hour
Routine letters written and routine telephone	£3.40 per item—(£3.55 per item for a fee-earner whose office is situated within legal aid area 1)

Civil Legal Aid—Proceedings under Part IV Family Law Act 1996
(applicable to certificates issued on or after November 1, 1997 and irrespective of venue)

	Non-Franchisees	*Franchisees*
Writing routine letters	£3.65 per item	£3.70 per item
Receiving routine letters	£1.85 per item	£1.85 per item
Routine telephone calls	£3.65 per item	£3.70 per item
All other preparation work including any work which was reasonably done arising out of or incidental to the proceedings: — interviews with client, witnesses, and other parties; — obtaining evidence; — preparation and consideration of, and dealing with, documents, negotiations and notices; — dealing with letters written and received and telephone calls which are not routine.	Where the proceedings were conducted in the divorce registry or in another court in the South Eastern Circuit at the time when the relevant work was done. £41 per hour All other circuits £38.75 per hour	£41.50 per hour £39.25 per hour
In addition to items above to cover the general care and conduct of the proceedings.	Plus 50%.	Plus 50%.
Travelling and waiting time in connection with the above.	£29.25 per hour	£29.50 per hour
Attending counsel in conference.	£32.50 per hour	£33 per hour
Travelling and waiting in connection with conferences.	£29.25 per hour	£29.50 per hour
Attending with counsel at the trial or hearing of any cause or the hearing of any summons or application at court, or other appointment.	£32.50 per hour	£33 per hour

689

	Non-Franchisees	Franchisees
Attending without counsel at any of the above (**new rate**)	£55.25 per hour	£56.25 per hour
Travelling and waiting in connection with attendances at court.	£29.25 per hour	£29.50 per hour

Taxation and Review of Taxation

	Non-Franchisees	Franchisees
Preparing the bill (where allowable) and completing the taxation (excluding preparing for and attending the taxation).	£32–£51	£32.50–£51.75
Preparing for and attending the taxation (including travelling and waiting).	Discretionary	Discretionary
Review by District Judge or Judge (including preparation).	Discretionary	Discretionary

Civil Legal Aid in the Magistrates' Court

The rates for civil legal aid for Magistrates' Court proceedings other than family proceedings are the same as for criminal legal aid.

Representation in Contempt Proceedings

Standard fee per day of appearance	£72.75
Division where solicitor and counsel/advocate both instructed:	
Advocate	£46.50
Solicitor	£26.25

Independent Social Workers

From April 1, 1996 onwards the fees payable to independent social workers are:

Preparation	£16.75 per hour
Travel	£11.17 per hour

Conciliation Reports

From April 1, 1996 onwards the amount allowable as a disbursement when a solicitor makes a referral to a recognised conciliation service under legal advice and assistance is £33.13 for franchisees and £33.00 for non-franchisees. This is broken down as to:

	Franchisees	Non-franchisees
Report	£23.35	£23.35
Solicitor's costs	£9.78	£9.65

Mileage

The mileage rate is 36p per mile.

Legal Aid Board Customer Service Standards

The text below is based on the Legal Aid Board's Customer Service Standards which were published in December 1993. This version has been updated and includes the 1998/99 performance targets.

Since the Legal Aid Board assumed responsibility for the administration of legal aid in 1989 we have set, and published through our Annual Reports, targets for the delivery of services and details of performance against those targets. The targets serve two key purposes: they inform you of the service that you can expect from us; and they are an important tool in monitoring and improving our performance. As part of our commitment to the principles of the Citizen's Charter we have decided to incorporate our performance targets into a wider statement of customer service standards.

This statement of service standards is a starting point upon which we intend to improve. We will review the standards annually in consultation with our customers and our aim will be both to improve on existing standards and to introduce new standards for areas not already covered.

TARGETS FOR 1998/99

Civil legal aid certificates

We will decide 75 per cent of civil legal aid certificates within 2 weeks and 90 per cent within 4 weeks.

Civil bills

We will pay 75 per cent of civil legal aid bills within 6 weeks and 90 per cent within 8 weeks.

Criminal bills

We will pay 95 per cent of standard fee claims within 4 weeks and 90 per cent of other criminal bills within six weeks.

Other bills

We will pay 90 per cent of other legal aid bills within 6 weeks.

Applications to amend or for prior authority in civil legal aid, criminal legal aid and ABWOR

We will decide 80 per cent of applications within 2 weeks and 95 per cent within 4 weeks.

Green form extensions

We will decide 90 per cent of applications for an extension of legal advice and assistance (a Green Form) within three working days.

Applications for criminal legal aid

We will decide reviews of applications for criminal legal aid in which the area office is able to make a delegated decision as follows: 80 per cent within 2 weeks and 95 per cent within 4 weeks. Area committee decisions will be dealt with as follows: 90 per cent within 4 weeks.

Appeals by assisted persons or applicants for legal aid

We will offer 90 per cent of appellants an area committee hearing of their appeal on a date within 8 weeks of the receipt of their appeal and 100 per cent within 10 weeks.

Emergency certificates

Emergency applications will continue to receive a high priority. We expect to provide an applicant with a decision within 24 hours of receipt by us. However, in exceptional cases it may take up to 48 hours to reach a decision.

Repayments to assisted persons*

We will repay monies in 75 per cent of cases within six weeks of receipt of any costs and/or damages due and having processed a bill.

Land charges*

We will deal with land charge matters as follows: 90 per cent of postponements will be processed within five working days; 90 per cent of redemptions will be processed

* Performance in these areas has been affected by the transition to our new Corporate Information System (CIS) but we will aim to achieve these targets by the application of additional resources.

within five working days; 90 per cent of vacations will be processed within 15 working days.

General correspondence

All general correspondence will be responded to as quickly as possible. Most will be responded to within one to two weeks and our aim is to respond to all correspondence within twenty working days of receipt. Urgent correspondence will be fast-tracked so that it is dealt with within a period commensurate with its urgency. We will measure performance in this area by reference to post contained in office backlogs.

CUSTOMER SERVICE

Our correspondence contains details of how to contact us. Most of the letters and certificates that we produce are of standard form and do not identify a particular sender as any one of a number of caseworkers will be able to help with an enquiry. Where an individual, non-standard, letter is sent it will either be signed by the individual who sent it or their name will be provided in the "who to contact" section at the top of the letter. All of our staff will give their names over the telephone.

Our work is such that we can deal with issues most quickly and effectively by letter or telephone rather than in meetings. If you would like a meeting to discuss a particular matter we will consider your request in a helpful and sympathetic manner and, where it is the best way to progress the issue, we will arrange this. When an applicant for legal aid or a legally aided person has to attend an area office, the office will provide them with information about what they can expect when they attend.

Our area offices are open between the hours of 9.00 am and 5.00 pm and a telephone service is available during those hours. Outside of opening hours a recorded message informs callers of how and when the office may best be contacted.

INFORMATION

We publish and make readily available information about the Legal Aid Board and the availability of legal aid. Our leaflets—"A Practical Guide to Legal Aid"; "How to Get Free or Low Cost Legal Help"; "If you need this ... Look for this" (a leaflet about franchising); "Criminal Legal Aid at the Police Station and in Court"; "Customer Service"; "Paying Back the Legal Aid Board - Statutory Charge" and "Representations—what we do when you think legal aid should not have been granted"—are available from your local area office.

Our area offices will display details of our performance targets, overall national performance and area office performance against those targets.

COMPLAINTS

We operate a comprehensive complaints procedure and will address any complaint about our performance promptly and effectively.

All complaints to area offices will be actioned within five working days. If a substantive response cannot be sent in that time an acknowledgement will be sent indicating when a substantive response may be expected.

If you wish to make a complaint you should, in the first instance, contact the office which is the subject of your complaint. If you do make a complaint you will receive an explanation and, if we are at fault, an apology and information on what we have done to put things right. (See also p. 695.)

FURTHER INFORMATION

The Board welcomes suggestions or comments about these standards and will be reviewing them in the light of the feed-back we get from the profession and other legal aid clients. If you would like to comment please write to Anne-Marie Roberts, Secretariat Department, Legal Aid Head Office.

Customer service

The text of the Legal Aid Board's customer service leaflet is reproduced below. Copies are available from the Board's offices.

The Legal Aid Board is proud to display the ISO9002 Quality Assurance logo. It demonstrates our commitment to providing an efficient and effective service for all our customers. If you think our standard of service falls below what you should reasonably expect, then we want to know. We have staff in each of our offices ready to deal with your concerns.

SERVICE STANDARDS

We aim to give the best possible service to our customers. Our work is subject to quality checks and we are committed to a process of continuous improvement.

One measure of our service relates to how quickly we deal with different areas of our work, for example, responding to letters. The following list details some of the main targets we have set our area offices. All of our targets are detailed in our Annual Report.

New applications for legal aid – 75% within 2 weeks

Correspondence – 100% within 4 weeks

Complaints (to area offices) – 100% within 10 days

Appeals to Area Committee – 90% within 8 weeks

WHEN THINGS GO WRONG

The Legal Aid Board has 13 area offices throughout England and Wales, in addition to a number of Head Office departments. Every week we deal with new applications, bills and letters from many thousands of people. When dealing with this volume of work it is inevitable that things will sometimes go wrong. When they do, we want you to tell us so we can do something about it and prevent similar problems occurring in the future.

If you are unhappy about the standard of our service, we want you to tell us what your concerns are and how we can help you. Please write to the local office dealing with your case marking your letter "Complaint" and address it to the Customer Services Manager.

The Customer Services Manager will arrange for a member of staff designated to deal with customer concerns, to investigate and reply to you within 10 working days (or sooner if the situation is urgent).

Alternatively, you can telephone us or visit the office and you will be put in touch with a member of staff who will be able to help you.

WHAT IF I AM NOT HAPPY ABOUT THE OUTCOME OF MY COMPLAINT?

There might be times when our response to your complaint does not fully satisfy you. If this happens, you should reply to the member of staff who dealt with your complaint raising your further concerns. Alternatively, you might wish to write to the Customer Services Manager directly.

If you are unable to resolve your concerns with your local office then you should contact our Customer Services Unit at Head Office. They will call for a report from the appropriate local office and review its handling of your complaint. They will reply to you within 15 working days.

WHEN IS A "COMPLAINT" NOT A COMPLAINT?

If you have been refused legal aid or you think legal aid has been given to someone who is not entitled to it, we have different procedures for dealing with the following two issues:

Appeals

If you are unhappy about a decision we have made which carries a right of appeal, as opposed to the standard of our service, then the appropriate course of action is to appeal against that decision. The letter notifying you of the decision will tell you if and how you can appeal. Your appeal will normally be reviewed by a member of staff who has the authority to overturn the original decision. If they agree with the original decision then they will refer the matter to the Area Committee which is made up of independent solicitors and barristers. A decision will normally be made by them within 8 weeks of receipt of the appeal. The Board has no power to overturn a decision of an Area Committee.

Representations against the grant of legal aid

If legal aid has been granted to someone who you think is not entitled to it you should write to the appropriate area office clearly marking your letter "Representation". Your letter should provide us with as much information as possible about why you think legal aid should not have been granted. You should also confirm whether you will allow us to show your letter to the person who has legal aid and/or their solicitor.

In appropriate circumstances, our staff will investigate your concerns and let you know the outcome. However:

i. Section 38 of the Legal Aid Act 1988 specifically forbids the disclosure of information supplied to the Board in connection with a person's case. This means we can usually tell you whether legal aid is to continue or be withdrawn, but we cannot provide details of the investigation itself.

ii. By their very nature, the investigations can sometimes take a long time. We would normally expect an outcome within about 10 weeks.

CONCERNS ABOUT YOUR SOLICITOR OR BARRISTER

If you have concerns about the service being provided by your solicitor or barrister then you should write to your solicitors. They will have their own complaints procedures. However, if you are not happy with their response then you can write to the Office for the Supervision of Solicitors or the Bar Council who are the respective bodies responsible for dealing with complaints about solicitors and barristers. Their addresses are on the back of this leaflet (*see page 745*).

PARLIAMENTARY OMBUDSMAN

It is the job of the Parliamentary Ombudsman to investigate complaints by members of the public about the way they have been treated by Government departments or other public sector bodies such as the Legal Aid Board. It is a free service and the Ombudsman has the power to recommend redress if he thinks the complaint is justified, by asking us to put right anything he finds wrong.

Any complaint referred to the Ombudsman must be referred via a Member of Parliament. The Ombudsman would normally expect the complainant to have used the complaints procedure provided by the Government department concerned before referring the matter to him via an MP. The address of the Parliamentary Ombudsman is on the back of this leaflet.

COMPENSATION

Sometimes the Board is able to offer compensation when something has gone wrong.

This is limited to cases where the Board has made an error and this has caused you direct financial loss. Applications for compensation should, initially, be addressed to the area office dealing with your case. Your letter should clearly set out the problem which has occurred and provide a detailed breakdown of the financial loss, and why it has been caused by the Board's error.

WHEN THINGS GO RIGHT

If you are pleased with the service you have received from the Legal Aid Board then we would like to know. It helps us to build upon our successes and provide positive feedback to our staff. Please contact the Customer Services Manager in the office dealing with your case.

LOCAL AREA OFFICES

For addresses, see page 745.

Customer Services Unit, Legal Department
85, Gray's Inn Road, London WC1X 8AA.   0171 813 1000 Extension 8410

Legal Aid Head Office
85, Gray's Inn Road, London WC1X 8AA.   0171 813 1000

Other Helpful Contacts
Office for the Supervision of Solicitors   01926 820 082
Victoria Court, 8 Dormer Place,
Leamington Spa, Warwickshire CV32 5AE

The Bar Council   0171 242 0082
3, Bedford Row, London WC1R 4DB

The Parliamentary Ombudsman   0171 217 3000
Millbank Tower, Millbank, London SW1P 4QP

Paying Back the Legal Aid Board— Statutory Charge

The text of the Legal Aid Board's leaflet about the statutory charge "Paying Back the Legal Aid Board" is reproduced below for information/reference. Copies are available from the area offices.

Over three million people got help through legal aid last year. Legal aid could help finance the expert advice you need. However, in some cases, where you get or defend money or property with the help of legal aid, you will have to repay all or some of your legal costs. In this way legal aid acts as a loan. The money you repay will be put towards your solicitor's bill. This is known as the statutory charge. The statutory charge helps to ensure that there is money available to help other people in need of legal help.

It is important that you understand the statutory charge before your case begins. This leaflet should answer most of your questions, but if in doubt ask your solicitor.

How Does the Statutory Charge Work?

The money or property you get with the help of legal aid will be used first to repay your legal costs to the Legal Aid Board and you will receive anything left over. For example, if you recovered £10,000 and the cost of your case was £2,000 you would have to repay £2,000 to the Legal Aid Board and you would be left with £8,000. Your solicitor cannot pay money out to you until the statutory charge has been dealt with.

Does the Statutory Charge Apply in Every Case?

No. The statutory charge does not apply in the following cases:

- *If you do not gain or hold on to the money or property in dispute.*
- *If you recover all your costs from the other side (if you only recover some of your costs the statutory charge applies only to the difference).*
- *Maintenance payments.*
- *To the first £2,500 of any money/property you gain or hold onto in divorce cases and most other family proceedings.*

When Does the Statutory Charge have to be Paid?

Normally the statutory charge must be paid as soon as the money or property comes through from the other side. Payments must be made through your solicitor and cannot be made to you directly.

If you recover a home or money to buy a home it may be possible to delay payment of the charge. If so, the charge will be registered on the house—rather like a mortgage—and interest will be added. You will then not have to repay the charge or the interest until the house comes to be sold. Your solicitor will explain how the interest is worked out.

Can the Statutory Charge be Reduced?

No, the Legal Aid Board cannot reduce the statutory charge. Neither can the Board say the statutory charge will not apply.

698

Since the statutory charge must be paid and it will tend to go up as your solicitor's bill goes up, you have a direct interest in ensuring (with the help of your solicitor) that costs do not rise unnecessarily. The more property that is in dispute, the bigger effect the statutory charge will have. It is in your interests to try to minimise the areas of dispute between you and the other side at an early stage. This is especially true if the other side also has legal aid or is unlikely to pay your costs.

Can I Object to the Amount of the Charge?

In cases where the statutory charge applies your solicitor will send you a copy of his/her bill and will tell you how to object if you do not agree with the bill. The Court or the Legal Aid Board will ensure that the costs paid to your solicitor are reasonable.

Other Areas of Expense

As well as the statutory charge you may have to pay a contribution to the Board towards your case while the case is running. If so, you will be told whether you have to pay a contribution at the beginning of your case when legal aid is first offered. If your financial position changes during your case your contribution may be put up or down. When working out your statutory charge you will be given credit for any contribution you have paid.

Asking for More Help

The legal aid scheme can at times be difficult to understand—don't be afraid to ask questions if there is anything you are uncertain about. Your solicitor can give you more details about everything discussed in this leaflet.

Legal Aid Board—Corporate Information System (CIS)

The Board has introduced a new computerised administration system in 1997/98. Some general information appears below.

Why do we need CIS?

- We are too reliant on paper-based systems.

- Our current computer systems are inconsistent, inflexible and unreliable and will cause major configuration problems when we reach 2000 AD.

- Our computer response times are unacceptably slow.

- We lack a national system accessible by *all* Area Offices.

- We lack a system capable of underpinning Legal Aid reform.

- More effective control of Legal Aid Fund expenditure is required.

- We need to improve the payment and collection of monies.

- Forms, documents and letters, many handwritten or illegible, lack clarity and existing systems prevent us making major changes.

What have we done to resolve these difficulties?

- We are implementing one, nationally accessible computer system providing:
  - up-to-the-minute, on-screen information to support enquiries and decision-making;
  - connections between civil, criminal and legal advice and assistance applications/schemes;
  - improved application and claim processing capabilities;
  - computer generated letters, documents and payments;
  - improved facts and figures storage to support generation of reports.

- New forms have been designed to provide us with more relevant information to speed up decision-making.

- Outgoing documents and letters have been simplified to help promote understanding of legal aid.

700

How will you be affected by these changes?

- **Legal Aid Case Reference Number**: Applicants will be given a *unique* reference which allows us to link all individual applications in any category type.

- **Legal Aid Supplier Number**: Practitioners have been allocated a *unique* identifier consisting of their legal aid office account number and their Law Society roll number. Counsel supplier numbers will remain the same.

- **Forms**: A number of existing forms have been amalgamated and some have been withdrawn altogether. All forms are now white with black text and can be easily photocopied. Each form is supported by checklist guidance.

- **Documents and letters**: The majority of certificates, documents and letters are computer generated and will be centrally printed. They look different but have been designed to promote clarity, quality and consistency.

- **Information Guidance**: When certain key events occur written supporting guidance will accompany outgoing documents or letters to aid understanding.

- **Contributions**: CIS will provide processing facilities to allow applicants to pay their contributions by direct debit.

- **Enquiries**: Up-to-the-minute, on screen information allows us to respond quickly and accurately to telephone and written enquiries. We no longer need to routinely retrieve paper files to deal with more detailed queries.

- **Further Information Policy**: Although we will still reject forms for basic errors, we *may telephone* in some cases for missing information which would help us to make a decision. If information cannot be provided within 24 hours, *only then* will these forms be rejected or refused because a decision cannot be made.

- **Franchise Monitoring Reports**: Monthly reports will be more detailed and informative.

Legal Aid Forms

N.B. all the Legal Aid Board's forms have been amended to allow for increased computerisation in the area offices. The table below shows new and old references.

New Form Reference (CIS)	Old Form Reference (pre-CIS)	Description
Application Form		
APP1	CLA1, CLA3	Application for legal aid (*Non-matrimonial*)
APP2	CLA2, CLA5, CLA3	Application for legal aid (*Matrimonial/Family*)
APP3	CLA5A	Application for legal aid (*Children non-means/merits*)
APP4	ABWOR1	Application for ABWOR
APP5	CRIM9	Application for review of refusal of *criminal* legal aid
APP6	CLA30, CLA31, ABWOR6	Application for amendment or prior authority (*CIVIL*)
APP7	CRIM9, CRIM10	Application for amendment or prior authority (*CRIMINAL*)
APP8	CLA38	Application for discharge
APP9*	NEW FORM	Notice of Appeal
APP10*	NEW FORM	Notice of application for review of assessment costs
APP11	FEA1	Faxed emergency application
APP11a	FEA1a	Faxed emergency means application
Administration		
ADMIN1	CLA36, CLA37	Preservation/recovery under the statutory charge and request to postpone enforcement
ADMIN2**	REP1	Application for registration as police station representative
ADMIN3	CLA29, CLA34	Application to suspend contributions and give undertaking
ADMIN4	NEW FORM	Payment of monies
ADMIN5	NEW FORM	Change of details

* These forms are generated by the Legal Aid Board CIS computer system.
** This form is available direct from Secretariat Department, Legal Aid Head Office.

New Form Reference (CIS)	Old Form Reference (pre-CIS)	Description
Costs Claim Forms		
CLAIM1	CLA16, CLA17, COSTS1	Claim for assessment of costs or payment of taxed costs (civil)
CLAIM2	CLA26, CLA32	Costs met in part or full by other party
CLAIM3	NEW FORM	Counsel's Fee Note—*CIVIL*
CLAIM4	CLA28, CLA28A, (Counsel's own)	Claim for payment on account—*CIVIL*
CLAIM5	ABWOR3	Claim for costs—*ABWOR*
CLAIM6	NEW FORM	Claim for payment on account—*ABWOR*
CLAIM7	CRIM13	Claim for lower standard fee
CLAIM8	CRIM14, CRIM15	Claim for higher or non standard fee
CLAIM9	CRIM11, CRIM12	Counsel's fee note—*CRIMINAL*
CLAIM10	GF1, GF3, GF4, GF5, GF7	Legal advice and assistance (application and claim)
CLAIM11	CLA35	Representation in contempt proceedings (forms available from the London area office)
CLAIM12	CRIM19	Claim for payment on account—*CRIMINAL* (franchised firms only)
CLAIM13	DSC	
CLAIM14	DSPS1	*PACE/CDS* claims
CLAIM15	DSPS2	
CLAIM16	DSPS1 (ABWOR only)	
Means Forms		
MEANS 1 and The Guide		Applicant not in receipt of income support or income-based Jobseeker's allowance.
MEANS 2		Applicant in receipt of income support or income-based Jobseeker's allowance.
MEANS 3		Applicant whose main home is outside the United Kingdom.
MEANS 4		Child applicant under 16.
MEANS 5A*		Change in capital.
L17		Statement of earnings by present employers.
L18		Self employed—declaration of income.
L30**		Information about a directorship.

* This form is sent from area offices when required.
** This form is sent from area offices to solicitors/applicants on request.

LEGAL AID FORMS CHECKLISTS

Presentation packs containing sample checklists are supplied to every legal aid practitioner in advance of the launch of the Board's Corporate Information System (CIS) in their local legal aid area office. The checklists are in the form of two booklets—one civil and the other non-civil. Each checklist details guidance on the completion of its respective form, when the form will be automatically rejected, and when and how further information may be requested. Each pack also contains an order form so that practitioners can order either or both checklist booklets according to their requirements. Checklists will be regularly updated, resulting in a better flow of information to the profession.

USING LEGAL AID FORMS

Legal aid forms for CIS and the associated checklists are now available on computer disk from a number of specialist organisations licensed by the Board to provide this service. The service also ensures that updates are promptly despatched to users.

The Board will also accept forms which have been created on computer systems by solicitors' firms and other organisations which deal with the Board as long as they have the same wording and are in exactly the same format as the originals.

Supplies of paper copies of forms and checklists will continue to be available from the Board until the end of November 1998, after which solicitors' firms and organisations not wishing to use the technological options described above may obtain a master pack of the forms from the Board from which to photocopy. The pack will also include the checklists. Holders of master packs will receive all updates to forms at the same time as they are available on disk.

To reduce waste, the Board will continue to accept part-forms where all of the pages of the form are not required to be completed in the circumstances of the particular case. Where this applies the form contains a box for the firm/organisation to declare which pages are being submitted and this must be completed for the part-forms to be accepted.

These arrangements apply only to the forms designed for CIS. Where the Board is developing its services through pilot projects and for a small number of other forms which are used infrequently the Board will continue to provide the necessary supplies direct to the firms/organisations that need them. Additionally, stocks of the old legal aid forms will continue to be made available from those of the Board's area offices which have not yet implemented CIS but will be withdrawn after the final roll out of the system.

MULTIPLE APPLICATIONS

If the solicitor is representing more than one child in proceedings, a separate APP2 form must be filled in for each child applicant. To reduce form-filling and copying of documents for practitioners the Board only requires one set of accompanying documents although a separate means form is required for each child. Multiple applications should be completed and submitted in the following way:

(i) fill in *one* APP2 leaving blank the applicant's name, signature and any other information which differs among the applicants. Do not sign the form at this stage;

(ii) write in print "ORIGINAL APPLICATION" in the top right hand corner of page 1;

(iii) photocopy the form the required number of times so that the words "ORIGINAL APPLICATION" appear on each.

(iv) write in the information particular to each child. The solicitor and if relevant the next friend or guardian ad litem should then sign each application. Any signatures must be original even on a photocopied form.

(v) The application forms must be sent together to the area office, the photocopied applications firmly attached behind the original. Only one set of supporting documents is required.

CIVIL LEGAL AID AND ABWOR—TABLE OF APPLICATION FORMS*

Form	Proceedings	Do I need a means form?
APP 3	*Children Act—* s.25—secure accommodation—child only s.31—care/supervision ⎫ s.43—child assessment ⎪ Child, s.44—emergency protection ⎬ parent or person with s.45—discharge/renewal of ⎪ parental emergency protection ⎭ responsibility	No No
APP 2	*Means tested only* applications under ss. 31, 43, 44 or 45 (by a party or person applying to be joined) *All other applications under the Children Act alone* *Adoption, wardship and s.20 or 27 Child Support Act 1991* *Matrimonial proceedings* *Children Act applications in other proceedings* *Matrimonial and Family Proceedings Act 1984* *Married Women's Property Act 1882* *Domestic Proceedings and Magistrates' Courts Act 1978*	Yes Yes
APP 1 (and emergency application if urgent)	All *other proceedings for which Civil Legal Aid is available—i.e.* non-matrimonial, non-Children Act	Yes
ABWOR 1	*ABWOR may be applied for if applicant financially eligible* Family Proceedings Court only —*Children Act 1989* residence/contact by parents, contact by grandparents, parental responsibility and financial provision for children (but only where relief sought is that which would have previously been sought under Guardianship of Minors Act 1971–73 or Part II of Children Act 1975) (Custodianship) (Note: If there is any doubt whether the proceedings will remain in the Family Proceedings Court, the APP 2 and appropriate means form should be used). —*Domestic Proceedings and Magistrates' Courts Act 1978* —*Any other court proceedings* listed in the Schedule to the Legal Advice and Assistance (Scope) Regulations 1989 *ABWOR must be applied for (i.e. only ABWOR available)* —Mental Health Review Tribunals, Parole Board, prison disciplinary proceedings, appeals under Fire Precautions Act and ABWOR within regulation 7(4) of the Legal Advice and Assistance (Scope) Regulations 1989.	No

* The Board's application forms have been amended to allow for increased computerisation—see the table on p. 702.

Financial Assessment Forms Checklist*

Relevant to forms MEANS1, MEANS2, MEANS3, MEANS4 AND MEANS5

- This checklist gives information about completing assessment forms. It should be referred to when checking that the client has correctly completed the forms.
- If a form is rejected, the reason will fall into one of three categories:

  Category A If this information is missing or completed incorrectly, we cannot process the application and it will be rejected. This will be counted as a reject under Franchise monitoring if it falls within a category which is monitored.

  Category B If this information is missing from the financial assessment form it will usually be rejected. In some cases the information may be obtained from accompanying documents or by phoning the solicitor or the applicant. If the application is returned, this will NOT be counted as a reject under Franchise monitoring.

  Category C These notes are for guidance only. Observing this guidance will help staff in the area office process the application and the means assessment as quickly as possible.

MEANS1—Initial assessment and further assessment

Category A

1. The client must sign and date the form.

2. If the applicant/assisted person is under 16, the form must be signed by the next friend, guardian ad litem or, where the rules of court allow the child to begin, prosecute or defend proceedings, by the solicitor. The signature must be the same as that on the legal aid application form.

3. No changes or additions must be made to the declaration.

4. **Initial assessments only:** The form must be dated no more than 2 months before the date the application was received unless it is a resubmitted form.

5. **Employed clients:** Form L17 must be sent for each job held by the client (and, if relevant, for each job held by their partner), unless it is an emergency application when they must send at least their latest wage slip. Form L17 must be signed by the employer, not by the client or their partner. A new L17 (not a copy of the original form) must be sent when reporting a change in income.

6. Company directors: a Form L30 must be completed for each directorship held by the client and their partner. L30 forms should be obtained from the Area Office.

7. Questions 1, 2, 3, 4 and 5 on page 2 (applicant's details) must be completed in full.

---

* Following the introduction of the new MEANS series of financial application forms, a revised checklist (CK3) has been introduced. This checklist will be used by the Board when considering whether to accept or reject an application. The general position is that the Board will aim to accept forms where this is consistent with fairness and protection of the legal aid fund.

Category B

8. Questions must be ticked "Yes" or "No". Answers such as "not known" will not be accepted. Full amounts and dates must be given when asked for. In some cases where the omission relates to a deduction claim by the applicant, further enquiries may be made or the deduction may not be allowed, rather than the form being rejected.

9. **Self-employed clients:** If the client or their partner is self-employed the following documents must be sent with the form:

    (a) A full set of trading accounts (for the last complete trading period) and associated balance sheet.

    (b) A completed Form L18.

    (c) An Inland Revenue calculation sheet and statement of account.

If the applicant gives an acceptable explanation as to why the above documents cannot be provided then the application will not be rejected.

Category C

10. In spouse/partner cases where there is no contrary interest, and both spouses/partners are applying, one form is acceptable as long as it has the original signatures and the financial information of both people.

MEANS2—Initial assessment and further assessments
People who receive Income Support/income-based Jobseeker's Allowance

Category A

1. The client must sign and date the form.
2. A national insurance number and full address of the Social Security office or Jobcentre must be given. Exceptionally, where the applicant states that they do not have a National Insurance number then the form shall be accepted.
3. No changes or additions must be made to the declaration.
4. The applicant's/assisted person's details must be completed in full.

Category B

5. The type of benefit received must be confirmed.
6. Questions must be answered in full. Answers such as "not known" will not be accepted. Dates must be given when asked for.

MEANS3—Initial assessment and further assessments
People whose main home is outside the United Kingdom

Category A

1. The client must sign and date the form.
2. If the applicant/assisted person is under 16, the form must be signed by the next friend, guardian ad litem or, where the rules of court allow the child to begin, prosecute or defend proceedings, by the solicitor. The signature must be the same as that on the legal aid application form.
3. The applicant's means must be certified by a responsible person on page 17.
4. The form must be signed on page 18 by a witness.
5. **Initial assessments only:** The form must be dated no more than 2 months before the date the application was received unless it is a resubmitted form.
6. **Employed clients:** A written statement from the applicant's/assisted person's employer (and if relevant, their partner's employer) must be attached for each job held.

7. Questions 1, 2, 3, 4, 5 and 7 on pages 2 and 3 (applicant's details) must be completed in full.

8. No changes or additions must be made to the declaration.

Category B

9. **Self-employed clients:** If the client or their partner is self-employed the following documents must be sent with the form:

(a) A full set of trading accounts (for the last complete trading period) and associated balance sheet.

(b) A completed Form L18, if the applicant pays U.K. tax.

(c) An Inland Revenue calculation sheet and statement of account, if the applicant pays U.K. tax.

If the applicant gives an acceptable explanation as to why the above documents cannot be provided then the application will not be rejected.

10. Questions must be ticked "Yes" or "No". Answers such as "not known" will not be accepted. Full amounts and dates must be given when asked for. In some cases where the omission relates to a deduction claim by the applicant, further enquiries may be made or the deduction may not be allowed, rather than the form being rejected.

MEANS4—Child applicant under 16 who has less than £2,500 capital and no regular income

Category A

1. The form must be signed and dated by the next friend, guardian, ad litem or, where the rules of court allow the child to begin, prosecute or defend proceedings, by the solicitor. The signature must be the same as that on the legal aid application form.

2. The form must be dated no more than 2 months before the date the application was received unless it is a resubmitted form.

3. No changes or additions must be made to the declaration.

Category B

4. The child applicant's details must be completed in full.

5. The name and correspondence address of the person applying on behalf of the child must be completed.

6. Questions 2 and 3 must be completed in full.

7. Questions must be ticked "Yes" or "No". Answers such as "not known" will not be accepted. Dates must be given when asked for.

MEANS5—Increase in capital

Category A

1. The client must sign and date the form.

2. Questions 1 to 6 must be completed.

3. All documents (e.g. savings books or bank statements) listed as being sent must be attached to the form.

4. If question 2 or question 3 is answered "yes", written proof (e.g. receipts or bills) must be attached.

5. No changes or additions must be made to the declaration.

Category B

6. The assisted person's details must be fully completed.

7. Questions must be ticked "Yes" or "No". Answers such as "not known" will not be accepted. Full amounts and dates must be given when asked for.

8. The solicitor's details must be given.

Notice of Issue of (Emergency) Certificate

(The Notes form part of the Notice)

LEGAL AID BOARD

LEGAL AID ACT 1988

Regulation 50 Civil Legal Aid (General) Regulations 1989

No.

In the

[[County Court] [Division]

Between   [Applicant] [Plaintiff] [Petitioner]

and

[Defendant] [Respondent]

TAKE notice that [an Emergency] [a Legal Aid] Certificate No.

dated the   day of   199 has been issued in Legal Aid Area No.

to   who since that date has been an assisted person.

The description/scope of legal aid is:

Appeal cases only—the limitation (if any) [costs limitations need not be disclosed] is:

Emergency certificates only—the emergency certificate [has] [has not] been granted for a specified period. [It will expire on]:

To:

From:

Signed:

Date:

Note to Assisted Person's Solicitor

1. This notice **must** be served in accordance with reg. 50 Civil Legal Aid (General) Regulations 1989.

Notes to Opponent or Opponent's Solicitor

1. An assisted person's solicitor must notify the Legal Aid Area Office which issued the assisted person's legal aid certificate if a legal aid certificate is issued to another party to the proceedings—reg. 70 Civil Legal Aid (General) Regulations 1989.

2. All monies payable to the assisted person must be paid to his/her solicitor or, if he/she is no longer represented by a solicitor, to the Legal Aid Board. This is so even if his/her certificate has been discharged or revoked. Only the solicitor or the Legal Aid Board is capable of giving a good discharge for monies so payable—reg. 87 Civil Legal Aid (General) Regulations 1989.

Notice approved by the Legal Aid Board.

710

Notice of Extension/Amendment of (Emergency) Certificate

(The Notes form part of the Notice)

LEGAL AID BOARD

LEGAL AID ACT 1988

Regulations 25 and 54 Civil Legal Aid (General) Regulations 1989

No.

In the

[[County Court] [Division]

Between   [Applicant] [Plaintiff] [Petitioner]

and

[Defendant] [Respondent]

TAKE notice that [the Emergency] [the Legal Aid] Certificate No.

dated the   day of   199   which was issued in Legal Aid Area No.

to

was amended on the   day of   199

The amended description/scope of legal aid is:

Appeal cases only—the amended limitation (if any) [costs limitations need not be disclosed] is:

Emergency certificates only—the period allowed for the duration of the emergency certificate has been extended. It will now expire on:

To:

From:

Signed:

Date:

Note to Assisted Person's Solicitor

1. This notice **must** be served in accordance with regs. 25 and/or 54 Civil Legal Aid (General) Regulations 1989.

Notes to Opponent or Opponent's Solicitor

1. An assisted person's solicitor must notify the Legal Aid Area Office which issued the assisted person's legal aid certificate if a legal aid certificate is issued to another party to the proceedings—reg. 70 Civil Legal Aid (General) Regulations 1989.

2. All monies payable to the assisted person must be paid to his/her solicitor or, if he/she is no longer represented by a solicitor, to the Legal Aid Board. This is so even if his/her certificate has been discharged or revoked. Only the solicitor or the Legal Aid Board is capable of giving a good discharge for monies so payable—reg. 87 Civil Legal Aid (General) Regulations 1989.

Notice approved by the Legal Aid Board.

Notice of Discharge or Revocation of (Emergency) Certificate
(The Notes form part of the Notice)

LEGAL AID BOARD

LEGAL AID ACT 1988

Regulation 82 Civil Legal Aid (General) Regulations 1989

No.

In the

[[County Court] [Division]

Between   [Applicant] [Plaintiff] [Petitioner]

and

[Defendant] [Respondent]

TAKE notice that [the Emergency] [the Legal Aid] Certificate No.

dated the   day of   199   which has been issued in Legal Aid Area No.

to

was [discharged] [revoked] on the   day of   199

To:

From:

Signed:

Date:

Note to Assisted Person's Solicitor

1. This notice **must** be served in accordance with reg. 82 Civil Legal Aid (General) Regulations 1989.

Note to Opponent or Opponent's Solicitor

1. All monies payable to the assisted person must be paid to his/her solicitor or, if he/she is no longer represented by a solicitor, to the Legal Aid Board. This is so even if his/her certificate has been discharged or revoked. Only the solicitor or the Legal Aid Board is capable of giving a good discharge for monies so payable—reg. 87 Civil Legal Aid (General) Regulations 1989.

Notice approved by the Legal Aid Board.

Legal Aid Area Committee Members' Handbook

1. FOREWORD

This handbook is to help area committee members by providing relevant information about area committees. Detailed technical information on the legal aid merits tests, authorities, costs, the statutory charge etc. is available [elsewhere] in the *Legal Aid Handbook* (which includes the Board's Notes for Guidance and decisions of the Costs Appeals Committee) and is, therefore, not repeated here as area committee members should have, and be familiar with, this publication.

The Notes for Guidance, and the decisions of the Costs Appeals Committee should be followed by area committees. The Legal Aid Board has the general function of administering the Legal Aid Act 1988 and appoints area committees to help in this regard. The function of area committees is to deal with appeals against decisions of area office staff who should also make their decisions with full regard to the Board's guidance and decisions. This does not interfere with an area committee's independence as an appeal body or prevent any area committee from disagreeing with any area office decision.

This handbook has been created by the Area Chairmen's Working Party which comprises five current or former area committee Chairmen or Vice Chairmen (one from each group of legal aid area offices). It is intended to be a living document which can change and improve. Feedback from area committee members will be very useful in helping this to happen. Please contact either your area committee Chairman or Vice-

Chairman or the Area Manager in charge of your area office with your suggestions.

2. WELCOME FROM THE CHAIRMAN OF THE LEGAL AID BOARD

I am very pleased to welcome you to the area committee. You have joined a group of about fifteen hundred skilled and experienced solicitors and barristers throughout England and Wales who help the Legal Aid Board administer the Legal Aid Act 1988. Legal aid administration is based on 13 area offices, covering defined geographical areas. The *Legal Aid Handbook* includes the addresses and telephone numbers of the area offices and shows the counties and London boroughs covered by each area office.

Each legal aid area has its own area committee with about 120 members (more in London). As legal aid is a national service, covering the whole of England and Wales, it is very important that area committees achieve a consistent quality of decision-making, wherever decisions are made. Every committee member's part in this is vital. You have been appointed to an area committee dealing with appeals from decisions made in one area office. You can help ensure that your committee's operations and decisions contribute to the nationally consistent quality of decision-making and appeals handling which legal aid's stakeholders deserve.

The preface to the *Legal Aid Handbook* refers to the need for consistency. The Act and Regulations contain many cases where the decision of the area committee is discretionary. It is in these areas particularly that variations occur. While the exercise of a discretion is always a matter of judgment for the person concerned, so that there is always room for variation between individuals, the Board takes the view that guidance on the factors to be taken into account when exercising a discretion should reduce unwarranted variations.

Each discretionary decision should be justifiable. Legal aid serves several "stakeholders", *i.e.* those with a legitimate interest in its operation. The stakeholders identified by the Board are the assisted person or potential assisted person, the judicial system, the legal profession and the taxpayer through the Government. Stakeholders may have conflicting interests, but each one has to be borne in mind when a decision is made. Sometimes, the decision the applicant wants may not be right for the court or taxpayer; for example, if legal aid is granted unreasonably. Similarly, an applicant may not be happy with a decision which saves the taxpayer money; for example, if legal aid is refused. This is unavoidable. The principle, however, is that the Board should be able to justify to its stakeholders each and every decision. In particular, every decision must be justifiable to the unsuccessful stakeholder.

3. INTRODUCTION BY THE CHIEF EXECUTIVE

This is a time of change for the legal aid service. Your contribution to the effective operation of the service as an experienced, independent lawyer, is greatly valued. Area committees perform an important public function. They consider most sensitive cases and applications and their decisions affect individual applicants, lawyers, the courts and all taxpayers.

This handbook is here to help you. It explains what area committees do and what will be expected of you. There should be no real surprises in this as it builds on the Board's information sheet for those applying to join a legal aid area committee.

This handbook explains the types of appeals which you will have to consider, showing those where appellants have a right of attendance and those relating to franchised firms. It also includes an outline of the role of the committee clerk/secretary and a section on the conduct of meetings and dealing with appellants.

We hope that this, together with your induction visit to your legal aid area office where you will meet staff and be shown the workings of the office, will help to give you a picture of the legal aid service and your role in it as an area committee member.

The need to be able to justify decision-making carries with it the obligation to have and to give clear and justifiable reasons for decisions. This handbook includes a section

715

on the importance of clear and justifiable reasons and, drawing on what has been learned from previous judicial reviews of area committee decisions, how you can help to minimise the likelyhood of judicial review.

4. ABOUT THE LEGAL AID BOARD

The Legal Aid Board is established under the Legal Aid Act 1988 "the Act" with the general function of securing that advice, assistance and representation are available in accordance with the Act and of administering the Act.

Legal aid expenditure represents about 15 per cent of the total money spent on all legal services in England and Wales. This makes the Board, by a multiple of many times, the largest purchaser of legal services in the U.K. These services are purchased with taxpayers' money.

To carry out its functions the Board employs about 1,300 staff throughout its 13 legal aid area offices and its central departments. The addresses and telephone numbers of these area offices are found in the *Legal Aid Handbook* along with details of the geographical areas covered by each area office.

Legal aid policy is for the Lord Chancellor. The Legal Aid Board is responsible to the Lord Chancellor for the performance of the legal aid service and sets policy on operational matters.

The Legal Aid Executive Board is responsible for the implementation of policy and for the day-to-day management of the legal aid service. The names of the members of both the Legal Aid Board and the Legal Aid Executive Board are set out in the *Legal Aid Handbook* (see page 744).

Each year the Board publishes a report on the operation and finance of the Legal Aid Act 1988 showing the Board's management/operational strategy and performance.

5. ABOUT THE AREA COMMITTEE

Area committees constitute an independent body to hear appeals from decisions made by the Board's staff in legal aid area offices.

Each area committee comprises about 120 solicitors and barristers from within the geographical area covered by a legal aid area office. The London committee has up to double this number of members.

Each area committee has a Chairman and one or two Vice-Chairmen who are elected at the area committee's Annual General Meeting.

At each AGM, the Area Manager will give an annual report on the work of the office and the developments in legal aid since the last meeting.

Each year, usually in May, the Board holds a conference for Area Chairmen and Vice-Chairmen. This enables area committee members, through their appointed Chairmen and Vice Chairmen, to exchange views with other committee members and with the Chairman, Chief Executive and other Board officials.

The Legal Aid Board has approved the Legal Aid Board Area Committee Arrangements which specify the legal aid areas, allocate statutory functions to staff in area offices and regulate the composition, powers and procedures of area committees. These Arrangements are found in the *Legal Aid Handbook* (see page 649).

Although the Arrangements provide for each area committee member to be appointed by the Board, the Board has devolved to Area Managers in consultation with Area Chairmen the power to appoint area committee members who fit criteria established by the Board. Prospective members who do not fit these criteria may still be appointed but their applications are considered by the Board itself.

Through your work as a member of the area committee and in your practice, you may well develop ideas as to how the legal aid service could be improved, or how better value for money could be achieved. If you do, please let us have your ideas either through your Area Chairman or Vice Chairman or by writing directly to the Area Manager at your area office.

6. WHAT THE AREA COMMITTEE DOES

The area committee determines appeals from decisions of the Board's staff. To do so the committee generally meets in sub-committees of three or four members. The Legal Aid Board Area Committee Arrangements set out the requirements for a quorum.

Each sub-committee has a Chairman who will normally have had several years' experience on the area committee. He or she will control the proceedings and will guide new members on procedure.

You will usually be asked to sit as an area sub-committee member between five and ten times a year depending on the number of appeals and the size of the area committee. Meetings are generally held in the afternoon and usually last between two and four hours, depending on the complexity of the appeals and the number of appellants who attend in person. In some areas, with a heavy appeals workload, meetings may occasionally last longer.

The front page of each appeals agenda will show the names of the sub-committee members, indicating who will be the chairman and the time, date and venue of the meeting. The Area Manager or his or her nominee (*e.g.* the leader of the area committee support team in the area office) is responsible for the administrative support provided by the area office to the area committee including the organisation of meetings and agendas and the nomination of chairmen for particular meetings.

The appeals agenda is sent out about a week before the meeting to allow you to prepare for it. The area office will try to avoid including in any agenda any case in which any member of a sub-committee may be concerned.

However, this will not always be possible. For example, the area office will not always know who are the appellants' opponents' solicitors or who all the prospective opponents may be. In addition, there may be (rarely) other reasons why an area sub-committee member should not see a particular appeal.

When you read your agenda, you should be alert to the possibility of its including an appeal which you should not determine because you have an interest in it. If you recognise such a case, you should stop reading it immediately. At the area sub-committee meeting, you should notify your interest and will be asked to withdraw while the appeal is determined by the other members of the sub-committee. The agenda will be indorsed to show that you took no part in the appeal.

In its *Guide to the Professional Conduct of Solicitors*, The Law Society says:

> "A solicitor member of an Area Legal Aid Committee may act (or continue to act) for the applicant in a case coming before that Committee, provided he or she declares an interest in the case and withdraws from the adjudication.
>
> Where a solicitor has adjudicated on an application submitted to a Legal Aid Committee, he or she must not act or continue to act for the opponent of the applicant. Even if the solicitor does not remember the details of the case, it would be undesirable for the solicitor to act. Adjudication by a member of a Legal Aid Committee should not inhibit the solicitor's partners or other members of the firm dealing with the matter."

Appeal agendas should be treated as strictly confidential. Committee members should not discuss, otherwise than in committee meetings, any matters relating to individual appeals. Section 38 of the Legal Aid Act 1988 makes it an offence for information furnished in connection with the case of a person seeking or receiving advice and assistance or representation to be disclosed otherwise than in accordance with the provisions of that section.

Area offices will try to schedule all meetings by sending out at least a three months schedule of meetings, at least one month before the first scheduled meeting, so that you can ensure that you will be available. If, on receiving your schedule you realise you are unable to attend any meeting, you should inform the area committee support team without delay so they can arrange for another member to attend in your place.

However, if you subsequently become unable to attend any scheduled meeting (or fail promptly to inform the support team of your unavailability) it is then your responsi-

717

bility to try to find another area committee member who will stand in for you. You should keep the support team informed and they may be able to help you. If, after you have received an agenda, you realise you will be unable to attend the meeting, you should immediately inform the support team and return the agenda to the area office or pass it to the area committee member who will be standing in for you.

The Bar Council requires attendance at area committees as a professional obligation to be fulfilled—that is, by appearing in person or by an alternative barrister member attending.

The Legal Aid Board Area Committee Arrangements set out the circumstances in which area committee members may be removed from office. The names of removed members will be given at the area committee AGM and notified to the local law society or the Bar Council, as appropriate.

7. FRANCHISING

Franchising is a major development in the legal aid service which area committee members should know about.

The Board's objectives in promoting franchising are to work in partnership with the profession to provide an accessible and quality assured legal aid service to clients giving improving value for money to the taxpayer. The essential elements of the scheme are:

(a) an improvement in the service offered by suppliers of legal services to their clients and the reduction of their administrative cost by:
  (i) delegating some powers that traditionally have been exercised with the Board;
  (ii) improving the working relationship between suppliers and the Board by appointment of a nominated liaison manager for each applicant;
  (iii) providing regular information about any perceived problems in the relationship between the Board and the supplier;
(b) specification of quality assurance standards that the Board would expect suppliers to achieve in order to ensure a good service to clients covering:
  (i) management, including case management; recruitment, training and supervision of staff; client care; accounting and forward planning;
  (ii) the handling of cases as assessed after the event by the auditing of legal aid files on a confidential basis; and
  (iii) work submitted to area offices,
(c) arrangements for audits by the Board to ensure that the standards are being achieved and maintained;
(d) the control of case costs;
(e) an effective appeal procedure where contracts have been refused, suspended or terminated;
(f) the continuous monitoring of the scheme involving the profession and others to ensure that it is achieving its objectives;
(g) obtaining the views of clients about franchised organisations.

Devolved powers

The delegated or "devolved" powers (see (a) (i) above) which traditionally have been exercised by the Board are set out below. Franchisees will have been granted one or more of these powers in one or more of the categories of work in which they hold the franchise.

Green form

(a) Self-authorisation of an application from a child or on behalf of a child or patient,
(b) Self-authorisation of an application from a client outside England and Wales,
(c) Self-authorisation of an application from a client who has previously received advice and assistance on the same matter from a solicitor,
(d) Self-granting of green form extensions.

ABWOR
- (a) Self-granting of approvals of ABWOR,
- (b) Self-granting of prior permissions for disbursements,
- (c) Self-granting of approval to instruct counsel.

Civil legal aid
- (a) Self-granting of emergency legal aid certificates.
- (b) Self-granting of some amendments to legal aid certificates.

In addition, though strictly they are not devolved powers, the franchise contract includes as devolved powers the power to accept telephone and postal applications for green form advice, the rights to claim for the cost of outward travel (but not travelling time) to attend on a client away from the office prior to the signature of a green form and the right to claim payments on account at enhanced legal aid rates. These "powers" are really special arrangements for franchisees created by regulations for franchising.

A devolved power exercised in a franchisee's office is just the same as a power exercised in an area office. Just as the regulations talk of powers being exercised and the decisions being made by an "Area Director" but allow the area office staff to make them, so the franchise contract allows franchisee's staff to make them. The only difference is the place that a decision is made. On making a decision, the franchisee could be sitting in the area office as part of that office.

At present, area offices quality control every exercise of a devolved power by a franchisee.

In green form cases, each bill sent to the area office for payment is quality controlled.

In ABWOR cases, when each self-grant of approval is sent to the area office (which must be within five working days of the exercise of the devolved power) it is quality controlled and other self-grants are quality controlled when the bill is sent to the area office for payment.

In civil legal aid cases, when each self-grant of an emergency certificate is sent to the area office (which must be within five working days of the exercise of devolved power) it is quality controlled and when civil bills are submitted for payment they are quality controlled—to see whether, if enhanced rate payments on account have been claimed, they have been properly claimed.

Grants and refusals

Franchising presently has little impact on the work of area committees.

If a franchised firm exercises devolved powers to grant an emergency legal aid certificate and the area office, on quality controlling the decision, takes the view that the grant was made outside the Board's guidelines on the exercise of devolved powers, the area office will nevertheless issue a certificate but will limit it to the work done to date or limit it to exclude specified future work. The area office will, at the same time, decide whether or not to grant a substantive certificate. There is no right of appeal against the area office's decision on the emergency certificate and the right of appeal against the area office's decision on the substantive certificate is the usual right of appeal against the refusal of legal aid.

Therefore, area committees will occasionally, receive appeals against the refusal of legal aid where an emergency certificate has previously been granted by a franchised firm but the area office has refused the substantive certificate. Area committees deal with these appeals in the same way as any other appeal against the refusal to grant legal aid.

Similar principles apply if a franchisee grants ABWOR. Again, the franchised firm must submit details to the area office within five working days of the exercise of their power and the area office will quality control the decision. If the area office disagrees with the decision to grant ABWOR, ABWOR may be withdrawn giving the usual right of appeal to the area committee against the withdrawal of ABWOR.

Franchised firms have the delegated power to decide against their client as well as in favour. This is unlikely often to arise as the firm is more likely informally to advise their client that it is not an appropriate case for the grant of an emergency certificate rather than formally to refuse to grant one—just as a non-franchised firm might give such advice.

Area committees will not be greatly affected by any franchised firm's decisions to refuse as the only delegated power given them, against which there is a right of appeal, is the power to refuse ABWOR. Nevertheless, in theory, area committees may have to deal with appeals against refusals of ABWOR where it was a franchised firm which made the refusal. Area committees should determine such appeals just as if the decision to refuse had been made by a member of the area office staff.

Prior authorities and costs

An important function of the area committee is to determine appeals against area offices' assessments of solicitors' legal aid, ABWOR and green form claims. Where devolved powers have been exercised, area offices should assess such claims on the basis that the grant of emergency legal aid or ABWOR was correct (whether or not the area office agreed with that decision on quality control).

Franchised firms can grant their own ABWOR prior permissions to obtain a report or an opinion of an expert, to tender expert evidence or to perform an act which is either unusual in its nature or involves an unusually large expenditure, and their own authorities to engage counsel. When such claims are submitted for payment, they should be assessed on the basis that the prior permissions or authorities were properly granted by the area office.

Similarly, area offices will assess franchised firms' green form claims on the basis that any devolved powers exercised by the franchised firm (including green form extensions) have been properly granted. This means that, save in exceptional circumstances, the area office will not challenge the reason behind a franchised firm's grant of a green form extension. This does not prevent costs from being assessed down. It may have been right to take certain steps but too much time may have been taken over them. It may have been right to obtain an expert's report but the expert's charges may have been excessive.

Devolved powers—late submissions and *ultravires*

Franchisees are obliged to submit details of their grant of emergency legal aid or ABWOR or of an amendment to a civil legal aid certificate to the area office within five working days. Any application submitted outside this period must be accompanied by a written explanation for the delay.

If it is considered that the explanation is not sufficient the area office franchise manager will discuss the case with the franchised firm's franchise representative. Very occasionally, after such a discussion, it may still be felt that the explanation is insufficient. In such a case, the emergency legal aid certificate or the ABWOR approval (though dated the date of the exercise of the devolved powers) will be endorsed with wording to restrict payment to the solicitor only for any work done from the date the decision details were submitted to the area office.

Where the area office makes this decision, the franchisee has, through the franchising specification, a right of appeal to the area committee.

Very occasionally, a franchisee may exercise a devolved power so as, for example, to make an *ultra vires*, grant of legal aid, *i.e.* a grant which is outside both the Board's and franchisee's powers. In such a case, the Board could not issue an emergency legal aid certificate (or ABWOR approval) because it has no power to do so. The Franchise specification provides a right of appeal against the Board's decision in such a case. When faced with such appeal, the area committee's role is to determine whether or not the grant was exercised outside the Board's and the franchised firm's powers.

Summary

    1. Appeal against an area office's full or partial refusal of civil legal aid (where a

franchised firm has previously granted an emergency certificate)—Appeal to be dealt with in the usual way (unaffected by the franchised firm's grant of the emergency certificate).

2. Appeal against a franchised firm's refusal of ABWOR—appeal to be dealt with in the usual way—as if the area office had refused ABWOR.
3. Appeal against withdrawal of ABWOR (where a franchised firm has previously granted ABWOR)—appeal to be dealt with in the usual way (unaffected by the franchised firm's previous grant of ABWOR).
4. Assessment of green form, ABWOR and civil legal aid bills carried out in the usual way and on the basis that the reasons for the exercise of any devolved powers were valid. Claims may be reduced if, for example, the time spent was, or the experts' fees were, excessive.
5. Late submissions of grants of emergency certificates or ABWOR approvals—area office intends not to pay for earlier work (right of appeal provided by franchising specification). These are expected to be very rare and guidance will be given on a case by case basis.
6. *Ultra vires* exercise of devolved powers (right of appeal provided by franchising specification). The area committee role is to determine whether or not the grant was *ultra vires* both the franchised firm's and the Board's powers. In such cases the agenda note will explain the reasons for the area office decision.

8. APPEALS, REVIEWS AND APPLICATIONS TO AREA COMMITTEES

Civil legal aid

Area committees may determine appeals against the following decisions:

(i) refusal of an application for a certificate or the terms upon which the certificate would be issued (reg. 35 CLA(G)R 1989);
(ii) refusal of an application for amendment of a certificate (reg. 57 CLA(G)R 1989);
(iii) discharge of a certificate on the merits or where the assisted person has been adjudicated bankrupt (reg. 81(2) CLA(G)R 1989);
(iv) discharge or revocation of a certificate for abuse of legal aid or failure to provide information when required (reg. 81(2) CLA(G)R 1989);
(v) devolved powers exercised *ultra vires* the Act or Regulations by franchised firm (Franchising Specification);
(vi) applications submitted late where franchised firms have exercised devolved powers (Guidance on the Exercise of Devolved Powers).

The above appeals are by way of reconsideration; the appellant may submit further information and the decision of the area committee is final. In all cases, except (ii) there is a right of attendance and representation. The area committee may dismiss the appeal or allow the appeal subject to such terms and conditions as it considers appropriate.

ABWOR

Area committees may determine appeals against the following decisions:

(i) refusal of an application for ABWOR (reg. 26 LAAR 1989);
(ii) refusal of an application for prior authority to incur expenditure (reg. 26 LAAR 1989);
(iii) withdrawal of ABWOR (reg. 26 LAAR 1989);
(iv) devolved powers exercised *ultra vires* the Act or Regulations by franchised firm (Franchising Specification);
(v) applications submitted late where franchised firms have exercised devolved powers (Guidance on the Exercise of Devolved Powers).

The above appeals are by way of reconsideration; the appellant may submit further information and the decision of the area committee is final. There is no right of attendance or of representation. The area committee may dismiss the appeal or allow the appeal subject to such terms and conditions as it considers appropriate.

Criminal reviews/renewals/authorities

Under the regulations, these go directly to the area committee. As the area office can, under the regulations, grant, it is only where the area office is not willing to grant that the area committee receives these cases.

(i) Area office declines to grant an application for a Criminal Legal Aid Order (review) (reg. 15 LACCP(G)R 1989).
(ii) Area office declines to amend a Legal Aid Order (renewal) (reg. 51(2) LACCP (G)R 1989).
(iii) Area office declines to grant an application for either prior authority for expenditure or to assign counsel (reg. 54 LACCP(G)R 1989).
(iv) Withdrawal of a Legal Aid Order.

Costs reviews, applications and requests to certify points of principle of general importance

The area committee may receive requests to review the reduction or disallowance of solicitors' costs and/or counsel's fees in respect of the following categories of claims for costs. The area committee may also be asked to certify points of principles of general importance (PPGI) and to authorise the carrying in of objections to taxations.

(i) Green form bills (reg. 29 LAAR 1989) (review or PPGI);
(ii) ABWOR bills (reg. 29 LAAR 1989) (review or PPGI);
(iii) court duty solicitor bills (reg. 29 LAAR 1989) (review or PPGI);
(iv) police station duty solicitor (PACE) bills (reg. 29 LAAR 1989) (review or PPGI);
(v) criminal bills (reg. 12 LACCP(C)R 1989—review) (reg. 13 LACCP(C)R 1989—PPGI);
(vi) civil assessed bills (reg. 105 CLA(G)R 1989) (review or PPGI);
(vii) civil taxed bills (reg. 113 CLA(G)R 1989) (authority to carry in objections to a taxation).

On a costs review, the area committee may confirm, increase or decrease the amount allowed on the original assessment.

A solicitor who is dissatisfied with any decision on the assessment of a claim for costs may send in further information and will be permitted to attend before the area committee and make oral representations.

9. COSTS REVIEWS

If, on receipt of the area office's assessment of costs, the solicitor or counsel is dissatisfied with it they may, within 21 days, apply to the area committee for a review of it.

Procedure

1. The area office assesses the claim for costs,
2. The area office issues a notice of assessment to the solicitor,
3. The solicitor or counsel dissatisfied with the decision makes representations within 21 days to the appropriate area committee,
4. The area committee reviews the assessment and may confirm, decrease or increase the amount assessed.

The relevant regulations

1. Green form bills—regulation 29 Legal Advice and Assistance Regulations 1989.
2. ABWOR bills—regulation 29 Legal Advice and Assistance Regulations 1989.
3. Court duty solicitor bills—regulation 29 Legal Advice and Assistance Regulations 1989.

4. Police station duty solicitor (PACE) bills—regulation 29 Legal Advice and Assistance Regulations 1989.
5. Criminal bills—regulation 12 of Legal Aid in Criminal and Care Proceedings (Costs) Regulations 1989.
6. Civil assessed bills—regulation 105 Civil Legal Aid (General) Regulations 1989.

General
Although the regulations provide no right of attendance on such reviews, the Legal Aid Board considers that the solicitor and/or counsel should be permitted to attend, at their own expense, to support their written representations. In any civil legal aid case, when a solicitor or counsel will attend, the assisted person will also be allowed to attend if he or she has a financial interest in the case.

On all costs reviews, the area committee determines the costs *de novo* after consideration of (a) the original claim submitted, (b) any further submissions made by the solicitor in writing and (c) any oral representations made by the solicitor or their representative at the committee meeting.

On the review the area committee may confirm, increase or decrease the amount allowed.

Area committees must in all cases state the reasons for their decisions referring, if necessary, to the relevant regulations and principles governing the assessment of costs.

10. POINTS OF PRINCIPLE OF GENERAL IMPORTANCE

A solicitor or counsel who is dissatisfied with the decision of an area committee on a review of a costs assessment may, within 21 days of the notification of the outcome of the review, make application to the area committee to certify a point of principle of general importance. The solicitor or counsel doing so must provide the exact wording of the point of principle they wish to be certified.

Procedure
Attendance on applications for certification of points of principle is not permitted.

On determining an application to certify a point of principle of general importance, the area committee will consider whether the result of the review raises a point of general importance to the profession. (This is a threshold requirement, comparable to the requirement that a point of law of public importance be certified for an appeal, which ensures that cases heard on appeal by the Costs Appeals Committee do not turn on their particular facts but raise issues of principle which are likely to affect other determinations in the future.)

If the area committee grants an application to certify a point of principle of general importance, a clear point of principle must be certified by the committee at the meeting. The solicitor or counsel may then, within 21 days of receipt of that certification, appeal in writing to the Legal Aid Board's Costs Appeals Committee.

If the area committee refuses an application, brief reasons for refusing must be given. These must refer to one or both limbs of the basis on which a point can be certified, *i.e.* (a) point of principle and/or (b) general importance.

Most points of principle are likely to arise in the interpretation and application of the regulations affecting the assessment of costs. If an application turns only on the facts of the case it is unlikely that any principle has arisen. If an application turns on very particular facts which are unlikely to arise again (and, even if they did, they would not be generally applicable) it will be unlikely to be of general importance.

In no circumstances may an application to certify a point of principle of general importance be made or considered at the same area committee meeting which dealt with the review of the assessment.

The relevant regulations
1. Green form bills—regulation 29 Legal Advice and Assistance Regulations 1989,
2. ABWOR bills—regulation 29 Legal Advice and Assistance Regulations 1989,
3. Court duty solicitor bills—regulation 29 Legal Advice and Assistance Regulations 1989,
4. Police station duty solicitor (PACE) bills—regulation 29 Legal Advice and Assistance Regulations 1989,
5. Criminal bills—regulation 13 of Legal Aid in Criminal and Care Proceedings (Costs) Regulations 1989,
6. Civil assessed bills—regulation 105 Civil Legal Aid (General) Regulations 1989.

Costs Appeals Committee
Decisions of the Legal Aid Board's Costs Appeals Committee are binding on the Board for costs assessment and are maintained in a manual of points of principle of general importance. A copy of the manual should be available to area committees when considering reviews of assessments and applications to certify points of principle of general importance—when it will be particularly important to check whether the point of principle has already been determined.

As well as dealing with appeals concerning points of principle of general importance, the Board's Costs Appeals Committee is also responsible, under regulation 114 Civil Legal Aid (General) Regulations 1989, for determining applications for authorities to have taxations reviewed.

Attendance on appeals to the Costs Appeals Committee is not permitted.

Examples of matters considered by the Costs Appeals Committee
Set out below are examples of points which have been considered by the Costs Appeals Committee to illustrate what types of matter are suitable for certification as raising points of principle of general importance. This is not, of course, a definitive or exhaustive list.

The Costs Appeals Committee also consider applications under regulations 114 and 115 Civil Legal Aid (General) Regulations 1989 for authorities to have taxations reviewed and to appeal from judges' taxation decisions.

Examples of points of principle of general importance
A. Whether applications for advice and assistance under the green form scheme have been made in accordance with the Regulations (see the Legal Advice and Assistance Regulations 1989) as to whether costs would be allowed under the green form.
B. The circumstances in which rota and panel Duty Solicitors can claim enhanced rates of remuneration payable for acting under the Advice at Police Stations Scheme (see the Legal Advice and Assistance at Police Stations (Remuneration) Regulations 1989) and the Duty Solicitor Arrangements 1997.
C. The principles governing the enforcement of time limits for submission of costs claims.
D. Whether work involved in file review in accordance with franchising specifications is fee earner work or whether it is part of good practice and borne under office overheads.
E. Payment for preparation of bills in legally aided cases.
F. The scope of limitations to legal aid certificates.
G. The principles governing enhanced rates in criminal cases—the broad average direct cost and how to define it.

11. CONDUCT OF MEETINGS

The Chairman of an appeal sub-committee has primary responsibility for the conduct of the meeting. Appellants and their representatives must be afforded a fair and reasonable opportunity to present their case. Justice must not only be done but be seen to be done. The reasonable appellant should leave the committee room feeling that he or she has had a fair hearing.

The Chairman should be courteous but firm. It will be necessary to be firm with a voluble appellant and to ensure that he keeps to the point but without hindering the reasonable presentation of his case. He or she may be nervous. Other nervous appellants may need to have further relevant information drawn out of them. Appellants will not know how to proceed and will look to the Chairman for guidance.

The decisions of the area committee are by a majority vote and, in the case of an equality of votes, the Chairman of the meeting has a second or casting vote.

Area committee meetings are confidential. As in court, no tape recording of the proceedings is permitted. Information for each area committee appeal is provided solely for the purpose of properly disposing of that appeal. Members of the press are not admitted.

Minutes are kept of each area sub-committee meeting. These usually comprise the secretary's appeal agenda, on each agenda note in which he or she will have endorsed the committee's decision and reasons for it with any other relevant note. The front page of the agenda records the names of the area committee members forming the sub-committee and the date and venue of the meeting.

When any appeal is being determined, any member must, if they discover they have an interest in any of the appeals, declare that interest and take no part in the decision-making. This must then be recorded in the minutes. Similarly, any member forming part of a dissenting minority may ask that his or her name appear on the minutes as dissenting. Except in so far as the procedure of any area committee is regulated by the Board, any such committee has the power to regulate its own procedure. The ruling of the Chairman of any committee or sub-committee on any matter of procedure arising at any meeting of such committee or sub-committee is final and conclusive.

For some of the appeals, the appellant will have the right of attendance before area committee and, in some of these cases, appellants will exercise that right. An appellant who does may either conduct the appeal himself, with or without the assistance of any person whom he may appoint for the purpose, or be represented by counsel or a solicitor or a legal executive. If someone other than a solicitor, counsel or legal executive, for example a trainee solicitor or a friend, attends to represent the appellant, the area committee has a discretion whether or not to hear them.

If an appellant appoints someone ostensibly for the purpose of assisting him with the appeal but the committee doubts that that is the true purpose of the appointment—for example because the appointee is a journalist—the committee may refuse to allow the appointee admission to the committee room.

Where an appellant has given notice that they will attend or be represented but no one is there at the appointed time, the committee should put back consideration of that appeal until either the person attends or until all other matters have been dealt with. The committee is providing a service to the appellant as well as the other stakeholders in legal aid.

When an appellant or his or her representative arrive at a legal aid office, they will have been asked to report to the reception (or some other identified point) where they will either be met and taken to a waiting area or there will be clear directions to enable them to go to the waiting area. Either the committee's clerk/secretary or some other member of the area office staff will take responsibility for noting the name of the person attending and the appeal for which they have come for—generally putting them at ease, for telling them when their appeal is likely to be heard and for dealing with any questions they may have about the procedure.

When appeals are heard elsewhere, the area office staff responsible for providing administrative support for the area committee will have made arrangements to ensure that appellants know that they have come to the right place and that there are sufficient facilities. The committee's clerk/secretary on the day is responsible for ensuring that the best arrangements that can be made at the time are made for putting these arrangements into effect. They should also, so far as is possible, note the name of the person attending and the appeal for which they have come and for explaining to that person the informality of the procedure and generally putting them at ease and for telling them when their appeal is likely to be heard.

All appellants, however, will have been sent a leaflet about the appeal procedure, how to get to the appeal venue and what to expect.

When dealing with appeals for appellants who do not attend or are not represented, Chairmen often find it effective to take a preliminary sounding to see whether there is likely to be any variation of views. If so, the merits of the case will need to be discussed in detail. If not, and all members have agreed to the decision (having already read the papers) the Chairman will nevertheless have to check that the reasons given for the decision are those of the committee as a whole. Even where an attendance is expected, it is usually useful for the chairman to take a preliminary sounding of views. This can help clarify any areas of concern and focus the questions which will be put.

Where an appellant attends in person or is represented, he or she will be shown into the committee room by the committee clerk/secretary. The Chairman of the committee should then introduce himself or herself and the committee members by name. Addresses or firm names need not be provided and names need to be provided only to appellants and their representatives (for example, they need not be provided to members of the press who may subsequently enquire).

Having provided a name, there is a small risk that an area committee member may be approached individually by a (former) appellant or their representative in connection with the appeal. In such case, the committee member should refer the person to the area office and notify the area office accordingly.

The Chairman should also explain what the committee have read and what the committee's role is. It is important not only that appellants receive a fair hearing but that they feel that they have received a fair hearing with all relevant points having been taken into account.

Handling of requests for adjournment

The Committee should always consider whether they wish to allow the appeal on the information available as this will avoid a further hearing. The Committee need only entertain requests for adjournments which they consider reasonable. If the request has no merit, the Committee may refuse to allow the adjournment, giving reasons and then proceed to deal with the appeal. The committee clerk/secretary may be able to provide information from the area office file which the committee should take into account when considering whether or not to grant an adjournment. Where an appeal has been badly prepared and an adjournment is requested to enable more information to be provided, this should generally be refused.

Running order and preview

The Chairman should decide how the meeting is to be run bearing in mind the following considerations:

(a) Appeals considered in the order in which they appear in the list increase the chances of attenders being seen on time and every effort should be made to ensure that people are seen on time.

(b) It is useful to preview cases. This may be done before each one is considered (and before the appellant or their representative come into the committee room) or at the start of the meeting. Some committees find it helpful to run through the agenda at the start of the meeting to identify items where members agree to grant. If there are any such items where the appellant is in attendance, those items may be dealt with first in order to avoid the attender and/or his representative waiting unnecessarily.

(c) Although those attenders with a right of attendance/representation have been given an attendance time, they do not know the running order. The order in which they should be seen should be decided with reference to any combination of the following:

(i) those represented by solicitor or counsel may be given priority, to save costs;

    (ii) appellants in person may be given priority because they may have had to take time off work;

   (iii) appellants with children may be given priority, particularly if there are no facilities for children in the reception area;

   (iv) those who arrive late take less priority;

    (v) cases which appear likely to involve lengthy representations may be left until later so as to avoid others having to wait.

Time allowed for representations

No predetermined time limit should be placed on the time for oral representations. However, the Chairman should indicate as soon as he or she is satisfied that the main arguments in support of an appeal have been conveyed and should invite the appellant and/or his/her representative to close. In extreme circumstances, the Chairman may have to call a halt to oral representation where the main arguments have been established but the appellant appears intent on continuing unnecessarily.

Committee members should not enter into any debate with appellants or their representatives which could suggest the committee's likely decision.

Poorly prepared appeals (insufficient information)

Applications which lack sufficient information to show a basis for granting legal aid will usually be refused by the area office even where the lack of information appears to be due to poor preparation by the solicitor rather than the merits of the case itself.

If on appeal sufficient information is still not provided, the committee should also dismiss the appeal. Where such an appeal is dismissed, the reasons for dismissal should specify, as far as possible, what information should have been supplied to enable the committee to reach a decision and should indicate that the appellant can reapply for legal aid. Only in very exceptional cases should the committee adjourn such cases.

Non-discrimination

Every member of the committee must be vigilant in ensuring that no remarks that could be construed as discriminatory or personally offensive, for any reason, are made, however inadvertently, at any time during the meeting. The Chairman has a particular responsibility to ensure this and, should any such remark be made, to take such steps as seem to him or her to be appropriate in the circumstances.

Care should be taken to try to pronounce the names of appellants properly. For some people the correct pronunciation of their name is an important matter.

The role of the committee clerk or secretary

The committee clerk or secretary is there to help the committee conduct its business. As well as making arrangements for appellants and their representatives who attend appeals, he or she will be able to provide information from the area office file for the committee. Where appeals are held in the area office, he or she will be able to call on staff with specialist legal aid knowledge—either legal or financial. Where meetings are held away from the office, the committee will generally be clerked by a member of the area office staff with such knowledge.

For obvious reasons, the committee clerk should not usually be the member of staff who made the original decision to refuse—though on occasion this may be unavoidable and where the original decision-maker and the clerk are one and the same, particular care must be taken by the clerk not to exceed his or her remit. It is important that the committee's decision should be, and be seen to be, independent of the area office. The clerk's role is limited to providing information to help the committee. Though this may occasionally extend to reminding the committee of a particular fact or issue which, from their discussion, they appear to have overlooked, more usually it should be limited to providing information when requested.

Having said this, there may be occasions when, for example, if the appeal agenda note has omitted to refer to a relevant Note for Guidance or to a relevant decision of the Board's Costs Appeals Committee, the committee clerk may draw this to the committee's attention. And either the committee clerk or other specialist members of staff may, when appropriate, be able to advise the committee about decisions of previous area committees and other matters of Board guidance, where this is relevant. This may be more likely to arise in costs appeals.

The committee may ask the clerk to express a view and this is in order but, where the clerk was the person who made the original decision to refuse, he or she should declare this.

Urgent items

As well as the items in the agenda sent to committee members in advance of the meeting, committees will usually have to deal with some urgent items presented on the day. These are likely to be criminal matters (for which the Board has set stringent targets) or civil matters where an emergency has arisen. The Chairman, perhaps with the assistance of the committee clerk/secretary, should determine the running order of these items.

Making and communicating decisions

Decisions should be made in the absence of appellants or their representatives, who should normally be told that the committee's decision will be communicated to them by the area office. In some cases, the committee will have decided to grant before hearing the appellant or representative. In such cases, the appellant or representative should be invited into the committee room to be told the committee's decision. Similarly, if an appeal has to be adjourned for administrative reasons, *e.g.* the committee is not quorate, the appellant or representative should be invited into the committee room for an explanation to be given.

There will also be occasions where the committee is able immediately to notify a favourable decision to the appellant or representative. Unfavourable decisions should never (except in the most exceptional circumstances) be communicated in this way.

Reasons for decisions

Public duty and public money—the need for reasons

As a member of an area committee, you perform an important public duty. Your decisions affect both access to justice and payments for legal services from public money.

Not only must area committees make consistent, fair and justifiable decisions, but those decisions must be seen to be so.

This means that every time an area committee considers a person's case and decides against them, it must identify the ground or grounds for its decision and give reasons for its decision which are accurate, clear, sound, meaningful and sufficient.

Fair treatment for the person concerned—the need for reasons

The quality of reasons is particularly important when an area committee refuses legal aid or refuses to amend, discharges or revokes a person's legal aid certificate. The person affected by the area committee's decision must know why it made its decision. It is also particularly important when a costs appeal concerns a large sum or affects a large number of cases.

Reasons also help when an area committee grants an appeal or review as the reasons can be relayed to the original decision maker as an aid to consistency. In these cases, however, reasons need only be brief.

Reasons should show that you have successfully come to grips with the main contentions advanced and explain why you have reached your decision. They should state any findings on contentious facts (with reasons) and any conclusions on law.

Better decision making

The discipline of having to provide accurate, clear, sound, meaningful and sufficient reasons for decisions, helps to ensure that the decisions are good ones.

Grounds and reasons

Legal aid may be refused and a legal aid certificate may be discharged or revoked only for the grounds set out in legal aid legislation. The relevant provisions are set out in section 15 of the Legal Aid Act 1988 and Parts IV, V and X of the Civil Legal Aid (General) Regulations 1989. Regard should also be had to the Notes for Guidance 7 "Civil legal aid merits test" and 13 "Discharge and revocation of certificates including representations".

If you decide to refuse legal aid or to discharge or revoke a legal aid certificate, you must identify on which ground or grounds you are doing so and only then go on to give reasons showing why that ground applies.

For example, if you decide that an application for legal aid should be refused because you are not satisfied that the appellant has reasonable grounds for taking proceedings (section 15(2) of the Legal Aid Act 1988, the "legal merits test") you should not only specify that ground as the one on which your decision is based but go on to say why, *e.g.*:

> "The Committee were not satisfied that you have reasonable grounds for taking proceedings. They noted the additional points made in your solicitor's letter of appeal dated xx/xx/xx but considered that you would not be able to establish that the proposed defendant had been negligent because the defects in your property, which the proposed defendant had failed to identify, were not ones that a competent surveyor could reasonably have been expected to identify."

For example, if you decide that an application for legal aid should be refused because it appears to you unreasonable the particular circumstances of the case that the appellant should be granted legal aid (section 15(3)(a) of the Legal Aid Act 1988, the "reasonableness" test) you should not only specify that ground as the one on which your decision is based but go on to say why, *e.g.*

> "It appeared to the Committee unreasonable that you should be granted legal aid in the particular circumstances of the case because your prospects of recovering any money from the proposed defendant are remote. The committee noted the additional points made in your solicitor's letter of appeal dated xx/xx/xx and the enclosures sent with it which showed that you have legal grounds for taking proceedings, but the enquiry agent's report shows that the proposed defendant is unemployed, lives in rented accommodation and does not appear to own any assets."

Reasons may often be most conveniently be linked to grounds by words such as "in particular", or "for example". The word "because" suggests that the reason stated is the only reason which is fine if that is the case—but it may not always be the case.

Length and detail of reasons

The length and detail of reasons should be appropriate to the case. In straightforward cases, short reasons may be all that is required. However, in a heavy and complex case, the committee's reasons have to be longer. Where there is a favourable counsel's opinion (or similar document) and the committee is making a decision to refuse, detailed reasons are required to explain clearly and fully why the committee disagreed with the opinion.

If a committee gives very brief reasons, the adequacy of the reasons may be a ground for judicial review. However, the most important aspect of reasons is not their length but that they are sufficiently detailed and full so that they give a fair account of why the committee made its decision.

Where a committee reaches legal conclusions it must be clear why those conclusions were reached. For example, expressing the view that a claim will fail or has no prospects of success clearly requires the committee to state what the weaknesses are in the case which led to that conclusion.

Where facts are in issue and the committee makes a finding of fact it should state that finding and why it has made it. (Where an appellant or his or her solicitor attend an appeal, the committee should ask to be addressed on any facts in issue and on any issues which concern the committee, whether or not they are in the papers before the committee.)

Previous reason

Area committees should never simply say that they are refusing an appeal or review for the reasons previously given by the area office, unless this is followed by words of explanation.

If an area committee merely adopts the reasons previously given by the area office, this gives the impression that there has been no real reconsideration of the case and that any further information has been ignored. Because it is an "easy option" it can lead to an area committee making a decision without properly having formed a collective view of their reasons for the decision. Furthermore, the reasons previously given may, because of developments in the case, be entirely inappropriate.

Where further information in support of an appeal has been received (since the area office decision) and considered, it should be specifically referred to in the committee's reasons.

Standard reasons

There is no objection to an area committee basing its expressed reasons on one of the Board's "standard" reasons which are intended to be an aid to (not a substitute for) the formulation and specification of reasons.

However, even where no further information has been submitted, what sufficed to explain a (first) refusal by an area office will rarely be appropriate to explain a decision on an appeal. Further words of explanation will almost always be required.

What is important is that the area committee's own reasons are expressed.

Discharges and revocations

In 1996 an area committee was judicially reviewed (*R. v. Legal Aid Board, ex p. Doran, The Times*, July 22, 1996 (Collins J. , QBD)) over a decision to revoke a legal aid certificate for failure to disclose a material fact. The judge in the case stressed the need for proper reasons to be given. (See NFG 13, para. 13–07/5).

Costs appeals (and other cases where there is no statutory obligation to state reasons

In 1998, an area committee was judicially reviewed (*R. v. Legal Aid Board, ex p. Rafina*, February 12, 1998, *New Law Journal*, February 27, 1998) over a decision on a green form costs appeal. The judgment makes it clear that, even where (as on costs appeals) regulations do not require reasons to be given, they must be given.

It is also clear, from the judgment, that when giving reasons, area committees must state any conclusions they reach on contested facts and any conclusions on issues of law.

Responsibility for reasons

It is the responsibility of each chair of an area committee appeals sub-committee to ascertain and specify the committee's reasons for its decisions. These reasons must be accurate, clear, sound, meaningful and sufficient.

It is the responsibility of each clerk of an appeals sub-committee to ensure that he or she correctly records reasons for the committee's decisions. If he or she:

    (a) thinks that the committee has merely adopted the area office's reasons; or

    (b) is not sure that the reasons he or she has recorded relate to an appropriate ground; or

(c) is not sure that the reasons are accurate, clear, sound. meaningful and sufficient;

he or she should raise this with the chair.

The Area Chairmen's Working Party believes that area committee members considering agenda items before a meeting, should, if they form a preliminary view of a case, ensure that they are clear about their reasons for that view and the statutory ground to which they relate. This should ensure a better informed discussion of the item and assist the provision of good quality reasons. It should also save time at the meeting.

Judicial review

If apparently inadequate or inappropriate reasons are given, the Board may be judicially reviewed. The Board's Legal Department will have conduct of the judicial review proceedings for the Board.

If the proceedings will be contested, the chair of the relevant appeals sub-committee will be required to swear an affidavit. If the Legal Department considers that the Board will lose the proceedings, it may concede them and agree either to the matter being considered afresh by the area office or an appeals sub-committee.

The provision of good quality reasons helps to avoid judicial review proceedings in the first place.

Summary

The Area Chairmen's Working Party and the Board ask for your help in improving the quality of reasons for decisions given by area committees.

Reasons must relate to grounds and be accurate, clear, sound, meaningful and sufficient. Where facts are contested and findings of fact are made, these must be stated with the reasons for the finding. Where conclusions on law are reached these must be stated.

12. JUDICIAL REVIEW

The decisions of area committees, being part of administrative law, are judicially reviewable.

In the GCHQ case, *Council of Civil Service Unions v. Minister for the Civil Service* [1985] A.C. 374, Lord Diplock divided the grounds of challenge through judicial review into illegality, irrationality and procedural impropriety.

"Illegality" This relates to the actions/decisions of the area committee and not to whether or not the area committee has got the law right when considering any particular case. An area committee's decision could be criticised under the heading of "illegality" if, for example, the merits tests relevant to an application for legal aid were wrongly applied, for example, by refusing legal aid on the basis that it was "unreasonable in the particular circumstances of the case" because an applicant had an (irrelevant) previous conviction for drink/driving.

"Irrationality" The courts expect powers and duties to be exercised reasonably and will interfere on the ground of irrationality if they consider a decision "is so outrageous in its defiance of logic or of accepted moral standards that no sensible person who had applied his mind to the question to be decided could have arrived at it"—*per* Lord Diplock in the GCHQ case. This is often called "Wednesbury unreasonableness", after the case of *Associated Provincial Picture Houses v. Wednesbury Corporation* [1948] 1 K.B. 223 [1947] 2 All E.R. 680.

In practice, courts very rarely make such an express finding; they are more likely, if there is a decision which they do not allow to stand, to find that the decision-maker has taken into account an irrelevant consideration or failed to take into account a relevant

731

consideration, or otherwise has directed his mind to the wrong question. Where it is not clear what questions a decision-maker has addressed his mind to, the courts may say that he must have addressed his mind to the wrong questions because, if he had addressed his mind to the right questions, and still reached the same conclusion, his decision would have been "Wednesbury unreasonable".

It is, therefore, important that an area committee's reasons show that the committee directed its mind to the right issues and to none of the wrong ones and that the reason given holds up to scrutiny. It is generally better to give one (or two) good reasons than to give two or three good reasons and one bad. Your reasons should also relate to the statutory criteria for the grant of legal aid.

At the end of each area committee meeting, or a few days later if it is sent to him, the Chairman will sign the agenda on behalf of the committee to confirm the committee's reasons. In any judicial review, this agenda would have to be produced by the Board as an exhibit to an affidavit sworn by the Chairman.

All the cases which area committees consider have already been considered by the Board's staff (the area office) and, in nearly all cases, a decision (with reasons), which the appellant was unhappy with, will have been made.

In many cases, area committees will agree with the original reasons given for the original decision but should take care not to fall into the trap of merely adopting the previous reasons because this is an easy option or because the committee considered them to be roughly right.

If an area committee adopts the previous reasons as its own, it must be sure that it wholly agrees with them and should, in every case where further information has been submitted since the original decision, make some reference to the area committee's having taken that further information into account and the extent to which (if at all) that further information affected the area committee's decision.

In some appeals, the area committee's decision will have been influenced by previous decisions of area committees or by the Board's general approach (endorsed by area committees) as, perhaps, set out in the Notes for Guidance. It is important that such guidelines do not unreasonably fetter an area committee's discretion.

It is legitimate for decision-makers to have guidelines as to how like cases are to be treated but the decision-maker must not allow the guidelines to close its mind to the circumstances of a particular case which might lead to the policy not being applied in that case. An area committee which fetters its discretion by failing to take account of the particular circumstances of an appeal before it may be subject to successful judicial review.

"Procedural Impropriety"   The decision may be quashed on judicial review if the decision-making body has not followed the procedures which it has established for itself, or if those procedures are unfair. Area committee procedures are quite straightforward so, in the ordinary case, there is little risk of an area committee falling foul of this potential head of challenge.

One possibility of challenge might arise if representations had been received from the opponent of an appellant and these were put before the area committee without the appellant (or his or her legal advisers) having an opportunity to comment on them. It is the Board's invariable practice to allow applicants and appellants to comment on representations made by their opponents or third parties.

Also under the heading of procedural impropriety is the question whether a person affected by a decision has been given a fair hearing. To protect the interests of appellants it is important that the area committee should give a full opportunity for representations to be made so that it can be fully acquainted with all the relevant consideration before making its decision. This is really all part of the area committee's general duty to act fairly.

Another form of procedural impropriety is bias. Here, it is the appearance or suspicion of bias which counts. Examples of bias in this context are potential conflicts of interest caused by having an interest (perhaps a financial interest) in the subject matter of the decision or being a friend or relative of the appellant or his or her opponent.

Area offices take particular care to try to avoid including in any agenda any case in which any member of a sub-committee may have an interest. However, while the area office will know who the appellant's current solicitors are, they will not necessarily know whether he or she has recently changed solicitors and, if so, who the new solicitors are, or know who the opponents (or potential opponent)'s solicitors are, or whether any members of the area sub-committee are friends or relatives of the appellant's opponent or potential opponent.

If an area committee member receives an agenda which includes a case in which he has an interest, he should not read that case or, if he has started to read it, he should stop reading it as soon as the interest is identified. He should then notify his interest at the committee meeting. Section 6 explains the steps which will be taken at the meeting.

"Legitimate expectation" This is another doctrine which has developed through judicial review. The GCHQ case is a well-known example of this. This is really part of the duty to act fairly and, in any particular case, it is necessary to look at the position as a whole to decide whether the circumstances are such that a person affected by a decision has acquired a legitimate expectation that the decision-maker should act towards him in a particular way.

A judicial review of an area committee decision is not an appeal. Even if the court does set aside a decision made, it will still be for an area committee, rather than the court, to make a fresh decision. This means that the same decision could be reached the second time round, without the second decision being amenable to judicial review. However when, on a judicial review, the court quashes a decision, it will usually indicate what factors it believes should be taken into account when the decision is made again, or what further steps should be taken before the decision is made again.

Particularly in complex cases, such as multi-party actions, it is easy to found an application for judicial review with the benefit of hindsight. With hindsight, an applicant might be able to point to an alleged misunderstanding between him and the committee for example as to the particular point which was concerning the committee. This might enable a challenge on the ground of procedural unfairness.

Possible ways to reduce this danger are:

(i) By the area office ensuring that, in correspondence leading up the hearing, nothing is said that could give the impression that only one particular aspect of the case is troubling the Board, if there is any possibility of a decision being taken on a different ground.

(ii) At the hearing, it may be necessary for the area committee specifically to draw to the attention of the appellants any ground which is particularly troubling them and which may form the basis of the decision. In the context of a multi-party action, it may be necessary expressly to make it clear that the applicants need to address the committee both of general issues and on individual cases before the committee.

(iii) Where a committee is formulating its reasons in a very complex case (such as a multi-party action) and are considering deciding the case on different grounds to those covered by the applicant, it may be necessary to adjourn and reconvene the committee to allow the applicant to answer any such points, or to write to the applicant explaining the concerns and asking them to respond before any final decision is taken.

(iv) Whenever an area committee wishes to depart from counsel's opinion on behalf of the appellant(s), particularly clear and detailed reasons must be given for the views reached.

ANNEX A–Board guidance on the Area Committee Arrangements

The Board would not expect any Chairman of an area committee to remove from office, under paragraph 25(2), any member of an area committee unless, at least once in the previous twelve months, the Chairman could have removed them from office under paragraph 25(2).

The Board would not expect any Chairman of an area committee to remove from office, under paragraph 25(2), any member of an area committee who, promptly after having been notified of the date of the meeting he was due to attend, had notified the area director in writing of his inability to attend.

Membership of an area committee is an important matter and the area committee system relies on members attending meetings to which they are called. However, the Board recognises that there will be occasions when area committee members are unable to attend. The Board expects area committee members who are called to four or fewer meetings not to miss more than one, and area committee members who are called to between five and ten meetings not to miss more than two. The Board expects that, in most cases, a committee member who has to miss a meeting will be able to make up for that by attending another—perhaps at short notice at the request of the area office.

ANNEX B–Board criteria and guidance on appointments to area committees and panels of chairs

Area committees—criteria

The criteria which prospective members of area committees must meet before they may be appointed by an area director in consultation with the chair of the appropriate area committee are set out below. (An area director in consultation with the chair of the appropriate area committee may set additional requirements.)

1. All applicants must have three years experience of legal aid work since qualifying.
2. An applicant who is a solicitor must not have any committee decisions currently recorded against them at the OSS (Note: such committee decisions are kept by the OSS for five years.)
3. An applicant who is a solicitor must not have any adverse Findings or Orders of the Solicitors Disciplinary Tribunal recorded against them. (Note: such committee decisions are kept by the OSS without time limit.)
4. An applicant who is a solicitor in private practice must hold a current practising certificate.
5. An applicant who is a barrister must be approved by the General Council of the Bar.

Area committees—guidance

In appointing members of area committees, area directors shall, so far as they consider practicable:

1. have regard to the desirability not only of retaining members with experience of area committee work, but also the desirability of bringing in new members;
2. ensure that area committees include members with broad, general legal experience and members with specialist legal experience; and
3. ensure that area committees include members from among groups who are in a minority in the legal profession such as women and members of ethnic minorities.

Panels of chairs—guidance

In maintaining panels of chairs, area directors shall have regard to:

1. experience of committee work;
2. experience of legal aid work;
3. understanding of legal aid legislation and the Board's guidance on it; and
4. ability to deal courteously and effectively with appellants.

Extracts from the Code of Conduct of the Bar of England and Wales

(Dated March 31, 1990 and incorporating Amendment No. 1 dated October 22, 1990, Amendment No. 2 dated March 16, 1991, Amendment No. 3 dated October 1, 1993, Amendment No. 4 dated March 12, 1994 and Amendment No. 5 dated April 14, 1997).

PART II—FUNDAMENTAL PRINCIPLES

Applicable to Practising Barristers
A practising barrister: **203**

    (a) must promote and protect fearlessly and by all proper and lawful means his lay client's best interests and do so without regard to his own interests or to any consequences to himself or to any other person (including his professional client or fellow members of the legal profession);

    (b) subject only to compliance with the specific provisions of Legal Aid Regulations owes his primary duty:

      (i) as between his lay client and his professional client; and
      (ii) as between the Legal Aid Fund and his lay client;
    to his lay client and must not permit the Legal Aid Fund or his professional client to limit his discretion as to how the interests of his lay client can best be served;

    (c) must act towards his lay client and his professional client at all times in good faith.

Applicable to Barristers in Independent Practice
A barrister in independent practice must comply with the "Cab-rank rule" and accord-   **209**
ingly except only as otherwise provided in paragraphs 501, 502 and 503 he must in any field in which he professes to practise in relation to work appropriate to his experience and seniority and irrespective of whether his client is paying privately or is legally aided or otherwise publicly funded:

    (a) accept any brief to appear before a court in which he professes to practise;

    (b) accept any instructions;

    (c) act for any person on whose behalf he is briefed or instructed;

and do so irrespective of (i) the party on whose behalf he is briefed or instructed (ii) the nature of the case and (iii) any belief or opinion which he may have formed as to the character reputation cause conduct guilt or innocence of that person.

PART V—BRIEFS AND INSTRUCTIONS TO PRACTISING BARRISTERS

Acceptance of Briefs and Instructions and Application of the "Cab-rank Rule"
A barrister in independent practice is not obliged to accept a brief or instructions: **502**

(a) requiring him to do anything other than during the course of his ordinary working year;

(b) other than at a fee which is proper having regard to the complexity length and difficulty of the case and to his ability experience and seniority and any brief or instructions in a legally aided matter shall for this purpose unless the Bar Council or the Bar in general meeting otherwise determines (either in a particular case or in any class or classes of case or generally) be deemed to be at a proper professional fee;

(c) if the expenses which will be incurred are likely to be unreasonably high in relation to the fee likely to be paid and are not to be paid additionally to such fee;

(d) save in the case of legal aid work:

(i) unless and until his fees are agreed;

(ii) if having required his fees to be paid before he accepts the brief or instructions to which the fees relate those fees are not paid.

503 A Queen's Counsel in independent practice is not obliged to accept a brief or instructions:

(a) to settle alone any document of a kind generally settled only by or in conjunction with a junior;

(b) to act without a junior if he considers that the interests of the lay client require that a junior should also be instructed.

Over-representation

503A.4 In cases involving several parties, a practising barrister must in the case of each brief and, if he is a barrister in independent practice, also in the case of all instructions, consider, on receipt of the brief or instructions and further in the event of any change of circumstances, whether, consistently with the proper and efficient administration of justice and having regard to all the circumstanes and any actual or potential conflict of interest, his client needs to be separately represented or advised or whether he could properly be jointly represented or advised with another party or, where there is more than one client, whether it is in all their interests to be jointly represented or advised.

503A.5(i) If the barrister considers that the client could properly be jointly represented or advised with another party, he must immediately advise the client accordingly.

503A.5(ii) If the barrister considers that it is not in the interests of all his clients that they should be jointly represented or advised, he must immediately advise the clients accordingly.

Withdrawal from a Case and Return of Brief or Instructions

504 A practising barrister must cease to act and if he is a barrister in independent practice must return any brief or instructions:

(c) if in any legally aided case (whether civil or criminal) it has become apparent to him that legal aid has been wrongly obtained by false or inaccurate information and action to remedy the situation is not immediately taken by his client;

(d) if the circumstances set out in Regulation 67 of the Civil Legal Aid (General) Regulations 1989 arise at a time when it is impracticable for the Area Committee to meet in time to prevent an abuse of the Legal Aid Fund.

NOTE: Paragraph 802.1 requires barristers to comply with the provisions of the Legal Aid Act 1974, the Legal Aid Act 1988 or any regulations made for giving effect to or for preventing abuses of either of those Acts. Any failure to do so constitutes professional misconduct rendering the barrister liable to disciplinary proceedings.

The General Council of the Bar's Legal Aid Guidelines

1 Introduction

1.1 These Guidelines are intended to assist barristers to comply with the provisions of the Legal Aid Act 1988 (and regulations made under the Act) when advising the Legal Aid Board on merits on behalf of an applicant for civil legal aid, or when acting on an assisted person's behalf.

1.2 They are derived in part from the *Legal Aid Handbook* (published annually) which every barrister instructed under the terms of a civil legal aid certificate should consult.

1.3 They are essentially statements of good practice and should not be rigidly applied. *They may, however, be taken into account when a wasted costs order is being considered against a barrister on the gound of his non-compliance with the Act, or in deciding whether or not a barrister has committed a disciplinary offence.* They should be read in conjunction with the Code of Conduct (see especially paragraphs 203(b), 504(c)(d) and 802.1(d)).

2 The statutory test

2.1 The statutory test for the grant of civil legal aid to an applicant who is financially eligible is *twofold*:

(1) The applicant must satisfy the Board that he has *reasonable grounds for taking, defending or being a party to the proceedings* (section 15(2)—the "legal merits" test); and

(2) Representation may be refused if it *is unreasonable for him to be granted representation* in the particular circumstances of the case (section 15(3)(a)—the "reasonableness test").

2.2 The test does not apply to certain public law proceedings under the Children Act 1989 (section 15 as amended).

"Legal merits"

2.3 Reasonable grounds for taking, defending or being a party to proceedings may be said to exist if (a) assuming the facts alleged are proved, there is a case which has *reasonable prospects of success* in law; *and* (b) assuming he *had the means* to pay the likely costs, *the applicant would be advised to take or defend the proceedings privately.*

2.4 When considering *merits*, it is important to remember that there is almost always an opposing point of view and that litigation is notoriously uncertain. Whilst it is no part of a barrister's duty to be over-cautious, he should not advise that legal aid be granted when the prospects of success are no more than slight.

2.5 A barrister should estimate the prospects of a successful outcome by reference to one of the following categories, namely: A. Very good (80 per cent); B. Good (60–80 per cent); C. Reasonable (50–60 per cent); D. Less than evens; or E. Impossible to say.

2.6 The *means* of the hypothetical private client being considered should be taken as *moderate but not excessive*. In other words, he would be able to meet the likely costs, albeit with some difficulty or as something of a sacrifice.

"Reasonableness"

2.7 Even if his case has legal merits, an applicant may be refused legal aid if it would not be reasonable for him to be granted it.

2.8 A common example of proceedings which it would be unreasonable for the Legal Aid Board to fund are those which are *not likely to be cost effective, i.e.* any benefit to be achieved does not justify the cost. Another example is where the application reveals *some illegal motive or conduct* on the part of the applicant *or abuse* of legal aid.

2.9 More specific examples are where:

(a) the applicant has other rights or facilities (such as trade union or insurance cover) making it unnecessary for him to apply for legal aid;

(b) the applicant is a victim of a crime of violence who could obtain compensation from the Criminal Injuries Compensation Board;

(c) the proceedings should be taken in a different court where the costs are likely to be lower; or

(d) the arguments on which the applicant relies will be put forward on behalf of another party whose interests in the proceedings are substantially the same.

3 Contents of barrister's opinion on merits

3.1 A barrister's written opinion on merits should:

(i) show that *both* (a) the legal merits and (b) the reasonableness tests (as outlined above) have been specifically and separately addressed by him before reaching a conclusion—a general statement that legal aid should be granted is not sufficient; it should estimate the prospects of a successful outcome by reference to one of the categories A to E mentioned in paragraph 2.5 above; in a case falling within category D or E, more explanation must be given if the Board are to be satisfied that legal aid should be granted;

(ii) where *factual issues* are involved (a) set out in sufficient detail, (although not necessarily at great length), the rival factual versions to enable the Board to assess their relative strengths, and (b) express a clear opinion as to whether the applicant's version has a reasonable prospect of being accepted by a court and why;

(iii) in a case where the applicant's own evidence is likely to be contested, and a *conference* would assist the barrister to form a view of his reliability as a witness, state whether a conference has been held and what emerged from it, or if none was held, indicate briefly why;

(iv) where *legal issues* or difficulties of law are involved (a) summarise those issues or difficulties in sufficient detail to enable the Board to come to a view about them without looking outside the opinion, and (b) express a clear view as to whether the applicant's case on the law has a reasonable prospect of being accepted by a court and why;

(v) draw attention to (a) any *lack or incompleteness of material* which in his opinion might bear on the reliability or otherwise of the applicant's version, and (b) any other factor which in his opinion could—whether now or in the future—materially affect his assessment of the outcome of the case;

(vi) in a case where *damages* are claimed, quantify at least the likely bracket for an award;

(vii) draw attention to the need for the legal representatives between them to *quantify the costs* likely to be incurred by the Fund in the light of the barrister's opinion (if favourable) assuming the proceedings are fully contested;

(viii) suggest or formulate for the Board any *limitation or condition* (whether as to the scope of the work that should be covered or as to the costs which should be expended) which in his opinion ought to be imposed on the grant of legal aid in order to safeguard the Fund;

(ix) confirm that the proceedings are in his view *cost-effective, i.e.* that the estimated costs of the proceedings are likely to be justified by the benefit to the client, having regard in particular to the statutory charge which may be created by virtue of section 16 of the Act.

4 Barrister's continuing duty to the Fund

4.1 A barrister is under a specific duty to comply with the provisions of the Legal Aid Acts 1974 and 1988 or any regulations made for giving effect to or preventing abuses of those Acts: para. 802.1(d) of the Code of Conduct. Since these are directed at ensuring that legal aid is granted and continued only in justifiable cases, it follows that a barrister acting under a legal aid certificate is under a duty to bring to the attention of the Legal Aid Board any matter which in his view might affect the assisted person's entitlement to legal aid, or the terms of his certificate, at whatever stage of the proceedings that might occur.

4.2 An example of when the duty may arise is whenever *proposals for settlement* are made by the other side. He should report to the Board any decision of the client which may cast doubt on the reasonableness of legal aid being continued contrary to his advice.

4.3 A further example is where a barrister finds that his legally assisted client has an interest in the proceedings which is or may become substantially the same as that of another party (see paragraph 2.9(d) above. A barrister should in those circumstances, after discussing the matter with his client, report it to the Board and advise whether in his opinion it is reasonable for legal aid to be continued.

Legal Aid and Solicitors' Professional Conduct

Except where otherwise stated, the Practice Rules and the other requirements of solicitors' professional conduct apply equally whether the client is in receipt of legal aid or not. This note sets out some of the main specific obligations solicitors have in respect of legal aid, and the areas where obligations differ depending upon whether or not the client is legally aided. References are to "The Guide to the Professional Conduct of Solicitors" 1996.

Availability of Legal Aid

It is a principle of professional conduct that:

"A solicitor is under a duty to consider and advise the client on the availability of legal aid where the client might be entitled to assistance under the Legal Aid Act 1988." (Principle 5.01)

Note 6 to that principle states:

"Legally aided clients must be treated in the same way as privately funded clients and the same standards of care apply."

Note 2 to that principle states:

"Failure to advise clients of their rights under the Legal Aid Act can amount to unbefitting conduct and may also lead to a claim in negligence against a solicitor for breach of duty owed to the client."

Note 5 to that principle states:

"Where a solicitor considers that legal aid is likely to be available to the client, the availability of an emergency certificate should also be borne in mind. A solicitor who commences work without legal aid cover runs the risk of being unable to recover his or her pre-certificate costs."

Note 4 to that principle states:

"The duty to advise applies not only at the outset of the retainer but also as the matter proceeds. It is the duty of a solicitor to ensure that any material change in the client's means of which the solicitor becomes aware is at once taken into consideration in the context of eligibility for legal aid."

Information to Legally Aided Clients

The written professional standards deal with giving clients advance information on costs. Some of these standards will not be appropriate for legally aided clients. Standard (e) (Principle 13.10) deals specifically with legally aided clients and states:

Where clients are legally aided they should be informed at the outset of a case and at appropriate stages thereafter:

    (i) of the effect of the statutory charge on the case;

    (ii) that if they lose the case they may still be ordered by the court to contribute to their opponent's costs even though their own costs are covered by legal aid;

(iii) that even if they win, their opponent may not be ordered to pay the full amount of their costs and may not be capable of paying what they have been ordered to pay;

(iv) of their obligations to pay any contribution assessed and of the consequences of any failure to do so.

Professional Responsibilities

There are three important differences between solicitors' professional responsibilities in the case of legal aid clients as compared with privately paying ones:

(i) *Payments to Witnesses*

Solicitors are normally professionally responsible for payment of the reasonable agreed fees and expenses of witnesses called to give evidence on behalf of the client. However, Note 3 to Principle 21.11 states:

"In legal aid cases, whether civil or criminal, a solicitor should draw the attention of the witnesses to the fact of legal aid and that the witness's fees and disbursements will have to be taxed or assessed, and that only such amounts can be paid to the witness. A solicitor should expressly disclaim personal responsibility for payment of fees beyond those allowed on taxation or assessment. It should be noted that:

(a) prior authority is not mandatory;

(b) Area Committees do not have the power to grant prior authority for the costs of tendering expert evidence in criminal cases;

(c) witness expenses are not payable under a criminal legal aid order unless the court directs that they may not be paid from Central Funds (see *Practice Direction on Costs in Criminal Proceedings*, May 3, 1991: [1991] 2 All E.R. 924)."

(ii) *Solicitors' Lien*

Notes 3 and 4 to Principle 5.05 state:

"3. Where the client is legally aided, the solicitor's costs are secured by a legal aid order or certificate and therefore it would be inappropriate to call for a professional undertaking from the successor solicitor to pay the costs except in respect of any outstanding pre-certificate costs.

4. A solicitor who has acted in a legally aided matter may call for an undertaking from the successor solicitor either:

(a) to return the papers promptly at the end of the matter to enable a bill of costs to be drawn up; or

(b) that the successor solicitor will include the former solicitor's costs in a bill to be taxed, collect those costs and pay them over to the former solicitor."

(iii) *Confidentiality*

Note 9 to Principle 16.02 makes it clear that a solicitor's general duty of confidentiality to the client (Principle 16.04) may be overridden by the regulations dealing with legal aid which, in certain circumstances, impose a duty on the solicitor to report to the Legal Aid Board information which is confidential and privileged.

Solicitors Accounts Rules 1998

At the time of going to press, the concurrence of the Master of the Rolls has not been given to the Solicitors Accounts Rules 1998. However, it is anticipated that it will be given. Rule 21, which concerns payments to legal aid practitioners is set out below.

Rule 21—Treatment of payments to legal aid practitioners

Payments from the Legal Aid Board

(1) Two special dispensations apply to payments from the Legal Aid Board:

> (a) An advance payment in anticipation of work to be carried out, although *client money*, may be placed in an *office account*, provided the Board instructs in writing that this may be done.
>
> (b) A payment for *costs* (interim and/or final) may be paid into an *office account* at a *bank* or *building society* branch (or head office) in England and Wales, regardless of whether it consists wholly of *office money*, or is mixed with *client money* in the form of:
>
>> (i) advance payments for *fees* or *disbursements*; or
>> (ii) money for unpaid *professional disbursements*;
>
> provided all money for payment of *disbursements* is transferred to a *client account* (or the *disbursements* paid) within 14 days of receipt.

Payments from a third party

(2) If the Legal Aid Board has paid any *costs* to a *solicitor* or a previously nominated *solicitor* in a matter ("green form" *costs*, advance payments or interim *costs*), or has paid *professional disbursements* direct, and *costs* are subsequently settled by a third party:

> (a) The entire third party payment must be paid into a *client account*.
>
> (b) A sum representing the payments made by the Board must be retained in the *client account*.
>
> (c) Any balance belonging to the *solicitor* must be transferred to an *office account* within 14 days of the *solicitor* sending a report to the Board containing details of the third party payment.
>
> (d) The sum retained in the *client account* as representing payments made by the Board must be:
>
>> (i) **either** recorded in the individual *client's* ledger account, and identified as the Board's money;
>> (ii) **or** recorded in a ledger account in the Board's name, and identified by reference to the *client* or matter;
>
> **and** kept in the *client account* until notification from the Board that it has recouped an equivalent sum from subsequent legal aid payments due to the *solicitor*. The retained sum must be transferred to an *office account* within 14 days of notification.

Notes

> (i) This rule deals with matters which specifically affect legal aid practitioners. It should not be read in isolation from the remainder of the rules which apply to all solicitors, including legal aid practitioners.
>
> (ii) Franchised firms can apply for advance payments on the issue of a certificate. The Legal Aid Board has issued instructions that these payments may be placed in office account.
>
> (iii) Rule 21(1)(b) deals with the specific problems of legal aid practitioners by allowing mixed or indeterminate payments (or even a payment consisting entirely of unpaid professional disbursements) to be paid into an office account, which for the purpose of rule 21(1)(b) must be an account at a bank or building society. However, it is always open to the solicitor to comply with rule 19(1)(a) to (c), which are the options for all solicitors for the receipt of costs.
>
> (iv) Solicitors are required by the Legal Aid Board to report promptly to the Legal Aid Board on receipt of costs from a third party. It is advisable to keep a copy of the report on the file as

      proof of compliance with the Board's requirements, as well as to demonstrate compliance with the rule.

    (v) A third party payment may also include unpaid professional disbursements or outstanding costs of the client's previous solicitor. This part of the payment is client money and must be kept in a client account until the solicitor pays the professional disbursement or outstanding costs.

(Practitioners are reminded that the Board has instructed that payments on account to franchised firms, *i.e.* advance payments in anticipation of work to be carried out (rule 21(1)(a)), may be paid into office account).

743

Members of Legal Aid Board and Executive Board

LEGAL AID BOARD

Sir Tim Chessells (Chairman)
Henry Hodge OBE (Deputy Chairman)

Diane Charnock	Steve Orchard
Jean Dunkley	Diana Payne
Philip Ely	Jim Shearer
Brian Harvey	David Sinker OBE
Peter Hollingworth	

EXECUTIVE BOARD

Steve Orchard
(*Chief Executive*)

Richard Buxton	Roger Hamilton
(*Operations Director*)	(*Policy and Legal Director*)

Brian Harvey	Nick Scholte
(*Director of Resources and Supplier Development*)	(*Business Systems Director*)

Addresses of Legal Aid Offices

You should write or telephone rather than attend in person. Offices are:

London (Area No. 1)
29-37 Red Lion Street
London WC1R 4PP

General enquiries Tel: 0171-813 5300
Fax: 0171-813 5312
Emergency civil applications
Tel: 0171-813 5301
Fax: 0171-813 5321
Group duty solicitor manager
Tel: 0171-813 5302
Franchising 0171-813 5303
Criminal applications 0171-813 5304
Green Form extensions 0171-813 5305
Customer Services Unit 0171-813 5314
DX 170 LON/CH'RY LN WC2

Brighton (Area No. 2)
3rd and 4th Floors
Invicta House
Trafalgar Place
Cheapside
Brighton BN1 4FR

Legal Customer Services Unit
Tel: 01273 699622
Finance Customer Services Unit
Tel: 01273 679929
Emergency applications by fax:
   01273-570201
Franchising Tel: 01273-670690
DX 2752 BRIGHTON-1

Reading (Area No. 3)
80 Kings Road
Reading RG1 4LT

Tel: 0118-9589696
Franchising Tel: 0118-9581620
Emergency applications by fax:
   0118-9584056
DX 4016 READING

Bristol (Area No. 4)
33-35 Queen Square
Bristol BS1 4LU

Switchboard Tel: 0117-921 4801
Applications and Amendments
   Tel: 0117-9087726
Means Assessment Tel: 0117-9087722
Civil Bills Tel: 0117-9087724
Criminal Authorities Tel: 0117-9087720
Green Form/ABWOR—0117-9087721
Franchising Tel: 0117-9304076
Finance Tel: 0117-9304082
Emergency applications by fax:
   0117-9252534
DX 7852 BRISTOL-1

Cardiff (Area No. 5)
Marland House
Central Square
Cardiff CF1 1PF

Tel: 01222-388971
Emergency applications by fax:
   01222-238959
Franchising Tel: 01222-344872
DX 33006 CARDIFF-1

Birmingham (Area No. 6)
Centre-City Podium
5 Hill Street
Birmingham B5 4UD

Tel: 0121-632 6541
Fax no. (to order forms
only): 0121-643 6220
Emergency applications by fax:
   0121-632 5078
DX 13041 BIRMINGHAM-1

Manchester (Area No. 7)
2nd Floor
Elisabeth House
16, St. Peter's Square
Manchester M2 3DA

Tel: 0161-228 1200
Emergency applications by fax:
  0161-228 0445; 0161-228 7047
DX 14343 MANCHESTER-1

Newcastle (Area No. 8)
Eagle Star House
Fenkle Street
Newcastle upon Tyne
NE1 5RU

Tel: 0191-232 3461
DX 61005 NEWCASTLE-u-TYNE-1

Leeds (Area No. 9)
City House
New Station Street
Leeds LS1 4JS

Tel: 0113-244 2851
Emergency applications by fax:
  0113-244 9820
DX 12068 LEEDS-1

Nottingham (Area No. 10)
1st Floor
Fothergill House
16 King Street
Nottingham NG1 2AS

Tel: 0115-955 9600
Franchising Tel: 0115-955 9613
GDSM Tel: 0115-955 9665
Emergency applications by fax:
  0115-956 0716
DX 10035 NOTTINGHAM-1

Cambridge (Area No. 11)
Kett House
Station Road
Cambridge CB1 2JT

Tel: 01223-366511
Office fax: 01223-222608
Emergency applications for Essex:
  01223-222608
Emergency applications for Herts/Beds/
Cambs/Norfolk/Suffolk.
  Fax: 01223-222609
Franchising Tel: 01223-222601
DX 5803 CAMBRIDGE-1

Chester (Area No. 12)
Pepper House, 2nd Floor
Pepper Row
Chester CH1 1DW

Tel: 01244-315455
Emergency applications by fax:
  01244-319036
DX 19981 CHESTER-1

Liverpool (Area No. 15)
Cavern Walks
8 Mathew Street
Liverpool L2 6RE

General enquiries: 0151-236 8371
Legal enquiries: 0151-243 3901
Civil Finance enquiries: 0151-243 3903
ABWOR/green form extensions:
  0151-243 3904
Criminal applications: 0151-243 3905
Emergency applications by fax:
  0151-227 2533
Franchising: 0151-243 3907
DX 14208 LIVERPOOL-1

**HEAD OFFICE (including Finance
Department):**
Legal Aid Board Head Office
85 Gray's Inn Road
London WC1X 8AA

Tel: 0171-813 1000
DX 328 LON/CH'RY LN WC2

Legal Aid Areas and Offices

This list is up to date as at July 1998.

Legal Aid Area	Counties, Unitary Authorities or Metropolitan Borough Councils covered	Local Authority Districts covered
(1) London London	Barnet Bexley Brent Bromley Camden Croydon Ealing Enfield Greenwich Hackney Hammersmith and Fulham Haringey Harrow Havering Hillingdon Hounslow Islington Kensington and Chelsea Kingston upon Thames Lambeth Lewisham London City Merton Newham Redbridge Richmond upon Thames Southwark Sutton Tower Hamlets Waltham Forest Wandsworth Westminster Barking and Dagenham	
(2) South Eastern Brighton	West Sussex Kent East Sussex Surrey Brighton and Hove Gillingham and Rochester	

Legal Aid Area	Counties, Unitary Authorities or Metropolitan Borough Councils covered	Local Authority Districts covered
(3) Southern Reading	Buckinghamshire Dorset Hampshire Isle of Wight Oxfordshire Bournemouth Bracknell Forest Milton Keynes Newbury Portsmouth Poole Reading Slough Southampton Windsor and Maidenhead Wokingham	
(4) South Western Bristol	City of Bristol Cornwall Gloucestershire Devon Wiltshire Somerset North Somerset South Gloucestershire Bath and North East Somerset Plymouth Thamesdown Torbay	
(5) South Wales Cardiff	Bridgend Caerphilly Cardiff Carmarthenshire Ceredigion Merthyr Tydfil Monmouthshire Neath Port Talbot Newport Pembrokeshire Rhondda, Cynon, Taff Swansea City Torfaen Vale of Glamorgan Blaenau Gwent The following districts in Powys:	Brecknock, Powys Radnor, Powys

Legal Aid Area	Counties, Unitary Authorities or Metropolitan Borough Councils covered	Local Authority Districts covered
(6) West Midlands Birmingham	Hereford and Worcester Warwickshire Birmingham Coventry Dudley Sandwell Solihull Walsall Wolverhampton Herefordshire	
	The following districts in Staffordshire:	Lichfield, Staffordshire South Staffordshire, Staffordshire Tamworth, Staffordshire Cannock Chase, Staffordshire
(7) North Western Manchester	Blackburn Bolton Bury Manchester Oldham Rochdale Salford Stockport Tameside Trafford Wigan	
	The following districts in Lancashire:	Burnley, Lancashire Chorley, Lancashire Hyndburn, Lancashire Lancaster, Lancashire Pendle, Lancashire Ribble Valley, Lancashire Rossendale, Lancashire
	The following districts in Cumbria:	South Lakeland, Cumbria Barrow-in-Furness, Cumbria
(8) Northern Newcastle	The following districts in Cumbria:	Carlisle, Cumbria Eden, Cumbria Allerdale, Cumbria Durham Hartlepool Middlesbrough

Legal Aid Area	Counties, Unitary Authorities or Metropolitan Borough Councils covered	Local Authority Districts covered
	The following districts in North Yorkshire:	Hambleton, North Yorkshire Richmondshire, North Yorkshire Ryedale, North Yorkshire Scarborough, North Yorkshire
	Northumberland Redcar and Cleveland Stockton-on-Tees Gateshead Newcastle upon Tyne North Tyneside South Tyneside Sunderland Darlington	
(9) North Eastern Leeds	Barnsley Bradford Calderdale Doncaster Kirklees Leeds Rotherham Sheffield Wakefield East Riding of Yorkshire City of Kingston upon Hull City of York	
	The following districts in North Yorkshire:	Craven, North Yorkshire Selby, North Yorkshire Harrogate, North Yorkshire
(10) East Midlands Nottingham	Derbyshire Leicestershire Lincolnshire North East Lincolnshire North Lincolnshire Northamptonshire Nottinghamshire Derby Leicester Rutland Nottingham	
(11) Eastern Cambridge	Essex Bedfordshire Norfolk Hertfordshire Cambridgeshire Suffolk Luton Peterborough Southend Thurrock	

750

Legal Aid Area	Counties, Unitary Authorities or Metropolitan Borough Councils covered	Local Authority Districts covered
(12) Chester and North Wales Chester	Cheshire	
	Conwy Denbighshire Flintshire Gwynedd Halton Isle of Anglesey Shropshire Stoke-on-Trent Warrington Wrekin Wrexham	
	The following districts in Staffordshire:	Newcastle-under-Lyme, Staffordshire Stafford, Staffordshire Staffordshire Moorlands, Staffordshire East Staffordshire, Staffordshire
	The following districts in Powys:	Montgomery, Powys
(15) Merseyside Liverpool	Blackpool Knowsley Liverpool Sefton St Helens Wirral	
	The following districts in Lancashire:	Fylde, Lancashire Preston, Lancashire South Ribble, Lancashire West Lancashire, Lancashire Wyre, Lancashire

751

Index

(There is a separate Table of Cases at page ix)

Costs—*cont.*
  assistance by way of representation
    and, 76–79, 342, 351–354,
    359–361
  attendance and, 204, 491–492, 540
  authority and, 167–171, 393–395, 536,
    551–552
  Bill of Costs and, 201
  blood tests, 77
  capital, 64
  care proceedings and, 202–203, 256
  certificates of general health, 77–78
  checking the bill and, 201
  children and, 203, 428–429
  Children Act 1989 proceedings and,
    135–136
  CIS and, 186–187, 193–195
  civil legal aid and, 295–296, 393–395,
    402–413, 436–438
  claims queries and, 192–195
  collecting court and, 550–551
  committals and, 257, 261–262
  compliance with formalities, 201
  computation of criminal final claim
    and, 543
  computer system and, 186–187,
    193–195
  conditional discharges, 78–79
  contempt proceedings and, 205, 457
  cost benefit and, 118–120
  contributions, 185–187
  Costs Appeals Committee, 259
  counsel and, 61, 76, 197–201,
    393–394, 423–424, 547–559,
    567–589
  counterclaims and, 184
  court orders, 257
  county courts and, 430
  cracked trials and, 259–260
  criminal legal aid and, 243, 244,
    253, 254, 257–259, 533–589
  Crown Court and, 485–486, 539–542
  custodianship proceedings, 77–78
  damages and, 185–187
  decisions, 76
  deductions and, 249
  deferment of, 415
  delay and, 254
  determination of, 253, 427, 431
  devolved powers, 61–62
  disallownce, 422–423
  disbursements, 77, 197, 205, 414–415,
    536–537
  discontinuance and, 259–260
  duty solicitors and, 51–53
  early payments, 541–542
  either way offences and, 260
  emergency applications and, 107–108
  enhancement of, 205–206, 459–460
  English law, 62
  enhanced rates and, 45, 202–203,
    246–247, 253–255
  enquiry agents and, 256, 260

Costs—*cont.*
  European Commission and, 205
  European Court of Justice and, 268
  exceptional circumstances and,
    202–206, 260
  expenses and, 187, 204
  expert, 72–74, 165–167, 169–170,
    238–241
  extension of limit and, 51
  failure to report significant changes
    and, 201
  financial eligibility and, 206–207, 172,
    427
  financial interest in assessment of
    bills, 189–191
  fixed and hourly fees and, 191–195,
    205–206
  foreign law, 62
  forms and, 187, 194–195
  franchising and, 6, 538–539
  fresh green forms, 60
  full and final settlement and, 192
  graduated fees and, 572–574
  granted after costs incurred, 415–416
  guardians *ad litem,* 428–429
  guilty pleas and, 573–574
  hardship and, 414–415, 542–543
  high cost cases and, 97–98, 121, 122
  hourly rates, 191–195, 205–206
  House of Lords and, 431, 555
  immigration, 61
  income, 64
  inquiries, 430–432
  inspection of original documents, 201
  inter partes, 185–187, 193
  interest, 186
  interim payments and, 536–541
  interpreters and, 52, 73, 202
  intervention, 426
  late claims and, 247–248
  Law Society,
    Children Panel, 202
    Medical Negligence Panel, 205–206
  legal advice and assistance and, 40,
    51–53, 56–64, 286–288
    agents, 56
    assessment of, 56–64
    attendance on behalf of a client, 62
    authority, 61
    capital and income details, 64
    counsel, 61
    duty solicitor rates and, 51–53
    expert's reports and, 57
    fresh green forms and, 60
    Immigration Appeal Tribunals and,
      61
    limit exceeded, 60
    misleading solicitors, 63
    mistakes, 63–64
    more than one solicitor and, 61
    non-solicitors and, 57
    payments, 58
    police stations and, 61